SOFTWARE ENGINEERING
A Practitioner's Approach

McGraw-Hill Series in Software Engineering and Technology

Consulting Editor

Peter Freeman, *University of California, Irvine*

Cohen: *Ada as a Second Language*
Fairley: *Software Engineering Concepts*
Howden: *Functional Program Testing and Analysis*
Jones: *Programming Productivity*
Kolence: *An Introduction to Software Physics: The Meaning of Computer Measurement*
Musa, Iannino and Okumoto: *Software Reliability: Measurement, Prediction and Application*
Pressman: *Software Engineering: A Practitioner's Approach*

SOFTWARE ENGINEERING
A Practitioner's Approach

Second Edition

Roger S. Pressman, Ph.D.

President, R.S. Pressman & Associates, Inc.
and
Adjunct Professor of Computer Engineering
University of Bridgeport

McGraw-Hill Book Company

New York   St. Louis   San Francisco   Auckland   Bogotá   Hamburg
London   Madrid   Mexico   Milan   Montreal   New Delhi   Panama
Paris   São Paulo   Singapore   Sydney   Tokyo   Toronto

This book was set in Times Roman by Publication Services.
The editor was Gerald A. Gleason;
the production supervisor was Phil Galea;
the cover was designed by Infield + D'Astolfo.
Project supervision was done by Publication Services.
R.R. Donnelley & Sons Company was the printer and binder.

SOFTWARE ENGINEERING
A Practitioner's Approach

Copyright © 1987, 1982 by McGraw-Hill, Inc. All rights reserved. Printed in the United States of America. Except as permitted under the United States Copyright Act of 1976, no part of this publication may be reproduced or distributed in any form or by any means, or stored in a data base or retrieval system, without the prior written permission of the publisher.

2 3 4 5 6 7 8 9 0 DOCDOC 8 9 2 1 0 9 8 7

Library of Congress Cataloging-in-Publication Data
Pressman, Roger S.
    Software engineering.

    Includes bibliographies and index.
      1. Electronic digital computers—Programming.
I. Title.
QA76.6.P73   1987   005.1   86-18549
ISBN 0-07-050783-X

ABOUT THE AUTHOR

Roger S. Pressman is a nationally recognized industry consultant in software engineering. He received a B.S.E. from the University of Connecticut, an M.S. from the University of Bridgeport, and a Ph.D. in Engineering from the University of Connecticut. He has had nearly two decades of industry experience, holding both technical and management positions with responsibility for the development of software for engineered products and systems.

In addition to his industry experience, Dr. Pressman was Bullard Associate Professor of Computer Engineering at the University of Bridgeport and Director of the University's Computer Aided Design and Manufacturing Center. He remains at the university as an adjunct Associate Professor of Computer Engineering.

Dr. Pressman is President of R.S. Pressman & Associates, Inc., a consulting firm specializing in management and technical problem solving in software engineering. Clients include many large corporations as well as smaller high technology companies. The firm specializes in software engineering training and has developed courses and other training products that have been used by over 10,000 industry professionals.

Dr. Pressman is author of many technical papers and another book, *Numerical Control and Computer Aided Manufacturing*. He is a member of the ACM, IEEE, and Tau Beta Pi, Phi Kappa Phi, Pi Tau Sigma, and Eta Kappa Nu.

TO MY PARENTS

CONTENTS

3   Software Project Planning

6   Software Design Fundamentals

7   Data Flow–Oriented Design

8 Data Structure–Oriented Design

9 Object-Oriented Design

10   Real-Time Design

11   Programming Languages and Coding

12 Software Quality Assurance

13 Software Testing Techniques

14 Software Testing Strategies

15 Software Maintenance and Configuration Management

PREFACE

In the five years since the first edition of *Software Engineering: A Practitioner's Approach,* software engineering has grown from infancy to early adolescence. Today, software engineering is recognized as a legitimate discipline and "software engineer" has replaced "programmer" as the job title of preference. Software engineering methods and procedures have been adopted successfully in a broad spectrum of industry applications. Managers and practitioners alike recognize the need for a more disciplined approach to software development.

But the problems that were described in the preface to the first edition remain with us. Many companies still develop software haphazardly. Many professionals and students are unaware of modern methods. In addition, debate and controversy about the true nature of the software engineering approach continue. The status of software engineering is a study in contrasts. Attitudes have changed, progress has been made, but much remains to be done before the discipline reaches maturity.

The second edition of *Software Engineering: A Practitioner's Approach* is intended to provide one element of a foundation from which the bridge from adolescence to maturity can be constructed. The second edition, like the first, is intended for both students and practitioners, maintaining the same format and style of the first edition. The book retains its appeal as a guide to the industry professional and a comprehensive introduction to the student at the upper level undergraduate or first year graduate level.

Like the first edition, software engineering methods are presented in the chronological sequence that they are applied during software development. However, the second edition is more than a simple update. The book has been restructured to emphasize new and important software engineering methods and techniques. Rather than maintaining a strict life cycle view, the second edition presents generic activities that are performed regardless of the software engineering paradigm that has been chosen.

Chapters that have been retained from the first edition have been expanded and revised to reflect current trends and techniques. Major new sections have been added to chapters on computer system engineering, software project planning, analysis methodologies, programming languages and coding, testing strategies and software maintenance.

New chapters on analysis and design fundamentals have been added to provide a foundation for the methods that are introduced in later chapters. In addition, new chapters present object-oriented design, real-time design, software test case design techniques, and software quality assurance. These chapters have been added to reflect new software engineering methods that are rapidly gaining acceptance in the industry. Many new examples, problems, and points to ponder have been added and the *Further Readings* sections (one of the more popular tidbits in the first edition) have been expanded and updated for every chapter.

The software engineering literature is expanding at an explosive rate. Once again, my thanks to the many authors who have provided additional insight, ideas, and commentary in the years since the first edition. Many have been referenced within the pages of each chapter. All deserve credit for their contribution to this rapidly evolving field. I also wish to thank the reviewers of the second edition: Robert Glass, Seattle University; Ernest H. Goldman, University of Bridgeport; Medi-Harandi, University of Illinois-Urbana-Champaign; Marvin Zelkowitz, University of Maryland; and John Musa, ATT Bell Labs. Their comment and criticism have been invaluable.

The content of the second edition of *Software Engineering: A Practitioner's Approach* has been shaped by the hundreds of industry professionals, university professors and students who have taken the time to communicate their suggestions, criticisms and ideas. In addition, my personal thanks go to our many industry clients, who certainly teach me as much or more than I can teach them.

Finally, to Barbara, Mathew, and Michael, my love and thanks for tolerating my travel schedule, understanding the evenings at the office, and encouraging the second edition of "the book."

Roger S. Pressman

PREFACE TO THE FIRST EDITION

In the brief history of the electronic digital computer, the 1950s and 1960s were decades of hardware. The 1970s were a period of transition and a time of recognition of software. The decade of software is now upon us. In fact, advances in computing may become limited by our inability to produce quality software that can tap the enormous capacity of 1980-era processors.

During the past decade we have grown to recognize circumstances that are collectively called the *software crisis*. Software costs escalated dramatically, becoming the largest dollar item in many computer-based systems. Schedules and completion dates were set but rarely kept. As software systems grew larger, quality became suspect. Individuals responsible for software development projects had limited historical data to use as guides and less control over the course of a project.

A set of techniques, collectively called *software engineering*, has evolved as a response to the software crisis. These techniques deal with software as an engineered product that requires planning, analysis, design, implementation, testing, and maintenance. The goal of this text is to provide a concise presentation of each step in the software engineering process.

The contents of this book closely parallel the software life cycle. Early chapters present the planning phase, emphasizing system definition (computer systems engineering), software planning, and software requirements analysis. Specific techniques for software costs and schedule estimation should be of particular interest to project managers as well as to technical practitioners and students.

In subsequent chapters emphasis shifts to the software development phase. The fundamental principles of software design are introduced. In addition, descriptions of two important classes of software design methodology are presented in detail. A variety of software tools are discussed. Comparisons among techniques and among tools are provided to assist the practitioner and student alike. Coding style is also stressed in the context of the software engineering process.

The concluding chapters deal with software testing techniques, reliability, and software maintenance. Software engineering steps associated with testing are described and specific techniques for software testing are presented. The current status of software reliability prediction is discussed and an overview of reliability models and program correctness approaches is presented. The concluding chapter considers both management and technical aspects of software maintenance.

This book is an outgrowth of a senior-level/first-year-graduate course in software engineering offered at the University of Bridgeport. The course and this text cover both management and technical aspects of the software development process. The chapters of the text correspond roughly to major lecture topics. In fact, the text is derived in part from edited versions of transcribed notes of these lectures. Writing style is therefore purposely casual and figures are derived from viewgraphs used during the course.

Software Engineering: A Practitioner's Approach may be used in a number of ways for various audiences. The text can serve as a concise guide to software engineering for the practicing manager, analyst, or programmer. It can also serve as the basic text for an upper-level undergraduate or graduate course in software engineering. Lastly, the text can be used as a supplementary guide for software development early in computer science or computer engineering undergraduate curricula.

The software engineering literature has expanded rapidly during the past decade. I gratefully acknowledge the many authors who have helped this new discipline evolve. Their work has had an important influence on this book and my method of presentation. I also wish to acknowledge Pat Duran, Leo Lambert, Kyu Lee, John Musa, Claude Walston, Anthony Wasserman, Marvin Zelkowitz, and Nicholas Zvegintzov, the reviewers of this book, and Peter Freeman, the series editor. Their thoughtful insights and suggestions have been invaluable during the final stages of preparation. Special thanks go to Leo Lambert and his colleagues from the Computer Management Operation, General Electric Company, who have allowed me to tap their broad collective experience during my long association with them. In addition, to the students at the University of Bridgeport and the hundreds of software professionals and their managers who have attended short courses that I have taught, my thanks for the arguments, the ideas, and the challenges that are essential in a field such as ours.

Finally, to Barbara, Mathew, and Michael, my love and thanks for tolerating the genesis of book number two.

Roger S. Pressman

CHAPTER
1

SOFTWARE
AND
SOFTWARE
ENGINEERING

On February 23, 1984, the front page of *Business Week* displayed the following headline in banner type: ''Software: The New Driving Force.'' Many technologists, upon reading the headline, smiled and commented that it was about ten years too late. But others recognized that this headline was a harbinger of a new understanding of the importance of computer software. Today, for the first time in the history of computing, software has surpassed hardware as the key element to the success of many businesses, products, and systems.

In essence software is often the key factor that *differentiates*. The completeness and timeliness of information provided by software (and related data bases) differentiates one company from its competitors. The design and ''human friendliness'' of a software product differentiates it from competing products with otherwise similar functions. The intelligence and function provided by embedded software often differentiates two similar industrial or consumer products. It is software that can make the difference.

1.1 THE IMPORTANCE OF SOFTWARE

During the first three decades of the computing era, the primary challenge was to develop computer hardware that reduced the cost of processing and storing data. Throughout the decade of the 1980s, advances in microelectronics have resulted in more computing power at increasingly lower cost.

Today the problem is different. The primary challenge is to reduce the cost and improve the quality of computer-based solutions—solutions that are implemented with software.

1

The power of yesterday's mainframe computer is available now on a single integrated circuit. The awesome processing and storage capabilities of modern hardware represent *computing potential*. Software is the mechanism that enables us to harness and tap this potential.

1.1.1 The Evolving Role of Software

The context in which software has been developed is closely coupled to four decades of computer system evolution. Better hardware performance, smaller size, and lower cost have precipitated more sophisticated computer-based systems. We've moved from vacuum tube processors to microelectronic devices. In popular books on "the computer revolution," Osborne [OSB79] characterized a "new industrial revolution"; Toffler [TOF80] called the advent of microelectronics part of "the third wave of change" in human history; and Naisbitt [NAI82] predicted that the transformation from an industrial society to an "information society" will have a profound impact on our lives.

Figure 1.1 depicts the evolution of software within the context of computer-based system application areas. During the early years of computer system development, hardware underwent continual change while software was viewed by many as an afterthought. Computer programming was a seat-of-the-pants art for which few systematic methods existed. Software development was virtually unmanaged unless schedules slipped or costs began to escalate. During this period a batch orientation was used for most systems. Notable exceptions were interactive systems such as the early American Airlines reservation system and real-time defense-oriented systems such as SAGE. For the most part, however, hardware was dedicated to the execution of a single program that in turn was dedicated to a specific application.

During the early years general-purpose hardware became commonplace. Software, on the other hand, was custom designed for each application and had a relatively limited distribution.

Product software (i.e., programs developed to be sold to one or more customers) was in its infancy. Most software was developed and ultimately used by the same person or organization. The same person wrote it, got it running, and if it failed, fixed it. Because job mobility was low, managers could rest assured that this person would be there when bugs were encountered. Because of this personalized software environment, design was an implicit process performed in one's head and documentation was often nonexistent.

Throughout the early years we learned much about the implementation of computer-based systems, but relatively little about computer system engineering. In fairness, however, we must acknowledge the many outstanding computer-based systems that were developed during this era. Some of these remain in use today and provide landmark achievements that continue to justify admiration.

The second era of computer system evolution (Figure 1.1) spanned the decade from the mid-1960s to the late 1970s. Multiprogramming, multi-user systems introduced new concepts of human-machine interaction. Interactive techniques opened a new world of applications and new levels of hardware and software sophistication. Real-time systems could collect, analyze, and transform data from multiple sources,

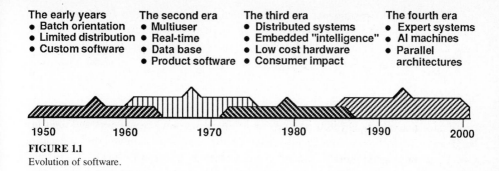

FIGURE 1.1
Evolution of software.

thereby controlling processes and producing output in milliseconds rather than minutes. Advances in on-line storage devices led to the first generation of data base management systems.

The second era was also characterized by the use of product software and the advent of "software houses." Software was developed for widespread distribution in a multidisciplinary market. Programs for mainframes and minicomputers were distributed to hundreds and sometimes thousands of users. Entrepreneurs from industry, government, and academia broke away to "develop the ultimate software package" and earn a bundle of money.

As the number of computer-based systems grew, libraries of computer software began to expand. In-house developed projects produced tens of thousands of program source statements. Software products purchased from the outside added hundreds of thousands of new statements. A dark cloud appeared on the horizon: All of these programs—all of these source statements— had to be corrected when faults were detected, modified as user requirements changed, or adapted to new hardware that was purchased. These activities were collectively called *software maintenance*. Effort spent on software maintenance began to absorb resources at an alarming rate. Worse yet, the personalized nature of many programs made them virtually unmaintainable. A *software crisis* had begun.

The third era of computer system evolution began in the mid-1970s and continues today. The distributed system—multiple computers, each performing functions concurrently and communicating with one another—greatly increased the complexity of computer-based systems. Global and local area networks, high band-width digital communications, and increasing demands for "instantaneous" data access put heavy demands on software developers.

The third era has also been characterized by the advent and widespread use of microprocessors and personal computers. The microprocessor is an integral part of a wide array of "intelligent" products including automobiles, microwave ovens, industrial robots, and blood serum diagnostic equipment. In many cases software technology is being integrated into products by technical staff who understand hardware but are often novices in software development.

The personal computer has been the catalyst for the growth of many software companies. While the software companies of the second era sold hundreds or thousands of copies of their programs, the software companies of the third era sell tens and even hundreds of thousands of copies. Personal computer hardware is rapidly becoming a commodity, while software provides the differentiating characteristic. In fact, as the rate of personal computer sales growth flattened during the mid-1980s, software product sales continued to grow. Many people in industry and at home spent more money on software than they did to purchase the computer on which the software runs.

The fourth era in computer software is just beginning. Authors such as Feigenbaum and McCorduck [FEI83] predict that "fifth generation" computers and their related software will have a profound impact on the balance of political and industrial power throughout the world. Already, *fourth generation techniques* (4GT) for software development (discussed later in this chapter) are changing the manner in which some segments of the software community build computer programs. Expert systems and artificial intelligence software have finally moved from the laboratory into practical application for wide-ranging problems in the real world.

As we move into the fourth era, the software crisis continues to intensify. The problems that characterize the crisis are discussed in Section 1.3. For now we can describe the software crisis in the following manner:

1. Hardware sophistication has outpaced our ability to build software that can tap hardware's potential.
2. Our ability to build new programs cannot keep pace with the demand for new programs.
3. Our ability to maintain existing programs is threatened by poor design and inadequate resources.

As a response to the software crisis, *software engineering* practices—the topic to which this book is dedicated—are being adopted throughout the industry.

1.1.2   An Industry Perspective

In the early days of computing, computer-based systems were developed using hardware-oriented management techniques. Project managers focused on hardware because it was the single largest budget item for system development. To control hardware costs managers instituted formal controls and technical standards. They demanded thorough analysis and design before something was built. They measured the process to determine where improvement could be made. Stated simply, they applied the controls, methods, and tools that we recognize as hardware engineering. Sadly, software was often little more than an afterthought.

In the early days, programming was viewed as an art form. Few formal methods existed and fewer people used them. The programmer often learned his or her craft by trial and error. The jargon and challenges of building computer software created a mystique that few managers cared to penetrate. The software world was virtually undisciplined—and many practitioners of the day loved it!

Today, the distribution of costs for the development of computer-based systems has changed dramatically. Software, rather than hardware, is often the largest cost item. For the past decade managers and many technical practitioners have asked the following questions:

- Why does it take so long to get programs finished?
- Why are costs so high?
- Why can't we find all errors before we give the software to our customers?
- Why do we have difficulty in measuring progress as software is being developed?

These, and many other questions, are a manifestation of the concern about software and the manner in which it is developed—a concern that has led to the adoption of software engineering practice.

1.2 SOFTWARE

Twenty years ago, less than 1 percent of the public could have intelligently described what "computer software" meant. Today, most professionals and many members of the public at large feel they understand software. But do they?

A textbook description of software might take the following form:

Software: (1) instructions (computer programs) that when executed provide desired function and performance; (2) data structures that enable the programs to adequately manipulate information; (3) documents that describe the operation and use of the programs.

There is no question other, more complete definitions could be offered, but we need more than a formal definition.

1.2.1 Software Characteristics

To gain an understanding of software (and ultimately of software engineering), it is important to examine the characteristics of software that make it different from other things that human beings build. When hardware is built, the human creative process (analysis, design, construction, testing) is ultimately translated into a physical form. If we build a new computer, our initial sketches, formal design drawings, and breadboarded prototype evolve into a physical product with VLSI chips, circuit boards, power supplies, etc.

Software is a *logical* rather than a *physical* system element. Therefore, software has characteristics that are considerably different than those of hardware:

Software is developed or engineered; it is not manufactured in the classical sense. Although some similarities exist between software development and hardware manufacture, the two activities are fundamentally different. In both activities high quality is achieved through good design, but the manufacturing phase for hardware can introduce quality problems that are nonexistent or easily corrected for software. Both activities are dependent on people, but the relationship between people applied and work accomplished is entirely different for software (see Chapter 3). Both activities require the construction of a "product," but the approaches are different.

Software costs are concentrated in engineering. This means software projects cannot be managed as if they were manufacturing projects.

Over the past five years, the concept of the "software factory" has been discussed in the literature (e.g., [MAN84], [TAJ84]). It is important to note that this term does not imply that hardware manufacturing and software development are equivalent. Rather, the software factory concept recommends the use of automated tools (see Section 1.5.4) for software development.

Software doesn't "wear out." Figure 1.2 depicts failure rate as a function of time for hardware. The relationship, often called the "bathtub curve," indicates that hardware exhibits relatively high failure rates early in its life. These failures are often attributable to design or manufacturing defects. When defects are corrected the failure rate drops to a lower, steady-state level for some period of time. As time passes, however, the failure rate rises again as hardware components suffer from the cumulative effects of dust, vibration, abuse, temperature extremes, and many other environmental maladies. Stated simply, the hardware begins to wear out.

Software is not susceptible to the environmental maladies that cause hardware to wear out. In theory, therefore, the failure-rate curve for software should take the form shown in Figure 1.3. Undiscovered defects will cause high failure rates early in the life of a program. However, once these are corrected, assuming other errors aren't introduced, the curve flattens as shown. Figure 1.3 is a gross oversimplification of actual failure models (see Chapter 12 for more information) for software. However, the implication is clear—software doesn't wear out. But it does *deteriorate*!

This seeming contradiction can best be understood by considering Figure 1.4. During its life software will undergo change (maintenance). As changes are made, it is likely that some new defects will be introduced, causing the failure rate curve to spike as shown in Figure 1.4. Before the curve can return to the original steady-state failure

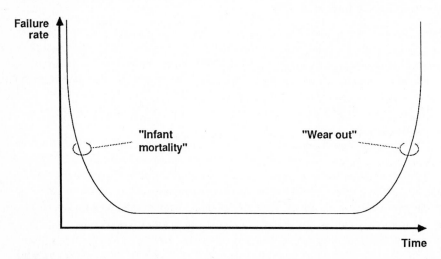

FIGURE 1.2
Failure curve for hardware.

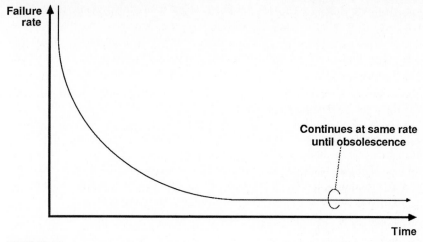

FIGURE 1.3
Failure curve for software (idealized).

rate, another change is requested, causing the curve to spike again. Slowly, the minimum failure rate level begins to rise; the software is deteriorating due to change.

Another aspect of wear illustrates the difference between hardware and software. When a hardware component wears out, it is replaced by a spare part. There are no software ''spare parts.'' Every software failure indicates an error in design or in the process through which design was translated into machine-executable code. Therefore, software maintenance involves considerably more complexity than hardware mainte-nance.

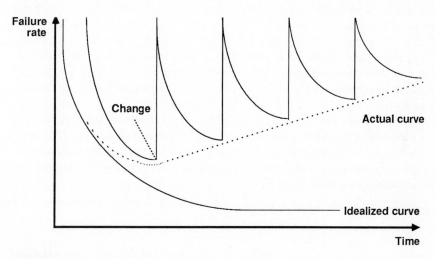

FIGURE 1.4
Actual failure curve for software.

Most software is custom built, rather than assembled from existing components. Consider the manner in which the control hardware for a microprocessor-based product is designed and built. The design engineer draws a simple schematic of the digital circuitry, does some fundamental analysis to assure that proper function will be achieved, and then goes to the shelf where catalogs of digital components exist. Each integrated circuit (IC or "chip") has a part number, a defined and validated function, a well-defined interface, and a standard set of integration guidelines. After each component is selected, it can be ordered off the shelf.

Sadly, software designers are not afforded the luxury described above. With few exceptions, there are no catalogs of software components. It is possible to order ready-made software, but only as a complete unit, not as components that can be reassembled into new programs.* Although much has been written about "software reusability" (e.g., [BIG84]), little tangible success has been achieved to date.

1.2.2 Software Components

Computer software is information that exists in two basic forms: non-machine-executable components and machine-executable components. For the purpose of our discussion in this chapter, only those software components leading directly to machine-executable instructions are presented. All software components comprise a *configuration*, discussed in later chapters.

The manner in which software is translated into machine-executable form is illustrated in Figure 1.5. The software design is translated into a language form that specifies software data structure, procedural attributes, and related requirements. The language form is processed by a translator that converts it into machine-executable instructions.

Ideally humans would communicate with computers using a natural language (e.g., English, Spanish, Russian). Unfortunately, large vocabularies, sophisticated grammars, and our use of context for understanding hamper human-computer communication via natural language. Research (e.g., [WIN83]) in semantic information processing and natural language recognition has laid the groundwork for the use of natural language as a communication medium with the computer. However, for the next few years, at least, language forms for the specification of programs are limited to *artificial languages*.

All programming languages are artificial languages. Each has a limited vocabulary, an explicitly defined grammar, and well-formed rules of syntax and semantics. These attributes are essential for machine translation. The language forms that are one component of software are characterized as machine level languages, high-order languages, and nonprocedural languages.

---

*This situation is beginning to change. For example, a number of firms currently offer reusable components for Ada programs. Others have begun to talk about creating catalogs of "software ICs" for object-oriented languages.

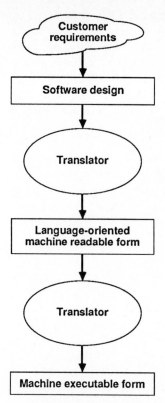

FIGURE 1.5
Software translation steps.

Machine level language, illustrated by the microprocessor assembler language excerpt in Figure 1.6, is a symbolic representation of the CPU instruction set. When a good software developer produces a maintainable, well-documented program, machine level language can make extremely efficient use of memory and "optimize" program execution speed. When a program is poorly designed and has little documentation, machine language tends to exacerbate the problems that will occur.

Even when machine level language does provide attractive execution speed and memory characteristics, it has a number of serious disadvantages:

1. Implementation time is protracted by the complexity of the language form and the low level of abstraction with which information is represented.
2. Resultant programs are difficult to read.
3. Testing is difficult.
4. Maintenance is extremely difficult.
5. Portability between different processors is not possible.

As we shall see in Chapter 3, software "productivity" is seriously impaired when machine level language is used. Because of the disadvantages associated with its use, this language form is likely to find only limited use during the next decade.

```
0000                                         ORG      0000
                                 ;
0000    F3                               DI
                                 ;
0001    3E00            START:           MVI      A,0
0003    47                               MOV      B,A
0004    D301            LOP1:            OUT      1
0006    3D                               DCR      A
0007    C20400                           JNZ      LOP1
000A    78                               MOV      A,B
000B    3D                               DCR      A
000C    CA1500                           JZ       CONT
000F    47                               MOV      B,A
0010    3E00                             MVI      A,0
0012    C30400                           JMP      LOP1
                                 ;
0015    3E00            CONT:            MVI      A,0
0017    D303            LOP2:            OUT      3
0019    3D                               DCR      A
001A    C21700                           JNZ      LOP2
001D    78                               MOV      A,B
001E    3D                               DCR      A
001F    CA2800                           JZ       NEXT
0022    47                               MOV      B,A
0023    3E00                             MVI      A,0
0025    C31700                           JMP      LOP2
                                 ;
0028    C30100          NEXT:            JMP      START
002B                                     END
```

FIGURE 1.6
Machine level language.

High-order languages allow the software developer and the program to be machine-independent. When a more sophisticated translator is used, the vocabulary, grammar, syntax, and semantics of a high-order language can be much more sophisticated than machine level languages. In fact high-order language compilers and interpreters produce machine level language as output.

Although hundreds of programming languages are in use today, fewer than ten high-order programming languages are widely used in the industry. Languages such as COBOL and FORTRAN remain in widespread use nearly 30 years after their introduction. Modern programming languages (languages that directly support modern design practices for procedural and data design) such as Pascal, C, and Ada[*] are being used widely. Specialized languages (designed for specific application domains), such as Smalltalk, APL, LISP and Prolog, are gaining wider acceptance as new application approaches move from the laboratory to practical use.

---

[*] Ada is a registered trademark of the U.S. Government (Ada Joint Program Office).

We have already alluded to the function of the programming language translator, that is, to transform a language form to machine-executable instructions. An assembler is the translator for machine level code and performs the relatively simple task of converting symbolic machine instructions to machine-executable instructions. An interpreter is a translator that transforms high-level languages on a statement-by-statement basis. As each language statement is encountered, it is converted to machine-executable code and executed. APL and BASIC are among the languages usually executed with an interpreter. The most common high-order language translator is the compiler. By evaluating a program globally, a compiler is capable of optimizing memory size and/or execution speed of the machine-executable instructions that it produces.

Machine-executable instructions are the bottom line of the software configuration. A hexadecimal or other specialized code is used to represent the binary pattern of bits that invokes specific CPU processing steps. Referring again to Figure 1.6, the machine-executable instructions (*machine code*) corresponding to machine level language (*assembler code*) are shown in the left-hand columns.

Machine code, assembler (machine level) languages, and high-level programming languages are often referred to as the first three generations of computer languages. With any of these languages, the programmer must be concerned with both the specification of the information structure and the control of the program itself. Hence, languages in the first three generations are termed *procedural languages*.

Over the past decade, a group of fourth generation or *non-procedural languages* have been introduced. Rather than requiring the software developer to specify procedural detail, the nonprocedural language implies a program by "specifying the desired result, rather than specifying action required to achieve that result" [COB85]. Support software translates the specification of result into a machine-executable program. To date, fourth generation languages (4GLs) have been used in data base applications and other business data processing areas. Further discussion of their application within the context of software engineering is presented later in this chapter.

1.2.3 Software Applications

Software may be applied in any situation for which a previously specified set of procedural steps (i.e., an algorithm) has been defined. (A notable exception to this rule is expert system software.) Information content and determinacy are important factors in determining the nature of a software application. Content refers to the meaning and form of incoming and outgoing information. For example many business applications make use of highly structured input data (a data base) and produce formatted "reports." Software that controls an automated machine (e.g., a numerical control) accepts discrete data items with limited structure and produces individual machine commands in rapid succession.

Information determinacy refers to the predictability of the order and timing of input data. An engineering analysis program accepts data that has a predefined order, executes the analysis algorithm(s) without interruption, and produces resultant data in report or graphical format. Such applications are determinate. A multi-user operating system, on the other hand, accepts inputs that have varied content and arbitrary timing;

executes algorithms that can be interrupted by external conditions; and produces output that varies as a function of environment and time. Applications with these characteristics are indeterminate.

It is somewhat difficult to develop meaningful generic categories for software applications. As software complexity grows, neat compartmentalization disappears. The following software areas indicate the breadth of potential applications.

SYSTEM SOFTWARE. System software is a collection of programs written to service other programs. Some system software (e.g., compilers, editors, and file management utilities) process complex, but determinate, information structures. Other systems applications (e.g., operating system components, drivers, telecommunications processors) process largely indeterminate data. In either case the systems software area is characterized by heavy interaction with computer hardware; heavy usage by multiple users; concurrent operation that requires scheduling, resource sharing, and sophisticated process management; complex data structures; and multiple external interfaces.

REAL-TIME SOFTWARE. Software that measures/analyzes/controls real-world events as they occur is called real-time. Elements of real-time software include a data gathering component that collects and formats information from an external environment, an analysis component that transforms information as required by the application, a control/output component that responds to the external environment, and a monitoring component that coordinates all other components so that real-time response (typically ranging from 1 millisecond to 1 minute) can be maintained. It should be noted that the term "real-time" differs from "interactive" or "timesharing." A real-time system *must* respond within strict time constraints. The response time of an interactive (or timesharing) system can normally be exceeded without disastrous results.

BUSINESS SOFTWARE. Business information processing is the largest single software application area. Discrete "systems" (e.g., payroll, accounts receivable/payable, inventory, etc.) have evolved into management information system (MIS) software that accesses one or more large data bases containing business information. Applications in this area restructure existing data in order to facilitate business operations or management decision making. In addition to conventional data processing tasks, business software applications also encompass interactive computing (e.g., point-of-sale transaction processing).

ENGINEERING AND SCIENTIFIC SOFTWARE. Engineering and scientific software has been characterized by "number crunching" algorithms. Applications range from astronomy to volcanology, from automotive stress analysis to space shuttle orbital dynamics, and from molecular biology to automated manufacturing. However, new applications within the engineering/scientific area are moving away from conventional numerical algorithms. Computer-aided design (CAD), system simulation, and other interactive applications have begun to take on real-time and even system software characteristics.

EMBEDDED SOFTWARE. Intelligent products have become commonplace in nearly every consumer and industrial market. Embedded software resides in read-only memory and is used to control products and systems for the consumer and industrial markets. Embedded software can perform very limited and esoteric functions (e.g., key pad control for a microwave oven) or provide significant function and control capability (e.g., digital functions in an automobile such as fuel control, dashboard displays, braking systems, etc.).

PERSONAL COMPUTER SOFTWARE. The personal computer (PC) software market has burgeoned over the past decade. Word processing, spreadsheets, computer graphics, entertainment, data base management, personal and business financial applications, and external network or data base access are only a few of hundreds of applications. In fact PC software continues to represent some of the most innovative software design in the software field.

ARTIFICIAL INTELLIGENCE SOFTWARE. Artificial intelligence (AI) software makes use of nonnumerical algorithms to solve complex problems that are not amenable to computation or straightforward analysis. Currently, the most active AI area is *expert systems*, also called knowledge-based systems [WAT85]. Other application areas for AI software are pattern recognition (image and voice), theorem proving, and game playing.

1.3 THE SOFTWARE CRISIS

The *software crisis* alludes to a set of problems encountered in the development of computer software. The problems are not limited to software that ''doesn't function properly.'' Rather, the software crisis encompasses problems associated with how we develop software, how we maintain a growing volume of existing software, and how we can expect to keep pace with a growing demand for more software. Although reference to a ''software crisis'' can be criticized for being melodramatic, the phrase does serve a useful purpose by highlighting real problems found in all areas of software development.

1.3.1 Problems

The software crisis is characterized by many problems, but managers responsible for software development concentrate on the ''bottom-line'' issues: (1) schedule and cost estimates are often grossly inaccurate; (2) the ''productivity'' of software people hasn't kept pace with the demand for their services; and (3) the quality of software is sometimes less than adequate. Cost overruns of an order of magnitude have been experienced. Schedules slip by months or years. Little has been done to improve the productivity of software practitioners. Error rates for new programs cause customer dissatisfaction and lack of confidence. Such problems are only the most visible manifestations of other software difficulties:

- We haven't taken the time to collect data on the software development process. With no historical data as a guide, estimation has been "seat-of-the-pants" with predictably poor results. With no solid indication of productivity, we cannot accurately evaluate the efficacy of new tools, techniques, or standards.
- Customer dissatisfaction with the "completed" system is encountered too frequently. Software development projects are frequently undertaken with only a vague indication of customer requirements. Communication between customer and software developer is often poor.
- Software quality is often suspect. We have only recently begun to understand the importance of systematic, technically complete software testing. Solid quantitative concepts of software reliability and quality assurance are only beginning to emerge [IAN84].
- Existing software can be very difficult to maintain. The software maintenance task devours the majority of all software dollars. Maintainability has not been emphasized as an important criterion for software acceptance.

We have presented the bad news first. Now for the good news: Each of the problems described above can be corrected. An engineering approach to the development of software, coupled with continuing improvement of techniques and tools, provides the key.

One problem (we could call it a fact of life) will remain. Software will absorb a larger and larger percentage of the overall development cost for computer-based systems. In the United States we spend close to 50 billion dollars each year on the development, purchase, and maintenance of computer software. We had better take the problems associated with software development seriously.

1.3.2   Causes

Problems associated with the software crisis have been caused by the character of software itself and by the failings of the people charged with software development. It is possible, however, that we have expected too much in too short a period of time. After all, our experience spans little more than 35 years.

The character of computer software was discussed briefly in the preceding section. To review, software is a logical rather than a physical system element; therefore, success is measured by the quality of a single entity rather than many manufactured entities. Software does not wear out. If faults are encountered, there is a high probability that each was inadvertently introduced during development and went undetected during testing. We replace "defective parts" during software maintenance, but we have few, if any, spare parts; i.e., maintenance often includes correction or modification to design.

The logical nature of software provides a challenge to the people who develop it. For the first time we have accepted the task of communicating with an alien intelligence—a machine. The intellectual challenge of software development is certainly one cause of the software crisis, but the problems discussed above have been caused by more mundane human failings.

Middle- and upper-level managers with no background in software are often given responsibility for software development. There is an old management axiom that states: "A good manager can manage any project." We should add: "...if he or she is willing to learn the milestones that can be used to measure progress, apply effective methods of control, disregard mythology, and become conversant in a rapidly changing technology." The manager must communicate with all constituencies involved with software development—customers, software developers, support staff, and others. Communication can break down because the special characteristics of software and the particular problems associated with its development are misunderstood. When this occurs, the problems associated with the software crisis are exacerbated.

Software practitioners (the past generation have been called *programmers*; this generation will earn the title *software engineer*) have had little formal training in new techniques for software development. In many organizations a mild form of anarchy reigns. Each individual approaches the task of "writing programs" with experience derived from past efforts. Some people develop an orderly and efficient approach to software development by trial and error, but many others develop bad habits that result in poor software quality and maintainability.

We all resist change. It is truly ironic, however, that while computing potential (hardware) experiences enormous change, the software people responsible for tapping that potential often oppose change when it is discussed and resist change when it is introduced. Maybe that is the real cause of the software crisis.

1.4 SOFTWARE MYTHS

Many causes of the software crisis can be traced to a mythology that arose during the early history of software development. Unlike ancient myths, which often provided humans lessons well worth heeding, software myths propagated misinformation and confusion. Software myths had a number of attributes that made them insidious; for instance, they appeared to be reasonable statements of fact (sometimes containing elements of truth), they had an intuitive feel, and they were often promulgated by experienced practitioners who "knew the score."

Today, most knowledgeable professionals recognize myths for what they are—misleading attitudes that have caused serious problems for managers and technical people alike. However, old attitudes and habits are difficult to modify, and remnants of software myths are still believed as we move toward the fifth decade of software.

The following sections examine some of the more common software myths and present corresponding statements of reality.

1.4.1 Management Myths

Managers with software responsibility, like managers in most disciplines, are often under pressure to maintain budgets, keep schedules from slipping, and improve quality. Like a drowning person who grasps at straws, a software manager often grasps at a software myth even if such a belief will lessen the pressure only temporarily.

Myth: Why should we change our approach to software development? We're doing the same kinds of programming now that we did ten years ago.

Reality: Although the application domain may be the same (and for many organizations it has changed substantially), the demand for greater productivity and quality and the criticality of software to strategic business objectives have increased substantially.

Myth: We already have a book that is full of standards and procedures for building software.

Reality: The book may very well exist, but is it used? Are software practitioners aware of its existence? Does it reflect modern software development practice? Is it complete? In many cases, the answer to all of these questions is ''no.''

Myth: Our people do have state-of-the-art software development tools; after all, we buy them the newest computers.

Reality: It takes much more than the latest model mainframe (or PC) to do high-quality software development. *Software tools* (programs that help in the creation of other programs) are more important than hardware for achieving good quality and productivity.

Myth: If we fall behind schedule, we can add more programmers and catch up (sometimes called the ''Mongolian horde concept'').

Reality: Software development is not a mechanistic process like manufacturing. In the words of Brooks [BRO75]: ''... adding people to a late software project makes it later.'' At first, this statement may seem counterintuitive. However, as new people are added, the need for learning and communication among staff can and does reduce the amount of time spent on productive development. People can be added, but only in a planned and well-coordinated manner.

1.4.2 Customer Myths

A *customer* who requests computer software may be a person at the next desk, a technical group down the hall, the marketing/sales department, or an outside company that requests software under contract. In many cases the customer believes myths about software because responsible managers and practitioners do little to correct misinformation. Myths lead to false expectations by the customer and, ultimately, dissatisfaction with the developer.

Myth: A general statement of objectives is sufficient to begin writing programs—we can fill in the details later.

Reality: Poor initial definition is the major cause of failed software efforts. A formal and detailed description of information domain, function, performance, interfaces, design constraints, and validation criteria is essential. These characteristics can be determined only after thorough communication between customer and developer.

Myth: Project requirements continually change, but change can be accommodated easily because software is flexible.

Reality: It is true that software requirements change, but the impact of change
varies with the time it is introduced. Figure 1.7 illustrates the impact of
change. If serious attention is given to initial definition, early requests for
change can be accommodated easily. The customer can review requirements and recommend modifications with relatively little impact on cost.
When changes are requested during software design, cost impact grows
rapidly. Resources have been committed and a design framework has been
established. Change can cause upheaval that requires additional resources
and major design modification, i.e., additional cost. Changes in function,
performance, interfaces, or other characteristics during implementation
(code and test) can have a severe impact on cost. Change, when requested
late in a project, can be an order of magnitude more expensive than the
same change requested earlier.

1.4.3   Practitioner's Myths

Myths that are still believed by software practitioners have been fostered by four decades of programming culture. As we noted earlier in this chapter, during the early days
of software, programming was viewed as an art form. Old ways and attitudes die hard.

Myth: There really aren't any methods for analysis, design, and testing that work;
I will just go to my terminal and begin coding.

Reality: Proven methods for analysis, design, and testing (described in later chapters) are being used throughout the industry. None of them are foolproof,
but the use of a methodology for software development is available to all.

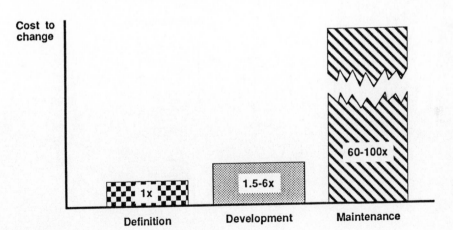

FIGURE 1.7
The impact of change.

Myth: Once we write the program and get it to work, our job is done.

Reality: Someone once said, "The sooner you begin 'writing code,' the longer it will take you to get done." Software development encompasses three generic activities (described in detail in Section 1.5): *definition, development,* and *maintenance*. In addition industry data [LIE80] indicate that between 50 and 70 percent of all effort expended on a program will be expended after it is delivered to the customer for the first time.

Myth: Until I get the program "running" I really have no way of assessing its quality.

Reality: One of the most effective software quality assurance mechanisms can be applied from the inception of a project—the *formal technical review*. Software review is a "quality filter" that has been found to be more effective than testing for finding certain classes of software defects.

Myth: The only deliverable for a successful project is the working program.

Reality: A working program is only one part of a *software configuration* that includes all elements illustrated in Figure 1.8. Documentation forms the foundation for successful development and, more importantly, provides guidance for the software maintenance task.

Myth: Once software is in use, maintenance is minimal and can be handled on a catch-as-catch-can basis.

Reality: A relatively small percentage of budget is allocated to maintenance, but to the dismay of many managers, over half of a budget is actually expended on maintenance [LIE80]. Therefore, software maintenance should be or-

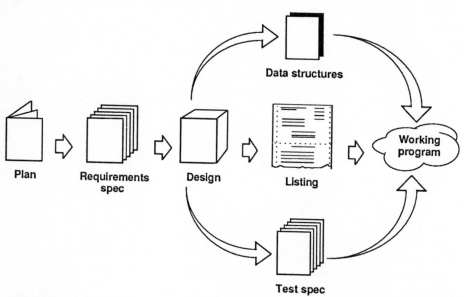

FIGURE 1.8
The software configuration.

ganized, planned, and controlled as if it were the largest project within an organization. It often is!

Many software professionals recognize the fallacy of the myths described above. Regrettably, habitual attitudes and methods foster poor management and technical practices even when reality dictates a better approach. Recognition of software realities is the first step toward formulation of practical solutions for software development.

1.5   SOFTWARE ENGINEERING PARADIGMS

The software crisis will not disappear overnight. Recognizing problems and their causes and debunking software myths are the first steps toward solutions. Then, the solutions themselves must provide practical assistance to the software developer, improve software quality, and finally, allow the "software world" to keep pace with the "hardware world."

There is no single best approach to a solution for the software crisis. However, by combining comprehensive methods for all phases in software development: better tools for automating these methods; more powerful building blocks for software implementation; better techniques for software quality assurance; and an overriding philosophy for coordination, control, and management, we can achieve a discipline for software development—a discipline called *software engineering*.

1.5.1   Software Engineering: A Definition

An early definition of software engineering was proposed by Fritz Bauer at the first major conference [NAU69] dedicated to the subject:

> The establishment and use of sound engineering principles in order to obtain economically software that is reliable and works efficiently on real machines.

Although many more comprehensive definitions have been proposed, all reinforce the importance of engineering discipline in software development.

Software engineering is an outgrowth of hardware and system engineering. It encompasses a set of three key elements—*methods, tools,* and *procedures*—that enable the manager to control the process of software development and provide the practitioner with a foundation for building high-quality software in a productive manner. In the paragraphs that follow, we briefly examine each of these elements.

Software engineering methods provide the technical "how to's" for building software. Methods encompass a broad array of tasks that include: project planning and estimation; system and software requirements analysis; design of data structure, program architecture, and algorithm procedure; coding; testing; and maintenance. Methods for software engineering often introduce a special language-oriented or graphical notation and a set of criteria for software quality.

Software engineering tools provide automated or semi-automated support for methods. Today, tools exist to support each of the methods noted above. When tools are integrated so that information created by one tool can be used by another, a system for the support of software development, called *computer-aided software engineering* (CASE), is established. CASE combines software, hardware, and a *software engineering data base* (a data structure containing important information about analysis, design, code, and testing) to create a software engineering environment (e.g., [HEN84]) analogous to CAD/CAE (computer-aided design/engineering) for hardware.

   Software engineering procedures are the glue that holds the methods and tools together and enables rational and timely development of computer software. Procedures define the sequence in which methods will be applied, the deliverables (documents, reports, forms, etc.) that are required, the controls that help assure quality and coordinate change, and the milestones that enable software managers to assess progress.

   Software engineering is composed of steps that encompass the methods, tools, and procedures discussed above. These steps are often referred to as *software engineering paradigms*. A paradigm for software engineering is chosen based on the nature of the project and application, the methods and tools to be used, and the controls and deliverables that are required. Three paradigms have been widely discussed (and debated) and are described in the following sections.

1.5.2   The Classic Life Cycle

Figure 1.9 illustrates the classic life cycle paradigm for software engineering. Sometimes called the ''waterfall model,'' the life cycle paradigm demands a systematic, sequential approach to software development that begins at the system level and progresses through analysis, design, coding, testing, and maintenance. Modeled after the conventional engineering cycle, the life cycle paradigm encompasses the following activities:

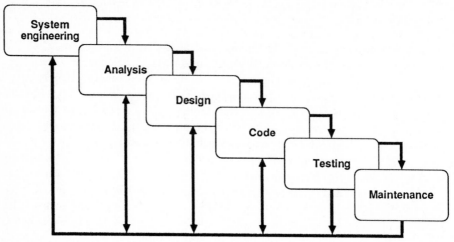

FIGURE 1.9
The classic life cycle.

System engineering and analysis. Because software is always part of a larger system, work begins by establishing requirements for all system elements and then allocating some subset of these requirements to software. This system view is essential when software must interface with other elements such as hardware, people, and data bases. System engineering and analysis encompass requirements gathering at the system level with a small amount of top-level design and analysis.

Software requirements analysis. The requirements gathering process is intensified and focuses specifically on software. To understand the nature of the program(s) to be built, the software engineer (''analyst'') must understand the information domain (described in Chapter 4) for the software, as well as required function, performance, and interfacing. Requirements for both the system and the software are documented and reviewed with the customer.

Design. Software design is actually a multistep process that focuses on three distinct attributes of the program: data structure, software architecture, and procedural detail. The design process translates requirements into a representation of the software that can be assessed for quality before coding begins. Like requirements, the design is documented and becomes part of the software configuration.

Coding. The design must be translated into a machine-readable form. The coding step performs this task. If design is performed in a detailed manner, coding can be accomplished mechanistically.

Testing. Once code has been generated, program testing begins. The testing process focuses on the logical internals of the software, assuring that all statements have been tested, and on the functional externals, that is, conducting tests to assure that defined input will produce actual results that agree with required results.

Maintenance. Software will undoubtedly undergo change after it is delivered to the customer (a possible exception is embedded software). Change will occur because errors have been encountered, because the software must be adapted to accommodate changes in its external environment (e.g., a change required because of a new operating system or peripheral device), or because the customer requires functional or performance enhancements. Software maintenance applies each of the preceding life cycle steps to an existing program rather than a new one.

The classic life cycle is the oldest and the most widely used paradigm for software engineering. However, over the past few years, criticism of the paradigm has caused even active supporters to question its applicability in all situations. Among the problems that are sometimes encountered when the classic life cycle paradigm is applied are:

1. Real projects rarely follow the sequential flow that the model proposes. Iteration always occurs and creates problems in the application of the paradigm.
2. It is often difficult in the beginning for the customer to state all requirements explicitly. The classic life cycle requires this and has difficulty accommodating the natural uncertainty that exists at the beginning of many projects.

3. The customer must have patience. A working version of the program(s) will not be available until late in the project time span. A major blunder undetected until the working program is reviewed can be disastrous.

Each of these problems is real. However, the classic life cycle paradigm has a definite and important place in software engineering work. It provides a template into which methods for analysis, design, coding, testing, and maintenance can be placed. In addition we shall see that the steps of the classic life cycle paradigm are very similar to the generic steps (Section 1.6) applicable to all software engineering paradigms. The classic life cycle remains the most widely used procedural model for software engineering. While it does have weaknesses, it is significantly better than a haphazard approach to software development.

1.5.3 Prototyping

Often a customer will define a set of general objectives for software, but will not identify detailed input, processing, or output requirements. In other cases the developer may be unsure of the efficiency of an algorithm, the adaptability of an operating system, or the form that human-machine interaction should take. In these and many other situations, a *prototyping* approach to software engineering may be best.

Prototyping is a process that enables the developer to create a model of the software to be built. The model can take one of three forms: a *paper prototype* that depicts human-machine interaction in a form that enables the user to understand how such interaction will occur, a *working prototype* that implements some subset of the function required of the desired software, or an existing program that performs part or all of the function desired but has other features to be improved upon in the new development effort.

The sequence of events for the prototyping paradigm is illustrated in Figure 1.10. Like all approaches to software development, prototyping begins with requirements gathering. Developer and customer meet and define the overall objectives for the software, identify whatever requirements are known, and outline areas where further definition is mandatory. A "quick design" then occurs. The quick design focuses on a representation of those aspects of the software visible to the user (e.g., input approaches and output formats). The quick design leads to the construction of a prototype. The prototype is evaluated by the customer/user and is used to refine requirements for the software to be developed. A process of iteration occurs as the prototype is "tuned" to satisfy the needs of the customer, while at the same time enabling the developer to understand better what needs to be done.

Ideally, the prototype serves as a mechanism for identifying software requirements. If a working prototype is built, the developer attempts to make use of existing program fragments or applies tools (e.g., report generators, window managers, etc.) that enable working programs to be generated quickly.

But what do we do with the prototype when it has served the purpose described above? Brooks [BRO75] provides an answer:

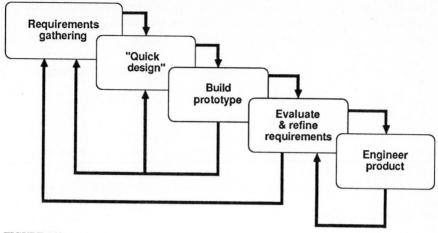

FIGURE 1.10
Prototyping.

In most projects, the first system built is barely usable. It may be too slow, too big, awkward in use, or all three. There is no alternative but to start again, smarting but smarter, and build a redesigned version in which these problems are solved....When a new system concept or new technology is used, one has to build a system to throw away, for even the best planning is not so omniscient as to get it right the first time.

The management question, therefore, is not whether to build a pilot system and throw it away. You *will* do that. The only question is whether to plan in advance to build a throwaway, or to promise to deliver the throwaway to customers....

The prototype can serve as "the first system"—the one Brooks recommends we throw away. But this may be an idealized view. Like the classic life cycle, prototyping as a paradigm for software engineering can be problematic for the following reasons:

1. The customer sees what appears to be a working version of the software, unaware that the prototype is held together "with chewing gum and baling wire," unaware that in the rush to get it working we haven't considered overall software quality or long term maintainability. When informed that the product must be rebuilt, the customer cries "foul" and demands that "a few fixes" be applied to make the prototype a working product. Too often software development management relents.

2. The developer often makes implementation compromises in order to get a prototype working quickly. An inappropriate operating system or programming language may be used simply because it is available and known; an inefficient algorithm may be implemented simply to demonstrate capability. After a time the developer may become familiar with these choices and forget the reasons why they were inappropriate. The less-than-ideal choice has now become an integral part of the system.

Although problems can occur, prototyping is an effective paradigm for software engineering. The key is to define the rules of the game at the beginning; that is, the customer and developer must both agree that the prototype is built to serve as a mechanism for defining requirements. It is then to be discarded (at least in part), and the actual software engineered with an eye toward quality and maintainability.

1.5.4   Fourth Generation Techniques

The term *fourth generation techniques* (4GT) encompasses a broad array of software tools that have one thing in common: each enables the software developer to specify some characteristic of software at a high level. The tool then automatically generates source code based on the developer's specification. There is little debate that the higher the level at which software can be specified to a machine, the faster a program can be built. The 4GT paradigm for software engineering focuses on the ability to specify software to a machine at a level that is close to natural language or in a notation that imparts significant function.

Currently, a software development environment supporting the 4GT paradigm includes some or all of the following tools: nonprocedural languages for data base query, report generation, data manipulation, screen interaction and definition, and code generation; high-level graphics capability; and spreadsheet capability. Each of these tools does exist, but only for very specific application domains. There is no 4GT environment available today that can be applied with equal facility to each of the software application categories described in Section 1.2.3.

The 4GT paradigm for software engineering is depicted in Figure 1.11. Like other paradigms, 4GT begins with a requirements gathering step. Ideally, the customer would describe requirements and these would be directly translated into an operational prototype; but this is unworkable. The customer may be unsure of what is required, may be ambiguous in specifying facts that are known, and may be unable or unwilling to specify information in a manner that a 4GT tool can consume. In addition current

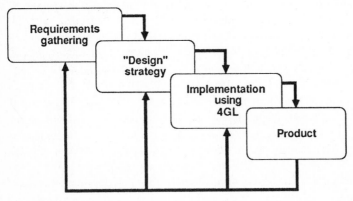

FIGURE 1.11
Fourth generation techniques.

4GT tools are not sophisticated enough to accommodate truly "natural" language and won't be for some time. At this time the customer-developer dialogue described for other paradigms remains an essential part of the 4GT approach.

For small applications, it may be possible to move directly from the requirements gathering step to implementation using a nonprocedural *fourth generation language* (4GL). However, for larger efforts it is necessary to develop a design strategy for the system, even if a 4GL is to be used. The use of 4GT without design (for large projects) will cause the same difficulties (poor quality, poor maintainability, poor customer acceptance) we have encountered in developing software using conventional approaches.

Implementation using a 4GL enables the software developer to describe desired results which are translated automatically into source code to produce those results. Obviously, a data structure with relevant information must exist and be readily accessible by the 4GL. A more detailed description of 4GL is contained in Chapter 11.

The last step in Figure 1.11 contains the word "product." To transform a 4GT implementation into a product, the developer must conduct thorough testing, develop meaningful documentation, and perform all other "transition activities" required in other software engineering paradigms. In addition the 4GT developed software must be built in a manner that enables maintenance to be performed expeditiously.

There has been much hyperbole and considerable debate surrounding the use of the 4GT paradigm (e.g., [COB85], [GRA85]). Proponents claim dramatic reductions in software development time and greatly improved productivity for people who build software. Opponents claim that current 4GT tools are not much easier to use than programming languages, that the source code produced by such tools is "inefficient," and that the maintainability of large software systems developed using 4GT is open to question.

There is some merit in the claims of both sides. Although it is somewhat difficult to separate fact from fancy (few controlled studies have been done to date), it is possible to summarize the current state of 4GT approaches:

1. With very few exceptions the current application domain for 4GT is limited to business information systems applications, specifically, information analysis and reporting keyed to large data bases. To date, 4GT has been used sparingly in the engineered products and systems application area.

2. Preliminary data collected from companies using 4GT seem to indicate that time required to produce software is greatly reduced for small and intermediate applications and that the amount of design and analysis for small applications is also reduced.

3. However, the use of 4GT for large software development efforts demands as much or more time for analysis, design, and testing (software engineering activities) thereby negating the substantial time saving achievable through the elimination of coding.

To summarize, fourth generation techniques are likely to become an increasingly important part of software development during the next decade. As Figure 1.12 illustrates, the demand for software will continue to escalate throughout the remainder of

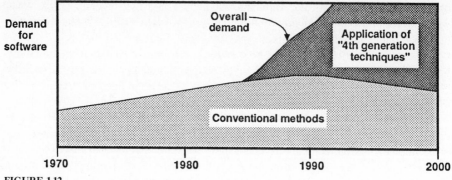

FIGURE 1.12
The changing nature of software.

this century, but conventional methods and paradigms are likely to contribute less and less to all software developed. Fourth generation techniques will fill the gap until fifth generation AI approaches are practical.

1.5.5 Combining Paradigms

The software engineering paradigms discussed in the preceding sections are often described as *alternative* approaches to software engineering rather than *complementary approaches*. In many cases the paradigms can and should be combined so the strengths of each can be utilized on a single project. An adversarial relationship need not exist!

Figure 1.13 illustrates how each of the three paradigms can be combined during a single software development effort. In all cases work begins with a requirements gathering step. The approach taken can follow the classic life cycle (system engineering and software requirements analysis) or can be the less formal problem definition used in prototyping. Regardless, customer-developer communication must occur.

The nature of the application will dictate the applicability of a prototyping approach. If the requirements for software function and performance are reasonably well

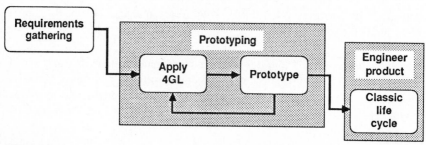

FIGURE 1.13
Combining paradigms.

understood, the specification approaches recommended by the classic life cycle paradigm may be applicable. On the other hand, if the software application demands heavy human-machine interaction or requires unproven algorithms or output/control techniques, a prototype may be in order. In such cases a 4GL can sometimes be used to develop the prototype rapidly. Once the prototype has been evaluated and refined, the design and implementation steps of the classic life cycle can be applied to engineer the software formally.

There is no need to be dogmatic about the choice of paradigms for software engineering; the nature of the application should dictate the approach to be taken. By combining approaches, the whole can be greater than the sum of the parts.

1.6 A GENERIC VIEW OF SOFTWARE ENGINEERING

The software development process contains three generic phases (Figure 1.14) regardless of the software engineering paradigm chosen. The three phases, *definition, development*, and *maintenance*, are encountered in all software development, regardless of application area, project size, or complexity.

The definition phase focuses on *what*. That is, during definition, the software developer attempts to identify what information is to be processed, what function and performance are desired, what interfaces are to be established, what design constraints exist, and what validation criteria are required to define a successful system. Thus, the key requirements of the system and the software are identified. Although the methods applied during the definition phase will vary depending upon the software engineering paradigm (or combination of paradigms) applied, three specific steps will occur in some form:

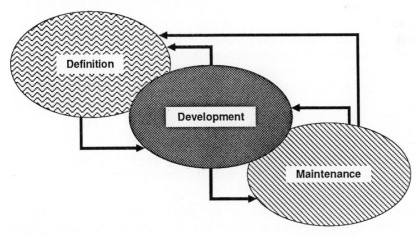

FIGURE 1.14
Paradigms: a generalized view.

System analysis. Already described in our discussion of the classic life cycle (Section 1.5.2), system analysis defines the role of each element in a computer-based system, ultimately allocating the role software will play.

Software project planning. Once the scope of the software is allocated, resources are allocated, costs are estimated, and work tasks and schedules are defined.

Requirements analysis. The scope defined for the software provides direction, but a more detailed definition of the information domain and function of the software is necessary before work can begin.

The development phase focuses on *how*. That is, during development, the software developer attempts to describe how data structure and software architecture are to be designed, how procedural details are to be implemented, how the design will be translated into a programming language (or nonprocedural language), and how testing will be performed. The methods applied during the development phase will vary depending upon the software engineering paradigm (or combination of paradigms) applied. However, three specific steps will occur in some form:

Software design. Design translates the requirements for the software into a set of representations (some graphical, others tabular or language-based) that describe data structure, architecture, and algorithmic procedure (each discussed in detail in Chapter 6).

Coding. Design representations must be translated into an artificial language (a conventional programming language or a nonprocedural language used in the context of the 4GT paradigm) that results in instructions executable by the computer. The coding step performs this translation.

Software testing. Once the software is implemented in machine-executable form, it must be tested to uncover defects in function, in logic, and in implementation.

The maintenance phase focuses on *change* that is associated with error correction, adaptations required as the software's environment evolves, and modifications due to enhancements brought about by changing customer requirements. The maintenance phase reapplies the steps of the definition and development phases, but does so in the context of existing software. Three types of change are encountered during the maintenance phase:

Correction. Even with the best quality assurance activities, it is likely that the customer will discover defects in the software. *Corrective maintenance* changes the software to correct defects.

Adaptation. Over time the original environment (e.g., CPU, operating system, peripherals) for which the software was developed is likely to change. *Adaptive maintenance* results in modification to the software to accommodate changes in its external environment.

Enhancement. As software is used, the customer/user will recognize additional functions that would provide benefit. *Perfective maintenance* extends the software beyond its original functional requirements.

The phases and related steps described in our generic view of software engineering are complemented by a number of *umbrella activities*. Reviews are conducted as each step is completed to assure that quality is maintained. Documentation is developed and controlled to assure that complete information about the system and software will be available for later use. Change control is instituted so that changes can be approved and tracked.

In the classic life cycle paradigm, the phases and steps described in this section are explicitly defined. In the prototyping and 4GT paradigms, some of the steps are implied but not explicitly identified. The approach to each step may vary from paradigm to paradigm, but an overall approach that demands definition, development, and maintenance remains invariant. One can conduct each phase with discipline and well-defined methods or muddle through each haphazardly. But they will need to be performed nonetheless. The remainder of this book is dedicated to a software development approach that emphasizes discipline and well-defined methods—an approach called *software engineering.*

1.7   SUMMARY

Software has become the key element in the evolution of computer-based systems and products. Over the past four decades software has evolved from a specialized problem solving and information analysis tool to an industry in itself. But early "programming" culture and history have created a set of problems that persist today. Software has become a limiting factor in the evolution of computer-based systems.

Software engineering is a discipline that integrates methods, tools, and procedures for the development of computer software. A number of different paradigms for software engineering have been proposed, each exhibiting strengths and weaknesses, but all have a series of generic phases in common. It is the steps of these generic phases and the methods that are applied in each step that make up the remainder of this book.

REFERENCES

[BIG84]   Biggerstaff, T. J., and A. J. Perlis (eds.), *Special Issue on Software Reusability, IEEE Trans. Software Engineering,* vol. SE-10, no. 5., September 1984.

[BRO75]   Brooks, F., *The Mythical Man-Month,* Addison-Wesley, 1975.

[COB85]   Cobb, R. H., "In Praise of 4GLs," *Datamation,* July 15, 1985, p. 92.

[FEI83]   Feigenbaum, E. A., and P. McCorduck, *The Fifth Generation,* Addison-Wesley, 1983.

[GRA85]   Grant, F. J., "The Downside of 4GLs," *Datamation,* July 15, 1985, pp. 99–104.

[HEN84]   Henderson, P. (ed.), *Software Engineering Symposium on Practical Software Development Environments, ACM Sigsoft Notes,* vol. 9, no. 3, May 1984.

[IAN84]   Iannino, A. et al., "Criteria for Software Reliability Model Comparisons," *IEEE Trans. Software Engineering*, vol. SE-10, no. 6, November 1984, pp. 687–691.

[LIE80]   Lientz, B., and E. Swanson, *Software Maintenance Management*, Addison-Wesley, 1980.

[MAN84]   Manley, J. H., "CASE: Foundation for Software Factories," *COMPCON Proceedings*, IEEE, September 1984, pp. 84–91.

[NAI82]   Naisbitt, J., *Megatrends*, Warner Books, 1982.

[NAU69]   Naur, P., and B. Randell (eds.), *Software Engineering: A Report on a Conference sponsored by the NATO Science Committee*, NATO, 1969.

[OSB79]   Osborne, A., *Running Wild—The Next Industrial Revolution*, Osborne/McGraw-Hill, 1979.

[TAJ84]   Tajima, D., and T. Matsubara, "Inside the Japanese Software Factory," *Computer*, vol. 17, no. 3, March 1984, pp. 34–43.

[TOF80]   Toffler, A., *The Third Wave*, Morrow Publishers, 1980.

[WAT85]   Waterman, D. A., *A Guide to Expert Systems*, Addison-Wesley, 1985.

[WIN83]   Winograd, T., *Language as a Cognitive Process*, Addison-Wesley, 1983.

PROBLEMS AND POINTS TO PONDER

1.1 Software is the differentiating characteristic in many computer-based products and systems. Provide examples of two or three products and at least one system in which software, not hardware, is the differentiating element.

1.2 In the 1950s and 1960s computer programming was an art form learned in an apprentice-like environment. How has this affected software development practices today?

1.3 Toffler [TOF80] and Naisbitt [NAI82] have discussed the impact of the "information era." Provide a number of examples (both positive and negative) that indicate the impact of software on our society.

1.4 Research the early history of software engineering starting with early papers on program design and continuing with attempts to develop a broader methodology. Write a paper on a topic of interest.

1.5 The myths described in this chapter are only the tip of the iceberg. List additional myths for each of the categories presented in Section 1.4.

1.6 Computer-aided software engineering (CASE) is a growing industry. Research three commercially available CASE products and provide a comparison using criteria that you develop. Revisit this problem after you've read the remaining chapters.

1.7 Which of the software engineering paradigms presented in this chapter would be most useful for your software applications? Why?

1.8 Provide five examples of software development projects amenable to prototyping. Name two or three applications more difficult to prototype.

1.9 Develop a paper prototype for a video game of your own invention.

1.10 Research two or three 4GLs and present a summary discussion. How broad is their applicability?

1.11 Many people argue that the term "maintenance" is incorrectly applied to software—that the activities associated with software maintenance aren't "maintenance" at all. What do you think?

1.12 Is there ever a case when the generic phases of the software engineering process don't apply? If so, describe it.

FURTHER READINGS

The current state of the art in software engineering can best be determined from monthly publications such as *IEEE Software, Computer,* and the *IEEE Transactions on Software Engineering*. The discipline is ''summarized'' every 18 months in the *Proceedings of the International Conference on Software Engineering*, sponsored by the IEEE and ACM.

A book by Werner Frank (*Critical Issues in Software*, Wiley-Interscience, 1983) presents a useful management guide to the economics of software development, software engineering strategies and software as it relates to business profitability. A recent feature in *Fortune* magazine (''A Growing Gap in Software,'' April 28, 1986) has done much to raise the consciousness of senior business managers.

The United States government has created a *Software Engineering Institute* (located at Carnegie-Mellon University) that has been chartered with the responsibility of sponsoring a software engineering monograph series. Practitioners from industry, government, and academia are contributing important new work.

Handbooks on software engineering have been published by McGraw-Hill and Van Nostrand Reinhold. The McGraw-Hill handbook (1986) was developed by General Electric Company and contains excellent descriptions of software documentation and standards. The Van Nostrand Reinhold handbook (1984) contains contributed chapters on many important topics that relate to software engineering.

CHAPTER
2

COMPUTER
SYSTEM
ENGINEERING

Four hundred and fifty years ago, Machiavelli said:

> ...there is nothing more difficult to take in hand, more perilous to conduct or more uncertain in its success, than to take the lead in the introduction of a new order of things....

During the last two decades of the twentieth century, computer-based systems are introducing a new order. Although technology has made great strides since Machiavelli spoke, his words continue to ring true.

Software engineering and hardware engineering fall within the broader category that we shall call *computer system engineering*. Each of these disciplines represents an attempt to bring order to the development of computer-based systems. Engineering techniques for computer hardware grew out of electronic design and have reached a state of relative maturity. Hardware design techniques are well-established, manufacturing methods are continually improved, and reliability is a realistic expectation rather than a modest hope.

Unfortunately, computer software still suffers from the Machiavellian description stated above. In computer-based systems software has replaced hardware as the system element most difficult to plan, least likely to succeed (on time and within cost), and most dangerous to manage. Yet the demand for software continues unabated as computer-based systems grow in number, complexity, and application.

Engineering techniques for producing computer software have only recently gained widespread acceptance. In the first chapter we discussed the evolution of a software culture that viewed computer programming as an art form. No engineering precedent existed and no engineering approach was applied. Times are changing!

2.1   COMPUTER-BASED SYSTEMS

The word *system* is possibly the most overused and abused term in the technical lexicon. We speak of political systems and educational systems, of avionics systems and manufacturing systems, of banking systems and subway systems. The word tells us little. We use the adjective describing *system* to understand the context in which the word is used. *Webster's Dictionary* defines *system* in the following way:

> ...1. a set or arrangement of things so related as to form a unity or organic whole; 2. a set of facts, principles, rules, etc., classified and arranged in an orderly form so as to show a logical plan linking the various parts; 3. a method or plan of classification or arrangement; 4. an established way of doing something; method; procedure....

Five additional definitions are provided in the dictionary, yet no precise synonym is suggested. *System* is a special word.

Borrowing from Webster's definition above, we define a *computer-based system* as:

> A set or arrangement of elements organized to accomplish some method, procedure, or control by processing information.

The elements of a computer-based system are depicted in Figure 2.1 and include the following:

Software. Computer programs, data structures, and related documentation that serve to effect the logical method, procedure, or control required.

Hardware. Electronic devices (e.g., CPU, memory) that provide computing capa-

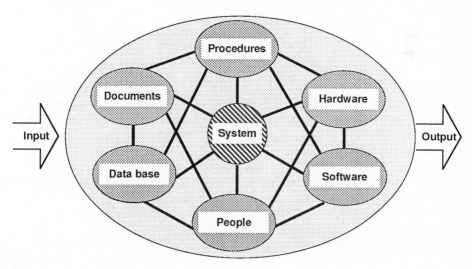

FIGURE 2.1
The elements.

bility, and electromechanical devices (e.g., sensors, motors, pumps) that provide external world function.

People. Individuals that are users and operators of hardware and software.

Data Base. A large, organized collection of information that is accessed via software and is an integral part of system function.

Documentation. Manuals, forms, and other descriptive information that portray the use and/or operation of the system.

Procedures. The steps that define the specific use of each system element or the procedural context in which the system resides.

One complicating characteristic of computer-based systems is that the elements composing one system may also represent one macro element of a still larger system. A *macro element* is a computer-based system that is one part of a larger computer-based system. As an example we consider a factory automation system, which is essentially the hierarchy of systems shown in Figure 2.2. At the lowest level of the hierarchy we have numerical control (NC) machines, robots, and data entry devices. Each is a computer-based system in its own right. The elements of the NC machines include electronic and electromechanical hardware (e.g., processor and memory, motors, sensors); software (for communications, machine control, interpolation); people (the machine operator); a data base (the stored NC program); documentation and procedures. A similar decomposition could be applied to the robots and data entry devices. Each is a computer-based system.

At the next level in the hierarchy, a *manufacturing cell* is defined. The manufacturing cell is a computer-based system possibly having elements of its own as well as integrating the macro elements NC machines, robots, and data entry devices.

To summarize, the manufacturing cell and its macro elements are each composed of system elements with the following generic labels: software, hardware, people, data

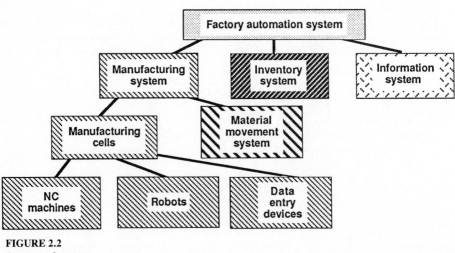

FIGURE 2.2
A system of systems.

base, procedures, and documentation. In some cases macro elements may share a generic element. For example the robot and the NC machine both might be managed by a single operator (the people element). In other cases generic elements are exclusive to one system.

The role of the system engineer (or system analyst) is to define the elements for a specific computer-based system in the context of the overall hierarchy of systems (macro elements). In the sections that follow, we examine the tasks that constitute computer system engineering.

2.2 COMPUTER SYSTEM ENGINEERING

Computer system engineering[*] is a problem-solving activity. Desired system functions are uncovered, analyzed, and allocated to individual system elements. The computer system engineer (called a *system analyst* in some application domains) begins with customer defined goals and constraints and derives a representation of function, performance, interfaces, design constraints, and information structure that can be allocated to each of the generic system elements described in the preceding section.

The genesis of most new systems begins with a rather nebulous concept of desired function. Therefore, the system engineer must *bound* the system by identifying the desired scope of function and performance. For example, it is not enough to say that the control software for the robot in the manufacturing automation system (discussed in Section 2.1) will ''respond rapidly if a parts tray is empty.'' The system engineer must define (1) what indicates an empty tray to the robot; (2) the precise time bounds (in seconds) in which software response is expected; and (3) what form the response must take.

Once function, performance, constraint, and interfaces are bounded, the system engineer moves on to the task called *allocation*. During allocation, function is assigned to one or more generic system elements (i.e., software, hardware, people, etc.). Often alternative allocations are proposed and evaluated.

To illustrate the process of allocation, we consider another macro element of the factory automation system—a conveyor line sorting system (CLSS). The system engineer is presented with the following (somewhat nebulous) statement of objectives for CLSS:

> CLSS must be developed such that boxes moving along a conveyor line will be identified and sorted into one of six bins at the end of the line. The boxes will pass by a sorting station where they will be identified. Based on an identification number printed on the side of the box (an equivalent bar code is provided), the

---

[*] The terms *computer system engineering* and *computer engineering* should not be confused. Computer engineering focuses exclusively on the design and implementation of computer hardware and its associated system software, while computer system engineering is applied to all products and systems that contain computers.

boxes will be shunted into the appropriate bins. Boxes pass in random order and are evenly spaced. The line is moving slowly.

CLSS is depicted schematically in Figure 2.3. Before continuing, make a list of questions that you would ask if you were the system engineer.
Among the many questions that should be asked and answered are the following:

1. How many different identification numbers must be processed and what is their form?
2. What is the speed of the conveyor line in feet/sec and what is the distance between boxes in feet?
3. How far is the sorting station from the bins?
4. How far apart are the bins?
5. What should happen if a box doesn't have an identification number or an incorrect number is present?
6. What happens when a bin fills to capacity?
7. Is information about box destination and bin contents to be passed elsewhere in the factory automation system? Is real-time data acquisition required?
8. What error/failure rate is acceptable?
9. What pieces of the conveyor line system currently exist and are operational?
10. What schedule and budgetary constraints are imposed?

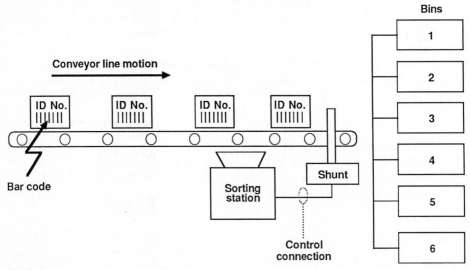

FIGURE 2.3
Example—a conveyor line sorting system.

Note that the above questions focus on function, performance, and information flow and content. The system engineer does not ask the customer *how* the task is to be done; instead, the engineer asks *what* is required.

Assuming reasonable answers, the system engineer develops a number of alternative allocations. Note that function and performance are assigned to different generic system elements in each allocation.

> **Allocation 1.** A sorting operator is trained and placed at the sorting station. He/she reads the box and places it into an appropriate bin.

Allocation 1 represents a purely manual (but nevertheless, effective) solution to the CLSS problem. The primary system element is people (the sorting operator). The person performs all sorting functions. Some documentation may be required in the form of a table relating identification number to bin location and a procedural description for operator training. Therefore, this allocation uses only the people and documentation elements.

> **Allocation 2.** A bar code reader and controller are placed at the sorting station. Bar code output passes to a programmable controller that controls a mechanical shunting mechanism. The shunt slides the box to the appropriate bin.

For allocation 2 hardware (bar code reader, programmable control, shunt hardware, etc.), software (for the bar code reader and programmable controller), and data base (a lookup table that relates box ID to bin location) elements are used to provide a fully automated solution. Any of these system elements may have corresponding manuals and other documentation, adding another generic system element.

> **Allocation 3.** A bar code reader and controller are placed at the sorting station. Bar code output passes to a robot arm that grasps a box and moves it to the appropriate bin location.

Allocation 3 makes use of generic system elements and one macro element—the robot. Like allocation 2, this allocation uses hardware, software, a data base, and documentation as generic elements. The robot is a macro element of CLSS and itself contains a set of generic system elements.

By examining the three alternative allocations for CLSS, it should be obvious that the same function can be allocated to different system elements. In order to choose the most effective allocation, a set of trade-off criteria should be applied to each alternative.

The following trade-off criteria govern the selection of a system configuration based on specific allocation of function and performance to generic system elements:

Project considerations. Can the configuration be built within pre-established cost and schedule bounds? What is the risk associated with cost and schedule estimates?

Business considerations. Does the configuration represent the most profitable solution? Can it be marketed successfully? Will ultimate payoff justify development risk?

Technical analysis. Does the technology exist to develop all elements of the system? Are function and performance assured? Can the configuration be adequately maintained? Do technical resources exist? What is the risk associated with the technology?

Manufacturing evaluation. Are manufacturing facilities and equipment available? Is there a shortage of necessary components? Can quality assurance be adequately performed?

Human issues. Are trained personnel available for development and manufacture? Do political problems exist? Does the customer understand what the system is to accomplish?

Environmental interfaces. Does the proposed configuration properly interface with the system's external environment? Are machine-to-machine and human-to-machine communication handled in an intelligent manner?

Legal considerations. Does this configuration introduce undue liability risk? Can proprietary aspects be adequately protected? Is there potential infringement?

We examine some of these issues in more detail later in this chapter.

It is important to note that the system engineer should also consider off-the-shelf solutions to the customer's problem. Does an equivalent system already exist? Can major parts of a solution be purchased from a third party?

The application of trade-off criteria results in the selection of a specific system configuration and the specification of function and performance allocated to hardware, software (and firmware), people, data bases, documentation, and procedures. Essentially, the scope of function and performance is allocated to each system element. The role of hardware engineering, software engineering, human engineering, and data base engineering is to refine scope and produce an operational system element that can be properly integrated with other system elements.

2.3   HARDWARE CONSIDERATIONS

Computer system engineering always allocates one or more system functions to computer hardware. In the following paragraphs, basic hardware components and applications are discussed. In addition, an overview of hardware engineering is presented.

2.3.1   The Hardware Element

The computer system engineer selects some combination of hardware components that make up one element of the computer-based system. Hardware selection, although by no means simple, is aided by a number of characteristics: (1) components are packaged as individual building blocks; (2) interfaces among components are standardized; (3) numerous off-the-shelf alternatives are available; and (4) performance, cost and availability are relatively easy to determine.

A hardware configuration evolves from the "building blocks" shown in Figure 2.4. Discrete components (i.e., integrated circuits and electronic components such as

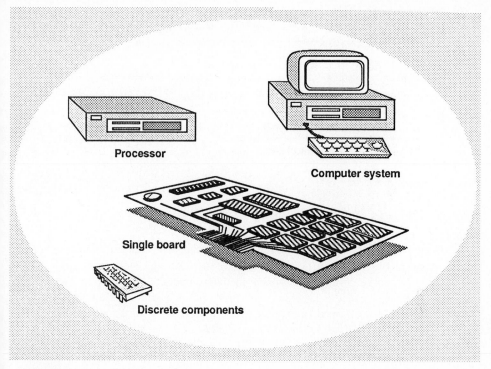

FIGURE 2.4
The hardware configuration.

resistors, capacitors, etc.) are assembled as a printed circuit (PC) board that performs a specific set of operations. Boards are interconnected to form system components (e.g., the processor and support chips, memory) that in turn are integrated into a hardware subsystem or system element. As very large scale integration (VLSI) becomes commonplace, functions once available on a set of PC boards with dozens of integrated circuits are now available on a single chip.

A complete discussion of hardware configuration is beyond the scope of this book and may be found in one of many references (e.g., [SEI82], [ZIS84]). For those readers who are unfamiliar with the subject, we shall briefly examine some of the more important elements of a hardware configuration.

The basic elements of a hardware configuration are found in all computer systems. The architecture of these elements, e.g., the manner in which the elements are organized and the communication paths among them, varies greatly. Figure 2.5 illustrates a simple hardware architecture. The *central processing unit* (CPU) performs arithmetic, logical, and control functions and interacts with other hardware components. Today, many architectures incorporate co-processors that perform specialized processing functions, thereby improving the perceived performance of the CPU. Elements of the architecture are interconnected by ''buses,'' communication paths that transmit instructions, data, and control information. It should be noted that a number

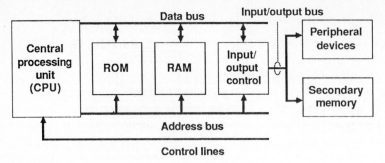

FIGURE 2.5
Typical hardware architecture.

of alternative machine architectures have been proposed (e.g., [MAR85], [SRI85]) and are being investigated for the "next generation."

Memory provides a storage medium for instructions and data and is accessed (directly or indirectly) via instructions executed by the CPU and its co-processors. Primary memory can be defined as a storage medium directly addressable by the CPU. *Random-access* (also called read-write) *memory* (RAM) is essential for all applications in which data are transformed and stored. Modern processors can address millions of bytes of primary memory. *Read-only memory* (ROM), as its name implies, can only be read by the CPU. Often called *firmware*, ROM is manufactured with instructions and/or data permanently (and unalterably) inscribed and maintains this information in the absence of electrical power. Other forms of read-only memory (e.g. PROM and EPROM) can be programmed using a relatively low-cost microprocessor development system. ROM is used extensively in consumer products, personal computers, and other microprocessor applications.

Secondary memory is a storage medium that has slower access time and greater capacity than primary memory. The most common secondary memory device is a rotating magnetic medium called a disk. Information access times for disks are typically in the millisecond range and capacity ranges from 400,000 bytes (low-capacity floppy disks) to over 1 billion bytes (large-capacity mainframe systems). Compact disk technologies, using optical rather than magnetic storage techniques, may offer the next step in low-cost, high-capacity secondary memory. Magnetic tape, the oldest form of secondary information storage, continues to be used as a relatively slow but inexpensive archival storage medium.

Selection of the memory component for a computer-based system can make or break both function and performance. Computer system engineers frequently err by specifying too little primary and/or secondary memory. The common penalties for insufficient memory are reduced function, poor performance, and very costly software. Because memory costs are decreasing rapidly, there is no legitimate excuse for under-specifying memory capacity for computer-based systems produced in small numbers. Issues associated with high-volume products are discussed later in this chapter.

Communications between the CPU and the outside world are handled by I/O or interface hardware. Among its many functions interface hardware accommodates specific communication protocol between I/O devices (peripherals) and the CPU; controls information transfer rates that may range from 10 to hundreds of thousands of characters (bytes) per second; satisfies interface standards (e.g., RS-232C, IEEE-488) for multivendor configurations; manages local-area network interfacing; and communicates directly with other system components.

Proper definition of interfaces is a key to successful computer system engineering. Selection of appropriate interface hardware has direct impact on ease of system integration, simplicity of I/O software, and efficiency of communication between the processor and the outside world.

2.3.2 Hardware Applications

During the first four decades of the computing era, discussions of computer hardware focused on the size of the machine. Today, the distinction between so-called mainframe, mini, and microcomputers is beginning to disappear, although the terminology is maintained for marketing purposes. Rather than attempting to categorize hardware by size, we consider computer hardware in the context of its application area. Applications for computer hardware may be divided into three broad categories: information processing, process-control and real-time applications, and embedded intelligence.

The vast majority of computer-based systems continue to apply hardware as a stand-alone information processor. Information is fed into the ''computer system''; analysis or transformation occurs; other information may be acquired; and results are produced. Primary input almost always originates from people and output is formatted for people. Specific applications include commercial data processing, engineering analysis and data base management, and a wide array of personal computer processing.

A process-control/real-time application integrates hardware as a mechanism for monitoring and control of real-world events. The hardware monitors process parameters and, using heuristics normally implemented in software, invokes analysis, control, or reporting. Monitoring is characterized by machine or transducer input. The hardware continuously monitors a process (transducer input), and produces control commands for the process (feedback control), while at the same time accepting data from human operators and supplying information to them. Typical process-control/real-time applications are exemplified by automated manufacturing (e.g., steel mills, petroleum refineries, chemical processing), system and instrumentation control, and real-time data analysis and reporting. It should be noted that computer hardware can be geographically separated from other system components in process-control/real-time applications.

A system has ''embedded intelligence'' when computer hardware is packaged within a larger product. Nearly all products that contain microprocessor hardware have embedded intelligence. Other applications include on-board flight control systems for aircraft, various weapons systems, consumer and industrial electronics, and automotive applications. In many cases, an embedded application takes on many real-time characteristics. Unlike more conventional computer hardware applications, the computer does not sit behind glass walls in an air-conditioned room; it is fully integrated with the rest of the product (system), going where the product goes and enduring the same environmental conditions (e.g., heat, humidity, and vibration).

2.3.3 Hardware Engineering

Hardware engineering for digital computers grew from precedents established by decades of electronic design. The hardware engineering process can be viewed in three phases: planning and specification; design and prototype implementation; and manufacturing, distribution, and field service. The phases are illustrated in Figure 2.6a, b, and c.

Once system engineering (system analysis and definition) has been conducted, functions are allocated to hardware. The first phase of hardware engineering (Figure 2.6a) includes *development planning* and *hardware requirements analysis*. Development planning is conducted to establish the scope of the hardware effort. That is, we ask the following questions:

- What classes of hardware best address the specified functions?
- What hardware is available for purchase; what are the sources, availability, and cost?
- What kinds of interfacing are required?
- What do we have to design and build; what are the potential problems and required resources?

From these questions and others, preliminary cost and schedule estimates for the hardware system element are established. These estimates are reviewed by appropriate managers and technical staff and modified if necessary.

Next we must establish a "road map" for hardware design and implementation. Hardware requirements analysis is conducted to specify precise functional, performance, and interface requirements for all components of the hardware element. In addition design constraints (e.g., size, environment) and test criteria are established. A *Hardware Specification* is often produced. Review and modification are to be encouraged at this stage.

The popular image of "shirt-sleeve" engineering is characterized by the second phase (Figure 2.6b). Requirements are analyzed, and a preliminary hardware configuration is designed. Technical reviews are conducted as the design evolves toward detailed engineering drawings (a design specification). Off-the-shelf components are acquired, custom components are built, and a prototype is assembled. The prototype is tested to assure that it meets all requirements.

The prototype often bears little resemblance to the manufactured product. Therefore, manufacturing specifications are derived. Breadboards become PC boards; EPROM or PROM become ROM; new packaging is designed; tooling and equipment are defined. Emphasis shifts from function and performance to ease of manufacture.

The third phase of hardware engineering makes few direct demands on the design engineer but does tax the abilities of the manufacturing engineer. Before production begins, quality assurance methods must be established, and a product distribution mechanism must be defined. Spare parts are placed in inventory and a field service or-

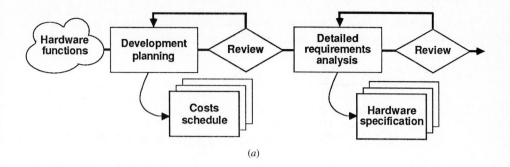

(a)

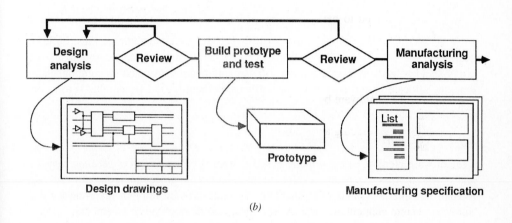

(b)

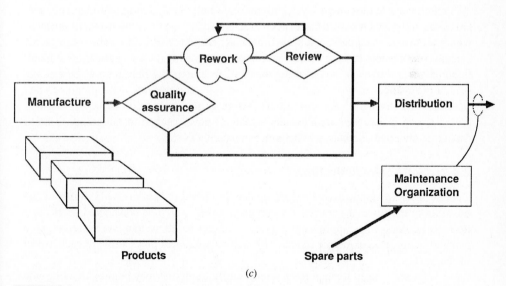

(c)

FIGURE 2.6
Hardware engineering (*a*) Phase I. (*b*) Phase II. (*c*) Phase III.

ganization is established for product maintenance and repair. The manufacturing phase of hardware engineering is illustrated in Figure 2.6c.

2.4 SOFTWARE CONSIDERATIONS

The characteristics of software and software engineering have been discussed in detail in Chapter 1. In this section we summarize our earlier discussion in the context of computer system engineering.

Function and performance are allocated to software during system engineering. In some cases function is simply the implementation of a sequential procedure for data manipulation; performance is not explicitly defined. In other cases function is the internal coordination and control of other concurrent programs, and performance is defined explicitly in terms of response and wait times.

To accommodate function and performance the software engineer must build or acquire a set of software components. Unlike hardware, software components are rarely standardized. In most cases the software engineer creates custom components to meet the allocated requirements of the software element for the system that is to be developed.

2.4.1 The Software Element

The software element of a computer-based system is composed of *application software* and *system software*. Application software implements the procedure required to accommodate information-processing functions. System software implements control functions that enable application software to interface with other system elements.

In Chapter 1 we described software as programs, data structures, and supporting documentation. At the lowest level, programs are built using a programming language. However, in many cases software is constructed from a set of components or *modules*, which perform some specific subfunction (e.g., sorting, matrix inversion, string concatenation). In most cases a module must be custom-built for the application at hand. In some cases, however, modules are acquired from existing libraries for reuse. Data structures (also called *data objects*) are also software components. Like modules, data structures are normally custom-built. However, a new generation of object-oriented programming languages (see Chapters 9 and 11) have resulted in the ability to build data structures in a manner that encourages reuse [COX85].

2.4.2 Software Applications

Generic software application areas have been described in Section 1.2.3. Software application in the broader context of a computer-based system is considered in this section. Regardless of its application area, a computer-based system can be represented using an input-process-output model. This software element plays a role in each aspect of the model.

Software is used to acquire incoming information that may be provided by some external source or by another system element (including macro elements). When a computer-based system requires an interactive human-machine interface, software implements the I/O "conversation." Prompting and data input mechanisms are implemented in software, displays and graphics are generated with software, and the logic that leads the user through the sequence of interactive steps is accomplished through software. When data are acquired from a device, software in the form of *drivers* accommodates the special characteristics of the hardware. Finally, software is used to establish interface to data bases, enabling a program to tap pre-existing data sources.

Software implements processing algorithms that are required to accomplish system function. In general a processing algorithm transforms input data and produces information or control for output to another system element or macro element. Today, the most common type of processing is the numerical or nonnumerical procedure in which all steps, loops, and conditions are predefined. However, a new category of processing algorithms, often called *expert system software*, is being introduced into some computer-based systems. Unlike conventional algorithms, expert systems software makes use of specified facts and rules for inference, enabling the software to exhibit human-like diagnostic abilities in a limited problem domain. Figure 2.7 [FOR84] illustrates the overall structure of an expert system.

To be of practical use in a computer-based system, software must output information or control to another system element or external source. To produce output, software must format data in a manner amenable to the output medium and then interface with the output device (e.g., printer, optical disc, CRT).

2.4.3   Software Engineering

Software engineering is a discipline for developing high-quality software for computer-based systems. In Chapter 1 we discussed software engineering in some detail and

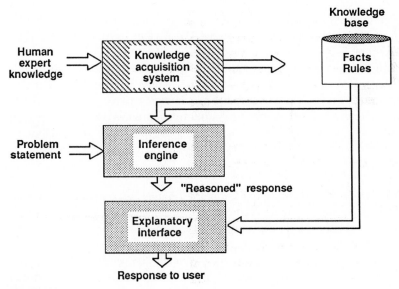

FIGURE 2.7
Typical expert system structure.

identified three software engineering paradigms—the classic life cycle, prototyping, and fourth generation techniques. Each is distinct, yet all have three phases in common. Like hardware, software is first defined, then developed, and finally maintained.

Figures 2.8, 2.9, and 2.10 illustrate the generic steps in the software engineering process. The figures illustrate the steps that must be accomplished and the various representations of software that are derived as it evolves from concept to realization.

DEFINITION PHASE. As we have already noted, software is always part of a larger computer-based system. Therefore, system engineering must occur prior to (or in conjunction with) software planning. System functions are to be allocated to software.

The definition phase of software engineering, depicted in Figure 2.8, begins with the software planning step. During this step a bounded description of the scope of software effort is developed; resources required to develop the software are predicted; cost and schedule estimates are established. The purpose of the software planning step is to provide a preliminary indication of project viability in relationship to cost and schedule constraints that may have already been established. A *Software Plan* is produced and reviewed by project management.

The next step in the definition phase is software requirements analysis and definition. During this step the system element allocated to software is defined in detail. Requirements are analyzed and defined in one of two ways. Formal information domain analysis may be used to establish representation of information flow and structure. These representations are then expanded to become a software specification. Alternatively, a prototype of the software is built and evaluated by the customer in an attempt to solidify requirements. Performance requirements or resource limitations are translated into software design characteristics. Global analysis of the software element defines validation criteria that will be used to demonstrate that requirements have been met.

Software requirements analysis and definition is a joint effort conducted by the software developer and the customer. A *Software Requirements Specification* is the deliverable document produced as a result of this step.

The definition phase culminates with a technical review of the *Software Requirements Specification* (or, in lieu of the specification, a software prototype) by the developer and the customer. Once acceptable requirements have been defined, the *Software Plan* is re-evaluated for correctness. Information uncovered during requirements analysis may impact estimates made during the planning. Deliverables developed during the definition phase serve as the foundation for the second phase in the process—software development.

DEVELOPMENT PHASE. The development phase (Figure 2.9) translates a set of requirements into an operational system element that we call software. At early stages of development a hardware engineer does not reach for a soldering iron: the software engineer should not reach for a compiler. Design must be accomplished first.

The first step of the development phase concentrates on design. The design process for software begins with a description of architectural and data design. That is, a modular structure is developed, interfaces are defined, and data structure is estab-

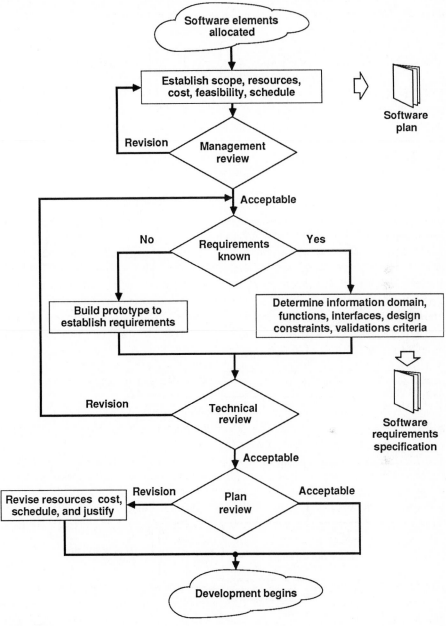

FIGURE 2.8
The definition phase.

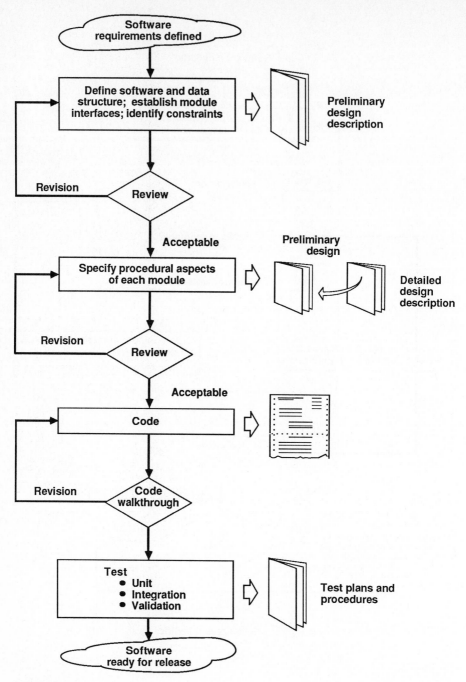

FIGURE 2.9
The development phase.

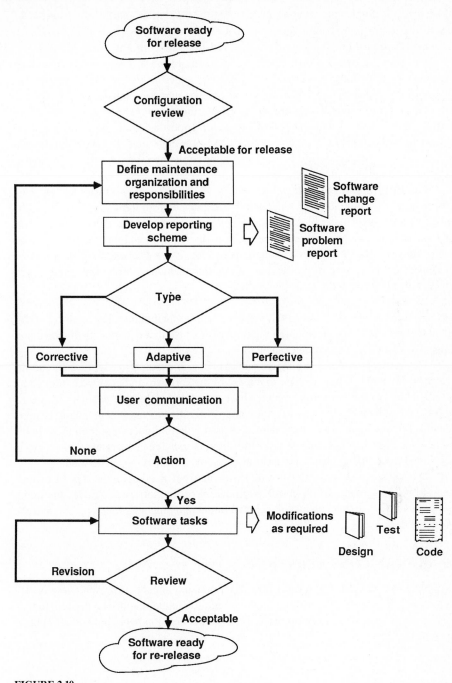

FIGURE 2.10
The maintenance phase.

lished. Design criteria are used to assess quality. This preliminary design step is reviewed for completeness and traceability to software requirements. A first draft *Design Document* [*] is delivered and becomes part of the software configuration.

Procedural aspects of each modular component of the software design are considered next. Each detailed procedural description is added to the *Design Document* after review. Finally, after design has been conducted, we come to coding, i.e., the generation of a program using an appropriate programming language. Software engineering methodology views coding as a consequence of good design. Code is reviewed for style and clarity but should otherwise be directly traceable to a detail design description. A source language listing for each modular component of software is the configuration deliverable for the coding step.

The final three steps of development are associated with software testing. Unit testing attempts to validate the functional performance of an individual modular component of software. Integration testing provides a means for the construction of the software architecture while at the same time testing function and interfaces. Validation testing verifies that all requirements have been met. A *Test Plan and Procedure* may be developed for the testing steps. Review of test documentation, test cases, and test results is always conducted.

MAINTENANCE PHASE. Nontrivial software will be maintained. Recognition of this fact is the first step toward lessening the impact of a task that devours 50–70 percent of budget for many large software organizations.

The software engineering maintenanc phase, illustrated in Figure 2.10 and described in Chapter 15, begins prior to release of the software and continues throughout its useful life. During software maintenance errors are corrected, adaptations are effected, and enhancements are implemented. After the development phase is completed, a *configuration review* is conducted to assure that all documentation is available and adequate for the maintenance tasks to follow. A maintenance organization is established, and a reporting scheme for error and system modifications is defined.

The tasks associated with software maintenance depend upon the type of maintenance to be performed. In all cases modification of the software includes the entire configuration (i.e., all documents developed in the planning and development phases), not just code.

2.5   HUMAN CONSIDERATIONS

A computer-based system almost always has a human element. A person may directly interact with hardware and software, conducting a dialogue that drives the function of the system; in all cases people are responsible for the development, support, or maintenance of the system.

---

[*]Today, a design document can be created with specialized software design tools (e.g., Nastec's *DesignAid*) and maintained in machine-readable form. In some cases design documentation, called *program design language*, is embedded directly into source code files.

Our perception of the human element in computer-based systems has changed in recent years. Early computer-based systems forced the user to communicate in ways easy to implement in hardware and software (if not always easy to understand in the human context). Today the phrase "user friendly" has taken on new meaning. Human engineering for computer-based systems is regarded as an important step in system development.

2.5.1 The Human Element

When people interact with others, a culturally defined set of rules, queues, and responses allows the interaction to proceed smoothly. Unfortunately, the conventions for person-to-person interaction are not present when human-machine interaction (HMI) is attempted.

Before a system engineer can allocate function to the human element, the interaction necessary to perform function must be specified. To do this, the "components" of the human element should be understood. Among many components that make up the human element are: human memory and knowledge representation, thinking and reasoning, visual perception, and human dialogue construction. A complete discussion of these topics is beyond the scope of this text (for more details, see [MON84]). However, a brief overview will aid our understanding of human engineering.

Human memory is crucial to HMI. A system user may have to remember commands, operating sequences, alternatives, error situations, and other arcane data. Human memory is itself a system that is currently believed to comprise *short-term memory* (STM) and *long-term memory* (LTM) [KLA80]. Sensory input (visual, auditory, tactile) enters a "buffer" and is then stored in STM where it can be reused immediately. The buffer's size and the length of time during which reuse can occur are limited. Knowledge is maintained in LTM and forms the basis for our learned response when HMI is conducted. Both semantic and syntactic information (knowledge) are stored in LTM. If the system engineer specifies a human-machine interface that makes undue demands on STM and/or LTM, the performance of the human element in the system will be degraded.

Most people do not apply formal inductive or deductive reasoning when confronted with a problem. Rather, we apply a set of heuristics (guidelines, rules, and strategies) based on our understanding of similar problems (see [GIL82]). In fact the heuristics we use tend to be domain-specific. That is, identical problems, encountered in entirely different contexts, might be solved by applying different heuristics. An HMI should be specified in a manner enabling the human to develop heuristics for interaction. In general these heuristics should remain consistent across different interaction domains.

Most HMI is accomplished through a visual medium (e.g., printed reports or graphics, CRT displays). To specify visual interaction properly, the system engineer should understand both the physical and cognitive constraints associated with visual perception. The eye and brain work together to receive and interpret visual information in terms of size, shape, color, orientation, movement, and other characteristics. Visual communication has a "parallel" quality: many discrete information items are presented simultaneously. Proper specification of visual communication is a key element of a user-friendly interface.

In addition to the above "components" of the human element, it is important to note individual skill level and sophistication of system users during the allocation process. An interface that is entirely acceptable to a degreed engineer might be completely inadequate for an unskilled worker. The proliferation of computer-based systems has spawned a phenomenon called "technofright" [DAR85]—an irrational fear of high-technology products and systems. As we broaden our understanding of the human element in computer-based systems and specify HMI in ways accommodating human needs, it is likely that the level of technofright will be greatly reduced.

2.5.2 HMI Applications

People interact with computer-based systems by using a human-machine interface. The components of the human element (memory, reasoning, visual perception) must be considered when function and performance are allocated to people. In this section we examine how hardware and software can be applied to accomplish effective human-machine interaction (HMI).

HMI hardware enables the user to communicate (a two way information transfer) with the computer-based system. Table 2.1 lists different categories of I/O devices and representative examples of each. The selection of a specific device may not occur during system analysis. However, the system engineer must be aware of the options available to hardware and software designers.

HMI software is the key to effective communication. Function and performance allocated to the human element must be considered in the design of HMI software. For example if the user is required to evaluate different data representations (e.g., text, a graph, and a spreadsheet) simultaneously, software that utilizes "windowing" may be necessary. If the user must recall many different commands, a menu-driven approach may be indicated. But what kind of windows or menu-driven approach? A description

TABLE 2.1
HMI input and output hardware

Category	Type	Examples
Text input	Input	Alphanumeric keyboard
Numeric input	Input	Key pad, alphanumeric keyboard
Command input	Input	Function key pad, keyboard
Picking	Input	Mouse, joystick, light pen, touch screen, tracker ball
Positioning	Input	Mouse, joystick, light pen, touch screen, tracker ball
Drawing	Input	Mouse, light pen, tablet
Digitizing	Input	Digitizer, video input
Audio	Input	Voice recognition system
Hardcopy	Output	Printer, plotter
Display	Output	CRT, plasma display, LCD display
Audio	Output	Voice synthesizer

of these details is often postponed until the requirements analysis step of software engineering.

2.5.3 Human Engineering

Human engineering is a multidisciplinary activity that applies knowledge derived from psychology and technology to specify and design high quality HMI. The human engineering process encompasses the following steps:

Activity Analysis. Each activity allocated to the human element is evaluated in the context of required interaction with other elements. An activity is subdivided into tasks, which are further analyzed in later steps.

Semantic Analysis and Design. The precise meaning of each action required of the user and produced by the machine is defined. The design of a ''dialog'' that communicates proper semantics is established.

Syntactic and Lexical Design. The specific form of actions and commands is identified and represented. Then the hardware and software implementation of each action or command is designed.

User Environment Design. Hardware, software, and other system elements are combined to form a user environment. The environment may include physical facilities (lighting, space management, etc.) as well as the HMI itself.

Prototyping. It is difficult, if not impossible, to formally specify an HMI without the use of a prototype. Prototyping enables the HMI to be evaluated from the human perspective, using active participation rather than passive evaluation. Prototyping results in evaluation and the iterative application of all human engineering steps noted above.

2.6 DATA BASE CONSIDERATIONS

Not all computer-based systems make use of a data base, but for those that do, this information store is often pivotal to overall function. *Data base engineering* (data base analysis, design, and implementation) is a technical discipline that is applied once the information domain of the data base has been defined. Therefore, the role of the system engineer is to define the information to be contained in a data base, the types of queries to be submitted for processing, the manner in which data will be accessed, and the capacity of the data base.

Although data base engineering is a topic for serious study in its own right (e.g., see [DAT86]), data analysis and design are also fundamental software engineering activities, regardless of the presence of a formal data base. These data base engineering topics, collectively called *data design*, are discussed in later chapters.

2.7 SYSTEM ANALYSIS

System analysis is an activity that encompasses most of the tasks we have collectively called computer system engineering. Confusion sometimes occurs because the term is often used in a context that alludes only to software requirements analysis activities (see Chapters 4 and 5). For the purposes of this discussion, system analysis focuses on all system elements—not just software.

System analysis is conducted with the following objectives in mind: (1) identify the customer's need; (2) evaluate the system concept for feasibility; (3) perform economic and technical analysis; (4) allocate functions to hardware, software, people, data base, and other system elements; (5) establish cost and schedule constraints; and (6) create a system definition that forms the foundation for all subsequent engineering work. Both hardware and software expertise (as well as human and data base engineering) are required to successfully attain the objectives listed above.

Although most industry professionals recognize that time and effort expended on system analysis pay important dividends later in the system development process, three questions still arise:

- *How much effort should be expended on analysis and definition for systems and software?* Definitive guidelines for analysis effort are difficult to establish. System size and complexity, application area, end use, and contractual obligations are only a few of the many variables affecting overall analysis effort. An oft-used rule of thumb is that 10–20 percent of all development effort should be applied to system analysis and that another 10–20 percent of software engineering effort should be applied to software requirements analysis.
- *Who does it?* An experienced, well-trained "analyst" should conduct most of the tasks. The analyst works in conjunction with management and technical staff of the customer and system developer. For very large projects, an analysis team may be formed to conduct each analysis task.
- *Why is it so difficult?* A nebulous concept must be transformed into a concrete set of tangible elements. Because communication content is exceptionally high during analysis, opportunity for misunderstanding, omission, inconsistency, and error abounds. Finally, the perception of the system may change as the activity progresses, thereby invalidating earlier work.

2.7.1   Identification of Need

The first step of the system analysis process involves the identification of need. The analyst (system engineer) meets with the customer or his representative. The customer may be a representative of an outside company, the marketing department of the analyst's company (when a product is being defined) or another technical department (when an internal system is to be developed).

Identification of need is the starting point in the evolution of a computer-based system. Figure 2.11 illustrates the inputs provided to the analyst as part of this step. To begin, the analyst assists the customer in defining the goals of the system (product): the information to be produced, the information to be provided, the functions and performance to be required. The analyst makes sure to distinguish between customer "needs" (features critical to success) and customer "wants" (features nice to have but not essential).

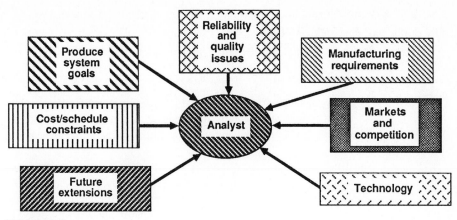

FIGURE 2.11
Inputs for the system analyst.

Once overall goals are identified, the analyst moves on to an evaluation of supplementary information: Does the technology exist to build the system? What special development and manufacturing resources will be required? What bounds have been placed on costs and schedule? If the new system is a product to be developed for sale to many customers, the following questions are also asked: What is the potential market for the product? How would this product compare with competitive products? What position will this product take in the overall product line of the company?

Information gathered during the needs identification step is specified in a *System Concept Document*. The original concept document is sometimes prepared by the customer before meetings with the analyst. Invariably, customer-analyst communication results in modifications to this document.

2.7.2 Feasibility Study

All projects are feasible—given unlimited resources and infinite time! Unfortunately, the development of a computer-based system is more likely plagued by a scarcity of resources and difficult (if not downright unrealistic) delivery dates. It is both necessary and prudent to evaluate the feasibility of a project at the earliest possible time. Months or years of effort, thousands or millions of dollars, and untold professional embarrassment can be averted if an ill-conceived system is recognized early in the definition phase.

The *feasibility study* concentrates on four primary areas of interest:

Economic feasibility. An evaluation of development cost weighed against the ultimate income or benefit derived from the developed system.

Technical feasibility. A study of function, performance, and constraints that may affect the ability to achieve an acceptable system.

Legal feasibility. A determination of any infringement, violation, or liability that could result from development of the system.

Alternatives. An evaluation of alternative approaches to the development of the system.

A feasibility study is not warranted for systems in which economic justification is obvious, technical risk is low, few legal problems are expected, and no reasonable alternative exists. However, if any of the preceding conditions fail, a study of that area should be conducted.

Economic justification is generally the "bottom-line" consideration for most systems (notable exceptions include national defense systems, systems mandated by law, and high-technology applications such as the space program). Economic justification includes a broad range of concerns that include cost-benefit analysis (discussed in the next section), long-term corporate income strategies, impact on other profit centers or products, cost of resources needed for development, and potential market growth.

Technical feasibility is frequently the most difficult area to assess at this stage of the system development process. Because objectives, functions, and performance are somewhat hazy, anything seems possible if the "right" assumptions are made. It is essential that the process of analysis and definition be conducted in parallel with an assessment of technical feasibility. In this way concrete specifications may be judged as they are determined.

The considerations that are normally associated with technical feasibility include:

Development risk. Can the system element be designed so that necessary function and performance are achieved within the constraints uncovered during analysis?

Resource availability. Are skilled staff who are competent available to develop the system element in question? Are other necessary resources (hardware and software) available to build the system?

Technology. Has the relevant technology progressed to a state that will support the system?

Developers of computer-based systems are optimists by nature. (Who else would be brave enough to attempt what we frequently undertake?) However, during an evaluation of technical feasibility, a cynical, if not pessimistic, attitude should prevail. Misjudgment at this stage can be disastrous.

Legal feasibility encompasses a broad range of concerns that include contracts, liability, infringement, and myriad other traps frequently unknown to technical staff. An excellent book [GEM81] by Michael Gemignani, a lawyer and computer scientist, is *must* reading for software engineers who assist in this area of feasibility study.

The degree to which alternatives are considered is often limited by cost and time constraints; however, a legitimate but "unsponsored" variation should not be buried.

The feasibility study may be documented as a separate report to upper management and included as an appendix to the *System Specification* (Section 2.9). Although the format of a feasibility report may vary, the following outline covers most important topics.

FEASIBILITY STUDY

1.0. Introduction
   A brief statement of the problem, the environment in which the system is to be implemented, and constraints that affect the project.
2.0. Management Summary and Recommendations
   A summary of important findings and recommendations for further system development.
3.0. Alternatives
   A presentation of alternative system configurations; criteria that were used in selecting the final approach.
4.0. System Description
   An abbreviated version of information contained in the *System Specification* or reference to the specification.
5.0. Cost-Benefit Analysis
   An economic justification for the system.
6.0. Evaluation of Technical Risk
   A presentation of technical feasibility.
7.0. Legal Ramifications
8.0. Other Project-Specific Topics

The feasibility study is reviewed first by project management (to assess content reliability) and by upper management (to assess project status). The study should result in a ''go/no-go'' decision. It should be noted that other go/no-go decisions will be made during the planning, specification, and development steps of both hardware and software engineering.

2.7.3 Economic Analysis

Among the most important information contained in a feasibility study is *cost-benefit analysis*—an assessment of the economic justification for a computer-based system project. Cost-benefit analysis delineates costs for project development and weighs them against tangible (i.e., measurable directly in dollars) and intangible benefits of a system.

Cost-benefit analysis is complicated by criteria that vary with the characteristics of the system to be developed, the relative size of the project, and the expected return on investment desired as part of a company's strategic plan. In addition many benefits derived from computer-based systems are intangible (e.g., better design quality through iterative optimization, increased customer satisfaction through programmable control, and better business decisions through reformatted and preanalyzed sales data). Direct quantitative comparisons may be difficult to achieve.

As we noted above, analysis of benefits will differ depending on system characteristics. To illustrate, consider the benefits for management information systems [KIN78] shown in Table 2.2. Most data processing systems are developed with "better information quantity, quality, timeliness, or organization" as a primary objective. Therefore, the benefits noted in Table 2.2 concentrate on information access and its impact on the user environment. The benefits that might be associated with an engineering-scientific analysis program or a microprocessor-based product could differ substantially.

TABLE 2.2
Possible information system benefits*

Benefits from contributions of calculating and printing tasks
    Reduction in per unit costs of calculating and printing (CR)
    Improved accuracy in calculating tasks (ER)
    Ability to quickly change variables and values in calculation programs (IF)
    Greatly increased speed in calculating and printing (IS)

Benefits from contributions to record-keeping tasks
    Ability to "automatically" collect and store data for records (CR, IS, ER)
    More complete and systematic keeping of records (CR, ER)
    Increased capacity for record keeping in terms of space and cost (CR)
    Standardization of record keeping (CR, IS)
    Increase in amount of data that can be stored per record (CR, IS)
    Improved security in records storage (ER, CR, MC)
    Improved portability of records (IF, CR, IS)

Benefits from contributions to record-searching tasks
    Faster retrieval of records (IS)
    Improved ability to access records from large data bases (IF)
    Improved ability to change records in data bases (IF, CR)
    Ability to link sites that need search capability through telecommunications (IF, IS)
    Improved ability to create records of records accessed and by whom (ER, MC)
    Ability to audit and analyze record-searching activity (MC, ER)

Benefits from contributions to system restructuring capability
    Ability to simultaneously change entire classes of records (IS, IF, CR)
    Ability to move large files of data about (IS, IF)
    Ability to create new files by merging aspects of other files (IS, IF)

Benefits from contributions of analysis and simulation capability
    Ability to perform complex, simultaneous calculations quickly (IS, IF, ER)
    Ability to create simulations of complex phenomena in order to answer "what if?" questions (MC, IF)
    Ability to aggregate large amounts of data in varous ways useful for planning and decision making (MC, IF)

Benefits from contributions to process and resource control
    Reduction of need for work force in process and resource control (CR)
    Improved ability to "fine tune" processes such as assembly lines (CR, MC, IS, ER)
    Improved ability to maintain continuous monitoring of processes and available resources (MC, ER, IF)

*Abbreviations: CR = cost reduction or avoidance; ER = error reduction; IF = increased flexibility; IS = increased speed of activity; MC = improvement in management planning or control.

Source: King and Schrems [KIN78], p. 23. Reprinted with permission.

Benefits of a new system are always determined relative to the existing mode of operation. As an example, we consider a computer-aided design (CAD) system that will replace elements of a manual engineering design process. The system analyst must define measurable characteristics for the existing system (manual design) and the proposed system (CAD). Choosing time to produce a finished detailed drawing (*t-draw*) as one of many measurable quantities, the analyst finds that a 4-to-1 reduction in *t-draw* will accrue from the CAD system. To further quantify this benefit, the following data are determined:

t-draw, average drawing time = 4 hours

c, cost per drawing-hour = $20.00

n, number of drawings per year = 8000

p, percentage of drawing to be done on CAD system = 60%

With the above data known, an estimate of yearly cost savings—the benefit—can be ascertained:

Drawing time cost savings = reduction × *t-draw* × *n* × *c* × *p* = $96,000 per year

Other tangible benefits from the CAD system would be treated in a similar fashion. Intangible benefits (e.g., better design quality and increased employee morale) can be assigned dollar values or used to support a ''go'' recommendation, if indicated.

Costs associated with the development of a computer-based system [KIN78] are listed in Table 2.3. The analyst can estimate each cost and then use development and on-going costs to determine a *return on investment*, a *break-even point*, and a *payback period*. The graph shown in Figure 2.12 illustrates these characteristics for the CAD

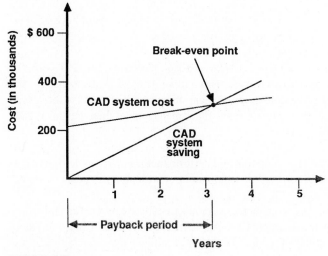

FIGURE 2.12
Cost-benefit analysis.

TABLE 2.3
Possible information system costs

Procurement costs
  Consulting costs
  Actual equipment purchase or lease costs
  Equipment installation costs
  Costs for modifying the equipment site (air conditioning, security, etc.)
  Cost of capital
  Cost of management and staff dealing with procurement

Start-up costs
  Cost of operating system software
  Cost of communications equipment installation (telephone lines, data lines, etc.)
  Cost of start-up personnel
  Cost of personnel searches and hiring activities
  Cost of disruption to the rest of the organization
  Cost of management required to direct start-up activity

Project-related costs
  Cost of applications software purchased
  Cost of software modifications to fit local systems
  Cost of personnel, overhead, etc., from in-house application development
  Cost for training user personnel in application use
  Cost of data collection and installing data collection procedures
  Cost of preparing documentation
  Cost of development management

Ongoing costs
  System maintenance costs (hardware, software, and facilities)
  Rental costs (electricity, telephones, etc.)
  Depreciation costs on hardware
  Cost of staff involved in information systems management, operation, and planning activities

Source: King and Schrems [KIN 78], p. 24. Reprinted with permission.

system example noted above. We assume that total cost savings per year have been estimated to be $96,000, total development (or purchase) cost is estimated to be $204,000, and annual costs are estimated to be $32,000.

From the graph shown in Figure 2.12, the payback period requires 3.1 years. In actuality return on investment is determined with a more detailed analysis that considers the time value of money, tax consequences, and other potential uses for the investment. Taking intangible benefits into account, upper management then decides if such economic results justify the system.

Another aspect of cost-benefit analysis considers incremental cost associated with added benefit (more or better function and performance). For computer-based systems, the incremental cost-benefit relationship can be represented as shown in Figure 2.13.

In some cases (curve AA') cost increases proportionally with benefits until some point A. After this point each additional benefit is exceedingly expensive. For example, consider a real-time polling function that has 500 milliseconds of idle time. New tasks can be added with relatively low cost; however, if total task execution approaches

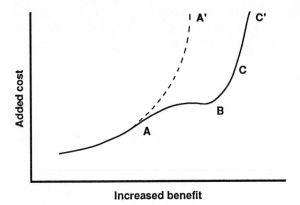

FIGURE 2.13
Incremental cost-benefit.

500 milliseconds, the cost to implement increases dramatically because overall performance must be improved.

In other cases (curve $ABCC'$) cost increases proportionally until A and then levels for added benefits (through B) before increasing dramatically (at C) for subsequent benefits. As an example, consider a single-user operating system that is enhanced incrementally to ultimately support multiple users. Once multi-user support is available, the rate of increase in cost for added multi-user functions may lessen somewhat. However, once processor capacity is reached, added features will require a more powerful processor and a large increment in cost.

The following excerpt [FRI77] may best characterize cost-benefit analysis:

> Like political rhetoric after the election, the cost-benefit analysis may be forgotten after the project implementation begins. However, it is extremely important because it has been the vehicle by which management approval has been obtained.

Only by spending the time to evaluate feasibility do we reduce the chances for extreme embarrassment (or worse) at later stages of a system project. Effort spent on a feasibility analysis that results in cancellation of a proposed project is not wasted effort.

2.7.4 Technical Analysis

During *technical analysis*, the analyst evaluates the technical merits of the system concept, while at the same time collecting additional information about performance, reliability, maintainability, and producibility. In some cases this system analysis step also includes a limited amount of research and design.

Technical analysis begins with an assessment of the technical viability of the proposed system. What technologies are required to accomplish system function and performance? What new material, methods, algorithms, or processes are required, and what is their development risk? How will these technology issues affect cost?

The tools available for technical analysis are derived from mathematical modeling and optimization techniques, probability and statistics, queuing theory, and control theory—to name a few. It is important to note, however, that analytical evaluation is not always possible.

Modeling (either mathematical or physical) is an effective mechanism for technical analysis of computer-based systems. Figure 2.14 illustrates the overall flow of information in the modeling process. A model is created based on observation of the real world or approximation based on system goals. The analyst assesses model behavior and compares it to real-world or expected system behavior, gaining insight into the technical viability of the proposed system.

Blanchard and Fabrycky [BLA81] define a set of criteria for the use of models during technical analysis of systems:

1. The model should represent the dynamics of the system configuration being evaluated in a way that is simple enough to understand and manipulate, and yet close enough to the operating reality to yield successful results.
2. The model should highlight those factors that are most relevant to the problem at hand, and suppress (with discretion) those that are not as important.

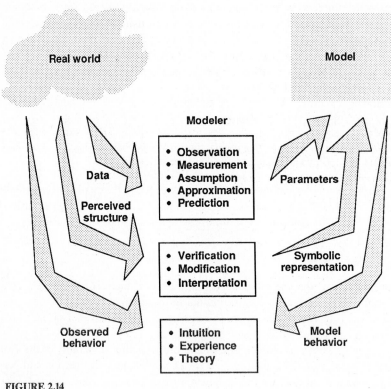

FIGURE 2.14
Modeling.

3. The model should be comprehensive by including *all* relevant factors and be reliable in terms of repeatability of results.

4. Model design should be simple enough to allow for timely implementation in problem solving. Unless the tool can be utilized in a timely and efficient manner by the analyst or the manager, it is of little value. If the model is large and highly complex, it may be appropriate to develop a series of models where the output of one can be tied to the input of another. Also, it may be desirable to evaluate a specific element of the system independently from other elements.

5. Model design should incorporate provisions for ease of modification and/or expansion to permit the evaluation of additional factors as required. Successful model development often includes a series of trials before the overall objective is met. Initial attempts may suggest information gaps which are not immediately apparent and consequently may suggest beneficial changes.

The results obtained from technical analysis form the basis for another ''go/no-go'' decision on the system. If technical risk is severe, if models indicate that desired function or performance cannot be achieved, if the pieces just won't fit together smoothly—it's back to the drawing board!

2.7.5   Allocation and Trade-Offs

Once the questions associated with the analysis task have been answered, alternative solutions are considered. Each system function with requisite performance and interface characteristics is allocated to one or more system elements.

For example, analysis of a new computer graphics system indicates that a major function is three-dimensional transformation of graphics images. Investigation of alternative solutions for the transformation function uncovers the following options:

1. All three-dimensional transformations are performed with the use of software.

2. ''Simple'' transformations (e.g., scaling and translation) are performed in hardware, while ''complex'' transformations (e.g., rotation and perspective) are performed in software.

3. All transformations are performed with the use of a geometry processor implemented in hardware.

Each of the above options represents a different *functional allocation* for the same graphics system function. One allocation is selected from among the alternatives. Criteria for selection are established and trade-offs evaluated.

The overall process for the evaluation of alternative system configurations is illustrated in Figures 2.15 and 2.16 [BLA81]. Referring to Figure 2.15, each system configuration alternative is evaluated according to a set of ''evaluation parameters'' (trade-off criteria) that have been ordered by importance (Figure 2.16). In general evaluation parameters are assessed with respect to economic factors (e.g., life-cycle cost). A trade-off area (Figure 2.17) is isolated when two or more system evaluation lower-order parameters (e.g., response time or display resolution) can be varied (in different allocations) and still achieve a desired higher-order parameter (e.g., cost or reliability).

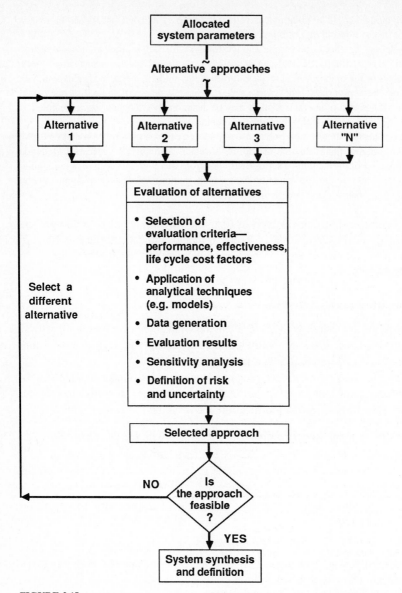

FIGURE 2.15
Evaluation of alternatives. (Reprinted with permission of Prentice-Hall, Inc., Englewood Cliffs, NJ.)

When a computer-based system is a product, the number of systems to be produced (volume) will have a significant impact on allocation. All functions allocated to
hardware represent a recurring incremental cost for each system that is manufactured.
The addition of a $3000 hardware component will have little cost impact if the system
product is a process-control system for a steel mill (volume, 3 to 5 systems per year)
priced at $3,000,000. A $3.00 IC added to an ''intelligent'' microwave oven (volume

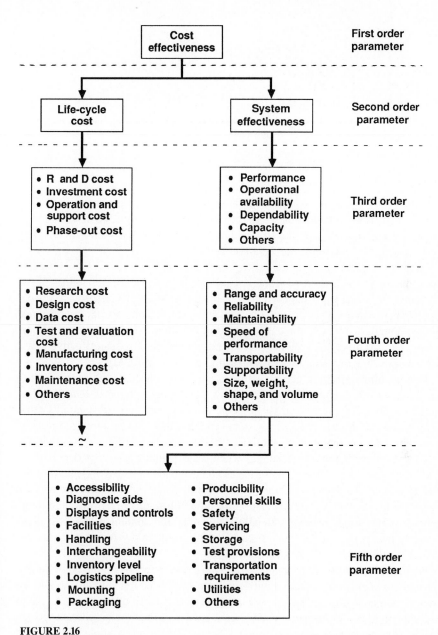

FIGURE 2.16
Order of evaluation parameters. (Reprinted with permission of Prentice-Hall, Inc., Englewood Cliffs, NJ.)

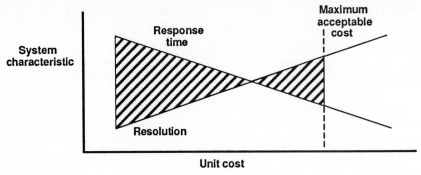

FIGURE 2.17
Trade-off area.

1 to 2 million products per year) can result in significant profit degradation. Software, as we have seen, is not manufactured and thus represents a one-time cost regardless of the number of systems to be produced. For large-volume products, software development cost, no matter how large, can be amortized.

In the context of the allocation task, *performance* alludes to processing speed or system response, RAM and ROM storage requirements, and system reliability. Speed critical functions are always allocated to a hardware element if (1) software cannot meet performance requirements and (2) hardware is available or can be designed within cost bounds. However, the development of a custom IC is still a relatively expensive process. At moderate volumes it is sometimes simpler and cost-effective to use a general-purpose microprocessor with supporting software in ROM.

Memory limitation has been an artificial and often unnecessary impediment to the development of computer-based systems. When system volume is relatively low, additional memory can often decrease software development cost substantially. However, when software is contained in a system (product) that is to be produced in large quantities, a constraint that dictates minimal memory may be justified. Fewer memory chips can result in substantial cost savings when large quantities are considered.

Reliability is the most costly performance characteristic to assess and the most difficult to guarantee. Hardware reliability theory is well established; data collected from prototype testing provide a good foundation for reliability estimates. Software reliability theory is in its formative stages. To help assure reliability in human critical systems (i.e., human life may be lost if the system fails) redundant hardware and software elements may be allocated to work in parallel.

The degree of *human decision making and interaction* depends on the environment in which the system will reside. Functions best performed by humans should be allocated to humans! This seemingly obvious guideline is often unheeded in a rush to automate. Techniques for human-machine interaction will undergo significant change during the next decade. Voice recognition systems already allow spoken input, and computer graphics already provides a visually pleasing mode of output. The human interface must be tuned to accommodate the higher communication bandwidth supported by these techniques.

Interface standardization and *adaptability* to product enhancement are representative of a second tier of trade-off criteria. These factors may serve as the arbiter when the trade-offs discussed above do not lead to a clear choice of allocation alternatives.

2.8 A SYSTEM ANALYSIS CHECKLIST

The process we call system analysis is a problem-solving activity that requires intensive communication between the customer and the system developer. Because system analysis is problem solving, it can best be understood by considering the topics that are addressed as the problem is analyzed. The following system analysis checklist provides insight into the attributes of the analysis task.

A SYSTEM ANALYSIS CHECKLIST*
Analysis Planning

Questions
1. Are the reasons for the analysis project clearly defined in writing?
2. Are the project limits defined (e.g., resources, time, and funds)?
3. Is the completion of the system scheduled?
4. Who will perform the analysis work? Does that person have any previous experience in this application area?
5. Who are the user participants? (The term ''user'' refers to the requester of the system as well as the people who will actually use it.)
6. Are objectives set for the new or modified system? If so, what are they, and who set them?
7. What priority has the organization set for the project?
8. What previous systems analysis work has been performed in this application area?
9. What is the status of current systems serving the application?
10. What (if any) special legal, security, or audit considerations must be observed in this system?

Deliverables
1. A narrative definition of the project boundaries
2. A tentative work plan for the analysis work
3. A user contact list
4. A tentative resource staffing list
5. A list of existing application systems
6. A priority impact statement concerning the relative importance of the system

---

*Adapted from Wenig, R., ''Systems Analysis Checklist,'' in *System Development Management*, Auerbach Publishers, Inc., 1981. With permission.

User Contacts

Questions
1. Are all user participants and organizational relationships identified?
2. Do users clearly understand the current system and its operation?
3. Are legitimate user complaints about the current system documented? Is the impact of the complaints fully documented?
4. How much time and effort are the users willing to put into the initial analysis work?
5. Are users identified as to who are supporters of, resistant to, and indifferent to the system?
6. Do users expect any specific benefits from the resulting system?
7. Is there clearly defined top-level support for the project? If so, who constitutes this support? How much power do they wield?
8. Who are the key decision makers in the user environment?
9. How many user locations are there? How many people will use the system at various levels? What is their level of computer system experience?

Deliverables
1. An organizational chart of all participating user areas, including their hierarchical relationships
2. A narrative describing the user's background and prior experience
3. Documentation of user problems with the existing system and the impact of these problems
4. A work plan of expected user participation in the analysis
5. A tentative statement of user expectations
6. A narrative on the political relationships and system support expectations of the major user participants
7. A brief history of previous data systems and procedures used in the application area
8. Identification of any other organizational systems or applications that interrelate with the proposed system

System Objectives

Questions
1. Are system objectives formally defined? Or are they loosely stated and subject to interpretation and/or later definition?
2. Will the new system have a major impact on the basic operations of the organization?
3. Will the new system replace an existing one? If so, how old is the current system? How many others preceded it?
4. Is the new system expected to cause relocation or removal of any work functions? If so, how sensitive is the issue? Who will help to combat any resistance?

5. Is an interim system required to satisfy immeuiate goals or to eliminate intolerable problems with the existing system?

6. Is a phased development and implementation approach feasible? Or is a one-time mass conversion required?

7. What cost can be justified? What resources can be allocated for this project?

8. How close to the state of the art is the new system expected to be?

9. How much time can users allocate for training and start-up? During what period of time?

Deliverables

1. A comprehensive statement of system objectives

2. A statement of general scope and level of project effort required, including tentative cost and resource estimates

3. A statement concerning the current system and procedures considered for change, elimination, and/or replacement

4. A general statement covering the expected project phasing and the overall team approach to the project

5. A tentative statement covering the levels and impact of anticipated organizational changes that will result from the system

6. A commentary on the roles and responsibilities of each participating user department and major user group in the desired system

Current System

Questions

1. What are the problems with the current system as evaluated by the users and the technical team? Do these evaluations agree?

2. How do other organizations perform similar functions? What is the current state of the art in the application area?

3. What other methods and procedures have been tried and/or used to service the application?

4. What is the detailed chronology of the current system's life?

5. What is the organization's history during the current system's life?

6. What development, maintenance, and operational costs are associated with the current system (including user efforts)?

7. Identify the name, rank, and organizational position of those who supported, built, and use the current system.

8. Identify one or more major situational failures that resulted from the current system.

Deliverables

1. A comprehensive narrative on the current system and its operation, history, and users

2. A ranked list of the current system's major faults and problems

3. A full cost analysis of the current system

4. A general statement on how the new system is related to those in other organizations or the state of the art

5. A complete collection of the documents, procedures, and other available details concerning the operation/content of the current system

Data Elements and Structures

Questions

1. Are the current data elements, files, forms, procedures, and so on thoroughly documented?

2. Are the current data elements and structures logical, consistent, and utilized?

3. How clean is the data base?

4. Do users have a list of new data elements they would like to see in the new system? Is it feasible to add these data elements?

5. How much redundancy exists between the current system's data base and that of other applications in the organization? Are any of the other applications a more logical repository for any elements of the data base?

6. Is there enough flexibility in the current data structure to meet the new system's needs?

7. How difficult will it be to convert the current data base to a new one? How much error testing will be necessary to achieve a clean conversion?

8. How much maintenance is normally done on the existing data base?

9. Can or should extensive data archives from this data base be converted?

10. How much of the current data base is actively used? By whom?

11. What significant faults or failures were encountered with the data files? How were they dealt with?

12. How many times and in what ways has the data base been modified?

Deliverables

1. A comprehensive set of format and content definitions of all data elements, files, and supporting data structures

2. An evaluation of current data base content, with emphasis on cleanliness, errors, unused areas, redundancy, conversion, and future use

3. A list of expected changes, additions, deletions, and other modifications to data elements and structures that are anticipated for the new system

4. A summary of the major uses of the data file and its elements

5. A list of faults and failures of the existing data files

User Interviews

Questions

1. Are all users identified?

2. Is there a formal interview plan for each user level covered?

3. Are lists of questions and objectives developed for the interviews at each user level?

4. Is top management supporting and publicizing the interviews, the interview team, and the overall expectations? Is top management making a strong pitch for interviewee cooperation?

5. Are all interviews scheduled during acceptable time periods?

6. Are the interviewers trained in effective interview techniques?

7. Are all scheduled interviews completed? Have canceled, interrupted, or forgotten interviews been rescheduled and conducted?

8. Have the interviewers taken adequate notes and written evaluations of each interview?

9. Have the interviewers compared notes, impressions, and other observations? Are these details documented?

10. Are interviewees given adequate feedback, such as summary reports, notes, and so on?

11. Have follow-up interviews been conducted when special problems or conditions are uncovered during initial interviews?

12. Has management been kept informed about the interview process, any problems uncovered, and uncooperative users?

Deliverables

1. A formal interview plan

2. Documentation of interview results

3. A report summarizing the interviews that includes both consensus answers and significant variances

4. An internal analysis of user attitudes and positions vis-à-vis the system

5. A management report covering interview findings and cooperation of the participants

6. Results of test interviews along with changes in questions, emphasis, and other interviewing guidelines

7. Explanation of any incomplete interviews

Research on Other Systems

Questions

1. What other organizations can be surveyed regarding their approach to the subject application?

2. What (if any) proprietary packages are available that might suit the application area?

3. What (if any) trade and industry associations study or catalog the systems work of others in the same field?

4. What (if any) formal literature is available on the subject application area?

5. How much time and effort should be spent in reviewing other systems?

6. Were the reviews of other systems productive? Should more time be spent on this activity?

7. Are field interviewers of other users and organizations necessary?

Deliverables

1. A list of organizations and sources to review for base knowledge on alternative approaches to the application

2. A narrative report detailing the ways other organizations are solving the application

3. A technical evaluation covering the current state-of-the-art application area

4. A summary report on contacts to other users and organizations

5. A follow-up plan for reviewing or tracking major developments in the industry

Alternative Propositions

Questions

1. How many application alternatives should be considered?

2. How much time and effort should be spent in evaluation of alternatives?

3. How detailed and complete should the considerations of each alternative be?

4. How will the alternatives be developed and documented?

5. Are formal requirements and evaluation criteria established for the alternatives?

6. Who will evaluate the alternatives? Will the users review the alternatives?

7. Are all logical alternatives being considered?

8. Are outside expert opinions being sought on the alternatives?

9. Are the alternatives considered consistent with those evaluated by other organizations?

Deliverables

1. Alternative design definitions

2. Positive and negative factors of each alternative

3. Evaluation reports from each group that studies the alternatives

4. Formal user presentation of the alternatives

5. Preliminary cost predictions for each alternative

6. A technology impact assessment for each alternative

7. A user impact assessment for each alternative

Selecting a Design Alternative

Questions

1. Are all alternatives fully reviewed and evaluated?

2. Are the alternatives ranked in terms of their ability to meet the system requirements criteria?

3. Is there a technical-management team with authority to select the most appropriate alternative?
4. Does one alternative clearly outrank the others?
5. Which alternative(s) do the users support?
6. Which alternative is best to implement in terms of time, cost, resources, and technical risk?
7. Which alternative uses the most advanced concepts?
8. Which alternative is likely to last the longest?

Deliverables
1. A detailed comparison of alternatives
2. A ranking of alternatives
3. A specific recommendation as to the alternative that is best to pursue
4. A report to the users on the alternative selected
5. A summary of reasons for rejecting other alternatives

Structural Analysis

Questions
1. Are all data elements, flows, and expected processing steps defined for the selected alternative?
2. Are procedural and organizational changes that the new system will generate defined and evaluated?
3. Are the content and uses of input files and outputs defined in a general way?
4. Are the equipment requirements for the new system estimated?
5. Is there a list of expected system modules?
6. Is there a tentative data conversion plan?
7. Is there an overall system flow being generated?
8. Are associated clerical procedures outlined?
9. What is the estimated volume of data and transactions?
10. Are the security and accuracy requirements of the data being considered?
11. Are testing procedures for the new approach thoroughly defined?
12. Is a preliminary system implementation plan available?

Deliverables
1. A report of the proposed system approach
2. A system flowchart
3. A user operations and responsibility flowchart
4. A detailed report on the analysis findings
5. A cost-benefit analysis report

6. A preliminary testing plan
7. A tentative implementation plan

Plans for the Next Phase

Questions

1. Are there work tasks and resource estimates for the general design work?
2. Is there a resource loading plan that shows requirements by work task?
3. Are user support tasks identified and planned? Are the users aware of them?
4. Are target dates set to obtain authorization to proceed with the next phase?
5. What is the expected completion date of the proposed work?

Deliverables

1. The work plan and the resource estimates
2. The user support plan
3. A narrative on the approach to managing the next phase

Management Presentations and Reviews

Questions

1. Are all levels of management in the technical and user areas briefed on the analysis results and recommendations?
2. Are the presentations clearly and logically formulated?
3. Are management's concerns and questions documented and answered?
4. Has the proposed alternative survived management's scrutiny?
5. Does the analysis team have any doubts about the project approach?
6. Have minority opinions and negative comments been properly addressed?

Deliverables

1. Presentation critiques and internal reviews
2. Presentation reports and visual aids
3. Authorization to proceed

The system analysis checklist contains a comprehensive set of questions with a distinct emphasis on activities associated with analysis of business data processing systems. It should be noted, however, that many of these same questions should be addressed during the analysis and definition of engineering and scientific systems, real-time systems, and microprocessor-based systems.

Among the many additional issues that could be included in the checklist are:

1. Hardware and software trade-offs that are encountered in the definition of microprocessor-based systems;

2. Hardware and software design issues (e.g., Is the design of the system to be driven by hardware characteristics or software requirements?);
3. Algorithm design and analysis considerations;
4. Performance, accuracy, and reliability;
5. The interrelation of all system elements and the communication among various development groups (e.g., hardware and software engineering);
6. The impact of a hardware technology that may change before the project development is complete.

These issues and many others become part of the analysis checklist for technical systems. Review of the system analysis task is essential, and the checklist format provides a means for guiding the review process and helping to assure the success of the analysis task.

2.9 THE SYSTEM SPECIFICATION

The *System Specification* is the first deliverable in the computer system engineering process. Each major section of the specification is described below.

SYSTEM SPECIFICATION

1.0. Introduction

The introductory section describes objectives of the system and the environment in which the system will operate. This section also contains an executive summary that specifies the scope of the system development process; feasibility and justification; resources required, and an overview of cost and schedule.

2.0. Functional Description

A description of each system function is provided in this section. The description includes a functional narrative that describes input information, tasks to be performed, resultant information, and additional interface data.

3.0. Allocation

Each function described in Section 2.0 of the specification is allocated to the appropriate system element. Hardware and software elements are described separately. Information, particularly existing data bases or files, is also described.

4.0. Constraints

Management and technical constraints that affect development of the system are described in this section. Typical categories include external environment, interfaces, design and implementation, resources, and cost or schedule. Constraints imply limitation. This section must be carefully reviewed to assure that successful implementation of the system is possible within limits specified.

5.0. Cost

Precise cost estimates may be impossible to determine at this stage of the computer system engineering process. Software planning and its hardware counterpart must be conducted to ascertain detailed cost estimates. However, cost bounds can, and normally are, established and noted in this section.

6.0. Schedule

A system development schedule may be predicated on an end date determined by customer (requester) demand, market impact, or external forces. Like cost, a detailed development schedule cannot be established without detailed software and hardware planning. Known chronological information (e.g., as specified in contract) is defined in this section.

2.10   SYSTEM DEFINITION REVIEW

Throughout the definition phase there is a natural tendency to short-circuit review and move quickly into development. Managers tend to become increasingly nervous when components are not being soldered and source code is not being written. Technical people want to move into the "creative engineering tasks" as soon as possible. Don't fall prey to these attitudes!

The *system definition review* evaluates the correctness of the definition contained in the *System Specification*. The review is conducted by both developer and customer to assure that (1) the scope of the project has been correctly delineated; (2) functions, performance, and interfaces have been properly defined; (3) analysis of environment and development risk justify the system; and (4) the developer and the customer have the same perception of system objectives. The system definition review is conducted in two segments. Initially, a management viewpoint is applied. Second, a technical evaluation of system elements and functions is conducted.

Key management considerations generate the following questions:

* Has a firm business need been established; does system justification make sense?
* Does the specified environment (or market) need the system that has been described?
* What alternatives have been considered?
* What is the development risk for each system element?
* Are resources available to perform development?
* Do cost and schedule bounds make sense?

Actually, the above questions should be raised and answered regularly during the analysis task. Each should be reexamined at this stage.

The level of detail considered during the technical stage of the system review varies with level of detail considered during the allocation task. The review should include the following issues:

* Does the functional complexity of the system agree with assessments of development risk, cost, and schedule?
* Is the allocation of functions defined in sufficient detail?

- Have interfaces among system elements and with the environment been defined in sufficient detail?
- Are performance, reliability, and maintainability issues addressed in the specification?
- Does the *System Specification* provide sufficient foundation for the hardware and software engineering steps that follow?

Parallel engineering paths begin once the system review has been completed. Hardware, human, and data base elements of a system are addressed as part of their corresponding engineering processes. For the remainder of this book we shall trace another path—software engineering.

2.11 SUMMARY

Computer system engineering is the first step in the evolution of a new computer-based system or product. Using the steps that we have called system analysis, the system engineer identifies the customer's needs, determines economic and technical feasibility, and allocates function and performance to software, hardware, people, and data bases—the key system elements. A system definition is created and forms the foundation for all the engineering work that follows.

System engineering demands intense communication between the customer and an analyst. The customer must understand system goals and be able to state them clearly. The analyst must know what questions to ask, what advice to give, and what research to do. If communication breaks down at this stage, the success of the entire project is in jeopardy.

REFERENCES

[BLA81]   Blanchard, B. S., and W. J. Fabrycky, *Systems Engineering and Analysis*, Prentice-Hall, 1981, p. 270.
[COX85]   Cox, B. J., "Software ICs and Objective-C," *Unix World*, Spring, 1985.
[DAR85]   Kneale, D., "Coping with Technofright, Technology in the Workplace," *The Wall Street Journal*, September 16, 1985, p. 98.
[DAT86]   Date, C. J., *An Introduction to Data Base Systems*, 4th ed., Addison-Wesley, 1986.
[FOR84]   Forsyth, R. (ed.), *Expert Systems*, Chapman and Hall, 1984.
[FRI77]   Fried, L., "Performing Cost Benefit Analysis," *System Development Management*, Auerbach Publishers, Pennsauken, NJ, 1977.
[GEM81]   Gemignani, M., *Law and the Computer*, CBI Publishing Co., Boston, 1981.
[GIL82]   Gilhooly, K. J., *Thinking:Directed, Undirected and Creative*, Academic Press, 1982.
[KIN78]   King, J., and E. Schrems, "Cost Benefit Analysis in Information Systems Development and Operation," *ACM Computing Surveys*, vol. 10, no. 1, March 1978, pp. 19–34.
[KLA80]   Klatzky, R. L., *Human Memory*, W.H. Freeman & Co., 2d ed., 1980.
[MAR85]   Martin, J. L. (ed.), "Complex Parallel Systems," *IEEE Software*, vol. 2, no. 4, July 1985.

[MON84]   Monk, A. (ed.), *Fundamentals of Human-Computer Interaction*, Academic Press, 1984.

[SEI82]   Seiwiorek, D. P., C. G. Bell, and A. Newell, *Computer Structures: Principles and Examples*, McGraw-Hill, 1982.

[SRI85]   Srini, V. P., "A Fault Tolerant Data Flow System," *Computer*, vol. 18, no. 3, March 1985.

[ZIS84]   Zissos, D., *System Design with Microprocessors*, 2d ed., Academic Press, 1984.

PROBLEMS AND POINTS TO PONDER

2.1 Develop a checklist of attributes to be considered when "feasibility" of a system is to be evaluated. Discuss the interplay among attributes and attempt to provide a method for grading each so that a quantitative "feasibility number" may be developed.

2.2 A system analyst can come from one of three sources: the system developer, the customer, or some outside organization. Discuss the pros and cons that apply to each source. Describe an "ideal" analyst.

2.3 Find as many single word synonyms as you can for the word "system." Good luck!

2.4 Attempt to draw the equivalent of Figure 2.1 for a system (preferably computer-based) with which you are familiar. Show major input and output, each system element, and the interconnectivity among elements.

2.5 Common system elements are hardware, software, and people. What other elements are frequently encountered in computer-based systems?

2.6 Research the accounting techniques that are used for detailed cost-benefit analysis of a computer-based system requiring some hardware manufacturing and assembly. Attempt to write a "cookbook" set of guidelines a technical manager could apply.

2.7 Develop the equivalent of Table 2.2 for engineering/scientific systems. Expand the table to encompass real-time and embedded applications.

2.8 Based on documents provided by your instructor, develop an abbreviated *System Specification* for one of the following computer-based systems:
   (*a*) A low-cost word processing system
   (*b*) A real-time data acquisition system
   (*c*) An electronic mail system
   (*d*) A university registration system
   (*e*) An engineering analysis system
   (*f*) An interactive reservation system
   (*g*) A system of local interest

2.9 Are there characteristics of a system that cannot be established at system definition? Describe the characteristics, if any, and explain why a consideration of them must be delayed until later in the definition phase.

2.10 Are there situations in which formal system specification can be abbreviated or eliminated entirely? Explain.

2.11 Your instructor will distribute a high level description of a computer-based system.
   (*a*) Develop a set of questions that an analyst should ask.
   (*b*) Propose at least two different allocations for the system based on answers to your questions provided by your instructor.
   (*c*) Compare your allocation to those derived by other students.

2.12 Develop a set of rules for the design of human-machine interfaces. Apply the HMI guidelines discussed in Section 2.5.

FURTHER READINGS

Because it is an interdisciplinary topic, computer system engineering is a difficult subject, and therefore, few really good books have been published. Books by Blanchard and Fabrycky [BLA81] and Athey (*Systematic Systems Approach*, Prentice-Hall, 1982) present the system engineering process (with a distinct engineering emphasis) and provide worthwhile guidance.

Books by Wetherbee (*Systems Analysis for Computer-Based Information Systems*, West Publishing, 1979) and Leeson (*Systems Analysis and Design*, SRA, 1981) provide useful discussions of the system analysis task as it is applied in the information systems world. Both books contain "case study" supplements that illustrate the problems, approaches, and solutions that may be applied during system analysis.

Many other textbooks have been published in the general area of system analysis and definition. Among the more recent additions to the literature:

Davis, W. S., *Systems Analysis and Design: A Structured Approach*, Addison-Wesley, 1983.
Menamin, S., and J. Palmer, *Essential Systems Analysis*, Yourdon Press, 1985.

For those readers actively involved in systems work or interested in a more sophisticated treatment of the topic, Gerald Weinberg's books (*An Introduction to General System Thinking* and *On the Design of Stable Systems*, Wiley Interscience, 1976, 1979) have become classics and provide an excellent discussion of "general systems thinking." Unlike many other texts with a distinct data processing orientation, Weinberg describes important and intellectually stimulating characteristics of systems and implicitly proposes a general approach to system analysis and design.

The Auerbach series, *System Development Management* (Auerbach Publishers, Inc., Pennsauken, NJ, updated yearly), provides an excellent treatment of system planning and definition for large scale information systems. Auerbach's pragmatic approach will be especially useful to industry professionals.

CHAPTER
3

SOFTWARE PROJECT PLANNING

In order to conduct a successful software development project, we must understand the scope of the work to be done, the resources to be required, the tasks to be accomplished, the milestones to be tracked, the effort (cost) to be expended, and the schedule to be followed. Software project planning, the first step in the software engineering process, provides that understanding.

Software project planning combines two tasks: research and estimation. Research enables us to define the scope of a software element in a computer-based system. Using the *System Specification* as a guide, each major software function can be described in a bounded fashion. A bounded, functional description, coupled with other data to be discussed later in this chapter, provides a target for estimation.

Whenever estimates are made, we look into the future and accept some degree of uncertainty as a matter of course. The second facet of software planning is estimation, and therefore, a characteristic of planning is uncertainty. To quote Frederick Brooks [BRO75]:

> ...our techniques of estimating are poorly developed. More seriously, they reflect an unvoiced assumption that is quite untrue, i.e., that all will go well.
>
> ...because we are uncertain of our estimates, software managers often lack the courteous stubbornness to make people wait for a good product.

Although estimating is as much art as it is science, software planning need not be conducted in a haphazard manner. Useful techniques for cost and schedule estimation do exist. Useful approaches to software project planning are available. Planning provides a road map for software development. We would be ill-advised to embark without it.

3.1 OBSERVATIONS ON ESTIMATING

A leading executive was once asked what single characteristic was most important in a project manager. His response: "...a person with the ability to know what will go wrong before it actually does...." We might add: "...and the courage to estimate when the future is cloudy ...."

Estimation of resources, cost, and schedule for a software development effort requires experience, access to good historical information, and the courage to commit to quantitative measures when qualitative data are all that exist. Estimation carries inherent risk. Factors that increase risk are illustrated in Figure 3.1. The axes shown in the figure represent characteristics of the project to be estimated. Project complexity has a strong effect on the uncertainty inherent in planning. Complexity, however, is a relative measure affected by familiarity with past effort. A real-time application might be perceived as "exceedingly complex" to a software group that has previously developed only batch applications. The same real-time application might be perceived as "run-of-the-mill" to a software group that has been heavily involved in high speed process control. A number of quantitative software complexity measures have been proposed (e.g., [MCC76]). Such measures are applied at the design or code level and are therefore difficult to use during software planning (before a design and code exist). However, other, more subjective assessments of complexity can be established early in the planning process (see Section 3.5).

Project size is another important factor that can affect the accuracy and efficacy of estimates. As size increases, the interdependency among various elements of the software grows rapidly. Problem decomposition, an important approach to estimating, becomes more difficult because decomposed elements may still be formidable. A corollary could be added to Murphy's Law: "If more things can fail, more things will fail."

The degree of project structure also has an effect on estimation risk. In this context structure refers to the ease with which functions can be compartmentalized and to the hierarchical nature of information that must be processed. Figure 3.1 uses the reciprocal measure of structure, i.e., as the degree of structure increases, the ability to estimate accurately is improved, and risk decreases.

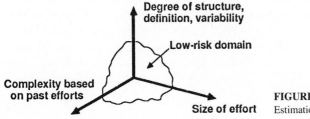

FIGURE 3.1
Estimation and risk.

The availability of historical information also determines estimation risk. Santayana once said, "Those who cannot remember the past are condemned to repeat it." By looking back we can emulate things that worked and improve areas where problems arose. When comprehensive *software metrics* (Section 3.5) for past projects are available, estimates can be made with greater assurance, schedules can be established to avoid past difficulties, and overall risk can be reduced.

Risk is measured by the degree of uncertainty in the quantitative estimates established for resources, cost, and schedule. If project scope is poorly understood or project requirements are subject to change, uncertainty and risk become dangerously high. The software planner should demand completeness of the function, performance, and interface definitions contained in the *System Specification*. The planner and, more importantly, the customer should recognize that any change in software requirements means instability in cost and schedule.

As a final observation on estimating, we consider the words of Aristotle (330 B.C.):

> ...it is the mark of an instructed mind to rest satisfied with the degree of precision which the nature of a subject admits, and not to seek exactness when only an approximation of the truth is possible....

3.2   PROJECT PLANNING OBJECTIVES

The software project manager is confronted with a dilemma at the very beginning of a development effort. Quantitative estimates are required, but solid information is unavailable. A detailed analysis of software requirements would provide necessary information for estimates, but analysis often takes weeks or months to complete. Estimates are needed "now."

The objective of software project planning is to provide a framework that enables the manager to make reasonable estimates of resources, cost, and schedule. These estimates are made within a limited time frame at the beginning of a software project and should be updated regularly as the project progresses.

As noted above the planning objective is achieved through a process of information discovery that leads to reasonable estimates. In the following sections each of the activities associated with software project planning is discussed.

3.3   SOFTWARE SCOPE

The first activity in software project planning is the determination of *software scope*. Function and performance allocated to software during computer system engineering should be assessed to establish a project scope that is unambiguous and understandable at the management and technical levels. A statement of software scope must be *bounded*. That is, quantitative data (e.g., number of simultaneous users, size of mailing list, maximum allowable response time) are stated explicitly; constraints and/or limitations (e.g., product cost restricts memory size) are noted; and mitigating factors (e.g., desired algorithms are well understood and available in Ada) are described.

The topics that are presented as part of software scope are illustrated in Figure 3.2. Software functions are evaluated and in some cases refined to provide more detail. Because both cost and schedule estimates are oriented functionally, some degree of decomposition is often useful. Performance considerations encompass processing time constraints, memory limitations for software, and special machine dependent features.

Function and performance must be evaluated together. The same function can precipitate a world of difference in development effort when considered in the context of different performance bounds. Reconsider, for example, the conveyor line sorting system (CLSS) discussed in Chapter 2. The software scope for CLSS (allocation 2) might be stated as follows:

CLSS software will receive input information from a bar code reader at time intervals that conform to the conveyor line speed. Bar code data will be decoded into box identification format. The software will do a look-up in a 1000-entry data base to determine proper bin location for the box currently at the reader (sorting station). A FIFO (first in, first out) list will be used to keep track of shunt positions for each box as it moves past the sorting station.

CLSS software will also receive input from a pulse tachometer that will be used to synchronize the control signal to the shunting mechanism. Based on the number of pulses that will be generated between the sorting station and the shunt, the software will produce a control signal to the shunt that will properly position the box....

The effort and cost required to develop CLSS software would be dramatically different if function remains the same (i.e., put boxes into bins) but performance varies. For instance if conveyor line average speed were increased by a factor of two and if boxes were no longer spaced evenly, software would become considerably more complex — thereby requiring more effort. Function and performance are intimately connected.

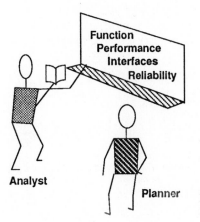

Function
Performance
Interfaces
Reliability

Analyst

Planner

FIGURE 3.2
Defining scope.

Software interacts with other elements of a computer-based system. The planner considers the nature and complexity of each interface to determine any effect on development resources, cost, and schedule. The concept of *interface* encompasses the following: (1) hardware (e.g., processor, peripherals) that executes the software and devices (e.g., machines, displays) indirectly controlled by the software; (2) software that already exists (e.g., data base access routines, subroutine packages, operating system) and must be linked to the new software; (3) people that make use of the software via terminals or other I/O devices; and (4) procedures that precede or succeed the software as a sequential series of operations. In each case the information transfer across the interface must be clearly understood.

The least precise aspect of software scope is a discussion of reliability. Software reliability measures are in the formative stage of development (see Chapter 12). Classic hardware reliability characteristics such as mean-time-between-failure (MTBF) are difficult to translate into the software domain. However, the general nature of the software may dictate special considerations to insure reliability. For example software for an air traffic control system or the Space Shuttle (both human rated systems) must not fail or human life may be lost. An inventory control system or word processor software should not fail, but the impact of failure is considerably less dramatic. Although it may not be possible to quantify software reliability as precisely as we would like, we can use the nature of the project to aid in formulating estimates of effort and cost to assure reliability.

If a *System Specification* has been properly developed, nearly all the information required for a description of software scope is available and documented before software project planning begins. In cases where a specification has not been developed, the planner must take on the role of system analyst to determine attributes and bounds that will influence estimation tasks.

3.4   RESOURCES

The second task of software planning is estimation of the resources required to accomplish the software development effort. Figure 3.3 illustrates development resources as a pyramid. At the foundation, tools—hardware and software—must exist to support the development effort. At a higher level, the primary resource—people—is al-

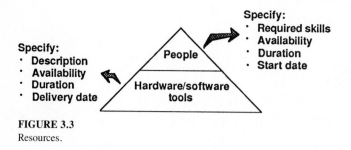

FIGURE 3.3
Resources.

ways required. Each resource is specified with four characteristics: description of the resource; a statement of availability; chronological date that the resource will be required; duration of time that the resource will be applied. The last two characteristics can be viewed as a *time window*. Availability of the resource for a specified window must be established at the earliest practical time.

3.4.1 Human Resources

Among the many problems posed by the software crisis, none is more ominous than the relative scarcity of capable human resources for software development. People are the primary software development resource.

The planner begins by evaluating scope and selecting the skills required to complete development. Both organizational position (e.g., manager, Senior Software Engineer, etc.) and specialty (e.g., telecommunications; data base; microprocessor) are specified. For relatively small projects (one person-year or less) a single individual may perform all software steps, consulting with specialists as required. For large projects, participation varies throughout the life cycle. Figure 3.4 illustrates typical project participation for each software engineering step.

Referring to the figure, management participation occurs early in the life cycle, tapers off to lower levels during the central steps of the development phase, and grows as project completion nears. Senior technical staff also participates actively during project planning, requirements analysis, design, and the final testing steps. Junior staff is most involved during later stages of design, coding, and early testing steps.

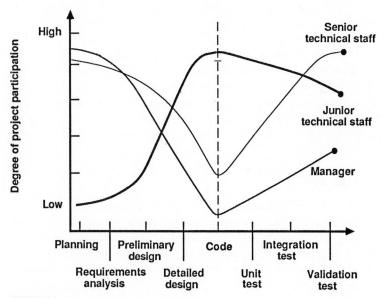

FIGURE 3.4
Management and staff participation.

The number of people required for a software project can be determined only after an estimate of development effort (e.g., person-months or person-years) is made. Techniques for estimating effort are discussed in Sections 3.6, 3.7, and 3.8.

3.4.2 Hardware Resources

Earlier in this book we referred to hardware as computing potential. Within the resource context hardware can also be a tool for software development.

Three hardware categories should be considered during software project planning: the development system, the target machine, and other hardware elements in the new system. The *development system* (also called the *host system*) is a computer and related peripherals that will be used during the software development phase. For example, a 32-bit computer may serve as the development system for a 16-bit microprocessor—the *target machine*—on which the software will eventually be executed. The development system is used because it can support multiple users, maintain large volumes of information that can be shared by software development team members, and support a rich assortment of software tools (to be discussed in the next section).

Except for very large projects the development system need not be specially acquired. Therefore, the *hardware resource* may be viewed as access to an existing computer rather than the purchase of a new computer. Because most development organizations have multiple constituencies that require development system access, the planner must carefully determine the time window required and verify that the resource will be available.

The *target machine* is a processor that executes software as part of the computer-based system. In most mainframe and minicomputer applications, the target machine and the development system are identical. Many microprocessor applications still require a separate microprocessor development system (MDS) that provides facilities for high-order language support, in-circuit emulation, and PROM programming.

Other hardware elements of the computer-based system may be specified as resources for software development. For example, software for a numerical control (NC) used on a class of machines may require a machine tool as part of the validation test step, or a software project for automated typesetting may need a phototypesetter at some point during development. Each hardware element must be specified by the planner.

3.4.3 Software Resources

Just as we use hardware as a tool to build new hardware, we use software to aid in the development of new software. The earliest application of software to software development was *bootstrapping*. A primitive assembler language translator was written in machine language and used to develop a more sophisticated assembler. Building on the capabilities of the previous version, software developers eventually *bootstrapped* high-level language compilers and other tools. Today a vast array of software tools are available. Figure 3.5 presents a hierarchy of software tools that are available today (*current tools*) or that will be available in the near term (*future tools*). Three broad categories of tools are available to the software engineer:

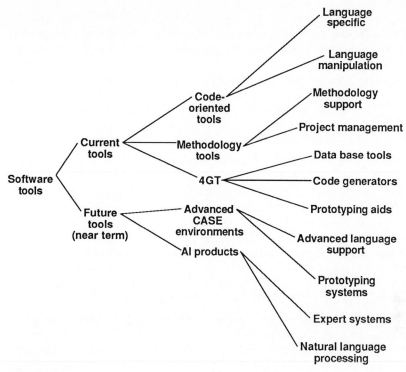

FIGURE 3.5
Categorizing software tools.

Code-oriented tools. Tools in this category are often the only tools available to software developers (a situation that is *not* ideal). Code-oriented tools include: programming language compilers, editors, linkers, and loaders; debugging aids; and a vast array of language-specific support.

Methodology tools. Just as a house builder needs a shovel to dig a foundation before a hammer and saw can be used to build a house, the software engineer needs methodology tools to analyze and design before coding. Tools in this category support project planning, requirements analysis, design, testing, configuration management, maintenance, and other activities. Among the tools in this category are *DesignAid* (Nastec Corporation), *Excelerator* (Index Technology), and *Teamwork* (Cadre Technologies, Inc.).

Fourth generation tools. The fourth generation techniques paradigm for software engineering was discussed in Chapter 1. To apply 4GT, a set of special tools must be available to enable the software developer to specify problems using data base query languages and other nonprocedural techniques. Among the many tools available in this category are NOMAD, FOCUS, INTELLECT (data base query) and GAMMA, HOS, TELON, TRANSFORM (code generators).

Tools in each of the above categories can be purchased off the shelf. In fact a new industry predicated on CASE (computer-aided software engineering) has spawned a number of companies dedicated to the integration of such tools into a *CASE workstation* environment.

Research in software tools and in the development of programming environments go hand-in-hand. Advanced software engineering environments are likely to use expert systems approaches to aid the analyst and designer in developing computer-based systems. A worthwhile survey of recent work can be found in [BAR84] and [HEN85].

Any discussion of the software resource would be incomplete without recognizing *reusability*, that is, the creation and reuse of software building blocks [JON84]. Such building blocks must be cataloged for easy reference, standardized for easy application, and validated for easy integration.

Most industry observers agree that improved software development productivity and product quality will bring an end to the software crisis. In such a world reusable software would abound. Software building blocks would be available to allow the construction of large packages with minimal "from scratch" development. Unfortunately, we have not yet achieved this ideal. Libraries of reusable software do exist for commercial applications, systems and real-time work, and engineering and scientific problems. However, few systematic techniques exist for making additions to a library, standard interfaces for reusable software are difficult to enforce, quality and maintainability issues remain unresolved, and, lastly, the developer is often unaware that appropriate software building blocks even exist.

Two "rules" should be considered by the software planner when reusable software is specified as a resource:

1. If existing software meets requirements, acquire it. The cost for acquisition of existing software will almost always be less than the cost to develop equivalent software.
2. If existing software requires "some" modification before it can be integrated properly with the system, proceed carefully. The cost of modifying existing software can sometimes be greater than the cost of developing equivalent software.

Ironically, software resources are often neglected during planning, only to become of paramount concern during the development phase of the software engineering process. It is far better to specify software resource requirements early. In this way technical evaluation of alternatives can be conducted and timely acquisition can occur.

3.5 METRICS FOR SOFTWARE PRODUCTIVITY AND QUALITY

Measurement is fundamental to any engineering discipline, and software engineering is no exception. Lord Kelvin once said:

> When you can measure what you are speaking about and express it in numbers, you know something about it; but when you cannot measure, when you cannot express it in numbers, your knowledge is of a meager and unsatisfactory kind: it may be the beginning of knowledge, but you have scarcely, in your thoughts, advanced to the stage of a science.

Over the past decade the software engineering community has taken Lord Kelvin's words to heart—but not without frustration and with more than a little controversy.

Software metrics refers to a broad range of measures for computer software (e.g., [ART85]). Within the context of software project planning, we are concerned with *productivity metrics*—measures of software development "output" as a function of effort applied. For planning purposes our interest is historical. What was software development productivity on past projects? How can past productivity data be extrapolated to the present? How can it help us estimate more accurately?

In the sections that follow, we first consider the broad range of software metrics in order to understand where productivity measures fit. Next, two important (and opposing) views on the measurement of software productivity are presented. Finally, we examine the practical problems of collecting metrics and using them for software project estimation.

3.5.1 Measuring Software

Measurement is commonplace in the hardware engineering world. We measure power consumption, weight, physical dimensions, temperature, voltage, signal-to-noise ratio—the list is almost endless. Unfortunately, measurement is far from commonplace in the software engineering world. We have trouble agreeing on what to measure and how to evaluate those measurements.

Software is measured for many reasons: (1) to indicate the quality of the product, (2) to assess the productivity of the people who produce the product, (3) to assess the benefits (in terms of productivity and quality) derived from new software engineering methods and tools, (4) to form a baseline for estimation, and (5) to help justify requests for new tools or additional training.

Measurements in the physical world can be categorized in two ways: *direct measures* (e.g., the length of a bolt) and *indirect measures* (e.g., the "quality" of bolts produced, measured by counting rejects). Software metrics can be categorized similarly. Figure 3.6 lists examples of direct and indirect measures of software. The cost and effort required to build software, the number of lines of code, and other direct measures

Direct measures

- Cost
- Effort
- LOC (lines of code)
- Speed
- Memory size
- Errors

Indirect measures

- Function
- Quality
- Complexity
- Efficiency
- Reliability
- Maintainability

FIGURE 3.6
Direct and indirect measures.

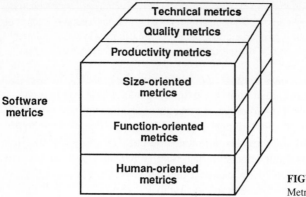

FIGURE 3.7
Metrics categorization.

are relatively easy to collect as long as specific conventions for measurement are established in advance. However, the quality and functionality of software, or its efficiency and maintainability, are more difficult to assess and can only be measured indirectly.

We can further categorize the software metrics domain as shown in Figure 3.7. As we have already noted, *productivity metrics* focus on the output of the software engineering process; *quality metrics* provide an indication of how closely software conforms to implicit and explicit customer requirements, and *technical metrics* focus on the character of the software (e.g, logical complexity, degree of modularity) rather than the process through which the software was developed. Referring again to the figure, we note that a second categorization can also be developed. *Size-oriented metrics* are used to collect direct measures of software engineering output and quality. *Function-oriented metrics* provide indirect measures and *human-oriented measures* collect information about the manner in which people develop computer software and human perceptions of the effectiveness of tools and methods.

3.5.2   Size-Oriented Metrics

Size-oriented software metrics are direct measures of software and the process by which it is developed. If a software organization maintains simple records, a table of size-oriented data, such as the one shown in Figure 3.8, can be created. The table lists each software development project completed over the past few years and the corresponding size-oriented data for that project. Referring to the table entry (Figure 3.8) for project aaa-01: 12.1 KLOC (thousand lines of code) were developed with 24 person-months of effort at a cost of $168,000. It should be noted that the effort and cost recorded in the table represent *all* software engineering activities (analysis, design, code, and test), *not* just coding. Further information for project aaa-01 indicates that 365 pages of documentation were developed, while 29 errors were encountered after release to the customer within the first year of operation. Three people worked on the development of software for project aaa-01.

From the rudimentary data contained in the table, a set of simple size-oriented productivity and quality metrics can be developed for each project. Averages can be computed for all projects. From Figure 3.8 we have:

$$productivity = KLOC/person\text{-}month$$

$$quality = error/KLOC$$

In addition other interesting metrics may be computed:

$$cost = \$ / KLOC$$

$$documentation = pgs.\ doc.\ / KLOC$$

Size-oriented metrics are controversial and are not universally accepted as the best way to measure the process of software development. Most of the controversy swirls around the use of lines of code (LOC) as a key measure. Proponents of the LOC measure claim that LOC is an "artifact" of all software development projects that can be easily counted, that many existing software estimation models use LOC or KLOC as a key input, and that a large body of literature and data predicated on LOC already exists. On the other hand opponents claim that LOC measures are programming language–dependent, that they penalize well-designed but shorter programs, that they cannot easily accommodate nonprocedural languages, and that their use in estimation requires a level of detail that may be difficult to achieve (i.e., the planner must estimate the LOC to be produced long before analysis and design have been completed).

3.5.3 Function-Oriented Metrics

Function-oriented software metrics are indirect measures of software and the process by which it is developed. Rather than counting LOC, function-oriented metrics focus

Project	Effort	$	LOC	Pgs.doc.	Errors	People
aaa-01	24	168	12.1	365	29	3
ccc-04	62	440	27.2	1224	86	5
fff-03	43	314	20.2	1050	64	6
•	•	•	•	•		
•	•	•	•	•		
•	•	•	•			

FIGURE 3.8
Size-oriented metrics.

on program "functionality" or "utility." Function-oriented metrics were first proposed by Albrecht [ALB79], who suggested a productivity measurement approach called the *function point* method. Function points are derived using an empirical relationship based on countable measures of software's information domain and subjective assessments of software complexity. The function point measure was originally designed to be applied to business information system applications. It may not be relevant to control-oriented or embedded applications in the engineered products and systems domain.

Function points are computed by completing the table shown in Figure 3.9. Five information domain characteristics are determined and counts are provided in the appropriate table location. Information domain values are defined in the following manner:

Number of user inputs. Each user input that provides distinct application-oriented data to the software is counted. Inputs should be distinguished from inquiries, which are counted separately.

Number of user outputs. Each user output that provides application-oriented information to the user is counted. In this context output refers to reports, screens, error messages, etc. Individual data items within a report are not counted separately.

Number of user inquiries. An inquiry is defined as an on-line input that results in the generation of some immediate software response in the form of an on-line output. Each distinct inquiry is counted.

Number of files. Each logical master file (i.e., a logical grouping of data that may be one part of a large data base or a separate file) is counted.

Number of external interfaces. All machine-readable interfaces (e.g., data files on tape or disk) that are used to transmit information to another system are counted.

Information domain item	Count	Weighting factor			FP
		Simple	Avg.	Complex	
Number of user inputs		3	4	6	
Number of user outputs		4	5	7	
Number of user inquiries		3	4	6	
Number of files		7	10	15	
Number of ext. interfaces		5	7	10	

Count times weighting factor = FP

FIGURE 3.9
Computing function points.

Once the above data have been collected, a complexity value is associated with each count. Organizations that use function-point methods develop criteria for determining whether a particular entry is simple, average, or complex. Nonetheless, the determination of complexity is somewhat subjective.

To compute function points (FP), the following relationship is used:

$$FP = \text{count.total} \times [0.65 + 0.01 \times \text{SUM}(F_i)]$$

where count.total is the sum of all WC entries obtained from the table in Figure 3.9. F_i ($i = 1$ to 14) are "complexity adjustment values" based on responses to questions [ART85] noted in Table 3.1. The constant values in the above equation and the weighting factors applied to information domain counts are determined empirically.

Once function points have been calculated, they are used in a manner analogous to LOC as a measure of software productivity, quality, and other attributes:

TABLE 3.1
Computing function points

Rate each factor on a scale of 0 to 5:

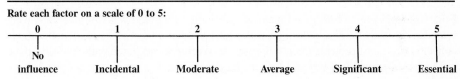

0	1	2	3	4	5
No influence	Incidental	Moderate	Average	Significant	Essential

F_i:

1. Does the system require reliable backup and recovery?

2. Are data communications required?

3. Are there distributed processing functions?

4. Is performance critical?

5. Will the system run in an existing, heavily utilized operational environment?

6. Does the system require on-line data entry?

7. Does the on-line data entry require the input transaction to be built over multiple screens or operations?

8. Are the master files updated on-line?

9. Are the inputs, outputs, files, or inquiries complex?

10. Is the internal processing complex?

11. Is the code designed to be reusable?

12. Are conversion and installation included in the design?

13. Is the system designed for multiple installations in different organizations?

14. Is the application designed to facilitate change and ease of use by the user?

$$\text{productivity} = \text{FP} / \text{person-month}$$

$$\text{quality} = \text{error} / \text{FP}$$

$$\text{cost} = \$ / \text{FP}$$

$$\text{documentation} = \text{pgs. doc.} / \text{FP}$$

among others.

The function-point metric, like LOC, is relatively controversial. Proponents claim that FP is programming language–independent, making it ideal for applications using conventional and nonprocedural languages, and that it is based on data more likely to be known early in the evolution of a project, thus making FP more attractive as an estimation approach. Opponents claim that the method requires some ''sleight of hand'' in that computation is based on subjective, rather than objective, data; that information domain information can be difficult to collect after-the-fact; and that FP has no direct physical meaning—it's just a number.

3.5.4   Reconciling Different Metrics Approaches

Both size- and function-oriented metrics have their strong and weak points. However, each can be used effectively during software project planning. LOC and FP data can be collected from past projects (recall Figure 3.8). Averages computed with historical data can be used in conjunction with LOC or FP *estimates* for new work (see Section 3.6) to provide estimates of cost and effort.

A number of studies have attempted to relate FP and LOC measures. To quote Albrecht and Gaffney [ALB83]:

> The thesis of this work is that the amount of function to be provided by the application (program) can be estimated from the itemization of the major components of data to be used or provided by it. Furthermore, this estimate of function should be correlated to both the amount of LOC to be developed and the development effort needed.

The investigators evaluated function points of 24 COBOL, PL/1, and a simple data base query language (a 4GL). For this rather limited sample, LOC and function points correlated well but varied for each programming language. Summarizing, the authors found the following (average) relationships:

Language	LOC/FP
COBOL	110
PL/1	65
4GL	25

A review of the above data indicates that one LOC of PL/1 provides almost twice the ''functionality'' (on average) as one LOC of COBOL. Furthermore, one LOC of a

4GL provides between two and four times the functionality of an LOC for a conventional programming language.

Any discussion of software productivity measurement invariably leads to a debate about the use of such data. Should the LOC/person-month (or FP/PM) of one group be compared to similar data from another? Should managers appraise the performance of individuals by using these metrics? The answer to these questions is an emphatic "No!" The reason for this response is that many factors influence productivity, making for "apples and oranges" comparisons that can be easily misinterpreted.

Basili and Zelkowitz [BAS78] define five important factors that influence software productivity:

People factors. The size and expertise of the development organization.

Problem factors. The complexity of the problem to be solved and the number of changes in design constraints or requirements.

Process factors. Analysis and design techniques that are used, languages available, and review procedures.

Product factors. Reliability and performance of the computer-based system.

Resource factors. Availability of development tools, hardware, and software resources.

The effect of these and other factors are best illustrated by the results of a landmark study conducted by Walston and Felix [WAL77]. The authors isolate 29 factors that affect productivity and attempt to show how productivity varies with each factor. Referring to Figure 3.10 reproduced from the study, factors are listed in the leftmost column; productivity [delivered source lines per person-month (DSL/PM)] is indicated in the central three columns, with factors varying from favorable to unfavorable; the rightmost column indicates the productivity variance for a particular factor. Referring to Figure 3.10, it can be seen that the productivity variance can be significant as factors change from favorable to unfavorable.

It should be noted that the factors listed in Figure 3.10 have complex interrelationships that are disregarded to simplify the data. However, the Walston and Felix data do provide a worthwhile qualitative feel for the relative impact of a particular factor on lines of code (LOC) productivity. It is likely that the same effects would be encountered for function points.

Function points and LOC have been found to be relatively accurate predictors of software development effort and cost. However, in order to use LOC and FP in the estimation techniques described in Section 3.6, a historical baseline of information must be established. In the next section guidelines for metrics data collection are presented.

3.5.5 Metrics Data Collection

To develop accurate estimates, a *historical baseline* must be established. The baseline consists of data collected from past software development projects and can be as simple as the table presented in Figure 3.8. To be an effective aid in cost and effort estima-

Question or variable	Response group mean productivity (DSL/PM)*			Productivity change (DSL/PM)*
Customer interface complexity	<Normal 500	Normal 295	>Normal 124	376
User participation in the definition of requirements	None 491	Some 267	Much 205	286
Customer originated program design changes	Few 297		Many 196	101
Customer experience with the application area of the project	None 318	Some 340	Much 206	112
Overall personnel experience and qualifications	Low 132	Average 257	High 410	278
Percentage of programmers doing development who participated in design of functional specifications	<25% 153	25-50% 242	>50% 391	238
Previous experience with operational computer	Minimal 146	Average 270	Extensive 312	166
Previous experience with programming languages	Minimal 122	Average 225	Extensive 385	263
Previous experience with application of similar or greater size and complexity	Minimal 146	Average 221	Extensive 410	264
Ratio of average staff size to duration (people/month)	<0.5 305	0.5–0.9 310	>0.9 173	132
Hardware under concurrent development	No 297		Yes 177	120
Development computer access, open under special request	0% 226	1–25% 274	>25% 357	131
Development computer access, closed	0–10% 303	11–85% 251	>85% 170	133
Classified security environment for computer and 25% of programs and data	No 289		Yes 156	133
Structured programming	0–33% 169	34–66% —	>66% 301	132
Design and code inspections	0–33% 220	34–66% 300	>66% 339	119
Top-down development	0–33% 196	34–66% 237	>66% 321	125
Chief programmer team usage	0–33% 219	34–66%	>66% 408	189
Overall complexity of code developed	<Average 314		>Average 185	129

FIGURE 3.10

Productivity variance: Variables that correlate significantly with programming productivity. (*Source:* Walston and Felix, ''A Method for Programming Measurement and Estimation,'' *IBM Systems Journal,* 1977, courtesy of the IBM Corporation.)

Question or variable	Response group mean productivity (DSL/PM)*			Productivity change (DSL/PM)*
Complexity of application processing	<Average 349	Average 345	>Average 168	181
Complexity of program flow	<Average 289	Average 299	>Average 209	80
Overall constraints on program design	Minimal 293	Average 286	Severe 166	107
Program design constraints on main storage	Minimal 391	Average 277	Severe 193	198
Program design constraints on timing	Minimal 303	Average 317	Severe 171	132
Code for real-time or interactive operation, or executing under severe timing constraint	<10% 279	10–40% 337	>40% 203	76
Percentage of code for delivery	0–90% 159	91–99% 327	100% 265	106
Code classified as non-mathematical application and I/O formating programs	0–33% 188	33–66% 311	67–100% 267	79
Number of classes of items in the data base per 1000 lines of code	0–15 334	16–80 243	>80 193	141
Number of pages of delivered documentation per 1000 lines of delivered code	0–32 320	33–88 252	>88 195	125

* DSL/PM = delivered source lines/person-month

FIGURE 3.10
(*continued*)

tion, baseline data must have the following attributes: (1) data must be reasonably accurate—''guestimates'' about past projects are to be avoided; (2) data should be collected for as many projects as possible; (3) measurements must be consistent (e.g., LOC must be interpreted consistently across all projects for which data are collected); and (4) applications should be similar to work that is to be estimated—it makes little sense to use a baseline for batch information system work to estimate a real-time microprocessor application.

The process for establishing a baseline is illustrated in Figure 3.11. Ideally, data needed to establish a baseline has been collected in an on-going manner. Sadly, this is rarely the case. Therefore, *data collection* requires a historical investigation of past projects to reconstruct required data. Once data have been collected (unquestionably the most difficult step), *metrics computation* is possible. Depending on the breadth of data collected, metrics can span a broad range of LOC or FP measures. Finally, computed

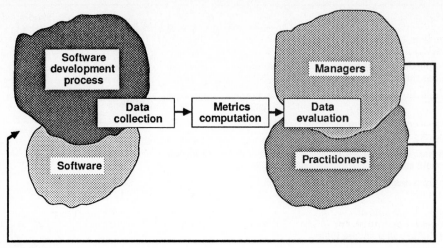

FIGURE 3.11
Software metrics collection process.

data must be evaluated and applied in estimation. *Data evaluation* focuses on the underlying reasons for the results obtained. Are the computed averages relevant to the project at hand? What extenuating circumstances invalidate certain data for use in this estimate? These and other questions must be addressed so that metrics data are not used blindly.

Figure 3.12a and b presents a spreadsheet model for collection and computation of historical software baseline data. Note that the model includes cost data, size-oriented data, and function-oriented data, enabling computation of both LOC and FP[*] oriented metrics. It should be noted that it is not always possible to collect all data requested in this model. If we apply such a model to a number of past projects, we will have established the foundation for software project estimation.

3.6   SOFTWARE PROJECT ESTIMATION

In the early days of computing, software costs represented a small percentage of the overall cost of a computer-based system. A sizable error in estimates of software cost had relatively little impact. Today, software is the most expensive element in many computer-based systems. A large cost-estimation error can make the difference between profit and loss. Cost overrun can be disastrous for the developer.

Software cost and effort estimation will never be an exact science. Too many variables—human, technical, environmental, political—can affect the ultimate cost of

---

[*]The computation of FP shown in this spreadsheet uses an experimental model that is somewhat different than FP computations described in Section 3.5.3.

software and the effort applied to develop it. However, software project estimation can be transformed from a black art into a series of systematic steps that provide estimates with an acceptable degree of risk.

In an earlier section we noted that estimation cannot be undertaken without risk. Any software project estimation technique (or set of techniques) should strive to provide the highest degree of reliability, i.e., the lowest risk of major estimation error.

To achieve reliable cost and effort estimates, a number of potential options arise:

1. Delay estimation until late in the project (obviously, we can achieve 100 percent accurate estimates after the project is complete!);
2. Use relatively simple "decomposition techniques" to generate project cost and effort estimates;
3. Develop an empirical model for software cost and effort;
4. Acquire one or more automated estimation tools.

Description	Units	Data
Cost data		
Labor cost	$/person-month	7744
Labor year	Hrs/year	1560
Size-oriented data		
Proj. name	Alphanumeric	HypoProj
Number of project staff	People	3
Effort	Person-hours	5200
Elapsed time	Months	13.0
Source lines delivered	KLOC	11.5
Source lines reused	Percent - %	8
Technical documentation	Pages	465
User documentation	Pages	122
No. of errors (1st year)	Errors	26
Maint. effort-modifications	Person-hours	810
Maint. effort-errors	Person-hours	740
Mean tie to repair	Hours	64
Function-oriented data		
Information domain		
No. programs or tasks	Programs, tasks	1
No. interactive commands	Commands	46
Data items per command	Data items (avg.)	2
No. distinct outputs	Outputs	28
No. distinct files	Files	4
No. system interfaces	Interfaces	1
Processing complexity		
Data transmission	Scale: 1 to 5	1
Distributed processing	Scale: 1 to 5	2
Performance	Scale: 1 to 5	3
Executive level functions	Scale: 1 to 5	2
System criticality	Scale: 1 to 5	1

FIGURE 3.12
(*a*) Metrics data collection model.

Description	Units	Data
Size-oriented metrics		
Productivity and cost metrics:		
Project name	Alphanumeric	HypoProj
Output	P-m/KLOC	3.5
Cost-all LOC	$/KLOC	$26,936
Cost excluding reused	$/KLOC	$29,278
Elapsed time	Months/KLOC	1.1
Documentation	Pages/KLOC	51
Documentation	Pages/p-m	15
Documentation	$/page	$528
Quality metrics:		
Defects	Errors/KLOC	2.3
Cost of errors	$/error	$141
Maint. errors/total maint.	Ratio	0.48
Maint. modss/total maint.	Ratio	0.52
Maint. effort/total effort	Ratio	0.30
Function-oriented metrics		
Info. flow complexity (IFC)		
Number of arrows in DFD	Arrow count	9
IFC.couple		1.33
IFC.size.e1		0.60
P		0.30
IFC.size.e2		1.64
IFC.size		2.24
IFC		3.57
Processing complexity	Avg. rating	1.80
Processing complexity	Computed	1.16
Modified function points	MFP	327
Program functionality	MFP/program	327
Program size	KLOC/program	11.5
Functionality per file	MFP/file	81.8
Function size ratio	MFP/KLOC	28.5
Function size	LOC/MFP	35
Productivity and cost metrics:		
Output	p-m/MFP	0.12
Cost	$/MFP	$946
Documentation	Pages/MFP	1.8
Elapsed time	Days/MFP	0.9
Quality metrics:		
Defects	Errors/MFP	0.079
Maint. effort-errors	P-m/MFP	2.474
Maint. effort-mods	P-m/MFP	2.261

FIGURE 3.12

(*b*) Metrics computation model.

Unfortunately, the first option, however attractive, is not practical: Cost estimates must be provided "up-front." However, we should recognize that the longer we wait, the more we know, and the more we know, the less likely we are to make serious errors in our estimates.

The remaining three options are viable approaches to software project estimation. Ideally, the techniques noted for each option should be applied in tandem, each used to cross-check the others. *Decomposition techniques* take a "divide and conquer" approach to software project estimation. By decomposing a project into major functions and related software engineering tasks, cost and effort estimation can be performed in a stepwise fashion. *Empirical estimation models* can be used to complement decomposition techniques and offer a potentially valuable estimation approach in their own right. A model is based on experience (historical data) and takes the form:

$$d = f(v_i)$$

where *d* is one of a number of estimated values (e.g., effort, cost, project duration) and v_i are selected independent parameters (e.g., estimated LOC or FP). *Automated estimation tools* implement one or more decomposition techniques or empirical models. When combined with an interactive human-machine interface, automated tools provide an attractive option for estimating. In such systems the characteristics of the development organization (e.g., experience, environment) and the software to be developed are described. Cost and effort estimates are derived from these data.

Each of the viable software cost-estimation options is only as good as the historical data used to seed the estimate. If no historical data exist, costing rests on a very shaky foundation. In Section 3.5 we examined the characteristics of software productivity data and how it could be used as a historical basis for estimation.

3.7 DECOMPOSITION TECHNIQUES

Humans have developed a natural approach to problem solving: if the problem to be solved is too complicated, we tend to subdivide it until manageable problems are encountered. We then solve each individually and hope that the solutions can be combined to answer the original problem.

Software project estimation is a form of problem solving, and in most cases the problem to be solved (i.e., developing a cost and effort estimate for a software project) is too complex to be considered in one piece. For this reason we decompose the problem, re-characterizing it as a set of smaller (and hopefully, more manageable) problems.

3.7.1 LOC and FP Estimation

In Section 3.5 lines of code (LOC) and function points (FP) were described as basic data from which productivity metrics could be computed. LOC and FP data are used in two ways during software project estimation: (1) as an *estimation variable* that is used to "size" each element of the software, and (2) as *baseline metrics* collected from past projects and used in conjunction with estimation variables to develop cost and effort projections.

LOC and FP estimation are distinct estimation techniques. Yet both have a number of characteristics in common. The project planner begins with a bounded statement of software scope and from this statement attempts to decompose software into small subfunctions that can each be estimated individually. LOC or FP (the estimation variable) is then estimated for each subfunction. Baseline productivity metrics (e.g., LOC/PM or FP/PM) are then applied to the appropriate estimation variable and cost or effort for the subfunction is derived. Subfunction estimates are combined to produce an overall estimate for the entire project.

The LOC and FP estimation techniques differ in the level of detail required for decomposition. When LOC is used as the estimation variable, function decomposition is absolutely essential and is often taken through considerable levels of detail. Because the data required to estimate function points are more macroscopic, the level of decomposition used when FP is the estimation variable is considerably less detailed. It should also be noted that LOC is estimated directly, while FP is determined indirectly by estimating the number of inputs, outputs, data files, inquiries, and external interfaces, as well as the fourteen *complexity adjustment values* described in Section 3.5.3.

Regardless of the estimation variable used, the project planner or technical consultant typically provides a range of values for each decomposed function. Using historical data or (when all else fails) intuition, the planner estimates an optimistic, most likely, and pessimistic LOC or FP value for each function. An implicit indication of the degree of uncertainty is provided when a range of values is specified.

The expected (or average) number of LOC or FP is computed in the next step of the estimation technique. The expected value for the estimation variable, E, can be computed as a weighted average of the optimistic (a), most likely (m), and pessimistic (b) LOC or FP estimates. For example,

$$E = (a + 4m + b) / 6$$

gives heaviest credence to the ''most likely'' estimate and follows a *beta probability distribution*.

We assume that there is a very small probability that the actual LOC or FP result will fall outside the optimistic or pessimistic values. Using standard statistical techniques, we can compute deviation of the estimates. However, it should be noted that a deviation based on uncertain (estimated) data must be used judiciously.

Once the expected value for the estimation variable has been determined, LOC or FP productivity data are applied. At this stage the planner can apply one of two different approaches.

1. The total estimation variable value for all subfunctions can be multiplied by the average productivity metric corresponding to that estimation variable. For example if we assume that 310 FP are estimated in total and that average FP productivity based on past projects is 5.5 FP/PM, then the overall effort for the project is:

   effort (PM) = 310 / 5.5 = 56 person-months

2. The estimation variable value for each subfunction can be multiplied by an *adjusted productivity value* that is based on the perceived level of complexity of the subfunction. For functions of average complexity, the average productivity metric is used. However, the average productivity metric is adjusted up or down (somewhat subjectively) based on higher or lower than average complexity for a particular subfunction. For example if average productivity is 490 LOC/PM, line of code estimates for subfunctions that are considerably more complex than average might be multiplied by 300 LOC/PM and simple functions by 650 LOC/PM.

It is important to note that average productivity metrics should be corrected to reflect inflationary effects, increased project complexity, new people, or other development characteristics.

Are the estimates correct? The only reasonable answer to this question is: "We can't be sure." Any estimation technique, no matter how sophisticated, must be cross-checked with another approach. Even then, common sense and experience must prevail. Other approaches to estimation are presented in later sections, but first, it is worthwhile to consider a brief example.

3.7.2 An Example

As an example of LOC and FP estimation techniques, let us consider a software package to be developed for a computer-aided design (CAD) application. Reviewing the *System Specification* we find that the software is to execute in a microcomputer-based work station and will interface with various computer graphics peripherals including a mouse, digitizer, high resolution color display, and high-resolution printer.

For the purposes of this example, LOC will be used as the estimation variable. It should be noted, however, that FP could also be used and would require estimates of the information domain values discussed in Section 3.5.3.

Evaluation of scope indicates that the following major functions are required for the CAD software:

- user interface and control facilities (UICF)
- two-dimensional geometric analysis (2DGA)
- three-dimensional geometric analysis (3DGA)
- data structure management (DSM)
- computer graphics display facilities (CGDF)
- peripheral control (PC)
- design analysis modules (DAM)

Following the decomposition technique, an estimation table, shown in Figure 3.13, is developed. A range of LOC estimates is developed. Viewing the first three columns of the table, it can be seen that the planner is fairly certain of LOC required for the peripheral control function (only 450 lines of code separate optimistic and pessimistic estimates). On the other hand, the three-dimensional geometric analysis function is a relative unknown as indicated by the 4000 LOC difference between optimistic and pessimistic values.

Calculations for expected value are performed for each function and placed in the fourth column of the table (Figure 3.14). By summing vertically in the expected value column, an estimate of 33360 lines of code is established for the CAD system.[*]

---

[*]It should be noted that the estimation precision implied by the three low-order significant digits (i.e., 360) is not attainable. Rounding off to the nearest 1000 LOC would be far more realistic. Low-order digits are maintained for calculation accuracy only.

Function	Optimistic	Most likely	Pessimistic	Expected	$/line	Line/month	Cost	Months
User interface control	1800	2400	2650					
2 – D geometric analysis	4100	5200	7400					
3 – D geometric analysis	4600	6900	8600					
Data structure management	2950	3400	3600					
Computer graphics display	4050	4900	6200					
Peripheral control	2000	2100	2450					
Design analysis	6600	8500	9800					

FIGURE 3.13
Estimation table.

Function	Optimistic	Most likely	Pessimistic	Expected	$/line	Line/month	Cost	Months
User interface control	1800	2400	2650	2340				
2 – D geometric analysis	4100	5200	7400	5380				
3 – D geometric analysis	4600	6900	8600	6800				
Data structure management	2950	3400	3600	3350				
Computer graphics display	4050	4900	6200	4950				
Peripheral control	2000	2100	2450	2140				
Design analysis	6600	8500	9800	8400				

Total 33360

FIGURE 3.14
Estimation table.

The remainder of the estimation table required for the decomposition technique is shown in Figure 3.15. Productivity metrics (derived from a historical baseline) are acquired for $/LOC and LOC/person-month. In this case the planner uses different values of productivity metrics for each function based on the degree of complexity. Values contained in the cost and months columns of the table are determined by multiplying or dividing expected LOC with $/LOC and LOC/person-month, respectively. The totals of these two columns are $657,000 and 145 person-months. In Section 3.8 we will see how the estimated effort can be used with an empirical model to derive an estimate for project duration (in chronological months).

3.7.3 Effort Estimation

Effort estimation is the most common technique for costing any engineering development project. A number of person-days, months, or years is applied to the solution of each project task. A dollar cost is associated with each unit of effort and an estimated cost is derived.

Like the LOC or FP technique, effort estimation begins with a delineation of software functions obtained from the project scope. A series of software engineering tasks—requirements analysis, design, code, and test—must be performed for each function. Functions and related software engineering tasks may be represented as part of a table illustrated in Figure 3.16.

The planner estimates the effort (e.g., person-months) that will be required to accomplish each software engineering task for each software function. These data make up the central matrix of the table in Figure 3.16. Labor rates (i.e., cost/unit effort) are applied to each of the software engineering tasks. It is very likely the labor rate will vary for each task. Senior staff are heavily involved in requirements analysis and early design tasks; junior staff (who are inherently less costly) are involved in later design tasks, code, and early testing.

Costs and effort for each function and software engineering task are computed as the last step. If effort estimation is performed independently of LOC or FP estimation, we now have two estimates for cost and effort that may be compared and reconciled. If both sets of estimates show reasonable agreement, there is good reason to believe that the estimates are reliable. If, on the other hand, the results of these decomposition techniques show little agreement, further investigation and analysis must be conducted.

3.7.4 An Example

To illustrate the use of effort estimation, we again consider the CAD software introduced in Section 3.7.2. The system configuration and all software functions remain unchanged and are indicated by project scope.

Referring to the completed effort estimation table shown in Figure 3.17, estimates of effort (in person-months) for each software engineering task are provided for each CAD software function (abbreviated to save space). Horizontal and vertical totals provide an indication of effort required. It should be noted that 75 person-months are

Function	Optimistic	Most likely	Pessimistic	Expected	$/line	Line/month	Cost	Months
User interface control	1800	2400	2650	2340	14	315	32,760	7.4
2 – D geometric analysis	4100	5200	7400	5380	20	220	107,600	24.4
3 – D geometric analysis	4600	6900	8600	6800	20	220	136,000	30.9
Data structure management	2950	3400	3600	3350	18	240	60,300	13.9
Computer graphics display	4050	4900	6200	4950	22	200	108,900	24.7
Peripheral control	2000	2100	2450	2140	28	140	59,920	15.2
Design analysis	6600	8500	9800	8400	18	300	151,200	28.0

Estimated LOC: 33360

Estimated project cost ($): $656,680

Estimated effort required (PM): 144.5

FIGURE 3.15
Estimation table.

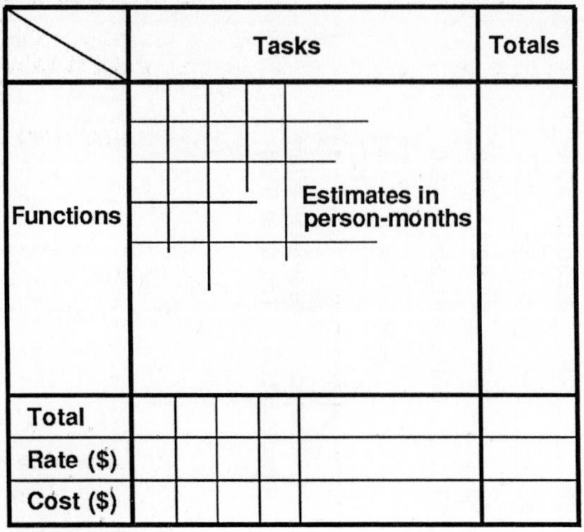

FIGURE 3.16
Develop a cost matrix.

Tasks / Functions	Requirements analysis	Design	Code	Test	Totals*
UICF	1.0	2.0	0.5	3.5	7
2DGA	2.0	10.0	4.5	9.5	26
3DGA	2.5	12.0	6.0	11.0	31.5
DSM	2.0	6.0	3.0	4.0	15
CGDF	1.5	11.0	4.0	10.5	27
PCF	1.5	6	3.5	5	16
DAM	4	14	5	7	30
Total*	14.5	61	26.5	50.5	152.5
Rate ($)	5200	4800	4250	4500	
Cost ($)	75,400	292,800	112,625	227,250	708,075

Estimated effort for all tasks

Estimated cost for all tasks

* All estimates are in person-months except where otherwise noted.

FIGURE 3.17
Effort estimation table.

expended on "front-end" development tasks (requirements analysis and design) indicating the relative importance of this work.

Labor rates are associated with each software engineering task and entered in the "Rate($)" row of the table. These data reflect "burdened" labor costs (i.e., labor costs that include company overhead). In this example it is assumed that labor costs for requirements analysis ($5200/person-month) will be 22 percent greater than costs for code and unit test. Unlike software productivity data, average labor rates can be accurately predicted in a software development organization.

Total estimated cost and effort for the CAD software are $708,000 and 153 person-months, respectively. Comparing these values to data derived using the lines of code technique, a cost variance of 7 percent and effort variance of 5 percent are found. We have achieved extremely close agreement.

What happens when agreement between estimates is poor? The answer to this question requires a reevaluation of information used to make the estimates. Widely divergent estimates can often be traced to one of two causes:

1. The scope of the project is not adequately understood or has been misinterpreted by the planner.
2. Productivity data used in LOC or FP estimation are inappropriate for the application, obsolete (in that they no longer accurately reflect the software development organization), or have been misapplied.

The planner must determine the cause of divergence and reconcile the estimates.

3.8 EMPIRICAL ESTIMATION MODELS

An *estimation model* for computer software uses empirically derived formulae to predict data that are a required part of the software project planning step. The empirical data that support most models are derived from a limited sample of projects. For this reason no estimation model is appropriate for all classes of software and in all development environments. Therefore, the results obtained from such models must be used judiciously.

Resource models consist of one or more empirically derived equations that predict effort (in person-months), project duration (in chronological months), or other pertinent project data. Basili [BAS80] describes four classes of resource models: static single-variable models, static multivariable models, dynamic multivariable models, and theoretical models.

The static single-variable model takes the form:

$$\text{resource} = c_1 \times (\text{estimated characteristic})^{c_2}$$

where the resource could be effort (E), project duration (D), staff size (S), or requisite lines of software documentation (DOC). The constants c_1 and c_2 are derived from data collected from past projects. The estimated characteristic is lines of source code, effort (if estimated), or other software characteristics.

As an example of a set of static single-variable models, we again consider the Walston and Felix [WAL77] study. Based on data collected from 60 software development projects ranging in size from 4000 to 467,000 source lines and 12 to 11,758 person-months, the following models were derived:

$$E = 5.2 \times L^{0.91}$$

$$D = 4.1 \times L^{0.36}$$

$$D = 2.47 \times E^{0.35}$$

$$S = 0.54 \times E^{0.06}$$

$$\text{DOC} = 49 \times L^{1.01}$$

Effort (in person-months), E, project duration (in calendar months), D, and pages of documentation, DOC, are modeled as a function of estimated number of source lines (in thousands), L. Alternatively, project duration and staffing requirements (people), S, may be computed from derived or estimated effort.

The above equations are environment and application specific and may not be applied generally. However, simple models like those above can be derived for a local environment if sufficient historical data are available. The basic COCOMO estimation model, presented in Section 3.8.1, is an example of a static single-variable model.

Static multivariable models, like their single-variable counterpart, make use of historical data to derive empirical relationships. A typical model in this category takes the form:

$$\text{resource} = c_{11} \times e_1 + c_{21} \times e_2 + \ldots$$

where e_i is the ith software characteristic and c_{i1}, c_{i2} are empirically derived constants for the ith characteristic.

A *dynamic multivariable model* projects resource requirements as a function of time. If the model is derived empirically, resources are defined in a series of time steps that allocate some percentage of effort (or other resource) to each step in the software engineering process. Each step may be further subdivided into tasks. A theoretical approach to dynamic multivariable modeling hypothesizes a continuous "resource expenditure curve" [BAS80], and from it, derives equations that model the behavior of the resource. The Putnam Model, a theoretical dynamic multivariable model, is discussed in Section 3.8.2.

3.8.1   The COCOMO Model

In his landmark book on "software engineering economics" [BOE81], Barry Boehm introduces a hierarchy of software estimation models bearing the generic name COCOMO, for *COnstructive COst MOdel*. Boehm's hierarchy of models takes the following form:

Model 1. The Basic COCOMO model is a static single-valued model that computes software development effort (and cost) as a function of program size expressed in estimated lines of code (LOC).

Model 2. The Intermediate COCOMO model computes software development effort as a function of program size and a set of "cost drivers" that includes subjective assessments of product, hardware, personnel, and project attributes.

Model 3. The Advanced COCOMO model incorporates all characteristics of the intermediate version with an assessment of the cost driver's impact on each step (analysis, design, etc.) of the software engineering process.

To illustrate the COCOMO model, we present an overview of the Basic and Intermediate versions. For a more detailed discussion, the reader is urged to study [BOE81].

The COCOMO models are defined for three classes of software projects. Using Boehm's terminology these are: (1) *organic mode*—relatively small, simple software projects in which small teams with good application experience work to a set of less than rigid requirements (e.g., a thermal analysis program developed for a heat transfer group); (2) *semi-detached mode*—an intermediate (in size and complexity) software project in which teams with mixed experience levels must meet a blend of rigid and less than rigid requirements (e.g., a transaction processing system with fixed requirements for terminal hardware and data base software); (3) *embedded mode*—a software project that must be developed within a set of tight hardware, software, and operational constraints (e.g., flight control software for aircraft).

The Basic COCOMO equations take the form:

$$E = a_b \, (\text{KLOC}) \, \exp(b_b)$$

$$D = c_b \, (E) \, \exp(d_b)$$

where E is the effort applied in person-months, D is the development time in chronological months and KLOC is the estimated number of delivered lines of code (in thousands) for the project. The coefficients a_b and c_b and the exponents b_b and d_b are given in Table 3.2.

The Basic model is extended to consider a set of "cost driver attributes" [BOE81] that can be grouped into four major categories:

1. *Product attributes*
   a. required software reliability
   b. size of application data base
   c. complexity of the product
2. *Hardware attributes*
   a. run-time performance constraints
   b. memory constraints
   c. volatility of the virtual machine environment
   d. required turnaround time

TABLE 3.2
Basic COCOMO model

Software project	a_b	b_b	c_b	d_b
Organic	2.4	1.05	2.5	0.38
Semi-detached	3.0	1.12	2.5	0.35
Embedded	3.6	1.20	2.5	0.32

3. *Personnel attributes*
   a. analyst capability
   b. software engineer capability
   c. applications experience
   d. virtual machine experience
   e. programming language experience
4. *Project attributes*
   a. use of software tools
   b. application of software engineering methods
   c. required development schedule

Each of the 15 attributes is rated on a six-point scale that ranges from "very low" to "extra high" (in importance or value). Based on the rating, an *effort multiplier* is determined from tables published by Boehm [BOE81], and the product of all effort multipliers is an *effort adjustment factor* (EAF). Typical values for EAF range from 0.9 to 1.4.

The Intermediate COCOMO model takes the form:

$$E = a_i \, (\text{KLOC}) \, \exp(b_i) \times \text{EAF}$$

where E is the effort applied in person-months and KLOC is the estimated number of delivered lines of code (in thousands) for the project. The coefficient a_i and the exponent b_i are given in Table 3.3.

COCOMO represents the most comprehensive empirical model for software estimation published to date. However, Boehm's own comments [BOE81] about COCOMO (and by extension all models) should be heeded:

> Today, a software cost estimation model is doing well if it can estimate software development costs within 20% of actual costs, 70% of the time, *and* on its own turf (that is, within the class of projects to which it has been calibrated).... This is not as precise as we might like, but it is accurate enough to provide a good deal of help in software engineering economic analysis and decision making.

3.8.2   Putnam Estimation Model

The Putnam Estimation Model [PUT78] is a dynamic multivariable model that assumes a specific distribution of effort over the life of a software development project. The model has been derived from manpower distributions encountered on large proj-

TABLE 3.3
Intermediate COCOMO model

Software project	a_i	b_i
Organic	3.2	1.05
Semi-detached	3.0	1.12
Embedded	2.8	1.20

ects (total effort of 30 person-years or more). However, extrapolation to smaller software projects is possible.

The distribution of effort for large software projects can be characterized as shown in Figure 3.18. The curves shown in the figure take on a classic shape that was first described analytically by Lord Rayleigh. Empirical data on system development, collected by Norden [NOR80], have been used to substantiate the curves. Hence, the distribution of effort shown in Figure 3.18 is often called the "Rayleigh-Norden Curve."

The Rayleigh-Norden Curve may be used to derive [PUT78] a "software equation" that relates the number of delivered lines of code (source statements) to effort and development time:

$$L = C_k\,K^{1/3}\,t_d^{4/3}$$

where C_k is a *state of technology constant* and reflects "throughput constraints that impede the progress of the programmer." Typical values might be: $C_k = 2000$ for a poor software development environment (e.g., no methodology, poor documentation and reviews, a batch execution mode); $C_k = 8000$ for a good software development environment (e.g., methodology in place, adequate documentation/reviews, interactive execution mode); $C_k = 11,000$ for an "excellent" environment (e.g., automated tools and techniques). The constant C_k can be derived for local conditions using historical data

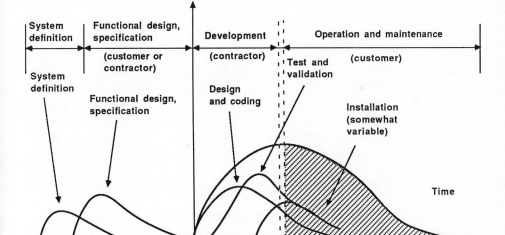

FIGURE 3.18
Effort distribution—large projects. (*Source*: L. Putnam, *Software Cost Estimating and Life Cycle Control*, IEEE Computer Society Press, 1980, p. 15. Reproduced with permission.)

collected from past development efforts. Rearranging the software equation (above), we can arrive at an expression for development effort K:

$$K = L^3 / (C_k^3 \, t_d^4)$$

where K is the effort expended (in person-years) over the entire life cycle for software development and maintenance, and t_d is the development time in years. The equation for development effort can be related to development cost by the inclusion of a burdened labor-rate factor ($/person-year).

Because of the high-order power relationship exhibited by the software equation, it can be shown [PUT78] that relatively small extensions in delivery date can result in a (projected) substantial saving in human effort applied to the project. Stated another way, the relationship between effort applied and chronological time to delivery is highly nonlinear.

3.8.3   Function Point Models

Both the COCOMO model and the Putnam model are predicated on estimates of the number of lines of code (LOC). Albrecht and Gaffney [ALB83] propose an estimation model based on the function point measure for software productivity (Section 3.5.3). However, the small number of completed projects that served as the basis for the model preclude its use in a general context.

To date few empirical models for function point estimation have been published and validated across a broad range of applications. However, there is no reason why such models could not be developed and it is likely that empirical models based on function points will begin to appear in the literature.

3.8.4   A Time-Study Model

Esterling [EST80] has proposed a productivity model that accounts for the *microscopic* characteristics of the work environment. At an individual level, the process of software development is affected by the number, n, of people interacting on a project and the characteristics of the environment in which these people interact. Esterling contends that meetings and other ''nonproductive'' activities occur during an eight-hour workday and that the most productive period occurs during overtime (time worked beyond the standard work week).

The parameters associated with Esterling's model include:

a average fraction of workday spent on administrative or other indirect work
t average duration of work interruptions (minutes)
r average recovery time after interruption (minutes)
k number of interruptions/workday from people working directly on the project
p number of interruptions/workday from other causes
i indirect (overhead) cost/person expressed as a fraction of base pay
d differential pay for overtime expressed as a fraction of base pay

Table 3.4, reproduced from Esterling [EST80], provides typical data for these parameters.

The productivity model consists of five equations. If g is the average number of overtime hours per workday and n is the number of people working on a project, Esterling develops an empirical relationship for the fraction, w, of useful working time (per workday per person):

$$w = 0.125 \times \left(8 - 8a + g - \frac{4r}{60} - \frac{p(t + r)}{60} - \frac{k(n - 1)(t + r)}{60}\right)$$

Using w the following equations are developed:

$$T = \frac{7}{5nw}$$

$$c = ns(gd + 8(1 + i))$$

$$e = \frac{nw}{c}$$

$$C = \frac{c}{nw}$$

where T = ratio of calendar time to person-days to complete project
c = labor cost per work day for an average base salary s
e = cost efficiency
C = project cost per person-day

Figure 3.19a,b,c, and d is reproduced from Esterling and illustrates the effect of number of people on the project variables described in the above equations. Project characteristics can be selected so that the cost-time product, CT, is minimized.

The *time study* nature of the required parameters make data difficult to collect and would hinder application of the model. In addition the model does not consider software characteristics explicitly. However, the Esterling model is a unique approach to software project estimation and can provide a useful indication of the efficacy of a local programming environment.

TABLE 3.4
Values for Esterling model parameters

Parameter	Range	Factory workers	Programmers		
			Optimistic	Typical	Pessimistic
a	0–0.5	0.0	0.05	0.10	0.15
t	1–20	3	3	5	10
r	5–10	0.5	0.5	2.0	8.0
k	1–10	1	2	3	4
p	1–10	1	1	4	10
i	1–3	0.2	0.2	0.5	1.0
d	1–2	1.5	1.0	1.0	1.5

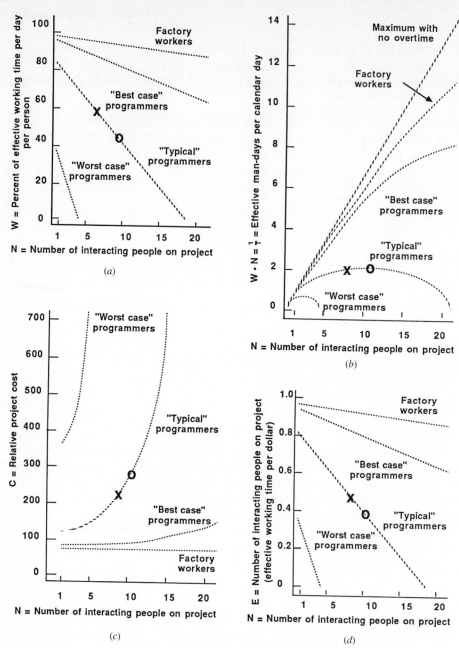

FIGURE 3.19

A time-study model. (*a*) The percent of effective working time per day per person. (*b*) The effective number of man-days per calendar-day. (*c*) The relative project costs. (*d*) The effective working time per dollar. In each case the horizontal axis is the number of interacting people on a project. The different curves are for the four sets of parameters given in Table 3.4. The X represents the point at which the project time-cost product, CT, is at a minimum; the O is the point at which the project completion time is minimized. The maxima in the curves indicates that there is some *n* for which the addition of more people can increase the project completion time (and cost) even ignoring learning curves for new people. (Reprinted with permission of DATA-MATION Magazine, copyright by Technical Publishing Co., 1980, all rights reserved)

116

3.9 AUTOMATED ESTIMATION TOOLS

The decomposition techniques and empirical estimation models described in the preceding sections can be implemented in software. These *automated estimation tools* allow the planner to estimate cost and effort and to perform "what if" analyses for important project variables such as delivery date or staffing. Although many automated estimation tools exist, all exhibit the same general characteristics and all require one or more of the following data categories:

1. A quantitative estimate of project size (e.g., LOC) or functionality (function point data);
2. Qualitative project characteristics such as complexity, required reliability, or business criticality;
3. Some description of the development staff and/or development environment.

From these data, the model implemented by the automated estimation tool provides estimates of effort required to complete the project, costs, staff loading, and, in some cases, development schedule and associated risk. In the paragraphs that follow we examine two representative tools.

SLIM [PUT80] is an automated costing system that is based on the Rayleigh-Norden curve for the software life cycle and the Putnam estimation model (described in Section 3.8.2). SLIM applies the Putnam software model, linear programming, statistical simulation, and PERT (a scheduling method) techniques to derive software project estimates. The system enables a software planner to perform the following functions in an interactive terminal-oriented session: (1) *calibrate* the local software development environment by interpreting historical data supplied by the planner; (2) create an *information model* of the software to be developed by eliciting basic software characteristics, personnel attributes, and environmental considerations; and (3) conduct software *sizing*—the approach used in SLIM is a more sophisticated, automated version of the LOC costing technique described in Section 3.8.2.

Once software size (i.e., LOC for each software function) has been established, SLIM computes size deviation—an indication of estimation uncertainty, a *sensitivity profile* that indicates potential deviation of cost and effort, and a *consistency check* with data collected for software systems of similar size.

The planner can invoke a linear programming analysis that considers development constraints on both cost and effort. Using the Rayleigh-Norden curve as a model, SLIM also provides a month-by-month distribution of effort and cost so that staffing and cash flow requirements can be projected.

ESTIMACS [RUB83] is a "macro-estimation model" that uses a function point estimation method enhanced to accommodate a variety of project and personnel factors. The ESTIMACS tool contains a set of models that enable the planner to estimate: (1) system development effort, (2) staff and cost, (3) hardware configuration, (4) risk, and (5) the effects of "development portfolio."

The system development effort model combines data about the user, the developer, the project geography (i.e., the proximity of developer and customer), and the number of "major business functions" to be implemented with the information domain data (see Section 3.5.3) required for function point computation. In addition the overall nature of the proposed system (e.g., on-line, batch, etc.), the application complexity, performance, and reliability are all taken into account.

Using data from the system development effort model, ESTIMACS can develop staffing and costs using "a customizable life cycle data base to provide work distribution and deployment information." [RUB83] The target hardware configuration is sized (i.e., processor power and storage capacity are estimated) using answers to a series of questions that help the planner evaluate transaction volume, windows of application, and other data. The level of risk associated with successful implementation of the proposed system is determined based on responses to a questionnaire that examines project factors such as size, structure, and technology. Finally, ESTIMACS takes the effects of other concurrent work, called the *development portfolio*, into account.

Like most automated estimating tools, ESTIMACS conducts a dialog with the planner, obtaining appropriate project and supporting information, and producing both tabular and graphical output. Both SLIM and ESTIMACS have been implemented on personal computers.

3.10   SOFTWARE PROJECT SCHEDULING

Scheduling for software development projects can be viewed from two rather different perspectives. In the first, an end-date for release of a computer-based system has already (and irrevocably) been established. The software organization is constrained to distribute effort within the prescribed time frame. The second view of software scheduling assumes that rough chronological bounds have been discussed, but that the end-date is set by the software organization. Effort is distributed to make best use of resources and an end-date is defined after careful analysis of the software element. Unfortunately, the first perspective is encountered far more frequently than the second.

Accuracy in scheduling can sometimes be more important than accuracy in costing. In a product-oriented environment, added cost can be absorbed by repricing or amortization over large numbers of sales. A missed schedule, however, can reduce market impact, create dissatisfied customers, and raise internal costs by creating additional problems during system integration.

When we approach software project scheduling, a number of questions must be asked. How do we correlate chronological time with human effort? What tasks and parallelism are to be expected? What milestones can be used to show progress? How is effort distributed throughout the software engineering process? Are scheduling analysis methods available and how do we physically represent a schedule? Each of these questions is addressed in the following sections.

3.10.1   People-Work Relationships

In a small software development project a single person can analyze requirements, perform design, generate, code and conduct tests. As the size of a project increases, more people must become involved. (We can rarely afford the luxury of approaching a ten person-year effort with one person working for ten years!)

There is a common myth that is still believed by many managers who are responsible for software development effort: ''If we fall behind schedule, we can always add more programmers and catch up later in the project.'' Unfortunately, adding people late in a project often has a disruptive effect on the project, causing schedules to slip even further.

From a quantitative standpoint, the reason for this seeming anomaly lies in the complex communication paths that must be established among software development staff. Although communication is absolutely essential to successful software development, every new communication path requires additional effort and therefore additional time.

As an example, consider four software engineers, each capable of producing 5000 LOC/year when working on an individual project. When these four engineers are placed on a team project, six potential communication paths are possible. Each communication path requires time that could otherwise be spent developing software. We shall assume that team productivity (when measured in LOC) will be reduced by 250 LOC/year because of time used for each communication path. Therefore, team productivity is $20,000 - 250 \times 6 = 18,500$ LOC/year—7.5 percent less than what we might expect.

The one-year project on which the above team is working falls behind schedule and with two months remaining, two additional people are added to the team. The number of communication paths escalates to 14. The productivity input of the new staff is the equivalent of $840 \times 2 = 1680$ LOC for the two months remaining before delivery. Team productivity now is $20,000 + 1680 - 250 \times 14 = 18,180$ LOC/year. The 250 LOC/year reduction for all paths was taken to reflect the learning curve required of new staff.

Although the above example is a gross oversimplification of real-world circumstances, it does serve to illustrate the contention that the relationship between the number of people working on a software project and overall productivity is not linear.

Based on the people-work relationship, are teams counterproductive? The answer is an emphatic ''no'' if communication serves to improve software quality and maintainability. In fact formal technical review (see Chapter 12) conducted by software development teams can lead to better software analysis and design, and, more importantly, can reduce the number of errors that go undetected until testing (thereby reducing test effort). Hence, productivity, when measured by time to project completion, can actually improve.

The Rayleigh-Norden model for large projects predicts a highly nonlinear relationship between chronological time to complete a project and effort. This leads to some interesting results. Recalling the CAD software example (Section 3.7), an estimated 33,000 LOC, 12 person-year effort could be accomplished with eight people working for 1.3 years. If, however, we extend the end date to 1.75 years, Putnam's software equation shows:

$$K = L^3 / C_k^3 \times t_d^4 = 3.8 \text{ person-years.}$$

This implies that by extending the end-date 6 months, we can reduce the number of people from eight to four! The validity of such results is suspect, but the implication is clear: benefit can be gained by using fewer people over a somewhat longer time span to accomplish the same objective.

3.10.2 Task Definition and Parallelism

When more than one person is involved in a software engineering project, it is likely that development activities will be performed in parallel. Figure 3.20 shows a schematic *task network* for a typical multiperson software engineering project. The network assumes that system engineering has occurred and that specific function has been allocated to software.

Requirements analysis and review are the first tasks to be performed and lay the foundation for the parallel tasks that follow. Once requirements have been identified and reviewed, preliminary design activities (architectural and data design) and test planning commence in parallel. The modular nature of well-designed software lends itself to the parallel development tracks for detail design, code, and unit testing, illustrated in Figure 3.20. As components of the software are completed, the integration testing task commences. Finally, validation testing readies the software for release to the customer.

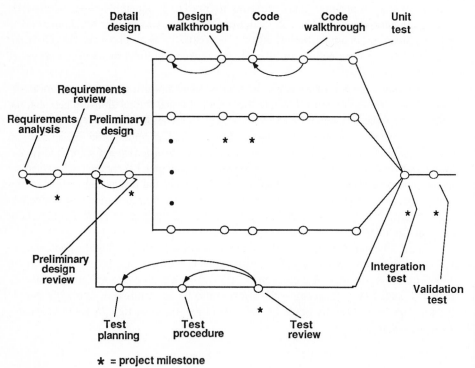

FIGURE 3.20
Parallelism.

Referring to the figure, it is important to note that *milestones* are spaced at regular intervals throughout the software engineering process, providing a manager with regular indications of progress. A milestone is reached once documentation produced as part of a software engineering task has been successfully reviewed.

The concurrent nature of software engineering activities leads to a number of important scheduling requirements. Because parallel tasks occur asynchronously, the planner must determine intertask dependencies to assure continuous progress toward completion. In addition the project manager should be aware of those tasks that lie on the *critical path*, that is, tasks that must be completed on schedule if the project as a whole is to be completed on schedule. These issues are discussed in more detail in Section 3.10.4.

3.10.3 Effort Distribution

Each of the software project estimation techniques discussed in this chapter leads to estimates of person-months (or years) required to complete software development. Figure 3.21 illustrates a recommended distribution of effort across the definition and development phases. This distribution, sometimes called the *40-20-40 rule*, emphasizes front-end analysis and design tasks and back-end testing. The reader can correctly infer that coding (20 percent of effort) is de-emphasized.

The 40-20-40 rule should be used as a guideline only. The characteristics of each project must dictate the distribution of effort. Effort expended on project planning rarely accounts for more than 2–3 percent of effort, unless the plan commits an organization to large expenditures with high risks. Requirements analysis may account for 10–20 percent of project effort. Effort expended on analysis or prototyping should increase in direct proportion to project size and complexity. A range of 20–30 percent of effort is normally applied to software design. Time expended for design review and subsequent iteration must also be considered.

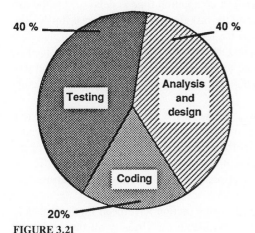

FIGURE 3.21
Distribution of effort.

Because of the effort applied to software design, code should follow with relatively little difficulty. A range of 10–20 percent of overall effort can be achieved. Testing and subsequent debugging can account for 30–50 percent of software development effort. The criticality of the software system element often dictates the amount of testing that is required. If software is human-rated (i.e., software failure can result in loss of life), even higher percentages may be considered.

3.10.4 Scheduling Methods

Scheduling of a software project does not differ greatly from the scheduling of any multitask development effort. Therefore, generalized project scheduling tools and techniques can be applied to software with little modification.

Program evaluation and review technique (PERT) and critical path method (CPM) are two project scheduling methods [WIE77] that can be applied to software development. Both techniques develop a *task network* description of a project; that is, a pictorial or tabular representation of tasks that must be accomplished from the beginning to the end of a project (Figure 3.20). The network is defined by developing a list of all tasks associated with a specific project and a list of orderings (sometimes called a restriction list) that indicates in what order tasks must be accomplished.

Both PERT and CPM provide quantitative tools that allow the software planner to: (1) determine the *critical path*—the chain of tasks that determines the duration of the project, (2) establish *most likely* time estimates for individual tasks by applying statistical models, and (3) calculate *boundary times* that define a time "window" for a particular task.

Boundary time calculations can be very useful in software project scheduling. Slippage in the design of one function, for example, can retard the further development of other functions. Riggs [RIG11] describes important boundary times that may be discerned from a PERT or CPM network: (1) the earliest time that a task can begin when all preceding tasks are completed in the shortest possible time; (2) the latest time for task initiation before the minimum project completion time is delayed; (3) the earliest finish—the sum of the earliest start and the task duration; (4) the latest finish—the latest start time added to task duration; (5) the total float—the amount of surplus time or leeway allowed in scheduling tasks so that the network critical path is maintained on schedule. Boundary time calculations lead to a determination of critical path and provide the manager with a quantitative method for evaluating progress as tasks are completed.

As a final comment on scheduling, we recall the Rayleigh-Norden curve representation of effort expended during the software life cycle (Figure 3.18). The planner must recognize that effort expended on software does not terminate at the end of development. Maintenance effort, although not easy to schedule at this stage, will ultimately become the largest cost factor. A primary goal of software engineering is to help reduce this cost.

The scheduling techniques described in this section have been implemented as automated project scheduling tools that are available for virtually all personal computers [DAU84]. Such tools are relatively easy to use and make the analysis methods described above available to every software project manager.

3.10.5   A Scheduling Example

This section presents a project scheduling example developed using an automated scheduling tool, *MacProject*, available for the Apple MacIntosh personal computer. The project task network, shown in Figure 3.22, is drawn interactively using the project scheduling tool. Rectangular boxes represent software engineering tasks and boxes with rounded edges are milestones. The starting date and duration for each task are specified above each task. In addition the planner specifies the resources (people) who will be working on each task and the costs of these resources.

Once project data are entered (in the form of the network diagram shown in Figure 3.22), *MacProject* automatically generates the following information: (1) a *Gantt Chart* (Figure 3.23) that describes tasks as a function of chronological date (note that *slack time* is shaded and milestones are shown as diamonds); (2) start and finish times (Figure 3.24) that enable a manager to track progress by task; (3) a resource allocation table (Figure 3.25); and (4) the critical path, noted in bold on the network representation (Figure 3.22).

Manual development of these scheduling charts would take at least two days. Using *MacProject*, the job was done in less than one hour.

3.11   SOFTWARE ACQUISITION

In many software application areas, it is often more cost effective to acquire rather than develop computer software. Software engineering managers are faced with a *make-buy* decision that can be further complicated by a number of acquisition options: (1) software may be purchased (or licensed) *off-the-shelf*; (2) off-the-shelf software may be purchased and then modified to meet specific needs, or (3) software may be custom-built by an outside contractor to meet the purchaser's specifications.

The steps involved in the acquisition of software are defined by the criticality of the software to be purchased and the end cost. In some cases (e.g., low-cost PC software), it is less expensive to purchase and experiment than to conduct a lengthy paper evaluation. For more expensive software packages, the following guidelines can be applied:

1. Develop a specification for function and performance of the desired software. Define measurable characteristics whenever possible.
2. Estimate the internal cost to develop and the delivery date.
3. Select three or four candidate software packages that best meet your specification.
4. Develop a *comparison matrix* that presents a head-to-head comparison of key functions. Alternatively, conduct *benchmark* tests to compare candidate software.
5. Evaluate each software package based on: past product quality, vendor support, product direction, reputation, etc.
6. Contact other users of the software and ask for opinions.

In the final analysis the make-buy decision should be made based on the following conditions: (1) Will the delivery date of the software product be sooner than that for internally developed software? (2) Will the cost of acquisition plus the cost of

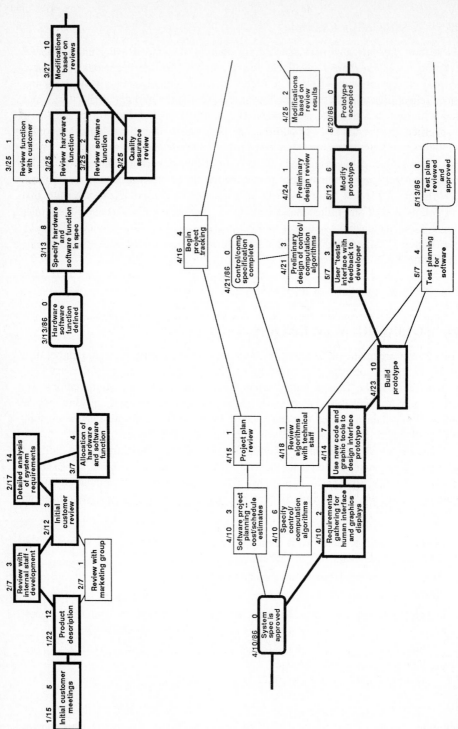

124

FIGURE 3.22

A typical task network for a software engineering project. Bold lines and boxes represent the "critical path." (Pages 124 and 125 should be read according to the date sequence contained at the top of each task box.)

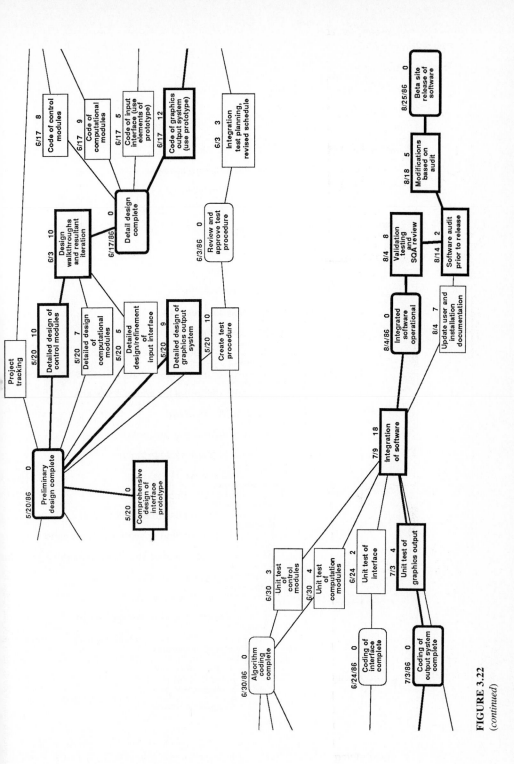

FIGURE 3.22
(*continued*)

125

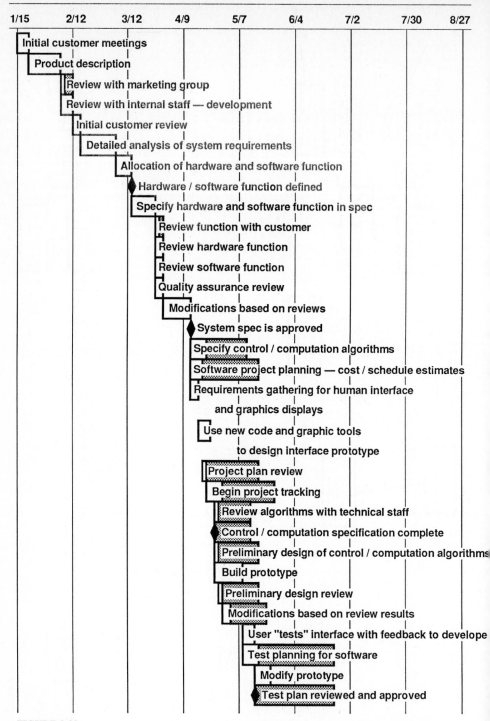

FIGURE 3.23

Gantt chart for software engineering project tasks. Shaded areas imply *slack time* and diamonds indicate milestones. (Continuation of Figure 3.23 on p. 127 would actually appear below the Figure on this page, with corresponding dates appropriately aligned.)

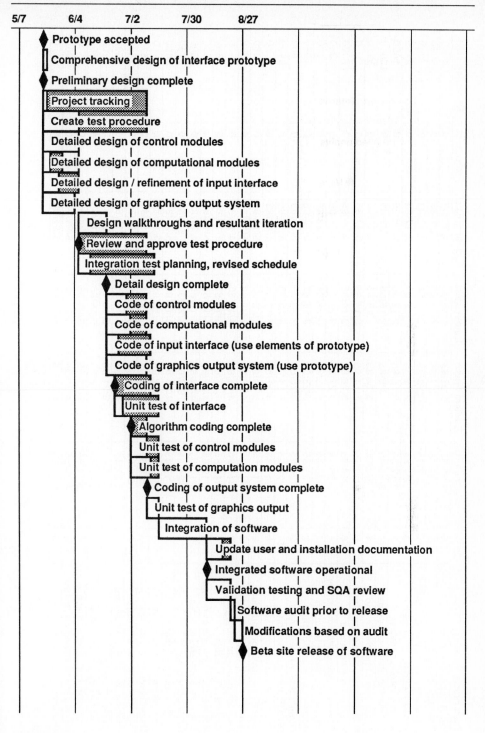

5/7 6/4 7/2 7/30 8/27

Prototype accepted
Comprehensive design of interface prototype
Preliminary design complete
Project tracking
Create test procedure
Detailed design of control modules
Detailed design of computational modules
Detailed design / refinement of input interface
Detailed design of graphics output system
Design walkthroughs and resultant iteration
Review and approve test procedure
Integration test planning, revised schedule
Detail design complete
Code of control modules
Code of computational modules
Code of input interface (use elements of prototype)
Code of graphics output system (use prototype)
Coding of interface complete
Unit test of interface
Algorithm coding complete
Unit test of control modules
Unit test of computation modules
Coding of output system complete
Unit test of graphics output
Integration of software
Update user and installation documentation
Integrated software operational
Validation testing and SQA review
Software audit prior to release
Modifications based on audit
Beta site release of software

FIGURE 3.23
(*continued*)

#	Task name	Days	Earliest start	Earliest finish	Latest start	Latest finish	Fixed cost	Resource cost
1	Initial customer meetings	5	1/15/85	1/22/85	1/15/85	1/22/85	0	1750
2	Product description	12	1/22/85	2/7/85	1/22/85	2/7/85	0	15000
3	Review with marketing group	1	2/7/85	2/8/85	2/11/85	2/12/85	0	350
4	Review with internal staff –	3	2/7/85	2/12/85	2/7/85	2/12/85	0	2700
5	Initial customer review	3	2/12/85	2/15/85	2/12/85	2/15/85	0	1050
6	Detailed analysis of system	14	2/15/85	3/8/85	2/15/85	3/8/85	0	13860
7	Allocation of hardware and	4	3/8/85	3/14/85	3/8/85	3/14/85	0	3960
8	Hardware/software function	0	3/14/85	3/14/85	3/14/85	3/14/85	0	0
9	Specify hardware and	8	3/14/85	3/26/85	3/14/85	3/26/85	0	7920
10	Review function with customer	1	3/26/85	3/27/85	3/27/85	3/28/85	0	350
11	Review hardware function	2	3/26/85	3/28/85	3/26/85	3/28/85	0	930
12	Review software function	2	3/26/85	3/28/85	3/26/85	3/28/85	0	1050
13	Quality assurance review	2	3/26/85	3/28/85	3/26/85	3/28/85	0	800
14	Modifications based on	10	3/28/85	4/11/85	3/28/85	4/11/85	0	9900
15	System spec is approved	0	4/11/85	4/11/85	4/11/85	4/11/85	0	0
16	Specify control/computation	6	4/11/85	4/19/85	5/2/85	5/10/85	0	3000
17	Software project planning	3	4/11/85	4/16/85	5/9/85	5/14/85	0	3375
18	Requirements gathering for	2	4/11/85	4/15/85	4/11/85	4/15/85	0	0
19	Project plan review	1	4/16/85	4/17/85	5/14/85	5/15/85	0	600
20	Review algorithms with technical	1	4/19/85	4/22/85	5/10/85	5/13/85	0	500
21	Use new code and graphic	7	4/15/85	4/24/85	4/15/85	4/24/85	0	6300
22	Build prototype	10	4/24/85	5/8/85	4/24/85	5/8/85	0	9750
23	Begin project tracking	4	4/17/85	4/23/85	5/15/85	5/21/85	0	2400
24	Control/comp. specification	0	4/22/85	4/22/85	5/13/85	5/13/85	0	0
25	User "tests" interface with	3	5/8/85	5/13/85	5/8/85	5/13/85	0	1575
26	Test planning for software	4	5/8/85	5/14/85	6/18/85	6/24/85	0	1600
27	Preliminary design of control	3	4/22/85	4/25/85	5/13/85	5/16/85	0	1500
28	Modify prototype	6	5/13/85	5/21/85	5/13/85	5/21/85	0	2700
29	Preliminary design review	1	4/25/85	4/26/85	5/16/85	5/17/85	0	900
30	Test plan reviewed and approved	0	5/14/85	5/14/85	6/24/85	6/24/85	0	0
31	Modifications based on review	2	4/26/85	4/30/85	5/17/85	5/21/85	0	1000
32	Prototype accepted	0	5/21/85	5/21/85	5/21/85	5/21/85	0	0

FIGURE 3.24
Task status table.

Resources Allocated for Tasks 34 – 62

#	Task						
34	Preliminary design complete						
35	Project tracking	sw mgr					
36	Create test procedure	sw engr #4					
37	Detailed design of control	sw engr #2	sw engr #5				
38	Detailed design of computation	sw engr #2	sw engr #6				
39	Detailed design/refinement of	sw engr #1					
40	Detailed design of graphics	sw engr #3					
41	Design walkthroughs and	sw engr #1	sw engr #2	sw engr #3	sw engr #4	sw engr #5	sw engr #6
42	Review and approve test	sw engr #1		sw engr #3			
43	Detail design complete						
44	Integration test planning, revised	sw engr #4	sw engr #1	sw engr #3			
45	Code of control modules	sw engr #2					
46	Code of computational modules	sw engr #5					
47	Code of input interface (use	sw engr #1					
48	Code of graphics output	sw engr #3					
49	Algorithm coding complete						
50	Coding of interface complete						
51	Coding of output system						
52	Unit test of control modules	sw engr #5					
53	Unit test of computation modules	sw engr #6					
54	Unit test of interface	sw engr #1					
55	Unit test of graphics output	sw engr #3					
56	Integration of software	sw engr #1	sw engr #2	sw engr #3			
57	Update user and installation	sw engr #5	sw engr #6				
58	Integrated software						
59	Validation testing and SQA	sw engr #1	sqa	marketing			
60	Software audit prior to	sqa					
61	Modifications based on audit	sw engr #5	sw engr #6				
62	Beta site release of	sw engr #6		sw engr #1			

FIGURE 3.25
Resource allocation table.

customization be less than the cost of developing the software internally? (3) Will the cost of outside support (e.g., a maintenance contract) be less than the cost of internal support? These conditions apply for each of the acquisition options noted above.

It is important to note that software engineering controls must be rigorously enforced when software development has been contracted to a third party. The customer must be sure that software engineering standards and practices are enforced, that formal technical reviews are conducted, and that appropriate documentation is developed.

3.12 ORGANIZATIONAL PLANNING

There are almost as many human organizational structures for software development as there are organizations that develop software. For better or worse, organizational structure cannot be easily modified by a software project planner. Concern with the practical and political consequences of organizational change are not within the software project planner's scope of responsibilities. However, organization of the people directly involved in a new software project can be considered at this time.

The following options are available for applying human resources to a project that will require n people working for k years:

1. n individuals are assigned to m different functional tasks, relatively little combined work occurs; coordination is the responsibility of a software manager who may have six other projects to be concerned with;
2. n individuals are assigned to m different functional tasks ($m < n$) so that informal "teams" are established; an *ad hoc* team leader may be appointed; coordination among teams is the responsibility of a software manager;
3. n individuals are organized into t teams; each team is assigned one or more functional tasks; each team has a specific organization; coordination is controlled by both the team and a software manager.

Although it is possible to voice pro and con arguments for each of the above approaches, there is a growing body of evidence (e.g., [SHN80]) that indicates that a formal team organization (option 3) is most productive.

The software development team approach has its origins in the *chief programmer team* concept first proposed by Harlan Mills and described by Baker [BAK72]. The organization of the software development team is illustrated in Figure 3.26. The nucleus of the team is composed of a *senior engineer* ("the chief programmer") who plans, coordinates, and reviews all technical activities of the team, *technical staff* (normally two to five people) who conduct analysis and development activities, and a *backup engineer* who supports the senior engineer in his or her activities and can replace the senior engineer with minimum loss in project continuity.

The software development team may be served by one or more specialists (e.g., telecommunications expert, data base designer), support staff (e.g., technical writers, clerical personnel), and a *software librarian*. The librarian serves many teams and performs the following functions: maintains and controls all elements of the software configuration, i.e., documentation, source listings, data, magnetic media; helps collect

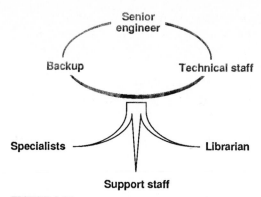

FIGURE 3.26
Software development team.

and format software productivity data; catalogs and indexes "revisable" software modules; and assists the teams in research, evaluation, and document preparation. The importance of a librarian cannot be overemphasized. The librarian acts as a controller, coordinator, and, potentially, an evaluator of the software configuration.

The primary goal of the software development team is to approach a project as a joint effort. The team fosters the concept of *egoless programming* [WEI71] in that "my program" becomes "our program." By helping to eliminate ego attachment to software, the team can foster more thorough review, increased learning through side-by-side work, and improved software quality.

In Section 3.10.1 we discussed people-work relationships. The increased communication inherent in any team project would seem to mitigate against improved development productivity when software development teams are used. However, a significant percentage of effort in the software engineering process must be expended on communication (e.g., planning, analysis, reviews) regardless of project organization. The team organization reduces communication effort and eliminates many time consuming misunderstandings that occur when people work alone. In addition the team organization encourages review, thereby improving software product quality.

Although it is not always practical to use software development teams (e.g., small, one-person projects or large highly compartmentalized efforts), the underlying concepts are sound and should be applied whenever needs warrant.

3.13 THE SOFTWARE PROJECT PLAN

Each step in the software engineering process should produce a deliverable that can be reviewed and that can act as a foundation for the steps that follow. The *Software Project Plan* is produced at the culmination of the planning step. It provides baseline cost and scheduling information that will be used throughout the software life cycle.

The *Software Project Plan* is a relatively brief document that is addressed to a diverse audience. It must (1) communicate scope and resources to software management, technical staff, and the customer; (2) define cost and schedule for management review; and (3) provide an overall approach to software development to all people associated with the project. The following document outline may be used as a guide.

Software Project Plan Outline

1. Scope
   a. Project objectives
   b. Major functions
   c. Other characteristics
   d. A development scenario
2. Resources
   a. Human resources
   b. Hardware resources
   c. Software resources
   d. Availability windows
3. Cost
4. Schedule
   a. Task network
   b. Gantt chart
   c. Task-resource table

A presentation of cost and schedule will vary with the audience to whom it is addressed. If the plan is used only as an internal document, the results of each costing technique can be presented. When the plan is disseminated outside the organization, a reconciled cost breakdown (combining the results of all costing techniques) is provided. Similarly, the degree of detail contained within the schedule section may vary with the audience and the formality of the plan.

The *Software Project Plan* need not be a lengthy, complex document. Its purpose is to help establish the viability of the software development effort. The plan concentrates on a general statement of *what* and a specific statement of *how much* and *how long*. Subsequent steps in the software engineering process will concentrate on definition, development, and maintenance.

3.14   SUMMARY

Software project planning occurs as a consequence of the function and performance allocations performed as a part of computer system engineering. During planning the scope of the software effort is established, and resources, cost, and schedule are estimated. Estimation is accomplished using one of a number of techniques that rely on historical productivity data for software development.

Each task associated with software project planning attempts to develop a systematic (rather than haphazard) approach to estimating. Risk will always exist. But by applying multiple estimation techniques and scheduling methods, the planner can minimize uncertainty and establish a road map for the conduct of software engineering.

REFERENCES

[ALB79]   Albrecht, A. J., "Measuring Application Development Productivity," *Proc. IBM Applic. Dev. Symposium*, Monterey, CA, October 1979, pp. 83–92.

[ALB83]   Albrecht, A. J., and J. E. Gaffney, "Software Function, Source Lines of Code and Development Effort Prediction: A Software Science Validation," *IEEE Trans. Software Engineering*, November 1983, pp. 639–648.

[ART85]   Arthur, L. J., *Measuring Programmer Productivity and Software Quality*, Wiley-Interscience, 1985.

[BAK72]   Baker, F. T., "Chief Programmer Team Management of Production Programming," *IBM Systems Journal*, vol. 11, no. 1, 1972, pp. 56–73.

[BAR84]   Barstow, D. R., H. E. Shrobe, and E. Sandewall, *Interactive Programming Environments*, McGraw-Hill, 1984.

[BAS78]   Basili, V., and M. Zelkowitz, "Analyzing Medium Scale Software Development," *Proc. 3rd Intl. Conf. Software Engineering*, IEEE, 1978, pp. 116–123.

[BAS80]   Basili, V., *Models and Metrics for Software Management and Engineering*, IEEE Computer Society Press, 1980, p. 4–9.

[BRO75]   Brooks, F., *The Mythical Man-Month*, Addison-Wesley, 1975.

[DAU84]   Dauphinais, B., and L. Darnell, "Project Management: One Step at a Time," *PC World*, September 1984, pp. 240–256.

[EST80]   Esterling, R., "Software Manpower Costs: A Model," *Datamation*, March 1980, pp. 164–170.

[HEN85]   Henderson, P. B., "Software Development/Programming Environments," *ACM Sigsoft Notes*, April 1985, p. 60ff.

[JON84]   Jones, T. C., "Reusability in Programming: A Survey of the State of the Art," *IEEE Trans. Software Engineering*, September 1984, pp. 488–493.

[MCC76]   McCabe, T., "A Complexity Measure," *IEEE Trans. Software Engineering*, December 1976, pp. 308–320.

[NOR80]   Norden, P., "Useful Tools for Project Management," *Software Cost Estimating and Life Cycle Control*, IEEE Computer Society Press, 1980, pp. 216–225.

[PUT78]   Putnam, L., "A General Empirical Solution to the Macro Software Sizing and Estimating Problem," *IEEE Trans. Software Engineering*, vol. 4, no. 4, 1978, pp. 345–361.

[RIG81]   Riggs, J., *Production Systems Planning, Analysis and Control*, 3d ed., Wiley, 1981.

[RUB83]   Rubin, H. A., "Macro-estimation of Software Development Parameters: The Estimacs System," *Softfair Proceedings*, IEEE, July 1983, p. 109–118.

[SHN80]   Shniederman, B., *Software Psychology*, Winthrop Publishers, 1980, pp. 124–132.

[WAL77]   Walston, C., and C. Felix, "A Method for Programming Measurement and Estimation," *IBM Systems Journal*, vol. 16, no. 1, 1977, pp. 54–73.

[WEI71]   Weinberg, G., *The Psychology of Computer Programming*, Van Nostrand, 1971, pp. 47–66.

[WIE77]   Wiest, J., and F. Levy, *A Management Guide to PERT/CPM*, 2d ed., Prentice-Hall, 1977.

PROBLEMS AND POINTS TO PONDER

3.1 Software project complexity is discussed briefly in Section 3.1. Develop a list of software characteristics (e.g., concurrent operation, graphical output, etc.) that affect the complexity of a program. Prioritize the list.

3.2 Consider a software project on which you have worked recently. Write a bounded description of the software scope and present it for criticism. Can the scope you have established be misinterpreted? Have you bounded the system?

3.3 Performance is an important consideration during planning. Discuss how performance can be interpreted differently depending upon the software application area.

3.4 In Section 3.4 we discuss human, software, and hardware resources. Are there others?

3.5 The *make-buy* decision is an important management prerogative. You are the manager of a software organization that has an average software development cost of $20.00/LOC. You are considering the purchase of a 5000 LOC software package that will cost $50,000. Initially, your technical staff indicates that no modifications will be required for the package to meet your specifications. However, your software development group wants to develop similar software in-house. Should you make or buy?

3.6 Reconsider the situation of Problem 3.5. After further study your technical group now finds that at least 1000 LOC will have to be modified or added to make the package viable. Should you make or buy? Carefully state any assumptions you have made in making your decision.

3.7 The Walston and Felix study [WAL77] is only one of a number of sources for software productivity data. Write a paper outlining the results of other studies (see Further Readings). Is there commonality among the results?

3.8 Collect software productivity data for 2–5 projects on which you have worked. Basic information should include cost (if applicable), LOC, effort (person-months), a complexity indicator (scale 1 to 10), and chronological time to completion. Combine your data with information from other students/colleagues. Use a statistical technique like multiple regression analysis to derive static single- and multi-variable cost/effort models for the combined data. Do the data correlate well? Do new data fit the model?

3.9 Using reference [PUT78] as a guide, write a brief paper outlining the derivation of Putnam's "software equation" discussed in Section 3.8.2.

3.10 How well do the data collected as part of Problem 3.8 fit the Putnam model? the COCOMO model?

3.11 Specify, design, and develop a program that implements the Esterling model discussed in Section 3.8.4. Using reference [EST80] as a guide, extend the program so that it can be used as a planning tool.

3.12 Given a project on which you are currently working or a project description assigned by your instructor, apply the lines of code costing technique described in Section 3.7. Develop a complete cost table using derived productivity data or "average data" specified by your instructor (e.g., $18.00/LOC average, 400 LOC/person-month average).

3.13 Using the results obtained in Problem 3.12, indicate potential deviation in cost and end-date; assign a probability estimate to these numbers.

3.14 For the project noted in Problem 3.12, apply the effort/task costing technique. Develop a table similar to Figure 3.17. Use a burdened rate structure for wages that averages $5000/person-month.

3.15 Given a project on which you are currently working or a project description assigned by your instructor, compute function point information and use the function point costing technique, described in Section 3.7. Assume $900/FP and 8 FP/person-month average.

3.16 Specify, design, and implement an abbreviated interactive software costing system. The system should incorporate modeling and the techniques described in Sections 3.7 and 3.8.

3.17 Are there circumstances under which people can be added late in a software project without incurring Brooks' Law?

3.18 Schedule a software project that you are currently working on or a project assigned by your instructor using a personal computer based project scheduling tool (e.g., the *Harvard Project Manager* for the IBM PC). What is the critical path?

3.19 Many software projects are so large that many software development teams must be formed. Recommend a management structure for coordinating multiple teams. What are some of the potential problems that can arise?

3.20 Develop a detailed questionnaire that can be used for the collection of software productivity data in a development organization. See reference [BAS80] for guidelines.

3.21 Suggest practical methods by which a manager can monitor compliance with costs and schedules defined in the software plan.

3.22 It seems odd that cost and schedule estimates are developed during software project planning—before detailed software requirements analysis has been conducted. Why do you think this is done? Are there circumstances when it should not be done?

FURTHER READINGS

A quasi-expert system for software project planning is described by Capers Jones (*Programming Productivity*, McGraw-Hill, 1986). Jones' estimating tool, SPQR, considers ten categories of information that are important for project estimation. Books on productivity by Arthur (*Programmer Productivity*, Wiley, 1983) and Parikh (*Programmer Productivity*, Reston, 1984) treat aspects of this broad subject.

Putnam's tutorial on software cost estimating [PUT80] and Boehm's book on software engineering economics [BOE81] respectively describe the SLIM and COCOMO estimation techniques. Boehm's book presents detailed project data and provides excellent quantitative insight into the process of estimation. An excellent book by DeMarco (*Controlling Software Projects*, Yourdon Press, 1982) provides valuable insight into the ''management, measurement, and estimation'' of software projects.

A major source for software productivity data is a large data base maintained by the Rome Air Development Center (RADC) at Griffiss Air Force Base in New York. Data from hundreds of software development projects have been entered in the data base. Belady and Lehman (''The Characteristics of Large Systems'' in *Research Directions in Software Technology*, MIT Press, 1979) provide other data for large projects.

A worthwhile anthology of important papers on software management is presented by Reifer (*Tutorial: Software Management*, IEEE Computer Society Press, 1981). Although a decade old, books by Gunther (*Management Methodology for Software Product Engineering*, Wiley, 1978) and Metzger (*Managing a Programming Project*, Prentice-Hall, 2d ed., 1980) remain important contributions to the software project management literature.

The management and motivation of software development people should not be overlooked. A classic text by Cougar and Zawacki (*Motivating and Managing Computer Personnel*, Wiley, 1980) presents important insight. A more recent book by Licker (*The Art of Managing Software Development People*, Wiley, 1985) presents pragmatic guidelines for both new and experienced managers.

CHAPTER

4

REQUIREMENTS ANALYSIS FUNDAMENTALS

A complete specification of software requirements is essential to the success of a software development effort. No matter how well-designed or well-coded, a poorly specified program will disappoint the user and bring grief to the developer.

The requirements analysis task is a process of discovery and refinement. The software scope, initially established during system engineering, is refined in detail. Alternative solutions are analyzed and allocated to various software elements.

Both the developer and customer take an active role in requirements specification. The customer attempts to reformulate a somewhat nebulous concept of software function and performance into concrete detail. The developer acts as interrogator, consultant, and problem solver.

Requirements analysis and specification may appear to be a relatively simple task, but appearances can be deceiving. Since communication content is very high, chances for misinterpretation or misinformation abound. The dilemma that confronts a software engineer may best be understood by repeating the statement of an anonymous (infamous?) customer: ''I know you believe you understood what you think I said, but I am not sure you realize that what you heard is not what I meant.''

4.1 REQUIREMENTS ANALYSIS

Requirements analysis is a software engineering task that bridges the gap between system level software allocation and software design (Figure 4.1). Requirements analysis enables the system engineer to specify software function and performance, indicate

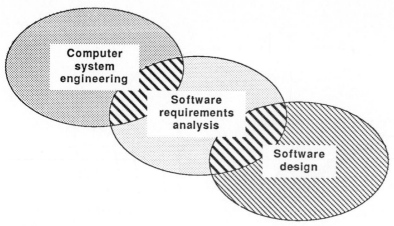

FIGURE 4.1
Overlap of the analysis task.

software's interface with other system elements, and establish design constraints that software must meet. Requirements analysis allows the software engineer (often called *analyst* in this role) to refine the software allocation and represent the *information domain* that will be treated by software. Requirements analysis provides the software designer with a representation of information and function that can be translated into data, architectural, and procedural design. Finally, the requirements specification provides the developer and the customer with the means to assess quality once software is built.

4.1.1 Analysis Tasks

Software requirements analysis may be divided into four areas of effort: (1) problem recognition, (2) evaluation and synthesis, (3) specification, and (4) review.

Initially, the *analyst* (discussed in Section 4.1.2) studies the *System Specification* (if one exists) and the *Software Project Plan*. It is important to understand software in a system context and to review the software scope that was used to generate planning estimates. Next, communication for analysis must be established so that problem recognition is ensured.

The communication paths required for analysis are illustrated in Figure 4.2. The analyst must establish contact with management and technical staff of the user/customer organization and the software development organization. The project manager can serve as a coordinator to facilitate establishment of communication paths. The goal of the analyst is recognition of the basic problem elements as perceived by the user/customer.

Problem evaluation and solution synthesis is the next major area of effort for analysis. The analyst must evaluate the flow and structure of information, refine all software functions in detail, establish system interface characteristics, and uncover de-

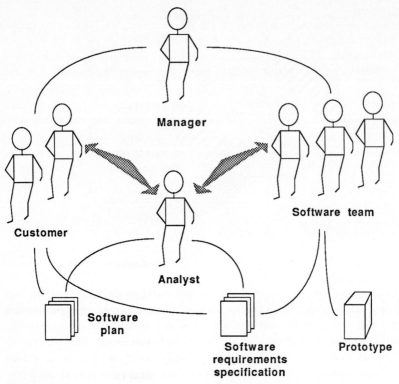

FIGURE 4.2
Communication for analysis.

sign constraints. Each of these tasks serves to describe the problem so that an overall approach or solution may be synthesized.

For example an inventory control system is required for a major supplier of plumbing supplies. The analyst finds that problems with the current manual system include: (1) inability to obtain the status of a component rapidly; (2) two- or three-day turnaround to update a card file; and (3) multiple re-orders to the same vendor because there is no way to associate vendors with components, etc. Once problems have been identified, the analyst determines what information is to be produced by the new system and what data will be provided to the system. For instance the customer desires a daily report that indicates what items have been taken from inventory and how many similar items remain. The customer indicates that inventory clerks will log the identification number of each part as it leaves the inventory area.

Upon evaluating current problems and desired information (input and output), the analyst begins to synthesize one or more solutions. An on-line terminal–based system will solve one set of problems, but does it fall within the scope outlined in the *Software Plan*? A data base management system would seem to be required, but is the user/customer's need for associativity justified? The process of evaluation and synthesis continues until both analyst and customer feel confident that software can be adequately specified for the development phase.

In Chapter 1 we noted that detailed specification may not be possible at this stage. The customer may be unsure of precisely what is required. The developer may be unsure whether a specific approach will properly accomplish function and performance. For these and many other reasons, an alternate approach to requirements analysis, called *prototyping*, may be conducted. We discuss prototyping later in this chapter.

The tasks associated with analysis and specification exist to provide a representation of software that can be reviewed and approved by the customer. In an ideal world the customer develops a *Software Requirements Specification* in its entirety. This is rarely the case in the real world. At best the specification is developed as a joint effort with developer and customer.

Once basic functions, performance, interfaces, and information are described, *validation criteria* are specified to demonstrate an understanding of a successful software implementation. These criteria serve as a basis for testing during software development. A formal requirements specification is written to define characteristics and attributes of the software. In addition a *Preliminary User's Manual* is drafted for cases in which a prototype has not been developed.

It may seem odd that a user's manual is developed so early in the software engineering process. In fact the draft-copy user's manual forces the analyst (developer) to take a user's view of the software (particularly important in interactive systems). The manual encourages the user/customer to review the software from a human engineering perspective and often elicits the comment: "The idea is OK, but this isn't the way I thought we would do this." Better to uncover such comments early in the process.

Requirements analysis documents (specification and user's manual) serve as the basis for a review conducted by the customer and the developer. The requirements review (discussed in Section 4.7) almost always results in modifications to function, performance, information representations, constraints or validation criteria. In addition the *Software Project Plan* is reassessed to determine whether early estimates remain valid given the additional knowledge obtained during analysis.

4.1.2 The Analyst

Entire textbooks have been dedicated to the role and duties of the *analyst*. Atwood [ATW77] provides a workable job description: "...the system analyst is expected to analyze and design systems of optimum performance. That is, the analyst must produce...an output that fully meets management objectives...." The analyst is known by a variety of aliases: *system analyst, system engineer, chief system designer, programmer/ analyst*, and so on. Regardless of job title, the analyst must exhibit the following character traits:

- The ability to grasp abstract concepts, reorganize into logical divisions, and synthesize "solutions" based on each division.
- The ability to absorb pertinent facts from conflicting or confused sources.
- The ability to understand the user/customer environments.

- The ability to apply hardware and/or software system elements to the user/customer environments.
- The ability to communicate well in written and verbal form.
- The ability "to see the forest for the trees."

It is probably the last trait that distinguishes truly outstanding analysts from the pack. Individuals who become mired in detail too early frequently lose sight of the overall software objective. Software requirements must be uncovered in a "top down" manner; major functions, interfaces, and information must be fully understood before successive layers of detail are specified.

The analyst's role is depicted in Figure 4.3. The analyst performs or coordinates each of the tasks associated with software requirements analysis (Section 4.1.1). During recognition tasks, she or he communicates with user/customer staff to ascertain characteristics of the existing environment. The analyst then calls upon development staff during the evaluation and synthesis tasks so that characteristics of the software are defined correctly. The analyst is generally responsible for the development of a *Software Requirements Specification* and also participates in all reviews.

It is important to note that the analyst must also understand each software engineering paradigm (Section 1.5) and appreciate the generic software engineering phases and steps that are applied regardless of the paradigm used. Many implicit software requirements (e.g., design for maintainability) are incorporated into a requirements specification only if the analyst understands software engineering.

4.2 PROBLEM AREAS

Requirements analysis is a communication intensive activity. When communication occurs, *noise* (e.g., misinterpretation, omission) on the communication path can cause difficulty for both analyst and customer. Among the problems that may be encountered

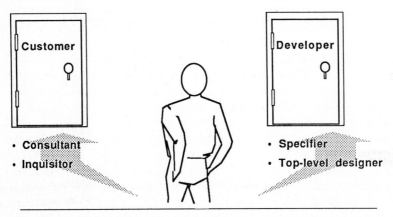

FIGURE 4.3
The role of the analyst.

during requirements analysis are difficulties associated with acquiring pertinent information, handling problem complexity, and accommodating changes that will occur during and after analysis.

The first two analysis tasks discussed in the preceding section—problem recognition and solution evaluation and synthesis—are predicated on the successful acquisition of information. Often customer-supplied information conflicts with requirements stated earlier by other people; function and performance conflict with constraints imposed by other system elements; or the perception of the goals of the system changes with time. What information should be collected and how should it be represented? Who supplies the various pieces of information? What tools and techniques are available to facilitate collection of information?

As the size of the problem grows, the complexity of the analysis task also grows. Each new information item, function, or constraint may have an effect on all other elements of the software. For this reason analysis effort grows geometrically as problem complexity increases. How can we eliminate inconsistency when specifying large systems? Is it possible to detect omissions? Can a large problem be effectively partitioned so that it becomes more manageable intellectually?

In coining "the first law of system engineering," Bersoff [BER80] said: "No matter where you are in the system life cycle, the system will change, and the desire to change it will persist throughout the life cycle." The changes alluded to in this statement are changes in requirements. Whether we talk about a system or just software, change will occur. In fact it is likely that changes will be requested even *before* we complete the analysis task. How are changes to other system elements coordinated with software requirements? How do we assess the impact of a change on other, seemingly unrelated, parts of the software? How do we correct errors in specification so that side effects are not generated?

There are many causes for the problems noted above and some good answers to the resultant questions. The underlying requirements analysis problems are attributable to many causes: (1) poor communication that makes information acquisition difficult; (2) inadequate techniques and tools that result in inadequate or inaccurate specification; (3) a tendency to short-cut the requirements analysis task, leading to an unstable design; and (4) a failure to consider alternatives before the software is specified. Although a software engineering approach to requirements analysis is not a panacea, application of fundamental analysis principles and systematic analysis methods will greatly reduce the impact of the problems noted above. For the remainder of this chapter and throughout Chapter 5, we discuss these principles and methods. In so doing we shall also answer the questions that accompany the statement of each problem.

4.3 ANALYSIS PRINCIPLES

Over the past decade, a number of software analysis and specification methods (discussed in Chapter 5) have been developed. Investigators have identified problems and their causes and developed rules and procedures to overcome them. Each analysis method has a unique notation and point of view. However, all analysis methods are related by a set of fundamental principles:

1. The information domain, as well as the functional domain, of a problem must be represented and understood.

2. The problem must be partitioned in a manner that uncovers detail in a layered (or hierarchical) fashion.

3. Logical and physical representations of the system should be developed.

By applying these principles, the analyst approaches a problem systematically. The information domain is examined so that function may be understood more completely. Partitioning is applied to reduce complexity. Logical and physical views of the software are necessary to accommodate the logical constraints imposed by processing requirements and the physical constraints imposed by other system elements.

4.3.1   The Information Domain

All software applications can be collectively called *data processing*. Interestingly, this term contains the key to our understanding of software requirements. Software is built to process *data*; to transform data from one form to another; that is, to accept input, manipulate it in some way, and produce output. This fundamental statement of objective is true whether we build batch software for a payroll system or real-time embedded software to control fuel flow to an automobile engine.

The information domain contains three different views of the data that are processed by computer programs: (1) information flow, (2) information content, and (3) information structure. To fully understand the information domain, each of these views should be considered.

Information flow represents the manner in which data changes as it moves through a system. Referring to Figure 4.4, input is transformed into intermediate data and further transformed into output. Along this transformation path (or paths), additional data may be introduced from existing *data stores* (e.g., a disk file or memory buffer). The transformations that are applied to the data are functions or subfunctions that a program must perform. Data moving between two transformations (functions) define the interface for each function.

Information content represents the individual data items that compose some larger item of information. For example *payroll record* is an information item that is composed of an employee number, a pay rate, year-to-date wages, year-to-date taxes, and so forth. The content of *payroll record* is defined by the items contained within it. To understand the processing that is to be applied to *payroll record*, we must first understand its information content.

Information structure represents the logical organization of various data items. Is data to be organized as an n-dimensional table or as a hierachical tree structure? Within the context of the structure, what data items are related to other data items? Is all information contained within a single information structure or are distinct structures used? How do data in one information structure relate to information in another structure? These questions and others are answered by an assessment of information structure. It should be noted that *data structure*, a related concept discussed later in this book, refers to the design and implementation of information structure with software.

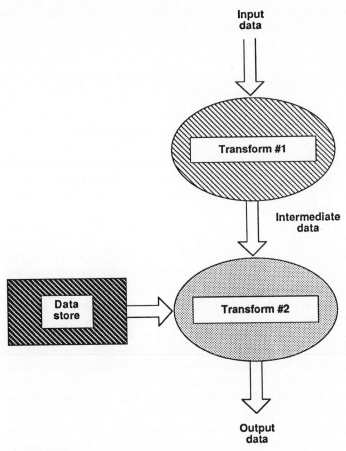

FIGURE 4.4
Information flow.

4.3.2 Partitioning

Problems are often too large and complex to be understood as a whole. For this reason, we tend to *partition* (divide) such problems into parts that can be easily understood and establish interfaces between the parts so that overall function can be accomplished. During requirements analysis, both the functional domain and the information domain of software can be partitioned.

In essence partitioning decomposes a problem into its constituent parts. Conceptually, we establish a hierarchical representation of function or information and then partition the uppermost element by (1) exposing increasing detail by moving vertically in the hierarchy or (2) functionally decomposing the problem by moving horizontally in the hierarchy. To illustrate these partitioning approaches, let us reconsider the conveyor line sorting system (CLSS) introduced in Chapter 2. The original problem statement is reproduced below:

CLSS must be developed such that boxes moving along a conveyor line will be identified and sorted into one of six bins at the end of the line. The boxes will pass by a sorting station where they will be identified. Based on an identification number printed on the side of the box (an equivalent bar code is provided), the boxes will be shunted into the appropriate bins. Boxes pass in random order and are evenly spaced. The line is moving slowly. CLSS is depicted schematically in Figure 2.3.

The software allocation for CLSS can be stated in the following paragraphs:

CLSS software will receive input information from a bar code reader at time intervals that conform to the conveyor line speed. Bar code data will be decoded into box identification format. The software will do a look-up in a 1000-entry data base to determine proper bin location for the box currently at the reader (sorting station). A FIFO list will be used to keep track of shunt positions for each box as it moves past the sorting station.

CLSS software will also receive input from a pulse tachometer that will be used to synchronize the control signal to the shunting mechanism. Based on the number of pulses that will be generated between the sorting station and the shunt, the software will produce a control signal to the shunt to properly position the box....

Requirements for CLSS software may be analyzed by partitioning the functional domain of the problem. Figure 4.5 illustrates a horizontal decomposition of CLSS software. The problem is partitioned by representing constituent CLSS software functions and moving horizontally in the functional hierarchy. Four major functions are noted on the first level of the hierarchy.

The subfunctions associated with a major CLSS function may be examined by exposing detail vertically in the hierarchy as illustrated in Figure 4.6. The function *decode box id and lookup bin location* is refined vertically to show increasing levels of functional detail.

The partitioning approach we have applied to CLSS functions can also be applied to the information domain. In fact partitioning of information flow (discussed

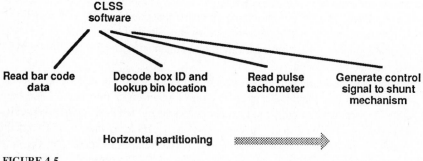

FIGURE 4.5
Horizontal partitioning.

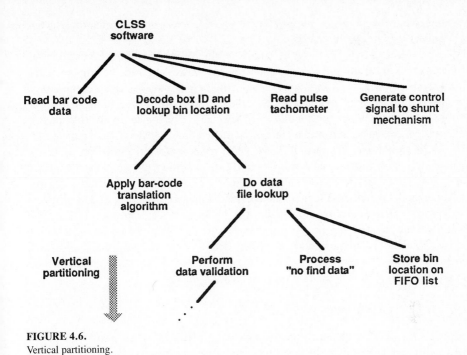

FIGURE 4.6.
Vertical partitioning.

in Chapter 5) will result in horizontal decomposition of software function. As the problem is partitioned, interfaces between functions are derived. Data items that move across an interface should be restricted to inputs required to perform the stated function and outputs required by other functions or system elements.

4.3.3   Logical and Physical Views

A logical view of software requirements presents the functions to be accomplished and information to be processed without regard to implementation details. For example the logical view of the CLSS function *read bar code data* does not concern itself with the physical form of the data or the type of bar code reader used. In fact it could be argued that *read data* would be a more appropriate name for this function since it disregards the input mechanism altogether. Similarly, a *logical data model* such as the *table* of CLSS box IDs is represented without regard to the underlying data structure used to implement the table. A logical representation of software requirements is an essential foundation for design.

The physical view of software requirements presents the real-world manifestation of processing functions and information structures. In some cases a physical representation is developed as the first step in software design. However, most computer-based systems are specified in a manner that dictates certain physical accommodations. The CLSS input device *is* a bar code reader, not a keyboard, switch, or digital encoder. Therefore, the analyst must recognize the constraints imposed by predefined system elements and consider the physical view of function and information structure when such a view is appropriate.

We have already noted that software requirements analysis should focus on *what* the software is to accomplish rather than on *how* processing will be implemented. However, the physical view should not necessarily be interpreted as a representation of *how*. Instead, the physical model represents the current mode of operation, that is, the existing or proposed allocation for all system elements. The logical model (of function or data) is generic in the sense that realization of function is not explicitly indicated.

McMenamin and Palmer [MCM84] have proposed a modeling approach that separates the *essence* of a system from its implementation details. The *essential model*, like the logical model, describes what a system must accomplish and includes descriptions of essential activities (functions) and essential memory (the overall data structure and content). The *incarnation model*, like the physical model, provides information about hardware constraints, specific operating system coupling, data base organization and access, and other implementation specific details. In many cases the analysis of a system alternates between specification of the essential model (to some level of detail) and specification of the incarnation (implementation) model.

4.4 OBJECT-ORIENTED ANALYSIS

Object-oriented software engineering techniques (e.g., [BOO82], [EVB86]) have generated widespread interest over the past few years. Object-oriented design techniques are presented in detail in Chapter 9; however, object-oriented approaches for problem definition and partitioning are well worth applying as part of software requirements analysis. In fact the definition of *objects* and *operations* is an excellent way to begin the analysis of both function and information domains. In addition an object-oriented view lends itself nicely to the partitioning principle that has already been discussed.

In the context of this discussion, an *object* may be viewed as an information item and an *operation* as a process or function that is applied to one or more objects. (It should be noted that extensions to this view are possible and are considered in Chapter 9.) Object-oriented analysis provides us with a simple, yet powerful, mechanism for identifying objects and operations.

The object-oriented analysis approach may be described in the following manner:

1. The allocated software (or entire system) is described using an *informal strategy* [BOO82]. The strategy is nothing more than an English language description of the solution for the problem to be solved by software represented at a consistent level of detail. The informal strategy may be stated in the form of a single, grammatically correct paragraph [EVB86].

2. Objects are determined by underlining each noun or noun clause and entering it in a simple table. Synonyms should be noted. If the object is required to implement a solution, then it is part of the *solution space*; otherwise, if an object is necessary only to describe a solution, it is part of the *problem space*.

3. Attributes of objects are identified by underlining all adjectives and then associating them with their respective objects (nouns).

4. Operations are determined by underlining all verbs, verb phrases, and predicates (a verb phrase indicating a conditional test) and relating each operation to the appropriate object.

5. Attributes of operations are identified by underlining all adverbs and then associating them with their respective operations (verbs).

To illustrate the object-oriented analysis approach, we again consider the CLSS software described earlier in this chapter. Using the software description as our informal strategy, we apply the first step:

> CLSS software will receive input information from a bar code reader at time intervals that conform to the conveyor line speed. Bar code data will be decoded into box identication format. The software will do a look-up in a 1000-entry data base to determine proper bin location for the box currently at the reader (sorting station). A FIFO list will be used to keep track of shunt positions for each box as it moves past the sorting station.
>
> CLSS software will also receive input from a pulse tachometer that will be used to synchronize the control signal to the shunting mechanism. Based on the number of pulses that will be generated between the sorting station and the shunt, the software will produce a control signal to the shunt to properly position the box....

A quick examination of the underlined nouns indicates that many of them reside in the problem space and are not necessary for the software implementation. Other nouns, such as *bar code data*, *bin location*, and *control signal*, reside in the solution space and are entered in Table 4.1. Following the object-oriented analysis procedure, all adjectives are underlined next and are placed in the table as shown.

Each of the objects represents an information item that must be processed by the software. To determine processing functions, we must isolate all operations. Following the analysis procedure:

TABLE 4.1
Objects and operations

Object	Attribute	Corresponding operation
Data	Bin code	Decode
Location	Bin	Determine
Signal	Control	Synchronize; produce
Input	Pulse tach	Receive
List	FIFO	Keep track
Positions	Shunt	Keep track
Intervals	Time	Conform
Format	Box id	Decode
Database	1000-entry	Do a lookup
Pulses	Tach	Generated

CLSS software will <u>receive</u> input information from a bar code reader at time intervals that <u>conform</u> to the conveyor line speed. Bar code data will be <u>decoded</u> into box identication format. The software will <u>do a look-up</u> in a 1000-entry data base to <u>determine</u> proper bin location for the box currently at the reader (sorting station). A FIFO list will be used to <u>keep track</u> of shunt positions for each box as it <u>moves</u> past the sorting station.

CLSS software will also <u>receive</u> input from a pulse tachometer that will be used to <u>synchronize</u> the control signal to the shunting mechanism. Based on the number of pulses that will be <u>generated</u> between the sorting station and the shunt, the software will <u>produce</u> a control signal to the shunt to properly position the box....

Some of the operations noted above belong in the solution space (e.g., *receive, look-up, produce*) while others are part of the problem space (e.g., *moves, synchronize*). Solution space operations are added to Table 4.1. For the CLSS informal strategy, no significant operation attributes are noted.

Referring to Table 4.1, it can be seen that object-oriented analysis provides the analyst with a simple mechanism for representing key items in the information domain and key functions in the function domain. Each item and function shown in the table can be further partitioned, and the analysis steps reapplied iteratively.

Many important and unique characteristics of object-oriented software engineering have been purposely omitted from this discussion. We shall return to this topic and consider many of these characteristics in Chapter 9.

4.5   SOFTWARE PROTOTYPING

Analysis should be conducted regardless of the software engineering paradigm applied. However, the *form* that analysis takes will vary. In some cases it is possible to apply fundamental analysis principles and derive a paper specification of software from which a design can be developed. In other situations *requirements gathering* is conducted, the analysis principles are applied, and a model of the software, called a *prototype*, is constructed for customer and developer assessment. Finally, there are circumstances that require the construction of a prototype at the beginning of analysis since the model is the only means through which requirements can be effectively derived. The model then evolves into production software.

Boar [BOA84] justifies the prototyping technique in this way:

> Most currently recommended methods for defining business system requirements are designed to establish a final, complete, consistent, and correct set of requirements before the system is designed, constructed, seen or experienced by the user. Common and recurring industry experience indicates that despite the use of rigorous techniques, in many cases users still reject applications as neither correct nor complete upon completion. Consequently, expensive, time-consuming, and divisive rework is required to harmonize the original specification with the definitive test of actual operational needs. In the worst case, rather than retrofit the delivered system, it is abandoned. Developers may build and test against specifications but users accept or reject against current and actual operational realities.

Although the above quote represents an extreme view, its fundamental argument is sound. In many (but not all) cases, the construction of a prototype, possibly coupled with systematic analysis methods, is an effective approach to software engineering.

4.5.1 A Prototyping Scenario

The prototyping paradigm for software engineering was introduced in Chapter 1. We shall expand this paradigm to indicate the individual steps in the prototyping process and the decision points that dictate how these steps are applied.

All software engineering projects begin with a request from a customer. The request can be in the form of a memo describing a problem, a report defining a set of business or product goals, a formal *Request for Proposal* from an outside agency or company, or a *System Specification* that has allocated function and performance to software as one element of a larger computer-based system. Assuming the a request for software exists in one of the forms noted above, the following steps may be applied to accomplish software prototyping.

STEP 1. *Evaluate the software request and determine whether the software to be developed is a good candidate for prototyping.* Not all software is amenable to prototyping. A number of prototyping *candidacy factors* [BOA84] can be defined: application area, application complexity, customer characteristics, and project characteristics.

In general any application that creates dynamic visual displays, interacts heavily with a human user, or demands algorithms or combinatorial processing that must be developed in an evolutionary fashion is a candidate for prototyping. However, these application areas must be weighed against application complexity. If a candidate application (one that has characteristics noted above) will require the development of tens of thousands of lines of code before any demonstrable function can be performed, it is likely to be too complex for prototyping. If, however, the complexity can be partitioned, it may still be possible to prototype portions of the software.

Because the customer must interact with the prototype in later steps, it is essential that (1) customer resources be committed to the evaluation and refinement of the prototype, and (2) the customer is capable of making requirements decisions in a timely fashion. Finally, the nature of the development project will have a strong bearing on the efficacy of prototyping. Is project management willing and able to work with the prototyping method? Are prototyping tools available? Do developers have experience with prototyping methods?

STEP 2. *Given an acceptable candidate project, the analyst develops an abbreviated representation of requirements.* Before construction of a prototype can begin, the analyst must represent both the information and functional domains of the problem and develop a reasonable approach to partitioning. The application of these fundamental analysis principles can be accomplished through requirements analysis methods described in Chapter 5.

STEP 3. *After the representation of requirements has been reviewed, a set of abbreviated design specifications are created for the prototype.* Design must occur before prototyping can commence. However, design for a prototype typically focuses on top level architectural and data design issues, rather than detailed procedural design.

STEP 4. *Prototype software is created, tested and refined.* Ideally, pre-existing software building blocks are used to create the prototype in a rapid fashion. Unfortunately, such building blocks rarely exist.* Alternatively, specialized prototyping tools (e.g., [KRU84], [TAT85]) can be used to assist the analyst/designer in representing the design and translating it into executable form.

Even if implementation of a working prototype is impractical, the prototyping scenario can still be applied. For human-interactive applications, it is often possible to create a *paper prototype* that depicts the human-machine interaction (queries, displays, decisions, etc.) using a series of *story board sheets*. Each story board sheet contains a representation of a screen image with narrative text that describes the interaction between machine and user. The customer reviews the story board sheets, obtaining a user's perspective of the operation of the software.

STEP 5. *Once the prototype has been tested, it is presented to the customer, who "test drives" the application and suggests modifications.* This step is the kernel of the prototyping approach. It is here that the customer can examine an implemented representation of software requirements, suggesting modifications that will make the software better meet actual needs.

STEP 6. *Steps 4 and 5 are repeated iteratively until all requirements are formalized or until the prototype has evolved into a production system.* The prototyping paradigm can be conducted with one of two objectives in mind: (1) the purpose of prototyping is to establish a set of formal requirements that may then be translated into production software through the use of software engineering methods and techniques, or (2) the purpose of prototyping is to provide a continuum that can lead to the evolutionary development of production software. Both approaches have merit and both create problems.

4.5.2 Prototyping Methods and Tools

For software prototyping to be effective, a prototype must be developed rapidly so that the customer may assess results and recommend changes. To conduct *rapid prototyping*, three generic classes of methods and tools are available: fourth generation techniques, reusable software components, formal specification and prototyping environments.

FOURTH GENERATION TECHNIQUES. Fourth generation techniques (4GT) encompass a broad array of data base query and reporting languages, program and application generators, and other very high-level, nonprocedural languages. Because 4GT enable the software engineer to generate executable code quickly, they are ideal for rapid prototyping. Unfortunately, the application domain for 4GT is currently limited to business information systems.

---

*Notable exceptions are Smalltalk and Lisp development environments.

REUSABLE SOFTWARE COMPONENTS. Another approach to rapid prototyping is to assemble, rather than build, the prototype by using a set of existing software components. A software component may be a data structure (or data base) or a software architectural component (i.e., a program) or a procedural component (i.e., a module) [JON84]. In each case the software component must be designed in a manner that enables it to be reused without any detailed knowledge of its internal workings.

It should be noted that an existing software product can be used as a prototype for a "new, improved" competitive product. In a way this is a form of reusability for software prototyping.

FORMAL SPECIFICATION AND PROTOTYPING ENVIRONMENTS. Over the past two decades a number of formal specification languages (see Chapter 5) have been developed to replace natural language specification techniques. Today, developers of these formal languages are in the process of developing interactive environments [RZE85] that (1) enable an analyst to interactively create a language-based specification of a system or software, (2) invoke automated tools that translate the language-based specification into executable code, and (3) enable the customer to use the prototype executable code to refine formal requirements. Specification languages such as PSL, RSL, IORL, GYPSY, OBJ, and many others are being coupled to interactive environments in an effort to achieve an *automated software engineering paradigm* (Figure 4.7) [BAL83]. Although still in early stages of development and application, such environments offer substantial hope for improved prototyping and software development productivity.

4.6 SPECIFICATION

There is no doubt that the mode of specification has much to do with a solution's quality. Software engineers who have been forced to work with incomplete, inconsistent,

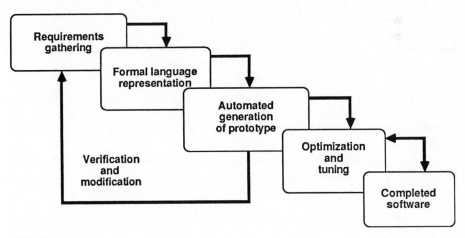

FIGURE 4.7
An *automated* software engineering paradigm.

or misleading specifications have experienced the frustration and confusion that invariably results. The quality, timeliness, and completeness of the software suffers as a consequence.

We have seen that software requirements may be analyzed in a number of different ways. Analysis techniques may lead to a paper specification that contains graphical and natural language descriptions of software requirements. Prototyping results in an *executable specification*, that is, the prototype serves as a representation of requirements. Formal specification languages lead to formal representations of requirements that may be verified or further analyzed.

4.6.1 Specification Principles

Specification, regardless of the mode through which we accomplish it, may be viewed as a representation process. Requirements are represented in a manner that ultimately leads to successful software implementation. Balzer and Goldman [BAL79] propose eight principles of good specification. Their discussion (included with permission of the IEEE) is reproduced below.

*   *   *

PRINCIPLE #1. Separate functionality from implementation.

First, by definition, a specification is a description of *what* is desired, rather than *how* it is to be realized (implemented). Specifications can adopt two quite different forms. The first form is that of mathematical functions: Given some set of input, produce a particular set of outputs. The general form of such specifications is find [*a/the/all*] result such that P(input), where P represents an arbitrary predicate. In such specifications, the result to be obtained has been entirely expressed in a *what* (rather than *how*) form. In part this is because the result is a mathematical function of the intput (the operation has well-defined starting and stopping points) and is unaffected by any surrounding environment.

PRINCIPLE #2. A process-oriented systems specification language is required.

Consider instead a situation in which the environment is dynamic and its changes affect the behavior of some entity interacting with that environment (as in an "embedded computer system"). Its behavior cannot be expressed as a mathematical function of its input. Rather, a process-oriented description must be employed, in which the *what* specification is achieved by specifying a model of the desired behavior in terms of functional responses to various stimuli from the environment.

Such process-oriented specifications, presenting a model of system behavior, have normally been excluded from formal specification languages, but they are essential if more complex dynamic situations are to be specified. In fact, it must be recognized that in such situations both the process to be automated and the environment in which it exists must be described formally. That is, the entire system of interacting parts must be specified, rather than just one component.

PRINCIPLE #3. A specification must encompass the system of which the software is a component.

A system is composed of interacting components. Only within the context of the entire system and the interaction among its parts can the behavior of a specific component be defined. In general, a system can be modeled as a collection of passive and active objects. These objects are interrelated and over time the relationships among the objects change. These dynamic relationships provide the stimulus to which the active objects, called agents, respond. The responses may cause further changes and, hence, additional stimuli to which the agents might respond.

PRINCIPLE #4. A specification must encompass the environment in which the system operates.

Similarly, the environment in which the system operates and with which it interacts must be specified.

Fortunately, this merely necessitates recognizing that the environment is itself a system composed of interacting objects, both passive and active, of which the specified system is one agent. The other agents, which are by definition unalterable because they are part of the environment, limit the scope of the subsequent design and implementation. In fact, the only difference between the system and its environment is that the subsequent design and implementation effort will operate exclusively on the specification of the system. The environment specification enables the system "interface" to be specified in the same way as the system itself rather than introducing another formalism.

It should be noted that the picture of system specification presented here is that of a highly intertwined collection of agents reacting to stimuli in the environment (changes to objects) produced by those agents. Only through the coordinated actions of the agents are the goals of the system achieved. Such mutual dependence violates the principle of separability (isolation from other parts of the system and environment). But this is a *design* principle, not one of specification. Design follows specification and is concerned with decomposing a specification into nearly separable pieces in preparation for implementation. The specification, however, must accurately portray the system and its environment as perceived by its user community in as much detail as required by the design and implementation phases. Since this level of required detail is difficult, if not impossible, to foresee in advance, specification, design, and implementation must be recognized as an iterative activity. It is therefore critical that technology exist for recovering as much of this activity as possible as the specification is elaborated and modified (during both initial development and later maintenance).

PRINCIPLE #5. A system specification must be a cognitive model.

The system specification must be a cognitive model rather than a design or implementation model. It must describe a system as perceived by its user community. The objects it manipulates must correspond to the real objects of that domain; the agents must model the individuals, organizations, and equipment in that domain; and the actions they perform must model those actually occurring in the domain. Furthermore, it must be possible to incorporate into the specification the rules or laws which govern the objects of the domain. Some of these laws proscribe certain states of the system (such as ''two objects cannot be at the same place at the same time''), and hence limit the behavior of the agents or indicate the need for further elaboration to prevent these states from arising. Other laws describe how objects respond when acted upon (e.g., Newton's laws of motion). These laws, which represent a ''physics'' of the domain, are an inherent part of the system specification.

PRINCIPLE #6. A specification must be operational.

The specification must be complete and formal enough that it can be used to determine if a proposed implementation satisfies the specification for arbitrarily chosen test cases. That is, given the results of an implementation on some arbitrarily chosen set of data, it must be possible to use the specification to validate those results. This implies that the specification, though not a complete specification of *how*, can act as a generator of possible behaviors among which must be the proposed implementation. Hence, in an extended sense, the specification must be operational....

PRINCIPLE #7. The system specification must be tolerant of incompleteness and augmentable.

No specification can ever be totally complete. The environment in which it exists is too complex for that. A specification is always a model—an abstraction—of some real (or envisioned) situation. Hence, it will be incomplete. Furthermore, as it is being formulated it will exist at many levels of detail. The operationality required above must not necessitate completeness. The analysis tools employed to aid specifiers and to test specifications must be capable of dealing with incompleteness. Naturally this weakens the analysis which can be performed by widening the range of acceptable behaviors which satisfy the specification, but such degradation must mirror the remaining levels of uncertainty.

PRINCIPLE #8. A specification must be localized and loosely coupled.

The previous principles deal with the specification as a static entity. This one arises from the dynamics of the specification. It must be recognized that although the main purpose of a specification is to serve as the basis for design and implementation of some system, it is not a precomposed static object, but a dynamic object which undergoes considerable modification. Such modification occurs in three main activities: formulation, when an initial specification is being created; development, when the specification is elaborated during the iterative process of design and implementation; and maintenance, when the specification is changed to reflect a modified environment and/or additional functional requirements.

With so much change occurring to the specification, it is critical that its content and structure be chosen to accommodate this activity. The main requirements for such accommodations are that information within the specification must be localized so that only a single piece (ideally) need be modified when information changes, and that the specification is loosely structured (coupled) so that pieces can be added or removed easily, and the structure automatically readjusted.

*   *   *

Although the principles espoused by Balzer and Goldman focus on the impact of specification on the definition of formal specification languages, their comments apply equally well to all forms of specification. However, principles must be translated into reality. In the next section we examine a set of guidelines for creating a specification of requirements.

4.6.2   Representation

Figure 4.8 is a classic example of a good specification representation. The drawing, taken from Galileo's work (circa 1638), is used to supplement text that describes his method for the analysis of the strength of a beam. Even without the accompanying text, the diagram helps us to understand what must be done.

FIGURE 4.8
Representation of a specification. (*Source*: Galileo's *Discorsi e Dimonstrazioni Matematiche intorno à due nuove scienze*, Leyden, 1638. From J.D. Bernal, *Science in History*, London Watts, 1969.)

We have already seen that software requirements may be specified in a variety of ways. However, if requirements are committed to paper (and they almost always should be) a simple set of guidelines is well worth following:

Representation format and content should be relevant to the problem. A general outline for the contents of a *Software Requirements Specification* can be developed. However, the representation forms contained within the specification are likely to vary with the application area. For example, a specification of a manufacturing automation system would use different symbology, diagrams, and language than the specification for a programming language compiler.

Information contained within the specification should be nested. Representations should reveal layers of information so that a reader can move to the level of detail required. Paragraph and diagram numbering schemes should indicate the level of detail being presented. It is sometimes worthwhile to present the same information at different levels of abstraction to aid in understanding.

Notational forms should be restricted in number and consistent in use. For example, the symbology shown in Figure 4.9 can be interpreted to mean at least three (and probably five or six) different things. Confusing or inconsistent notation, whether graphical or symbolic, degrades understanding and fosters errors.

Representations should be revisable. The content of a specification will change. Ideally, automated tools should be available to update all representations that are affected by each change. Pragmatically, paper and pencil methods can be eliminated with good desk-top publishing systems.

Investigators have conducted numerous studies (e.g., [SHE81]) on human factors associated with specification. There appears to be little doubt that symbology and arrangement affect understanding. However, software engineers appear to have individual preferences for specific symbolic and diagrammatic forms. Familiarity often lies at the root of a person's preference, but other more tangible factors such as spacial arrangement, easily recognizable patterns, and degree of formality often dictate an individual's choice.

4.6.3 Software Requirements Specification Outline

The *Software Requirements Specification* is produced at the culmination of the analysis task. The function and performance allocated to software as part of system engineering are refined by establishing a complete information description, a detailed functional

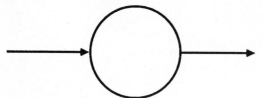

FIGURE 4.9
A symbol with multiple interpretations.

description, an indication of performance requirements and design constraints, appropriate validation criteria, and other data pertinent to requirements. The National Bureau of Standards, IEEE (Standard No. 830-1984), and the U.S. Department of Defense have all proposed formats for software requirements specifications (as well as other software engineering documentation). For our purposes, however, the following simplified outline may be used as a framework for the specification:

Software Requirements Specification

1. Introduction
   a. System reference
   b. Business objectives
   c. Software project constraints
2. Information description
   a. Information flow representation
   b. Information content representation
   c. Information structure representation
   d. System interface description
3. Functional description
   a. Functional partitioning
   b. Functional description
      (1) Processing narrative
      (2) Restrictions/limitations
      (3) Performance requirements
      (4) Design constraints
      (5) Supporting diagrams
4. Validation criteria
   a. Performance bounds
   b. Classes of tests
   c. Expected software response
   d. Special considerations
5. Bibliography
6. Appendix

The *Introduction* states the goals and objectives of the software, describing it in the context of the computer-based system. Actually, the introduction may be nothing more than the software scope of the planning document.

The *Information description* provides a detailed description of the problem the software must solve. Information flow, content, and structure are documented. Hardware, software, and human interfaces are described for external system elements and internal software functions.

A description of each function required to solve the problem is presented in the *Functional description*. A processing narrative is provided for each function, design constraints are stated and justified, performance characteristics are stated, and one or more diagrams are included to represent graphically the overall structure of the software and the interplay among its functions and other system elements.

The fourth section of the *Software Requirements Specification* is probably the most important, and, ironically, the most neglected. Validation may be best explained by the following short fable:

> A much-harried software development manager, D.O. Loop, is about to embark on a major project. Suddenly, an evil-looking gremlin appears on Loop's desk.
> "I'll deliver the system you want, free of charge," sneers the gremlin.
> "Great!" says Loop. "When can you have it for me?"
> "Tomorrow," says the gremlin as he disappears.
> Loop's enthusiasm dissipates rapidly. Can he trust the gremlin to deliver, and, more importantly, how will he recognize a successful system if it is dropped on his desk tomorrow?

Mr. Loop's last question is the concern of the *Validation criteria* section of the *Software Requirements Specification*. How do we recognize a successful implementation? What classes of tests must be conducted to validate function, performance, and constraints? We neglect this section because completing it demands a thorough understanding of software requirements—something that we often do not have. The validation criteria section acts as an implicit review of information and functional requirements. It is essential that time and attention be given to this section.

Finally, the *Software Requirements Specification* includes a *Bibliography* and *Appendix*. The bibliography contains references to all documents that relate to the software. These include other definition phase documentation, technical references, vendor literature, and standards. The appendix contains information that supplements the specification. Tabular data, detailed description of algorithms, charts, graphs, and other material are presented as appendices.

In many cases the *Software Requirements Specification* may be accompanied by an executable prototype (that in some cases may replace the specification), a paper prototype, or a *Preliminary User's Manual*. The *Preliminary User's Manual* presents the software as a black box. That is, heavy emphasis is placed on user input and resultant output. The manual can serve as a valuable tool for uncovering problems at the human-machine interface.

4.7   SPECIFICATION REVIEW

A review of the *Software Requirements Specification* (and/or prototype) is conducted by both software developer and customer. Because the specification forms the foundation of the development phase, extreme care should be taken in conducting the review.

The format of the review may best be understood by considering some of the questions that must be answered:

• Do stated goals and objectives for software remain consistent with system goals and objectives?
• Have important interfaces to all system elements been described?

- Is information flow, content, and structure adequately defined for the problem domain?
- Are diagrams clear; can each stand alone without supplementary text?
- Do major functions remain within scope and has each been adequately described?
- Are design constraints realistic?
- What is the technological risk of development?
- Have alternative software requirements been considered?
- Have validation criteria been stated in detail? Are they adequate to describe a successful system?
- Do inconsistencies, omissions, or redundancy exist?
- Is the customer contact complete?
- Has the user reviewed the user manual or prototype?
- How are the *Software Project Plan* estimates affected?

Once the review is complete, the *Software Requirements Specification* is "signed off" by both customer and developer. The specification becomes a "contract" for software development. Changes in requirements requested after the specification is finalized will still occur. But the customer should note that each after-the-fact change is an extension of software scope and therefore can increase cost and/or protract the schedule.

Even with the best review procedures in place, a number of common specification problems persist. The specification is difficult to "test" in any meaningful way, and therefore inconsistency or omissions may pass unnoticed. During the review, changes to the specification may be recommended. It is extremely difficult to assess the global impact of a change; that is, how does a change in one function affect requirements for other functions? Automated specification tools have been developed to help solve these problems and are discussed in the next chapter.

4.8 SUMMARY

Requirements analysis is the first technical step in the software engineering process. It is at this point that a general statement of software scope is refined into a concrete specification that becomes the foundation for the development phase.

Analysis must focus on both the functional and information domains of a problem. To better understand what is required, the problem is partitioned and represented in both logical and physical views. Object-oriented analysis enables the analyst to begin the partitioning process by isolating key objects and operations that the software must implement.

In many cases, it is not possible to completely specify a problem at an early stage. Prototyping offers an alternative approach that results in an executable model of the software from which requirements can be refined. To properly conduct prototyping, special tools and techniques are required.

The *Software Requirements Specification* is developed as a consequence of analysis. Review is essential to assure that developer and customer have the same perception of the system. Unfortunately, even with the best.of methods, the problem is that the problem keeps changing.

REFERENCES

[ATW77]   Atwood, J. W., *The Systems Analyst*, Hayden, 1977.

[BAL79]   Balzer, R., and N. Goodman, "Principles of Good Software Specification," *Proc. on Specifications of Reliable Software*, IEEE, 1979, pp. 58–67.

[BAL83]   Balzer, R., T. E. Cheatham, and C. Green, "Software Technology in the 1990s: A New Paradigm," *Computer*, vol. 16, no. 11, November 1983, pp. 39–45.

[BER80]   Bersoff, E. H., V. D. Henderson, and S. G. Siegel, *Software Configuration Management*, Prentice-Hall, 1980, p. 43.

[BOA84]   Boar, B., *Application Prototyping*, Wiley-Interscience, 1984.

[BOO82]   Booch, G., "Object Oriented Design," *Ada Letters*, vol. 1, no. 3, March/April 1982, pp. 64–76.

[EVB86]   *Object Oriented Design Handbook*, EVB Software Engineering, Rockville, MD, 1986.

[JON84]   Jones, T. C., "Reusability in Programming: A Survey of the State of the Art," *IEEE Trans. Software Engineering*, vol. SE-10, no. 5, September 1984, pp. 488–494.

[KRU84]   Kruchten, P., E. Schonberg, and J. Schwartz, "Software Prototyping Using the SETL Programming Language," *Software*, vol. 1, no. 4, October 1984, pp. 66–76.

[MCM84]   McMenamin, S., and J. Palmer, *Essential Systems Analysis*, Yourdon Press, 1984.

[RZE85]   Rzepka, W., and Y. Ohno, eds., "Requirements Engineering Environments," *Computer*, vol. 18, no. 4, special issue, April 1985.

[SHE81]   Shepard, S., E. Kruesi, and B. Curtis, "The Effects of Symbology and Spacial Arrangement on the Comprehension of Software Specifications," *Proc. 5th Intl. Conf. on Software Engineering*, IEEE, 1981, pp. 207–214.

[TAT85]   Tate, G., and T. Docker, " A Rapid Prototyping System Based on Data Flow Principles," *Software Engineering Notes*, ACM SIGSOFT, vol. 10, no. 2, April 1985, pp. 28–35.

PROBLEMS AND POINTS TO PONDER

4.1 Software requirements analysis is unquestionably the most communication-intensive step in the software engineering process. Why does the communication path frequently break down?

4.2 There are frequently severe political repercussions when software requirements analysis (and/or system analysis) begins. For example, workers may feel that job security is threatened by a new automated system. What causes such problems? Can the analysis task be conducted so that politics is minimized?

4.3 Discuss your perceptions of the ideal training and background for a systems analyst.

4.4 Throughout this chapter we refer to the "customer." Describe the "customer" for information systems developers, for builders of computer-based products, for systems builders. Be careful here—there may be more to this problem than you first imagine!

4.5 Is it fair to say that a *Preliminary User Manual* is a form of prototype? Explain your answer.

4.6 Why does a customer always react in a manner that is described by the "first law of system engineering" (Section 4.2)?

The following product description will be used for problems 4.7–4.15. If your instructor wishes, another problem may be substituted:

Assume that you work for a consumer products company that is building a microprocessor-based *Home Security System* (HSS) that receives input from entry (burglar) sensors, smoke sensors, temperature sensors (for situations when the furnace is broken and no one is home), and flood sensors (for basement flooding) and is capable of generating alarms, turning on selected lights, and calling owner-defined telephone numbers. HSS is owner-programmable; that is, the owner can set the limits for some sensors, program phone numbers and delay times, and control system function from a centralized control station located in the home.

4.7 Acting first as the "customer," derive a set of product requirements for HSS. Then, acting as an analyst, apply basic analysis principles to the problems that follow. *Note*: If time permits, talk to a few people who own security systems. This "market" will give you some insight into desirable features.

4.8 Analyze the information domain for HSS. Represent (using any notation that seems appropriate) information flow in the system, information content, and any information structure that is relevant.

4.9 Partition the functional domain for HSS. First perform horizontal partitioning; then perform vertical partitioning.

4.10 Create logical and physical representations of the HSS system.

4.11 Using the object-oriented analysis approach, write an informal strategy for HSS, then identify objects and operations that are relevant to this problem. Use a table similar to Table 4.1.

4.12 Build a paper prototype (or a real prototype) of HSS software. Be sure to depict owner interaction and overall system function.

4.13 Try to identify software components of HSS that might be "reusable" in other products or systems. Attempt to categorize these components.

4.14 Develop a written specification for HSS using the outline provided in Section 4.6.3. Be sure to apply the questions that are described for the specification review.

4.15 How did your requirements differ from others who attempted a solution for HSS? Who built a "Chevy"—who built a "Cadillac?"

FURTHER READINGS

Information domain analysis is a fundamental principle of requirements analysis. An issue of *Computer* magazine (IEEE, January 1986) has been dedicated to "data engineering" and presents a number of excellent articles on analysis and design of the information domain. A special issue of the *IEEE Transactions on Software Engineering* (February 1986) presents other important work in analysis methods, formal specification, and prototyping. The IEEE publication *Data Base Engineering* covers a broad range of topics that relate to information domain analysis and design methods as well as data base applications and research.

Gehani and McGettrick (*Software Specification Techniques*, Addison-Wesley, 1986) have edited an important anthology of papers on software analysis topics, ranging from basic principles of specification to advanced specification and design environments. Barstow et al. (*Interactive Programming Environments*, McGraw-Hill, 1984) present contributed chapters that describe advanced software analysis, prototyping, and design environments that are likely to find their way into industry application over the next few years.

Boar's book on application prototyping [BOA84] is one of the few dedicated to the subject. Although prototyping is presented with a definite information systems flavor, many topics are applicable across all application domains.

The *Software Engineering Standards Application Workshop* from the IEEE (proceedings available on an approximately bi-annual schedule) reports on developments in specification standardization and the impact of standards on software engineering procedures and methods. A handbook developed by the General Electric Company (*Software Engineering Handbook*, McGraw-Hill, 1986) contains an appendix with detailed outlines for specifications and other software engineering documentation.

CHAPTER
5

REQUIREMENTS ANALYSIS METHODS

A requirements analysis methodology combines systematic procedures and a unique notation to analyze the information and functional domain of a software problem; it provides a set of heuristics for partitioning the problem and defines a mode of representation for both logical and physical views. In essence, software requirements analysis methods enable the software engineer to apply fundamental analysis principles within the context of a well-defined approach.

Most requirements analysis methods are *information driven*. That is, the method provides a mechanism for representing the information domain. From this representation, function is derived and other software characteristics are developed. We have already noted that the information domain is characterized by three attributes: data flow, data content, and data structure. A requirements analysis method makes use of one or more of these attributes.

Liskov and Berzins [LIS86] have stated:

> Every program performs some task correctly. What is of interest to computer scientists [and software engineers and their managers] is whether a program performs its intended task. To determine this, a precise and independent description of the desired program behavior is needed. Such a description is called a *specification*.

The role of requirements analysis methods is to assist the analyst in deriving "a precise and independent description" of the software element of a computer-based system.

5.1 REQUIREMENTS ANALYSIS METHODOLOGIES

Requirements analysis methodologies enable an analyst to apply fundamental analysis principles (Chapter 4) in a systematic fashion. In the sections that follow, we examine some of the common characteristics of all methods and present an overview of the choices available to the analyst.

5.1.1 Common Characteristics

Although each method introduces new notation and analysis heuristics, all methods can be evaluated in the context of the following common characteristics: (1) mechanism for information domain analysis, (2) approach for functional representations, (3) definition of interfaces, (4) mechanisms for problem partitioning, (5) support for abstraction, and (6) representation of physical and logical views.

Although information domain analysis is conducted differently with each methodology, some common threads can be recognized. All methods address (either directly or indirectly) data flow and data content or structure. In most cases data flow is characterized in the context of transformations (functions) that are applied to change input into output. Data content may be represented explicitly by using a dictionary mechanism or implicitly by first addressing the hierarchical structure of data.

Functions are typically described as information transforms or processes. Each function may be represented using specific notation (e.g., a circle or box). A description of the function may be developed using natural language text, a procedural language with informal syntax rules, or a formal specification language.

A description of interfaces is generally an outgrowth of information and function representations. Flow of data into and out of a specific function can be matched with information flows to other functions. Interfaces are derived from an examination of information flow.

Problem partitioning and abstraction are accomplished through a *layering* process that enables the analyst to represent the information domain and the functional domain at different levels of abstraction. For example, all methods enable an analyst to represent a function such as *compute all payroll taxes* and to represent and manipulate the function at this level of abstraction. In addition, all methods provide a mechanism for partitioning *compute all payroll taxes* into a set of functions, such as *compute withholding tax, compute FICA, compute state tax,* and *compute city tax*. Each of these functions may be represented at a lower level of abstraction using a function-descriptive notation (e.g., a procedural language).

Most analysis methods allow the analyst to evaluate the physical representation of a problem prior to deriving the logical solution. In general, the same notation is used to represent both views.

5.1.2 Representative Methods and Tools

Many requirements analysis approaches have been proposed in the literature. A smaller, but still significant, number are being used in industry applications on a regular basis. Table 5.1 contains a list of some of the more common analysis methods and

TABLE 5.1
Requirements analysis methods and tools

Method/tool name	Information source	Category*
Data Structured Systems Development	Ken Orr & Associates Topeka, KS	M, T
DesignAid	Nastec Corporation Southfield, MI	T
Excelerator	Index Technology, Inc. Cambridge, MA	T
Higher Order Software (HOS)	HOS, Inc. Cambridge, MA	M, T
Information Engineering Workbench	Knowledgeware, Inc. Ann Arbor, MI	T
Jackson System Development	[JAC83]	M, T
Logical Construction of System (LCS)	[WAR81]	M
PSL/PSA	ISDOS, Inc. Ann Arbor, MI	F, T
Software Requirements Engineering Methodology (SREM) and (SYSREM)	[ALF85]	F, T
Structured Analysis (SA)	[DEM79], [GAN82]	M, T
Structured Analysis and Design Technique (SADT)	Softech, Inc. Waltham, MA	M, T
Structured Analysis Tools	Tektronix Beaverton, OR	T
System Development Methodology (SDM)	CAP Gemini Vienna, VA	M, T
Technology for Automated Generation of Systems (TAGS)	[SEI85]	F, T

*M—manual analysis technique, T—automated tool, F—formal specification language

tools, along with a reference or pointer to an organization that can provide additional information.

The methods and tools listed in Table 5.1 can be divided into three broad analysis categories: data flow–oriented analysis, data structure–oriented analysis, and language-based formal specification. Methods and tools in the first two categories were originally developed for manual application and have been upgraded with a variety of support tools including some of the stand-alone tools listed in Table 5.1. Support tools for language-based formal specification environments have been created to establish computer-aided requirements engineering [RZE85].

5.2 DATA FLOW–ORIENTED ANALYSIS METHODS

Information is transformed as it *flows* through a computer-based system. The system accepts input in a variety of forms; applies hardware, software, and human elements to

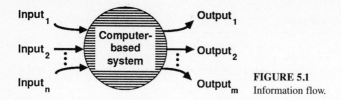

FIGURE 5.1
Information flow.

transform input into output; and produces output in a variety of forms. Input may be a control signal transmitted by a transducer, a series of numbers typed by a human operator, a packet of information transmitted on a network link, or a voluminous data file retrieved from secondary storage. The transform(s) may comprise a single logical comparison, a complex numerical algorithm, or the rule-inference approach of an expert system. Output may light a single LED or produce a 200-page report. In effect a data flow model can be applied to any computer-based system regardless of size or complexity.

One technique for representing information flow through a computer-based system is illustrated in Figure 5.1. The overall function of the system is represented as a single information transform, noted as a *bubble* in the figure. One or more inputs, shown as labeled arrows, drive the transform to produce output information. It should be noted that the model may be applied to the entire system or to the software element only. The key is to represent the information fed into and produced by the transform.

5.2.1 Data Flow Diagrams

As information moves through software, it is modified by a series of transformations. A *data flow diagram* (DFD) is a graphical technique depicting information flow and the transforms that are applied as data move from input to output. The basic form of a DFD is illustrated in Figure 5.2. The diagram is similar in form to other activity-flow diagrams (e.g., production flow diagrams [RIG81]) and has been incorporated into analysis and design techniques proposed by Yourdon and Constantine [YOU78], De-Marco [DEM79], and Gane and Sarson [GAN82]. It is also known as a *data flow graph* or a *bubble chart*.

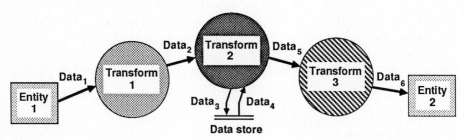

FIGURE 5.2
A data flow diagram (DFD).

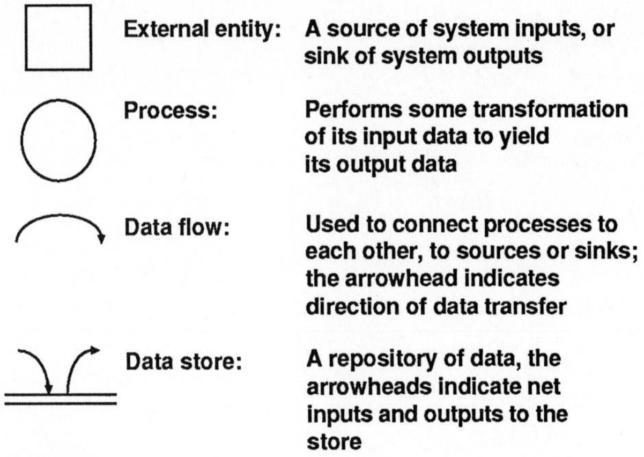

External entity: **A source of system inputs, or sink of system outputs**

Process: **Performs some transformation of its input data to yield its output data**

Data flow: **Used to connect processes to each other, to sources or sinks; the arrowhead indicates direction of data transfer**

Data store: **A repository of data, the arrowheads indicate net inputs and outputs to the store**

FIGURE 5.3
DFD symbology.

The DFD may be used to represent a system or software at any level of abstraction. In fact, DFDs may be partitioned into *levels* that represent increasing information flow and functional detail. A level 01 DFD, also called a *fundamental system model*, represents the entire software element as a single bubble with input and output data indicated by incoming and outgoing arrows, respectively. Additional transforms and information flow paths are represented as the level 01 DFD is partitioned to reveal more detail.

DFD symbology[*] is illustrated in Figure 5.3. A rectangle is used to represent an *external entity*, that is, a system element (e.g., hardware, a person) or another system that produces information for transformation by the software or receives information produced by the software. A circle or oval represents a *process* or *transform* that is applied to data and changes it in some way. An arrow represents one or more data items. All arrows on a data flow diagram should be labeled. The double line represents a *data store*—stored information that is used by the software. The exceptional simplicity of DFD symbology is one reason why data flow–oriented analysis techniques are the most widely used.

As a simple example of a data flow diagram, consider information flow for a typical telephone call (Figure 5.4a). The level 01 DFD for a telephone call indicates that output is the sound of the caller's voice received by the listener. Input to the telephone call is the caller's voice and a keyed phone number. Figure 5.4b illustrates a level 02 refinement of the level 01 DFD. In this figure, more information about both information flow and process function (transforms) is provided. The caller's action of depressing the keypad is transformed by associated electronics into a series of audible frequen-

---

[*]Extensions to DFD symbology have been proposed for the analysis of real-time systems. These are discussed in Chapter 10.

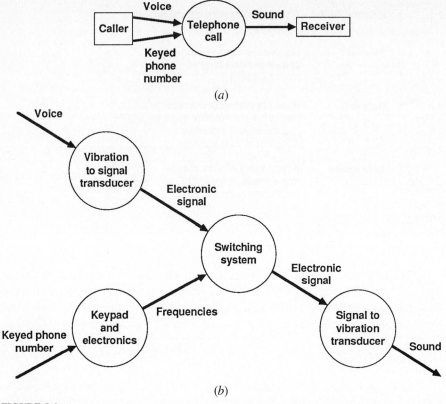

FIGURE 5.4
Example—a telephone call DFD. (*a*) Level 01 data flow diagram. (*b*) Level 02 data flow diagram.

cies (tones). The frequencies flow to a switching system that performs requisite routing and establishes a link from sender to receiver. The human voice is transformed by a vibration transducer that produces a signal as output. The switching system moves the voice signal to a receiver that transforms it back to sound.

Although the above example is a gross oversimplification, the flow of information, represented by the data flow diagram, is easy to discern. Each transform in the diagram (the bubbles) could be refined still further to provide greater detail about keypad processing, transducers, or the switching system. That is, the diagram may be layered to show any desired level of detail.

It is important to note that no explicit indication of the sequence of events (e.g., is keying done before or after voice input?) is supplied by the diagram. Procedure or sequence may be implicit in the diagram, but explicit procedural representation is generally delayed until software design.

As we noted earlier, each of the bubbles may be refined or layered to depict more detail. Figure 5.5 illustrates this concept. A fundamental model for system F indicates the primary input as A and ultimate output as B. We refine the F model into transforms f_1 to f_7. Note that *information flow continuity* must be maintained, that is, input and out-

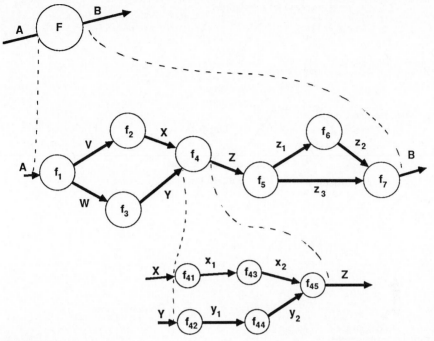

FIGURE 5.5
Information flow refinements.

put to the refinement must remain the same. Further refinement of f_4 depicts detail in the form of transforms f_{41} to f_{45}. Again, the input (X,Y) and output (Z) remain unchanged.

As a further illustration of the use of data flow diagrams, we consider information flow for a *patient monitoring system* (PMS) to be installed in a hospital. PMS, illustrated with a level 01 DFD model in Figure 5.6, monitors the vital signs of all patients in a ward, maintains records by updating a patient log, notifies nursing staff if anything goes awry, and produces a patient report upon request.

Conducting requirements analysis for the system, we can refine information flow into a level 02 DFD as shown in Figure 5.7. The level 01 model has been refined to show four major functions: local monitoring performed by a bedside monitor, central monitoring performed at the nurse's station, patient log update, and generation of reports at the nurses station. Information sources and sinks remain unchanged. The nurse becomes both a source and a sink for information. The patient log file has been refined to depict new data flow among the transforms (functions). An internal file, *patient bounds*, is shown and used to indicate safe bounds (limits) for vital signs. Even without a supporting narrative, a reader of the PMS data flow diagram can discern the overall operation of the system.

PMS data flow is further refined to level 03 in Figure 5.8. The *central monitoring* bubble of Figure 5.7 has been refined to indicate greater detail. Note that continuity of information remains unchanged, i.e., all incoming and outgoing arrows in the original

A distributed, microprocessor based *patient monitoring system*
is to be developed for a hospital.

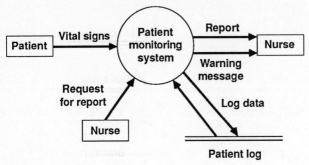

FIGURE 5.6
An example: PMS.

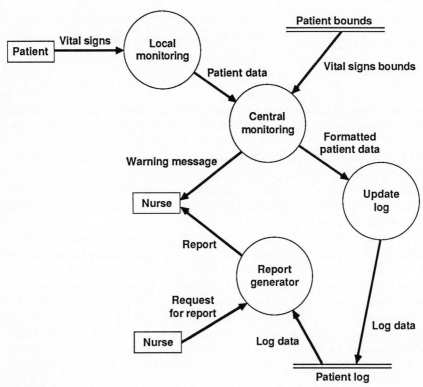

FIGURE 5.7
Refining the model.

170

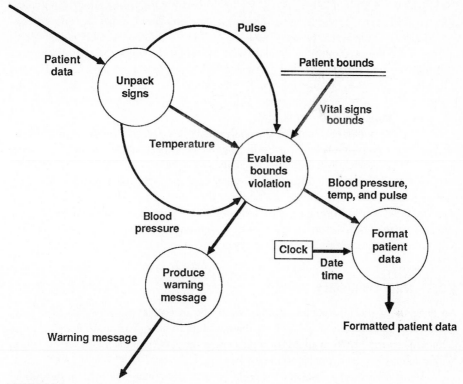

FIGURE 5.8
Information flow in central monitoring.

central monitoring bubble (and all relevant files) appear in the refined data flow diagram. Refinement does, however, indicate an internal clock that supplies the date/time information used as part of patient record keeping. Examining Figure 5.8, we see that a patient's vital signs are unpacked and compared with bounding values. Bounds violation results in a warning message. In all cases patient data is combined with clock data for log update preparation.

Figures 5.6, 5.7, and 5.8 depict three distinct layers of information flow. Each layer indicates that progressively more detailed requirements analysis is being conducted.

The data flow diagram is a graphical tool that can be very valuable during software requirements analysis. However, the diagram can cause confusion if its function is confused with that of a flowchart. A data flow diagram depicts information flow without explicit notation of control[*] (e.g., conditions or loops). It is not a flowchart with rounded edges!

---

[*]Extensions to DFDs do support control notation. See Chapter 10 for details.

A few simple guidelines can aid immeasurably during derivation of software-oriented data flow: (1) the level 01 data flow diagram should depict the software/system as a single bubble; (2) primary input/output/files should be carefully noted; (3) all arrows and bubbles should be labeled (with meaningful names); (4) *information flow continuity* must be maintained; and (5) one bubble at a time should be refined. There is a natural tendency to overcomplicate the data flow diagram. This occurs when the analyst attempts to show too much detail too early or represents procedural aspects of the software in lieu of information flow.

During requirements analysis the analyst may discover that certain aspects of the system "are subject to change" or "will be enhanced in the future" or are vaguely defined by the customer. Alternatively, an analyst may be working on existing software that is about to undergo modification. In either case the data flow diagram allows easy isolation of the *domain of change* as shown in Figures 5.9 and 5.10. By clearly understanding the flow of information across the domain of change boundary, better preparation can be made for future modification, or current modification can be conducted without upsetting other elements of the system.

5.2.2 Data Dictionary

An analysis of the information domain would be incomplete if only data flow were considered. Each arrow of a data flow diagram represents one or more items of information. Therefore, some method for representing the *content* of each DFD arrow (information item) must be available to the analyst.

The *data dictionary* has been proposed as a quasi-formal grammar for describing the content of information items and has been defined in the following manner [PAG80]:

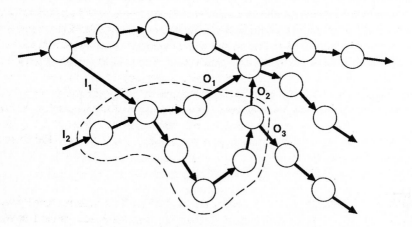

Dashed line identifies the "domain of change"

FIGURE 5.9
Data flow diagrams for existing systems.

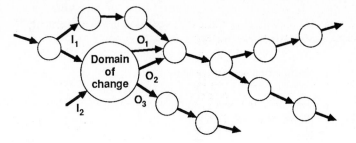

FIGURE 5.10
Remodel with domain of change isolated.

...the data dictionary contains definitions of all data mentioned in the DFD, in a process specification and in the data dictionary itself. Composite data (data that can be further divided) is defined in terms of its components; elementary data (data that cannot be further divided) is defined in terms of the meaning of each of the values that it can assume. Thus, the data dictionary is composed of definitions of data flows, files [data stores], and data used within processes [transforms]....

Data dictionary notation, illustrated in Figure 5.11, enables the analyst to represent *composite data* in one of the three fundamental ways that it can be constructed: (1) as a *sequence* of data items, (2) as a *selection* from among a set of data items, or (3) as a *repeated grouping* of data items. Each data item entry that is represented as part of a sequence, selection, or repetition may itself be another composite data item that needs further refinement within the dictionary.

To illustrate the use of the data dictionary, let us return to the DFD for the telephone call shown in Figure 5.4. Referring to the figure, the data item *keyed phone number* is specified as input. But what exactly is a keyed phone number? It could be a seven-digit local number, a four-digit extension, or a 25-digit long-distance carrier sequence. The data dictionary provides us with a precise definition of keyed phone number for the DFD in question:

keyed phone number = [local extension | outside number | 0]

The above data dictionary statement may be read: *keyed phone number* is composed of either a *local extension* or an *outside number* or 0 (for operator). *Local extension* and *out-*

Data construct	Notation	Meaning
	=	Is composed of
Sequence	+	And
Selection	[|]	Either - or
Repetition	$\{\}^n$	n repetitions of
	( )	Optional data

FIGURE 5.11
Data dictionary notation.

side number represent composite data and must be refined further in other data dictionary statements. The numeral 0 is elementary data and needs no further refinement.

Continuing the data dictionary entries for *keyed phone number*:

keyed phone number	= [local extension | outside number | 0]
local extension	= [2001 | 2002 | ... | 2999 | conference set]
outside number	= 9 + [local number | long distance no.]
local number	= prefix + access number
long distance no.	= (0) + area code + local number
conference set	= $\{\# + \text{local extension} + \#(\#)\}_2^6$

The data dictionary is expanded until all composite data items have been represented as elementary items or until all composite items are represented in terms that would be well known and unambiguous to all readers (e.g., *area code* is generally understood to mean a three-digit number with a 0 or 1 as the second digit).

The data dictionary defines information items unambiguously. Although we might assume that the phone call represented by the DFD in Figure 5.4 could accommodate a 25-digit long-distance carrier access number, the data dictionary for the DFD tells us that such numbers are not part of the data that may be input. In addition the data dictionary can provide information about function that may not be immediately obvious from an examination of the DFDs. For example, conference calling capability is implied by the entry for *conference set*, where between two and six extensions may be keyed (delimited by #) until two # signs are entered in a row. Each of these extensions, we infer, would be part of a conference call. It is important to note, however, that further information (external to the data dictionary) would have to be provided about conference calling capability.

For large computer-based systems, the data dictionary grows rapidly in size and complexity. In fact it is extremely difficult to maintain a data dictionary manually. For this reason a number of automated data dictionary systems are available. In addition, new *computer-aided software engineering* workstations support automated generation of DFDs and direct coupling and management of associated data dictionaries.

5.2.3   Functional Descriptions

Once the information domain has been represented (using DFDs and the data dictionary), the analyst describes each function (transform) represented using natural language or some other stylized notation. One such notation is called *structured English* (also called process or program design language (PDL)). Structured English incorporates basic procedural constructs—sequence, selection and repetition—with English language phrases so that concise procedural descriptions can be developed for functions represented within a DFD. To illustrate the use of structured English, we consider the data flow diagram shown in Figure 5.12. This DFD represents the flow of information that occurs when a functional description is generated for the transform of a DFD. A functional description of the DFD bubble follows:

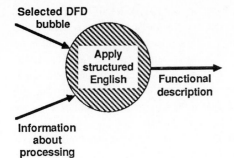

Selected DFD bubble

Apply structured English

Functional description

Information about processing

FIGURE 5.12
Generating a functional description.

```
procedure: Apply Structured English
      select DFD bubble, call it target.bubble;
      do while target.bubble needs further refinement
           if target.bubble is multifunctional
                 then decompose as required;
                       select new target.bubble;
                 else no further refinement needed;
           endif
      enddo
      use procedure statement to name target.bubble;
      describe sequence of process tasks;
      repeat until all process tasks have been described
            case of processing task logic:
            case: process task includes a sequence
                  state sequence of steps;
            case: process task is a condition
                  use if-then-else to describe condition;
            case: process task includes repetition
                  use do while or repeat until to describe;
            case: process task includes a number of cases
                  use case of to describe;
            endcase
      endrep
      review structured English that has been generated;
      modify as required using procedure Apply Structured English;
end procedure
```

Structured English can often be combined with natural language descriptions to provide a complete functional description. During software design the functional description is refined to provide additional procedural detail.

5.3   DATA STRUCTURE–ORIENTED METHODS

We have already noted that the information domain for a software problem encompasses data flow, data content, and data structure. Data structure–oriented analysis methods represent software requirements by focusing on data structure rather than data flow. Although each data structure–oriented method has a distinct approach and notation, all have some characteristics in common: (1) each assists the analyst in identifying key information *objects* (also called *entities* or *items*) and *operations* (also called *actions* or *processes*); (2) each assumes that the structure of information is hierarchical; (3) each requires that the data structure be represented using the sequence, selection, and repetition constructs discussed in Section 5.2.2; and (4) each provides a set of steps for mapping a hierarchical data structure into a program structure.

Like their data flow–oriented counterparts, data structure–oriented analysis methods lay the foundation for software design. In every case an analysis method may be extended to encompass architectural and procedural design for software.

In the sections that follow, an overview of two important data structure–oriented analysis methods is presented.

5.4 DATA STRUCTURED SYSTEMS DEVELOPMENT

Data Structured Systems Development (DSSD), also called the Warnier-Orr methodology, evolved from pioneering work on information domain analysis conducted by J. D. Warnier ([WAR74], [WAR81]). Warnier developed a notation for representing information hierarchy using the three constructs for sequence, selection, and repetition and demonstrated that the software structure could be derived directly from the data structure.

Orr ([ORR77], [ORR81]) has extended Warnier's work to encompass a somewhat broader view of the information domain that has evolved into *Data Structured Systems Development*. DSSD considers information flow and functional characteristics as well as data hierarchy.

5.4.1 Warnier Diagrams

The *Warnier diagram* [WAR74] enables the analyst to represent information hierarchy in a compact manner. The information domain is analyzed and the hierarchical nature of the output is represented. To illustrate, let us consider an automated composition system used by a newspaper to prepare each day's edition. The general organization of the paper takes the following form.

Front Section
    Headline news
    National news
    Local news
Editorial Section
    Editorials
    Columns
    Letters to the editor
    Satirical cartoon

Second Section
    Sports news
    Business news
    Classified

The newspaper outline shown above is an information hierarchy. The Warnier diagram may be used to represent the hierarchy at any level of detail. In Figure 5.13a, the newspaper information hierarchy is represented using Warnier notation. The brace ({) is used to differentiate levels of the information hierarchy. All names contained within a brace represent a *sequence* of information items (each item may be a composite of other items or an elementary item). The notation next to some names represents *repetition*, that is, the number of times the particular item appears in the hierarchy. For example, 1 to c columns will appear in the editorial section, while a cartoon may or may not be present (appears 0 to 1 times).

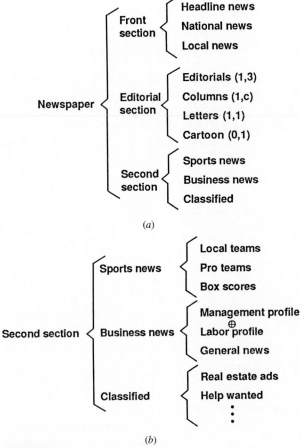

(a)

(b)

FIGURE 5.13
(*a*) Warnier diagram. (*b*) Refined diagram.

The Warnier diagram may be used to further partition the information domain by refining composite data items. Figure 5.13b illustrates refinement for the second section. The *exclusive-or* symbol ($\oplus$) indicates a conditional occurrence (*selection*) of an information item; in this case, the business news section will contain either a management profile or a labor profile but not both.

5.4.2 The DSSD Approach

Rather than beginning analysis by examining information hierarchy, DSSD first examines the *application context*, that is, how data move between producers and consumers of information from the perspective of one of the producers or consumers. Next, *application functions* are assessed with a Warnier-like representation that depicts information items and the processing that must be performed on them (this is similar in concept to the data flow diagram). Finally, *application results* are modeled using the Warnier diagram. Using this approach, DSSD encompasses all attributes of the information domain: data flow, content, and structure.

To illustrate DSSD notation and to provide an overview of the analysis method, we present a simple example. A mail/phone order business, called *The Software Store*, sells personal computer software. A computer-based order processing system is to be specified for the business.

To illustrate the overall flow of information for *The Software Store*, refer to the data flow diagram in Figure 5.14 (Note: The DFD is not part of the DSSD method, but has been used because it is an already familiar analysis notation.) Phone orders are received by a sales clerk who records the order and builds an order file that is composed of the data items shown in Figure 5.14. An order number is assigned to a particular

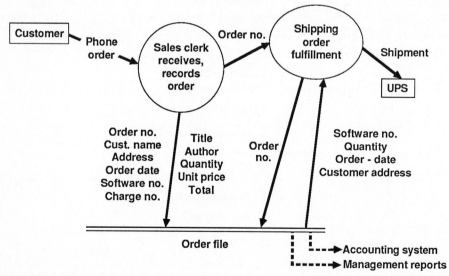

FIGURE 5.14
The Software Store—an example.

order and passed to the shipping department, which prepares shipment using information in the order file. Other business functions (e.g., accounting) have access to the order file.

5.4.3 Application Context

To determine the DSSD *application context*, the problem must be stated in a manner that enables us to answer three questions:

1. What are the information items that must be processed?
2. Who/what are the producers and consumers of information?
3. How does each producer/consumer view information in the context of other constituencies?

DSSD proposes an *entity diagram* as a mechanism for answering these questions.

The entity diagram uses a notation that is, regrettably, very similar to the data flow diagram. However, similar symbols have different meanings. The circle in an entity diagram depicts a producer or consumer (a person, a machine, another system) of information. The five producers and consumers of information for *The Software Store* are shown in Figure 5.15a. An entity diagram for the *sales: order receiving* department is illustrated in Figure 5.15b. All interfaces between *sales: order receiving* and other constituencies are shown from the point of view of *sales: order receiving*. Entity diagrams for other producers and consumers of information are shown in Figure 5.15c, d, and e.

After each entity diagram is reviewed for correctness, a *combined entity diagram* (Figure 5.16) is created for all producers and consumers of information. Those entities that fall within the bounds of the proposed system (an automated order processing system) are indicated by identifying an *application boundary*. The detail within the application boundary may be hidden (temporarily) as illustrated in Figure 5.17. Information

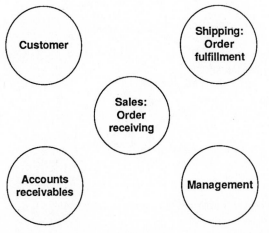

FIGURE 5.15
(*a*) Producers and consumers of information.

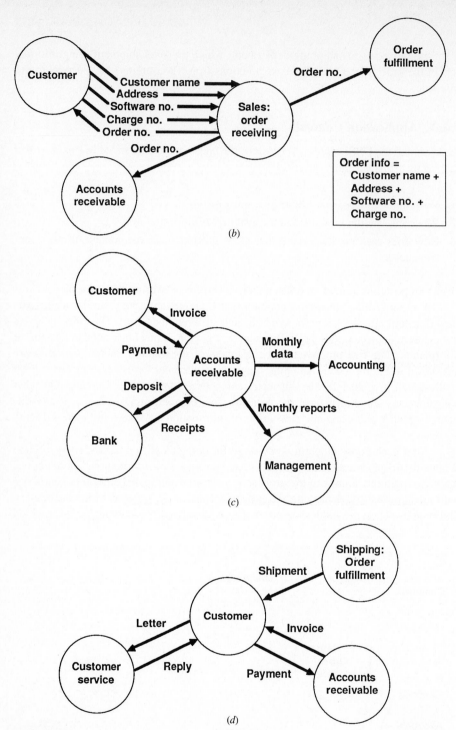

FIGURE 5.15

(*b*) Entity diagram for *sales: order receiving.* (*c*) Entity diagram for *accounts receivable.* (*d*) Entity diagram for *customer.*

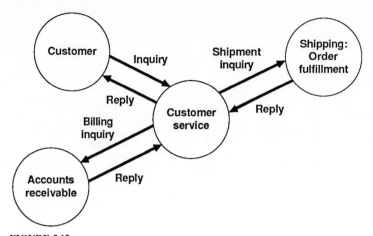

FIGURE 5.15
(*e*) Entity diagram for *customer service*.

moving across the application boundary must be processed by the automated order processing system.

5.4.4 Application Functions

The functions that must be implemented to accomplish the automated order processing system can be discerned by examining information flow across the application boundary. The sequence in which data items move across the boundary is noted as shown in Figure 5.17. Using a Warnier-like notation called an *assembly line diagram* (ALD), DSSD provides a mechanism for coupling information and the processes (transforms or functions) applied to it. Conceptually, the ALD plays the same role as the data flow diagram.

An assembly line diagram is developed by beginning with the last numbered information flow (Figure 5.17) and working backward toward the first numbered flow. The information flow item is derived by combining the preceding numbered information item with the procedure that creates the desired item. An ALD for the order processing system is shown in Figure 5.18. Read left to right, the monthly report (based on monthly data to accounting) is derived by taking bank receipt information and applying a report generation process. The plus sign indicates the coupling between process and information. Receipts information is derived from a bank deposit (information) and the associated function that processes the deposit, producing a receipt. A similar progression occurs until we reach *Order Info*, the first input in the sequence (Figure 5.17).

Each process in the ALD is refined by developing a processing narrative that addresses output, action, frequency of action, and input. A Warnier-Orr diagram, de-

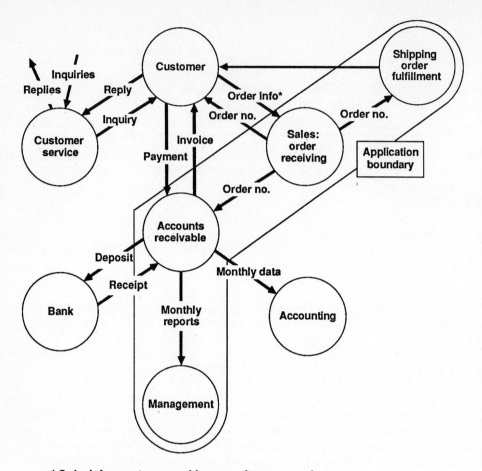

* Order info = customer + address + software no. + charge no.

FIGURE 5.16
A combined entity diagram.

scribed in the next section, may be used to represent procedural details for each process.

5.4.5 Application Results

DSSD requires the analyst to build a *paper prototype* of the desired output for the system. The prototype identifies primary system output and the organization of information items that compose the output. Once a prototype has been created, the information hierarchy may be modeled using a *Warnier-Orr diagram*—essentially a Warnier diagram (Section 5.4.1) with small variations in notation and format.

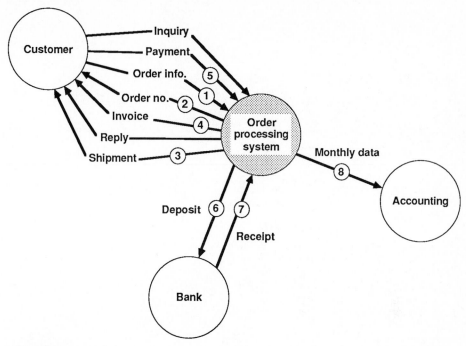

FIGURE 5.17
An application-level entity diagram.

To illustrate the use of paper prototyping and the Warnier-Orr diagram in the derivation of application results, we consider the *monthly report* generated as output from the automated order processing system for *The Software Store*. Figure 5.19a shows a paper prototype for the report, and Figure 5.19b illustrates a Warnier-Orr diagram of the corresponding information hierarchy.

5.4.6   Physical Requirements

DSSD notation that includes entity, assembly line, and Warnier-Orr diagrams is used to model software requirements from the logical view. Physical requirements must also be determined as part of analysis. Among the physical requirements that must be considered are:

Performance. Some applications demand strict run-time performance constraints. These might include defined execution time limits for specific algorithms and response-time bounds for interactive systems.

Reliability. Processes may have to be designed and implemented in a manner that assures specific reliability as measured by mean-time-between-failures or availability (see Chapter 12).

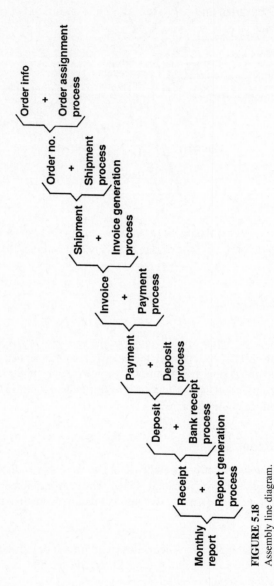

FIGURE 5.18
Assembly line diagram.

184

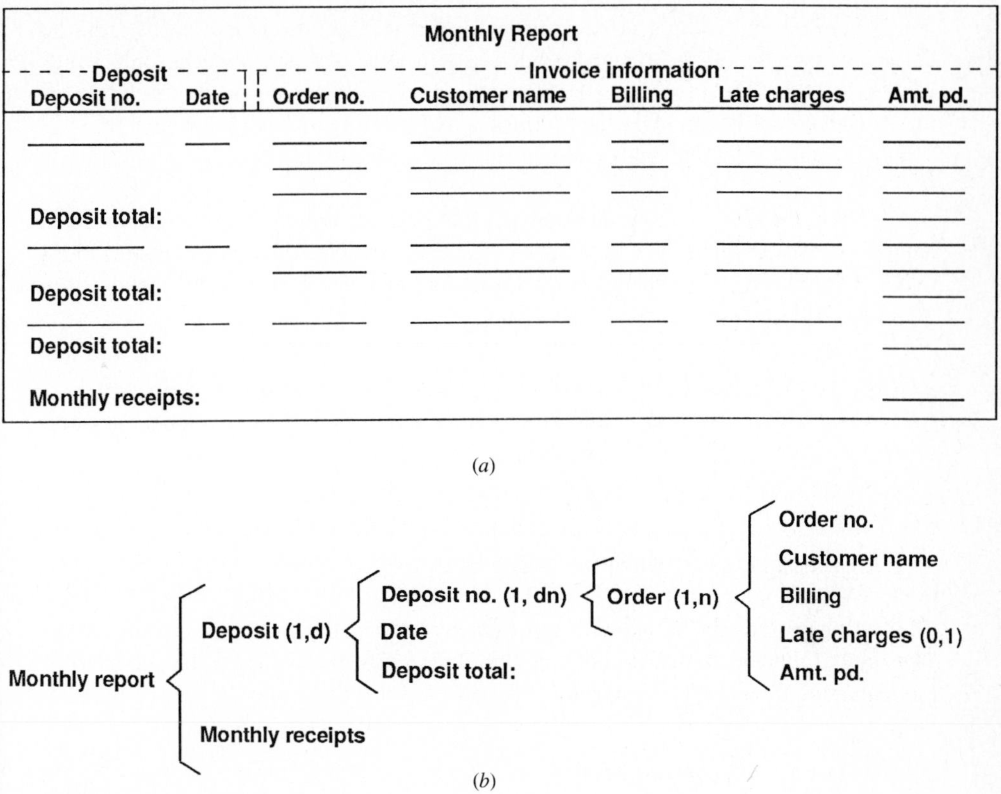
Monthly Report
Deposit
Invoice information
Deposit no.
Date
Order no.
Customer name
Billing
Late charges
Amt. pd.
Deposit total:
Deposit total:
Deposit total:
Monthly receipts:
(a)
Monthly report
Deposit (1,d)
Monthly receipts
Deposit no. (1, dn)
Date
Deposit total:
Order (1,n)
Order no.
Customer name
Billing
Late charges (0,1)
Amt. pd.
(b)

FIGURE 5.19
(*a*) Paper prototype. (*b*) Warnier-Orr diagram for application results.

Security. The degree to which system and information access is protected may be a system constraint and can have a profound effect on the manner in which the system is implemented.

Hardware. Characteristics of the host processor(s) must be noted when software is coupled to such hardware in nonstandard ways. Similarly, operating system characteristics must be noted.

Interfaces. Interface protocol with external data bases, devices, networks, and communication links may constrain the system.

These physical constraints, when coupled with the logical requirements derived using DSSD, provide the analyst with a method and notation for deriving software requirements.

5.5 JACKSON SYSTEM DEVELOPMENT

Jackson System Development (JSD) evolved out of work conducted by M. A. Jackson ([JAC75], [JAC83]) on information domain analysis and its relationship to program and system design. Similar in some ways to Warnier's approach and DSSD, JSD focuses on models of the "real world" information domain. In Jackson's words [JAC83]: "The developer begins by creating a model of the reality with which the system is concerned, the reality which furnishes its [the system's] subject matter...."

To conduct JSD the analyst applies the following steps:

Entity action step. Using an approach that is quite similar to the object-oriented analysis technique described in Chapter 4, *entities* (people, objects, or organizations that a system needs to produce or use information) and *actions* (the events that occur in the real world that affect entities) are identified.

Entity structure step. Actions that affect each entity are ordered by time and represented with *Jackson diagrams* (a treelike notation described later in this section).

Initial model step. Entities and actions are represented as a process model; connections between the model and the real world are defined.

Function step. Functions that correspond to defined actions are specified.

System timing step. Process scheduling characteristics are assessed and specified.

Implementation step. Hardware and software are specified as a design.

The last three steps in JSD are closely aligned with system or software design. Therefore, in this chapter we discuss only the first three steps, postponing a consideration of the remaining three until Chapter 8.

5.5.1   The Entity Action Step

The entity action step begins with a brief (usually one paragraph) natural language statement of the problem. As an example we shall analyze requirements for a software-based control system for the *University Shuttle Service* (USS) described below:

> A large university is spread over two campuses which are over a mile apart. To help students who must travel between campuses to get to lectures on time, the university plans to install a shuttle service.
>
> The shuttle service makes use of only one high-speed shuttle, which travels over tracks between a station at each campus. Each station has a call button that students can use to request transport to the other station. When students arrive at a station, they push the call button. If the shuttle is already there, they board it and depart for the other station. If the shuttle is in transit, they must wait for it to stop at the other station, board students (if any), and return. If the shuttle is at the other station, it leaves to come and pick up the students who pushed the button. The shuttle will wait at a station until the next request for service (a button is pushed) occurs.

Entities are selected by examining all nouns in the description. After review of the above description, the following candidate entities are chosen: *university, campus, students, lectures, shuttle, station, button*. We are not directly concerned with *campus, lec-*

tures, students, or *stations*—all of these lie outside the model boundary and are rejected as possible entities. University is merely a collective term for both campuses, so we reject it as a possible entity. We select *shuttle* and *button*.

An action occurs at a specific point in time and is applied to an entity. Actions are selected by examining all verbs in the description. Candidate actions are: *travels, arrive, push, board, leaves, waits.* We reject *travels* because it refers to student and student has not been selected as an entity. *Waits* is rejected because it represents a state, rather than an action. We select *arrive, push,* and *leaves.*

It should be noted that by rejecting candidate entities and actions, we have bounded the scope of the system to be developed. For example, by rejecting *student,* we have precluded later enhancements such as the generation of information on how many students used the shuttle system today. However, the list of entities and actions may be modified as analysis continues.

5.5.2 The Entity Structure Step

When used in the context of JSD, the *structure* of an entity describes the entity's history by considering the impact of actions over time. To represent entity structure, Jackson has introduced the diagrammatic notation illustrated in Figure 5.20. Actions are applied to an entity as a sequence, as part of an either-or selection, or repetitively (an iteration).

The entity structure for *shuttle* and *button* are shown in Figure 5.21a and b. In the structure diagram shown in Figure 5.21a, the shuttle begins and ends its history at station 1. The actions that affect the entity are arrivals and departures. The diagram indicates that the shuttle begins at station 1, spends its time moving back and forth be-

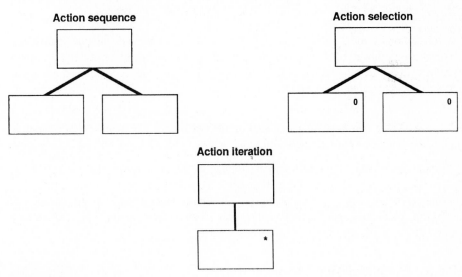

FIGURE 5.20
Structure diagram notation.

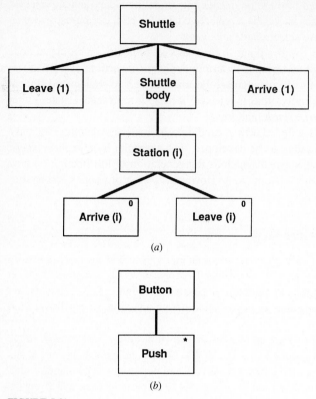

FIGURE 5.21
(*a*) Structure diagram for the *shuttle* entity. (*b*) Structure diagram for the *button* entity.

tween stations 1 and 2, and ultimately returns to station 1. We indicate that an arrival at a station is followed by a departure from the same station by representing both actions (*arrive(i)* and *leave(i)*) with the same station index i. Notes may accompany the diagram to specify constraints that cannot be represented directly by JSD notation. For example:

> The value of i must be 1 or 2 and in any two successive occurrences of station, the value of i must change.

A single repetitive action (*push*) may be applied to the entity *button* (Figure 5.21b).

The structure diagram presents a *time-ordered* specification of the actions performed on or by an entity. For this reason it is a more precise representation of the real world than a simple list of actions and entities. A structure diagram is created for each entity and may be accompanied by narrative text.

5.5.3 The Initial Model Step

The first two steps of JSD are concerned with "an abstract description of the real world" [JAC83]. Entities and actions are selected and related to each other through structure diagrams. The initial model step begins by constructing a specification of the system as a model of the real world. The specification is created with a *system specification diagram* (SSD) using symbology illustrated in Figure 5.22. A *data stream connection* occurs when one process transmits a stream of information (e.g., writes records) and the other process receives the stream (e.g., reads records). Arrowheads represent the direction of information flow, the circle represents the data stream which is assumed to be placed in a FIFO buffer of unlimited capacity. A *state vector connection* occurs when one process directly inspects the state vector of another process. Arrowheads represent the direction of information flow and the diamond indicates the state vector. This connection is common in process control applications in which it is necessary to check the state of some electromechanical device. By convention the suffix 0 represents a real-world process and the suffix 1 represents a system model process.

The system specification diagram for USS is illustrated in Figure 5.23. Whenever possible, we prefer to connect model processes with real-world entities by data streams because direct correspondence between the behavior of the model and the real world is assured. In our example the call button emits a pulse when pressed. This can be transmitted to the *button-1* process as a data stream connection. However, we shall assume that the sensors that detect arrival or departure of the shuttle do not emit a pulse, but do close an electric switch. The state of the switch (on/off) can be accessed. Hence, a state vector connection is required.

The internal details of model processes are specified using what Jackson calls *structure text*. Structure text represents the same information as structure diagrams (Figure 5.20)—sequence, selection, repetition—but does so in a textual format. The structure text for *button-1* is:

```
BUTTON-1
    read BD;
    PUSH-BDY itr while BD
        PUSH;
        read BD;
    PUSH-BDY end
BUTTON-1 end
```

Data stream

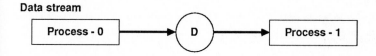

State vector

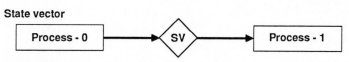

FIGURE 5.22
SSD notation.

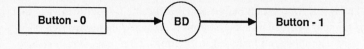

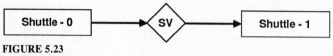

FIGURE 5.23
An SSD for USS.

The structure of BUTTON-1 corresponds identically to the structure of BUTTON-0, with the addition of *read* operations that connect the real world to the system.

As noted earlier, the *shuttle-1* process cannot be connected to its real-world counterpart by a data stream connection. Instead, we must interrogate the switches that are turned on/off by the arrival/departure of the shuttle at a station. The system process must inspect the real-world entity frequently enough to ensure that no actions pass undetected. This is accomplished by executing a *getsv* (get state vector) operation that obtains the state vector of the real-world entity. It is likely that the system process will obtain each value of the state vector a number of times before it is changed, and the model process can be elaborated to show these "in transit" values of the state vectors. A structure text description of *shuttle-1* follows:

```
SHUTTLE-1 seq
    getsv SV;
    WAIT-BDY itr while WAIT1
        getsv SV;
    WAIT-BDY end
    LEAVE (1);
    TRANSIT-BDY1 itr while TRANSIT1
        getsv SV;
    TRANSIT-BDY1 end
    SHUTTLE-BDY1 itr
        STATION seq
            ARRIVE (i);
            WAIT-BDY itr while WAITi
                getsv SV;
            WAIT-BDY end
            LEAVE (i);
            TRANSIT-BDY itr while TRANSITi
                getsv SV;
            TRANSIT-BDY end
        STATION end
    SHUTTLE-BDY end
    ARRIVE (1);
SHUTTLE-1 end
```

The state values WAIT and TRANSIT represent appropriate values of the arrival and departure switch. The real-world process SHUTTLE-0 produces a change of state in the switch, and the system process SHUTTLE-1 executes *getsv* operations to sense this change. Figure 5.24 illustrates the structure text for SHUTTLE-1 as a structure diagram.

JSD continues with additional steps that allow the analyst to make the transition to software design. We postpone a discussion of these until Chapter 8. It is important to note, however, that the three JSD steps presented in this section provide an analysis and specification approach that is unique and, potentially, quite powerful.

5.6 AUTOMATED TOOLS FOR REQUIREMENTS ANALYSIS

The software requirements analysis methods presented in the preceding sections were originally developed to be applied manually. However, manual application of structured analysis, DSSD, or JSD can be cumbersome and error prone when large systems are to be analyzed. Today, each of these methods, along with a class of techniques specifically designed for automated processing, is available in a "computer-aided"

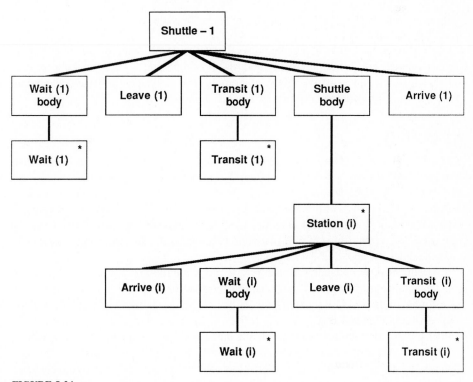

FIGURE 5.24
Structure diagram corresponding to structure text.

format. Automated analysis tools are a first step toward computer-aided software engineering and are already improving the quality and productivity of the analyst.

Automated tools for requirements analysis may be categorized in a number of different ways. Some tools have been designed to automate the generation and maintenance of what was originally a manual method, and these tools typically make use of a graphical notation for analysis. This class of tools produces diagrams, aids in problem partitioning, maintains a hierarchy of information about the system, and applies heuristics to uncover problems with the specification. More importantly, such tools enable the analyst to update information and track the connections between new and existing representations of the system. For example, Nastec's CASE 2000 system (Figure 5.25) enables the analyst to generate data flow diagrams and a data dictionary (Section 5.2) and maintain these in a data base that can be analyzed for correctness, consistency, and completeness. In fact the true benefit of this, and of most automated requirements tools, is in the "intelligent processing" that the tool applies to the problem specification.

Another class of automated requirements analysis tools makes use of a special notation (in most cases this is a *requirements specification language*) that is processed in an automated manner. Requirements are described with a specification language that combines keyword indicators with a natural language (e.g., English) narrative. The specification language is fed to a processor that produces a requirements specification and, more importantly, a set of diagnostic reports about the consistency and organization of the specification.

In the sections that follow, we present an overview of some of the more important automated tools for requirements analysis. It is important to note that the tools presented below are representative. Many other tools exist, and an entirely new generation of "expert" or knowledge-based analysis tools is on the horizon.

5.6.1 SADT

SADT (a trademark of Softech, Inc.) is a structural analysis and design technique that has been widely used as a tool for system definition, software requirements analysis, and system/software design [ROS77, ROS85]. Originally developed as a manual method, SADT consists of procedures that allow the analyst to decompose software (or system) functions; a graphical notation, the SADT *actigram* and *datagram*, that communicates the relationships of information to function within software; and project control guidelines for applying the methodology.

Using SADT, the analyst develops a model comprising many hierarchically defined actigrams and datagrams. A format for this notation is shown in Figure 5.26, and an example of an SADT actigram of the early steps of the definition phase of software engineering is depicted in Figure 5.27 [FRE80]. Each box within the actigram can be further refined in much the same way that a data flow diagram undergoes refinement.

The SADT methodology encompasses automated tools that support analysis procedures and a well-defined organizational harness through which the tools are applied. Reviews and milestones are specified, allowing validation of developer/customer communication. Staff responsibilities are similar to those found on the chief programmer team (Chapter 3), stressing a team approach to analysis, design, and review.

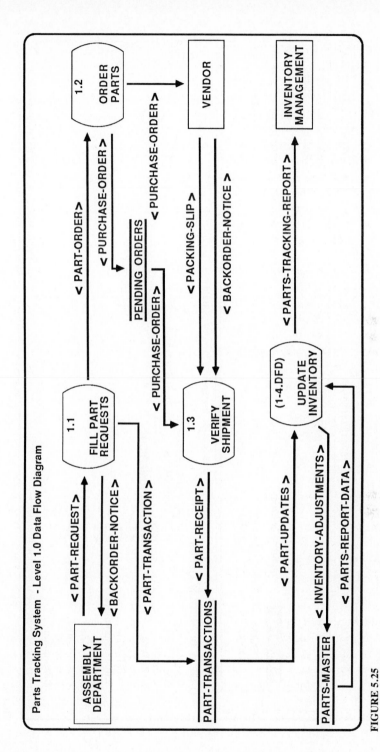

FIGURE 5.25
(a) Automated analysis tools. (Courtesy of Nastec Corporation.)

193

REPORT FORMAT - Parts Tracking Report	AUTHOR: J. King	DATE: 8/17/84	PAGE 1 of 1	REPORT NUMBER: PT100R01
PROJECT: Parts Tracking System	PROGRAM ID: PT100P00		FREQUENCY: Daily	DP REVIEWERS: S. Bishop

```
          1         2         3         4         5         6         7         8         9         1
                                                                                                    0
1234567890123456789012345678901234567890123456789012345678901234567890123456789012345678901234567890123

1
2
3
4  REPORT: PT100R01                          PARTS TRACKING REPORT                    DATE: MM/DD/YY
5                                                                                     PAGE:    99999
6
   PART NUMBER    QUANTITY IN STOCK   UNIT PRICE   REORDER POINT   QUANTITY ON ORDER   QUANTITY ON BACK-ORDER
7
8  XXXXX          999,999             999.99       99,999          99,999              99,999
   XXXXX          999,999             999.99       99,999          99,999              99,999
```

DesignAid: Interactive Inquiry/Update

OBJECT DEFINITION FIELDS
  Object Name   < PART-NUMBER >
  Object Type   < DATA REQMT >
  Alias Of   < >
  Data Type   < ALPHANUMERIC >
  Data Size   < 5 >
  Initial Value   < >
  Value Constraints < >
  Locked?   < >
  Date Defined   < 10/17/84 >
  Last Modified   < >
  Defined By   < Jim >
  Description

< User required part identification number >

Press GO to execute
Press PAGE! to view Relation Menu

FIGURE 5.25

(b) Data dictionary tool. (Courtesy of Nastec Corporation.)

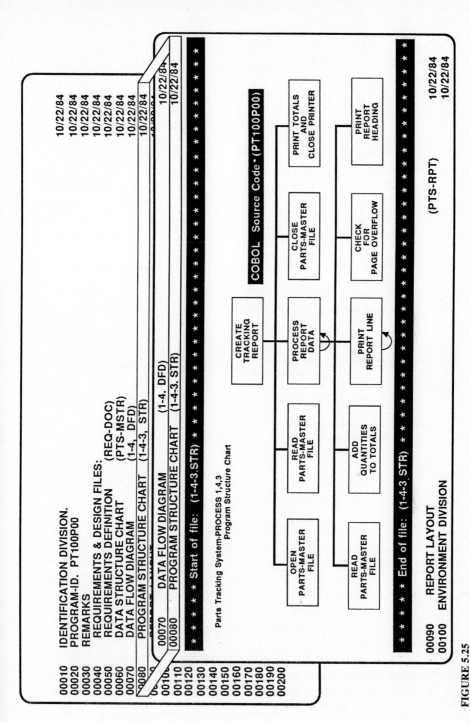

FIGURE 5.25

(c) Design representation tool. (Courtesy of Nastec Corporation.)

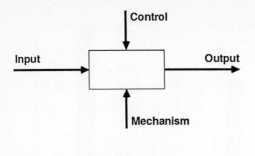

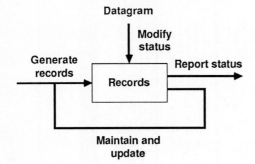

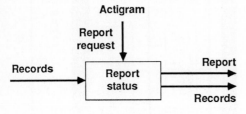

Maintain and update	**FIGURE 5.26** SADT diagrammatic notation.

5.6.2 SREM

SREM (Software Requirements Engineering Methodology) [ALF85] is an automated requirements analysis tool that makes use of a *requirements statement language* (RSL) to describe "elements, attributes, relationships and structures." *Elements* (in SREM terminology) comprise a set of objects and concepts used to develop a requirements specification. *Relationships* between objects are specified as part of RSL, and *attributes* are used to modify or qualify elements. *Structures* are used to describe information flow. These RSL primitives are combined with narrative information to form the detail of a requirements specification.

The power of an automated requirements tool may be measured by the support software that has been developed to analyze the specification. SREM applies a *requirements engineering and validation system* (REVS). REVS software uses a combination of reports and computer graphics to study information flow, determine consistency in the

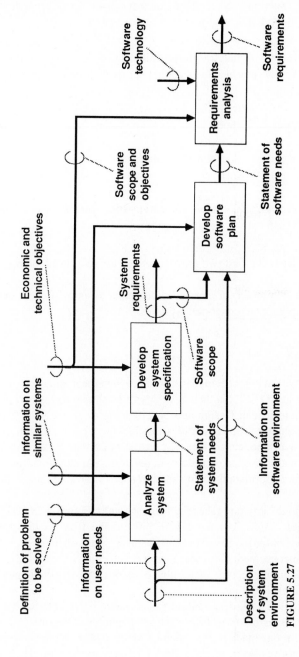

FIGURE 5.27

Actigram of the definition phase.

197

use of information throughout the system, and simulate dynamic interrelationships among elements.

Like SADT (Section 5.6.1), SREM incorporates a set of procedures that guide the analyst through the requirements step. The procedures include:

1. *Translation*. An activity that transforms initial software requirements described in a *System Specification* into a more detailed set of data descriptions and processing steps.

2. *Decomposition*. An activity that evaluates information at the interface to the software element and results in a complete set of computational (functional) requirements.

3. *Allocation*. An activity that considers alternative approaches to the requirements that have been established; trade-off studies and sensitivity analyses are conducted.

4. *Analytical feasibility demonstration*. An activity that attempts to simulate critical processing requirements to determine feasibility.

RSL is used heavily in the first two procedures and REVS is used to accomplish procedures 3 and 4.

SREM was developed for embedded computer systems. Recent extensions provide support for distributed concurrent systems.

5.6.3 PSL/PSA

PSL/PSA (Problem Statement Language/Problem Statement Analyzer) was developed by the ISDOS project [TEI77] at the University of Michigan and is part of a larger system called Computer Aided Design and Specification Analysis Tool, CADSAT. PSL/PSA provides an analyst with capabilities that include: (1) description of information systems regardless of application area; (2) creation of a data base containing descriptors for the information system; (3) addition, deletion, and modification of descriptors; and (4) production of formatted documentation and a variety of reports on the specification.

The PSL model structure takes the form shown in Figure 5.28. The model is developed using PSL descriptors for system information flow, system structure, data structure, data derivation, system size and volume, system dynamics, system properties, and project management. Tools have been developed [NAS86] to enable other representations of requirements (e.g., data flow diagrams and data dictionary) to be translated into a PSL representation.

Once a complete PSL description for the system is established, a problem statement analyzer (PSA) is invoked. PSA produces a number of reports that include a record of all modifications made to the specification data base, reference reports that present data base information in varying formats, summary reports that provide project

arameters: DBxPSADB.DBF INPUT=# SOURCE-LISTING NOCROSS-REFERENCE UPDATE
DATA-BASE-REFERENCE

```
INE    S T M T                                              ID FIELD
  1  >  /# This top-down PSL program describes the following aspect of
  2  >      the example payroll processing system:
  3  >
  4  >           Data Structure
  5  >
  6  >
  7  >  INPUT employee-information;
  8  >    CONSISTS OF operation-code, required-information;
  9  >
 10  >  ELEMENT operation-code;
 11  >    VALUES ARE 1 THRU 3;
 12  >
 13  >  GROUP required-information;
 14  >
 15  >  INPUT time-cards;
 16  >    CONSISTS OF a-time-card;
 17  >
 18  >  GROUP a-time-card;
 19  >    CONSISTS OF employee-number, regular hours, overtime-hours;
 20  >
 21  >  OUTPUT cheque;
 22  >    CONSISTS OF employee-name, net-pay, deduction-stub;
 23  >
 24  >  GROUP employee-name;
 25  >    CONSISTS OF last-name, initials;
 26  >
 27  >  GROUP deduction-stub;
 28  >    CONSISTS OF gross-pay, income-tax, unemployment-insurance,
 29  >                canada-pension, union-dues, net-pay;
 30  >
 31  >  SET old-master-file, new-master-file;
 32  >    CONSISTS OF number-of-employees master-file-record;
 33  >    SUBSETTING-CRITERIA ARE province;
 34  >
 35  >  ENTITY master-file-record;
 36  >    CONSISTS OF record-key, employee-number, employee-name,
 37  >                hourly-wage, tax-code;
 38  >    IDENTIFIED BY record-key;
 39  >
 40  >  ELEMENT hourly-wage;
 41  >    VALUES ARE 5 THRU 20;
 42  >
 43  >  ELEMENT employee-number, last-name, tax-code,
 44  >          regular-hours, overtime-hours, gross-pay, income-tax,
 45  >          unemployment-insurance, canada-pension, union-dues,
 46  >          net-pay, record-key, province;
 47  >
 48  >  EOF
```

FIGURE 5.28

PSL source listing. (*Source: PSL/PSA Primer*, ISDOS Project, University of Michigan, reproduced with permission.)

management information, and analysis reports that evaluate characteristics of the data base.

5.6.4   TAGS

TAGS (Technology for the Automated Generation of Systems) was developed by Teledyne Brown Engineering, Inc. [SEI85] as an automated approach to the application of system engineering methods. Like SREM and PSL/PSA, TAGS is composed of three key components: a specification language called *Input/Output Requirements Language* (IORL), a set of software tools for requirements analysis and IORL processing, and an underlying TAGS methodology.

Unlike SREM and PSL/PSA, the TAGS specification language was designed to accommodate both graphical and textual representations created by the analyst using an interactive tool. The highest level of IORL representation is a *schematic block diagram* (SBD). SBDs identify primary system components and the data interfaces between them. Each system component in an SBD may be refined by representing input/output relationships, timing, and other supplementary information.

The IORL specification is analyzed using a variety of software tools. These include a *diagnostic analyzer* that helps to uncover static errors (e.g., syntax errors, range violations) in the specification and a *simulation compiler* that aids in uncovering dynamic errors by simulating the system modeled with IORL. The combined output of the analyzer and compiler is Ada programming language source code, which is used to create the system simulation.

5.6.5   Analysis Tools—A Summary

The automated approach to requirements analysis provided by SADT, SREM, PSL/PSA, TAGS, and other tools is not a panacea, but it does provide benefits that include:

- improved documentation quality through standardization and reporting
- better coordination among analysts in that the data base is available to all
- gaps, omissions, and inconsistency are more easily uncovered through cross-reference maps and reports,
- the impact of modifications can be more easily traced
- maintenance costs for the specification are reduced

The perceptive reader will note that these tools have many characteristics in common. Each demands a formal method (either graphical or textual) of specification; each provides automated or semi-automated mechanisms for analyzing the specification; each creates a data base that represents requirements in terms of system information, components, and processes; and each is used to aid the analyst but must rely on information provided by the analyst and customer.

Today's automated analysis tools are the harbinger of more advanced tools that will encompass software design and, ultimately, the automatic generation and verification of software. Knowledge-based (expert) systems are likely to be applied to requirements analysis tasks. However, the definition of the knowledge base (facts, rules, and necessary inferences to perform analysis) will remain a significant challenge into the foreseeable future.

5.7 DATA BASE REQUIREMENTS

Requirements analysis for a data base incorporates tasks identical to software requirements analysis. Extensive contact with the customer is necessary; identification of functions and interfaces is essential; specification of information flow, structure, and associativity is required; and a formal requirements document must be developed.

A complete discussion of data base analysis is beyond the scope of this book. Texts by Weiderhold [WEI83] and Date [DAT86] will provide the reader with an excellent foundation in this topic. Our goal in this section is to provide an overview of the topics to be considered when a data base is to be created or used as part of a software development project.

5.7.1 Data Base Characteristics

The term *data base* has become one of many catch-words in the computing field. Although many elegant definitions exist, we shall define a data base as: *a collection of information organized in a way that facilitates access, analysis, and reporting.*

A data base contains information entities that are related via organization and association. The logical architecture of a data base is defined by a *schema* that represents definitions of relationships among information entities. The physical architecture of a data base depends upon the host hardware configuration. However, both schema (logical description) and organization (physical description) must be tuned to satisfy functional and performance requirements for access, analysis, and reporting.

A large number of data base management systems (DBMS) are available for purchase. These systems contain a variety of *query languages* for data manipulation and access, 4GLs for application development, and requisite file management software.

5.7.2 Analysis Steps

The flow of events for data base analysis is illustrated in Figure 5.29. Before an evaluation of data base requirements can commence, the analyst must understand the global objectives and scope of the system for which the data base is to be developed. A complete and highly refined information model is then developed.

The information model includes a comprehensive data dictionary that defines all data items in terms of the information that is used to develop the item. For example, profit (a dollar quantity) could be defined using other derived quantities:

profit = (sales + other income) − (operating expense + debt service + taxes)

The next steps in data base analysis define the logical and physical characteristics of the data base. With the information model and system specification as a guide,

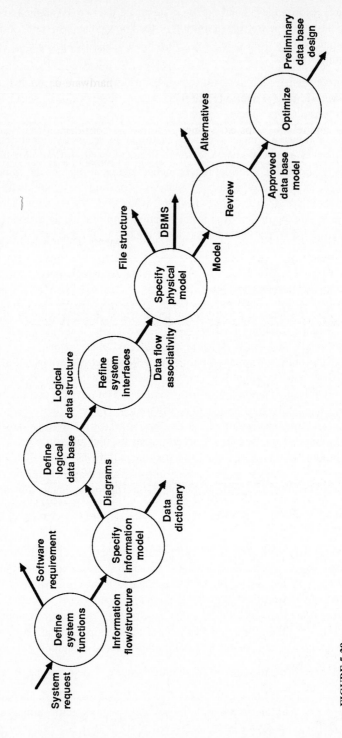

FIGURE 5.29
Data base analysis steps.

the analyst, working in conjunction with a data base designer, defines a logical data organization. The logical organization must accommodate requirements for data access, modification, associativity, and other system-oriented concerns. Once the logical data organization is established, physical organization may be developed. The physical data base organization defines file structure, record formats, hardware-dependent processing features, and DBMS characteristics. Finally, a complete review of the schema and physical characteristics is conducted.

Complex interrelationships exist among the factors considered during data base analysis. Referring to Figure 5.30, we see that no single factor can be changed without potential impact on other factors. The trade-offs that can impact the final data base design include specialization versus generalization, degree of associativity, potential for expansion, and operational characteristics.

The degree of information associativity and the potential for expansion (of both size and information content) are actually elements of a broader issue—the degree of specialization assigned to the data base during requirements analysis and design. A specialized data base addresses specific information requirements of a system. The information structure is designed to accommodate required associativity and predicted expansion. A generalized data base is amenable to a broader class of information requirements. However, generality is achieved at the expense of more software processing at the information interface, more overhead associated with adaptability to a broader range of problems, and greater internal complexity in data structure organization.

Operational characteristics follow from the preceding trade-offs. Data base structure, size, and logical design can have a significant impact on physical organization, hardware, access methods, and performance. The impact of these and other characteristics on organization, hardware, and software is summarized in Figure 5.31.

5.7.3 Normalization

We have already seen that information domain analysis requires the definition of data content. Each information item is listed (a data dictionary may be used) and ultimately organized in logical file structures. However, it is often possible to simplify the organi-

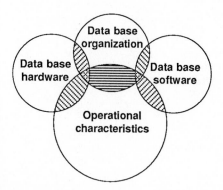

FIGURE 5.30
Analysis considerations.

	Organization	Hardware	Software
As size goes up	Structure must have low overhead	Multiple devices may be required	Performance of searches/sorts/ compression is critical
As content becomes complex	Structure overhead increases	Performance becomes critical	Software becomes more complex
If cost must be minimal	Organization must be simple	Single device should be used	Acquire a simple DBMS
If performance is critical	Organization should be tailored to application	High speed devices are essential	Custom DBMS should be acquired; designed

FIGURE 5.31
Interrelationships.

zation of such files, thereby facilitating the design of a data base. A technique called *normalization* is used to simplify the logical data structure.

The normalization process identifies redundant data that may exist in the logical data structure, determines unique *keys* needed to access data items, and helps to establish necessary relationships between data items. Three levels of normalization, called *normal forms*, can be achieved. To illustrate the normalization process, we revisit *The Software Store* example (Figure 5.14). Figure 5.32a lists each data item that is part of the information domain for *The Software Store's* order processing system. To normalize

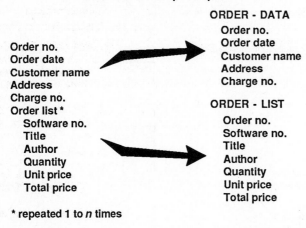

**Steps 1 and 2: List data elements/group
for the *Software Shop* example**

Order no.
Order date
Customer name
Address
Charge no.
Order list *
  Software no.
  Title
  Author
  Quantity
  Unit price
  Total price

* repeated 1 to *n* times

ORDER - DATA
Order no.
Order date
Customer name
Address
Charge no.

ORDER - LIST
Order no.
Software no.
Title
Author
Quantity
Unit price
Total price

(a)
Unnormalized structure.

(b)
Two normalized structures.

FIGURE 5.32
Normalization.

this list, all repeating groups of data (in this case, the list of software ordered, *order list* may occur a number of times if different products are ordered) are separated so that no file has any repeating groups (Figure 5.32b). This level of simplification is called *first normal form* (1NF). We may represent this 1NF data structure in the following manner:

ORDER-LIST (order-no, software-no, title, author, quantity, unit-price, total-price)

ORDER-DATA (order-no, order-date, customer-name, address, charge-no)

The above data files are sometimes termed *relations*.

Further normalization can be accomplished by identifying key and non-key data items. A *key data item* is used to identify one or more other non-key items. For example, *software-no*, a key data item, uniquely identifies *title, author, unit-price*. In this example, *software-no* and *order-no* are key data items. For the relations above, *quantity* is termed *fully functionally dependent* because it can be obtained only if both key data items (order-no and software-no) for the relation are known. The non-key item *title* is not fully functionally dependent because we need to know only one key, *software-no*, to access it.

To achieve *second normal form* (2NF), relations must be reorganized so that all non-key data items are fully functionally dependent. Examples of 2NF relations follow:

ORDER-DATA (order-no, order-date, customer-name, address, charge-no)

ORDER-LIST (order-no, software-no, quantity, total-price)

SOFTWARE-INFO (software-no, title, author, unit-price)

Third normal form (3NF) simplification can be achieved if all conditions for 2NF are met and no non-key data item can be derived from a combination of other non-key data items in any of the relations. For example, *total-price* can be computed as the sum of the products of *unit-price* and *quantity*. Therefore, it need not be maintained in the relations. Examples of 3NF relations are:

ORDER-DATA (order-no, order-date, customer-name, address, charge-no)

ORDER-LIST (order-no, software-no, quantity)

SOFTWARE-INFO (software-no, title, author, unit-price)

The normalization process simplifies data structures and removes redundancy and unnecessary data items from a data base.

5.7.4 Capacity Analysis

Data base analysis requires an examination of the projected use of the data base, as well as its contents and organization. In this section we present a brief overview of a rudimentary capacity analysis technique—the *transaction matrix*.

The transaction matrix is used to identify all requests for data base access (transactions) and relate each request to information categories or items (elements) within the data base. In effect the transaction matrix helps the analyst to answer questions such as:

- What combinations of data elements are required for each major transaction?
- What combination of data should be grouped within the same physical record/block?
- Can transactions be modified to: (1) reduce frequency of access? (2) eliminate redundant requests for information? (3) improve projected performance?

The transaction matrix takes the form shown in Figure 5.33. Each transaction is characterized by type, frequency of access, and use (read, modify, add, delete). Data elements that are required for each transaction are noted in the bottom half of the table.

To illustrate the use of a transaction matrix, we recall the *The Software Store* example (Sections 5.4.2 and 5.7.3). Assuming that the 3NF relations presented in the last section describe the data base, a set of five transactions can be defined:

T1   List all software information for each order.
T2   Get customer name, address, etc., given order no.
T3   List price information given software no.
T4   Compute total sales for a particular date.
T5   Compare total sales ($) on one date with the same information from another date.

Based on these transactions, a matrix (Figure 5.34) is created. Referring to the figure, each transaction is characterized by type (e.g., batch, O/L (on-line)), frequency of access, and use. Characteristic data elements are listed in the lower part of the matrix. The relationship of each element to each transaction is also shown. By examining the lower right-hand quadrant of the matrix, the analyst may be able to organize information in a way that optimizes transaction processing.

5.7.5 Data Diagramming

Normalization of data files and subsequent analysis of data base capacity must be coupled with an effective technique for representing the relationship between data ob-

Characteristic	Transactions
Type	On-line, batch, software originated, human source
Frequency	Number of transactions/month
Use	Read, modify, add, delete
Data element list	Relationship to each transaction

FIGURE 5.33
The transaction matrix.

Transaction	T_1	T_2	T_3	T_4	T_5
Type	Batch	On-line	On-line	Batch	On-line
Frequency	200	600	1000	10	5
Use	R	R	R	R	R
Order no.	RK	RK		RK	RK
Order date	R			RK	RK
Customer name	R	R			
Address	R	R			
Charge no.	R				
Software no.	RK		RK		
Quantity	R			R	R
Title	R				
Author	R				
Unit price	R		R	R	R

R = read; K= key data element

FIGURE 5.34
Transaction matrix for *The Software Store* data base.

jects. The *entity relationship diagram* [CHE76] and its subsequent extensions [MAR85] are often used as a graphical tool to represent data relationships.

Basic notation for entity relationship diagrams is shown in Figure 5.35. Each box represents a data object. The connecting lines indicate an association between data objects that is specified by the symbology shown. The vertical bar that appears on a connecting line may be viewed as a ''1.'' The circle implies ''0.''

A simple entity relationship diagram for *The Software Store* example (Section 5.7.3) is illustrated in Figure 5.36. Referring to the diagram, a customer is associated with one customer number, name, and address and one or more orders. Each order may be associated with an order number, date, and charge number, as well as one or more software numbers. Orders can also be associated with customer numbers. Each software number is associated with a title, an author (note that the author data item may not be present), and a unit price.

It should be noted that additional notation can be introduced and considerably more sophisticated entity relationship models can be developed. The interested reader should refer to Martin and McClure [MAR85].

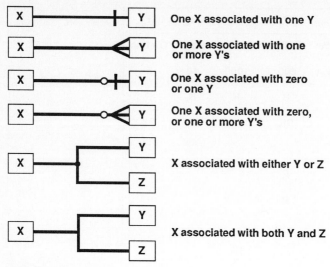

FIGURE 5.35
Entity relationship notation.

5.8 SUMMARY

Requirements analysis methodologies provide a systematic approach to problem analysis. Although each method has a unique set of procedures and symbology, all provide mechanisms for assessment and representation of the information domain, partitioning of the functional domain, and modeling procedures for both the physical and logical world.

Three major methodological categories have evolved: data flow–oriented methods, data structure–oriented methods, and language-based methods. Data flow methods focus on an assessment of how data move through the information domain but

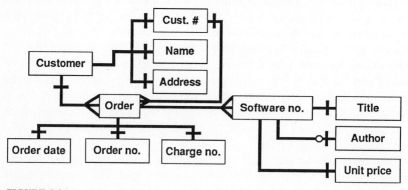

FIGURE 5.36
Entity relationship diagram for *The Software Store*.

also provide procedures for isolating data content and processing function. Data structure–oriented methods identify information items and actions (processes) and model these according to the information hierarchy (structure) of the problem. Language-based methods use a formal specification language to model the system, enabling automated processing to uncover inconsistency, omissions, and other errors.

Because software and a data base are often allocated as part of a computer-based system, methods for data base requirements analysis must also be applied by the analyst. The procedures for data base analysis are analogous to those applied for software requirements analysis. However, specialized activities, such as normalization and capacity analysis, must also be conducted.

We conclude our discussion of requirements analysis methodologies with the words of Gehani and McGettrick [GEH86]:

> There are important benefits which stem from writing specifications, i.e., stating in precise terms the intended effect of a piece of software. For then it is possible to talk about such issues as the correctness of an implementation, a measure of the consistency between that specification and the effect of the program. The range of benefits are actually wider than this: they relate to methods of programming, to possible approaches to verification and validation of programs, and even to the management and control of large software projects.

REFERENCES

[ALF85]   Alford, M., "SREM at the Age of Eight; The Distributed Computing Design System," *Computer*, vol. 18, no. 4, April 1985, pp. 36–46.

[CHE76]   Chen, P. P., "The Entity-Relationship Model—Toward a Unifying View of Data," *ACM Trans. on Data Base Systems*, vol. 1, no. 1, March 1976, pp. 9–36.

[DAT86]   Date, C. J., An Introduction to Database Systems, 4th ed., Addison-Wesley, 1986.

[DEM79]   DeMarco, T., *Structured Analysis and System Specification*, Prentice-Hall, 1979.

[FRE80]   Freeman, P., "Requirements Analysis and Specification," *Proc. Intl. Computer Technology Conf.*, ASME, San Francisco, August, 1980.

[GAN82]   Gane, T. and C. Sarson, *Structured System Analysis*, McDonnell Douglas, 1982.

[GEH86]   Gehani, N., and D. McGettrick, eds., *Software Specification Techniques*, Addison-Wesley, 1986, p. 1.

[JAC75]   Jackson, M. A., *Principles of Program Design*, Academic Press, 1975.

[JAC83]   Jackson, M. A., *System Development*, Prentice-Hall, 1983.

[LIS86]   Liskov, B. H., and V. Berzins, "An Appraisal of Program Specifications," *Software Specification Techniques*, N. Gehani and A. T. McGettrick, eds., Addison-Wesley, 1986, p. 3.

[MAR85]   Martin, J., and C. McClure, *Diagramming Techniques for Analysts and Programmers*, Prentice-Hall, 1985.

[NAS86]   *SafeSpan: A PSL/PSA Bridge*, Nastec Corporation, Southfield, MI, 1986.

[ORR77]   Orr, K. T., *Structured Systems Development*, Yourdon Press, New York, 1977.

[ORR81]   Orr, K. T., *Structured Requirements Definition*, Ken Orr & Associates, Inc., Topeka, KS, 1981.

[PAG80]   Page-Jones, M., *The Practical Guide to Structured Systems Design*, Yourdon Press, New York, 1980, p. 75.

[RIG81]   Riggs, J., *Production Systems: Planning, Analysis and Control*, 3d ed., Wiley, 1981.

[ROS77]   Ross, D., and K. Schoman, "Structured Analysis for Requirements Definition," *IEEE Trans. Software Engineering*, vol. 3, no. 1, January 1977, pp. 6–15.

[ROS85]   Ross, D., "Applications and Extensions of SADT," *Computer*, vol. 18, no. 4, April 1985, pp. 25–35.

[RZE85]   Rzepka, W., and Y. Ohno, eds., "Requirements Engineering Environments," *Computer*, vol. 18, no. 4, special issue, April 1985.

[SEI85]   Sievert, G. E., and T. A. Mizell, "Specification-based Software Engineering with TAGS," *Computer*, vol. 18, no. 4, April 1985, pp. 56–65.

[TEI77]   Teichroew, D., and E. Hershey, "PSL/PSA: A Computer Aided Technique for Structured Documentation and Analysis of Information Processing Systems," *IEEE Trans. Software Engineering*, vol. 3, no. 1, 1977, pp. 41–48.

[WAR74]   Warnier, J. D., *Logical Construction of Programs*, Van Nostrand Reinhold, 1974.

[WAR81]   Warnier, J. D., *Logical Construction of Systems*, Van Nostrand Reinhold, 1981.

[WEI83]   Weiderhold, G., *Database Design*, 2d ed., McGraw-Hill, 1983.

[YOU78]   Yourdon, E., and L. Constantine, *Structured Design*, Yourdon Press, 1978.

PROBLEMS AND POINTS TO PONDER

5.1 Recalling the fundamental analysis principles discussed in Chapter 4, indicate how data flow diagramming techniques accomplish each fundamental. That is, how are DFDs and the data dictionary used to analyze the information domain, partition and build logical and physical models of a system?

5.2 Redo Problem 5.1, but this time focus on DSSD.

5.3 Redo Problem 5.1, but this time focus on JSD.

5.4 Draw a fundamental system model (level 01 DFD) for five systems with which you are familiar. The systems need not be computer-based. Using a few paragraphs for each system, describe input-processing-output for each system.

5.5 Using the systems described in Problem 5.4, refine each into three to seven major functions (transforms) and develop a data flow diagram for each. Remember to specify all information flow by labeling all arrows between bubbles. Use meaningful names for each transform.

5.6 Select one of the systems described in Problems 5.4 and 5.5 and develop a data dictionary for it. Be sure that all information flows are described.

5.7 Select a computer-based system with which you are familiar. Develop a detailed set of data flow diagrams for the system, beginning with the fundamental system model and ending with detailed representations of all functions. Sources, sinks, and all information files should be shown. Next, create a data dictionary and structured English processing narrative for each function.

5.8 Discuss the difference between information flow and information structure. Are there systems in which there is no information flow? Are there systems in which there is no information structure?

5.9 Complete the data flow diagrams for the PMS described in section 5.2.1. Make appropriate assumptions about the system. Also, represent the information content for PMS using a data dictionary or Warnier diagram.

5.10 Reconsider the PMS example in the text by representing it using:

(*a*) DSSD notation

(*b*) JSD notation

Discuss how each of these techniques enables you to represent additional information that cannot be directly represented using DFDs.

5.11 Recalling the Home Security System (HSS) described as part of Problems 4.7 to 4.15, develop representations of HSS using:

(a) data flow techniques

(b) DSSD

(c) JSD

Which approach do you feel does the most complete job? Why?

5.12 Present a tutorial on requirements analysis techniques for data base systems. Use references provided at the end of this chapter and other sources as appropriate.

5.13 Select a data base with which you are familiar (or a description of a data base provided by your instructor). Develop a transaction matrix for the major information elements of the data base.

5.14 The department of public works for a large city has decided to develop a "computerized" pot hole tracking and repair system (PHTRS). As pot holes are reported they are assigned an identifying number, stored by street address, size (on a scale of 1 to 10), location (middle, curb, etc.), district (determined from street address), and repair priority (determined from the size of the pot hole). Work order data are associated with each pot hole and include pot hole location and size, repair crew identifying number, number of people on crew, equipment assigned, hours applied to repair, hole status (work in progress, repaired, temporary repair, not repaired), amount of filler material used, and cost of repair (computed from hours applied, number of people, material, and equipment used). Finally, a damage file is created to hold information about damage reported due to the pot hole and includes citizen's name, address, phone number, type of damage, and dollar amount of damage. PHTRS is an on-line system; queries are to be made interactively.

Making appropriate assumptions, develop a first normal form file structure for PHTRS and then apply normalization techniques to create 2NF and 3NF representations.

5.15 Use data flow–oriented analysis to represent the PHTRS described in Problem 5.14.

5.16 Use DSSD to represent the PHTRS described in Problem 5.14.

5.17 Software for a microcomputer-based word processing system is to be developed. The system will make use of a full screen editing format. Do a few hours of research on the application area and develop a list of questions that you, as an analyst, would ask a requester. Attempt to structure your questions so that major topics are addressed in a rational sequence. Represent the system using the analysis notation of your choice (i.e., DFDs, DSSD, JSD).

5.18 Software for a real-time test monitoring system for gas turbine engines is to be developed. Proceed as in Problem 5.17.

5.19 Software for a manufacturing control system for an automobile assembly plant is to be developed. Proceed as in Problem 5.17.

5.20 Software for a new operating system to support a 32-bit microcomputer for multi-user, interactive applications is to be developed. Proceed as in Problem 5.17.

5.21 Write a paper on the latest progress in the area of automated requirements analysis tools. Use recent conference proceedings and journal articles/papers as your primary source of information.

FURTHER READINGS

DeMarco's text [DEM79] on system analysis remains one of the best expositions of the data flow–oriented approach. Jackson's book [JAC83] contains a number of interesting examples and is must reading for anyone who intends to apply the JSD method. The DSSD methodology is described in a multivolume set of manuals that can be obtained from Ken Orr & Associates, Inc. in Topeka, Kansas.

Automated specification tools and formal specification languages are generating substantial interest. Gehani and McGettrick [GEH86] survey the current state of the art. IEEE *Computer* magazine (April 1985) dedicated an entire issue to formal specification languages and tools.

A number of important conference proceedings contain valuable papers on analysis methods and automated tools:

Third International Workshop on Software Specification and Design, IEEE, August 1985.
Compsac86, IEEE, October 1986.
Ninth International Conference on Software Engineering, IEEE, April 1987.

A book by James Martin (*System Design from Provably Correct Constructs*, Prentice-Hall, 1985) describes an approach called HOS that enables a software engineer to specify and design computer-based systems using a set of functional primitives. Although not yet fully proven in practice, HOS concepts are an indication of one attempt to achieve ''reusability'' in analysis and design.

CHAPTER
6

SOFTWARE
DESIGN
FUNDAMENTALS

Design is the first step in the development phase for any engineered product or system. It may be defined as: "...*the process of applying various techniques and principles for the purpose of defining a device, a process or a system in sufficient detail to permit its physical realization*" [TAY59].

The designer's goal is to produce a model or representation of an entity that will later be built. The process by which the model is developed combines: intuition and judgment based on experience in building similar entities, a set of principles and/or heuristics that guide the way in which the model evolves, a set of criteria that enables quality to be judged, and a process of iteration that ultimately leads to a final design representation.

Computer software design, like engineering design approaches in other disciplines, changes continually as new methods, better analysis, and broader understanding evolve. Unlike mechanical or electronic design, software design is at a relatively early stage in its evolution. We have given serious thought to software design (as opposed to "programming" or "writing code") for little more than two decades. Therefore, software design methodology lacks the depth, flexibility, and quantitative nature normally associated with more classical engineering design disciplines. However, techniques for software design do exist, criteria for design quality are available, and design notation can be applied.

This chapter presents fundamental concepts that are applicable to all software design. Chapters 7 through 10 examine a variety of software design methods.

6.1 THE DEVELOPMENT PHASE AND SOFTWARE DESIGN

A development phase must be instituted regardless of the software engineering paradigm applied. Once software requirements have been established, the development phase comprises three distinct steps: *design, code generation* (either manual or automatic), and *testing*. Each step transforms information in a manner that ultimately results in validated computer software.

The flow of information during the development phase is illustrated in Figure 6.1. Software requirements, manifested by information domain, functional and performance requirements, feed the design step. Using one of a number of design methodologies (discussed in later chapters), data design, architectural design, and procedural design are conducted. *Data design* focuses on the definition of data structures. *Architectural design* defines the relationship among major structural elements of the program. *Procedural design* transforms structural elements into a procedural description of

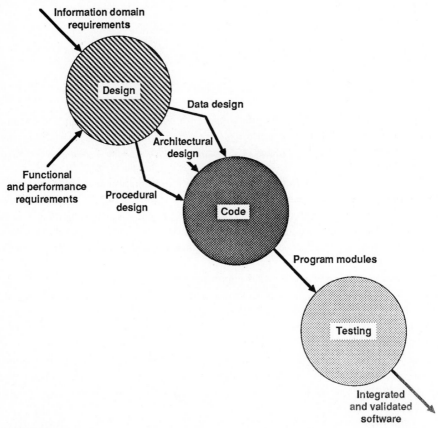

FIGURE 6.1
The development phase.

the software. Source code is generated and testing is conducted to integrate and validate the software.

The development phase absorbs 75 percent or more of the cost of software engineering (excluding maintenance). It is here that we make decisions that will ultimately affect the success of software implementation and, equally important, the ease with which software will be maintained. These decisions are made during software design, making it the pivotal step in the development phase. But why is design so important?

The importance of software design can be stated with a single word—*quality*. Design is the place where quality is fostered in software development. Design provides us with representations of software that can be assessed for quality. Design is the only way that we can accurately translate a customer's requirements into a finished software product or system. Figure 6.2 provides still another view. Software design serves as the foundation for all development and maintenance phase steps that follow. Without design, we risk building an unstable system—one that will fail when small changes are made; one that may be difficult to test; one whose quality cannot be assessed until late in the software engineering process, when time is short and many dollars have already been spent.

6.2 THE DESIGN PROCESS

Software design is a process through which requirements are translated into a representation of software. Initially the representation depicts a holistic view of software. Subsequent refinement leads to a design representation that is very close to source code.

From a project management point of view, software design is conducted in two steps. *Preliminary design* is concerned with the transformation of requirements into data and software architecture. *Detail design* focuses on refinements to the architectural representation that lead to detailed data structure and algorithmic representations for software. The relationship between the management and technical perceptions of design is shown in Figure 6.3.

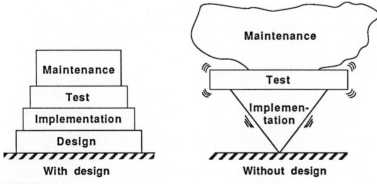

FIGURE 6.2
The importance of design.

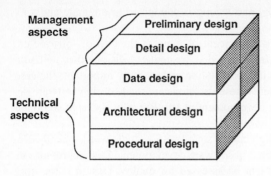

Management aspects

Preliminary design

Detail design

Data design

Technical aspects

Architectural design

Procedural design

FIGURE 6.3
Relationship between technical and management aspects of design.

6.2.1 Design and Software Quality

Throughout the design process, the quality of the evolving design is assessed with a series of *formal technical reviews* (described in Chapter 12). In order to evaluate the quality of a design representation, we must establish criteria for good design. Later in this chapter we discuss design quality criteria in some detail. For the time being, we present the following guidelines:

1. A design should exhibit a hierarchical organization that makes intelligent use of control among the elements of software.
2. A design should be modular; that is, the software should be logically partitioned into elements that perform specific functions and subfunctions.
3. A design should contain a distinct and separable representation of data and procedure.
4. A design should lead to modules (e.g., subroutines or procedures) that exhibit independent functional characteristics.
5. A design should be derived using a repeatable method that is driven by information obtained during software requirements analysis.

The above characteristics of a good design are not achieved by chance. The software engineering design process encourages good design through the application of fundamental design principles, systematic methodology, and thorough review.

6.2.2 The Evolution of Software Design

The evolution of software design is a continuing process that has spanned the past three decades. Early design work concentrated on criteria for the development of modular programs [DEN73] and methods for refining software architecture in a top-down manner [WIR71]. Procedural aspects of design definition evolved into a philosophy called *structured programming* ([DAH71], [MIL72]). Later work proposed methods for the translation of data flow [STE74] or data structure ([JAC75], [WAR74]) into a design definition. More recent work ([COX86], [EVB86]) proposes an *object-oriented* approach to design derivation.

Many design methodologies growing out of the work noted above are being applied throughout the industry. Like the analysis methods presented in the preceding chapter, each software design method introduces unique heuristics and notation as well as a somewhat parochial view of what characterizes design quality. Yet each of these methodologies (described in detail in Chapters 7 through 10) have a number of common characteristics: (1) a mechanism for the translation of information domain representation into design representation, (2) a notation for representing functional components and their interfaces, (3) heuristics for refinement and partitioning, and (4) guidelines for quality assessment.

Regardless of the design methodology used, a software engineer should apply a set of fundamental concepts to data, architectural, and procedural design. Each of these concepts is considered in the sections that follow.

6.3   Design Fundamentals

A set of fundamental software design concepts has evolved over the past three decades. Although the degree of interest in each concept has varied over the years, each has stood the test of time. Each provides the software designer with a foundation from which more sophisticated design methodologies can be applied. Each helps the software engineer to answer the following questions:

- What criteria can be used to partition software into individual components?
- How is function or data structure detail separated from a conceptual representation of software?
- Are there uniform criteria that define the technical quality of a software design?

M.A. Jackson once said: "The beginning of wisdom for a computer programmer [software engineer] is to recognize the difference between getting a program to work, and getting it *right*" [JAC75]. Fundamental software design concepts provide the necessary framework for "getting it right."

6.3.1   Refinement

Stepwise refinement is an early top-down design strategy proposed by Niklaus Wirth [WIR71]. The architecture of a program is developed by successively refining levels of procedural detail. A hierarchy is developed by decomposing a macroscopic statement of function in a stepwise fashion until programming language statements are reached. An overview of the concept is provided by Wirth [WIR71]:

> In each step (of the refinement), one or several instructions of the given program are decomposed into more detailed instructions. This successive decomposition or refinement of specifications terminates when all instructions are expressed in terms of any underlying computer or programming language....As tasks are refined, so the data may have to be refined, decomposed, or structured, and it is natural to refine the program and the data specifications in parallel.

Every refinement step implies some design decisions. It is important that...the programmer be aware of the underlying criteria (for design decisions) and of the existence of alternative solutions....

The process of program refinement proposed by Wirth is analogous to the process of refinement and partitioning that is used during requirements analysis. The difference is in the level of detail that is considered, not in the approach.

Refinement is actually a process of *elaboration*. We begin with a statement of function (or description of information) that is defined at a high *level of abstraction*. That is, the statement describes function or information conceptually but provides no information about the internal workings of the function or the internal structure of the information. Refinement causes the designer to elaborate on the original statement, providing more and more detail as each successive refinement (elaboration) occurs.

6.3.2   Software Architecture

Software architecture alludes to two important characteristics of a computer program: (1) the hierarchical structure of procedural components (modules) and (2) the structure of data. Software architecture is derived through a partitioning process that relates elements of a software solution to parts of a real-world problem implicitly defined during requirements analysis. The evolution of software and data structure begins with a problem definition. Solution occurs when each part of the problem is solved by one or more software elements. This process, symbolically represented in Figure 6.4, represents a transition between software requirements analysis and design.

Referring to Figure 6.5, it can be seen that a problem may be satisfied by many different candidate structures. A software design methodology (Chapters 7 through 10) may be used to derive structure, but because each is based on different underlying concepts of "good" design, each design method will result in a different structure for the same set of software requirements. There is no easy answer to the question, "Which is best?" We have not yet advanced to that stage of science. However, there are characteristics of a structure that can be examined to determine overall quality. We discuss these later in this chapter.

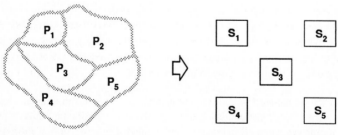

"Problem" to be solved via software   **Software "solution"**

FIGURE 6.4
Evolution of structure.

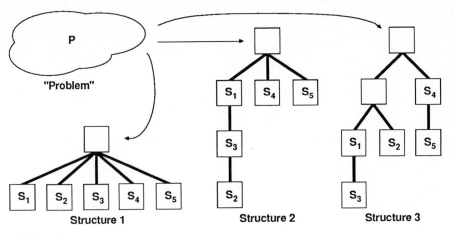

FIGURE 6.5
Different structures.

6.3.3   Program Structure

Program structure represents the organization (often hierarchical) of program components (modules) and implies a hierarchy of control. It does not represent procedural aspects of software such as sequence of processes, occurrence/order of decisions, or repetition of operations.

Many different notations are used to represent program structure. The most common is the treelike diagram, often called a *structure chart*, shown in Figure 6.6. However, other notations, such as Warnier-Orr and Jackson diagrams (Chapter 5), may also be used with equal effectiveness. In order to facilitate later discussions of structure, we define a few simple measures and terms. Referring to Figure 6.6, *depth* and *width* provide an indication of the number of levels of control and overall span of control, respectively. *Fan-out* is a measure of the number of modules that are directly controlled by another module. *Fan-in* indicates how many modules directly control a given module.

The control relationship among modules is expressed in the following way: a module that controls another module is said to be *superordinate* to it, and, conversely, a module controlled by another is said to be *subordinate* to the controller [YOU78]. For example, referring to Figure 6.6, module M is superordinate to modules a, b, and c. Module h is subordinate to module e and is ultimately subordinate to module M. Width-oriented relationships (e.g., between modules d and e), although possible to express in practice, need not be defined with explicit terminology.

6.3.4   Data Structure

Data structure is a representation of the logical relationship among individual elements of data. Because the structure of information will invariably affect the final procedural

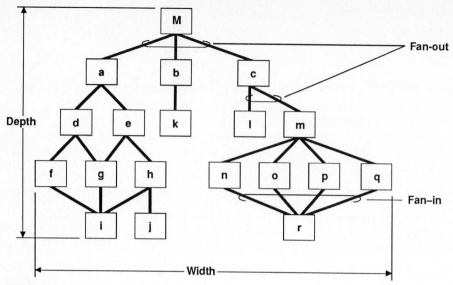

FIGURE 6.6
Structure terminology.

design, data structure is as important as program structure to the representation of software architecture.

Data structure dictates the organization, methods of access, degree of associativity, and processing alternatives for information. Entire texts (e.g., [AHO83], [KRU84]) have been dedicated to these topics and a complete discussion is beyond the scope of this book. However, it is important to understand the classic methods available for organizing information, and the concepts that underlie information hierarchies.

The organization and complexity of a data structure are limited only by the ingenuity of the designer. There are, however, a limited number of classic data structures that form the building blocks for more sophisticated structures. These classic data structures are illustrated in Figure 6.7.

A scalar item is the simplest of all data structures. As its name implies, a scalar item represents a single element of information that may be addressed by an identifier; that is, access may be achieved by specifying a single address in storage. The size and format of a scalar item may vary within bounds that are dictated by a programming language. For example, a scalar item may be: a logical entity one bit long, an integer or floating point number that is 8 to 64 bits long, or a character string that is hundreds or thousands of bytes long.

When scalar items are organized as a list or contiguous group, a sequential vector is formed. Vectors are the most common of all data structures and open the door to variable indexing of information. To illustrate we consider a simple Pascal example:

```
type G = array [1..100] of integer;
```
.
.
.

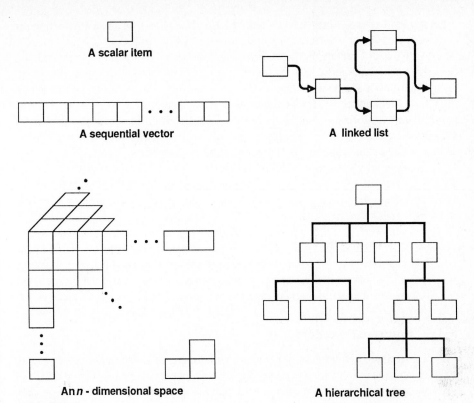

FIGURE 6.7
Classic data structures.

```
procedure S (var T:G; n: integer; sum: integer)
var i: integer
begin
    sum : = 0;
    for i : = 1 to n do
        sum : = sum + t[i]
end;
```

A sequential vector (array) of 100 scalar integer items, G, is defined. Access to each element of G is *indexed* in the procedure S so that elements of the data structure are referenced in a defined order.

When the sequential vector is extended to two, three, and, ultimately, an arbitrary number of dimensions, an *n-dimensional* space is created. The most common n-dimensional space is the two-dimensional matrix. In most programming languages an n-dimensional space is called an *array*.

Items, vectors, and spaces may be organized in a variety of formats. A *linked list* is a data structure that organizes noncontiguous scalar items, vectors, or spaces in a manner (called *nodes*) that enables them to be processed as a list. Each node contains the appropriate data organization (e.g., a vector) and one or more pointers that indicate the address in storage of the next node in the list. Nodes may be added at any point in the list by redefining pointers to accommodate the new list entry.

Other data structures incorporate or are constructed using the fundamental data structures described above. For example, a *hierarchical data structure* is implemented using multilinked lists that contain scalar items, vectors, and, possibly, *n*-dimensional spaces. A hierarchical structure is commonly encountered in applications that require information categorization and associativity. Categorization implies a grouping of information by some generic category (e.g., all subcompact automobiles or all 32-bit microcomputers that support the UNIX operating system).

Associativity implies the ability to associate information from different categories; e.g., find all entries in the microcomputer category that cost less than $1,000.00 (cost subcategory), run at 12 MHz (cycle time subcategory), and are made by U.S. vendors (vendor subcategory).

It is important to note that data structures, like program structure, can be represented at different levels of abstraction. For example, a *stack* is a conceptual model of a data structure that can be implemented as a vector or a linked list. Depending on the level of design detail, the internal workings of *stack* may or may not be specified. We discuss data abstraction in more detail in Section 6.3.7.

6.3.5   Software Procedure

Program structure defines control hierarchy without regard to the sequence of processing and decisions. Software procedure (Figure 6.8) focuses on the processing details of each module individually. Procedure must provide a precise specification of processing, including sequence of events, exact decision points, repetitive operations, and even data organization/structure.

There is, of course, a relationship between structure and procedure. Processing indicated for each module must include a reference to all modules subordinate to the module being described. That is, a procedural representation of software is layered as illustrated in Figure 6.9.

6.3.6   Modularity

The concept of modularity in computer software has been espoused for almost four decades. Architecture, as it has been described in Section 6.3.2, embodies modularity; that is, software is divided into separately named and addressable elements, called *modules*, that are integrated to satisfy problem requirements.

It has been stated that ''modularity is the single attribute of software that allows a program to be intellectually manageable'' [MYE78]. Monolithic software (i.e., a large program composed of a single module) cannot be easily grasped by a reader. The number of control paths, span of reference, number of variables, and overall complexity would make understanding close to impossible. To illustrate this point, consider the following argument based on observations of human problem solving.

Let $C(x)$ be a function that defines the perceived complexity of a problem x, and $E(x)$ be a function that defines the effort (in time) required to solve a problem x. For two problems, p_1 and p_2, if

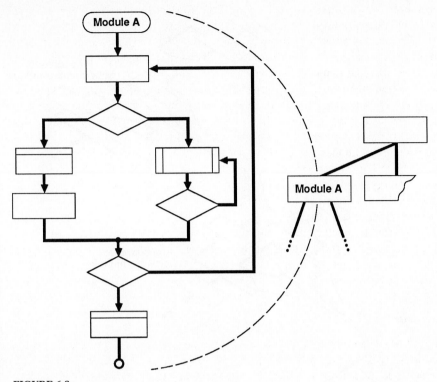

FIGURE 6.8
Procedure within a module.

$$C(p_1) > C(p_2) \qquad (6.1a)$$

it follows that

$$E(p_1) > E(p_2) \qquad (6.1b)$$

As a general case, this result is intuitively obvious. It does take more time to solve a difficult problem.

Another interesting characteristic has been uncovered through experimentation in human problem solving. That is,

$$C(p_1 + p_2) > C(p_1) + C(p_2) \qquad (6.2)$$

Inequality (6.2) implies that the perceived complexity of a problem that combines p_1 and p_2 is greater than the perceived complexity when each problem is considered separately. Considering Inequality (6.2) and the condition implied by Inequality (6.1), it follows that

$$E(p_1 + p_2) > E(p_1) + E(p_2) \qquad (6.3)$$

This leads to a ''divide and conquer'' conclusion—it's easier to solve a complex problem when you break it into manageable pieces. The result expressed in Inequality (6.3)

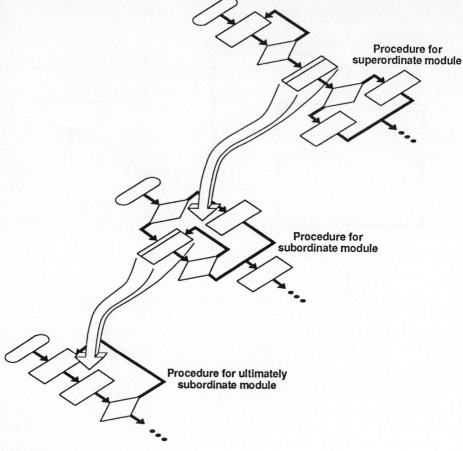

Procedure for superordinate module

Procedure for subordinate module

Procedure for ultimately subordinate module

FIGURE 6.9
Procedure is layered.

has important implications with regard to modularity and software. It is, in fact, an argument for modularity.

It is possible to conclude from Inequality (6.3) that if we subdivide software indefinitely, the effort required to develop it will become negligibly small! Unfortunately, other forces come into play, causing this conclusion to be (sadly) invalid. Referring to Figure 6.10, the effort (cost) to develop an individual software module does decrease as the total number of modules increases. Given the same set of requirements, more modules mean smaller individual size. However, as the number of modules grows, the effort (cost) associated with interfacing the modules also grows. These characteristics lead to the total cost or effort curve shown in the figure. There is a number, M, of modules that would result in minimum development cost, but we do not have the necessary sophistication to predict M with assurance.

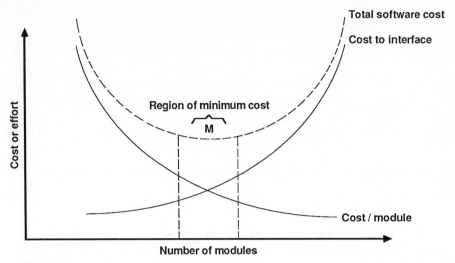

FIGURE 6.10
Modularity and software cost.

The curves shown in Figure 6.10 do provide useful guidance when modularity is considered. We should modularize, but care should be taken to stay in the vicinity of *M*. Undermodularity or overmodularity should be avoided. But how do we know "the vicinity of *M*"? How modular should we make software? The size of a module will be dictated by its function and application. In Section 6.4, design measures that help determine the appropriate number of modules for software are presented.

It is important to note that a system may be designed modularly, even if its implementation must be "monolithic." There are situations (e.g., real-time software, microprocessor software) in which relatively minimal speed and memory overhead introduced by subprograms (i.e., subroutines, procedures) is unacceptable. In such situations software can and should be designed with modularity as an overriding philosophy. Code may be developed "in-line." Although the program source code may not look modular at first glance, the philosophy has been maintained, and the program will provide the benefits of a modular system.

6.3.7 Abstraction

When we consider a modular solution to any problem, many *levels of abstraction* can be posed. At the highest level of abstraction, a solution is stated in broad terms using the language of the problem environment. At lower levels of abstraction, a more procedural orientation is taken. Problem-oriented terminology is coupled with implementation-oriented terminology in an effort to state a solution. Finally, at the lowest level of abstraction, the solution is stated in a manner that can be directly implemented. Wasserman [WAS83] provides a useful definition:

> ...the psychological notion of "abstraction" permits one to concentrate on a problem at some level of generalization without regard to irrelevant low level details; use of abstrac-

tion also permits one to work with concepts and terms that are familiar in the problem environment without having to transform them to an unfamiliar structure....

Each step in the software engineering process is a refinement in the level of abstraction of the software solution. During system engineering, software is allocated as an element of a computer-based system. During software requirements analysis, the software solution is stated in terms "that are familiar in the problem environment." As we move from preliminary to detail design, the level of abstraction is reduced. Finally, the lowest level of abstraction is reached when source code is generated.

To illustrate software defined by three different levels of abstraction, we consider the following problem: Develop software that will perform all functions associated with a two-dimensional drafting system for low-level computer-aided design applications.

ABSTRACTION 1. The software will incorporate a computer graphics interface that will enable visual communication with the draftsperson and a digitizer interface that replaces the drafting board and square. All line and curve drawing, all geometric computations, and all sectioning and auxiliary views will be performed by the CAD software.

At this level of abstraction, the solution is stated in terms of the problem environment.

ABSTRACTION 2.

```
CAD software tasks:
    user interaction task;
    2-D drawing creation task;
    graphics display task;
    drawing file management task;
end.
```

At this level of abstraction, each of the major software tasks associated with the CAD software is noted. Terms have moved away from the problem environment but are still not implementation-specific.

Now, to illustrate a third level of abstraction we concentrate on the 2-D drawing creation task:

ABSTRACTION 3.

```
procedure: 2-D drawing creation;
    repeat until (drawing creation task terminates)
    do while (digitizer interaction occurs)
        digitizer interface task;
        determine drawing request case;
```

```
        line: line drawing task;
        circle: circle drawing task;

        .

        .

        .

end;
do while (keyboard interaction occurs)
    keyboard interaction task;
    process analysis/computation case;
        view: auxiliary view task;
        section: cross sectioning task;

    .

    .

    .

    end;

.

.

.

    end repetition;
end procedure.
```

At this level of abstraction, a preliminary procedural representation exists. Terminology is now software-oriented (e.g., the use of constructs such as *do while*) and an implication of modularity begins to surface.

The concepts of stepwise refinement and modularity are closely aligned with abstraction. As the software design evolves, each level of modules in program structure represents a refinement in the level of abstraction of the software.

Data abstraction, like procedural abstraction, enables a designer to represent a *data object* at varying levels of detail and, more importantly, specify a data object in the context of those operations (procedures) that can be applied to it. Continuing the CAD software example above, we could define a data object called *drawing*. The object *drawing* connotes certain information with no further expansion when it is considered in the context of the drafting system. The designer, however, might specify *drawing* as an *abstract data type*. That is, the internal details of *drawing* are defined:

```
TYPE drawing IS STRUCTURE DEFINED
    number IS STRING LENGTH (12);
    geometry DEFINED ...
    notes IS STRING LENGTH (256);
    BOM DEFINED ...
END drawing TYPE;
```

In the design language description above, drawing is defined in terms of its constituent parts. In this case the data abstraction *drawing* is itself composed of other data abstractions: *geometry* and *BOM* (bill of materials).

Once the type *drawing* (an abstract data type) has been defined, we can use it to describe other data objects without reference to the internal details of *drawing*. For example, at another location in the data design, we might say:

blue-print IS INSTANCE OF drawing

or

schematic IS INSTANCE OF drawing

implying that *blue-print* and *schematic* take on all the characteristics of *drawing* as defined above. This typing process is called *instantiation*.

Once a data abstraction is defined, a set of operations that may be applied to it is also defined. For example, we might identify operations such as *erase, save, catalog,* and *copy* for the abstract data type *drawing*. By definition (literally), each of these procedures can be specified without the need to define details of *drawing* every time the procedure is invoked.

A number of programming languages (e.g., Ada, Modula, Smalltalk) provide mechanisms for creating abstract data types. For example, the Ada *package* is a programming language mechanism that provides support for both data and *procedural* abstractions [HAB83]. The original abstract data type is used as a template or generic data structure from which other data structures can be *instantiated*.

Control abstraction is the third form of abstraction used in software design. Like procedural and data abstraction, control abstraction implies a program control mechanism without specifying internal details. An example of a control abstraction is the *synchronization semaphore* [KAI83] used to coordinate activities in an operating system. The concept of the control abstraction is discussed in Chapter 10.

6.3.8 Information Hiding

The concept of modularity leads every software designer to a fundamental question: "How do we decompose a software solution to obtain the best set of modules?" The principle of *information hiding* [PAR72] suggests that modules be "characterized by design decisions that (each) hides from all others." In other words, modules should be specified and designed so that information (procedure and data) contained within a module is inaccessible to other modules that have no need for such information.

Hiding implies that effective modularity can be achieved by defining a set of independent modules that communicate with one another only that information necessary to achieve software function. Abstraction helps to define the procedural (or informational) entities that compose the software. Hiding defines and enforces access constraints to both procedural detail within a module and any local data structure used by the module [ROS75].

The use of information hiding as a design criteria for modular systems provides its greatest benefits when modifications are required during testing and, later, software maintenance. Because most data and procedure are hidden from other parts of the software, inadvertent errors introduced during modification are less likely to propagate to other locations within the software.

6.4 EFFECTIVE MODULAR DESIGN

The design fundamentals described in the preceding section all serve to precipitate modular designs. In fact modularity has become an accepted approach in all engineering disciplines. A modular design reduces complexity (see Section 6.3.6), facilitates change (a critical aspect of software maintainability), and results in easier implementation by encouraging parallel development of different parts of a system.

6.4.1 Module Types

Abstraction and information hiding are used to define modules within a software architecture. Both of these attributes must be translated into module operational features characterized by: time history of incorporation, activation mechanism, and pattern of control.

Time history of incorporation refers to the time at which a module is included within a source language description of the software. For example a module defined as a *compile time macro* is included as in-line code by the compiler via a reference made in developer-supplied code. A conventional subprogram (e.g., a subroutine or procedure) is included via generation of branch and link code.

Two *activation mechanisms* are encountered. Conventionally, a module is invoked by reference (e.g., a ''call'' statement). However, in real-time applications a module may be invoked by interrupt; that is, an outside event causes a discontinuity in processing that results in the passage of control to another module. Activation mechanics are important because they can affect program structure.

The *pattern of control* of a module describes the manner in which it is executed internally. Conventional modules have a single entry and exit and are executed sequentially as part of one user task. More sophisticated patterns of control are sometimes required. For example, a module may be *reentrant*. That is, a module is designed so that it does not in any way modify itself or the local addresses that it references. Therefore, the module may be used for more than one task concurrently.

Within a software structure, a module may be categorized as:

- a *sequential* module that is referenced and executed without apparent interruption by the applications software,
- an *incremental* module that can be interrupted prior to completion by applications software and subsequently restarted at the point of interruption or,
- a *parallel* module that executes simultaneously with another module in concurrent multiprocessor environments.

Sequential modules are most commonly encountered and are characterized by compile time macros and conventional subprograms—subroutines, functions, or procedures. Incremental modules, often called *coroutines,* maintain an entry pointer that allows the module to restart at the point of interruption. Such modules are extremely useful in interrupt-driven systems. Parallel modules, sometimes called *conroutines,* are encountered when high-speed computation (e.g., pipeline processing) demands two or more CPUs working in parallel.

A typical control hierarchy may not be encountered when coroutines or conroutines are used. Such nonhierarchical or *homologous* structures require special design approaches that are in the early stages of development.

Another module type is encountered in programming languages such as Modula and Ada. The Modula *module* and the Ada *package* (see Chapter 11) are program components that combine data abstractions and procedural elements in a manner that encourages modular data and architectural design.

6.4.2 Functional Independence

The concept of *functional independence* is a direct outgrowth of modularity and the concepts of abstraction and information hiding. In landmark papers on software design Parnas [PAR72] and Wirth [WIR71] allude to refinement techniques that enhance module independence. Later work by Stevens, Myers, and Constantine [STE74] solidified the concept.

Functional independence is achieved by developing modules with "single-minded" function and an "aversion" to excessive interaction with other modules. Stated another way, we want to design software so that each module addresses a specific subfunction of requirements and has a simple interface when viewed from other parts of the software structure.

It is fair to ask why independence is important. Software with effective modularity, i.e., independent modules, is easier to develop because function may be compartmentalized and interfaces may be simplified (consider ramifications when development is conducted by a team). Independent modules are easier to maintain (and test) because: secondary effects caused by design/code modification are limited, error propagation is reduced, and reusable modules are possible. To summarize, functional independence is a key to good design, and design is the key to software quality.

Independence is measured using two qualitative criteria: cohesion and coupling. *Cohesion* is a measure of the relative functional strength of a module. *Coupling* is a measure of the relative interdependence among modules.

6.4.3 Cohesion

Cohesion is a natural extension of the information hiding concept described in Section 6.3.8. A cohesive module performs a single task within a software procedure and requires little interaction with procedures being performed in other parts of a program. Stated simply, a cohesive module should do (ideally) just one thing.

Cohesion may be represented as a "spectrum" (shown in Figure 6.11). We always strive for high cohesion, although the mid-range of the spectrum is often acceptable. The scale for cohesion is nonlinear. That is, low-end cohesiveness is much "worse" than middle-range, which is nearly as "good" as high-end cohesion. In prac-

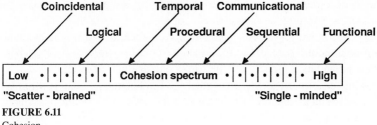

FIGURE 6.11
Cohesion.

tice a designer need not be concerned with categorizing cohesion in a specific module. Rather, the overall concept should be understood and low levels of cohesion should be avoided when modules are designed.

To illustrate (somewhat facetiously) the low end of the spectrum, we relate the following story:

> In the late 1960s most DP managers began to recognize the worth of modularity. Unfortunately many existing programs were monolithic, e.g., 6–20,000 lines of undocumented FORTRAN with one 2500-line subroutine! To bring his environment to the state of the art, a manager asked his staff to modularize such a program that underwent maintenance continuously. This was to be done ''in your spare time.''
>
> Under the gun, one staff member asked (innocently) the proper length for a module. ''Seventy-five lines of code,'' came the reply. She then obtained a red pen and a ruler, measured the linear distance taken by 75 lines of source code and drew a red line on the source listing, then another, and another. Each red line indicated a module boundary.
>
> This technique is akin to developing software with coincidental cohesion!

A module that performs a set of tasks that relate to each other loosely, if at all, is *coincidentally cohesive*. A module that performs tasks that are related logically (e.g., a module that produces all output regardless of type) is *logically cohesive*. When a module contains tasks that are related by the fact that all must be executed within the same time span, the module exhibits *temporal cohesion*.

As an example of low cohesion, consider a module that performs error processing for an engineering analysis package. The module is called when computed data exceed prespecified bounds. It performs the following tasks: (1) computes supplementary data based on original computed data, (2) produces an error report (with graphical content) on the user terminal, (3) performs follow-up calculations requested by the user, (4) updates a data base, and (5) enables menu selection for subsequent processing. Although the preceding tasks are loosely related, each is an independent functional entity that might best be performed as a separate module. Combining the functions into a single module can only serve to increase the likelihood of error propagation when a modification is made to one of the processing tasks noted above.

Moderate levels of cohesion are relatively close to one another in their degree of module independence. When processing elements of a module are related and must be executed in a specific order, *procedural cohesion* exists. When all processing elements concentrate on one area of a data structure, *communicational cohesion* is present. High cohesion is characterized by a module that performs one distinct procedural task.

The following excerpt from Stevens, et al. [STE75] provides a set of simple guidelines for establishing the degree of cohesion (called ''binding'' in this reference):

A useful technique in determining whether a module is functionally bound is writing a sentence describing the function (purpose) of the module and then examining the sentence. The following tests can be made:

1. If the sentence has to be a compound sentence, contains a comma, or contains more than one verb, the module is probably performing more than one function; therefore, it probably has sequential or communicational binding.
2. If the sentence contains words relating to time, such as ''first,'' ''next,'' ''then,'' ''after,'' ''when,'' ''start,'' etc., then the module probably has sequential or temporal binding.
3. If the predicate of the sentence doesn't contain a single specific object following the verb, the module is probably logically bound. For example, Edit All Data has logical binding: Edit Source Statement may have functional binding.
4. Words such as ''initialize,'' ''clean-up,'' etc., imply temporal binding.

Functionally bound modules can always be described by way of their elements using a compound sentence. But if the above language is unavoidable while still completely describing the module's function, then the module is probably not functionally bound.

As we have already noted, it is unnecessary to determine the precise level of cohesion. Rather it is important to strive for high cohesion and recognize low cohesion so that software design can be modified to achieve greater functional independence.

6.4.4   Coupling

Coupling is a measure of interconnection among modules in a program structure. Like cohesion, coupling may be represented on a spectrum as shown in Figure 6.12. Coupling depends on the interface complexity between modules, the point at which entry or reference is made to a module, and the data that pass across the interface.

In software design, we strive for lowest possible coupling. Simple connectivity among modules results in software that is easier to understand and less prone to a ''ripple effect'' [STE75] caused when errors occur at one location and propagate through a system.

Figure 6.13 provides examples of modules residing in a structure with low coupling. Modules 1 and 2 are subordinate to different modules. Each is unrelated and therefore no direct coupling occurs. Module 3 is subordinate to module 2 and is accessible

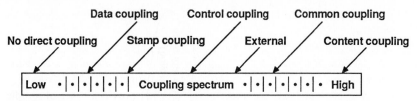

FIGURE 6.12
Coupling spectrum.

via a conventional argument list through which data are passed. As long as a simple argument list is present (i.e., simple data are passed; a one-to-one correspondence of items exists), low coupling (*data coupling* on the spectrum) is exhibited in this portion of structure. A variation of data coupling, called *stamp coupling*, is found when a portion of a data structure (rather than simple arguments) is passed via a module interface.

At moderate levels, coupling is characterized by the passage of control between modules. *Control coupling* is very common in most software designs and is illustrated in Figure 6.14. In its simplest form, control is passed via a "flag" on which decisions are made in a subordinate or superordinate module.

Relatively high levels of coupling occur when modules are tied to an environment external to software. For example, I/O couples a module to specific devices, formats, and communication protocols. *External coupling* is essential, but should be limited to a small number of modules within a structure. High coupling also occurs when a number of modules reference a global data area. *Common coupling*, as this mode is called, is shown in Figure 6.15. Modules C, E, and N each access a data item in a global data area (e.g., a disk file, Fortran COMMON, external data types in the C programming language). Module C reads the item, invoking E which recomputes and updates the item. Let us assume that an error occurs and E updates the item incorrectly. Much later in processing, module N reads the item, attempts to process it, and fails, causing the software to abort. The apparent cause of abort is module N; the actual cause, module E. Diagnosing problems in structures with considerable common coupling is time consuming and difficult. However, this does not mean that the use of global data is necessarily "bad." It does mean that a software designer must be aware of the potential consequences of common coupling and take special care to guard against them.

The highest degree of coupling, *content coupling*, occurs when one module makes use of data or control information maintained within the boundary of another module. Secondarily, content coupling occurs when branches are made into the middle of a module. This mode of coupling can and should be avoided.

The coupling modes discussed above occur because of design decisions made when structure was developed. Variants of external coupling, however, may be introduced during coding. For example, compiler coupling ties source code to specific (and often nonstandard) attributes of a compiler; operating system coupling ties design and

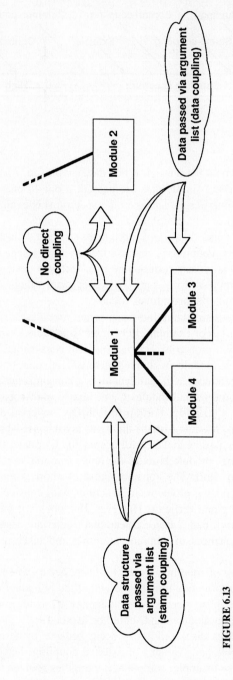

FIGURE 6.13
Low coupling.

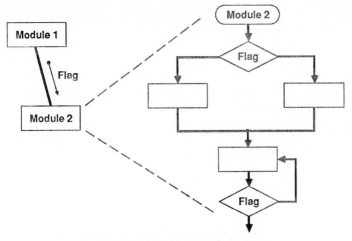

**Control coupling occurs when module 1
passes control data to module 2.**

FIGURE 6.14
Moderate coupling.

resultant code to operating system (OS) ''hooks'' that can create havoc when OS changes occur.

6.5 DATA DESIGN

Data design is the first (and some would say the most important) of the three design activities conducted during software engineering. The impact of data structure on program structure and procedural complexity causes data design to have a profound influence on software quality. Each of the design methodologies presented in this book

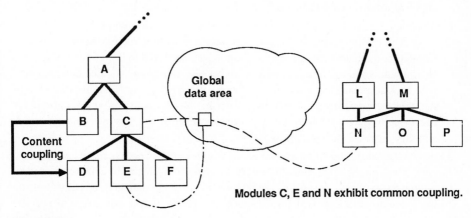

Modules C, E and N exhibit common coupling.

FIGURE 6.15
High coupling.

(Chapters 7–10) makes some attempt to address data design issues. The concepts of information hiding and data abstraction provide the foundation for an approach to data design.

The process of data design is summarized by Wasserman [WAS80]:

> The primary activity during data design is to select logical representations of data objects (data structures) identified during the requirements definition and specification phase. The selection process may involve algorithmic analysis of alternative structures in order to determine the most efficient design or may simply involve the use of a set of modules (a "package") that provide the desired operations upon some representation of an object.
>
> An important related activity during design is to identify those program modules that must operate directly upon the logical data structures. In this way the scope of effect of individual data design decisions can be constrained.

Regardless of the design techniques used, well-designed data can lead to better program structure, modularity, and reduced procedural complexity.

Wasserman [WAS80] has proposed a set of principles that may be used to specify and design data. In actuality the design of data is often encountered as part of the requirements analysis task described in Chapters 4 and 5. Recalling that requirements analysis and design often overlap, we consider the following set of principles [WAS80] for data specification:

1. *The systematic analysis methods applied to software should also be applied to data.* We spend much time and effort deriving, reviewing, and specifying software requirements and preliminary design. Representations of data flow and structure should also be developed and reviewed, alternative data organizations should be considered, and the impact of data design on software design should be evaluated. For example, specification of a multiringed linked list may nicely satisfy data requirements but may also lead to an unwieldy software design. An alternative data organization may lead to better results.

2. *All data structures and the operations that are to be performed on each should be identified.* The design of an efficient data structure must take the operations to be performed on the data structure into account (e.g., see [AHO83]). For example, consider a data structure made up of a set of diverse data elements. The data structure is to be manipulated in a number of major software functions. Upon evaluation of the operation performed on the data structure, an abstract data type is defined for use in subsequent software design. Specification of the abstract data type may simplify software design considerably.

3. *A data dictionary should be established and used to define both data and software design.* The concept of a data dictionary has been introduced in Chapter 5. A data dictionary explicitly represents the relationships among data and the constraints on the elements of a data structure. Algorithms that must take advantage of specific relationships can be more easily defined if a dictionary-like data specification exists.

4. *Low level data design decisions should be deferred until late in the design process.* A process of stepwise refinement may be used for the design of data. That is, overall data organization may be defined during requirements analysis, refined during preliminary design work, and specified in detail during the detail design step. The top-down approach to data design provides benefits that are analogous to a top down approach to software design—major structural attributes are designed and evaluated first so that the architecture of the data may be established.

5. *The representation of a data structure should be known only to those modules that must make direct use of the data contained within the structure.* The concept of information hiding and the related concept of coupling provide important insight into the quality of a software design. Principle 5 alludes to the importance of these concepts as well as "the importance of separating the logical view of a data object from its physical view" [WAS80].

6. *A library of useful data structures and the operations that may be applied to them should be developed.* Data structures and operations should be viewed as a resource for software design. Data structures can be designed for reusability. A library of data structure *templates* (abstract data types) can reduce both specification and design effort for data.

7. *A software design and programming language should support the specification and realization of abstract data types.* The implementation (and corresponding design) of a sophisticated data structure can be made exceedingly difficult if no means exist for direct specification of the structure. For example, implementation (or design) of a linked list structure or a multilevel, heterogeneous array would be difficult if the target programming language was FORTRAN because the language does not support direct specification of these data structures.

The principles described above form a basis for a data design approach that can be integrated into both the definition and development phases of the software engineering process. As we have noted elsewhere in this book, a clear definition of information is essential to successful software development.

6.6 ARCHITECTURAL DESIGN

The primary objective of *architectural design* is to develop a modular program structure and represent the control relationships between modules. In addition architectural design melds program structure and data structure and defines interfaces enabling data to flow throughout the program.

To understand the importance of architectural design, we present a brief story from everyday life:

You have saved your money, purchased a beautiful piece of land, and decided to build the house of your dreams. Having no experience in such matters, you visit a builder and explain your desires (e.g., number and size of rooms, contemporary styling, spa (of course!), cathedral ceilings, lots of glass, etc.). The builder listens carefully, asks a few questions, and then tells you that he'll have a design in a few weeks.

As you anxiously await his call, you conjure up many different (and outrageously expensive) images of your new house. What will he come up with? Finally, the phone rings and you rush to his office.

Pulling out a large manila folder, the builder spreads a diagram of the plumbing for the second floor bathroom in front of you and proceeds to explain it in great detail.

"But what about the overall design!" you say.

"Don't worry," says the builder, "we'll get to that later."

Does the builder's approach seem a bit unusual? Does our hero feel comfortable with the builder's final response? Of course not. Anyone would first want to see a sketch of the house, a floor plan, and other information that would provide an *architectural view*. Yet many software developers act like the builder in our story. They concentrate on the "plumbing" (procedural details and code) to the exclusion of the software architecture.

The design methods presented in the following chapters encourage the software engineer to concentrate on architectural design before worrying about the plumbing. Although each method has a different approach to architectural derivation, all recognize the importance of a holistic view of software.

6.7 PROCEDURAL DESIGN

Procedural design occurs after data and program structure have been established. In an ideal world the procedural specification required to define algorithmic details would be stated in a natural language such as English. After all, members of a software development organization all speak a natural language (in theory, at least), people outside the software domain could more readily understand the specification, and no new learning would be required.

Unfortunately, there is one small problem. Procedural design must specify procedural detail unambiguously, and a lack of ambiguity in a natural language is unnatural. Using a natural language, we can write a set of procedural steps in too many different ways. We frequently rely on context to get a point across. We often write as if a dialogue with the reader were possible (it isn't). For these and many other reasons, a more constrained mode for representing procedural detail must be used.

6.7.1 Structured Programming

The foundations of procedural design were formed in the early 1960s and were solidified with the work of Edsgar Dijkstra and his colleagues ([BOH66], [DIJ65], [DIJ76]). In the late 1960s Dijkstra and others proposed the use of a set of existing logical constructs from which any program could be formed. The constructs emphasized "maintenance of functional domain." That is, each construct had a predictable logical structure, was entered at the top and exited at the bottom and enabled a reader to follow procedural flow more easily.

The constructs, introduced earlier in the context of data representation (Chapter 5), are *sequence, condition*, and *repetition*. Sequence implements processing steps essential in the specification of any algorithm, condition provides the facility for selected processing based on some logical occurrence, and repetition provides for looping. These three constructs are fundamental to *structured programming*—an important design technique in the broader field that we have learned to call software engineering.

The structured constructs were proposed to limit the procedural design of software to a small number of predictable operations. Complexity metrics (Chapter 12) indicate that the use of the structured constructs reduces program complexity and thereby enhances readability, testability, and maintainability. The use of a limited number of logical constructs also contributes to a human understanding process that psychologists call *chunking*. To understand this process, consider the way in which you are reading this page. You do not read individual letters, but rather recognize patterns or chunks of letters that form words or phrases. The structured constructs are logical chunks that allow a reader to recognize procedural elements of a module rather than reading the design or code line by line. Understanding is enhanced when readily recognizable logical forms are encountered.

Any program, regardless of application area or technical complexity, can be designed and implemented using only the three structured constructs. It should be noted, however, that dogmatic use of only these constructs can sometimes cause practical difficulties. Section 6.7.2 considers this issue in further detail.

6.7.2   Graphical Design Tools

"A picture is worth a thousand words," but as Carl Machover (a leading computer graphics expert) says, "it's rather important to know which picture and which thousand words." There is no question that graphical tools, such as the flowchart or box diagram, provide excellent pictorial patterns that readily depict procedural detail. However, if graphical tools are misused, the wrong picture may lead to the wrong software.

The *flowchart* is the most widely used graphical representation for procedural design. Unfortunately, it is the most widely abused method as well.

The flowchart is quite simple pictorially. A box indicates a processing step, a diamond represents a logical condition, and arrows show the flow of control. Figure 6.16 illustrates the three structured programming constructs discussed in Section 6.7.1. Sequence is represented as two processing boxes connected by a line (arrow) of control. Condition, also called *if-then-else*, is depicted as a decision diamond, which, if true, causes *then-part* processing to occur and, if false, invokes *else-part* processing. Repetition is represented using two slightly different forms. The *do-while* tests a condition and executes a *loop task* repetitively as long as the condition holds true. A *repeat-until* executes the loop task first, then tests a condition and repeats the task until the condition fails. The selection (or *select-case*) construct shown in the figure is actually an extension of the *if-then-else*. A parameter is tested by successive decisions until a true condition occurs and a *case-part* processing path is executed.

The structured constructs may be nested within one another as shown in Figure 6.17. Referring to the figure, a *repeat-until* forms the *then-part* of an *if-then-else* (en-

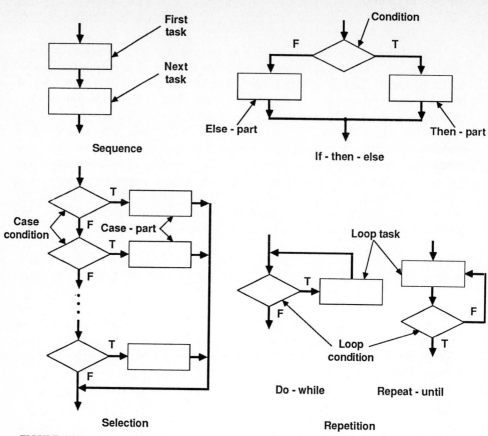

FIGURE 6.16
Flowchart constructs.

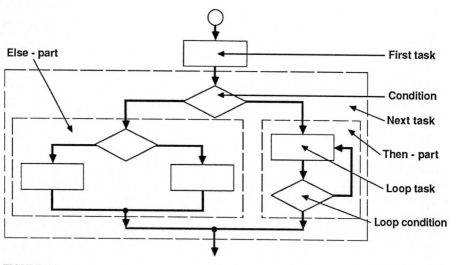

FIGURE 6.17
Nesting constructs.

closed by the outer dashed boundary). Another *if-then-else* forms the *else-part* of the larger condition. Finally, the condition itself becomes the second block in a sequence. By nesting constructs in this manner, a complex logical schema may be developed. It should be noted that any one of the blocks in Figure 6.17 could reference another module, thereby accomplishing *procedural layering* implied by program structure.

A more detailed structured flowchart is shown in Figure 6.18. As an exercise, the reader should attempt to box each construct. Upon completion of the exercise, two things will be apparent. The entire procedure is constructed using the constructs shown

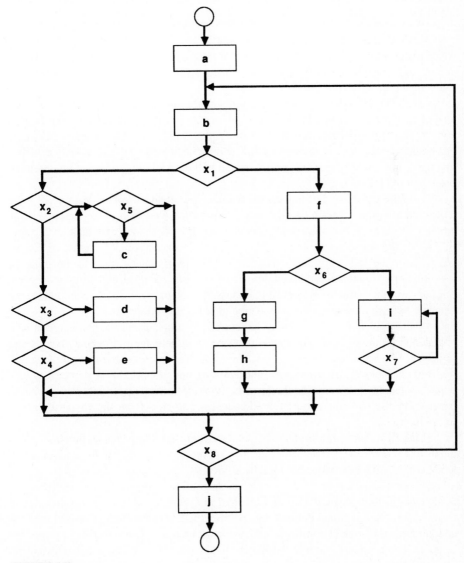

FIGURE 6.18
A structured flowchart.

in Figure 6.16, and as the constructs are "boxed," boundaries of the boxes never cross. That is, all constructs have a single entry and a single exit.

The use of only structured constructs can at times introduce complications in logical flow. For example, assume that as part of process i (Figure 6.18) a condition, z, may arise that requires an immediate branch to process j. A direct branch violates the logical constructs by escaping from the functional domain of the repeat-until of which process i is a part. To implement the above branch without violation, tests for condition z must be added to x_7 and x_8. These tests would occur repeatedly, even if the occurrence of z is rare. We have introduced additional complication and execution inefficiency.

In general the dogmatic use of only the structured constructs can introduce inefficiency when an escape from a set of nested loops or nested conditions is required. More importantly, additional complication of all logical tests along the path of escape can cloud software control flow, increase error possibilities and impair readability and maintainability. What can we do?

The designer is left with two options: (1) the procedural representation is redesigned so that the "escape branch" is not required at a nested location in the flow of control; or (2) the structured constructs are violated in a controlled manner; that is, a constrained branch out of the nested flow is designed. Option 1 is obviously the ideal approach, but option 2 can be accommodated without violating the spirit of structured programming [KNU75].

Another graphical design tool, the *box diagram*, evolved from a desire to develop a procedural design representation that would not allow violation of the structured constructs. Developed by Nassi and Shneiderman [NAS73] and extended by Chapin [CHA75], the diagrams (also called *Nassi-Shneiderman charts*, *N-S charts*, or *Chapin charts*) have the following characteristics: (1) *functional domain* (that is, the scope of repetition or an if-then-else) is well defined and clearly visible as a pictorial representation, (2) arbitrary transfer of control is impossible, (3) the scope of local and/or global data can be easily determined, and (4) recursion is easy to represent.

The graphical representation of structured constructs using the box diagram is illustrated in Figure 6.19. The fundamental element of the diagram is a box. To represent sequence, two boxes are connected bottom to top. To represent an *if-then-else*, a condition box is followed by a *then-part* and *else-part* box. Repetition is depicted with a bounding pattern that encloses the process (*do-while-part* or *repeat-until-part*) to be repeated. Finally, selection is represented using the graphical form shown at the bottom of the figure.

Like flowcharts, a box diagram is layered on multiple pages as processing elements of a module are refined. A "call" to a subordinate module can be represented by a box with the module name enclosed by an oval.

Figure 6.20 illustrates the use of a box diagram to represent a flow of control that is identical to the one shown in the flowchart in Figure 6.18. To illustrate the relative ease with which functional domain may be discerned, refer to the repeat-until loop for condition x_8. All logical constructs contained within the loop are readily apparent because of the boundary pattern. Note that an escape from the loop can only be implemented in one way—via strict adherence to the structured constructs. In fact there is no mechanism for violation of the constructs.

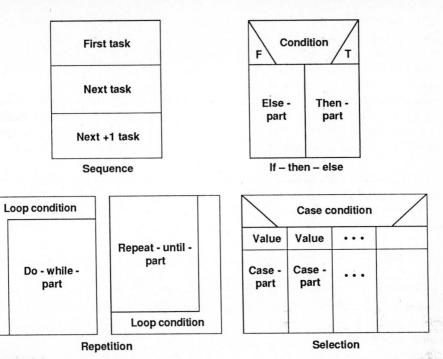

FIGURE 6.19
Box diagram constructs.

6.7.3 Tabular Design Tools

In many software applications, a module may be required to evaluate a complex combination of conditions and select appropriate actions based on these conditions. *Decision tables* provide a tool that translates actions and conditions (described in a processing narrative) into a tabular form. The table is difficult to misinterpret and may even be used as machine-readable input to a *table driven* algorithm. In a comprehensive treatment of this design tool, Ned Chapin states [HUR83]:

> Some old software tools and techniques mesh well with new tools and techniques of software engineering. Decision tables are an excellent example. Decision tables preceded software engineering by nearly a decade, but fit so well with software engineering that they might have been designed for that purpose.

Decision table organization is illustrated in Figure 6.21. Referring to the figure, darker lines divide the table into four quadrants. The upper left-hand quadrant contains a list of all conditions. The lower left-hand quadrant contains a list of all actions that are possible based on combinations of conditions. The right-hand quadrants form a matrix that indicates condition combinations and the corresponding actions that will occur for a specific combination. Therefore, each column of the matrix may be interpreted as a processing *rule*.

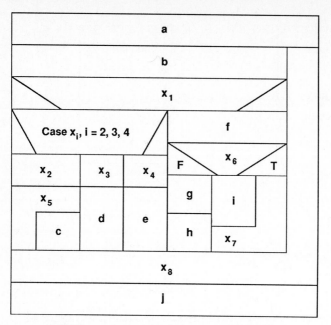

May be used to indicate a subprogram reference (i.e., a call to module A).

FIGURE 6.20
Box diagram.

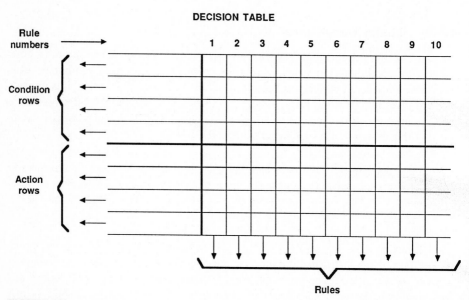

FIGURE 6.21
Decision table nomenclature.

The following steps are applied to develop a decision table:

1. List all actions that can be associated with a specific procedure (or module).
2. List all conditions (or decisions made) during execution of the procedure.
3. Associate specific sets of conditions with specific actions, eliminating impossible combinations of conditions. alternatively, develop every possible permutation of conditions.
4. Define *rules* by indicating what action(s) occurs for a set of conditions.

To illustrate the use of a decision table consider the following excerpt from a processing narrative for a public utility billing system:

> ...if the customer account is billed using a fixed rate method, a minimum monthly charge is assessed for consumption of less than 100 KWH (kilowatt-hours). Otherwise, computer billing applies a Schedule A rate structure. However, if the account is billed using a variable rate method, a Schedule A rate structure will apply to consumption below 100 KWH, with additional consumption billed according to Schedule B.

Figure 6.22 illustrates a decision table representation of the preceding narrative. Each of the five rules indicates one of five viable conditions (e.g., a "T" (true) in both fixed-rate and variable-rate account makes no sense in the context of this procedure).

As a general rule, the decision table can be effectively used to supplement other procedural design tools. It is possible to systematically evaluate the completeness and consistency [HUR83] of a table and to simplify complex alternatives using an approach described in Chapter 8.

		1	2	3	4	5
Conditions	Fixed rate account	T	T	F	F	F
	Variable rate account	F	F	T	T	F
	Consumption < 100 KWH	T	F	T	F	
	Consumption ≥ 100 KWH	F	T	F	T	
Actions	Minimum monthly charge	X				
	Schedule A billing		X	X		
	Schedule B billing				X	
	Other treatment					X

FIGURE 6.22
Resultant decision table.

6.7.4 Program Design Language

Program design language (PDL), called structured English or pseudocode in earlier chapters, is "a pidgin language in that it uses the vocabulary of one language (i.e., English) and the overall syntax of another (i.e., a structured programming language)" [CAI75]. In this chapter PDL is used as a generic reference for a design language. It should be noted, however, that PDL is sometimes used to describe a specific design language developed by Caine, Farber, and Gordon [CAI75].

At first glance PDL looks like Pascal or Ada. The difference between PDL and a real high-order programming language lies in the use of narrative text (e.g., English) embedded directly within PDL statements. Given the combined use of narrative text embedded directly into a syntactical structure, PDL cannot be compiled (at least not yet). However, PDL "processors" currently exist to translate PDL into a graphical representation (e.g., a flowchart) of design and to produce nesting maps, a design operation index, cross reference tables, and a variety of other information.

A program design language may be a simple transposition of a language such as Pascal, or it may be a product purchased specifically for procedural design. Regardless of origin, a design language should have the following characteristics:

- a fixed syntax of *keywords* that provide for all structured constructs, data declaration, and modularity characteristics
- a free syntax of natural language that describes processing features
- data declaration facilities that should include both simple (scalar, array) and complex (linked list or tree) data structures
- subprogram definition and calling techniques that support various modes of interface description

Today, a high-order programming language is often used as the basis for a PDL. For example, Ada-PDL is widely used in the Ada community as a design definition tool. Ada language constructs and format are mixed with English narrative to form the design language.

As an example PDL, we consider a design language modeled after any of the more common "structured" programming languages. A basic PDL syntax should include:

- subprogram definition
- interface description
- data declaration and typing
- techniques for block structuring
- condition constructs
- repetition constructs
- I/O constructs

The format and semantics of the example PDL are presented in the paragraphs below.

During earlier discussions of design, we emphasized the importance of data structure on both a local (per module) and global (program-wide) scale. PDL contains a construct that enables a designer to represent both local and global data structure:

TYPE ‹variable-name› IS ‹qualifier-1› ‹qualifier-2›

where:

‹variable-name›	is a variable contained within a module or declared for global use among modules;
‹qualifier-1›	indicates the specific data structure and includes keywords such as: SCALAR ARRAY LIST STRING STRUCTURE
‹qualifier-2›	indicates how variable names are to be used in the context of a module or program.

PDL also allows the specification of abstract data types [MOR80] that are problem-specific. For example,

TYPE table.1 IS INSTANCE OF symboltable

would be useful in the procedural design of modules for a compiler. The abstract data type *symboltable* would be defined in terms of other data types at some other location in the design.

Referring back to the CAD system example presented in Section 6.3.7, we can use PDL to define a *drawing* that must be globally available to many modules. A drawing is composed of different data types in a specific hierarchy and is therefore characterized as a *heterogeneous structure*. Using PDL:

```
TYPE drawing IS STRUCTURE DEFINED
    number IS STRING LENGTH (12);
    geometry DEFINED
        lines: (x,y) start; (x,y) end; line.type;
        circle: (x,y) center, radius, arc.angle;
        point: (x,y);
        curve: (x[i], y[i]) for i > 2;
    notes IS STRING LENGTH (256);
    BOM DEFINED
        part.sequence IS LIST;
            part.no: STRING format aa-nnnnnn;
            pointer IS PTR;
END drawing TYPE;
```

It is important to note that the above description of *drawing* is *not* a programming language description. The designer should follow the overall syntax of the PDL but can define the constituent parts of drawing in whatever manner is appropriate (and informative). Obviously, the translation of PDL into programming language source code must follow a precise syntax.

The procedural elements of PDL are *block structured*. That is, pseudocode may be defined in blocks that are executed as a single entity. A block is delimited in the following manner:

```
BEGIN ‹block-name›
     ‹pseudocode statements›;
END
```

where ‹blockname› may be used (but is not required) to provide a mode for subsequent reference to a block and ‹pseudocode statements› are a combination of all other PDL constructs. For example:

```
BEGIN ‹draw-line-on-graphics-terminal›
     get end-points from display list;
     scale physical end-points to screen coordinates;
     DRAW a line using screen coordinates;
END
```

The above block makes use of pseudocode statements that describe appropriate processing. The use of a specialized keyword, DRAW, illustrates the manner in which a PDL may be customized to address a specific application.

The condition construct in PDL takes a classic if-then-else form:

```
IF ‹condition-description›
     THEN ‹block or pseudocode statement›;
     ELSE ‹block or pseudo-code statement›;
ENDIF
```

where ‹condition-description› indicates the logical decision that must be made to invoke either *then-part* or *else-part* processing. For example, the following PDL segment describes a decision sequence for a payroll system:

```
IF year.to.date.FICA < maximum
     THEN BEGIN
          calculate FICA.deduction (see formula no.30-1);
          IF (year.to.date.FICA + FICA.deduction) > maximum
               THEN set FICA.deduction = maximum −
               year.to.date.FICA;
               ELSE skip;
          ENDIF
     END
     ELSE set FICA.deduction = 0;
ENDIF
```

Two nested IFs are shown in the PDL segment above. The *then-part* of the outer IF contains a block that combines the inner IF with pseudocode statements. ELSE skip indicates that *else-part* processing is skipped. The ENDIF is used to indicate unambiguous termination of the construct and is particularly useful when nested IFs are represented. The END following the first ENDIF terminates the block that processes FICA information.

The selection (or *select-case*) construct, actually a degenerate set of nested IFs, is represented:

```
CASE OF ‹case-variable-name›:
    WHEN‹case-condition-1›SELECT‹block or pseudocode statement›;
    WHEN‹case-condition-2›SELECT‹block or pseudocode statement›;
    .
    .
    WHEN‹last-case-condition›SELECT‹block or pseudocode statement›;
    DEFAULT: ‹default or error case: block or pseudocode statement›;
ENDCASE
```

In general this construct tests a specific parameter, the *case-variable*, against a set of conditions. Upon satisfaction of a condition, a block or individual pseudocode statement is invoked. As an example of the CASE construct in PDL, we consider a segment for system I/O processing:

```
CASE OF communication-status-bits (csb):
    WHEN csb = clear-to-send SELECT
        BEGIN
            select channel path;
            initiate message transmission;
        END
    WHEN csb = clear-to-receive SELECT initiate buffer management;
    WHEN csb = busy SELECT set queuing bit;
    DEFAULT: process csb content error;
ENDCASE
```

PDL repetition constructs include *pre-test* and *post-test loops* as well as an *indexing loop*:

```
DO WHILE condition-description
    block or pseudocode statement;
ENDDO
REPEAT UNTIL condition-description
    block or pseudocode statement;
ENDREP
DO FOR ‹index = index list, expression, or sequence›
    ‹block or pseudocode statement›;
ENDFOR
```

In addition to standard loop constructs, PDL supports two keywords, NEXT and EXIT, that enable the designer to specify constrained exits from loops. There are situations (as discussed in Section 6.7.2) in which an escape from nested loops is required. The PDL constructs EXIT and NEXT provide constrained violation of purely structured constructs as shown in Figure 6.23. Referring to the figure, EXIT causes a branch to the statement immediately following the repetition construct in which it is contained. NEXT causes a loop processing cycle to be discontinued but restarts repetition on the next loop cycle. By labeling outer loops, EXIT and NEXT can be used to escape from nesting as shown by

ELSE NEXT loop-y

that causes a branch to an outer loop labeled *loop-y*.

As an example of PDL repetition constructs, consider the following analysis loop that tests for convergence of two calculated values:

```
epsilon := 1.0;
no-of-tries := 0;
DO WHILE (epsilon > 0.001 AND no-of-tries <100)
    calculate value-1 := f(x,y,z);
    calculate value-2 := g(x,y,z);
    epsilon := ABSVAL (value-1 – value-2);
    increment no-of-tries by 1; update x, y, z;
ENDDO
```

It should be noted that the loop condition must be defined so that escape from the loop is guaranteed. The *no-of-tries* counter is established for this purpose.

Subprograms and corresponding interfaces are defined using the following PDL constructs:

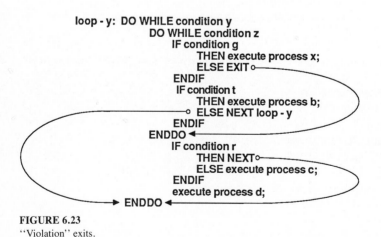

FIGURE 6.23
''Violation'' exits.

```
PROCEDURE ‹subprogram-name› ‹attributes›
INTERFACE ‹argument-list›
    ‹blocks and/or pseudocode statements›;
END
```

where ‹attributes› of a subprogram describe its reference characteristics (e.g., an INTERNAL or EXTERNAL module) and other implementation (programming language) dependent attributes (if any). INTERFACE is used to specify a module argument list that contains identifiers for all incoming and outgoing information.

Input/output specification is highly variable among design languages. Typical forms include:

```
READ/WRITE TO ‹device› ‹I/O-list›
```

or

```
ASK ‹query› ANSWER ‹response-options›
```

where ‹device› indicates the physical I/O device (e.g., CRT, disk, printer, tape) and ‹I/O list› contains variables to be transmitted. ASK-ANSWER is used for human interactive design in which a question-answer format is appropriate. For example:

```
ASK "select processing option" ANSWER "cost," "schedule";
```

I/O specification is frequently expanded to include special characteristics such as audio output or graphical display.

It should be noted that PDL can be extended to include keywords for multitasking and/or concurrent processing, interrupt handling, interprocess synchronization, and many other features. The applications for which PDL is to be used should dictate the final form of the design language.

6.7.5   A PDL Example

To illustrate the use of PDL, we present a more detailed example of a procedural design for home alarm system monitoring software. The home alarm system in question monitors alarms for fire, smoke, burglar, water, and temperature (e.g., furnace breaks while home owner is away during the winter), produces an alarm bell and calls a monitoring service, generating a voice-synthesized message. In the PDL that follows, we illustrate some of the important constructs that have been discussed in Section 6.7.4. Recall that PDL is not a programming language. The designer can adapt as required with no concern for syntax errors. However, the design for the monitoring software would have to be reviewed (do you see any problems?) and further refined before code could be written.

```
PROCEDURE security.monitor;
INTERFACE RETURNS system.status;
```

```
TYPE signal IS STRUCTURE DEFINED
    name IS STRING LENGTH VAR;
    address IS HEX device location;
    bound.value IS upper bound SCALAR;
    message IS STRING LENGTH VAR;
END signal TYPE;
TYPE system.status IS BIT (4);
TYPE alarm.type DEFINED
    smoke.alarm IS INSTANCE OF signal;
    fire.alarm IS INSTANCE OF signal;
    water.alarm IS INSTANCE OF signal;
    temp.alarm IS INSTANCE OF signal;
    burglar.alarm IS INSTANCE OF signal;
TYPE phone.number IS area code + 7-digit number;
        .
        .
        .
initialize all system ports and reset all hardware;
CASE OF control.panel.switches (cps):
    WHEN cps = "test" SELECT
        CALL alarm PROCEDURE WITH
            "on", test.time in seconds;
    WHEN cps = "alarm-off" SELECT
        CALL alarm PROCEDURE WITH
            "off";
    WHEN cps = "new.bound.temp" SELECT
        CALL keypad.input PROCEDURE;
    WHEN cps = "burglar.alarm.off" SELECT
        deactivate signal [burglar.alarm];
        .
        .
        .
    DEFAULT none;
ENDCASE
REPEAT UNTIL activate.switch is turned off
    reset all signal.values and switches;
    DO FOR alarm.type = smoke, fire, water, temp, burglar;
        READ address[alarm.type] signal.value;
        IF signal.value > bound [alarm.type]
            THEN phone.message = message[alarm.type];
                set alarm.bell to "on" for alarm.time seconds;
                PARBEGIN
                    CALL alarm PROCEDURE WITH
                        "on", alarm.time in seconds;
                    CALL phone PROCEDURE WITH
                        message [alarm.type], phone.number;
                ENDPAR
            ELSE skip
        ENDIF
```

```
ENDFOR
ENDREP
END security.monitor
```

Note that the designer for the security.monitor procedure has used a new construct, PARBEGIN...ENDPAR, which specifies a *parallel block*. All tasks specified within the PARBEGIN block are executed in parallel. In this case, implementation details are not considered.

6.7.6 Comparison of Design Notations

In this chapter we have presented a number of procedural design notations. Any comparison must be predicated on the premise that any notation for procedural design, if used correctly, can be an invaluable aid in the design process; conversely, even the best notation, if poorly applied, adds little to understanding. With this thought in mind, we examine criteria that may be applied to compare notations.

A design notation should lead to a procedural representation that is easy to understand and review. In addition the notation should enhance ''code to'' ability so that code does, in fact, become a natural by-product of design. Finally, the design representation must be easily maintainable so that design always correctly represents the program.

The following attributes of design notations have been established in the context of the general characteristics described above:

Modularity. A design notation should support the development of modular software (e.g., direct specification of procedures and block structuring) and provide a means for interface specification.

Overall simplicity. A design notation should be relatively simple to learn, relatively easy to use, and generally easy to read.

Ease of editing. The procedural design may require modification during the design step, during software testing, and, finally, during the maintenance phase of the software engineering process. The ease with which a design representation can be edited can help facilitate each of these software engineering steps.

Machine readability. Computer-aided software engineering environments are being adopted throughout the industry. A notation that can be input directly into a computer-based development system offers enormous potential benefits.

Maintainability. Software maintenance is the most costly phase of the software life cycle. Maintenance of the software configuration nearly always means maintenance of the procedural design representation.

Structure enforcement. The benefits of a design approach that uses structured programming concepts have already been discussed. A design notation that enforces the use of only the structured constructs promotes good design practice.

Automatic processing. A detail design contains information that can be processed to give the designer new or better insights into the correctness and quality of a design. Such insight can be enhanced with reports provided via an automatic processor.

Data representation. The ability to represent local and global data is an essential element of detail design. Ideally, a design notation should represent such data directly.

Logic verification. Automatic verification of design logic is a goal that is paramount during software testing. A notation that enhances the ability to verify logic greatly improves testing adequacy.

"Code-to" ability. The software engineering step that follows procedural design is coding. A notation that is converted easily to source code reduces effort and error.

A natural question that arises in any discussion of design notations is: "What notation is really the best, given the attributes noted above?" An answer to this question is admittedly subjective and open to debate. However, it appears that program design language offers the best combination of characteristics. PDL may be embedded directly into source listings, thereby improving documentation and making design maintenance less difficult. Editing can be accomplished with any text editor or word processing system, automatic processors already exist, and the potential for "automatic code generation" is good.

However, it does not follow that other design notations are necessarily inferior to PDL or are "not good" in specific attributes. The pictorial nature of flowcharts and box diagrams provide a perspective on control flow that many designers prefer. The precise tabular content of decision tables is excellent for table-driven applications. And many other design representations (e.g., see [PET81]) not presented in this book offer their own unique benefits. In the final analysis the choice of a design notation may be more closely related to human factors [SHE81] than to technical attributes.

6.8 DESIGN DOCUMENTATION

The document outline that follows can be used as a model for a *Design Specification.* Each section is composed of numbered paragraphs that address different aspects of the design representation.

Design Specification

1.0 Scope
    1.1 System objectives
    1.2 Hardware, software, and human interfaces
    1.3 Major software functions
    1.4 Externally defined data base
    1.5 Major design constraints, limitations
2.0 Reference documents
    2.1 Existing software documentation
    2.2 System documentation
    2.3 Vendor (hardware or software) documents
    2.4 Technical reference
3.0 Design description
    3.1 Data description

      3.1.1 Review of data flow

      3.1.2 Review of data structure

  3.2 Derived program structure

  3.3 Interfaces within structure

4.0 Modules

  For each module:

  4.1 Processing narrative

  4.2 Interface description

  4.3 Design language (or other) description

  4.4 Modules used

  4.5 Data organization

  4.6 Comments

5.0 File structure and global data

  5.1 External file structure

      5.1.1 Logical structure

      5.1.2 Logical record description

      5.1.3 Access method

  5.2 Global data

  5.3 File and data cross reference

6.0 Requirements cross reference

  (see Figure 6.24)

7.0 Test provisions

  7.1 Test guidelines

Requirement paragraph \ Module name	Module A	Module B	Module C	...	Module Z	
Paragraph 3.1.1	✓				✓	
Paragraph 3.1.2		✓	✓			
Paragraph 3.1.3		✓				
⋮						
Paragraph 3.m.n			✓		✓	

FIGURE 6.24

Requirements cross reference.

The documentation outline presents a complete design description of software. The numbered sections of the *Design Specification* are completed as the designer refines his or her representation of the software.

The overall scope of the design effort is described in Section 1.0 (section numbers here refer to *Design Specification* outline). Much of the information contained in this section is derived from the *System Specification*, and other software definition phase documents. Specific references to supporting documentation are made in Section 2.0.

Section 3.0, the design description, is completed as part of preliminary design. We have noted that design is *information-driven*; that is, flow and/or structure of data will dictate the architecture of software. In this section, data flow diagrams or other data representations, developed during requirements analysis, are refined and used to derive software structure. Because information flow is available, interface descriptions may be developed for elements of the software.

Sections 4.0 and 5.0 evolve as preliminary design moves into detail design. Modules—separately addressable elements of software such as subroutines, functions, or procedures—are initially described with an English language processing narrative. The processing narrative explains the procedural function of a module. Later, a procedural design tool is used to translate the narrative into a structured description.

A description of data organization is contained in Section 5.0. File structures maintained on secondary storage media are described during preliminary design, global data (e.g., Fortran COMMON) are assigned, and a cross reference that connects individual modules to files or global data is established.

Section 6.0 of the *Design Specification* contains a *requirements cross reference*. The purpose of this cross reference matrix is to establish that all requirements are satisfied by the software design and to indicate which modules are critical to the implementation of specific requirements.

The first stage in the development of test documentation is contained in Section 7.0 of the design document. Once software structure and interfaces have been established we can develop guidelines for testing individual modules and integrating the entire package. In some cases a detailed specification of test procedure occurs in parallel with design. In such cases this section may be deleted from the *Design Specification*.

Design constraints, such as physical memory limitations or the necessity for high performance, may dictate special requirements for assembling or packaging of software. Special considerations caused by the necessity for program overlay, virtual memory management, high-speed processing, or other factors may cause modification in design derived from information flow or structure. Requirements and considerations for software packaging are presented in Section 8.0. Secondarily, this section describes the approach that will be used to transfer software to a customer site.

Sections 9.0 and 10.0 of the *Design Specification* contain supplementary data. Algorithm descriptions, alternative procedures, tabular data, excerpts from other documents, and other relevant information are presented as a special note or as a separate appendix. It may be advisable to develop a *Preliminary Operations/Installation Manual* and include it as an appendix to the design document.

6.9 SUMMARY

Design—the first activity in the development phase—is the technical kernel of software engineering. During design, progressive refinements of data structure, program structure, and procedural detail are developed, reviewed, and documented. Design results in representations of software that can be assessed for quality.

A number of fundamental software design concepts have been proposed over the past three decades. Refinement provides a mechanism for representing successive layers of functional detail. Program and data structure contribute to an overall view of software architecture, while procedure provides the detail necessary for algorithm implementation. Modularity (in both program and data) and the concept of abstraction enable the designer to simplify and reuse software components. Information hiding and functional independence provide heuristics for achieving effective modularity.

Software design can be viewed from either a technical or project management perspective. From the technical point of view, design comprises three activities: data design, architectural design, and procedural design. From the project management viewpoint, the design evolves through preliminary and detail design.

Design tools, coupled with structured programming concepts, enable the designer to represent procedural detail in a manner that facilitates translation to code. Graphical, tabular, and textual tools are available.

We conclude our discussion of design fundamentals with the words of Glenford Myers [MYE78]:

> ...we try to solve the problem by rushing through the design process so that enough time will be left at the end of the project to uncover errors that were made because we rushed through the design process...

The moral is: *don't rush through it!* Design is worth the effort.

We have not concluded our discussion of design. In the chapters that follow, a number of important software design methods are introduced. These methods, combined with the fundamentals in this chapter, form the basis for a complete view of software design.

REFERENCES

[AHO83]   Aho, A. V., J. Hopcroft, and J. Ullmann, *Data Structures and Algorithms*, Addison-Wesley, 1983.

[BOH66]   Bohm, C., and G. Jacopini, "Flow Diagrams, Turing Machines and Languages with only Two Formation Rules," *CACM*, vol. 9, no. 5, May 1966, pp. 366–371.

[CAI75]   Caine, S., and K. Gordon, "PDL—A Tool for Software Design," *Proc. National Computer Conference*, AFIPS Press, 1975, pp. 271–276.

[CHA74]   Chapin, N., "A New Format for Flowcharts," *Software—Practice and Experience*, vol. 4, no. 4 , 1974, pp. 341–357.

[COX86]   Cox, B., *Object-Oriented Programming*, Addison-Wesley, 1986.

[DAH72]   Dahl, O., E. Dijkstra, and C. Hoare, *Structured Programming*, Academic Press, London, 1972.

[DEN73]   Dennis, J., "Modularity," *Advanced Course on Software Engineering*, F. L. Bauer, ed. Springer-Verlag, New York, 1973, pp. 128–182.

[DIJ65]   Dijkstra, E., "Programming Considered as a Human Activity," *Proc. 1965 IFIP Congress*, North Holland Publishing Co., 1965.

[DIJ76]   Dijkstra, E., "Structured Programming," in *Software Engineering, Concepts and Techniques*, J. Buxton et al., eds. Van Nostrand Reinhold, 1976.

[EVB86]   *Object-Oriented Design Handbook*, EVB Software Engineering, Rockville, MD, 1986.

[HAB83]   Haberman, N., and D. E. Perry, *Ada for Experienced Programmers*, Addison-Wesley, 1983.

[HUR83]   Hurley, R. B., *Decision Tables in Software Engineering*, Van Nostrand Reinhold, 1983.

[JAC75]   Jackson, M., *Principles of Program Design*, Academic Press, 1975.

[KAI83]   Kaiser, S. H., *The Design of Operating Systems for Small Computer Systems*, Wiley-Interscience, 1983, p. 594ff.

[KRU84]   Kruse, R. L., *Data Structures and Program Design*, Prentice-Hall, 1984.

[MIL72]   Mills, H. D., "Mathematical Foundations for Structured Programming," Technical Report FSC 71-6012, IBM Corp., Federal Systems Division, Gaithersburg, Maryland, 1972.

[MOR80]   Morris, J., "Programming by Successive Refinement of Data Abstractions," *Software—Practice and Experience*, vol. 10, no. 4, April 1980, pp. 249–263.

[MYE78]   Myers, G., *Composite Structured Design*, Van Nostrand, 1978.

[NAS73]   Nassi, I., and B. Shneiderman, "Flowchart Techniques for Structured Programming," SIGPLAN Notices, ACM, August 1973.

[PAR72]   Parnas, D. L., "On Criteria to Be Used in Decomposing Systems into Modules," *CACM*, vol. 14, no. 1, April 1972, pp. 221–227.

[PET81]   Peters, L. J., *Software Design: Methods and Techniques*, Yourdon Press, New York, 1981.

[ROS75]   Ross, D., J. Goodenough, and C. Irvine, "Software Engineering: Process, Principles and Goals," *Computer*, vol. 8, no. 5, May 1975.

[SHE81]   Shepard, S., and E. Kruesi, "The Effects of Symbology and Spacial Arrangement of Software Specifications in a Coding Task," *Proc. Trends and Applications 1981: Advances in Software Technology*, IEEE, Gaithersburg, MD, 1981.

[STE74]   Stevens, W., G. Myers, and L. Constantine, "Structured Design," *IBM Systems Journal*, vol. 13, no. 2, 1974, pp. 115–139.

[TAY59]   Taylor, E. S., "An Interim Report on Engineering Design," Massachusetts Institute of Technology, Cambridge, MA, 1959.

[WAR74]   Warnier, J., *Logical Construction of Programs*, Van Nostrand Reinhold, 1974.

[WAS80]   Wasserman, A., "Principles of Systematic Data Design and Implementation," in

Software Design Techniques, P. Freeman and A. Wasserman, eds. 3d ed., IEEE Computer Society Press, 1980, p. 287–293.

[WAS83]   Wasserman, A., "Information System Design Methodology," *Software Design Techniques*, P. Freeman and A. Wasserman, eds., 4th ed., IEEE Computer Society Press, 1983, p. 43.

[WIR71]   Wirth, N., "Program Development by Stepwise Refinement," *CACM*, vol. 14, no. 4, 1971, pp. 221–227.

[YOU78]   Yourdon, E., and L. Constantine, *Structured Design*, Yourdon Press, 1978.

PROBLEMS AND POINTS TO PONDER

6.1 Do you design software when you "write" a program? What makes software design different from coding?

6.2 Apply a "stepwise refinement approach" to develop three different levels of procedural abstraction for one or more of the following programs:

(*a*) Develop a check writer that, given a numeric dollar amount, will print the amount in words that is normally required on a check.

(*b*) Iteratively solve for the roots of a transcendental equation.

(*c*) Develop a simple round-robin scheduling algorithm for an operating system.

6.3 Is there a case when inequality (6.2) may not be true? How might such a case affect the argument for modularity?

6.4 When should a modular design be implemented as monolithic software? How can this be accomplished? Is performance the only justification for implementation of monolithic software?

6.5 Describe the concept of abstraction for software in your own words.

6.6 Develop at least five levels of abstraction for one of the following software problems:

(*a*) a full screen editor

(*b*) a 3-D transformation package for computer graphics applications

(*c*) a BASIC language interpreter

(*d*) a three degree of freedom robot controller

(*e*) any problem mutually agreeable to you and your instructor

As the level of abstraction decreases, your focus may narrow so that at the last level (source code) only a single task need be described.

6.7 Obtain the original Parnas paper [PAR72] and summarize the software example that he uses to illustrate decomposition of a system into modules. How is information hiding used to achieve the decomposition?

6.8 Discuss the relationship between the concept of information hiding as an attribute of effective modularity and the concept of module independence.

6.9 Review some of your recent software development efforts and grade each module (on a scale of 1 (low) to 7 (high). Bring in samples of your best and worst work.

6.10 A number of high-level programming languages support the internal procedure as a modular construct. How does this construct affect coupling? How does it affect information hiding?

6.11 How are the concepts of coupling and software portability related? Provide examples to support your discussion.

6.12 An enormous literature has evolved on the topic of structured programming. Write a brief paper that highlights the published arguments—pro and con—about the exclusive use of structured constructs.

Problems 6.13–6.21 may be represented using any one (or more) of the design tools that have been presented in this chapter. Your instructor may assign specific tools to specific problems.

6.13 Develop a procedural design for modules that implement the following sorts: Shell-Metzner sort; heapsort; BSST (tree) sort. Refer to a book on data structures if you are unfamiliar with these sorts.

6.14 Develop a procedural design for an interactive user interface that queries for basic income tax information. Derive your own requirements and assume that all tax computations are performed by other modules.

6.15 Develop a procedural design for a garbage collection function for a variable partitioned memory management scheme. Define all appropriate data structures in the design representation. Refer to a book on operating systems for more information.

6.16 Develop a procedural design for a program that accepts an arbitrarily long text as input and produces a list of words and their frequency of occurrence as output.

6.17 Develop a procedural design of a program that will numerically integrate a function f in the bounds a to b.

6.18 Develop a procedural design for a generalized Turing machine that will accept a set of quadruples as program input and produce output as specified.

6.19 Develop a procedural design for a program that will solve the Towers of Hanoi problem. Most books on artificial intelligence discuss this problem in some detail.

6.20 Develop a procedural design for all or major portions of an LR parser for a compiler. Refer to one or more books on compiler design.

6.21 Develop a procedural design for an encryption/decryption algorithm of your choosing.

6.22 Write a one- or two-page argument for the procedural design tool that you feel is best. Be certain that your argument addresses the criteria presented in Section 6.7.6.

FURTHER READINGS

An excellent survey of software design is contained in an anthology edited by Freeman and Wasserman (*Software Design Techniques*, 4th ed., IEEE, 1983). In addition to papers on every important aspect of design, this tutorial reprints many of the "classic" papers that have formed the basis for current trends in software design.

A good discussion of software design fundamentals can be found in books by Myers [MYE78], Peters [PET81], and Fairley (*Software Engineering Concepts*, McGraw-Hill, 1985). An extremely thorough treatment of design representation techniques can be found in a book by Martin and McClure (*Diagramming Techniques for Analysts and Programmers*, Prentice-Hall, 1985).

Mathematically rigorous treatments of computer software and design fundamentals may be found in books by Jones (*Software Development: A Rigourous Approach*, Prentice-Hall, 1980) and Wulf (*Fundamental Structures of Computer Science*, Addison-Wesley, 1981). Each of these texts helps to supply a necessary theoretical foundation for our understanding of computer software.

Fundamental design concepts and what others call "programming" are so closely related that no meaningful distinction can be made. Many excellent books on computer programming (particularly recent books on Pascal, Ada, and C (see Chapter 11 for references) contain many fine examples of good design practice.

Software Tools in Pascal by Kernighan and Plauger (Addison-Wesley, 1981) was written with the premise that "good programming (detailed design) is not learned from generalities, but by seeing ... significant programs.'' The authors provide programming guidance and examples that are invaluable to the student and practitioner alike. Zelkowitz, Shaw, and Gannon (*Principles of Software Engineering and Design*, Prentice-Hall, 1979) dedicate about 80 percent of their book to issues that relate to procedural design. A number of extensive examples are presented.

   Structured Programming—Theory and Practice (R. Linger, H. Mills, and B. Witt, Addison-Wesley, 1979) remains a definitive treatment of the subject. The text contains a good PDL as well as detailed discussions concerning the ramifications of structured programming with regard to program correctness.

CHAPTER

7

DATA FLOW– ORIENTED DESIGN

Design has been described as a multistep process in which representations of data structure, program structure, and procedure are synthesized from information requirements. This description is extended by Freeman [FRE80]:

> ...design is an activity concerned with making major decisions, often of a structural nature. It shares with programming a concern for abstracting information representation and processing sequences, but the level of detail is quite different at the extremes. Design builds coherent, well planned representations of programs that concentrate on the interrelationships of parts at the higher level and the logical operations involved at the lower levels....

As we have noted in the preceding chapter, design is information driven. Software design methodologies are derived from consideration of the information domain.

A data flow–oriented design method is presented in this chapter. The objective of the method is to provide a systematic approach for the derivation of program structure (Section 6.3.3)—a global view of software and the underpinning of preliminary design.

262

7.1 DESIGN AND INFORMATION FLOW

The representation of information flow is one element of the requirements analysis activity that we call information domain analysis (Chapter 4). Beginning with a *fundamental system model* (Chapter 5), information may be represented as a continuous flow that undergoes a series of transforms (processes) as it evolves from input to output. The *data flow diagram* (DFD) is used as a graphical tool to depict information flow. Data flow–oriented design defines a number of different mappings that transform information flow into program structure.

7.1.1 Contributors

Data flow–oriented design (and software design generally) has its origins in earlier design concepts that stressed modularity [DEN73], top-down design [WIR71], and structured programming ([DAH72], [LIN79]). However, the data flow–oriented design approach extended these procedural techniques by explicitly integrating information flow into the design process. Stevens, Myers, and Constantine [STE74] were early proponents of software design based on the flow of data through a system. Early work was refined and presented in books by Myers [MYE78] and Yourdon and Constantine [YOU78]. The methods presented in this chapter are a synthesis of this material.

7.1.2 Areas of Application

Each software design methodology has strengths and weaknesses. An important selection factor for a design method is the breadth of applications to which it can be applied. Data flow–oriented design is amenable to a broad range of application areas. In fact, because all software can be represented by a data flow diagram, a design method that makes use of the diagram could theoretically be applied in every software development effort.

A data flow–oriented approach to design is particularly useful when information is processed sequentially and no formal hierarchical data structure exists. For example, microprocessor control applications, complex numerical analysis procedures, process control, and many other engineering and scientific software applications fall into this category. Extensions to data flow–oriented design, such as DARTS [GOM84], adapt the approach to real-time, interrupt-driven applications and are presented in detail in Chapter 10. Data flow–oriented design techniques are also applicable in data processing applications and can be effectively applied even when hierarchical data structures do exist.

There are cases, however, in which a consideration of data flow is at best a side issue. In such applications (e.g., data base systems, expert systems, object-oriented interfaces), design methods described in Chapters 8 and 9 may be more appropriate.

7.2 DESIGN PROCESS CONSIDERATIONS

Data flow–oriented design allows a convenient transition from information representations (the data flow diagram (DFD) contained in a *Software Requirements Specification*) to a design description of program structure. The transition from information flow to structure is accomplished as part of a five-step process: (1) the type of information flow is established, (2) flow boundaries are indicated, (3) DFD is mapped into program structure, (4) control hierarchy is defined by *factoring*, and (5) resultant structure is refined using design measures and heuristics. The information flow type is the driver for the mapping approach required in step 3. In the following paragraphs we examine two flow types.

7.2.1   Transform Flow

Recalling the fundamental system model (level 01 data flow diagram), information must enter and exit software in an ''external world'' form. For example, data typed on a terminal keyboard, tones on a telephone line, and pictures on a computer graphics display are all forms of external world information. Such externalized data must be converted into an internal form for processing.

The time history of data flow can be illustrated in Figure 7.1. Information enters the system along paths that transform external data into an internal form and is identified as *incoming flow*. At the kernel of the software, a transition occurs. Incoming data are passed through a *transform center* and begin to move along paths that now lead ''out'' of the software. Data moving along these paths are called *outgoing flow*. When a segment of a data flow diagram exhibits these characteristics, *transform flow* is present.

7.2.2   Transaction Flow

The fundamental system model implies transform flow; therefore, all data flow can be placed in this category. However, information flow is often characterized by a single data item, called a *transaction*, that triggers other data flow along one of many paths. When a DFD takes the form shown in Figure 7.2, *transaction flow* is present.

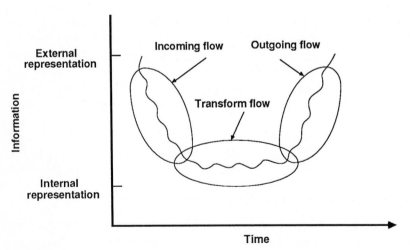

FIGURE 7.1
Flow of information.

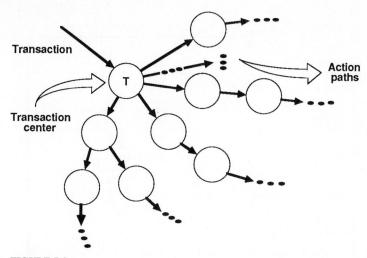

FIGURE 7.2
Transaction flow.

Transaction flow is characterized by data moving along an incoming path that converts external world information into a transaction. The transaction is evaluated, and, based on its value, flow along one of many *action paths* is initiated. The hub of information flow from which many action paths emanate is called a *transaction center*.

It should be noted that within a DFD for a large system, both transform and transaction flow may be present. For example, in a transaction-oriented flow, information flow along an action path may have transform flow characteristics.

7.2.3   A Process Abstract

The overall approach to data flow–oriented design is illustrated in Figure 7.3. Design begins with an evaluation of a detailed data flow diagram. The information flow category (i.e., transform or transaction flow) is established and flow boundaries that delineate the transform or transaction center are defined. Based on the location of boundaries, transforms (the DFD ''bubbles'') are mapped into program structure as modules. The precise mapping and definition of modules is accomplished by distributing control top-down in the structure (called *factoring*) and applying guidelines for effective modularity described in Chapter 6.

Figure 7.3 illustrates a step-by-step approach to design. However, variation and adaptation can and do occur. Above all, software design demands human judgment that can often transcend the ''rules'' of a method.

7.3   TRANSFORM ANALYSIS

Transform analysis is a set of design steps that allows a DFD with transform flow characteristics to be mapped into a predefined template for program structure. In this section, transform analysis is described by applying design steps to an example system.

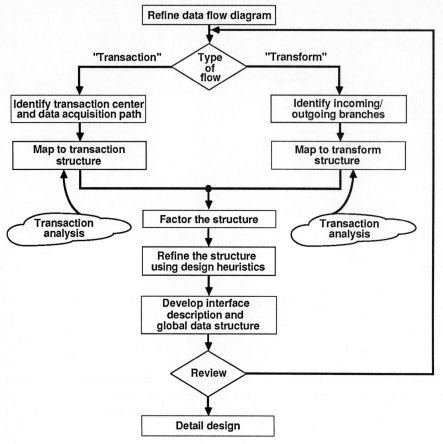

FIGURE 7.3
Data flow–oriented design.

Many good examples of transform analysis have been drawn from commercial data processing applications [YOU78]. As a change of pace, we consider an application from the domain of embedded microprocessor-based systems.

7.3.1 An Example

The era of ''intelligent'' products is upon us. Home entertainment products, appliances, cameras, tools—the list is endless—each require software development. In such products, software is embedded in ROM and becomes a permanent part of the device. As an example of transform analysis in data flow–oriented design, we consider an integrated digital dashboard for an automobile.

Depicted in Figure 7.4, our hypothetical dashboard will perform the following functions:

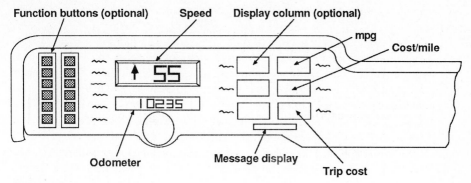

FIGURE 7.4
A design example.

- microprocessor interface via A/D (analog/digital) with transducers at engine, drive train, and chassis locations
- data displayed on LED panels
- indicators for miles per hour (mph), odometer, miles per gallon (mpg), cost/mile, trip cost, and other optional features
- an *overspeed* indicator that rings a chime synchronized to differentiate between current speed (if greater than 55) and 55 mph
- motorist-selectable functions via button array (to be discussed later)

Each of the above features and others would have to be thoroughly evaluated and documented during software requirements analysis. Based on this analysis, level 01 and 02 (Figure 7.5a and b) data flow diagrams and corresponding data dictionaries (Figure 7.5a) are developed.

7.3.2 Design Steps

The above example will be used to illustrate each step in transform analysis. The steps begin with a re-evaluation of work done during requirements analysis and then move to the development of program structure.

Step 1. Review the fundamental system model. The fundamental system model encompasses the level 01 DFD and supporting information. In actuality the design step begins with an evaluation of both the *System Specification* and the *Software Requirements Specification*. Both documents describe information flow and structure at the software interface. Figure 7.5a and b depict top-level data flow for the digital dashboard.

Step 2. Review and refine data flow diagrams for the software. Using information obtained from a *Software Requirements Specification*, a level 03 data flow diagram derived for the digital dashboard is shown in Figure 7.5c. Incoming data flow at the upper left is a converted rotation signal that is read and converted into signals per second. Time average and change in signal (measured in signals per second (sps)) are used to drive speedometer functions and to indicate acceleration or deceleration, respectively.

Once average sps is converted to rpm, speed (in mph) is developed and used to ring a synchronous chime (if speeding), to generate mph display and is also used as one data item to compute fuel consumption in miles per gallon (mpg). The odometer function also uses rpm as incoming data. All of these functions lead to a display on the dashboard.

Acceleration and deceleration are indicated by an arrow to the left of the speed display (Figure 7.4). An up arrow indicates acceleration, a bar indicates steady speed, and a down arrow indicates deceleration. Finally, a second incoming path collects fuel flow data, converting it to gallons per hour for fuel efficiency calculation and display.

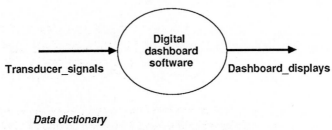

Data dictionary

transducer_signals=rotation_signal + fuel_flow_signal

dashboard_displays=mph_display + arrow + mpg_
display + odometer + chime

rotation_signal = ...

(a)

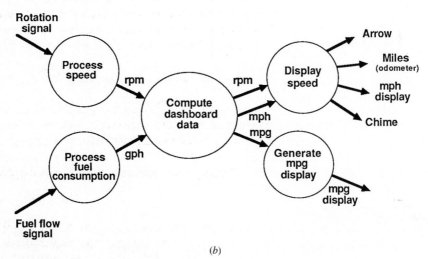

(b)

FIGURE 7.5

(a) Digital dashboard software—level 01 DFD. (b) Digital dashboard software—level 02 DFD.

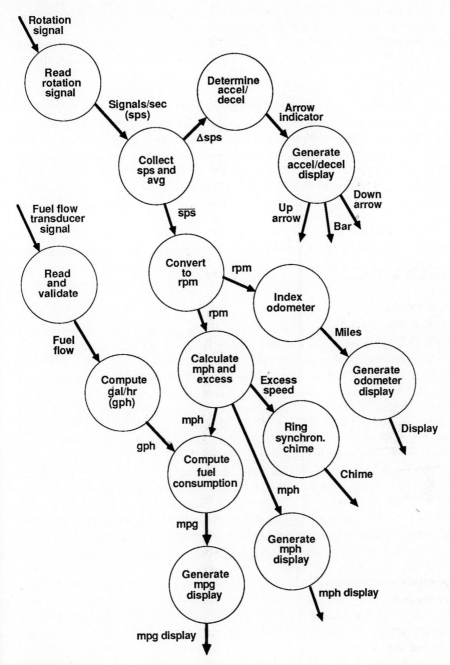

FIGURE 7.5
(c) Digital dashboard software—level 03 DFD.

Each transform in the data flow diagram shown in Figure 7.5c exhibits relatively high *cohesion* (Chapter 6). That is, the process implied by a transform performs a single, distinct function. Therefore, the DFD in Figure 7.5c contains sufficient detail for a "first cut" at the design of program structure and we proceed without further refinement.

Step 3. Determine whether the DFD has transform or transaction characteristics. In general, information flow within a system can always be represented as transform. However, when an obvious transaction characteristic (Figure 7.2) is encountered, a different design mapping is recommended. In this step, the designer selects a global (software-wide) flow characteristic based on the prevailing nature of the DFD. In addition, local regions of transform or transaction flow are isolated. These *subflows* can be used to refine program structure derived from a global characteristic described above.

Evaluating the dashboard DFD (Figure 7.5c), we see data entering the software along two incoming paths and exiting along five outgoing paths. No distinct transaction center is implied (although the transform *calculate mph and excess* could be perceived as such). Therefore, an overall transform characteristic will be assumed for information flow.

Step 4. Isolate the transform center by specifying incoming and outgoing flow boundaries. In the preceding section incoming flow was described as a path in which information is converted from external to internal form; outgoing flow is converted from internal to external form. Incoming and outgoing flow boundaries are open to interpretation; that is, different designers may select slightly different points in the flow as boundary locations. In fact, alternative design solutions can be derived by varying the placement of flow boundaries. Although care should be taken when boundaries are selected, a variance of one bubble along a flow path will generally have little impact on the final program structure.

Flow boundaries for the digital dashboard example are illustrated in Figure 7.6. The transforms (bubbles) that make up the transform center lie within the two boundaries that run from top to bottom in the figure. An argument can be made to re-adjust a boundary (e.g., an incoming flow boundary separating *read and validate* and *compute gal/hr (gph)* could be proposed). The emphasis in this design step should be on selecting reasonable boundaries rather than lengthy iteration on placement of divisions.

Step 5. Perform "first-level factoring." Program structure represents a top-down distribution of control. *Factoring* results in a program structure in which top-level modules perform decision making and low-level modules perform most input, computational, and output work. Middle-level modules perform some control and do moderate amounts of work.

When transform flow is encountered, a DFD is mapped to a specific structure that provides control for incoming, transform, and outgoing information processing. This *first-level factoring* is illustrated in Figure 7.7. A control module, C_m, resides at the top of the program structure and serves to coordinate the following subordinate control functions:

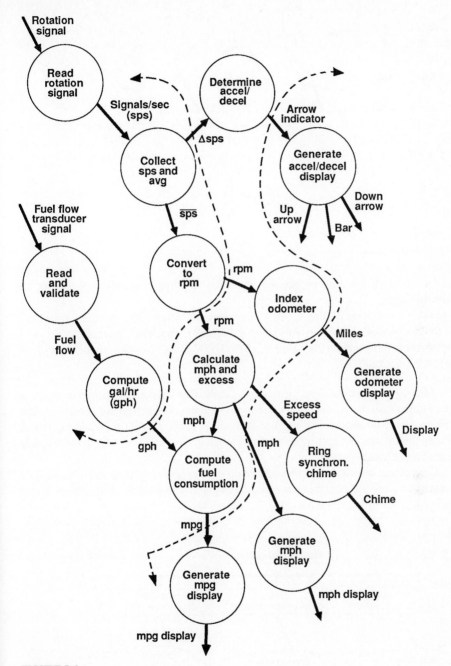

FIGURE 7.6
Digital dashboard software—level 03 DFD with flow boundaries.

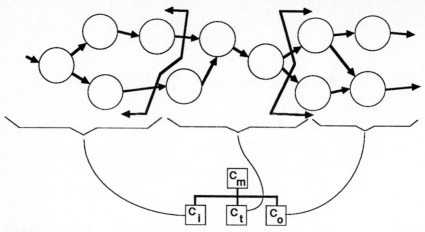

FIGURE 7.7
Transaction mapping.

- an incoming information processing controller, C_i, that coordinates receipt of all incoming data,
- a transform center controller, C_t, that supervises all operations on data in internalized form (e.g., a module that invokes various "number crunching" procedures),
- an outgoing information processing controller, C_o, that coordinates production of output information.

Although a three-pronged structure is implied by Figure 7.7, complex flows in large systems may dictate two or more control modules for each of the generic control functions described above. The number of modules at the first level should be limited to the minimum that can accomplish control functions and still maintain good coupling and cohesion characteristics.

Continuing the digital dashboard example, first-level factoring is illustrated as a structure in Figure 7.8. Each control module is given a name that implies the function of the subordinate modules it controls.

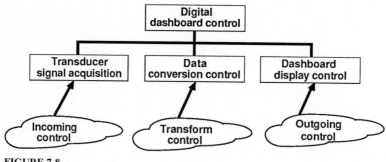

FIGURE 7.8
First-level factoring.

Step 6. Perform "second level factoring." *Second-level factoring* is accomplished by mapping individual transforms (bubbles) of a DFD into appropriate modules within the program structure. Beginning at the transform center boundary and moving outward along incoming and then outgoing paths, transforms are mapped into subordinate levels of the software structure. The general approach to second-level factoring is illustrated in Figure 7.9.

Although Figure 7.9 illustrates a one-to-one mapping between DFD transforms and software modules, different mappings frequently occur. Two or even three bubbles can be combined and represented as one module (recognizing potential problems with cohesion) or a single bubble may be expanded to two or more modules. Practical considerations and measures of design quality dictate the outcome of second-level factoring.

Program structure derived from the incoming flow paths of the DFD (Figure 7.6) are shown in Figure 7.10. A simple one-to-one mapping of bubbles to modules can be observed by following flow backward from the transform center boundary. Review and refinement may lead to changes in this structure, but it can serve as a "first-cut" design.

Second-level factoring for the transform center of digital dashboard software is shown in Figure 7.11. Each data conversion or calculation transform of the DFD is mapped into a module subordinate to the transform controller. Finally, outgoing flow is mapped into program structure as illustrated in Figure 7.12. Factoring is again accomplished by moving outward from the transform center boundary.

Each of the modules shown in Figures 7.10, 7.11, and 7.12 represents an initial design of program structure. Although modules are named in a manner that implies function, a brief processing narrative should be written for each. The narrative describes:

- information that passes into and out of the module (an interface description);
- information that is retained by a module, e.g., data stored in a local data structure;

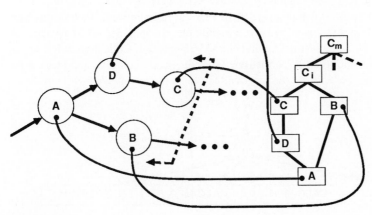

FIGURE 7.9
Second-level factoring.

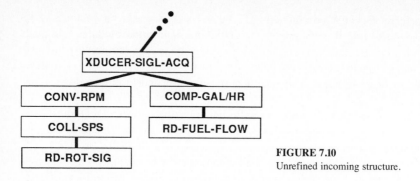

FIGURE 7.10
Unrefined incoming structure.

- a procedural narrative that indicates major decision points and tasks;
- a brief discussion of restrictions and special features (e.g., file I/O, hardware-dependent characteristics, special timing requirements).

The narrative serves as a first generation *Design Specification*. However, further refinement and additions occur regularly during this period of design.

Step 7. Refine the "first-cut" program structure using design measures and heuristics. A first-cut program structure can always be refined by applying concepts of module independence. Modules are *exploded* or *imploded* to produce sensible factoring, good cohesion, minimal coupling, and, most importantly, a structure that can be implemented without difficulty, tested without confusion, and maintained without grief.

Refinements are dictated by practical considerations and common sense. There are times, for example, when the controller for incoming data flow is totally unnecessary, when some input processing is required in a module that is subordinate to the transform controller, when high coupling due to global data cannot be avoided, or when optimal structural characteristics (see Section 7.7) cannot be achieved. Software requirements coupled with human judgment is the final arbiter.

Many modifications can be made to the first-cut structure developed for the digital dashboard example. Among many possibilities: (1) modules CONV-RPM and COLL-SPS in the incoming structure branch can be imploded. Collection of transducer signals and conversion to an RPM measure are sequentially cohesive and make sense

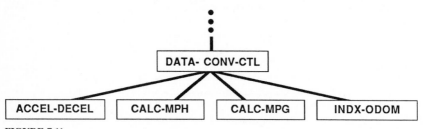

FIGURE 7.11
Unrefined transform structure.

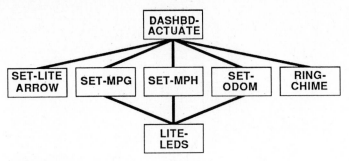

FIGURE 7.12
Unrefined outgoing structure.

in this context; (2) module ACCEL-DECEL can be placed subordinate to CALC-MPH—this arrangement reduces coupling by simplifying information transfer through the transform controller, DATA-CONV-CTL; (3) module SET-LITE-ARROW can also be placed subordinate to SET-MPH to conform to structural change above.

The refined software structure for the digital dashboard is shown in Figure 7.13. Design constraints (e.g., memory limitations or run-time performance) may dictate further revisions. For example, RD-ROT-SIGNAL and CONV-RPM could be imploded (at the expense of relatively low cohesion) or DATA-CONV-CTL could be removed and control functions performed by DIG-DASH-CTL.

The objective of the preceding seven steps is to develop a global representation of software. That is, once structure is defined, we can evaluate and refine software architecture by viewing it as a whole. Modifications made at this time require little additional work, yet can have a profound impact on software quality and maintainability.

The reader should pause for a moment and consider the difference between the design approach described above and the process of "writing programs." If code is the only representation of software, the developer will have great difficulty evaluating or refining at a global or holistic level and will, in fact, have difficulty "seeing the forest for the trees."

7.4 TRANSACTION ANALYSIS

In many software applications, a single data item triggers one or a number of information flows that affect a function implied by the triggering data item. The data item, called a *transaction*, and its corresponding flow characteristics were discussed in Section 7.2.2. In this section we consider design steps used to treat transaction flow.

7.4.1 An Example

Transaction analysis will be illustrated by considering an extension of the digital dashboard software presented in the previous section. The basic dashboard system has optional features that include an "electronic key" and a "function selection/display" facility. An ignition start-up sequence of numbers is keyed via a button array (Figure

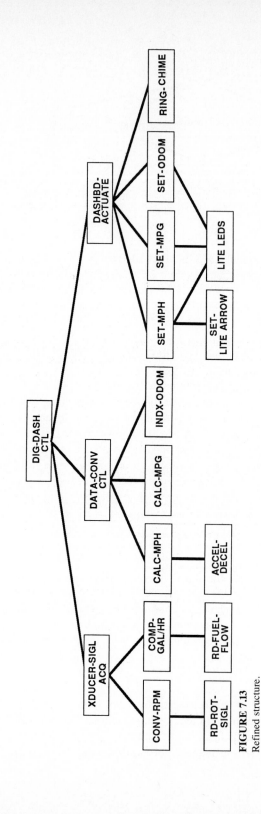

FIGURE 7.13
Refined structure.

7.4) and replaces the ignition key. The array is also used to initiate the following functions:

Button	Function selected
1	Initiate ignition start-up sequence
2	Activate radar detector (only available where legal!)
3	Activate display of various engine functions including oil pressure, temperature, etc.
4	Display trip computer data
5	Enter trip computer data
6	Cancel previous key (clear)

Applying the data flow analysis techniques described in Chapter 5, level 01 and 02 data flow diagrams and corresponding data dictionaries are developed (Figure 7.14a and b). Further refinement results in the level 03 DFD shown in Figure 7.14c.

Referring to Figure 7.14c, the array button or "function key" hit is a primary input that drives subsequent flow. After the key is validated, flow moves along one of a number of paths that are entered upon determination of which button was pressed. In the figure, paths for buttons 1 and 2 are shown in detail, while other paths are indicated with single shaded transforms (of course, these bubbles would have to be refined) to simplify the drawing.

It should be noted that information flow along both paths 1 and 2 incorporates additional incoming data. Each path also produces displays, messages, and/or alarms.

7.4.2 Design Steps

Design steps for transaction analysis are similar and in some cases identical to steps for transform analysis (Section 7.3). A major difference lies in the mapping of DFD to program structure.

Step 1. Review the fundamental system model.

Step 2. Review and refine data flow diagrams for the software.

Step 3. Determine whether the DFD has transform or transaction characteristics. Steps 1, 2, and 3 are identical to corresponding steps in transform analysis. The DFD shown in Figure 7.14c has a classic transaction flow characteristic. However, flow along each of the information paths emanating from the *invoke keyboard function* bubble appears to have transform flow characteristics. Therefore, flow boundaries must be established for both flow types.

Step 4. Identify the transaction center and the flow characteristics of each action path. The location of the transaction center can be immediately discerned from the DFD. The transaction center lies at the origin of a number of information paths that flow radially from it. For dashboard flow shown in Figure 7.14c, the *invoke keyboard function* bubble is the transaction center.

The incoming path (i.e., the flow path along which a transaction is received) and all action paths must also be isolated. Boundaries that define a reception (incoming) path and action paths are shown in Figure 7.15. Each action path must be evaluated for its individual flow characteristic. For example, the radar detection path (shown en-

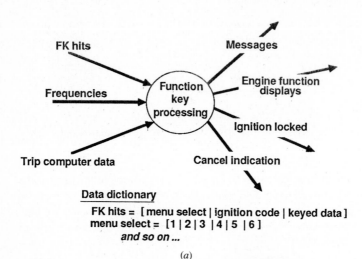

Data dictionary

FK hits = [menu select | ignition code | keyed data]
menu select = [1 | 2 | 3 | 4 | 5 | 6]
and so on ...

(*a*)

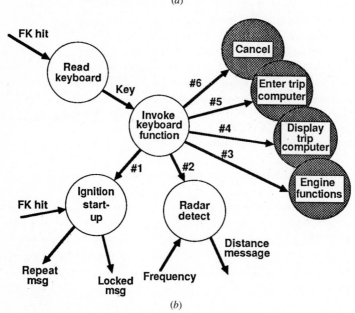

(*b*)

FIGURE 7.14
(*a*) Dashboard function key processing—level 01 DFD. (*b*) Dashboard function key processing—level 02 DFD.

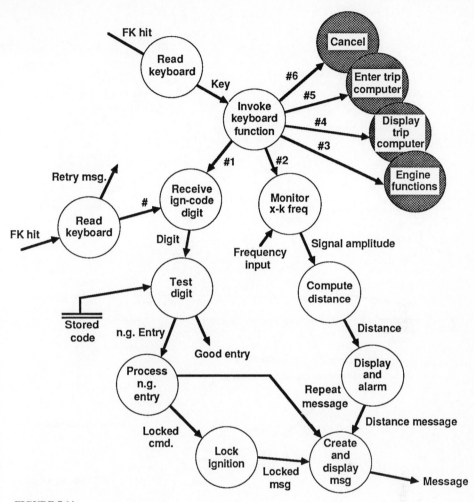

FIGURE 7.14

(c) Dashboard function key processing—level 03 DFD.

closed by a shaded area in Figure 7.15) has transform characteristics. Incoming, transform, and outgoing flow are indicated with dashed boundaries.

Step 5. Map the DFD into a software structure amenable to transaction processing. Transaction flow is mapped into a program structure that contains an incoming branch and a dispatch branch. Structure for the incoming branch is developed in much the same way as transform analysis. Starting at the transaction center, bubbles along the incoming path are mapped into modules. The structure of the dispatch branch contains a dispatcher module that controls all subordinate action modules. Each action flow path of the DFD is mapped to a structure that corresponds to its specific flow characteristics. This process is illustrated in Figure 7.16.

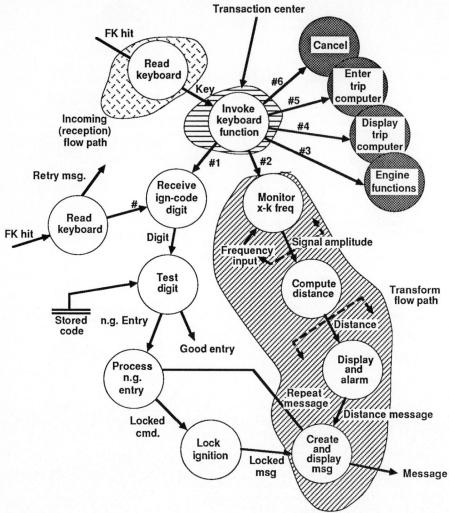

FIGURE 7.15
Isolating the flow regimes—level 03 DFD.

Considering the digital dashboard flow, first-level factoring for step 5 is shown in Figure 7.17. Module READ-KEYBD performs all reception operations passing the transaction (a function key hit) via the transaction controller, FUNC-KEY-CTL, to the dispatcher module, INVOKE-KEYBD-FUNCTION. Subordinate to the dispatcher, modules IGN-CODE-EVALUATION, RADAR-DETECT, and others act as control modules for each action.

Step 6. Factor and refine the transaction structure and the structure of each action path. Each action path of the data flow diagram has its own information flow characteristics. We have already noted that transform or transaction flow may be encountered.

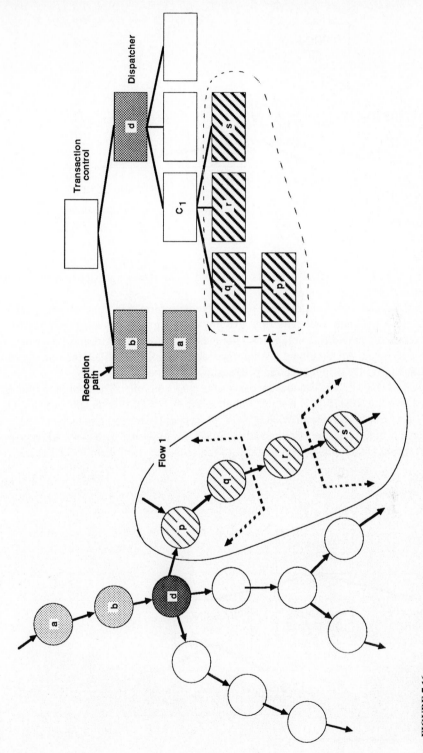

FIGURE 7.16
Transaction mapping.

281

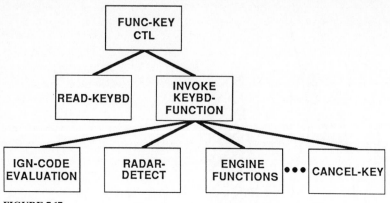

FIGURE 7.17
Map the transaction structure.

The action path related *substructure* is developed using the design steps discussed in this and the preceding sections.

As an example, consider the radar detector information flow shown (inside shaded area) in Figure 7.15. The flow exhibits classic transform characteristics. Frequencies are monitored (incoming flow) producing input to a transform center when a signal is received. An alarm and warning message (outgoing flow) are then produced. The structure for the resultant action path is shown in Figure 7.18.

A RADAR-DETECT module serves as the main controller. The incoming flow is mapped into a MONITOR X-K FREQ module. Module COMPUTE DISTANCE performs transform functions and WARNING-CTL acts as the outgoing branch controller. To maintain high cohesion, two modules, DISPLAY MSG and RING-ALARM, perform reporting functions as subordinates to the outgoing controller. The DFD trans-

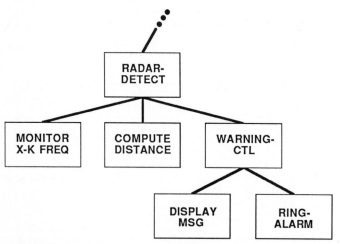

FIGURE 7.18
Develop action path structure.

form *create and display message* is mapped into a utility module (i.e., a module called by two or more modules) that is used by two action flow structures.

The overall software structure is illustrated in Figure 7.19. Ignition code and radar detection functions are factored to illustrate development of action branches. It should be noted that within each transform substructure input is acquired and output is produced. The DISPLAY-MSG module is subordinate to two action paths, exhibiting *fan-in*, a common feature of transaction structures.

Step 7. Refine the "first-cut" software structure using design measures and heuristics. This step for transaction analysis is identical to the corresponding step for transform analysis. In both design approaches, criteria such as module independence, practicality (efficacy of implementation and test), and maintainability must be carefully considered as structural modifications are proposed.

7.5 DESIGN HEURISTICS

Once a program structure is developed using data flow–oriented design, effective modularity can be achieved by applying the concepts introduced in Chapter 6 and manipulating the resultant structure according to the following set of heuristics (guidelines).

I. Evaluate the preliminary program structure to reduce coupling and improve cohesion. Once program structure has been developed, modules may be *exploded* or *imploded* with an eye toward improving module independence (Figure 7.20). The processing description of each module is examined to determine if a common process component can be exploded from two or more modules and redefined as a separate cohesive module. When high coupling is expected, modules can sometimes be imploded to reduce passage of control, reference to global data, and interface complexity.

II. Attempt to minimize structures with high fan-out; strive for fan-in as depth increases. The structure shown on the left-hand side of Figure 7.21, does not make effective use of factoring. In general, a more reasonable distribution of control is shown in the right-hand structure of the figure. The structure takes an oval shape, indicating a number of layers of control and highly utilitarian modules at lower levels.

III. Keep scope of effect of a module within the scope of control of that module. The *scope of effect* of a module *m* is defined as all other modules that are affected by a decision made in module *m*. The *scope of control* of module *m* is all modules that are subordinate and ultimately subordinate to module *m*. Figure 7.22 illustrates a violation of heuristic III and a modification that satisfies the heuristic.

IV. Evaluate module interfaces to reduce complexity and redundancy and improve consistency. Module interface complexity is a prime cause of software errors. Interfaces should be designed to pass information simply and should be consistent with the function of a module. Interface inconsistency (i.e., seemingly unrelated data passed via an argument list or other technique) is an indication of low cohesion. The module in question should be re-evaluated.

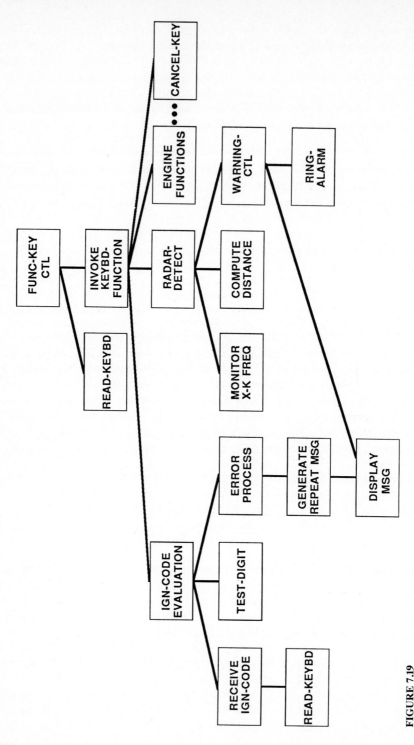

FIGURE 7.19
Dashboard function key processing — program structure.

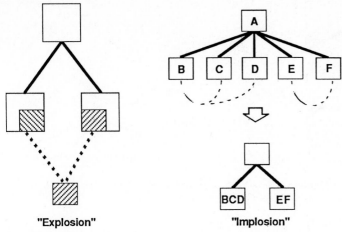

"Explosion" "Implosion"

FIGURE 7.20
Explosion and implosion.

V. Define modules whose function is predictable, but avoid modules that are overly restrictive. A module is predictable when it can be treated as a black box; that is, the same external data will be produced regardless of internal processing details. Modules that have internal "memory" can be unpredictable unless care is taken in their use. The procedural flow shown in Figure 7.23 illustrates a module that "remembers" an internal flag and uses the flag to select processing options. Because the flag is invisible to superordinate modules, confusion can arise.

A module that restricts processing to a single subfunction exhibits high cohesion and is viewed with favor by a designer. However, a module that arbitrarily restricts size of a local data structure, options within control flow, or modes of external interface will invariably require maintenance to remove such restrictions.

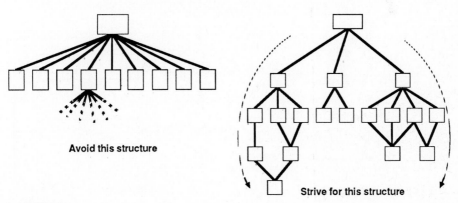

Avoid this structure **Strive for this structure**

FIGURE 7.21
Fan-in and fan-out.

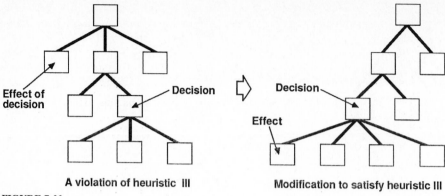

A violation of heuristic III   **Modification to satisfy heuristic III**

FIGURE 7.22
Scope of effect and control.

VI. Strive for single-entry, single-exit modules, avoiding "pathological connections." This design heuristic warns against content coupling (Chapter 6). Software is easier to understand, and therefore easier to maintain, when modules are entered at the top and exited at the bottom. *Pathological connection* refers to branches or references into the middle of a module.

VII. Package software based on design constraints and portability requirements. *Packaging* alludes to the techniques used to assemble software for a specific processing environment. Design constraints sometimes dictate that a program "overlay" itself in memory. When this must occur, the design structure may have to be reorganized to group modules by degree of repetition, frequency of access, and interval between

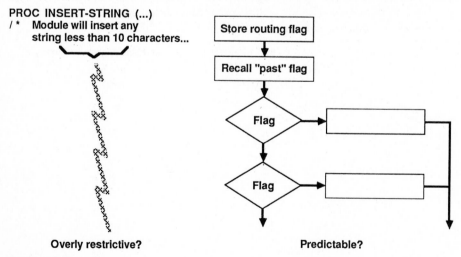

Overly restrictive?   **Predictable?**

FIGURE 7.23
Restrictive and predictable modules.

calls. In addition, optional or "one-shot" modules may be separated in the structure so that they may be overlaid effectively. An excellent discussion of packaging considerations for software design is presented in Yourdon and Constantine [YOU78].

7.6 DESIGN POSTPROCESSING

Successful application of transform or transaction analysis is supplemented by additional documentation that is required as part of preliminary design. After program structure has been developed and refined, the following tasks must be completed:

- A processing narrative is developed for each module.
- An interface description is provided for each module.
- Local and global data structures are defined.
- All design restrictions/limitations are noted.
- A preliminary design review (PDR) is conducted.
- "Optimization" is considered (if required and justified).

A processing narrative is (ideally) an unambiguous, bounded description of processing that occurs within a module. The narrative describes processing tasks, decisions, and I/O. The following narrative might be used for the RADAR-DETECT module shown in Figure 7.18:

> RADAR-DETECT is a control module for the radar detection function. The module invokes monitoring of X-K band frequencies, polling a monitoring module for occurrence of signal. If an occurrence is detected, RADAR-DETECT first invokes a distance computation and then passes control to warning generation modules.

The narrative serves as a top-level procedural description that will subsequently be refined during detailed procedural design.

An interface description provides a list of all data that enter and exit a module. The description should include data that move across an argument list, external world I/O, and information items acquired from global data areas. In addition, subordinate and superordinate modules are noted. As an example, consider an interface description (using the program design language introduced in Chapter 6) for a digital dashboard module, CALC-MPG:

```
PROCEDURE calc-mph;
    INTERFACE ACCEPTS:
        TYPE miles-per-hour IS NUMERIC,
        TYPE gallons-per-hour IS NUMERIC;
    INTERFACE RETURNS:
        TYPE miles-per-gallon IS NUMERIC;
    * no external I/O or global data used *
    * called by: data-conv-ctl *
    * calls: no subordinate modules *
```

The design of data structures can have a profound impact on program structure and the procedural details for each module. (Design techniques driven by data structure rather than data flow are discussed in Chapter 8.) Both local and global data structures must be defined after program structure has been established.

Warnier diagrams (Chapter 5) may be used to represent the organization of data. Figure 7.24 illustrates local data required for module DISPL-TRIP-COMP of the digital dashboard system.

Restrictions and/or limitations for each module are also documented. Typical topics for discussion include: restriction of data type or format, memory or timing limitations, bounding values or quantities of data structures, special cases not considered, and specific characteristics of an individual module.

The purpose of a restrictions/limitations section is to reduce the number of errors introduced because of ''assumed'' functional characteristics. As an example, consider the following excerpt from restrictions/limitations of module RING-CHIME: ''…chime frequency is a function of automobile speed….chime frequency has a lower limit of 0.5 Hz at 56 mph and an upper limit of 3.0 Hz at 80 mph….'' This excerpt specifies bounding values that restrict the function of the module.

Once design documentation has been developed for all modules, a preliminary design review is conducted (see Chapter 12 for review guidelines). The review emphasizes traceability to software requirements, quality of program structure, interface descriptions, data structure descriptions, implementation and test practicality, and maintainability.

7.7   DESIGN OPTIMIZATION

Any discussion of design optimization should be prefaced with the following comment: ''Remember that an 'optimal design' that does not work has questionable merit.'' The software designer should be concerned with developing a representation

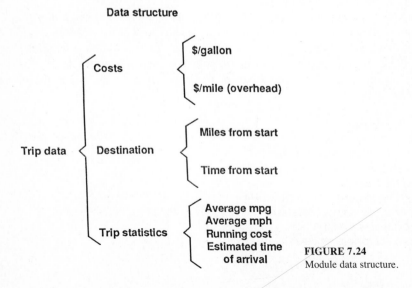

FIGURE 7.24
Module data structure.

of software that will meet all functional and performance requirements and merit acceptance based on design measures and heuristics.

Refinement of program structure during the early stages of design is to be encouraged. Alternative representations may be derived, refined, and evaluated for the "best" approach. This approach to optimization is one of the true benefits derived by developing a representation of software architecture.

It is important to note that structural simplicity often reflects both elegance and efficiency. Design optimization should strive for the smallest number of modules consistent with effective modularity and the least complex data structure that adequately serves information requirements.

For time-critical applications, it may be necessary to "optimize" during detailed design and possibly during coding. The software developer should note, however, that a relatively small percentage (typically 10–20 percent) of a program often accounts for a large percentage (50–80 percent) of all processing time. It is not unreasonable to propose the following approach for time-critical software:

1. Develop and refine program structure without concern for time-critical optimization.
2. During detail design, select modules suspected to be "time hogs" and carefully develop procedures (algorithms) for time efficiency.
3. Code in a high-order programming language.
4. Instrument the software to isolate modules that account for heavy processor utilization.
5. If necessary, redesign or recode in machine-dependent language to improve efficiency.

This approach follows a dictum that will be further discussed in a later chapter: "Get it to work, then make it fast."

7.8 SUMMARY

Data flow–oriented design is a methodology that uses information flow characteristics to derive program structure. A data flow diagram is mapped into program structure using one of two design analysis techniques—transform analysis or transaction analysis.

Transform analysis is applied to an information flow that exhibits distinct boundaries between incoming and outgoing data. The DFD is mapped into a structure that allocates control to input, processing, and output along three separately factored module hierarchies.

Transaction analysis is applied when an information item causes flow to branch along one of many paths. The DFD is mapped into a structure that allocates control to a substructure that acquires and evaluates a transaction. Another substructure controls all potential processing actions based on a transaction.

The techniques presented in this chapter lead to a preliminary design description of software. Modules are defined, interfaces are established, and data structure is developed. These design representations form the basis for all subsequent development work.

REFERENCES

[DAH72]   Dahl, O., E. Dijkstra, and C. Hoare, *Structured Programming*, Academic Press, 1972.

[DEN73]   Dennis, J. B., "Modularity," *Advanced Course on Software Engineering*, F. L. Bauer, ed., Springer-Verlag, New York, 1973, pp. 128–182.

[FRE80]   Freeman, P., "The Context of Design," *Software Design Techniques*, P. Freeman and A. Wasserman, eds., IEEE Computer Society Press, 3d ed., pp. 2–4.

[GOM84]   Gomaa, H., "A Software Design Method for Real Time Systems," *CACM*, vol. 27, no. 9, September 1984, pp. 938–949.

[LIN79]   Linger, R. C., H. D. Mills, and B. I. Witt, *Structured Programming*, Addison-Wesley, 1979.

[MYE78]   Myers, G., *Composite Structured Design*, Van Nostrand, 1978.

[STE74]   Stevens, W., G. Myers, and L. Constantine, "Structured Design," *IBM System Journal*, vol. 13, no. 2, 1974, pp. 115–139.

[WIR71]   Wirth, N., "Program Development by Stepwise Refinement," *CACM*, vol. 14, no. 4, 1971, pp. 221–227.

[YOU78]   Yourdon, E., and L. Constantine, *Structured Design*, Yourdon Press, 1978.

PROBLEMS AND POINTS TO PONDER

7.1 Write a paper that tracks the progress of software design methodologies from 1970 to the present. A starting point for reference material can be the contributors noted in Section 7.1.1.

7.2 Some designers contend that all data flow may be treated as transform-oriented. Discuss how this contention will affect the software structure that is derived when a transaction-oriented flow is treated as transform. Use an example flow to illustrate important points.

7.3 If you have not done so, complete Problem 5.9. Use the design methods described in this chapter to develop a program structure for the PMS.

7.4 Propose an approach to the design of real-time software applications that makes use of data flow–oriented techniques. To begin your discussion, list problems with real-time systems (e.g., interrupt-driven) that make direct application of data flow–oriented design somewhat unwieldy. Compare your approach to the one proposed in Chapter 10.

7.5 Using a data flow diagram and a processing narrative, describe a computer-based system that has distinct transform flow characteristics. Define flow boundaries and map the DFD into a program structure using the technique described in Section 7.3.

7.6 Using a data flow diagram and a processing narrative, describe a computer-based system that has distinct transaction flow characteristics. Define flow boundaries and map the DFD into a program structure using the technique described in Section 7.4.

7.7 Using requirements that are derived from a classroom discussion, complete the DFDs and architectural design for the digital dashboard example presented in Sections 7.3 and 7.4. Assess the functional independence of all modules. Document your design.

7.8 For readers with a background in compiler design: Develop a DFD for a simple compiler, assess its overall flow characteristic, and derive a program structure using the techniques described in this chapter. Provide processing narratives for each module.

7.9 How does the concept of *recursive modules* (i.e., modules that invoke themselves) fit into the design philosophy and techniques presented in this chapter?

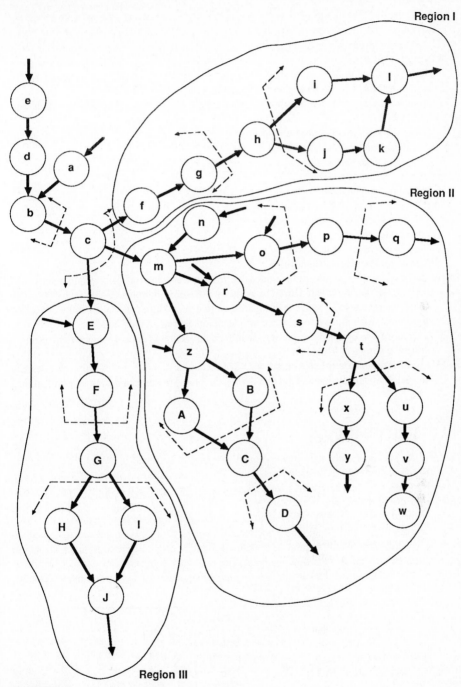

FIGURE 7.25
Problem 7.10.

7.10 Using the DFD in Figure 7.25, apply transaction analysis to the DFD and derive a program structure. The overall flow characteristic should be assumed to be transaction flow (with transaction center at transform c). Flow in region I is transform; flow in region II is transaction, with transform subflows as shown; flow in region III is transform. Your program structure should have modules that correspond on a one-to-one basis with the transforms in the figure. It will be necessary to derive a number of control modules.

7.11 Discuss the relative merits and difficulties of applying data flow–oriented design in the following areas:

(*a*) embedded microprocessor applications

(*b*) engineering/scientific analysis

(*c*) computer graphics

(*d*) operating system design

(*e*) business applications

(*f*) data base management system design

(*g*) communications software design

(*h*) compiler design

(*i*) process control applications

(*j*) artificial intelligence applications

7.12 Given a set of requirements provided by your instructor (or a set of requirements for a problem on which you are currently working) develop a complete design including all design documentation. Conduct a design review (Chapter 12) to assess the quality of your design. This problem may be assigned to a team rather than an individual.

7.13 The data flow–oriented design approach does not address (directly) a key element in the design of software. What is it?

7.14 List at least three attributes of software that sometimes require optimization and describe how a systematic design method that derives program structure can assist in such optimization.

FURTHER READINGS

A complete presentation of data flow–oriented design may be found in Myers [MYE78], Yourdon and Constantine [YOU78], and Page-Jones (*The Practical Guide to Structured Systems Design*, Yourdon Press, 1980). These books are dedicated to design alone and provide a comprehensive tutorial in the data flow approach. Each text contains numerous examples and all are strongly recommended for those readers who intend to actively apply the data flow method.

To gain further insight into the modern application of data flow–oriented analysis and design, it is worthwhile to survey product literature for automated software tools and workstation environments that support data flow methods. The following companies are a small sample of vendors of computer-aided software engineering tools that address data flow–oriented methods:

Company	Software tool
Cadre Technologies, Inc.	*Teamwork/SA, SD, RT*
Index Technology Corporation	*Excelerator*
Interactive Development Environments, Inc.	*Rapid/USE, DFE, SCE*
Knowledge, Inc.	*Information Engineering Workbench*
Nastec Corporation	*DesignAid*
Promod, Inc.	*Promod*

CHAPTER 8

DATA STRUCTURE–ORIENTED DESIGN

The intimate relationship between software and data can be traced to the origins of computing. The original concept behind the stored program computer is that programs could be viewed as data and data interpreted as programs. The structure of information, called *data structure*, has been shown to have an important impact on the complexity and efficiency of algorithms designed to process information.

As software design methods have evolved over the past decade, one school of thought holds that:

> The identification of the inherent data structure (for a computer-based system) is vital, and the structure of data (input and output) can be used to derive the structure (and some details) of a program [PET77].

In many areas of application, a distinct, hierarchical information structure exists. Input data, internally stored information (i.e., a data base), and output data may each have a unique structure. Data structure–oriented design makes use of these structures as a foundation for the development of software.

8.1 DESIGN AND DATA STRUCTURE

Data structure affects the design of both the structural and procedural aspects of software. Repetitive data are always processed with software that has control facilities for repetition; alternative data (i.e., information that may or may not be present) precipitate software with conditional processing elements; a hierarchical data organization frequently has a remarkable resemblance to the program structure of the software that uses the data. In fact the structure of information is an excellent predictor of program structure.

Data structure–oriented design transforms a representation of data structure into a representation of software. Like data flow–oriented techniques (Chapter 7), developers of data structure–oriented design have defined a set of "mapping" procedures that use information (data) structure as a guide.

8.1.1   Contributors

The origins of data structure–oriented design can be found in technical discussions on the "fundamentals of data structures" (e.g., [TRE76]), computer algorithms [HOR78], the structure of control and data [WUL81], and the concept of data abstractions [GUT77]. More pragmatic treatments of software design and its relationship to data structure have been proposed by Jackson ([JAC75], [JAC83]), Warnier ([WAR74], [WAR81]), and Orr ([ORR81], [HAN83]).

Jackson System Development methodology takes the view that "paralleling the structure of input data and output (report) data will ensure a quality design" [JAC75]. More recent extensions to the methodology focus on the identification of information entities and the actions that are applied to them and are quite similar in some respects to the object-oriented design approach described in Chapter 9. Jackson emphasizes practicality, developing pragmatic techniques to transform data into program structure.

Logical Construction of Programs (LCP), developed by J.D. Warnier [WAR74], provides a rigorous method for software design. Drawing upon the relationship between data structure and procedural structure, Warnier develops a set of techniques that accomplish a mapping from input/output data structure to a detailed procedural representation of software.

Data Structured Systems Development (DSSD), also called the Warnier-Orr Methodology ([ORR81], [HAN83]), is an extension of LCP and adds strong analysis as well as design capabilities. The DSSD approach provides a notation and procedures for deriving data structure, program structure, and detailed procedural design of program components (modules). In addition, DSSD provides a notation that enables the designer to examine data flow between sources and receivers of information and through processes that transform information.

A technique called Logical Construction of Software [CHA80] is representative of a synthesis of both data flow– and data structure–oriented design approaches. The developers of the method contend that "logical design can be described explicitly if the software is viewed as a system of data sets and data transforms" [CHA80].

8.1.2   Areas of Application

Data structure–oriented design may be successfully applied in applications that have a well-defined, hierarchical structure of information. Typical examples include:

- *Business Information Systems applications*. Input and output have distinct structure (e.g., input files, output reports); the use of a hierarchical data base is common.
- *Systems applications*. The data structure for operating systems comprises many tables, files, and lists that have well-defined structure.
- *CAD/CAM/CAE applications*. Computer-aided design/manufacturing/engineering systems require sophisticated data structures for information storage, translation, and processing.

In addition, applications from the engineering/scientific domain, computer-aided instruction, combinatorial problem solving, and many other areas may be amenable to data structure–oriented design.

In general, data structure–oriented design is more difficult to learn and more complicated to apply than data flow–oriented techniques (Chapter 7). However, the data structure–oriented school of design offers a richer and potentially more powerful approach to software design.

8.1.3 Data Structure versus Data Flow Techniques

Before considering differences between data structure– and data flow–oriented design, it is important to note that both begin with analysis steps that lay the foundation for subsequent design steps; both are information driven; both attempt to transform information into a software representation; both are based on separately derived concepts of "good" design.

Data structure–oriented design does not make explicit use of a data flow diagram. Therefore, transform and transaction flow classifications have little relevance to the data structure–oriented design method. More importantly, the ultimate objective of data structure–oriented methods is to produce a procedural description of the software. The concept of program modular structure is not explicitly considered. Modules are considered a byproduct of procedure, and the idea of module independence is given little emphasis.

Data structure–oriented design makes use of a hierarchical diagram to represent information structure. Therefore, the emphasis during software requirements analysis must be placed on these modes of representation.

It should be noted that a third important school of thought, object-oriented design (OOD) methods, has gained widespread attention in recent years and is presented in Chapter 9. OOD represents a third alternative for software design, borrowing certain ideas from its data flow– and data structure–oriented predecessors, while adding many new and important concepts of its own.

8.2 DESIGN PROCESS CONSIDERATIONS

Software requirements analysis remains the foundation for data structure–oriented design. The description of the information domain (data structure, content, and flow) contained in the *Software Requirements Specification* foreshadows software architecture to be developed during design. Each design method provides a set of "rules" that enable the designer to transform data structure into a representation of software.

Each data structure–oriented method has its own set of rules. However, the following design tasks are always conducted: (1) data structure characteristics are evaluated; (2) data are represented in terms of elementary forms such as sequence, selection, and repetition; (3) data structure representation is mapped into a control hierarchy for software; (4) software hierarchy is refined using guidelines defined as part of a method; and (5) a procedural description of software is ultimately developed.

A clean division between architectural and procedural design steps (as they have been described as part of the software design process) is not as evident in data structure–oriented methods. Jackson, Warnier, and Orr move quickly to a procedural representation.

8.3 JACKSON SYSTEM DEVELOPMENT

Like most software design methodologies, Jackson System Development (JSD) is actually a continuum of technical steps that support software analysis and design. In Chapter 5 the analysis-oriented steps of JSD were presented. The reader is urged to review Section 5.5 before continuing with this section.

To conduct JSD the analyst and designer conduct the following steps:

- *Entity action step*. Using an approach that is quite similar to the object-oriented analysis technique described in Chapter 4, *entities* (people, objects, or organizations that a system needs to produce or use information) and *actions* (the events that occur in the real world that affect entities) are identified.
- *Entity structure step*. Actions that affect each entity are ordered by time and represented with *Jackson diagrams*.
- *Initial model step*. Entities and actions are represented as a process model; connections between the model and the real world are defined.
- *Function step*. Functions that correspond to defined actions are specified.
- *System timing step*. Process scheduling characteristics are assessed and specified.
- *Implementation step*. Hardware and software are specified as a design.

The first three steps in JSD have been described in Section 5.5. To summarize, the *entity action step* begins with a brief English language statement of a problem from which entities (nouns) and actions (verbs) are chosen. Only those entities and actions that have direct relationship to the software solution are chosen for further evaluation.

The *entity structure step* creates a Jackson diagram that describes a time-ordered specification of the actions performed on or by an entity. The Jackson diagram, depicted in Figure 8.1 (for the *University Shuttle Service* example introduced in Section 5.5), is created for each entity (*shuttle* and *button* entities in the case of Figure 8.1) and is often accompanied by narrative text.

The *initial model step* begins the construction of a specification of the system as a model of the real world. The specification is created with a system specification diagram (SSD) using symbology that is illustrated in Figure 8.2. A *data stream connection* occurs when one process transmits a stream of information (e.g., writes records) and the other process receives the stream (e.g., reads records). Arrowheads

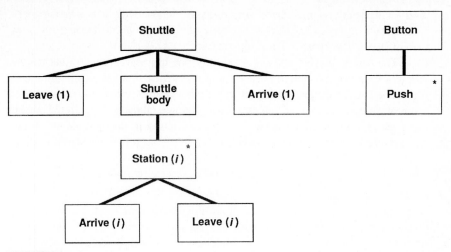

FIGURE 8.1
Jackson structure diagrams.

represent the direction of information flow, and the circle represents the data stream, which is assumed to be placed in a FIFO buffer of unlimited capacity. A *state vector connection* occurs when one process directly inspects the state vector of another process. Arrowheads represent the direction of information flow and the diamond indicates the state vector. This connection is common in process control applications in which it is necessary to check the state of some electromechanical device. By convention the suffix 0 represents a real-world process and the suffix 1 represents a system-model process.

8.3.1 JSD Design Steps

In order to discuss design steps for Jackson System Development, we continue the University Shuttle Service (USS) example presented in Section 5.5. Reproducing the problem statement:

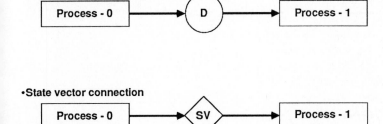

FIGURE 8.2
SSD notation.

A large university is spread over two campuses which are more than a mile apart. To help students who must travel between campuses to get to lectures on time, the university plans to install a shuttle service.

The shuttle service makes use of only one high-speed shuttle that travels over tracks between a station at each campus. Each station has a call button that students can use to request transport to the other station. When students arrive at a station, they push the call button. If the shuttle is already there, they board it and depart for the other station. If the shuttle is in transit, they must wait for it to stop at the other station, board students (if any), and return. If the shuttle is at the other station, it leaves to pick up the students who pushed the button. The shuttle will wait at a station until the next request for service (a pushed button) occurs.

Entities are selected by examining all nouns in the description. After review, the following candidate entities are chosen: *university, campus, students, lectures, shuttle, station, button*. We are not directly concerned with *campus, lectures, students*, or *stations* — all of these lie outside the model boundary and are rejected as possible entities. *University* is merely a collective term for both campuses, so we reject it as a possible entity. We select *shuttle* and *button*. Using a similar analysis, we select *arrive, push, and leave* as actions that affect *shuttle* and *button*.

The Jackson structure diagram for *shuttle* and *button* are shown in Figure 8.1. The system specification diagram for USS is illustrated in Figure 8.3. Finally, the initial model step for USS is conducted as described in the following discussion (reproduced from Section 5.5.3).

Whenever possible, we prefer to connect model processes with real-world entities by data streams so that direct correspondence between the behavior of the model and the real world is assured. In our example the call button emits a pulse when pressed. This can be transmitted to the *button-1* process as a data stream connection. However, we shall assume that the sensors that detect arrival or departure of the shuttle do not emit a pulse but do close an electric switch. The state of the switch (on/off) can be accessed. Hence, a state vector connection is required.

The internal details of model processes are specified using what Jackson calls *structure text*. Structure text represents the same information as structure diagrams (Fig-

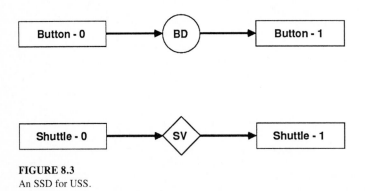

FIGURE 8.3
An SSD for USS.

ure 8.4)—sequence, selection, repetition—but does so in a textual format. The structure text for *button-1* is:

```
BUTTON-1
    read BD;
    PUSH-BDY itr while BD
        PUSH;
        read BD;
    PUSH-BDY end
BUTTON-1 end
```

The structure of BUTTON-1 corresponds exactly to the structure of BUTTON-0, with the addition of *read* operations that connect the real world to the system.

As noted earlier, the SHUTTLE-1 process cannot be connected to its real-world counterpart by a data stream connection. Instead, we must interrogate the switches that are turned on/off by the arrival/departure of the shuttle at a station. The system process must inspect the real-world entity frequently enough to ensure that no actions pass undetected. This is accomplished by executing a *getsv* (get state vector) operation that obtains the state vector of the real-world entity. It is likely that the system process will obtain each value of the state vector a number of times before it is changed, and the model process can be elaborated to show these "in transit" values of the state vectors. A structure text description of SHUTTLE-1 follows:

```
SHUTTLE-1 seq
    getsv SV;
    WAIT-BDY itr while WAIT1
        getsv SV;
```

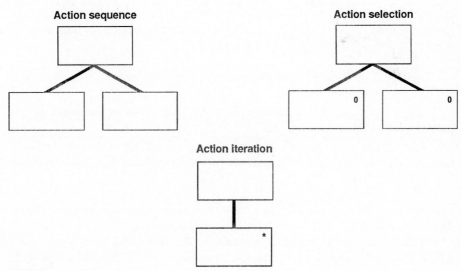

FIGURE 8.4
Structure diagram notation.

```
    WAIT-BDY end
    LEAVE (1);
    TRANSIT-BDY1 itr while TRANSIT1
        getsv SV;
    TRANSIT-BDY1 end
    SHUTTLE-BDY1 itr
        STATION seq
            ARRIVE (i);
            WAIT-BDY itr while WAITi
                getsv SV;
            WAIT-BDY end
            LEAVE (i);
            TRANSIT-BDY itr while TRANSITi
                getsv SV;
            TRANSIT-BDY end
        STATION END
    SHUTTLE-BDY end
    ARRIVE (1);
SHUTTLE-1 end
```

The state values WAIT and TRANSIT represent appropriate values of the arrival and departure switch. The real-world process SHUTTLE-0 produces a change of state in the switch, and the system process SHUTTLE-1 executes *getsv* operations to sense this change. Figure 8.5a illustrates the structure text for SHUTTLE-1 as a structure diagram.

8.3.2 The Function Step

The purpose of the JSD function step is to expand the system specification diagram by connecting newly defined function processes to the model processes by data or vector streams. JSD recognizes three kinds of functions:

Embedded functions. This function is achieved by allocating (write) operations to a model process structure text.

Imposed functions. This function inspects the state vector of the model process and produces output results.

Interactive functions. This function inspects the state vector of the model process, writes a data stream to affect the actions of the model process, and includes operations to write results.

The outputs of the function processes are system outputs and may be reports, commands to hardware devices, or any other outgoing information.

To illustrate the function step, we consider the USS example and examine the model of the shuttle. In the shuttle there is a light panel used to indicate arrival at the station by lighting a display message. The lamps are switched on/off by the lamp commands LON(i) and LOFF(i). A function must be embedded into the shuttle process model to write a command to lamp(i) when the shuttle arrives at station(i); another command must be generated to switch lamp(i) off when the shuttle leaves station(i). Thus, as the shuttle travels between stations, it outputs a data stream consisting of lamp commands. The SSD that represents this situation is shown in Figure 8.5b.

To implement the lamp commands, the structure text for SHUTTLE-1 is modified as follows:

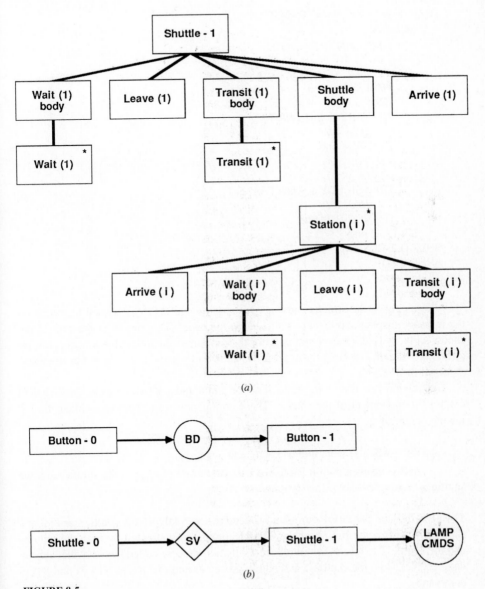

(a)

(b)

FIGURE 8.5
(a) Structure diagram corresponding to structure text. (b) Updated SSD.

```
SHUTTLE-1 seq
    LON(1);
    getsv SV;
    WAIT-BDY itr while WAIT1
        getsv SV;
    WAIT-BDY end
    LOFF(1);
    LEAVE (1);
    TRANSIT-BDY1 itr while TRANSIT1
        getsv SV;
    TRANSIT-BDY1 end
    SHUTTLE-BDY1 itr
        STATION seq
            ARRIVE (i);
            LON(i);
            WAIT-BDY itr while WAITi
                getsv SV;
            WAIT-BDY end
            LOFF(i);
            LEAVE (i);
            TRANSIT-BDY itr while TRANSITi
                getsv SV;
            TRANSIT-BDY end
        STATION end
    SHUTTLE-BDY end
    ARRIVE (1);
SHUTTLE-1 end
```

Referring to the structure text above, a command (LON) is issued to switch on the message display announcing station 1 on the panel. This occurs at the start of the shuttle's life, before it leaves station 1 for the first time. Each time the sensors indicate arrival at a station, we light the appropriate lamp and when the shuttle leaves, the lamp is turned off (LOFF).

A second function is to produce motor commands, START and STOP, that will control the movement of the shuttle. These commands are to be issued under the following conditions:

STOP—when sensors indicate arrival at a station.

START—when a button is pushed (the first time) to request the shuttle, and the shuttle is waiting at one of the stations.

The need to issue the STOP command is determined solely by the shuttle's arrival at a station. However, the timing of the START command is affected by both the buttons and the shuttle. Therefore, we introduce a function process called *mcontrol* that acts on data received from the shuttle-1 and button processes and that issues START and STOP commands.

The connection between the shuttle-1 process and *mcontrol* will be by data stream S1D. This means that the shuttle-1 process cannot miss the arrival of the shuttle, as may occur if the state vector were periodically inspected.

The structure text for the shuttle-1 process is reproduced once more, this time amended for lamp and motor control:

```
SHUTTLE-1 seq
    LON(1)
    getsv SV;
    WAIT-BDY itr while WAIT1
        getsv SV;
    WAIT-BDY end
    LOFF(1);
    LEAVE (1);
    TRANSIT-BDY1 itr while TRANSIT1
        getsv SV;
    TRANSIT-BDY1 end
    SHUTTLE-BDY1 itr
        STATION seq
            ARRIVE (i);
            write arrive to S1D;
            LON(i);
            WAIT-BDY itr while WAITi
                getsv SV;
            WAIT-BDY end
            LOFF (i);
            LEAVE (i);
            TRANSIT-BDY itr while TRANSITi
                getsv SV;
            TRANSIT-BDY end
        STATION end
    SHUTTLE-BDY end
    ARRIVE (1);
    write arrive to S1D;
SHUTTLE-1 end
```

It is necessary to ensure that the shuttle-1 process executes *getsv* SV operations, and that *mcontrol* reads its arrival records with sufficient frequency to stop the shuttle in time. Timing constraints, scheduling, and implementation are considered in JSD steps that follow.

To complete the USS example, we return to the model for the button entity. The original model, button-1, is an accurate statement of button actions, but it is now necessary to distinguish between the first push requesting a journey and subsequent pushes before the journey actually starts. A new level-2 process, button-2, is described to accommodate these requirements and is depicted with a Jackson structure diagram in Figure 8.6.

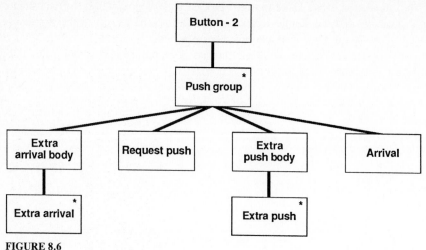

FIGURE 8.6
University shuttle service—function step.

A function process inspects the state vector of button-2 to determine whether there is an outstanding request for a journey. The *mcontrol* function informs button-2 when a request has been serviced, i.e., when the shuttle has arrived at the station where the request was made. It does this by passing the arrival records it receives from shuttle-1. Thus, an interactive function for the button-2 process is defined.

Structure text for the button-2 process follows:

```
BUTTON-2 seq
    request := no;
    read MBD and B1D;
    BUTTON-BDY itr
        PUSH-GROUP seq
            EXTRA-AR-BDY itr while (ARRIVAL)
                read MBD and B1D;
            EXTRA-AR-BDY end
            RQ-PUSH seq
                request := yes;
                read MBD and B1D;
            RQ-PUSH end
            EXTRA-RQ-PUSH itr while
                read MBD and B1D;
            EXTRA-RQ-PUSH end
            ARRIVAL seq
                request := no;
                read MBD and B1D;
            ARRIVAL end
        PUSH-GROUP end
    BUTTON-BDY end
BUTTON-2 end
```

The input to button-2 consists of two data streams, merged in a manner that is termed a *rough merge*. A rough merge occurs when the reading process simply accepts the next record that occurs in a data stream. Therefore, the order in which records are processed is dependent on two potentially asynchronous writing processes. For this example, the rough merge is sufficient. However, JSD provides other types of merging that would introduce less indeterminacy into the system [JAC83].

Figure 8.7 shows a system specification diagram that reflects all changes imposed as part of the function step. An embedded function within shuttle-1 generates lamp commands, and a new function process, *mcontrol*, imposes an interactive function on button-2 and produces motor commands for the shuttle. The double lines on MBD output implies a "one to many" connection. The structure of the *mcontrol* process is derived by examining input and output data structures (Sections 8.3.4 and 8.3.5).

8.3.3   System Timing Step

In this JSD step, the designer specifies timing constraints imposed on the system. The earlier design steps produce a system composed of sequential processes that communicate by data streams and direct inspection of state vectors. The relative scheduling of processing is indeterminate.

One mechanism that can be used to synchronize processes is the *time grain marker* (TGM). The TGM is a data record indicating the occurrence of a particular interval of time and can be used to enable the passage of time to affect the actions of a process.

The timing constraints for the University Shuttle Service example might include:

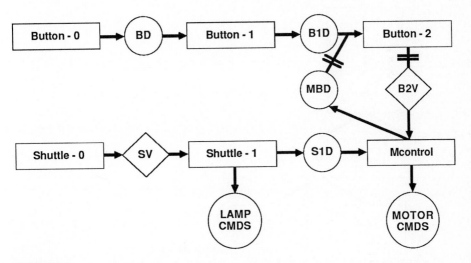

FIGURE 8.7
SSD, extended for functions 1 and 2.

1. the time within which the STOP command must be issued based on the shuttle forward speed and braking power
2. response times for switching the panel lamps on/off

For the USS example, there is no need to introduce any special synchronization mechanism. To some extent, the interchange of data has already imposed some degree of synchronization.

8.3.4   The Implementation Step

The implementation step of JSD draws on earlier work [JAC75] to derive remaining program or process structure from problem data structure. In this section and the one following, an overview of the Jackson's program design approach is presented. The mappings associated with this approach are the reason that this design methodology has been categorized as data structure–oriented.

The essence of the implementation step may be stated by paraphrasing Jackson: "Problems should be decomposed into hierarchical structures of parts that may be represented by three structural forms." The "structural forms" that Jackson alludes to are sequence, condition, and repetition—in actuality, *procedural constructs* (in the terminology of this book) that are the foundation of the structured programming philosophy (Chapter 6).

Data structure notation is a variation of the Jackson structure diagram and is illustrated in Figure 8.8. Referring to the figure, a collection of data, A, is composed of multiple occurrences (denoted by *) of data substructure B. B includes multiple occurrences of C and another substructure D that contains data item E or F (alternative

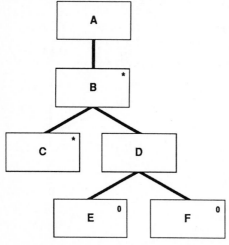

* = multiple occurrences; ⁰ = selection

FIGURE 8.8
Data structure notation.

data are denoted by an O). Jackson's block diagram representation of information hierarchy may be applied to input, output, or data base structures with equal facility.

As a more concrete example of this notation, we consider software to be developed for a credit card accounting system (grossly simplified) shown in Figure 8.9. A *payment-file*, containing customer numbers (CNO), payment date (DATE), and amount paid (AMT) is to be reconciled with a customer master file that contains CNO and outstanding balance. The payment file is presorted into customer number groupings (CNO-GROUP) so that all payments by an individual are contained within a single record. The data structure for both files, described in Jackson notation, is shown in the figure.

An output report format for the credit card accounting system and the resultant data structure diagram are shown in Figure 8.10. The report implies a hierarchy that includes customer data (CUST-DATA) and master totals. Substructures indicate information contained within the hierarchy.

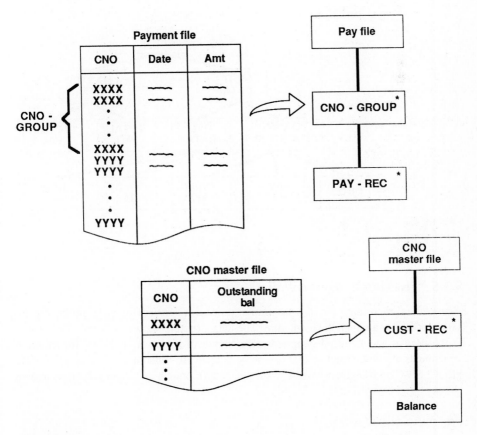

FIGURE 8.9
Credit card billing system.

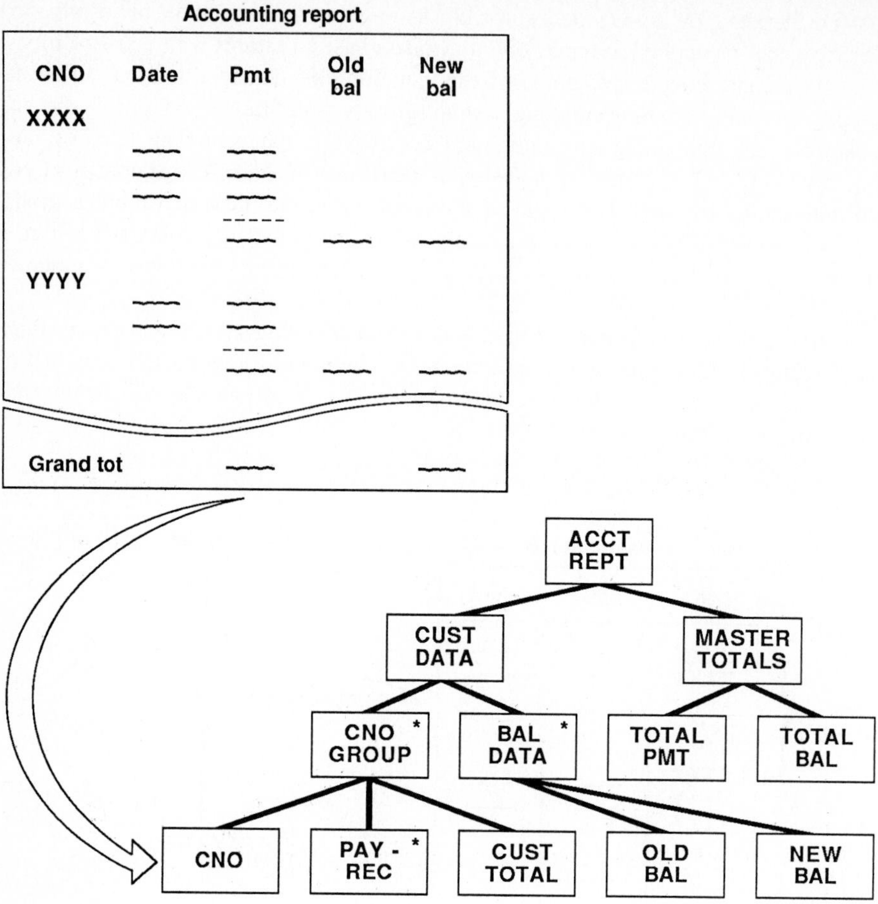
Accounting report
CNO
Date
Pmt
Old bal
New bal
XXXX
YYYY
Grand tot
ACCT REPT
CUST DATA
MASTER TOTALS
CNO GROUP *
BAL DATA *
TOTAL PMT
TOTAL BAL
CNO
PAY - REC *
CUST TOTAL
OLD BAL
NEW BAL

FIGURE 8.10
System output.

8.3.5 Procedural Representation

A procedural representation of a program or process is derived directly from the organization of its hierarchical data structure. The data structure shown in Figure 8.10 results in the derivation of the program structure shown in Figure 8.11. Using the program structure as a guide, structure text can be developed. To illustrate, structure text for the PROCESS-CUST-DATA (process customer data) branch of Figure 8.11 is shown below.

```
PROCESS-CUST-DATA seq
    open PAY-FILE;
    open C-M-F;
    PROCESS CNO-GROUP iter until eof:PAY-FILE;
```

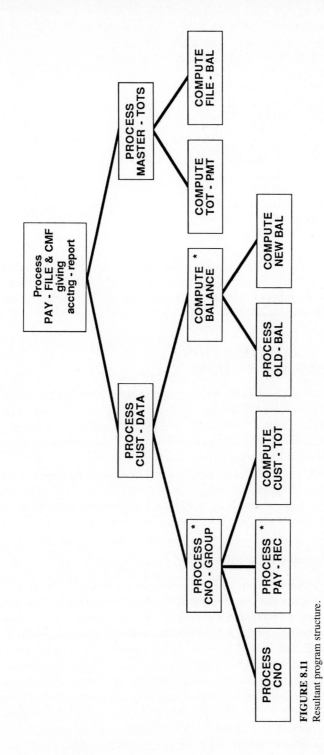

FIGURE 8.11
Resultant program structure.

```
      read PAY-FILE;
      PROCESS-CNO (read C-M-F, finds old balance)
      PROCESS-PAY-REC iter until end: CNO-GROUP;
          write report line;
          compute total payments;
          read PAY-FILE;
      end PROCESS-PAY-REC
      COMPUTE-CUST-TOTAL;
      COMPUTE-BALANCE seq
          PROCESS-OLD-BAL;
          COMPUTE-NEW-BAL;
          write report line;
      end COMPUTE-BALANCE
   end PROCESS-CNO-GROUP
end PROCESS-CUST-DATA
```

Jackson's methodology supports a number of supplementary techniques that broaden its applicability and enrich the overall design approach. A complete discussion of each of these techniques is best left to Jackson himself. The interested reader should refer to [JAC75] and [JAC83].

8.4 LOGICAL CONSTRUCTION OF PROGRAMS AND SYSTEMS

Warnier [WAR74], like Jackson, was among the early investigators who recognized the relationship between data and program structure. Logical Construction of Programs and the more recent Logical Construction of Systems (collectively referred to as LCP) were developed to define a set of "rules" and "laws" that govern the structure of information and the resultant organization of derived software.

LCP presents procedures for analysis and design. Beginning with formal representation of data structure, the method leads to the derivation of procedure and culminates with systematic methods for pseudocode generation, verification, and optimization. In the sections that follow, a number of important aspects of LCP are presented.

8.4.1 The Warnier Diagram

Data structure notation used in LCP is the *Warnier diagram* (introduced in Chapter 5). Like Jackson's hierarchical diagram, the Warnier representation of data depicts hierarchy as well as explicit repetitive and conditional information. Basic diagram characteristics are illustrated in Figure 8.12. Referring to the figure, a data file contains three record types (1, 2, and 3) that are encountered 4 times, 0 or 1 time, and n times, respectively. Data record 1 contains items a, b, and c. Data record 2 contains item f and an item g that may or may not be present (occurs 0 or 1 time). Data record 3 always contains item e and may contain n items comprising m occurrences of element i.

A "rule" stated by Warnier indicates that "any set of information must be subdivided into subsets...."[WAR74]. The Warnier diagram accomplishes this subdivision with additional specification of the number of occurrences of data ele-

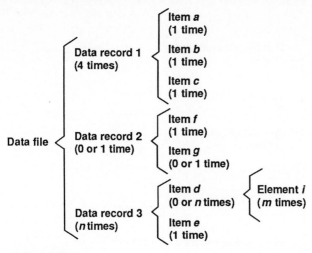

FIGURE 8.12
The Warnier diagram.

ments. In addition, data that appear conditionally are indicated with a ''(0 or 1 time)'' qualifier.

8.4.2 LCP Design Approach

The LCP design approach begins with specification of both input and output data structures with the use of Warnier diagrams. Like other design methods, a thorough evaluation of software requirements is a precursor to a derivation of a software representation. Warnier takes the classic view that "programs, like data (input) and results, are information files." Therefore, the next step of LCP is to represent software processing with the Warnier diagram.

A processing hierarchy for a program is derived from the structure of input data. For example, the data file shown in Figure 8.12 can be processed by a program such as that illustrated in Figure 8.13. Note that a bar above an entry in the diagram indicates a *not* condition, e.g., the bar above "*process g*" indicates that g may not be processed.

The Warnier diagram representation of software may be transformed into a more conventional flowchart representation shown in Figure 8.14. Examining the flowchart, we see that repetition in the data structure is translated into a *repeat-until* construct and conditional occurrence into the *if-then-else* construct. It is possible to interpret each box of the flowchart as a module. However, Warnier takes a procedural view that circumvents program structure and direct definition of modules.

As an example of the LCP design approach, applied through the development of a flowchart representation, we consider an application discussed in Warnier's text[*] [WAR74]:

---

[*]Figures 8.15–8.25 have been reproduced from [WAR74] with permission of Van Nostrand Reinhold Co., copyright 1974, Les Editions d'Organisation.

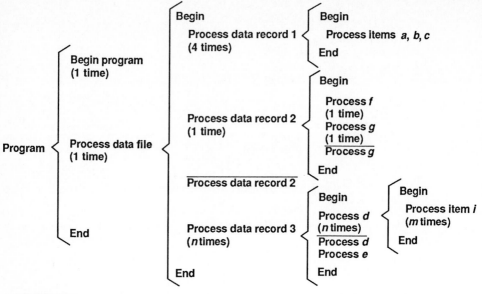

FIGURE 8.13
LCP processing hierarchy.

A periodic report of customer's accounts is to be produced. The input file contains for each customer a header record followed by "movement" (transaction) records. In other words, there are 0, 1 or many movements (transactions) for each customer.

The overall organization of an output report for the above application and a description of input records are given in Figure 8.15. The "code" field of the second input record indicates whether a movement (MVT) is a credit or a debit.

Warnier diagrams that describe the information hierarchy of the output report and the input data records are shown in Figure 8.16. It should be noted that the output diagram implies the conditional occurrence of levels 4 and 5. (A customer may have initiated no transactions.) The input records (Figure 8.15) are included in the Warnier diagram. Again, levels 4 and 5 occur only when a transaction has been made.

Processing hierarchy is developed from the input information structure. A Warnier diagram representation of the program is shown in Figure 8.17. A flowchart derived from the diagram is shown in Figure 8.18. The numbers to the left of each processing block in the flowchart are used in the development of *detailed organization*.

8.4.3 Detailed Organization

Logical construction of programs attempts to extend design methodology into a domain that other methods avoid. Warnier has developed a technique, called *detailed organization*, in which a set of detailed instructions can be systematically developed from the logical organization of the program (e.g., Figures 8.17 and 8.18). Of course, other

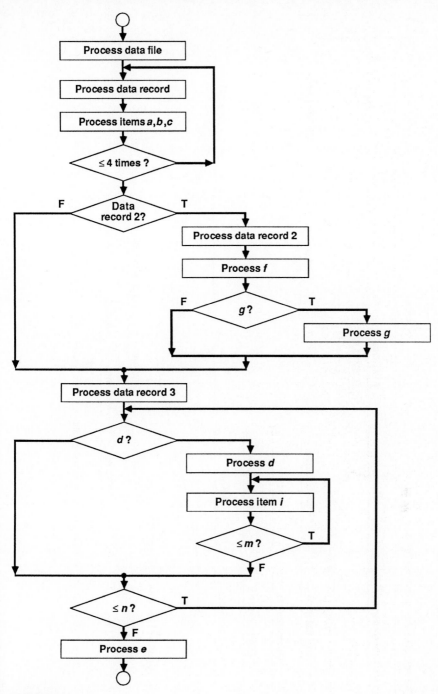

FIGURE 8.14
Flowchart representation.

313

The layout of the output report is:

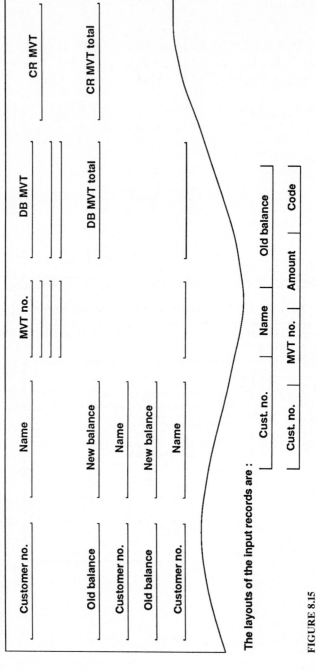

The layouts of the input records are :

FIGURE 8.15

An example. (Reprinted with permission of Van Nostrand Reinhold, Company, copyright 1974, Les Éditions d'Organisatio

314

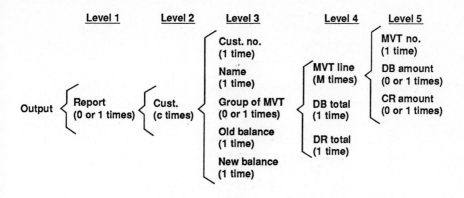

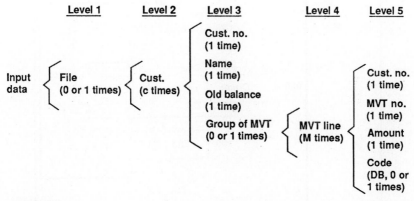

FIGURE 8.16
Information structure. (Reprinted with permission of Van Nostrand Reinhold, Company, copyright 1974, Les Editions d'Organisation.)

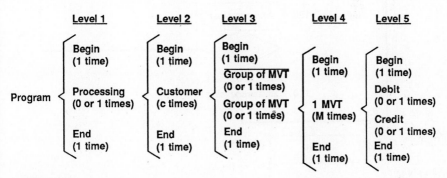

FIGURE 8.17
Processing hierarchy. (Reprinted with permission of Van Nostrand Reinhold, Company, copyright 1974, Les Editions d'Organisation.)

315

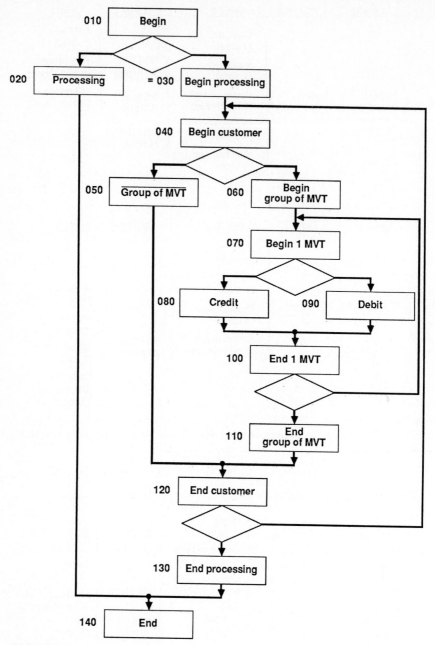

FIGURE 8.18
Resultant flowchart. (Reprinted with permission of Van Nostrand Reinhold, Company, copyright 1974, Les Editions d'Organisation.)

design methods set a foundation for specification of detailed instructions, but Warnier has proposed a step-by-step process for deriving such instructions.

Warnier defines the following types (or classes) of instructions:

- Input and input preparation
- Branching and branching preliminaries
- Calculations
- Output and output preparation
- Subprogram (module) calls

A detailed organization is developed by generating lists of instructions by type. The instruction is written and correlated to the appropriate processing block with a numeric indication (e.g., the number to the left of each block in Figure 8.18). A list for each instruction type is prepared.

After instruction lists are prepared, instructions with the same processing block identifier are grouped and organized in an input-processing-output sequence. For the customer accounts software discussed in Section 8.4.2, the corresponding instruction lists are shown in Figure 8.19. An example of sorted instructions is illustrated in Figure 8.20.

Detailed organization provides the designer with a technique for developing a detail design description in a systematic way. The nonsequential nature of the approach may seem a bit unusual (bizarre!), but the method does work.

8.4.4 Complex Structures

As the logical organization of a program becomes complex, additional design techniques are required to represent, and, ultimately, simplify conditions and corresponding processing. LCP recommends the usage of *Boolean algebra* and/or *Karnaugh mapping* to help reduce logical complexity, thereby aiding the designer in specification of detailed organization.

Although a detailed discussion of logical simplification techniques is beyond the scope of this text,* we shall consider a brief example [WAR74] to illustrate Warnier's approach. A tabular representation of four data items, A, B, C, and D, and corresponding processing actions V, W, X, Y, Z, and $\overline{R}$ (not R) is given in Figure 8.21. This *truth table* indicates under what circumstances processing actions will be executed. For example, from the third row, actions V and Y will be executed when data item C is encountered. It is possible to execute V under eight different sets of conditions and to execute Y under two different sets of conditions. Applying Boolean algebra, we obtain:

---

*For further information, see works by Warnier [WAR74], Bartee [BAR77], and Roth [ROT79].

List of branch instructions:
- 010 – if not end of file ($\overline{\text{EOF}}$)   030
- 020 –   140
- 040 – if Cust No read = Cust No processed   060
- 050 –   120
- 070 – if code DB   090
- 080 –   100
- 100 – if Cust No read = Cust No processed   070
- 120 – if not end of file ($\overline{\text{EOF}}$)   040

Preparation of branch instructions:
- 040 – transfer Cust No to Reference Cust No field

Calculations:
- 040 – Transfer old balance to working field
- 060 – Clear debit total field
- 060 – Clear credit total field
- 090 – Add debit to debit total
- 080 – Add credit to credit total
- 110 – Subtract debit total from working field
- 110 – Add credit total to working field

Outputs:
- 030 – Spaces to print area
- 040 – Transfer old balance to reference field
- 040 – Edit cust. heading
- 040 – Output and restore print area
- 070 – Edit MVT No
- 090 – Edit debit amount
- 080 – Edit credit amount
- 100 – Output and restore print area
- 110 – Edit debit total
- 110 – Edit credit total
- 120 – Edit old balance from reference field
- 120 – Edit new balance from reference field
- 120 – Output and restore print area

Inputs:
- 010 : read
- 040 : read
- 100 : read

FIGURE 8.19

Instruction lists. (Reprinted with permission of Van Nostrand Reinhold, Company, copyright 1974, Les Editions d'Organisation.)

$$V = \overline{A} \cdot \overline{B} \cdot C \cdot \overline{D} + \overline{A} \cdot \overline{B} \cdot C \cdot D + \overline{A} \cdot B \cdot C \cdot \overline{D} + \overline{A} \cdot B \cdot C \cdot D$$
$$+ A \cdot \overline{B} \cdot C \cdot \overline{D} + A \cdot \overline{B} \cdot C \cdot D + A \cdot B \cdot C \cdot \overline{D} + A \cdot B \cdot C \cdot D$$

where in Boolean notation "·" indicates *logical and* and " + " indicates *logical or*. Applying rules of logic simplification, we obtain the equations shown below:

$$\begin{aligned} V &= \overline{A} \cdot \overline{B} \cdot C(\overline{D} + D) + \overline{A} \cdot B \cdot C(\overline{D} + D) + A \cdot \overline{B} \cdot C(\overline{D} + D) + A \cdot B \cdot C(\overline{D} + D) \\ &= \overline{A} \cdot \overline{B} \cdot C + \overline{A} \cdot B \cdot C + A \cdot \overline{B} \cdot C + A \cdot B \cdot C \\ &= \overline{A} \cdot C(\overline{B} + B) + A \cdot C(\overline{B} + B) \\ &= \overline{A} \cdot C + A \cdot C = C(\overline{A} + A) \\ &= C \end{aligned}$$

The sorted list of instructions:

010 – Read
      If $\overline{EOF}$ 030
020 –   140
030 – Spaces to print area
040 – Cust No to Reference Cust No
      Old balance to working field
      Old balance to ref field
      Edit Cust No
      Print and restore print area
      Read
      If Cust No = Ref. Cust No   060
050 –   120
060 – Clear debit total
      Clear credit total
070 – Edit MVT No
      If code DB   090

080 – Add credit to CR total
      Edit credit   100
090 – Add debit to DB total
      Edit debit
100 – Print and restore print area
      Read
      If Cust No = ref Cust No   070
110 – Subtract DB total from
      working field
      Add CR total to working field
      Edit DB total
      Edit CR total
120 – Edit old balance
      Edit new balance
      Print and restore print area
      If $\overline{EOF}$ 040

FIGURE 8.20

Sorted instructions. (Reprinted with permission of Van Nostrand Reinhold, Company, copyright 1974, Les Editions d'Organisation.)

and similarly

$$X = A \cdot \overline{B} \cdot C \cdot \overline{D} + A \cdot \overline{B} \cdot C \cdot D$$
$$= A \cdot \overline{B} \cdot C(\overline{D} + D)$$
$$= A \cdot \overline{B} \cdot C$$

Therefore, V will be executed whenever C is encountered, and X will be executed when A and C are present and B is not present.

From the table in Figure 8.21, the following additional simplifications can be made for other processing actions:

$$V = C$$
$$W = C \cdot A$$
$$X = C \cdot A \cdot \overline{B}$$
$$Y = C \cdot \overline{A} \cdot \overline{B}$$
$$Z = C \cdot \overline{A} \cdot B$$
$$\overline{R} = \overline{C}$$

Using these simplified logical conditions, a Warnier diagram for processing hierarchy can be developed as shown in Figure 8.22.

The LCP approach to logical simplification requires a fairly rigorous evaluation of actions and conditions. However, redundant tests are eliminated from the procedure, thereby improving the efficiency of the software design. These techniques, called *complex alternative structure evaluation* by Warnier, may be combined with techniques discussed earlier in this section to develop composite solutions for complex sets of software requirements.

	DATA ABCD	V	W	X	Y	Z	$\overline{R}$
	0000						X
	0001						X
	0010	X			X		
	0011	X			X		
	0100						X
Complex	0101						X
Alternatives	0110	X				X	
	0111	X				X	
	1000						X
	1001						X
	1010	X	X	X			
	1011	X	X	X			
	1100						X
	1101						X
	1110	X	X				
	1111	X	X				

FIGURE 8.21
A truth table. (Reprinted with permission of Van Nostrand Reinhold, Company, copyright 1974, Les Editions d'Organisation.)

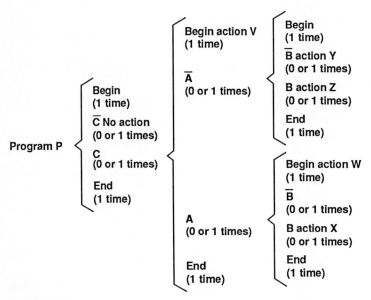

FIGURE 8.22
Resulting program structure. (Reprinted with permission of Van Nostrand Reinhold, Company, copyright 1974, Les Editions d'Organisation.)

320

Logical simplification may also be used during maintenance of existing, "unstructured" software. Many older programs have rambling control flow that is difficult to understand and impossible to maintain. Warnier suggests an approach for *restructuring* such programs with the use of complex alternative structures:

1. Develop a flowchart for the software.
2. Write a Boolean expression for each processing sequence.
3. Compile a truth table.
4. Reconstruct the software, using techniques for complex alternative structures; add modifications as required.

As an example [WAR74], we consider the unstructured flowchart and resultant truth table shown in Figures 8.23 and 8.24. Maintenance requires that the modifications ("amendments") shown in Figure 8.24 be applied. After amending the truth table and simplifying, a Warnier diagram for processing hierarchy may be developed by using the simplification techniques described above. This leads to the structured procedural design shown in Figure 8.25.

Logical construction of programs offers a second data structure–oriented design methodology. Using a set of rules developed from computer science foundations, LCP

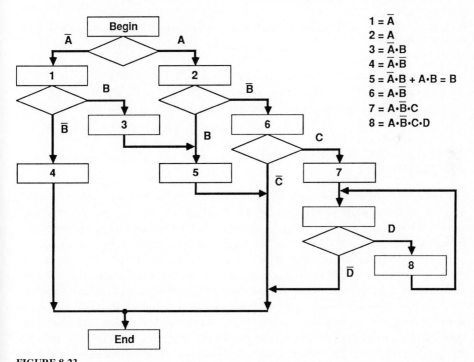

$$1 = \overline{A}$$
$$2 = A$$
$$3 = \overline{A} \cdot B$$
$$4 = \overline{A} \cdot \overline{B}$$
$$5 = \overline{A} \cdot B + A \cdot B = B$$
$$6 = A \cdot \overline{B}$$
$$7 = A \cdot \overline{B} \cdot C$$
$$8 = A \cdot \overline{B} \cdot C \cdot D$$

FIGURE 8.23

An unstructured program. (Reprinted with permission of Van Nostrand Reinhold, Company, copyright 1974, Les Editions d'Organisation.)

E ABCD	1	2	3	4	5	6	7	8
0 0 0 0	X			X				
0 0 0 1	X			X				
0 0 1 0	X			X				
0 0 1 1	X			X				
0 1 0 0	X		X		X			
0 1 0 1	X		X		X			
0 1 1 0	X		X		X			
0 1 1 1	X		X		X			
1 0 0 0		X				X		
1 0 0 1		X				X		
1 0 1 0		X				X	X	
1 0 1 1		X				X	X	X
1 1 0 0		X			X			
1 1 0 1		X			X			
1 1 1 0		X			X			
1 1 1 1		X			X			

The amendments required for this program subset are the following:
  • **action 9 = A. This action must be executed at the end of the processing of A.**
  • **action 10 = A.B.C.D. This action must be executed once for the group D at the end, but not at all if D contains no elements**

FIGURE 8.24
Resultant truth table. (Reprinted with permission of Van Nostrand Reinhold, Company, copyright 1974, Les Editions d'Organisation.)

developer Jean Warnier proposes a rigorous design approach that is driven by information hierarchy. He offers a set of techniques that extend software design into detailed procedural specification, logic simplification, and even restructuring of existing software.

8.5 DATA STRUCTURED SYSTEMS DEVELOPMENT

Data Structured Systems Development (DSSD) extends the basic concepts developed by Warnier into a more comprehensive methodology for the analysis and design of computer-based systems. In Chapter 5 the analysis-oriented steps of DSSD were presented. The reader is urged to review Section 5.4 before continuing with this section.

The DSSD design procedure is described using Warnier diagram notation in Figure 8.26. Input to the DSSD design procedure is requirements analysis information that includes the application context, function description, and application results (see Sections 5.4.3 through 5.4.5). The diagrams and data contained in these representations are used as the foundation for DSSD logical and physical design. The logical design focuses on outputs, interfaces, and procedural design of software. The physical design evolves from the logical design and focuses on the ''packaging'' of the software to best achieve desired performance, maintainability, and other design constraints imposed by the system environment.

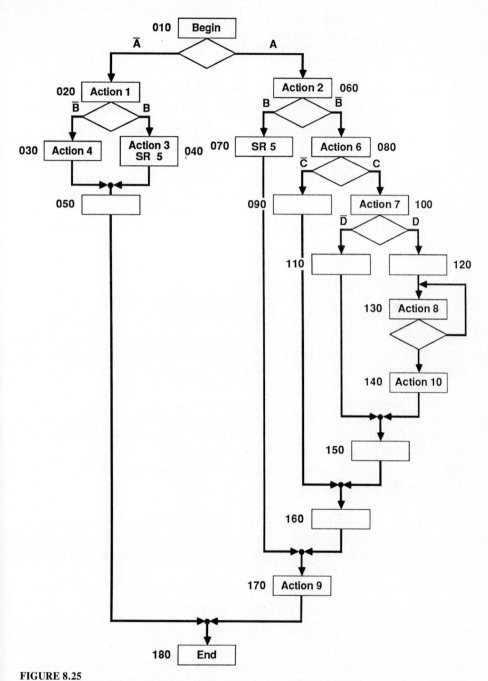

FIGURE 8.25
Amended, structured program. (Reprinted with permission of Van Nostrand Reinhold, Company, copyright 1974, Les Editions d'Organisation.)

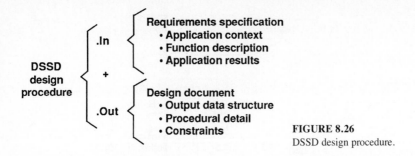

FIGURE 8.26
DSSD design procedure.

DSSD is one of the most thoroughly documented and comprehensive design methods. The procedures for both logical and physical design are described in step-by-step fashion in guidebooks that can be obtained from Ken Orr & Associates, Inc. To illustrate the DSSD approach, we present a much simplified version proposed by Hansen [HAN83].

8.5.1 A Simplified Design Approach

The logical design process can be divided into two activities: the derivation of *logical output structure* (LOS) and the resultant definition of *logical process structure* (LPS). A simplified approach [HAN83] has been proposed for the derivation of LOS. In this approach the data items that are part of the information domain of a problem are organized hierarchically in much the same way that Jackson and Warnier approach design. A four-step process is applied to derive LOS:

1. The problem statement or related requirements information is evaluated and all distinct data items (called *atoms*) that cannot be subdivided further are listed.
2. The frequency of occurrence of each atom is specified.
3. Data items that can be subdivided (called *universals*) are evaluated.
4. A diagrammatic representation of LOS is developed.

To illustrate the four-step process described above, we introduce a brief example. A "Daily Machine Tool Usage Report" (Figure 8.27) is generated as part of a large automated manufacturing information system. The simplified DSSD design approach will be used to derive LOS and LPS.

8.5.2 Derivation of Logical Output Structure

The logical output structure (LOS) is a hierarchical representation of data items that compose output from a computer-based system. The first step in the derivation of LOS is to isolate all atoms (data items that cannot be subdivided). This can be accomplished by reviewing the problem statement or, in the case of the tool usage report example, examining the format of the prototype report (Figure 8.27) itself. Next, the frequency of occurrence of each atom should be noted as shown in Figure 8.28.

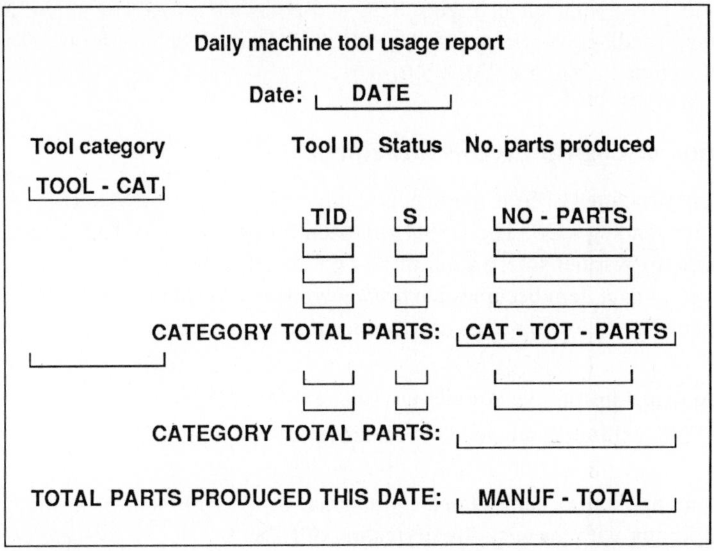

Daily machine tool usage report

Date: |___ DATE ___|

Tool category   Tool ID   Status   No. parts produced

|TOOL - CAT|

|TID| |S| |NO - PARTS|

     |__| |__| |_____|
     |__| |__| |_____|
     |__| |__| |_____|

        CATEGORY TOTAL PARTS: |CAT - TOT - PARTS|
|_____|

     |__| |__| |_____|
     |__| |__| |_____|

        CATEGORY TOTAL PARTS: |_____|

TOTAL PARTS PRODUCED THIS DATE: |___ MANUF - TOTAL ___|

FIGURE 8.27
Report prototype.

Once all atoms and their frequency have been defined, the designer begins an examination of *universals*. Universals are data items or categories that are composed of other universals and atoms. For our example universals would be: *report* (occurs a single time), *tools-category* (occurs *t* times per report), and *tool-id* (occurs *s* times per *tool-category*).

Data Element (Atom)	Frequency	Details
HEADING	1 / report	Daily machine tool usage report
DATE	1 / report	
COLUMN - HEAD	1 / report	Tool category, Tool ID, ...
TOOL - CAT	1 / tool category	
TID	1 / tool - id	
S	1 / tool - id	
NO PARTS	1 / tool - id	
SUBTOTAL - HEAD	1 / tool category	Category total parts
CAT - TOT - PARTS	1 / tool category	
TOTAL - HEAD	1 / report	Total parts produced this date
MANUF - TOTAL	1 / report	

FIGURE 8.28
Atoms and frequencies.

Using information contained in Figure 8.28 and collected as part of universal analysis, a Warnier-Orr diagram (Section 5.4.1) for the ''Daily Machine Tool Usage Report'' can be developed (Figure 8.29).

8.5.3   Derivation of Logical Process Structure

The logical process structure (LPS) is a procedural representation of software required to process the corresponding LOS. The DSSD approach for derivation of LPS is similar in many respects to Warnier's derivation of an LCP detailed organization (Section 8.4.3). Each universal data item becomes a *repetition* construct to which processing instructions are added. The following steps are conducted to derive LPS:

1. All atoms are stripped from the Warnier-Orr diagram for LOS.
2. BEGIN and END delimiters are added to all universals (repetitions).

If steps 1 and 2 are applied to our example, a diagram of the form shown in Figure 8.30 results. Continuing with the steps for derivation of LPS:

3. All initialization and termination instructions or processes are defined.
4. All computational or nonnumeric processing is specified.

Applying steps 3 and 4 results in the expanded Warnier-Orr diagram shown in Figure 8.31.

5. All output instructions and processes are specified.
6. All input instructions and processes are specified.

Application of steps 5 and 6 completes the specification of LPS and is shown in Figure 8.32.

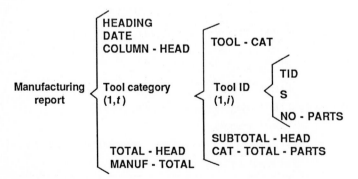

FIGURE 8.29
Warnier-Orr notation for LOS.

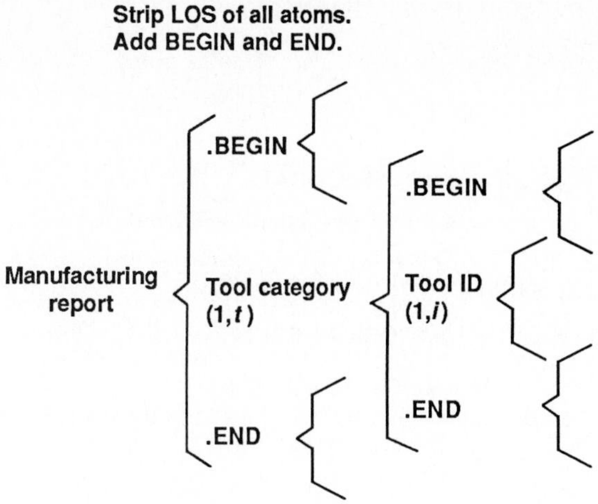

Strip LOS of all atoms.
Add BEGIN and END.

FIGURE 8.30
Transforming LOS to LPS.

8.5.4 Complex Process Logic

In many cases the procedural nature of a LPS is considerably more complicated than the example presented in the preceding sections. DSSD provides a notation for handling computational and conditional processing—*complex process logic*.

To illustrate the use of complex process logic, we consider a different example:

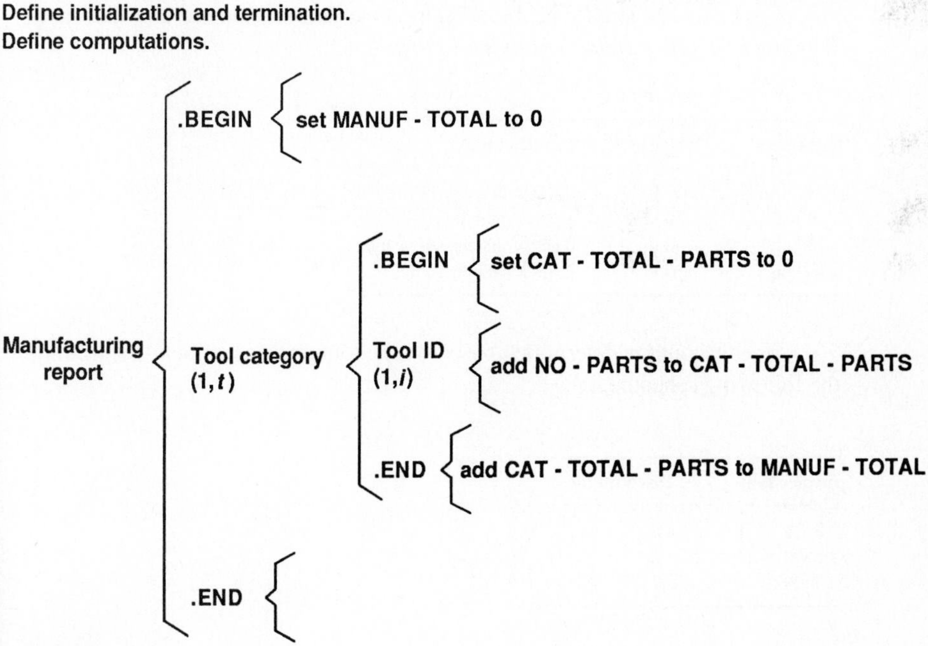

Define initialization and termination.
Define computations.

FIGURE 8.31
Deriving LPS.

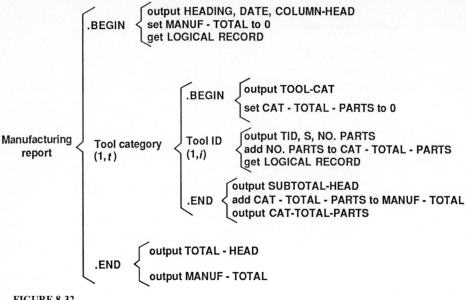

FIGURE 8.32
Complete LPS.

A mail order business computes total amount payable on orders by adding the cost of all items ordered and the shipping cost and subtracting any discounts. Shipping cost is determined from the following table:

Distance	Weight	Fee schedule
≤100 mi.	≤50 lb.	$0.01 \times$ distance $\times$ weight
≤100 mi.	>50 lb.	$1.10 \times$ weight
>100 mi.	≤50 lb.	$0.02 \times$ distance $\times$ weight
>100 mi.	>50 lb.	$2.35 \times$ weight

The discount is determined based on the total invoice amount according to the following schedule:

Invoice total	Discount factor
<$100	0%
<$500	1%
≥$500	2%

The processing required to model the computation of the total amount payable is shown in Figure 8.33. Arithmetic operators are represented in boxes to distinguish

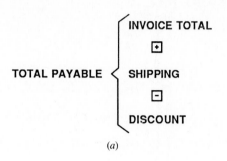

(a)

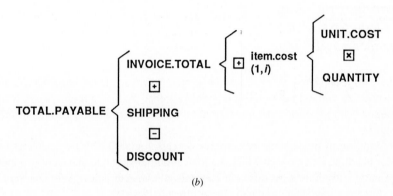

(b)

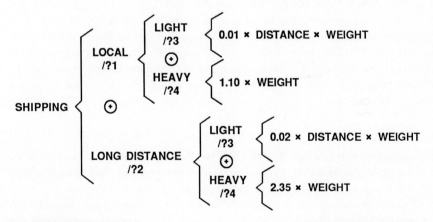

?1/ IF DISTANCE ≤ 100 mi   ?3/ IF WEIGHT ≤ 50 lb

?2/ IF DISTANCE > 100 mi   ?4/ IF WEIGHT > 50 lb

(c)

FIGURE 8.33
Process logic. (a) First level. (b) Second level. (c) Third level.

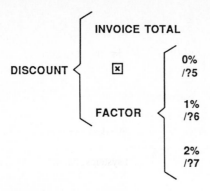

?5/ IF INVOICE TOTAL < $100

?6/ IF INVOICE TOTAL < $500

?7/ IF INVOICE TOTAL ≥ $500

FIGURE 8.33
(*d*) Third level.

them from logical operators. It should be noted, however, that arithmetic operators may be specified without boxes when it is unlikely that confusion might occur. A footnote symbol, /?*n*, where *n* is the footnote number, is used to qualify certain specified processing.

In addition to procedures for complex process logic, DSSD also provides techniques for handling situations in which the logical output structure and a corresponding physical output structure have different hierarchical characteristics. A *melding* process [HAN83] enables the design to handle these *structure clashes*.

DSSD, like Jackson System Development, and Logical Construction of Programs, offers a complete methodology for software analysis and design. Because each of these data structure–oriented methods provides a mechanism for derivation of detailed procedural design, each is amenable to automatic source code generation. In fact, recent extensions to DSSD may soon result in an automatic code generation system that is predicated on an accurate representation of logical and physical output and process structures.

8.6   SUMMARY

Data structure–oriented design, like all major software design methods, focuses on the information domain. However, rather than concentrating on data flow, data structure–oriented methods use information structure as the driver for design derivation.

Three important design methods—Jackson System Development, Logical Construction of Programs, and Data Structured System Development—have been presented in this chapter. All are remarkably similar in many respects, but each approaches the software design process from a somewhat different point of view. Jackson has introduced a set of preliminary notation that has little to do with data structure, concentrating instead on process modeling and control. Process design and implementation continue to depend on data structure representation. Warnier (LCP) takes a more rigorous view of data structure and focuses much attention on the description of detailed procedural design. Orr (DSSD) incorporates subtle elements of data flow techniques (during analysis) and adapts from both LCP and (to a lesser extent) JSD for his design procedures.

Orr [ORR81] provides a worthwhile summary for all the design methods presented in this chapter (and throughout this book):

> Bad systems are complex, hard to change, hardware and software dependent and monolithic. Moreover, they are large, costly and time-consuming to develop.
>
> Unfortunately, knowing what a bad system looks like does not necessarily provide a clear guide for developing a good one. Over the last twenty years, many methodologies were developed that aimed at avoiding the creation of bad systems, but not until the 1970s did approaches appear that defined what a good system should look like.

Each of the three data structure–oriented design methods presented in this chapter are "children" of the 1970s. Each introduces important ideas about the nature of good design and specific methods for achieving it. As these methods have matured, their singular focus on data structure has been broadened as our understanding of "what a good system should look like" evolves.

REFERENCES

[BAR77] Bartee, T., *Digital Computer Fundamentals*, 4th ed., McGraw-Hill, 1977.

[CHA80] Chand, D. R., and S. B. Yadav, "Logical Construction of Software," *CACM*, vol. 23, no. 10, October 1980, pp. 546–555.

[GUT77] Guttag, J., "Abstract Data Types and the Development of Data Structures," *CACM*, vol. 20, no. 6, June 1977, pp. 396–404.

[HAN83] Hansen, K., *Data Structured Program Design*, Ken Orr & Associates, Inc., Topeka, KS, 1983.

[HOR78] Horowitz, E., and S. Sahni, *Fundamentals of Computer Algorithms*, Computer Science Press, 1978.

[JAC75] Jackson, M., *Principles of Program Design*, Academic Press, 1975.

[JAC83] Jackson, M., *System Development*, Prentice-Hall, 1983.

[MYE78] Myers, G., *Composite Structured Design*, Van Nostrand Reinhold, 1978.

[ORR81] Orr, K., *Structured Requirements Definition*, Ken Orr & Associates, Inc., Topeka, KS, 1981.

[PET77] Peters, L. J., and L. L. Tripp, "Comparing Software Design Methodologies," *Datamation*, November 1977.

[ROT79] Roth, C., *Fundamentals of Logic Design*, 2d ed., West Publishing, 1979.

[TRE76] Tremblay, J. P., and P. G. Sorenson, *An Introduction to Data Structures with Applications*, McGraw-Hill, 1976.

[WAR74] Warnier, J. D., *Logical Construction of Programs*, Van Nostrand Reinhold, 1974.

[WAR81] Warnier, J. D., *Logical Construction of Systems*, Van Nostrand Reinhold, 1981.

[WUL81] Wulf, W., et al., *Fundamental Structures of Computer Science*, Addison-Wesley, 1981.

PROBLEMS AND POINTS TO PONDER

8.1 In this chapter we have introduced three important design techniques. Using the references as a guide, do some research and construct a table that indicates similarities and differences between the methods. Comparison criteria should include: representation of data, methods for representing procedural design, special notation and features, and so forth.

8.2 You have been asked to design inventory control software for an auto dealership that markets both new and used cars. Among other items, the system should maintain a list of each car on the lot, its year of manufacture, date of purchase, amount paid, wholesale value, asking price, condition, and repair cost. The car dealer can get any of this information online and generate reports that categorize cars by maker, age, cost, asking price, and so on. Expanding upon these requirements, provide a complete description of a data structure that will support the inventory system.

8.3 Apply one or more of the design techniques presented in this chapter to the auto inventory data structure described in Problem 8.2. It will be necessary to review Chapter 5 and first apply the analysis "front-end" before you move into design.

8.4 You have been hired to develop a microprocessor-based controller for a state-of-the-art elevator system for a high-rise office building. The elevators (there are n of them) must respond to rider commands for service. Commands include: (1) buttons pressed outside the elevator on each floor of the building, (2) buttons pressed inside the elevator to indicate a destination floor, and (3) an emergency command (generated by the fire detection system) that returns all elevators to the ground floor and disables the system. The controller must generate door open/close commands and coordinate elevators so that only one idle elevator moves to respond to a request for service. Using these comments as a starting point, derive additional requirements and develop a design for the system using JSD.

8.5 Explain how modules are defined as part of the Jackson Design Method. Can program structure and procedure be separated using Jackson's approach?

8.6 Recalling the Home Security System (HSS) introduced in problem sets for earlier chapters (Problems 4.7 to 4.15 and 5.11), apply JSD and DSSD design techniques to requirements derived in Problem 5.11.

8.7 Apply JSD to the PHTRS system described in Problem 5.14. Derive requirements and develop a design.

8.8 Apply LCP to the PHTRS system described in Problem 5.14. Derive requirements and develop a design.

8.9 Apply DSSD to the PHTRS system described in Problem 5.14. Derive requirements and develop a design.

8.10 Given a set of requirements provided by your instructor or requirements of a project on which you are currently working, apply the LCP approach and attempt to derive a procedural design. Show Warnier diagrams for input and output data and the program itself. Use a structured flowchart to define procedure.

8.11 For those readers unfamiliar with Boolean simplification: Obtain an introductory text in logic design (e.g., [ROT79]). Review chapters on Boolean algebra and simplification and prepare a brief summary of important concepts and theorems. Reread Section 8.4.4 of this book and show how expressions for W, Y, Z, and R were derived.

8.12 A word processor produces an output file that contains formatting information for document production. All documents contain header information that includes margin specification, line spacing, font selection, etc. The text file may or may not contain other margin modification information but always contains paragraph indicators, end-of-text-block indicators, and other text specific commands. Use the DSSD approach to define the output data structure and the resultant program procedural organization for document production software. Optionally, continue development by developing detailed organization using a known word processing system as a guide.

8.13 Select a fairly complex module that was not developed using the structured constructs (these are normally not difficult to find!). Apply Warnier's simplification approach to generate a structured representation of the same program.

8.14 Search the literature for comparisons of software design methods and write a short paper summarizing criteria for comparison and recommendations of the authors.

8.15 A major class project: Define full specifications and develop an ''automated design tool'' that would assist in the application of a data flow–/data structure–oriented design technique. The tool should be interactive, mechanize some or all of the design mappings, and provide graphical output as well as other reports that might help the designer assess his/her design. The tool should also support ''hooks'' for analysis tools and programming languages.

FURTHER READINGS

Books by Jackson [JAC83], Warnier [WAR81], and Hansen [HAN83] are required reading for those readers interested in data structure–oriented design. King and Pardoe (*Program Design Using JSP*, Wiley, 1985) provide a worthwhile summary of Jackson's program design approach that can be used to complement [JAC83].

A survey of data structure–oriented design would not be complete without reference to design techniques for data bases and data base management systems. Worthwhile papers are reprinted in *Software Design Techniques*, *Software Design Strategies*, and *Data Base Engineering*—all IEEE tutorials. Among many good texts on data base design are:

Date, C. J., *An Introduction to Data Base Systems*, 4th ed., Addison-Wesley, 1986.
Perkinson, R. C., *Data Analysis*, QED Information Sciences, 1984.
Weiderhold, G., *Data Base Design*, 2d ed., 1983.

Comprehensive documentation for the DSSD method can be obtained from Ken Orr & Associates in Topeka, KS. Orr has developed a set of automated tools that support the DSSD methodology.

CHAPTER
9

OBJECT-ORIENTED DESIGN

Object-oriented design (OOD), like other information-oriented design methodologies, creates a representation of the real-world problem domain and maps it into a solution domain that is software. Unlike other methods, OOD results in a design that interconnects data objects (data items) and processing operations in a way that modularizes information and processing rather than processing alone.

The unique nature of object-oriented design lies in its ability to build upon three important software design concepts: abstraction, information hiding, and modularity (Chapter 6). All design methods strive for software that exhibits these fundamental characteristics, but only OOD provides a mechanism that enables the designer to achieve all three without complexity or compromise.

Wiener and Sincovec [WIE84] summarize OOD methodology in the following manner:

> No longer is it necessary for the system designer to map the problem domain into predefined data and control structures present in the implementation language. Instead, the designer may create his or her own abstract data types and functional abstractions and map the real-world domain into these programmer-created abstractions. This mapping, incidentally, may be much more natural because of the virtually unlimited range of abstract types that can be invented by the designer. Furthermore, software design becomes decoupled from the representational details of the data objects used in the system. These representational details may be changed many times without any fallout effects being induced in the overall software system.

It is premature to call object-oriented design a comprehensive methodology. However, the concepts that are embodied in OOD represent an important and unique view of software design.

9.1 ORIGINS OF OBJECT-ORIENTED DESIGN

Objects and operations are not a new programming concept, but object-oriented design is. In the very earliest days of computing, assembly languages enabled programmers to use machine instructions (operators) to manipulate data items (operands). The level of abstraction that was applied to the solution domain was very low.

As high-order programming languages (e.g., FORTRAN, ALGOL, COBOL) appeared, objects and operations in the real-world problem space could be modeled by predefined data and control structures that were available as part of the high-order language. In general, software design (whenever it was explicitly considered) focused on the representation of procedural detail using the programming language of choice. Design concepts such as stepwise refinement of function, procedural modularity, and, later, structured programming were introduced.

During the 1970s, concepts such as abstraction and information hiding were introduced, and data driven design methods emerged, but software developers still concentrated on process and its representation. At the same time, modern high-order languages (e.g., Pascal) introduced a much richer variety of data structures and types.

While conventional high-order languages (languages out of the FORTRAN and ALGOL tradition) were evolving during the late 1960s and 1970s, researchers were hard at work on a new class of simulation and prototyping languages such as SIMULA and Smalltalk. In these languages, data abstraction was emphasized and real-world problems were represented by a set of *data objects* to which a corresponding set of *operations* were attached. The use of these languages was radically different from the use of more conventional languages.

The approach that we call object-oriented design has evolved over the past 15 years. Early work in software design (Section 6.6.2) laid the foundation by establishing the importance of abstraction, information hiding, and modularity to software quality. In some respects, data structure–oriented design methods such as *Data Structured Systems Development (DSSD)* and *Jackson System Development (JSD)* (Chapter 8) can be viewed as object-oriented.

During the 1980s the rapid evolution of the programming languages Smalltalk and Ada caused increased interest in OOD. In an early discussion of methods to achieve object-oriented design, Abbott [ABB83] showed "how the analysis of the English statement of the problem and its solution can be used to guide the development of both the visible part of a useful package [a package holds both data and the procedures that operate on it] and the particular algorithm for a given problem." Booch [BOO83] expanded upon Abbott's work and helped to popularize the concept of object-oriented design. Today OOD is being used in software design applications that range from computer graphics animation [LOR86] to telecommunications [LOV85].

9.2 OBJECT-ORIENTED DESIGN CONCEPTS

Like other design methods, OOD introduces a new set of terminology, notation, and procedures for the derivation of a software design. In this section we concentrate on OOD terminology in an attempt to understand the underlying concepts that guide all object-oriented design.

9.2.1 Objects, Operations, and Messages

Software function is accomplished when a data structure (of varying levels of complexity) is acted upon by one or more processes according to a procedure defined by a static algorithm or dynamic commands. To accomplish object-oriented design, we must establish a mechanism for: (1) the representation of data structure, (2) the specification of process, and (3) the invocation procedure.

An *object* is a component of the real world that is mapped into the software domain. In the context of a computer-based system, an object is typically a producer or consumer of information or an information item. For example, typical objects might be: machines, commands, files, displays, switches, signals, alphanumeric strings, or any other person, place, or thing. When an object is mapped into its software realization, it consists of a private data structure and processes, called *operations* or *methods*, that may legitimately transform the data structure. Operations contain control and procedural constructs that may be invoked by a *message*—a request to the object to perform one of its operations. The software realization of an object is illustrated in Figure 9.1.

Referring to the figure, a real-world object (a dictionary) is to be mapped into a software realization for a computer-based system. The software realization of *dictionary* exhibits a private data structure and related operations. The data structure might take the form depicted by the Warnier-Orr diagram in Figure 9.2. Entries in the dictionary are composed of the word, a pronunciation guide, and one or more definitions. A picture or diagram may also be contained within an entry. The object *dictionary* also contains a set of operations (e.g., *add-word*, *find-word*) that can process the elements of the data structure described above. The *private part* of an object is the data structure and the set of operations for the data structure.

An object also has a *shared part* that is its interface. *Messages* move across the interface and specify what operation on the object is desired, but not *how* the operation is to be performed. The object that receives a message determines how the requested operation is to be implemented.

By defining an object with a private part and providing messages to invoke appropriate processing, we achieve *information hiding*; that is, details of implementation are hidden from all program elements outside the object. Objects and their operations provide inherent *modularity*; that is, software elements (data and process) are grouped together with a well-defined interface mechanism (in this case, messages).

9.2.2 Classes, Instances, and Inheritance

Many objects in the physical world have reasonably similar characteristics and perform reasonably similar operations. If we look at the manufacturing floor of a heavy equip-

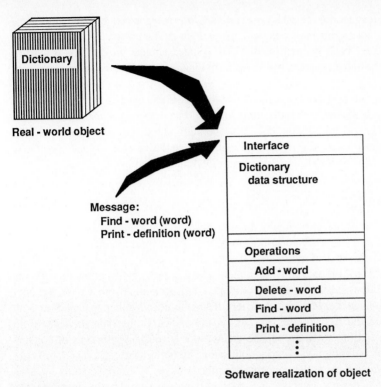

FIGURE 9.1
Objects.

ment manufacturer, we see milling machines, drill presses, and jig borers. Although each of these objects is different, all belong to a larger *class* called metal cutting tools. All objects in the metal cutting tools class have attributes in common (e.g., all use electric motors) and perform common operations (e.g., all perform metal cutting). Therefore, by categorizing a ''hobber'' as a member of the class *metal cutting machines*, we know something about its attributes and the operations it performs even if we don't know what its detailed function is.

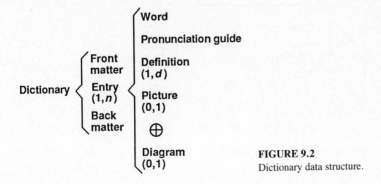

FIGURE 9.2
Dictionary data structure.

Software realizations of real-world objects are categorized in much the same way. All objects are members of a larger *class* and *inherit* the private data structure and operations that have been defined for that class. Stated another way, a *class* is a set of objects having the same characteristics. An individual object is therefore an *instance* of a larger class.

As an example of the relationship between objects and classes, we reconsider the *dictionary* object described in the preceding section. The object *dictionary* is an instance of the class *books* and inherits the data and operation characteristics of *books*. Therefore, *books* becomes a *data abstraction* that enables us to define each instance in a facile manner. Using the program design language (PDL) introduced in Chapter 6,

TYPE dictionary IS INSTANCE OF books;

implies *inheritance* of the attributes of books. Referring to Figure 9.3, other objects (e.g., brochures, reports, encyclopedia) can be defined as instances of books.

The use of classes and inheritance is crucially important in modern software engineering. *Reusability* of program components is achieved by creating objects (instances) that build on existing attributes and operations inherited from a class. We only need to specify how the new object differs from the class, rather than defining all characteristics of the new object. In fact, many industry observers believe (e.g., [COX85]) that reusable software will be created not by building libraries of conventional procedures (subprogram libraries) but rather by building a catalog of "software ICs"—objects created using the concepts described above.

Unlike other design concepts that are programming language–independent, the implementation of classes and objects varies with the programming language to be used. For this reason, the preceding generic discussion may require modification in the context of a specific programming language. For example, Ada implements the object

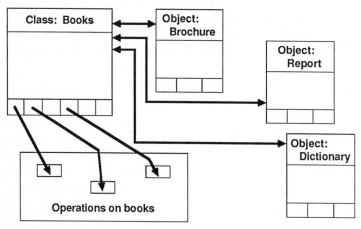

FIGURE 9.3
Objects, classes, and inheritance.

as a *package* and achieves instances through the use of data abstractions and typing. The Smalltalk programming language, on the other hand, implements each of the concepts described above directly, making it a true object-oriented programming language.

9.2.3 Object Descriptions

A design description of an object (an instance of a class) can take one of two forms [GOL83]:

1. A *protocol description* that establishes the interface of an object by defining each message that the object can receive and the related operation that the object performs when it receives the message, and
2. An *implementation description* that shows implementation details for each operation implied by a message that is passed to an object. Implementation details include information about the object's private part, that is, internal details about the data structure and procedural details that describe operations.

The protocol description is nothing more than a set of messages and a corresponding comment for each message. For example, a portion of the protocol description for the object *dictionary* (described earlier) might be:

MESSAGE → *add-word:* word *described as:* description;

Adds *word* to the dictionary with a definition contained in *description*.

MESSAGE ;› *find-word:* word;

Finds a word contained in the dictionary.

MESSAGE ;› *modify-definition:* word *with:* new definition;

Modifies the definition of an existing word by replacing it with *new definition*.

For a large system with many messages, it is often possible to create message categories. For example, message categories for the *dictionary* object might be editing messages and look-up messages.

An implementation description of an object provides the internal ("hidden") details that are required for implementation but are not necessary for invocation. That is, the designer of the object must provide an implementation description and must therefore create the internal details of the object. However, another designer or implementor who uses the object or other instances of the object requires only the protocol description but not the implementation description.

An implementation description consists of the following information: (1) a specification of the object's name and reference to class, (2) a specification of private data structure with an indication of data items and types, and (3) a procedural description of each operation or, alternatively, pointers to such procedural descriptions. The implementation description must contain sufficient information to provide for proper handling of all messages described in the protocol description.

Cox [COX85] characterizes the difference between the information contained in the protocol description and that contained in the implementation description in terms of "users" and "suppliers" of services. A user of the "service" provided by an object must be familiar with the protocol for invoking the service, that is, for specifying *what* is desired. The supplier of the service (the object itself) must be concerned with *how* the service is to be supplied to the user, that is, with implementation details. This concept, called *encapsulation*, is summarized as follows [COX85]:

> [An object] delivers encapsulation, whereby a data structure and a group of procedures for accessing it can be put into service such that the users of that capability can access it through a set of carefully documented, controlled and standardized interfaces. These encapsulated data structures, called objects, amount to active data that can be requested to do things by sending them messages.

9.3 OBJECT-ORIENTED DESIGN METHODS

Although OOD concepts described in the preceding section have been around for some time, the first attempts to describe a methodology for creating an object-oriented design did not surface until the early 1980s. Both Abbott [ABB83] and Booch [BOO83] contend that OOD begins with a natural language (e.g., English) description of the solution strategy for the software realization of a real-world problem. From this description, the designer can isolate objects and operations.

The work of Abbott and Booch has been refined by EVB Software Engineering, Inc. [EVB86], and a step-by-step method for OOD has evolved. In the sections that follow, we present one OOD method that is based on the work of these investigators and another method that has evolved from the work of Cox [COX86] and others.

At its current stage of evolution, OOD methodology combines elements of all three design categories discussed earlier in this book: data design, architectural design, and procedural design. By identifying objects, data abstractions are created. By defining operations, modules are specified and a structure for the software is established. By developing a mechanism for using (e.g., generating messages) the objects, interfaces are described.

Booch [BOO83] proposes the following steps for OOD:

1. Define the problem.
2. Develop an informal strategy for the software realization of the real-world problem domain.
3. Formalize the strategy using the following substeps:
   a. Identify objects and their attributes
   b. Identify operations that may be applied to objects
   c. Establish interfaces by showing the relationship between objects and operations.
   d. Decide on detailed design issues that will provide an implementation description for objects.
4. Reapply steps 2, 3, and 4 recursively until a complete design is created.

It should be noted that the first two steps are actually performed during software requirements analysis. In fact a preview of this approach (as it applied to analysis) was presented in Chapter 4 (Section 4.4).

9.4   PROBLEM DEFINITION

Problem definition is simply another term for requirements analysis. To adequately define the problem, computer system engineering should be applied in order to allocate function to the software element of a system. Next, software requirements analysis methods should be applied to identify the information domain and partition the problem. The analysis principles described in Chapter 4 and any one of the analysis methods described in Chapter 5 may be used to accomplish this step of OOD.

The application of requirements analysis principles and methods will enable the analyst and the designer to perform two necessary substeps [EVB86]: (1) stating the problem and (2) analyzing and clarifying known constraints. The software realization of the real-world problem, regardless of its size or complexity, should be stated in a single, grammatically correct sentence. Obviously, the level of abstraction may be very high, but a single problem statement ''allows software engineers working on the project to have a single, unified, understanding of the problem'' [EVB86].

To illustrate the problem definition step of OOD (and all subsequent steps), we introduce a simple example:

A numerical control (NC) for machine tools is to be developed. The NC is ''programmed'' with machine instructions and produces control commands for the machine tool's servosystem. In addition the NC contains a CRT display and keyboard for operator interaction.

In this example, we develop a design for NC software using object-oriented design.

Problem definition begins with system engineering. Hardware, software, human, data base, and other elements are allocated. The role of NC software is refined during software requirements analysis and is illustrated in Figure 9.4. The level 01 data flow diagram (Chapter 5) in the figure provides us with a view of information flow as well as data sources and sinks. In reality this DFD could be refined to levels 02 and 03. For our purposes, however, we make use of the top-level DFD only.

The first task for OOD problem definition is to write a one-sentence statement of the problem. Using the DFD (Figure 9.4) as a guide, we can state: *Develop a numerical control for a machine tool that reads NC blocks and operator commands and produces machine servosystem control commands and a CRT display.*

The next task for problem definition is to analyze and clarify known constraints. Information generated during analysis (e.g., DFDs and a data dictionary) provides the basis from which this task is accomplished. Analysis and clarification is accomplished by evaluating the information domain of the problem, partitioning, and assessing both real-world (physical) and software (logical) views. In addition, performance issues and validation criteria may be specified. It is possible that the original statement of the problem may be changed as analysis and clarification of constraints unfold.

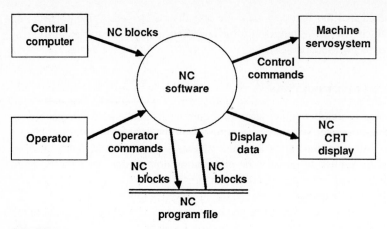

FIGURE 9.4
Analysis representation—an NC system.

To assist in analysis and clarification of constraints, the information domain content for NC software (Figure 9.4) is depicted in an abbreviated data dictionary:

NC.blocks = n.code + *(g.code)* + *x* + *y* + *z* + (s.code) + eob
operator commands = [insert.block|display.pgm|exec.pgm]
NC.program.file = program.number + {NC.blocks} ^{k}
control commands = position.cmds + special.cmds
display.data = listing of NC program file + (echo of inserted NC block from operator)
n.code = N + three-digit number
g.code = G + two-digit number between 01 and 99
x = X + four-digit coordinate for x axis
y = Y + four-digit coordinate for y axis
z = Z + four-digit coordinate for z axis
s.code = S + two-digit number between 00 and 32
eob = ascii control character for end of block
    … and so on.

The data dictionary serves two roles: (1) to define data content and (2) to implicitly provide a degree of functional partitioning.

The work performed as part of the problem definition step of OOD is software requirements analysis. Requirements can be established through the application of analysis methods (Chapter 5), paper (or executable) prototyping, and thorough customer-developer interaction.

9.5   AN INFORMAL STRATEGY

The next step in OOD is to write an informal strategy for the solution of the problem stated in the problem description. As a general rule, the informal strategy has the following characteristics: (1) it is written as a single, straightforward paragraph; (2) it is written at the same level of abstraction, that is, the level of detail should remain consistent throughout the paragraph; (3) it is focused on *what* must be done to solve the problem, rather than the procedural details of *how* the solution is accomplished; (4) it does not have to contain all information uncovered during requirements analysis. The quality of the informal strategy may be assessed by asking the following question: "If a solution is implemented that exactly follows the strategy stated in this paragraph, will the problem be solved?"

An informal strategy for the NC software described in the preceding section is stated in the following paragraph:

> A central computer transmits NC blocks to a numerical control that contains software which reads each NC block and stores it in an NC program file. NC blocks are read from the NC program file and decomposed into control words for position and special functions. Control words are processed and encoded into position control commands and special control commands that are sent to the machine servosystem. Operator commands are input to the NC software via a keyboard interface. Operator commands enable the operator to insert an NC block into an existing NC program file, to display an NC program file on a CRT, and to execute an NC program.

Note that the paragraph attempts to repeat the same terms to describe information and processing rather than using synonyms. In addition the informal strategy is described using system-level terminology rather than an arcane software vocabulary. Finally, the paragraph does not delve into *how* NC blocks are decomposed or *how* control words are processed and encoded. The discussion focuses on what must be done.

9.6 FORMALIZING THE STRATEGY

It is at this point that OOD actually begins. Our goal is to identify objects, operations, and their interrelationships so that a design can be derived. As described in Section 9.3, formalization is composed of four substeps [BOO83]. In the paragraphs that follow, we describe each and then apply it to the NC software example.

9.6.1 Objects and Their Attributes

The identification of objects lies at the core of OOD. Abbott [ABB83] provides a worthwhile discussion:

> Object orientation emphasizes the importance of precisely identifying the objects and their properties to be manipulated by a program before starting to write the details of those manipulations. Without this careful identification, it is almost impossible to be precise about the operations to be performed and their intended effects.
>
> The nouns and noun phrases in the informal strategy are good indicators of the objects and their classifications (i.e., data types) in our problem solution.

Therefore, our focus during this formalization substep is to isolate all nouns and noun phrases contained in the informal strategy.

A brief digression into noun categories is worthwhile at this point. A *common noun* is the name of a *class* of beings or things. For example, vehicle is a common noun that describes a class of things for moving other things. *Proper nouns* are the names of specific beings or things. For example, Porsche 928, Chevy van, and Sherman tank are all proper nouns or noun phrases within the class that we have called vehicle. A *mass* or *abstract* noun is the name of a quantity, an activity or a measure. For example, *traffic* is a mass noun that refers to a collection of proper nouns within the class implied by the common noun *vehicle*.

In the context of object-oriented design (and this substep of formalization), a common noun will often represent a class of objects (a data abstraction). A proper noun will represent an instance of a class. A mass or abstract noun (including units of measurement) will serve to indicate constraining characteristics or problem-specific groupings for objects or classes. It is important to note, however, that context and semantics must be used to determine noun categories. A word can be a common noun in one context, a proper noun in another, and, in some cases, a mass or abstract noun in a third context.

To illustrate the identification of objects, we return to our threaded example—NC Software. The informal strategy is repeated below with all noun and nouns phrases underlined:

A central computer transmits NC blocks to a numerical control that contains software which reads each NC block and stores it in an NC program file. NC blocks are read from the NC program file and decomposed into control words for position and special functions. Control words are processed and encoded into position control commands and special control commands that are sent to the machine servosystem. Operator commands are input to the NC software via a keyboard interface. Operator commands enable the operator to insert an NC block into an existing NC program file, to display an NC program file on a CRT, and to execute an NC program.

After all nouns and noun phrases are identified, an *object table* (Table 9.1) can be completed. The table lists each noun as an object; identifies whether the object falls within the *problem space* (objects outside the bounds of software) or the *solution space* (objects that will be directly created by software) and provides for a description of the attributes of an object. An attribute can be determined by examining all the adjectives in the informal strategy and associating each with an object. In addition, attributes may be discerned from the analysis and classification of problem constraints (step 2 of the OOD method).

It is important to note that not all nouns and noun phrases will be of interest in the final software realization of the solution. Some objects, as already noted, will reside outside the bounds of the software solution space. Other objects, although relevant to the problem, may be redundant or extraneous when the solution is refined. By

TABLE 9.1
Object table

Object	Space	Comment
Central computer	P	
NC blocks	S	
Numerical control	P	
Software	S	For NC
NC program file	S	Composed of NC blocks
Control words	S	For position and special functions
Functions	P	Activities performed by the machine servosystem
Position control commands	S	
Special control commands	S	
Machine servosystem	P	
Operator commands	S	
Keyboard interface	S	
Operator	P	
CRT	P	
NC program	S	Synonymous with NC program file

P = problem space, S = solution space

building the object table, potential objects are assessed and the final set of objects is determined [EVB86].

9.6.2 Operations Applied to Objects

Once objects in the solution space have been identified, the designer selects the set of operations that act on the objects. Operations are identified by examining all the verbs stated in the informal strategy.

Verbs connote actions or occurrences. In the context of OOD formalization, we consider not only verbs but also *descriptive verb phrases* and *predicates* (e.g., is-equal-to) as potential operations. For example, read, compute, is-less-than, determine-the-difference-between, and keep-track-of would all be candidate operations.

Table 9.2 lists all operations (verbs) contained in the informal strategy and shows how each relates to the objects defined in Table 9.1. Referring to the *object-operation table* (Table 9.2), there are many cases in which one operation refers to two or more objects. To which object should we attach the operation? The *Object Oriented Design Handbook* [EVB86] presents some guidelines for completing this substep:

If only one object is necessary for an operation to occur, then that is the object upon which the operation operates....

If two or more objects are required for an operation to occur, then the software engineer must determine which object's underlying implementation (private part) must be known to the operation....

If an operation requires knowledge of more than one type [object], then the operation is not *functionally cohesive* and should be rejected as part of the informal strategy....

TABLE 9.2
Object-operation table

Object	Space	Operations
Central computer	P	Transmits
NC blocks	S	Read, store, read-from-NC-program-file, decompose, insert-into-existing-file,
Numerical control	P	Contains
Software	S	Reads, stores, display, decompose, process, encode, sent
NC program file	S	Stores-in, read-from, display, execute
Control words	S	Processed, encoded
Functions	P	Decomposed-into
Position control commands	S	Sent-to-servosystem
Special control commands	S	Sent-to-servosystem
Machine servosystem	P	
Operator commands	S	Are-input-via-a-keyboard
Keyboard interface	S	
Operator	P	
CRT	P	
NC program	S	Synonymous with NC program file

P = problem space, S = solution space

The above guidelines help us to assess each potential operation and determine to which object it should be attached. For example, consider the phrase from the NC software informal strategy *"insert an NC block into...NC program file."* The insert operation requires two objects: *NC block* and *NC program file*. The *insert* operation must have access to the internal structure of the *NC program file* in order to add blocks to it. However, it need not have detailed knowledge of the internal structure of an *NC block*. Therefore, the operation *insert* is attached to the object NC program file.

Applying the guidelines noted above to the operations shown in Table 9.2, we can derive a refined version of the *object-operation table* shown in Table 9.3. In this table each operation has been attached to a single object and those objects and operations that exist in the problem space (outside the scope of the software) have been removed. In addition, redundant, extraneous, or abstract objects (e.g., the object *software* (See Table 9.1) encompasses all other objects and their operations and adds nothing to a design solution) have been removed; synonymous operations have been combined; and the names of operations have been expanded to make them more descriptive of processing function.

Each object listed in Table 9.3 should have at least one operation that acts on it. However, there are often cases in which an object seems to stand alone; that is, there is no apparent operation that requires information about the object's underlying implementation. Alternatively, we may encounter an operation that appears to apply to no object in the table. This situation may occur for a variety of reasons: (1) the informal strategy is incomplete and an important operation or object has been omitted; (2) an object or operation that belongs in the problem space has been allocated to the solution

TABLE 9.3
Object-operation table—refined

Object	Space	Operations
NC blocks	S	Read-from-central-computer
		Read-from-NC-program-file
		Decompose-into-control-words
NC program file	S	Insert-into-existing-file
		Stores-in
		Read-from
		Display-on-CRT
		Execute
Control words	S	Processed
		Encoded
Position control commands	S	Send-to-servosystem
Special control commands	S	Send-to-servosystem
Operator commands	S	Are-input-via-a-keyboard

P = problem space, S = solution space

space (or vice versa); (3) an operation shown in the object-operation table does require knowledge of the "stand alone" object, but this relationship has gone unrecognized; (4) the informal strategy has been written at different levels of abstraction, that is, low-level objects or operations are specified but only high-level operations or objects are discussed. In summary, it is crucially important to write, edit, review, and re-edit the informal strategy discussed in Section 9.5. Objects and operations should be discussed at a consistent level of abstraction.

It is often necessary to associate *attributes* to both objects and operations. An attribute helps us to understand the characteristics of the object or operation. As an example, consider the following excerpt from an informal strategy:

An out-of-bounds condition produces a multipitch alarm that is transmitted immediately to the operator station.

Table 9.4 lists all objects and operations and their attributes, based on the above statement of informal strategy.

Referring to Table 9.4, adjectives and adverbs become attributes of objects and operations, respectively. At the level of abstraction presented in the informal strategy, each of the attributes would have to be more completely defined. For example, what

TABLE 9.4
Object-operation table with attributes

Object	Space	Attribute	Operation	Space	Attribute
Condition	S	Out-of-bounds	Produces	S	–
Alarm	S	Multipitch	Produces	S	–
			Transmitted	S	Immediately
Station	P	Operator	Transmitted	S	–

does *immediately* mean—10-millisecond response or 10-second response? What does *out-of-bounds* imply? How many tones does *multipitch* refer to? Each of the attributes presented in the informal strategy must be bounded. However, bounding may be postponed until the strategy is restated at a lower level of abstraction. We note the attributes at this level as a reminder that further refinement and bounding is necessary.

In some cases the object attributes may be directly combined in the name of the object. This occurs only when the informal strategy is stated at a relatively high level of abstraction. For example, *NC Program File*, *control words*, and *position control command* (Table 9.3) embody attributes for the objects *file*, *word*, and *command*, respectively. As these objects and their respective operations are refined, the attributes may have to be stripped from the object and specified in detail.

9.6.3 Program Components and Interfaces

An important aspect of software design quality is *modularity*, that is, the specification of *program components* (modules) that are combined to form a complete program. OOD defines the object as a program component that is itself linked to other components (e.g., private data, operations). But defining objects and operations is not enough. We must also identify the *interfaces* that exist between objects and the overall structure (considered in an architectural sense) of the objects.

Although a *program component* is a design abstraction, it should be represented in the context of the programming language with which the design is to be implemented. To accommodate OOD the programming language to be used for implementation should be capable of creating the following program component (modeled after Ada):

```
PACKAGE program-component-name IS
     TYPE specification of data objects
        .
        .
        .
     PROC specification of related operations
        .
        .
        .

PRIVATE
     data structure details for objects
PACKAGE BODY program-component-name IS
     PROC operation.1 (interface description) IS
        .
        .
        .
     END
     PROC operation.n (interface description) IS
        .
        .
        .
     END
END program-component-name
```

Referring to the Ada-like PDL (program design language) shown above, a program component is specified by indicating both data objects and operations. The *specification part* of the component indicates all data objects (declared with the TYPE statement) and the operations (PROC for *procedure*) that act on them. The private part (PRIVATE) of the component provides otherwise hidden details of data structure and processing. In the context of our earlier discussion, the PACKAGE is conceptually similar to objects discussed in Section 9.2.

The first program component to be identified should be the highest-level module from which all processing originates and all data structures evolve. Referring once again to the NC Software example considered in preceding sections, we can define the highest-level program component as:

PROCEDURE nc-software

Using Table 9.3 as a guide, the *nc-software* component can be coupled with the following packages:

```
PACKAGE nc-program-file IS
    TYPE nc.program.file structure
    PROC insert-into-existing-file
    PROC stores-in
    PROC display-on-CRT
    PROC read-from
    PROC execute
END nc-program-file

PACKAGE nc-blocks IS
    TYPE nc-block-structure
    PROC read-from
    PROC decompose
END nc-blocks

PACKAGE control-words IS
    TYPE control-words
    PROC process
    PROC encode
END control-words

PACKAGE commands IS
    TYPE operator-command
    TYPE control-command
    PROC send
    PROC input
END commands
```

Data objects and corresponding operations are specified for each of the program components for NC Software. It should be noted that no attempt has been made to specify information about the private part of the data objects or details of the operations. These implementation details are considered later.

Once program components have been identified, we are ready to examine the evolving design and critically assess the need for changes. It is likely that a review of the "first-cut" definition of packages will result in modifications that add new data objects or return to earlier OOD steps (i.e., the informal strategy) to assess the completeness of operations that have been specified.

To illustrate the modifications that may occur as a result of the review of the first-cut design, consider the *nc-blocks* package. A review of the informal strategy and Table 9.3 indicates that an NC block may originate from the central computer, an NC program file, or the machine operator. Yet there appears to be no differentiation in the *nc-blocks* package. To accommodate this situation, the designer suggests the following approach:

> All NC blocks, regardless of origination, are read and placed into an nc-block-buffer. The point of origin for an NC block is indicated with an origination-pointer. The buffer is read and appropriate follow-on processing occurs.

The approach noted above considers the informal strategy at a lower level of abstraction. Implementation issues (e.g., buffers, pointers) are specified and two different read operations are indicated. In addition an *origination-pointer* is defined so that the original *read* can be properly conducted. Modification to the *nc-blocks* package might be:

```
PACKAGE nc-blocks IS
    TYPE nc-block-structure
    TYPE nc-block-buffer
    TYPE origination-pointer
    PROC read-from
    PROC decompose
END nc-blocks
```

The interface to the *read-from* procedure must contain an origination pointer so that proper reading can occur.

9.6.4   Graphical Representations for OOD

The program components defined in the preceding section can be represented graphically to help establish interface connections and to provide easily recognized patterns for design representation. Booch [BOO83] proposes the notation, sometimes called *Booch diagrams*, for program components shown in Figure 9.5. In the figure, a program component (object) is represented as a box that can be divided into a specification part (visible to the outside) and a private part (also called a *body part*) that is hidden from the outside. The free-form "cloud" represents implementation details that are part of the private part or package body and are not yet specified.

A package is represented by the notation shown in Figure 9.6. Data objects are noted by rounded rectangles, while operations that act on the objects are notated by normal rectangles. Again, the "cloud" shape is used to represent currently undefined implementation details.

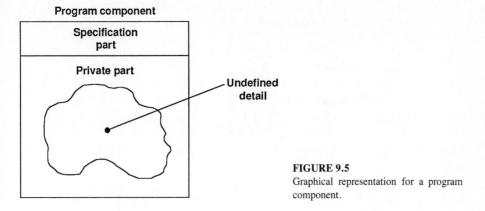

FIGURE 9.5
Graphical representation for a program component.

Figure 9.7 illustrates the use of Booch diagrams to represent the dependencies among program components. The connecting arrows imply dependency; that is, the package or component at the origin of the arrow depends on the package or program component at the tip of the arrow. In Figure 9.7 the highest-level program component, X, depends on the objects and operations contained in package 1 and package 2 to satisfy its function. Package 2 depends on objects and operations contained in package 3 and package 4.

Using Booch diagrams, a graphical representation of NC Software example may be developed. Based on the program component description contained in Section 9.6.3, Figure 9.8 is drawn. In the figure the highest-level program component, *nc-software*, is shown to depend on the packages *nc-blocks* and *commands*. The package *nc-blocks* depends upon the objects and operations of *nc-program-file* and the package *control-words*. The package *nc-program-file* also depends on *commands*, which in turn depends on the objects and operations in the package *control-words*.

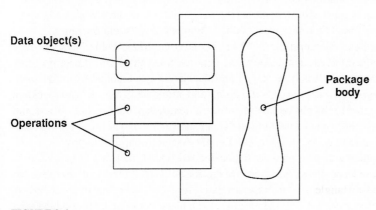

FIGURE 9.6
Package (object) notation.

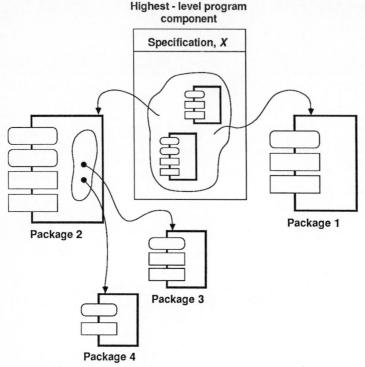

**Highest - level program
component**

FIGURE 9.7
Program components and interfaces, and Booch diagram [BOO83].

Examining the figure, we see that operations associated with NC blocks are contingent upon the availability of the NC program file and the operations that manipulate it. Decomposition of an NC block in preparation for command output to the machine servosystem requires control word information. Similarly, the actual generation of servosystem commands must also depend on the availability of control words. Operator commands are processed by directly accessing command objects and operations.

Another graphical notation for OOD has been proposed by Wiener and Sincovec [WEI84]. Called the *modular design chart*, the notation takes the form shown in Figure 9.9. The dependencies between packages are shown via quasi-communication pathways on a *software bus*. Package specifications and implementation details (package bodies) are connected to the bus in a manner that indicates dependencies of objects and operations. Figure 9.9 is a reasonable facsimile of the Booch diagram in Figure 9.7.

The use of graphical notation for OOD is not essential, but it does provide an indication of dependency among packages (objects and operations) that is lacking in a PDL representation. The Booch diagram or the modular structure chart is typically used to represent program components at a relatively high level of abstraction. When implementation detail design commences, the graphical notation is abandoned and PDL is used as the design representation.

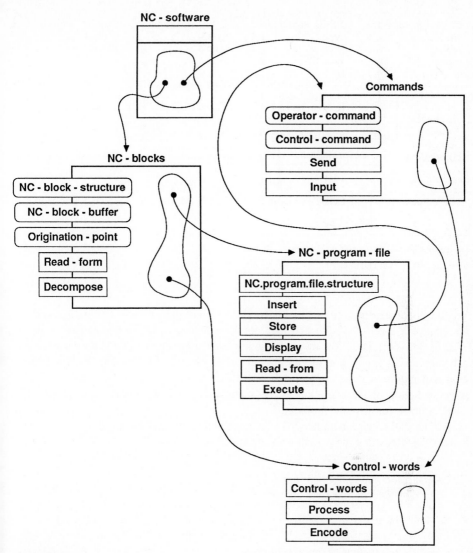

FIGURE 9.8
NC software design representation.

9.6.5   Implementation Detail

The detail design step of OOD is similar in many respects to detail design for any software design methodology. Interfaces are described in detail; data structures are refined and specified; algorithms are designed for each program unit using fundamental design concepts such as stepwise refinement and structured programming. The key difference for OOD is that the process described in Sections 9.5 and 9.6 may be applied

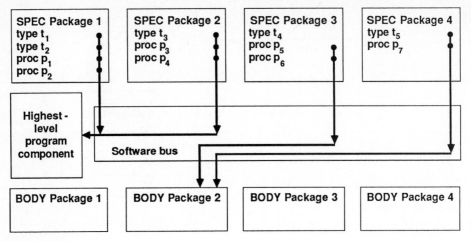

FIGURE 9.9
Modular design chart [WIE84].

recursively at any time. In fact, recursive definition of the solution strategy is essential to achieve a level of design and data abstraction from which implementation detail may be derived. The following guideline has been suggested [EVB86] for determining when recursive application of OOD is necessary: "If the implementation of an operation will require a large (greater than 200 lines) amount of code, then one takes the stated function of the operation as the statement of a new problem and repeats the OOD process for this new problem."

The PDL design template for a package can be used as the starting point for detail design. Recalling the overall package structure:

```
PACKAGE program-component-name IS
     TYPE specification of data objects
          .
          .
          .
     PROC specification of related operations
          .
          .
          .
PRIVATE
     data structure details for objects
PACKAGE BODY program-component-name IS
     PROC operation.1 (interface description) IS
          .
          .
          .
     END
```

```
PROC operation.n (interface description) IS
    .
    .
    .
END
END program-component-name
```

Detail design completes all information required to fully implement data structure and types contained in the PRIVATE portion of the package and all procedural detail contained in the PACKAGE BODY.

To illustrate the detail design of a program component, we reconsider the *control-words* package defined as part of the NC Software example. To this point in the OOD process *control-words* may be represented with the following package skeleton:

```
PACKAGE control-words IS
    TYPE control-words
    PROC process
    PROC encode
PRIVATE
    … control-words data structure
PACKAGE BODY control-words IS
    PROC process
        … procedural detail
    END
    PROC encode
        … procedural detail
    END
END control-words
```

The first step is to define the interfaces for each of the operations attached to control words and to identify internal structure for data objects. We use the PDL notation introduced in Chapter 6 and combine it with the PDL for representing packages introduced earlier in this chapter:

```
PACKAGE control-words IS
    TYPE control-words IS PRIVATE;
    PROC process (nc-block: IN ; control-words: OUT);
    PROC encode (control-words: IN; command; OUT);
PRIVATE
    TYPE control-words IS STRUCTURE DEFINED
        word-type IS STRING LENGTH (1);
        value IS INTEGER;
    END control-words TYPE;
END control-words
```

The next step requires stepwise refinement of each operation associated with the *control-words* package. To begin the refinement, we develop a processing narrative (an informal strategy) for *process* and *encode*:

The *process* operation accepts an NC block field as input and tests to determine the field type and whether the value contained in the field falls within pre-established bounds for the servosystem. If data are within bounds, *process* produces a control word corresponding to the NC block field. If data are out-of-bounds, a special control word indicating error condition is produced.

The *encode* operation accepts a control word and converts it to the absolute coordinate system of the machine. All special commands and operator commands are passed unchanged. All positioning control words must be converted so that *x* and *y* values are represented within the range 0 to 32768. The *encode* operation produces a command that consists of a letter command code and the appropriate special, operator or positioning command.

The processing narrative for *process* and *encode* introduces a new (and lower) level of abstraction. Additional lower-level data objects (e.g., NC block field) are introduced and specific information about each operation's algorithm is provided.

```
PACKAGE BODY control words IS
.
.
.

    PROC encode (control-words: IN; commands: OUT);
        – – a control word can take on values that range
        – – from –100.00 < = x,y < = + 100.00 where command
        – – value 0 corresponds to –100.0 and command value
        – – + 100.0 corresponds to 32678.
        TYPE scale-factor is SCALAR FLOAT;
        TYPE s-min, s-max, c-min, c-max IS INTEGER;
        command [1] = control-words [word-type];
        s-max : = 100;
        s-min : = –100;
        c-max : = 32768;
        c-min : = 0;
        scale-factor : = float.convert ((s-max – s-min)/
                    (s-max – s-min));
        IF control-words [word-type] <>κ "x" OR
           control-words [word-type] <> "y"
               THEN commands [2..] = control-word [value];
               ELSE commands [2..] = scale-factor *
                    control-words [value];
        ENDIF
    END encode
```

The PDL representation of the *encode* operation can be translated into the appropriate implementation language.

9.7 AN ALTERNATIVE APPROACH

The object-oriented design method presented in Sections 9.3 to 9.6 is oriented toward software development in programming languages such as Ada. The method does not explicitly address a number of important object-oriented concepts (e.g., inheritance, messages) that can serve to make OOD even more powerful. This section describes an alternative approach to OOD that has evolved from software development in programming languages such as Smalltalk—languages that directly support abstraction, inheritance, messages, and all other OOD concepts.

William Lorensen [LOR86a] has done an excellent job of summarizing an alternative approach to OOD. The remainder of this section (reproduced with the permission of General Electric Co., Corporate Research and Development Center) contains an excerpt from his discussion of object-oriented design.

9.7.1 Design Steps

The OOD approach described in this section is appropriate for preliminary design. The primary objective is to define and characterize abstractions in a manner that results in a definition of all important objects, methods (operations), and messages. Lorensen [LOR86a] suggests the following approach:

1. *Identify the data abstractions for each subsystem.*
   These data abstractions are the classes of the system. Working from the requirements document, the abstraction process should be performed top-down when possible, although many times the abstractions are mentioned explicitly in the requirements. Often the classes correspond to physical objects within the system being modeled. If this is not the case, the use of analogies, drawn from the designer's experience on past system designs, is helpful. This is, by far, the most difficult step in the design process and the selection of these abstractions influences the entire system architecture.

2. *Identify the attributes for each abstraction.*
   The attributes become the *instance variables* (methods for manipulating data) for each class. Many times, if the classes correspond to physical objects, the required instance variables are obvious. Other instance variables may be required to respond to requests from other objects in the system. Defer the specification of the data structures containing the attributes until the detailed design stage.

3. *Identify the operations for each abstraction.*
   The operations are the methods (or procedures) for each class. Some methods access and update instance variables, while others execute operations singular to the class. Do not specify the details of the methods' implementations now, only the functionalities. If the new abstraction inherits from another class, inspect the methods of that class to see if any need to be overridden by the new class. Defer the internal design of methods until the detailed design stage, where more conventional design techniques can be used.

4. *Identify the communication between objects.*
   This step defines the messages that objects send to each other. Here, define a correspondence between the methods and the messages that invoke the methods. Even if an object-oriented implementation is not planned, messages help the design team to communicate and can be used in the next step to write scenarios. The

design team decides on this protocol with consistency in message naming as a primary consideration.

5. *Test the design with scenarios*.

Scenarios, consisting of messages to objects, test the design's ability to match the system's requirements. Write a scenario to satisfy each user level function in the requirements specification.

6. *Apply inheritance where appropriate*.

If the data abstraction process in step 1 is performed top-down, introduce inheritance there. However, if abstractions are created bottom-up (often because the requirements directly name the abstractions), apply inheritance here, before going to another level of abstraction. The goal is to reuse as much of the data and/or methods that have already been designed. At this step, common data and operations often surface and these common instance variables and methods can be combined into a new class. This class may or may not have meaning as an object by itself. If its sole purpose is to collect common instance variables and methods, it is called an *abstract class*.

The designer repeats these steps at each level of abstraction. Through successive refinements of the design, the designer's view of the system changes depending on the needs at the moment. Each level of abstraction is implemented at a lower level until a point is reached where the abstraction corresponds to a primitive element in the design. New levels of abstraction should provide some attribute or operation that cannot be expressed at the previous lowest level. For example, the abstraction of geometric primitives might start with a polygon, with a rectangle defined at the next level of abstraction, followed by a square.

9.7.2 A Design Example

As an example of the OOD method described above, we consider a simple CAD tool to view and manipulate a variety of primitives in two dimensions. This CAD tool has the following requirements, described in a narrative form:

> The tool allows users to create and manipulate 2D polygons, splines, and conics on a color graphics terminal. Using a graphics input device such as a mouse, the user can move, rotate, scale, and color the primitives.

This is, indeed, a vague requirements definition, but it contains enough information for us to begin the design process. Here, we'll concentrate on the design of conic support. A conic is a second order implicit curve of the form,

$$ax^2 + bxy + cy^2 + dx + ey + f = 0$$

Conics embrace circles, ellipses, hyperbolas, and parabolas.

Pass 1

1. *Identify the data abstractions for each subsystem.*

   Abstractions for geometric systems are particularly easy to derive. The requirements say that the tool will have three different primitives, but first we look for things that are common to all primitives. Our initial class hierarchy is shown in Figure 9.10. The highest class in the diagram is called *object*, performing functions that are appropriate to all classes. The *primitive* class is an abstract class, acting as a place holder for data and methods that can be used by classes lower in the hierarchy.

2. *Identify the attributes for each abstraction.*

   At least one attribute of all primitives is obvious, color. If we think about geometric objects in general, other attributes come to mind such as position, orientation, texture, scale, opacity, etc. We know from the requirements that the user will move, scale, and rotate the primitives, so position, scale factors, and orientation are appropriate instance variables.

3. *Identify the operations for each abstraction.*

   Requirements documents often explicitly mention operations. Here, our tool requirements specify create, move, scale, and rotate operations. We'll also need methods to access instance variables. A summary of methods for primitives follows:

create_primitive	creates a primitive
set_position	sets the x,y position
get_position	gets the x,y position
add_position	increments the x,y position
set_orientation	sets the angle of rotation
get_orientation	gets the angle of rotation
add_orientation	increments the angle of rotation
set_scale	sets x,y scale factor
get_scale	gets the x,y scale
add_scale	increments the x, y scale
set_color	sets the color
get_color	gets the color

4. *Identify the communication between objects.*

   Now we can specify the inter-object protocol by associating messages with the methods defined above:

FIGURE 9.10
Initial class hierarchy.

new!	create_primitive
position =	set_position
position?	get_position
position +	add_position
orientation =	set_orientation
orientation?	get_orientation
orientation +	add_orientation
scale =	set_scale
scale?	get_scale
scale +	add_scale
color =	set_color
color?	get_color

5. *Test the design with scenarios.*

We match the requirements with simple scenarios that show how each requirement will be met:

Create a primitive:
       primitive new! name = aPrimitive
Move:
       aPrimitive position = (1,2)
Rotate:
       aPrimitive orientation = 30
Scale:
       aPrimitive scale = (10,1)
Set color:
       aPrimitive color = (1,0,0)

6. *Apply inheritance where appropriate.*

Since we only have one level of inheritance so far, we skip this step for now.

Pass 2

Now we repeat the six steps again to add further abstractions.

1. *Identify the data abstractions for each subsystem.*

The polygons, conics, and splines are types of primitives. This level of abstraction is shown in Figure 9.11.

2. *Identify the attributes for each abstraction.*

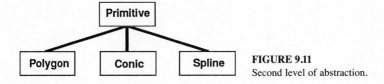

FIGURE 9.11
Second level of abstraction.

Here we'll go through the remaining steps for the conic only. Six coefficients specify a conic and become instance variables.

3. *Identify the operations for each abstraction.*
   We add new operations to set and retrieve the six coefficients:

   set_coefficients   sets the coefficients
   get_coefficients   gets the coefficients

   Also, since the conic has a different data structure than the primitive, we need a method to create a conic:

   create_conic   create a conic

4. *Identify the communication between objects.*

   new!   create_conic
   coefficients = set_coefficients
   coefficients?   get_coefficients

5. *Test the design with scenarios.*

   Create a conic:
        Conic new! name = aConic
   Modify a conic:
        aConic coefficients = (1,0,3,2.5,3,0)
   Move:
        aConic position = (1,2)
   Rotate:
        aConic orientation = 30
   Scale:
        aConic scale = (10,1)
   Set color:
        aConic color = (1,0,0)

6. *Apply inheritance where appropriate.*
   No inheritance is appropriate since we're proceeding in a top-down mode.

Pass 3
One more pass through the design will complete the process for now.

1. *Identify the data abstractions for each subsystem.*
   Six coefficients specify a conic, but this is not a convenient way for users to specify shape. We note, however, that circles and ellipses have parameters that a user can easily specify, either numerically or graphically. As long as we're at it,

we might as well add hyperbolas and parabolas, so we introduce a new level of abstraction in Figure 9.12.

2. *Identify the attributes for each abstraction.*
Here we'll go through the remaining steps for the circle. An additional attribute of a circle is its radius.

3. *Identify the operations for each abstraction.*

set_radius   sets the radius of the circle
get_radius   gets the radius of the circle

The circle is a restriction of a conic, so we provide a creation method that maintains the restriction.

create_circle   create a circle

Since a circle inherits methods from a conic, we must look at the conic's methods to see if there are any we need to override. For example, in the conic equation, the circle has some of the coefficients set to zero. If we let a circle inherit the *set_coefficients* method from a conic, we might create what we think is a circle but is actually a general conic. We need to override the conic's *set_coefficients* method. The conic's *get_coefficients* method is still valid however.

set_coefficients   set conic coefficients for a circle

4. *Identify the communication between objects.*

new!   create_circle
radius =   set_radius
radius?   get_radius
set_coefficients   set_coefficients

5. *Test the design with scenarios.*

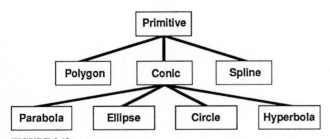

FIGURE 9.12
Third level of abstraction.

[EVB86]   *Object-Oriented Design Handbook*, EVB Software Engineering, Inc., Rockville, MD, 1986.

[GOL83]   Goldberg, A., and D. Robson, *Smalltalk-80: The Language and Its Implementation*, Addison-Wesley, 1983.

[LOR86]   Lorensen, W., "An Object-Oriented Graphics Animation System," General Electric Corporate Research & Development, Technical Information Series report, 1986.

[LOR86a]   Lorensen, W., Object-Oriented Design, *CRD Software Engineering Guidelines*, General Electric Co., 1986.

[LOV85]   Love, T., "Message Object Programming: Experiences with Commercial Systems," Productivity Products International, Sandy Hook, CT, 1985.

[WIE84]   Wiener, R., and R. Sincovec, *Software Engineering with Modula-2 and Ada*, Wiley, 1984.

PROBLEMS AND POINTS TO PONDER

9.1 From your everyday experience, select five classes of objects and provide at least five instantiations of objects for each class.

9.2 Do some research on object-oriented programming languages (e.g., Smalltalk) and explain why a programming language such as FORTRAN would not be suited to object-oriented applications.

9.3 Specify, design, and implement a tool that will parse all nouns, noun phrases, verbs, and verb phrases from an English language paragraph. The output of the tool should create a partially complete object-operation table. *Note*: This is not a simple problem!

9.4 OOD tends to be programming language–dependent. Why?

9.5 Apply OOD techniques to the Conveyor Line Sorting System described in Chapter 2 (Section 2.2).

9.6 Apply OOD techniques to the Patient Monitoring System (PMS) described in Chapter 5 (Section 5.2.1).

9.7 Apply OOD techniques to the microprocessor-based elevator controller described in Problem 8.4.

9.8 Apply OOD techniques to the Home Security System described in Chapter 6 (Section 6.7.5).

9.9 You are responsible for the development of an electronic mail (E-mail) system to be implemented on a PC network. The E-mail system will enable users to create letters to be mailed to another user or to a distribution or specific address list. Letters can be read, copied, stored, etc. The E-mail system will make use of existing word processing capability to create letters. Using this description as a starting point, derive a set of requirements and apply OOD techniques to create a top-level design of the E-mail system.

9.10 A small island nation has decided to build an air traffic control (ATC) system for its only airport. The system is specified as follows:

All aircraft landing at the airport must have a transponder that transmits aircraft type and flight data in high-density packed format to the ATC ground station. The ATC ground station can query an aircraft for specific information. When the ATC ground station receives data, they are unpacked and stored in an aircraft data base. A computer graphics display is created from the stored information and displayed for an air traffic controller. The display is updated every 10 seconds. All information is analyzed to determine if "dangerous situations" are present. The air traffic controller can query the data base for specific information about any plane displayed on the screen.

Using OOD, create a design for the ATC system. Do not attempt to implement it!

9.11 Using Booch [BOO83] as a guide, develop a detailed representation of the ATC system (Problem 9.10) using Booch diagrams.

9.12 Using Wiener and Sincovec [WIE84] as a guide, develop a detailed representation of the ATC system (Problem 9.10) using modular design charts.

FURTHER READINGS

The object-oriented design literature is expanding rapidly. Books by Booch [BOO83] and Goldberg and Robson [GOL83] are recommended for those who intend to pursue OOD more fully. A book by Cox (*Object Oriented Programming*, Addison-Wesley, 1986) describes object-oriented techniques using a C language dialect. *System Design with Ada* (Prentice-Hall, 1984) by Buhr presents another design approach for OOD that couples data flow and program structure charts with a notation that is similar to the Booch diagram.

An *IEEE Transactions on Software Engineering* special issue on software design (vol. SE-12, no. 2, February 1986) contains an excellent paper by Booch on "object-oriented development." A paper by Tarumi et al. (*Compsac-85 Proceedings*, IEEE, October 1985) discusses the topic further. A paper by Stefik and Bobrow ("Object-Oriented Programming: Themes and Variations," *The AI Magazine*, vol. 6, no. 4, 1986, pp. 40–62) presents a worthwhile overview of OOD and contains an interesting discussion of the history of object-oriented methods. A recent issue of *BYTE* magazine (August 1986) was dedicated to object-oriented languages and contains eight excellent articles on both languages and object-oriented techniques.

CHAPTER
10

REAL-TIME
DESIGN

The design of *real-time* computing systems is the most challenging and complex task that can be undertaken by a software engineer. By its very nature, software for real-time systems makes demands on analysis, design, and testing techniques that are unknown in other application areas.

Real-time software is highly coupled to the external world. That is, real-time software must respond to the problem domain (the real world) in a time frame dictated by the problem domain. Because real-time software must operate under rigorous performance constraints, software design is often driven by hardware as well as software architecture, operating system characteristics as well as application requirements, programming language vagaries as well as design issues.

In his book on real-time software, Robert Glass [GLA83] provides a useful introduction to the subject of real-time systems:

> The digital computer is becoming ever more present in the daily lives of all of us. Computers allow our watches to play games as well as tell time, optimize the gas mileage of our latest generation cars, and sequence our appliances.... [In industry, computers control machines, coordinate processes, and increasingly, replace manual skills and human recognition with automated systems and "artificial intelligence."]
>
> All these computing interactions—be they helpful or intrusive—are examples of real-time computing. The computer is controlling something that interacts with reality on a timely basis. In fact, timing is the essence of the interaction.... An unresponsive real-time system may be worse than no system at all.

No more than a decade ago, real-time software development was considered a black art, applied by anointed wizards who jealously guarded their closed world. Today, there just are not enough wizards to go around. Yet, there is no question that the engineering of real-time software requires special skills. In this chapter we examine real-time software and discuss at least some of the skills required to build it.

10.1   SYSTEM CONSIDERATIONS

Like any computer-based system, a real-time system must integrate hardware, software, human, and data base elements to properly achieve a set of functional and performance requirements. In Chapter 2 we examined the allocation task for computer-based systems and indicated that the system engineer must allocate function and performance among the system elements. The problem for real-time systems is proper allocation. Real-time performance is often as important as function, yet allocation decisions that relate to performance are often difficult to make with assurance. Can a processing algorithm meet severe timing constraints, or should we build special hardware to do the job? Can an off-the-shelf operating system meet our need for efficient interrupt handling, multitasking, and communication, or should we build a custom executive? Can specified hardware coupled with proposed software meet performance criteria? These and many other questions must be answered by the real-time system engineer.

A comprehensive discussion of all elements of real-time systems is beyond the scope of this book. Among a number of good sources of information are [FOS81], [MEL83], and [SAV85]. However, it is important that we understand each of the elements of a real-time system before focusing on software analysis and design issues.

"Real-Time Systems" [HIN83] appeared in the Special Series on System Integration published in *Electronic Design* magazine. The article considers real-time issues from a system point of view and serves as a worthwhile introduction to other topics in this chapter. Major excerpts (edited to conform to the format and style of this book) from the article are presented in the next section.

10.2   REAL-TIME SYSTEMS*

Real-time systems generate some action in response to external events. To accomplish this function, they perform high-speed data acquisition and control under severe time and reliability constraints. Because these constraints are so stringent, real-time systems are frequently dedicated to a single application.

Until recently the major consumer of real-time systems was the military. Today, however, significant decreases in hardware costs make it possible for most companies to afford real-time systems (and products) for diverse applications that include process

---

*Based on an article, "Real-Time Systems" by H.J. Hinden and W.B. Rausch-Hinden [HIN83]. Reproduced with permission of *Electronic Design* and Hayden Publishing.

control, industrial automation, medical and scientific research, computer graphics, local and wide-area communications, aerospace systems, computer-aided testing, and a vast array of industrial instrumentation.

10.2.1 Integration and Performance Issues

Putting together a real-time system presents the system engineer with difficult hardware and software decisions. [The allocation issues associated with hardware for real-time systems are beyond the scope of this book (see [SAV85] for additional information).] Once the software element has been allocated, detailed software requirements are established and a fundamental software design must be developed. Among many real-time design concerns are: coordination between the real-time tasks, processing of system interrupts, I/O handling to ensure that no data are lost, specifying the system's internal and external timing constraints, and ensuring the accuracy of its data base.

Each real-time design concern for software must be applied in the context of system *performance*. In most cases the performance of a real-time system is measured as one or more time-related characteristics, but other measures such as fault tolerance may also be used.

Some real-time systems are designed for applications in which only the response time or the data transfer rate is critical. Other real-time applications require optimization of both parameters under peak loading conditions. What is more, real-time systems must handle their peak loads while performing a number of simultaneous tasks.

Since the performance of a real-time system is determined primarily by the system response time and its data transfer rate, it is important to understand these two parameters. System *response time* is the time within which a system must detect an internal or external event and respond with an action. Often, event detection and response generation are simple. It is the processing of information about the event to determine an appropriate response that may involve complex, time-consuming algorithms.

Among the key parameters that affect response time are *context switching* and *interrupt latency*. Context switching involves the time and overhead needed to switch among tasks, and interrupt latency is the time lag before the switch is actually possible. Other parameters that affect response time are the speed of computation and of access to mass storage.

The *data transfer rate* indicates how fast serial or parallel, as well as analog or digital, data must be moved into or out of the system. Hardware vendors often quote timing and capacity values as performance characteristics. However, hardware specifications for performance are usually measured in isolation and are often of little value in determining overall real-time system performance. Therefore, I/O device performance, bus latency, buffer size, disk performance, and a host of other factors, although important, are only part of the story of real-time system design.

Real-time systems are often required to process a continuous stream of incoming data. Design must assure that no data are missed. In addition a real-time system must respond to events that are asynchronous. Therefore, the arrival sequence and data volume cannot be easily predicted in advance.

Although all software applications must be reliable, real-time systems make special demands on reliability, restart, and fault recovery. Because the real world is being monitored and controlled, loss of monitoring or control (or both) is intolerable in many circumstances (e.g., an air traffic control system). Consequently, real-time systems contain restart and fault-recovery mechanisms and frequently have built-in redundancy to ensure backup.

The need for reliability, however, has spurred an ongoing debate about whether *on-line* systems, such as airline reservation systems and automatic bank tellers, also qualify as real-time. On the one hand such on-line systems must respond to external interrupts within prescribed response times on the order of one second. On the other hand nothing catastrophic occurs if an on-line system fails to meet response requirements; instead, only system degradation results.

10.2.2   Interrupt Handling

One characteristic that serves to distinguish real-time systems from any other type is *interrupt handling*. A real-time system must respond to external stimuli—*interrupts*—in a time frame dictated by the external world. Because multiple stimuli (interrupts) are often present, priorities and priority interrupts must be established. In other words the most important task must always be serviced within predefined time constraints regardless of other events.

Interrupt handling entails not only storing information so that the computer can correctly restart the interrupted task, but also avoiding deadlocks and endless loops. The overall approach to interrupt handling is illustrated in Figure 10.1. Normal processing flow is "interrupted" by an event that is detected by processor hardware. An *event* is any occurrence that requires immediate service and may be generated by either hardware or software. The state of the interrupted program is saved (i.e., all register contents, control blocks, etc. are saved), and control is passed to an interrupt service routine that branches to software appropriate for handling the interrupt. Upon completion of interrupt servicing, the state of the machine is restored and normal processing flow continues.

In many situations, interrupt servicing for one event may itself be interrupted by another, higher-priority event. Interrupt priority levels (Figure 10.2) may be established. If a lower-priority process is accidentally allowed to interrupt a higher-priority one, it may be difficult to restart the processes in the right order and an endless loop may result.

To handle interrupts and still meet the system time constraints, many real-time operating systems make dynamic calculations to determine whether the system goals can be met. These dynamic calculations are based on the average frequency of occurrence of events, the amount of time it takes to service them (if they can be serviced), and the routines that can interrupt them and temporarily prevent their servicing.

If the dynamic calculations show that it is impossible to handle the events that can occur in the system and still meet the time constraints, the system engineer must

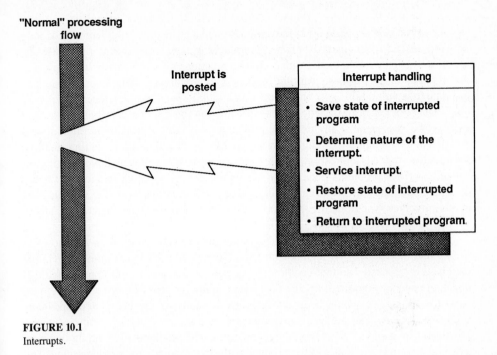

FIGURE 10.1
Interrupts.

decide on a scheme of action. One possible scheme involves buffering the data so that it can be processed quickly when the system is ready.

10.2.3 Real-Time Data Bases

Like many data-processing systems, real-time systems often are coupled with a data base management function. However, *distributed data bases* would seem to be a pre-

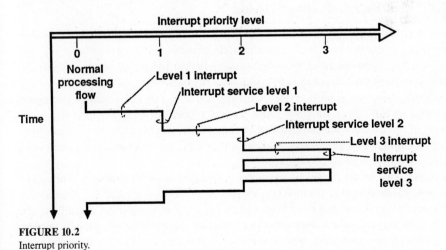

FIGURE 10.2
Interrupt priority.

ferred approach in real-time systems because multitasking is commonplace and data are often processed in parallel. If the data base is distributed and not centralized, individual tasks can access their data faster, more reliably, and with fewer bottlenecks. The use of a distributed data base for real-time applications divides input/output "traffic" and shortens queues of tasks waiting for access to a data base. Moreover, a failure of one data base will rarely cause the failure of the entire system if redundancy is built in.

The performance efficiencies achieved through the use of a distributed data base must be weighed against any potential problems associated with data partitioning and replication. Although data redundancy improves response time by providing multiple information sources, replication requirements for distributed files also produce logistical and overhead problems since all the file copies must be updated. In addition the use of distributed data bases introduces the problem of *concurrency control*. Concurrency control involves synchronizing the data bases so that all copies have the correct, identical information free for access.

The conventional approach to concurrency control is based on what are known as *locking* and *time stamps*. At regular intervals, the following tasks are initiated: (1) the data base is "locked" so that concurrency control is assured; no I/O is permitted; (2) updating occurs as required; (3) the data base is unlocked; (4) files are validated to assure that all updates have been correctly made; and (5) the completed update is acknowledged. All locking tasks are monitored by a master clock (i.e., time stamps). The delays involved in these procedures, as well as the problems of avoiding inconsistent updates and deadlock, mitigate against the widespread use of distributed data bases.

Some techniques, however, have been developed to speed updating and to solve the concurrency problem. One of these, called the *exclusive-writer protocol*, maintains the consistency of replicated files by allowing only a single, exclusive writing task to update a file. It therefore eliminates the high overhead of locking or time stamp procedures.

10.2.4 Real-Time Operating Systems

Choosing a real-time operating system (RTOS) for a specific application is no easy chore. Some operating system classifications are possible, but most do not fit into neat categories with clear-cut advantages and disadvantages. Instead, there is considerable overlap in capabilities, target systems, and other features.

Some real-time operating systems are applicable to a broad range of system configurations, while others are geared to a particular board or even microprocessor, regardless of the surrounding electronic environment. An RTOS achieves its capabilities through a combination of software features and (increasingly) a variety of microcoded capabilities implemented in hardware.

Today, two broad classes of operating systems are used for real-time work: (1) a dedicated RTOS designed exclusively for real-time applications and (2) general purpose operating systems that have been enhanced to provide real-time capability. The use of a *real-time executive* makes real-time performance feasible for a general purpose operating system. Behaving like application software, the executive performs a number of operating system functions—particularly those that affect real-time performance—faster and more efficiently than the general purpose operating system.

All operating systems must have a priority scheduling mechanism, but an RTOS must provide a *priority mechanism* that allows high-priority interrupts to take precedence over less important ones. Moreover, because interrupts occur in response to asynchronous, nonrecurring events, they must be serviced without first taking time to swap in a program from disk storage. Consequently, to guarantee the required response time, a real-time operating system must have a mechanism for *memory locking*, that is, keeping at least some programs in main memory so that swapping overhead is avoided.

To determine which kind of real-time operating system best matches an application, measures of RTOS quality can be defined and evaluated. Context switching time and interrupt latency (discussed earlier) determine interrupt-handling capability, the most important aspect of a real-time system. Context switching time is the time the operating system takes to store the state of the computer and the contents of the registers so that it can return to a processing task after servicing the interrupt.

Interrupt latency, the maximum time lag before the system gets around to switching a task, occurs because in an operating system there are often nonreentrant or critical processing paths that must be completed before an interrupt can be processed.

The length of these paths (the number of instructions required before the system can service an interrupt) indicates the worst-case time lag. The worst case occurs if a high-priority interrupt is generated immediately after the system enters a critical path between an interrupt and interrupt service. If the time is too long, the system may miss an unrecoverable piece of data. It is important for the designer to know the time lag so that the system can compensate for it.

Many operating systems perform multitasking, or concurrent processing, another major requirement for real-time systems. But to be viable for real-time operation, the system overhead must be low in terms of switching time and memory space used.

10.2.5 Real-Time Languages

Because of the special requirements for performance and reliability demanded of real-time systems, the choice of a programming language is important. Many general purpose programming languages (e.g., C, Pascal, Modula-2) can be used effectively for real-time applications. However, a class of so-called "real-time languages" (e.g., Ada, Jovial, HAL/S, Chill, and others) is often used in specialized military and communications applications. (We shall discuss the general characteristics of some of these languages in Chapter 11.)

A combination of characteristics makes a real-time language different from a general purpose language. These include the multitasking capability, constructs to directly implement real-time functions, and modern programming features that help ensure program correctness.

A programming language that directly supports multitasking is important because a real-time system must respond to asynchronous events occurring simultaneously. Although many RTOSs provide multitasking capabilities, embedded real-time software often exists without an operating system. Instead, embedded applications are written in a language that provides sufficient run-time support for real-time program execution. Run-time support requires less memory than an operating system, and it can be tailored to an application, thus increasing performance.

A real-time system that has been designed to accommodate multiple tasks must also accommodate intertask synchronization [KAI83]. A programming language that directly supports synchronization primitives such as SCHEDULE, SIGNAL, and WAIT greatly simplifies the translation from design to code. The SCHEDULE command schedules a process based on time or an event; SIGNAL and WAIT commands manipulate a special flag, called a *semaphore*, that enables concurrent tasks to be synchronized.

Finally, features that facilitate reliable programming are necessary because real-time programs are frequently large and complex. These features include modular programming, strongly enforced data typing, and a host of other control and data definition constructs.

10.2.6   Task Synchronization and Communication

A multitasking system must furnish a mechanism for the tasks to pass information to each other as well as to ensure their synchronization. For these functions, operating systems and languages with run-time support commonly use queuing semaphores, mailboxes, or message systems. Semaphores supply synchronization and signaling but contain no information. Messages are similar to semaphores except that they carry associated information. Mailboxes, on the other hand, do not signal information but instead contain it.

Queuing *semaphores* are software primitives that help manage traffic. They provide a method of directing several queues—for example, queues of tasks waiting for resources, data base access, or devices, as well as queues of resources and devices. The semaphores coordinate (synchronize) waiting tasks with whatever they are waiting for without letting tasks or resources interfere with each other.

In a real-time system, semaphores are commonly used to implement and manage *mailboxes*. Mailboxes are temporary storage places (also called *message pools* or *buffers*) for messages sent from one process to another. One process produces a piece of information, puts it in the mailbox, and then signals a consuming process that there is a piece of information in the mailbox for it to use.

Some approaches to real-time operating systems or run-time support systems view mailboxes as the most efficient way to implement communications between processes. Typical of this approach is Intel's iRMX real-time operating system, which provides a memory-based mailbox that in effect allows the transfer of data. However, by furnishing a place to send and receive pointers to that data, it eliminates the need to transfer all of the data—thus saving time and overhead.

A third approach to communication and synchronization among processes is a *message system*. With a message system, one process sends a message to another. The latter is then automatically activated by the run-time support system or operating system to process the message. Such a system incurs overhead because it transfers the actual information, but it provides greater flexibility and ease of use.

Rather than handling task synchonrization dynamically (via semaphores), some real-time systems approach task synchronization statically. That is, the overall flow of processing is analyzed and if flow is predominantly cyclical, with few asynchronous events, task synchronization can be handled with a real-time "cyclic executive," in which processing algorithms model the system's cyclic behavior [MAC83].

10.3 ANALYSIS OF REAL-TIME SYSTEMS

In the preceding section, the authors discussed a set of dynamic attributes that cannot be divorced from the functional requirements of a real-time system:

- interrupt handling and context switching
- response time
- data transfer rate and throughput
- resource allocation and priority handling
- task synchronization and intertask communication

Each of these performance attributes can be specified, but it is extremely difficult to verify if system elements will achieve desired responses, if system resources will be sufficient to satisfy computational requirements, or if processing algorithms will execute with sufficient speed.

The analysis of real-time systems requires modeling and simulation that enables the system engineer to assess "timing and sizing" issues. Although a number of techniques have been proposed in the literature (e.g., [DAS85], [TAI85], and [YET85]), it is fair to state that analytical approaches for the analysis and design of real-time systems are still in their infancy.

10.3.1 Mathematical Tools for Real-Time System Analysis

A set of mathematical tools that enable the system engineer to model real-time system elements and assess timing and sizing issues has been proposed by Thomas McCabe [MCC85]. Based loosely on data flow analysis techniques (Chapter 5), McCabe's approach enables the analyst to model both hardware and software elements of a real-time system; represent control in a probabilistic manner; apply network analysis, queuing and graph theory, and a Markovian mathematical model [GRO85] to derive system timing and resource sizing. Unfortunately, the mathematics involved lies outside the interests of many readers of this book, making a detailed explication of McCabe's work difficult. However, an overview of the technique will provide a worthwhile view of an analytical approach to the engineering of real-time systems.

McCabe's real-time analysis technique is predicated on a data flow model of the real-time system. (Later in this chapter, we examine how data flow diagrams can be used as one element of real-time software design.) However, rather than using a DFD in the conventional manner, McCabe [MCC85] contends that the transforms (bubbles) of a DFD can be represented as process states of a Markov chain (a probabilistic queuing model), and that data flows themselves can be represented as transitions between the process states. The analyst can assign transition probabilities to each data flow path. Referring to Figure 10.3, a value,

$$0 < P_{ij} \leqslant 1.0$$

may be specified for each flow path, where P_{ij} represents the probability that flow will occur between process i and process j. The processes correspond to information transforms (bubbles) in the DFD.

Each process in the DFD-like model can be given a "unit cost" that represents the estimated (or actual) execution time required to perform its function and an "entrance value" that depicts the number of system interrupts corresponding to the process. The model is then analyzed using a set of mathematical tools that compute: (1) the expected number of visits to a process, (2) the time spent in the system when processing begins at a specific process, and (3) the total time spent in the system.

To illustrate the McCabe technique on a realistic example, we consider a DFD for an electronic countermeasures system shown in Figure 10.4. The data flow diagram takes the standard form, but data flow identification has been replaced by P_{ij}. A queue network model derived from the DFD is shown in Figure 10.5. The values lambda (λ_i) correspond to the arrival rate (arrivals per second) at each process. Depending on the type of queue encountered, the analyst must determine statistical information such as the mean service rate (mean run-time per process), variance of service rate, variance of arrival rate and so forth.

The arrival rates for each process are determined using the flow path probabilities, P_{ij}, and the arrival rate into the system, λ_{in}. A set of flow balance equations are derived and solved simultaneously to compute the flow through each process. For the example shown in Figure 10.5, the following flow balance equations result [MCC85]:

$$\lambda_1 = \lambda_{in} + \lambda_4 \qquad\qquad \lambda_5 = P_{25}\lambda_2 + \lambda_3$$
$$\lambda_2 = P_{12}\lambda_1 \qquad\qquad\qquad \lambda_6 = \lambda_5$$
$$\lambda_3 = P_{13}\lambda_1 + P_{23}\lambda_2 \qquad \lambda_7 = P_{67}\lambda_6$$
$$\lambda_4 = P_{64}\lambda_6$$

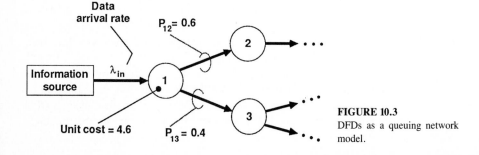

Data arrival rate

$P_{12} = 0.6$

Information source λ_{in}

Unit cost = 4.6 $P_{13} = 0.4$

FIGURE 10.3
DFDs as a queuing network model.

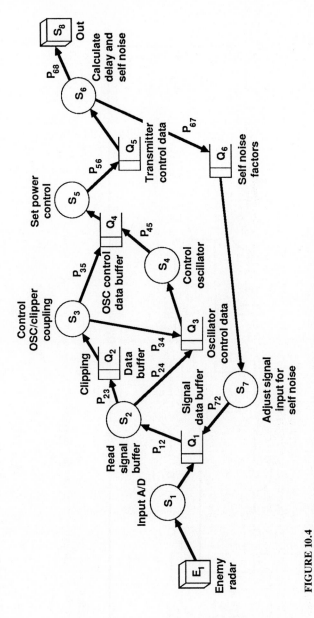

FIGURE 10.4
Example DFD (modified) for real-time analysis (with permission of McCabe & Associates).

377

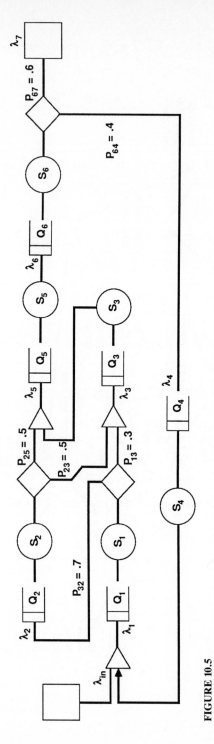

FIGURE 10.5
Queuing network model derived from data flow diagram (with permission of McCabe & Associates).

378

For the P_{ij} shown and an arrival rate of $\lambda_{in} = 5$ arrivals per second, the above equations can be solved [MCC85] to yield:

$$\lambda_1 = 8.3 \qquad \lambda_5 = 8.3$$
$$\lambda_2 = 5.8 \qquad \lambda_6 = 8.3$$
$$\lambda_3 = 5.4 \qquad \lambda_7 = 5.0$$
$$\lambda_4 = 3.3$$

Once the arrival rates have been computed, standard queuing theory can be used to compute system timing. Each subsystem (a queue, Q, and a server, S) may be evaluated using formulae that correspond to the queue type. For (m/m/1) queues [KLI75]:

utilization: $\rho = \lambda/\mu$

expected queue length: $N_q = \rho^2/(1 - \rho)$

expected number in subsystem: $N_s = \rho_1/(1 - \rho)$

expected time in queue: $T_q = \lambda/(\mu(\mu - \lambda))$

expected time in subsystem: $T_s = 1/(\mu - \lambda)$

where μ is completion rate (completions/sec). Applying standard queuing network reduction rules, illustrated in Figure 10.6, the original queuing network (Figure 10.5) derived from the data flow diagram (Figure 10.4) can be simplified by applying the steps shown in Figure 10.7. The total time spent in the system is 2.37 seconds.

Obviously, the accuracy of McCabe's analysis approach is only as good as estimates for flow probability, arrival rate, and completion rate. However, significant benefit can be achieved by taking a more analytical view of real-time systems during analysis. To quote McCabe [MCC85]: "By changing such variables as arrival rates, interrupt rates, splitting probabilities, priority structure, queue discipline, configurations, requirements, physical implementation and variances we can easily show the [system engineer] what effect it will have on the system at hand. These iterative methodologies are necessary to fill a void in real-time specification modeling."

10.3.2 Formal Analysis Methods for Real-Time Systems

The mathematical tools proposed by McCabe are only one of a number of formal methods for the analysis and specification of real-time systems. In Chapter 5, automated tools for requirements analysis (e.g., SADT, SREM, PSL/PSA, and TAGS) were discussed. Each of these tools, in its own fashion, is applicable to the specification of real-time and embedded systems.

As a brief example of one of these tools, we consider an extension of the SREM methodology (Section 5.6.2), called SYSREM (System Requirements Engineering Methodology) [ALF85]. SYSREM has been developed to address the specific analysis and specification problems imposed by real-time, embedded systems. Because SYS-

a) Series rule — The arrivals are served by the subsystem in series.

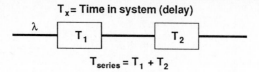

T_x = Time in system (delay)

$$T_{series} = T_1 + T_2$$

b) Parallel rule — The arrivals are served by the subsystem in parallel.

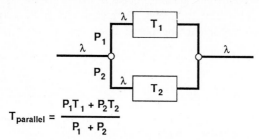

$$T_{parallel} = \frac{P_1T_1 + P_2T_2}{P_1 + P_2}$$

P_1 = probability of entering the server 1 system.
P_2 = probability of entering the server 2 system.

c) Looping rule — A server with delay $T(\lambda\mu)$ and a "feed - back" loop with looping probability P.

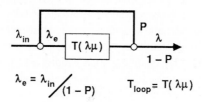

$$\lambda_e = \lambda_{in} \Big/ (1 - P) \qquad T_{loop} = T(\lambda\mu)$$

FIGURE 10.6
Queuing network reduction rules [MCC85].

REM provides a specification language through which system function and performance can be modeled, automated validation and simulation can be conducted. Alford
[ALF85] describes the key features of the tool:

1. *Both sequential processing and concurrency are represented.* Both may be decomposed to provide increasing layers of process and data structure detail.
2. *Control functions are derived as an integral part of the decomposition process.* When
   concurrent functions are defined, a mechanism for coordinating the function must
   also be established.
3. *Performance, as well as the information and functional domains, is decomposed.* That
   is, a performance index (e.g., maximum allowable response time) is established

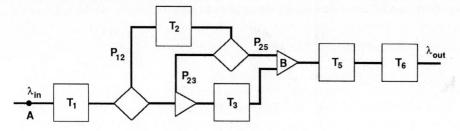

Step 1. Further abstracted queuing network

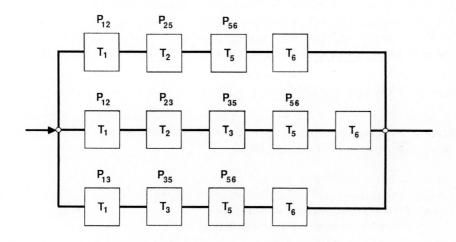

Step 2. Equivalent queuing network showing all possible paths through the network

$$T_{system}$$

Step 3. Final reduction

FIGURE 10.7
Simplifying the queuing network.

for a high-level function. As the function is decomposed, the performance indices associated with each subfunction are defined. Overall performance can be determined by investigating each of the decomposed performance indices.

4. *Component allocation is achieved.* Both sequential and concurrent functions are allocated to components of the real-time system.

5. *Interface designs are derived.*

6. *Error handling and fault recovery are defined.* An additional layer of function is modeled to handle errors and provide fault detection and recovery.

7. *Concurrency issues are exposed early.*

SYSREM is by no means the only available tool for the analysis and design of real-time systems. For an overview of recent work in this area, see [WHI85].

It is fair to ask whether the mathematical tools described in Section 10.3.1 and the formal methodology discussed above are actually design, rather than analysis, techniques. For real-time systems, the distinction is sometimes blurred. The analyst must consider design issues, or allocation will be stilted. Simulation helps the analyst and the designer to assure that architectural decisions are implementable, that performance has a good likelihood of being achieved, and that concurrency will achieve its desired effect. In summary, techniques like those discussed above set the stage for further design work and are an essential element in the engineering of real-time systems.

10.4 SOFTWARE DESIGN METHODS

The design of real-time software must incorporate all of the fundamental concepts (see Chapter 6) associated with high-quality software. In addition, real-time software poses a set of unique problems for the designer:

- representation of interrupts and context switching
- concurrency as manifested by multitasking and multiprocessing
- intertask communication and synchronization
- wide variations in data and communication rates
- representation of timing constraints
- special requirements for error handling and fault recovery
- asynchronous processing
- necessary and unavoidable coupling with operating systems, hardware, and other external system elements

Over the past two decades, a number of real-time software design methods have been proposed to grapple with some or all of these problems. Some design methods extend one of the three classes of design methodology already discussed in this book (i.e., data flow [MEL85], data structure [JAC83], and object-oriented [BOO83] methodologies). Others introduce an entirely separate approach, using finite-state machine models or message passing systems [WIT85], Petri nets [VID83], or a specialized language [STE84] as a basis. For the remainder of this chapter, we consider examples of representative methods.

10.5 A DATA FLOW–ORIENTED DESIGN METHOD

Data flow–oriented design methods (Chapter 7) are the most widely used in the industry. Yet the data flow diagram, data dictionary, and other notation normally associated with the methodology do not adequately support the real-time design problems noted in Section 10.4.

Hassan Gomaa ([GOM84], [GOM86]) has developed extensions to data flow representations that provide the mechanics for real-time software design. Gomaa's approach, called DARTS (Design Approach for Real-Time Systems) allows real-time system designers to adapt data flow techniques to the special needs of real-time applications. The following sections are adapted from Gomaa's work.

10.5.1 Requirements of a Real-Time Systems Design Method

Data flow–oriented design techniques (discussed in detail in Chapter 7) provide a worthwhile foundation for real-time design. Data flow diagrams [DEM79] depict information flow between system functions (or tasks), and mapping techniques [YOU78] enable the designer to derive a program structure from data flow characteristics. Design quality measures such as modularity and functional independence (Chapter 6) are reinforced with data flow–oriented methods.

The DARTS real-time software design method builds on the notation and approach for data flow–oriented design of conventional software. To support real-time design, data flow methods must be extended by providing: (1) a mechanism for representing task communication and synchronization, (2) a notation for representing state dependency, and (3) an approach that ''connects'' conventional data flow methods to the real-time world.

Because most real-time systems spawn multiple tasks that either share a single processor or execute simultaneously on distributed processors, mechanisms must be available to synchronize tasks and provide communication between tasks. Synchronization occurs through *mutual exclusion* or *cross stimulation*. Mutual exclusion is applied when two tasks may access a shared data area at the same time. Semaphores are used to *exclude* one task from accessing the data while another is using (reading or writing) the same data. Cross stimulation is implemented when one task signals another (waiting) task that it has completed some activity and the signaled task may proceed.

Task communication occurs when one task must transmit information to another task. *Message communication* [HAN73] is a common communication approach. When a *producer task* sends a message to a *consumer task* and then waits for a response from the consumer task, communication is *closely coupled*. When producer and consumer tasks continue processing at their own rates and use a message queue to buffer messages, communication is *loosely coupled*.

To implement message communication, Gomaa [GOM84] describes three different approaches:

1. A real-time operating system may provide intertask communication primitives (e.g., [KUN85]).
2. Task communication mechanisms may be implemented within the context of a programming language (e.g., Ada).

3. A special communication handler may be created using synchronization primitives provided by the operating system [SIM79].

The DARTS approach provides a notation that supports both closely and loosely coupled communication.

10.5.2 DARTS

The DARTS design method begins with the application of fundamental software analysis principles (i.e., information domain analysis, problem partitioning) applied in the context of data flow notation. Data flow diagrams are created, a corresponding data dictionary is defined and interfaces between major system functions (transforms) are established (see Chapters 5 and 7).

Gomaa [GOM84] describes the DARTS approach in the following manner:

> The DARTS design method can be thought of as extending the Structured Analysis/Structured Design method by providing an approach for structuring the system into tasks as well as a mechanism for defining the interfaces between tasks. In this sense, it draws on the experience gained in concurrent processing. As with other design methods, DARTS is intended to be iterative.

Once DFDs and a data dictionary have been created, the system must be examined from a different point of view. DFDs do not depict the asynchronous and concurrent tasks that implement the data flow. Therefore, we need an approach that identifies real-time system tasks in the context of system functions (transforms) drawn on a DFD. Transforms are grouped into real-time tasks. Data flow between newly defined tasks defines intertask communication requirements. Gomaa [GOM84] defines the following criteria for determining whether DFD transforms should be defined as a separate task or grouped with other transforms into a single task:

Dependency on I/O. Depending on input or output, a transform is often constrained to run at a speed dictated by the speed of the I/O device with which it is interacting. In this case, the transform needs to be a separate task.

Time-critical functions. A time-critical function needs to run at a high priority and therefore needs to be a separate task.

Computational requirements. A computationally intensive function (or set of functions) can run as a lower-priority task consuming spare CPU cycles.

Functional cohesion. Transforms that perform a set of closely related functions can be grouped together into a task. Since the data traffic between these functions may be high, having them as separate tasks will increase system overhead, whereas implementing each function as a separate module within the same task ensures functional cohesion both at the module and task levels.

Temporal cohesion. Certain transforms perform functions that are carried out at the same time. These functions may be grouped into a task so that they are executed each time the task receives a stimulus.

Periodic execution. A transform that needs to be executed periodically can be structured as a separate task that is activated at regular intervals.

Once tasks have been defined, DARTS provides a mechanism for communication handling between tasks by defining two classes of "task interface modules" [GOM84]: *task communication modules* (TCM) and *task synchronization modules* (TSM). A TCM is spawned by a communicating task and uses operating system synchronization primitives to assure proper access to data. TCMs are divided into two categories:

Message communication modules (MCMs) support message communication and implement appropriate mechanisms for managing a message queue (for loosely coupled communication) and synchronization primitives (for closely coupled communication). DARTS notation for intertask communication that is implemented by an MCM is illustrated in Figure 10.8a.

Information hiding modules (IHMs) provide access to a data pool or data store. The IHM implements the data structure as well as the access methods that enable other tasks to gain access to the data structure. Figure 10.8b illustrates DARTS notation for communication implemented by an IHM.

When control rather than data is to be passed between tasks, the task synchronization module (TSM) comes into play. One task may signal another that an event has occurred, or a task may wait for such a signal. The DARTS notation for task synchronization is shown in Figure 10.8c. A TSM may be viewed as a "supervisory module" that manages control and coordination as events occur.

10.5.3   Task Design

A real-time system task is a program that may be designed using conventional methods. That is, a task may be viewed as a sequential process implemented with a hierarchically organized program structure. Each module in the program structure may be designed using the structured programming philosophy.

Therefore, the DFD that represents data flow within a task boundary may be mapped into a program structure using conventional transform or transaction mapping techniques (Chapter 7). However, for real-time systems, control is dependent on both the input provided to the task and the current state of the system (i.e., what has happened to place the system in its current state of operation). For this reason control is *state-dependent*.

Gomaa [GOM84] suggests a mechanism for handling this situation:

An alternative is to have one module, a *state transition manager* (STM), maintain both the current state of the system and a state transition table defining all legal and illegal state transitions. A task that needs to process a transaction calls the STM with the desired action as an input parameter.

The STM then checks the state transition table to determine whether the desired action is legal, given the current state of the system. If the transaction is legal, the STM

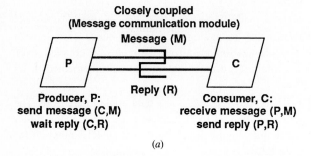

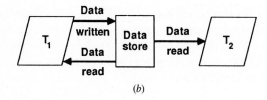

(b)

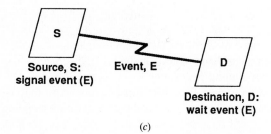

FIGURE 10.8

(a) Message communication. *(b)* Information hiding module. *(c)* Task synchronization.

changes the state of the system, if necessary, and then returns a positive response to the calling task. Otherwise, it returns a negative response. In some designs, it may be necessary for the STM to return a valid action in addition to a positive response (e.g., when the valid action to be taken also depends on the current state of the system).

In DARTS, the STM is designed as a TCM of the IHM type. It maintains a data structure, namely the *state transition table*, which is hidden from the calling tasks. The module also contains the access procedures that check the validity of task requests and perform the state transitions. As with other TCMs, the STM runs in the task that invokes it.

10.5.4   Example of the DARTS Design Method

As an abbreviated example of the DARTS method, we consider the top-level design of software for an air traffic control system (ATCS) illustrated in Figure 10.9. ATCS must acquire information from transponders of aircraft within its control area. Transponder data must be analyzed to determine aircraft identification type, bearing, altitude, and so forth. Data are placed in a data base from which displays are created for air traffic controllers. Controllers can query the data base for supporting information.

The system must operate under extremely rigid performance and reliability constraints: (1) data acquisition *must* be conducted at prespecified intervals, (2) analysis *must* be performed within specified execution time constraints, (3) the data base *must* be updated at defined intervals, and (4) controller interaction should not impede any other system functions.

The DARTS approach begins with the derivation of level 01 and 02 data flow diagrams (Figure 10.10a and b). In addition, the analyst would create a data dictionary (not shown in this example) for all important data items. These DFDs make no explicit reference to the real-time nature of ATCS or to the different tasks that are required to implement ATCS.

Examining the level 02 DFD and applying the task definition criteria discussed in Section 10.5.2, a set of system tasks may be defined:

- data acquisition task
- data analysis task
- data base I/O task
- display task
- air traffic controller interaction task

It should be noted that each of these tasks may be further subdivided into other concurrent tasks. For our purposes, however, further refinement is not attempted.

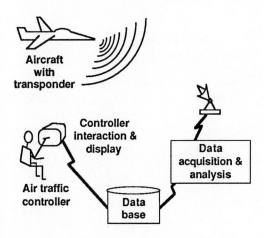

FIGURE 10.9
Air traffic control system (ATCS).

A state transition diagram (or table) may be created to illustrate the communication and events that cause the system to move from one state to the next. The notation for a state transition diagram is illustrated in Figure 10.11.[*] State 1 receives input x and produces output y until an input p is received (p can be data or control). Upon receipt of p an output item q is produced and control passes to state 2. A tabular representation of the state transition diagram is also shown in Figure 10.11.

In the ATCS example, system states correspond to real-time tasks. Referring to Figure 10.12, the data acquisition state continues receiving transponder data until (1) an internal clock (timer) signals that analysis and data base I/O must be conducted or (2) the buffer containing ''raw aircraft profile'' data fills. In either case, control is transferred to the data analysis state, which continues until interrupted by a timer, which returns control to the acquisition task, or until data analysis is complete. In the latter case, control is passed to the data base I/O state which receives a data stream from the analysis task and produces logical records for the data base. Controller interaction and data display (Figure 10.12) occur concurrently, with state transition illustrated as shown.

Returning to the level 02 DFD for ATCS, the real-time tasks are superimposed on the data flow, using dashed boundaries to delineate tasks (Figure 10.13). Finally, the notation depicted in Figure 10.8 is used to create a representation of control and communication between tasks (Figure 10.14).

Level 03 DFDs may be created for each of the tasks depicted in Figure 10.14. These DFDs may then be mapped into a program structure using transform or transaction mappings. The modules defined within the program structure for each task may be designed using conventional methods.

The DARTS approach extends data flow notation by enabling the designer to represent state transition, intertask communication, and concurrency. In addition the use

---

[*]Another view of state transition diagrams is presented in Section 10.6.1.

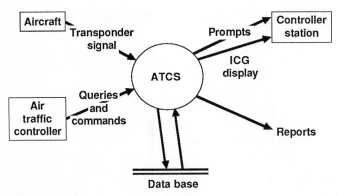

FIGURE 10.10
ATCS: level 01 DFD.

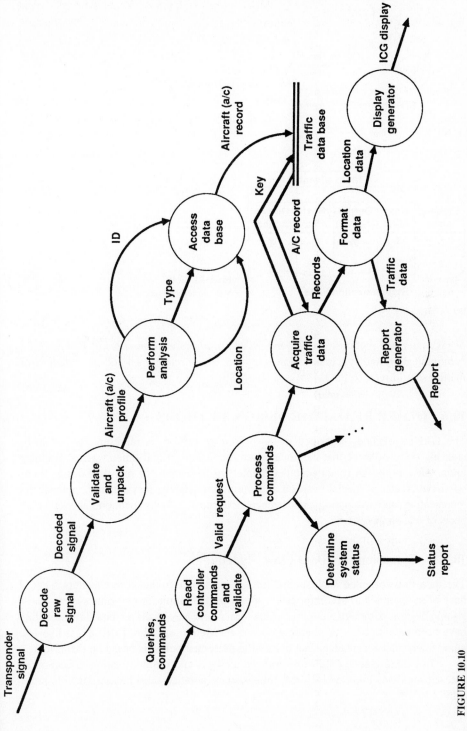

FIGURE 10.10
(b) ATCS: level 02 DFD.

389

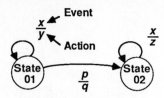

State transition diagram

	Input (Event)			
	x		**p**	
Present state	**Next state**	**Output (Action)**	**Next state**	**Output (Action)**
1	1	*y*	2	*q*
2	2	*z*	-	-

State transition table

FIGURE 10.11
State representations.

of task interface modules (TCMs and TSMs) provides a means for implementing the communication and synchronization activities. Those readers who desire further information should refer to [GOM84] and [GOM86].

10.6   OTHER REAL-TIME DESIGN METHODS

The DARTS method, described in the preceding section, is representative of an increasing body of work that has focused on the design of real-time systems. Building upon software design fundamentals (Chapter 6), developers of real-time design methods have created a special notation and, more importantly, a systematic approach for representing and evaluating concurrency, interrupts, synchronization, and other aspects of real-time systems.

10.6.1   Extensions for Data Flow Modeling

The data flow–oriented analysis and design methods introduced in Chapters 5 and 7 have been extended to accommodate a specialized notation for real-time system analysis and design. Although a number of notational schemes based on data flow modeling have been developed, a technique proposed by Mellor and Ward [MEL85] is likely to gain widespread acceptance. The discussion presented below is based on their work.

To extend classic data flow–oriented analysis and design notation to accommodate the demands imposed by a real-time system, notation must be developed to represent:

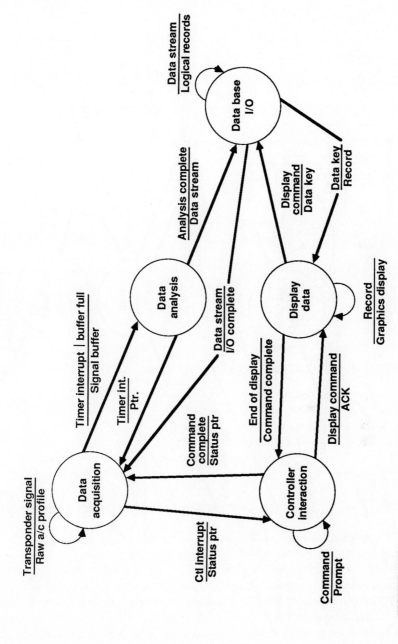

FIGURE 10.12
ATCS: simplified state diagram.

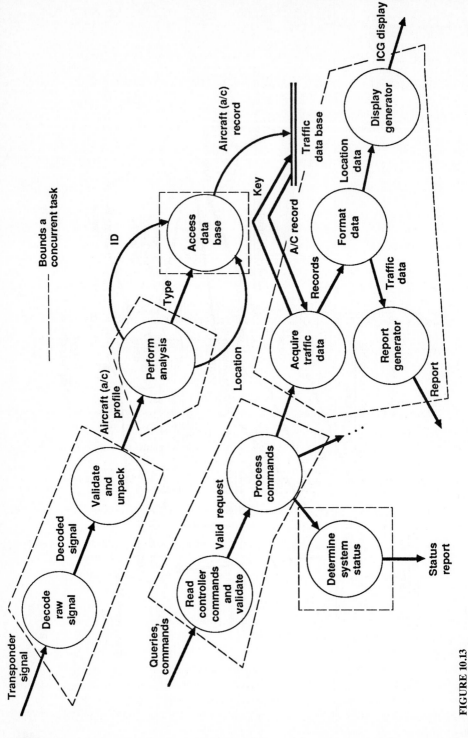

FIGURE 10.13
Superimposing tasks.

392

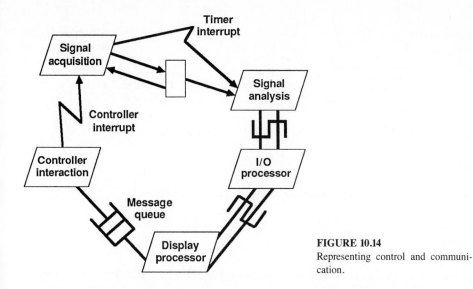

FIGURE 10.14
Representing control and communication.

- information flow that is gathered or produced on a time-continuous basis
- control information passed throughout the system and associated control processing
- multiple instances of the same transformation
- system states and the mechanism that causes transition between states

In a significant percentage of real-time applications, the system must monitor *time-continuous* information generated by some real-world process. For example, a real-time test monitoring system for gas turbine engines might be required to monitor turbine speed, combustor temperature, and a variety of pressure probes on a continuous basis. Conventional data flow notation does not make a distinction between discrete data and time-continuous data. That is, an examination of a data flow diagram (Chapter 5) provides no indication of the time continuity of data flow. An extension to conventional data flow notation, shown in Figure 10.15, provides a mechanism for representing time-continuous data flow. The double-headed arrow is used to represent time-continuous flow while a single-headed arrow is used to indicate discrete data flow. In the figure, temperature is measured continuously while a single value for *temperature set points* is also provided. The process shown in the figure produces a time-continuous output, *correction level value*.

The distinction between discrete and time-continuous data flow has important implications for both the system engineer and the software designer. During the creation of the logical model for a system, the system engineer will be better able to isolate those processes that may be performance-critical (it is often likely that the input and output of time-continuous data will be performance-sensitive). As the physical or implementation model is created, the designer must establish a mechanism for collection of time-continuous data. Obviously, the digital system collects data in a quasicontinuous fashion using techniques such as high-speed polling. The notation indicates

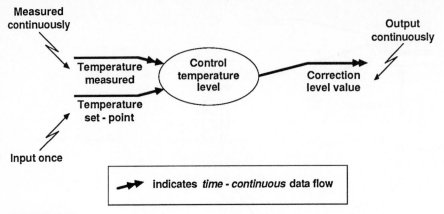

FIGURE 10.15
Data flow and time.

where analog-to-digital hardware will be required and which transforms are likely to demand high-performance software.

In conventional data flow–oriented representations, control or *event flows* are not represented explicitly. In fact, the analyst is cautioned to specifically exclude the representation of control flow from the data flow diagram. This exclusion is overly restrictive when real-time applications are considered and for this reason, a specialized notation for representing event flows and control processing has been developed. Continuing the convention established for data flow diagrams, data flow is represented using a solid arrow. Control flow, however, is represented using a dashed or shaded arrow.

Referring to Figure 10.16, a transform process named *display speed* accepts a discrete value, *speed value*, and produces another discrete output, *speed display. Display speed* also receives an event flow, *metric switch set*, that controls whether an English or metric conversion algorithm is used within the data transform. In many real-time applications, a significant percentage of all information flow can be associated with control and event processing.

Figure 10.17 illustrates a top-level view of a control process for a manufacturing cell. As components are placed on fixtures, a status bit is set within a *parts status buffer* that indicates the presence or absence of each component. Event information contained

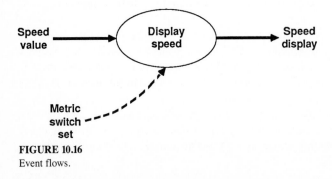

FIGURE 10.16
Event flows.

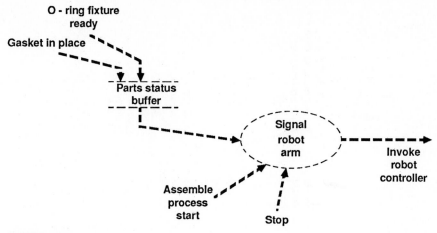

FIGURE 10.17
Event flows and control transformation.

within the *parts status buffer* is passed to a control process, *signal robot arm*, that also receives other event flows as shown in the figure. The output of the control process is a control signal that invokes a robot controller.

The control flow represented in Figure 10.17 is expanded in Figure 10.18 to illustrate combined event and data flow. Referring to Figure 10.18, the output of the control process described in the preceding paragraph is used to trigger a robot control system illustrated with a level 01 data flow diagram. It is important to note that expansion of the robot control system may result in the representation of additional event flows and control processes. These may be combined with data transformation processes and conventional data flows.

In some situations multiple instances of the same control or data transformation process may occur in a real-time system. For example, a number of parts status buffers may be monitored so that different robots can be signaled at the appropriate time. In addition, each robot may have its own robot control system. Figure 10.19 illustrates the notation that can be used to represent multiple *equivalent instances* of the same process.

The use of *state diagrams* (or state transition tables) as a notation scheme for real-time design was introduced in Section 10.5. The state diagrammatic representation that is used to extend data flow–oriented methods takes on a form that is slightly different from the one introduced earlier. System states (an externally observable mode of behavior) are represented using rectangles as illustrated in Figure 10.20. The important benefit of this notation is that the state diagrammatic form is less easily confused with data flow notation. State transition is represented by arrows that contain information about the event that triggers the transition and the action produced as a result of the transition.

By combining conventional data flow–oriented notation (data flow diagram, data dictionary, structured English, and decision trees and tables) with the real-time extension discussed above, a method for the analysis and design of real-time systems can be proposed:

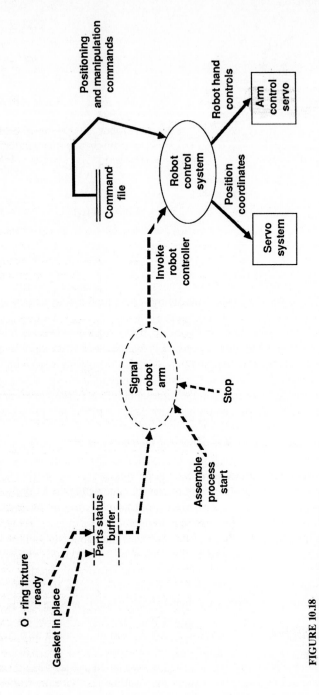

FIGURE 10.18
Combining data and control transformations.

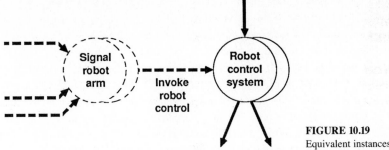

FIGURE 10.19
Equivalent instances.

1. *Develop a level 01 data flow diagram that includes all primary data and event flows and shows all information sources, sinks, and data stores.* For some real-time applications, event flows may be more important than data flow in the level 01 characterization of a system. For this reason, all top-level event flows should be represented.

2. *Create an event list that describes each major event associated with the system.* The event list would include control-oriented activities such as "power switch activated" or "temperature reaches set point value" and command-oriented events such as "operator requests current status display" or "user provides calibration value." The event list is used to refine the level 01 flow model and as a source of information for the creation of state diagrams.

3. *Refine the flow model to level 02 and 03 detail.* The guidelines proposed in Chapter 5 apply equally well to the refinement of real-time systems. It should be noted, however, that both data flow and event flow are refined.

4. *Create a state diagrammatic representation.* The event list can assist greatly in the creation of the state diagram. Like the flow model, the state diagram can be created at a number of different levels with each subsequent level elaborating on information contained in the preceding level.

5. *Review flow models and state diagrams to assure that each represents the function and flow of a system consistently.* The flow models for a real-time system imply the struc-

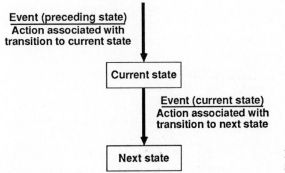

FIGURE 10.20
State transition diagrams.

ture of the state diagram and, to some extent, the state diagram implies system flow. Representations of each should be consistent.

6. *Use conventional notation to describe data objects and procedural content for the system.* A detailed description of data objects can be provided with a data dictionary. A processing narrative for both data and control transformations can be developed using structured English (or PDL), decision trees or decision tables.

7. *Program architecture can be derived using transform and transaction mappings.* These mappings, introduced in Chapter 7, can be applied to data flow models at any reasonable level of detail. When multiple tasks or processes are present, the mapping is applied to the flow model for each task or process individually.

8. *Review all representations and iterate as required.*

It is important to note that notational schemes for real-time design are still evolving. For example, Boeing Commercial Aircraft Company [BOE85] has proposed data flow–oriented extensions for real-time design that differ somewhat from those presented in this section. However, the Boeing extensions (derived from the work of Derek Hatley [HAT84]) provide a notation that addresses the same issues as those discussed in this chapter. At this time, it is difficult to predict which, if any, notational schemes will be adopted broadly throughout the industry.

10.6.2   Alternative Approaches

Another extension to data flow–oriented design, called Mascot [SIM79], provides features that are similar to DARTS. Using an information flow representation of concurrent processes, Mascot provides for the representation of intercommunication data areas that permit definition of interprocess communication. In addition, Mascot allows the designer to specify interfaces and coordinate communication with synchronizing primitives.

Other design methods for real-time systems emphasize ''state machine'' representations for software. An interesting approach proposed by Delfino [DEL84], called Hierarchical Software State Machines (HSSM), creates a state diagram representation of software. HSSM provides a notation and approach in which interfaces between state machines, inputs (called messages) to state machines, processes performed by state machines and associated interrupts, multitasking, and synchronization are used in the design of a real-time application. Related work can be found in [LAN79].

A comprehensive real-time design technique, originally based on the modeling of systems with Petri Nets (e.g., [PET81]) but now extended to encompass a specialized real-time design language and automated processor, is called *Galileo* [VID83]. Using a language called GTL, the designer creates the basic building blocks of a real-time system. A design language processor, GACOT, allows ''the interactive composition of Galileo networks, the marking of initial state situations and the observation of dynamic behavior with different speeds on the building blocks of the network'' [VID83].

Many other approaches to the specification and design of real-time systems are available. SADT, SREM, and TAGS (discussed briefly in Chapter 5) have been applied to real-time applications. SARA, a real-time design method developed at UCLA by Gerald Estrin [EST78], provides a language and graphical conventions for the representation of concurrency and a simulator for design validation. ESPRESO, another language-based tool, provides facilities for the formal specification of concurrent systems. Software engineering environments for real-time design, such as SARTOR [MOK85], enable the designer to describe a real-time system using either event-action or graph models.

10.7 SUMMARY

The design of real-time software encompasses all aspects of conventional software design while at the same time introducing a new set of design criteria and concerns. Because real-time software must respond to real-world events in a time frame dictated by those events, all classes of design (architectural, procedural, and data design) become more complex.

It is difficult, and often impractical, to divorce software design from larger system-oriented issues. Because real-time software is either clock or event driven, the designer must consider function and performance of hardware and software. Interrupt processing and data transfer rate, distributed data bases and operating systems, specialized programming languages, and synchronization methods are just some of the concerns of the real-time system designer.

The analysis of real-time systems encompasses both mathematical modeling and simulation. Queuing and network models enable the system engineer to assess overall response time, processing rate, and other timing and sizing issues. Formal analysis tools provide a mechanism for real-time system simulation.

Software design for real-time systems can be predicated on a conventional design methodology. For example the DARTS approach extends data flow–oriented design by providing a notation and approach that address real-time system characteristics.

Software design for real-time systems remains a challenge. Progress has been made and methods do exist, but a realistic assessment of the state of the art suggests much remains to be done.

REFERENCES

[ALF85]   Alford, M., "SREM at the Age of Eight; The Distributed Computing Design System," *Computer*, vol. 18, no. 4, pp. 36–46.

[BOE85]   *Structured Methods Standard*, Boeing Commercial Aircraft Co., Document No. D6-53036, Seattle, 1985.

[BOO83]   Booch, G., *Software Engineering with Ada*, Benjamin-Cummings, 1983.

[DAS85]   Dasarathy, B., "Timing Constraints of Real-Time Systems: Constructs for Expressing Them, Methods for Validating Them," *IEEE Trans. Software Engineering*, vol. SE-11, no. 1, January 1985, pp. 80–86.

[DEL84]   Delfino, A. B., "Hierarchical Software State Machines," course notes, University of Santa Clara, February 1984.

[DEM79]   DeMarco, T., *Structured Analysis and System Specification*, Prentice-Hall, 1979.

[EST78]   Estrin, G., "SARA Aided Design for Software for Concurrent Systems," *AFIPS Conference Proceedings*, Anaheim, CA, 1978, 325–336.

[FOS81]   Foster, C. C., *Real Time Programming—Neglected Topics*, Addison-Wesley, 1981.

[GLA83]   Glass, R. L., *Real-Time Software*, Prentice-Hall, 1983.

[GOM84]   Gomaa, H., "A Software Design Method for Real Time Systems," *CACM*, vol. 27, no. 9, September 1984, pp. 938–949.

[GOM86]   Gomaa, H., "Software Development of Real-Time Systems," *CACM*, vol. 29, no. 7, July 1986, pp. 657–668.

[GRO85]   Gross, D., and C. M. Harris, *Fundamentals of Queueing Theory*, 2d ed., Wiley, 1985.

[HAN73]   Brinch Hansen, P., "Concurrent Programming Concepts," *Computing Surveys*, vol. 5, no. 4, December 1973, pp. 223–245.

[HAT84]   Hatley, D. J., "The Use of Structured Methods in the Development of Large Software Based Systems," Digital Avionics Systems Conference, Baltimore, December 1984.

[HIN83]   Hinden, H. J., and W. B. Rauch-Hinden, "Real-Time Systems," *Electronic Design*, 6 January 1983, pp. 288–311.

[JAC83]   Jackson, M., *System Development*, Van Nostrand Reinhold, 1983.

[KAI83]   Kaiser, S. H. *The Design of Operating Systems for Small Computer Systems*, Wiley-Interscience, 1983.

[KLI75]   Kleinrock, L., *Queueing Systems, Volume 1: Theory*, Wiley, 1975.

[KUN85]   Kung, A., and R. Kung, "GALAXY: A Distributed Real-Time Operating System Supporting High Availability," *Proc. Real-Time Systems Symposium*, IEEE, December 1985, pp. 79–87.

[LAN79]   Landau, J. V., "State Description Techniques Applied to Industrial Machine Control," *Computer*, vol. 12, no. 4, February 1979, pp. 32–40.

[MAC83]   MacLaren, L., "Evolving Toward Ada in Real-Time Systems," *Real Time Software*, R. Glass, ed., Prentice-Hall, 1983.

[MCC85]   McCabe, T. J., et al., "Structured Real-Time Analysis and Design," *COMPSAC-85*, IEEE, October 1985, pp. 40–51.

[MEL83]   Mellichamp, D. A., ed., *Real Time Computing*, Van Nostrand Reinhold, 1983.

[MEL85]   Mellor, S. J., and P. T. Ward, *Structured Development for Real-Time Systems*, Yourdon Press, 3 vols., 1985, 1986.

[MOK85]   Mok, A. K., "SARTOR—A Design Environment for Real-Time Systems," *COMPSAC-85*, IEEE, October 1985, pp. 174–179.

[PAR72]   Parnas, D. L., "On Criteria to Be Used for Decomposing Systems into Modules," *CACM*, vol. 15, no. 12, December 1972, pp. 1053–1058.

[PET81]   Peterson, J. L., *Petri-Net Theory and the Modeling of Systems*, Prentice-Hall, 1981.

[SAV85]   Savitsky, S., *Real-Time Microprocessor Systems*, Van Nostrand Reinhold, 1985.

[SIM79]   Simpson, H. R., and K. L. Jackson, "Process Synchronization in Mascot," *The Computer Journal*, vol. 22, no. 4, 1979.

[STE84]   Steusloff, H. U., "Advanced Real-Time Languages for Distributed Industrial Process Control," *Computer*, vol. 17, no. 2, February 1984, pp. 37–46.

[TAI85]   Tai, K. C., and C. Y. Din, "Validation of Concurrency in Software Specification and Design," *Proc. Third Intl. Workshop on Software Specification and Design*, IEEE, London, August 1985, pp. 223–227.

[VID83]   Vidondo, F., "GALILEO: Design Language for Real-Time Systems," *Proc. ITT Conf. on Programming Productivity and Quality*, ITT Corporation, June 1983, pp. 198–210.

[WHI85]   White, S. M., and J. Z. Lavi, "Embedded Computer System Requirements Workshop," *Computer*, vol. 18, no. 4, April 1985, pp. 67–70.

[WIT85]   Witt, B. I., "Communicating Modules: A Software Design Model for Concurrent Distributed Systems," *Computer*, vol. 18, no. 1, January 1985, pp. 67–77.

[YET85]   Yetongon, K. T., B. R. Hewston, and T. L. Booth, "Performance Analysis Techniques and Tools to Aid the Design of Distributed Software Systems," *COMPSAC-85*, IEEE, October 1985, pp. 166–173.

[YOU78]   Yourdon, E., and L. Constantine, *Structured Design*, Prentice-Hall, 1978.

PROBLEMS AND POINTS TO PONDER

10.1 List five examples of computer-based real-time systems. Indicate what "stimuli" feed the system and what devices or situations the system controls or monitors.

10.2 Obtain information on a commercial real-time operating system (RTOS) and write a short paper that presents a discussion of RTOS internals. What special features are present, how are interrupts handled, and how does the RTOS effect task synchronization?

10.3 Write a brief comparison of the real-time constructs in the programming languages Ada and Modula-2. Do these constructs provide distinct benefits over other languages such as C or Pascal?

10.4 Provide three examples in which semaphores would be an appropriate task synchronization mechanism.

10.5 The analysis technique for real-time systems presented in Section 10.3 assumes a knowledge of queuing models. Do some research using the references indicated, and:

(*a*) Describe how Figure 10.5 was derived from Figure 10.4.

(*b*) Show how the flow balance equations are derived from Figure 10.5.

10.6 For those readers who are familiar with queuing models and Markov analysis: Making appropriate assumptions about arrival rates and service times, attempt to apply McCabe's real-time analysis method [MCC85] to the air traffic control system described in Section 10.5.4.

10.7 Get information on one or more formal analysis tools for real-time systems (Section 10.3.2). Write a paper that outlines its use in the specification and design of a real-time system.

10.8 Using the DARTS approach presented in Section 10.5.2, develop a design representation for the digital dashboard software described in Chapter 7 (Sections 7.3 and 7.4). (*Note*: The presentation in Chapter 7 did not explicitly assume real-time characteristics. You will have to make a number of assumptions about the requirements of this system before you proceed.)

FURTHER READINGS

Glass's anthology [GLA83] is a useful source of information on real-time software and its design. An advanced discussion of the theory of real-time control can be found in a chapter by Larsen et al. in the Van Nostrand Reinhold *Handbook of Software Engineering* (Vick and Ramamoorthy, eds., 1984). Savitsky [SAV85] presents a discussion of both hardware and software aspects of real-time systems.

For readers who are involved in the design of distributed systems, a book by Liebowitz and Carson (*Multiple Processor Systems for Real-Time Applications*, Prentice-Hall, 1985) presents a thorough treatment of this difficult subject. Other advanced discussions of distributed real-time systems can be found in papers by Shina, Perry and Toueg, and Indurkhya et al. in the *IEEE Transactions on Software Engineering* (March 1986).

A three-volume set by Mellor and Ward [MEL85] is an excellent guide to real-time design for those individuals who have adopted data flow–oriented design techniques for other software applications. The Boeing Company has proposed a set of recommendations for another data flow–oriented design approach to real-time systems that is based on a design approach proposed by Hatley [HAT84]. Hatley's method uses both state representations and data flow notation to represent key elements of a real-time software design.

The *Proceeding of the National Conference on Methodologies and Tools for Real-Time Systems* (Washington, March 1986) contains papers on TAGS, SREM, PAMELA, EPOS, DSDM, and other automated tools for the design of real-time systems.

CHAPTER
11

PROGRAMMING
LANGUAGES
AND
CODING

All software engineering steps that have been presented to this point are directed toward a final objective: to translate representations of software into a form that can be "understood" by the computer. We have (finally) reached the coding step—a process that transforms design into a programming language. Gerald Weinberg [WEI71] expressed the true meaning of coding when he wrote: "...when we talk to our computers, unhappily, we are usually speaking in different tongues...."

Readers of this book may live to see the day when the above quotation is proved incorrect. Requests for computer processing services may be coded (or spoken) in a natural language, such as English. Already a set of so-called *fourth generation techniques* is changing our understanding of the term "programming language." Rather than coding, developers of some classes of management information systems can now describe desired results, rather than desired procedure, in a *nonprocedural language*. More conventional programming language source code is then generated automatically.

However, the vast majority of software applications still reside beyond the reach of fourth generation approaches. For the time being, we code using artificial languages such as Ada, FORTRAN, Pascal, C, COBOL, or assembler language.

When considered as a step in the software engineering process, coding is a natural consequence of design. However, programming language characteristics and coding style can profoundly affect software quality and maintainability. This chapter does

403

not aspire to teach the reader to code. Rather, topics associated with programming languages and coding are presented in the broader context of software engineering.

11.1 THE TRANSLATION PROCESS

The coding step translates a detail design representation of software into a programming language realization. The translation process continues when a compiler accepts *source code* as input and produces machine-dependent *object code* as output. Compiler output is further translated into *machine code*—the actual instructions that drive hardwired or microcoded logic in the central processing unit.

The initial translation step—from detail design to programming language—is a primary concern in the software engineering context. ''Noise'' can enter the translation process in many ways. Improper interpretation of a detail design specification can lead to erroneous source code [SHE81]. Programming language complexity or restrictions can lead to convoluted source code that is difficult to test and maintain. More subtly, characteristics of a programming language can influence the way we think, propagating unnecessarily limited software designs and data structures.

For example, a design directed at a target FORTRAN implementation would be less likely to use a linked-list data structure, because FORTRAN does not directly support such a structure. If the target language were C or Pascal (both of which provide direct support for linked lists), this structure would be a more feasible alternative.

Language characteristics have an impact on the quality and efficiency of translation. In the next section, we evaluate language characteristics by considering two different views of programming languages.

11.2 PROGRAMMING LANGUAGE CHARACTERISTICS

Programming languages are a vehicle for communication between humans and computers. The coding process—communication via a programming language—is a human activity. As such, the psychological characteristics of a language have an important impact on the quality of communication. The coding process may also be viewed as one step in a software engineering methodology. The engineering characteristics of a language have an important impact on the success of a software development project. Finally, technical characteristics of a language can influence the quality of design (recall that practicality often dictates that detail design be directed toward a specific programming language). Therefore, technical characteristics can affect both human and software engineering concerns.

11.2.1 A Psychological View

In his book *Software Psychology*, Ben Shneiderman [SHN80] observed that the role of the software psychologist is to ''focus on human concerns such as ease of use, simplicity in learning, improved reliability, reduced error frequency and enhanced user satisfaction, while maintaining an awareness of machine efficiency, software capacity, and hardware constraints.'' Software engineering is an intensely human activity. We still have much to learn about the human aspects of computer-based system development.

Another software psychologist, Gerald Weinberg [WEI71] relates a story that bears repeating (in paraphrased form) when we consider characteristics of programming languages:

> It is impossible to begin a discussion of psychological principles of programming language design without recalling the story of ''The Genius Tailor.'' It seems that a man had gone to the tailor to have a suit made cheaply, but when the suit was finished and he went to try it on, it didn't fit him at all.
>
> Complaining that the jacket was too big in back, the right arm was too long, one pant leg was too short and three buttons were missing, the man was justifiably upset.
>
> ''No problem,'' said the tailor, ''just hunch your back, bend your arm, walk with a limp, and stick your fingers through the button holes and you'll look just fine!''
>
> The man contorted his body to fit the suit and feeling duped by the tailor, he left. He had not walked one block when he was approached by a stranger.
>
> ''Who made that suit for you?'' asked the stranger. ''I'm in the market for a new suit myself.''
>
> Surprised, but pleased at the compliment, the man pointed out the tailor's shop.
>
> ''Well, thanks very much,'' said the stranger, hurrying off. ''I do believe I'll go to that tailor for my suit. Why, he must be a genius to fit a cripple like you!''

Weinberg suggests that we could extend this parable to a story of the genius programming language designer. The designers of programming languages often make us contort our approach to a problem so that the approach will fit the constraints imposed by a specific programming language. Because human factors are critically important in programming language design, the psychological characteristics of a language have a strong bearing on the success of design to code translation and implementation.

A number of psychological characteristics [WEI71] occur as a result of programming language design. Although these characteristics are not measurable in any quantifiable way, we recognize their manifestation in all programming languages. We discuss each characteristic briefly in the paragraphs that follow.

Uniformity indicates the degree to which a language uses consistent notation, applies seemingly arbitrary restrictions, or supports exceptions to syntactic or semantic rules. For example, FORTRAN uses parentheses as a delimiter for array indices, as a modifier for arithmetic precedence, and as a delimiter for a subprogram argument list. This multi-use notation has led to more than a few subtle errors.

Ambiguity in a programming language is perceived by the programmer. A compiler will always interpret a statement in one way, but the human reader may interpret the statement differently. Here lies psychological ambiguity. For example, psychological ambiguity arises when arithmetic precedence is not obvious:

$$X = X_1/X_2 * X_3$$

One reader of the source code might interpret the above as $X = (X_1/X_2)*X_3$ while another reader might ''see'' $X = X_1/(X_2 * X_3)$. Another potential source of ambiguity is nonstandard use of identifiers that have default data types. For example, in FORTRAN an identifier KDELTA would be assumed (by default) to have *integer* characteristics. However, an explicit declaration, REAL KDELTA, could cause confusion due to psychological ambiguity.

A lack of uniformity and the occurrence of psychological ambiguity normally occur together. If a programming language exhibits the negative aspects of these characteristics, source code is less readable and translation from design is more error-prone.

Compactness of a programming language is an indication of the amount of code-oriented information that must be recalled from human memory. Among the language attributes that measure compactness are:

- the degree to which a language supports the structured constructs (Chapter 6) and logical "chunking"
- the kinds of keywords and abbreviations that may be used
- the variety of data types and default characteristics
- the number of arithmetic and logical operators
- the number of built-in functions

APL is an exceptionally compact programming language. Its powerful and concise operators allow relatively little code to accomplish significant arithmetic and logical procedures. Unfortunately, the compactness of APL also makes the language difficult to read and understand, and can lead to poor uniformity (e.g., the use of *monadic* and *dyadic* forms for the same operator symbol).

The characteristics of human memory have a strong impact on the way in which we use language. Human memory and recognition may be divided into *synesthetic* and *sequential* domains [KLA80]. Synesthetic memory allows us to remember and recognize things as a whole. For example, we recognize a human face instantly; we do not consciously evaluate each of its distinct parts prior to recognition. Sequential memory provides a means for recalling the next element in a sequence (e.g., the next line in a song, given preceding lines). Each of these memory characteristics affects programming language characteristics called *locality* and *linearity*.

Locality is the synesthetic characteristic of a programming language. Locality is enhanced when statements may be combined into *blocks*, when the structured constructs may be implemented directly, when design and resultant code is highly modular and cohesive (Chapter 6). A language characteristic that supports or encourages discontinuous processing (e.g., ON-condition processing in PL/1 or ERR= in extended versions of FORTRAN) violate locality.

Linearity is a psychological characteristic that is closely associated with the concept of maintenance of functional domain. That is, human perception is facilitated when a linear sequence of logical operations is encountered. Extensive branching (and to some extent, large loops) violates the linearity of processing. Again, direct implementation of the structured constructs aids programming language linearity.

Our ability to learn a new programming language is affected by *tradition*. A software engineer with a background in FORTRAN or PL/1 would have little difficulty learning C or Pascal. The latter languages have a tradition established by the former. Constructs are similar, form is compatible, and a sense of programming language "format" is maintained. However, if the same individual were required to learn APL or Lisp, tradition would be broken and time on the learning curve would be longer.

Tradition also affects the degree of innovation during the design of a new programming language. Although new languages are proposed frequently, new language forms evolve slowly. For example, Pascal is a close relative of ALGOL. However, a major innovation in the Pascal language [JEN74] is an implementation of user-defined data types, a form that does not exist in earlier languages tied to Pascal by tradition. Ada, a language that has also grown out of the ALGOL-Pascal tradition, extends beyond both languages with a wide variety of innovative structures and typing.

The psychological characteristics of programming languages have an important bearing on our ability to learn, apply, and maintain them. In summary a programming language colors the way we think about programs and inherently limits the ways in which we communicate with a computer. Whether this is good or bad remains an open question.

11.2.2   A Syntactic/Semantic Model

Shneiderman [SHN80] has developed a *syntactic-semantic model* of the programming process that has relevance in a consideration of the coding step. When a programmer applies software engineering methods (e.g., requirements analysis, design) that are programming language–independent, semantic knowledge is tapped. Syntactic knowledge, on the other hand, is language-dependent, concentrating on the characteristics of a specific language.

Of these knowledge types, semantic knowledge is the more difficult to acquire and the more intellectually demanding to apply. All software engineering steps that precede coding make heavy use of semantic knowledge. The coding step applies syntactic knowledge that is "arbitrary and instructional" and learned by rote [SHN80]. When a new programming language is learned, new syntactic information is added to memory. Potential confusion may occur when the syntax of a new programming language is similar but not equivalent to the syntax of another language. It should be noted, however, that a new programming language can serve to force the software engineer to learn new semantic information as well. For example, the Ada programming language has caused many software engineers to rethink their approach to design and implementation of software-based systems.

When arguments about the compelling need to "generate code" arise, the listener should realize that a software crisis has not been caused by a lack of syntactic knowledge. The problem lies in the scope of our semantic knowledge and our ability to apply it. The goal of software engineering is to expand knowledge of the semantics of software development.

11.2.3   An Engineering View

A software engineering view of programming language characteristics focuses on the needs of a specific software development project. Although esoteric requirements for source code may be derived, a general set of engineering characteristics can be established: (1) ease of design to code translation, (2) compiler efficiency, (3) source code portability, (4) availability of development tools, and (5) maintainability.

The coding step begins after a detail design has been defined, reviewed, and modified if necessary. In theory, source code generation from a detail design specification should be straightforward. *Ease of design to code translation* provides an indication of how closely a programming language mirrors a design representation. As we discussed in Section 11.1, a language that directly implements the structured constructs, sophisticated data structures, specialized I/O, bit manipulation capabilities, and string handling will make translation from design to source code much easier (if these attributes are specified in design).

Although rapid advances in processor speed and memory density have begun to mitigate the need for ''super-efficient code,'' many applications still require fast, ''tight'' (low memory requirement) programs. An on-going criticism of high-order language compilers is directed at an inability to produce fast, tight executable code. Languages with optimizing compilers may be attractive if software performance is a critical requirement. Stack-oriented languages, such as FORTH, have been developed specifically to enhance a program's run-time performance; i.e., such languages produce fast, tight machine-executable code.

Source code portability is a programming language characteristic that may be interpreted in three different ways:

1. Source code may be transported from processor to processor and compiler to compiler with little or no modification.

2. Source code remains unchanged even when its environment changes (e.g., a new version of an operating system is installed).

3. Source code may be integrated into different software packages with little or no modification required because of programming language characteristics.

Of the three interpretations of portability, the first is by far the most common. Standardization (by ISO—International Standards Organization—and/or ANSI—American National Standards Institute) continues to be a major impetus for the improvement of programming language portability. Unfortunately, most compiler designers succumb to a compelling urge to provide ''better'' but nonstandard features for a standardized language. If portability is a critical requirement, source code must be restricted to the ISO or ANSI standard, even if other features exist.

Availability of development tools can shorten the time required to generate source code and can improve the quality of the code. Many programming languages may be acquired with a suite of tools that include: debugging compilers, source code formatting aids, built-in editing facilities, tools for source code control, extensive subprogram libraries in a variety of application areas, cross-compilers for microprocessor development, macroprocessor capabilities, and others. In fact the concept of a good ''software development environment'' (e.g., [WAS81a], [BAR84], [WIL86]) that includes both conventional and automated tools has been recognized as a key contributor to successful software engineering.

Maintainability of source code is critically important for all nontrivial software development efforts. Maintenance cannot be accomplished until software is understood. Earlier elements of the software configuration (i.e., design documentation) provide a foundation for understanding, but ultimately source code must be read and modified according to changes in design. Ease of design to code translation is an important element in source code maintainability. In addition, self-documenting characteristics of a language (e.g., allowable length of identifiers, labeling format, data type/structure definition) have a strong influence on maintainability.

11.2.4 Choosing a Language

The choice of a programming language for a specific project must take into account both engineering and psychological characteristics. However, the problem associated with choice may be moot if only one language is available or dictated by a requester. Mack [MAC80] suggests a general philosophy when a programming language must be chosen:

> ...the art of choosing a language is to start with the problem, decide what its requirements are, and their relative importance, since it will probably be impossible to satisfy them all equally well (with a single language)...available languages should be measured against a list of requirements....

Among the criteria that are applied during an evaluation of available languages are: (1) general application area, (2) algorithmic and computational complexity, (3) environment in which software will execute, (4) performance considerations, (5) data structure complexity, (6) knowledge of software development staff, and (7) availability of a good compiler or cross-compiler. Application area of a project is a criterion that is applied most often during language selection. As we noted in Chapter 1, a number of major software application areas have evolved and de facto standard languages may be selected for each.

C is often the language of choice for the development of systems software, while languages such as Ada, C, and Modula-2 (along with FORTRAN and assembly language) are encountered in real-time applications. COBOL is the language for business applications, but the increasing use of fourth generation languages may someday displace it from its pre-eminent position. In the engineering/scientific area, FORTRAN remains the predominant language (although ALGOL, PL/1, and Pascal have wide usage). Embedded software applications make use of the same languages applied in systems and real-time applications. The predominant language for personal computer users is BASIC, but the language is rarely used by the developers of personal computer software products—more likely choices are Pascal or C. Artificial intelligence applications make use of languages such as Lisp or PROLOG, although other, more conventional, programming languages are used as well.

The proliferation of "new and better" programming languages continues. Although many of these languages are attractive, it is sometimes better to choose a "weaker" (old) language that has solid documentation and support software, is familiar to everyone on the software development team, and has been successfully applied in the past. However, new languages should be thoroughly evaluated and a transition from old to new should occur to combat the psychological resistance to change that is encountered in all organizations.

11.2.5 Programming Languages and Software Engineering

Regardless of the software engineering paradigm, programming language will have an impact on project planning, analysis, design, coding, testing, and maintenance. But the role of a programming language must be kept in perspective. Languages do provide the means for human-to-machine translation; however, the quality of the end result is more closely tied to software engineering activities that precede and follow coding.

During the project planning step, a consideration of the technical characteristics of a programming language is rarely undertaken. However, planning for support tools associated with resource definition may require that a specific compiler (and associated software) or programming environment be specified. Cost and schedule estimation may require learning curve adjustments because of staff inexperience with a language.

Once software requirements have been established, the technical characteristics of candidate programming languages become more important. If complex data structures are required, languages with sophisticated data structure support (e.g., Pascal or Ada) would merit careful evaluation. If high-performance, real-time capability is paramount, a language designed for real-time application (e.g., Ada) or memory-speed efficiency (e.g., FORTH) might be specified. If many output reports and heavy file manipulation are specified, languages like COBOL or RPG might fit the bill. Ideally, software requirements should precipitate the selection of a language that best fits the processing to be accomplished. In practice, however, a language is often selected because ''it's the only one we have running on our computer!''

The quality of a software design is established in a manner that is independent of programming language characteristics. (A notable exception is object-oriented design, Chapter 9.) However, language attributes do play a role in the quality of an implemented design and affect (both consciously and unconsciously) the way that design is specified.

In Chapter 6 we discussed a number of qualitative and quantitative measures of good design. The concepts of modularity and module independence were emphasized. Technical characteristics of many programming languages can affect these design concepts during the implementation of the design. To illustrate, consider the following examples:

> Modularity is supported by nearly all modern programming languages. COBOL, for example, supports a hierarchy of function that integrates various levels of procedural abstraction (Chapter 6) with the modularity concept. The hierarchy consists of divisions, sections, paragraphs, sentences, and finally words. Each of these terms has a precise meaning in the language and helps to emphasize a modular implementation.

Module independence can be enhanced or subverted by language characteristics. For example, the Ada *package* supports the concept of information hiding while the use of internal procedures in PL/1 can lead to extensive global data that increase module coupling.

Data design (discussed in Chapter 6) can also be influenced by language characteristics. A new class of programming languages (e.g., Ada, CLU, Smalltalk, and others) supports the concept of abstract data types—an important tool in data design and specification. Other, more common languages, such as Pascal, allow the definition of user-defined data types and direct implementation of linked lists and other data structures. These features provide the designer with greater latitude during the preliminary and detail design steps.

In some cases, design requirements can be satisfied only when a language has special characteristics. Per Brinch Hansen [HAN78] describes a set of language characteristics essential for implementation of a design that specifies distributed processes that are executing concurrently and must communicate and coordinate with one another. Languages such as concurrent Pascal, Ada, or Modula-2 can be used to satisfy such designs.

The effect of programming language characteristics on the steps that compose software testing is difficult to assess. Languages that directly support the structured constructs tend to reduce the cyclomatic complexity (Chapter 12) of a program, thereby making it somewhat easier to test. Languages that support the specification of external subprograms and procedures (e.g., FORTRAN) make integration testing much less error-prone. On the other hand, some technical characteristics of a language can impede testing. For example, block structuring in ALGOL can be specified in a manner that causes a loss of intermediate data when exit from a block occurs, thereby making the status of a program more difficult to assess.

Like testing, the effect of programming language characteristics on software maintenance is not fully understood. There is no question, however, that technical characteristics that enhance code readability and reduce complexity are important for effective maintenance. Further discussion of software maintenance is postponed until Chapter 15.

11.3 PROGRAMMING LANGUAGE FUNDAMENTALS

The technical characteristics of programming languages span an enormous number of topics that range from the theoretical (e.g., formal language theory and specification) to the pragmatic (e.g., functional comparisons of specific languages). In this section a brief discussion of programming language fundamentals is presented. For more detailed discussions of programming language technology, the reader should refer to [LED81] or [PRA84].

For the purposes of our discussion, programming language fundamentals will be presented within the context of three broad topics: data typing, subprogram mechanisms, and control structures. All programming languages can be characterized with respect to these topics, and the overall quality of a specific programming language can be judged by evaluating strengths and weaknesses related to each topic.

11.3.1 Data Types and Data Typing

Today, the merits of a modern programming language are judged by more than the syntax and breadth of its procedural constructs. *Data typing* and the specific data types supported by a programming language are an important aspect of language quality.

Pratt [PRA84] describes data types and data typing as "... a class of data objects together with a set of operations for creating and manipulating them." A data object inherits a set of fundamental attributes of the data type to which it belongs. A data object can take on a value that resides within the range of legitimate values for the data type and can be manipulated by operations that apply to the data type.

Simple data types span a wide range that includes *numeric* types (e.g., integer, complex, floating point numbers); *enumeration* types (e.g., user-defined data types found in Pascal); *Boolean* types (e.g., true or false); and *string* types (e.g., alphanumeric data). More complex data types encompass data structures that run the gamut from simple, one-dimensional arrays (vectors) to list structures to complex heterogeneous arrays and records.

The operations that may be performed on a particular data type and the manner in which different types may be manipulated in the same statement are controlled by *type checking*, implemented within the programming language compiler or interpreter. Fairley [FAI85] defines five levels of type checking that are commonly encountered in programming languages:

Level 0:   typeless
Level 1:   automatic type coercion
Level 2:   mixed mode
Level 3:   pseudostrong type checking
Level 4:   strong type checking

Typeless programming languages have no explicit means for data typing and therefore do not enforce type checking. Languages[*] such as BASIC, APL, Lisp and even COBOL fall into this category. Although each language does enable the user to define data structures, the representation of data contained within each data object is predefined.

---

[*]References to programming languages in this chapter assume "typical" or ANSI standard implementations. It is entirely possible that other versions of a language may exhibit characteristics that contradict our discussion.

Automatic type coercion is a type-checking mechanism that allows the programmer to mix different data types but then converts operands of incompatible types, thus allowing requested operations to occur. For example, PL/1 assigns a numeric value of 0 to the Boolean value *false* and a numeric value of 1 to the Boolean value *true*. Hence arithmetic operations (normally applied to numeric data types) can be applied to Boolean data types in PL/1.

Mixed mode type conversion is similar in many respects to automatic type coercion. Different data types within the same type category (e.g., two different numeric types) are converted to a single target type so that a specified operation can occur. FORTRAN's mixed mode arithmetic (a feature that is best avoided) enables integers and real numbers to be used in a single programming language statement.

Strong type checking occurs in programming languages that will permit operations to be performed only on data objects that are of the same, prespecified data type. Operators, operands, and subprogram (module) interfaces are checked for type compatibility at compile time, at load time, and at run time. Ada compilers perform strong type checking.

Pseudostrong type checking has all of the characteristics of strong type checking but is implemented in a manner that provides one or more loopholes [FAI85]. For example, although Pascal checks interface compatibility within a single compiled program, it does not do so for separately compiled procedures (modules)—a loophole in the enforcement of strong type checking.

11.3.2 Subprograms

A *subprogram* is a separately compilable program component that contains a data and control structure. Throughout this book, we have referred to a *module* as a generic manifestation of a subprogram. Depending on the programming language, a subprogram may be called a subroutine, procedure, function, or any of a number of specialized names. Regardless of its name, the subprogram exhibits a set of generic characteristics: (1) a specification section that includes its name and interface description, (2) an implementation section that includes data and control structure, and (3) an *activation mechanism* that enables the subprogram to be invoked from elsewhere in the program.

In conventional programming languages, each subprogram is an entity in itself, operating on data in a manner dictated by a larger program's control structure. In object-oriented programming languages, the classic view of the subprogram is replaced with the *object*—a language form that combines data structure and control structure in a unique way (Chapter 9).

11.3.3 Control Structures

At a fundamental level, all modern programming languages enable the programmer to represent sequence, condition, and repetition—the structured programming logical constructs. Most modern languages provide a syntax for direct specification of *if-then-*

else, *do-while*, and *repeat-until* (as well as *case*). Other languages, such as Lisp and APL, require the programmer to emulate the constructs within the syntax bounds of the language.

In addition to the basic procedural constructs of structured programming, other control structures may be present. *Recursion* creates a second activation of a subprogram during the first activation. That is, the subprogram invokes or activates itself as part of the defined procedure. *Concurrency* provides support for the creation of multiple tasks, the synchronization of tasks, and general communication between tasks. This language feature is invaluable when real-time or systems applications are undertaken. *Exception handling* is a programming language feature that traps user-defined or system error conditions and passes control to an exception handler for processing.

11.4   LANGUAGE CLASSES

There are hundreds of programming languages that have been applied at one time or another to serious software development efforts. Even a detailed discussion of the five most common languages is beyond the scope of this book. The reader is referred to Pratt [PRA84] and Ledgard [LED81] for thorough surveys and comparisons of the most common programming languages. In this section, four generations of programming languages are described and representative languages from each generation are discussed.

Any categorization of programming languages is open to debate. In many cases, one language might legitimately reside in more than one category. For the purposes of this book, we develop general language generations that correspond roughly to the historical evolution of programming languages. Figure 11.1 illustrates this categorization.

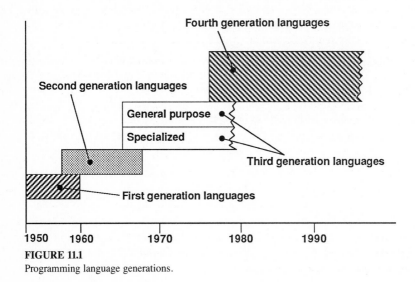

FIGURE 11.1
Programming language generations.

11.4.1 First Generation Languages

The first language generation hearkens back to the days of machine-level coding. (Substantial work with first generation languages continues to this date.) Machine code and its more human-readable equivalent, assembler language, represent the first language generation. These machine-dependent languages exhibit the lowest level of abstraction with which a program can be represented.

There are as many assembler languages as there are processor architectures with custom instruction sets. From a software engineering viewpoint, such languages should be used only when a high-order language cannot meet requirements or is not supported. To help justify the preceding statement, consider recent developments in the design of processor hardware. A number of modern processors (e.g., P-code machines, Intel IAPX-432, the Symbolics Lisp Machine, and others) do not support assembler language. Instead, such machines are programmed directly in a high order language — Ada in the case of the IAPX-432, Lisp in the case of the Symbolics machine. This development underlines the fact that hardware manufacturers are beginning to recognize the severe disadvantages (from a software engineering viewpoint) of using assembler language.

11.4.2 Second Generation Languages

Second generation languages were developed in the late 1950s and early 1960s and serve as the foundation for all modern (third generation) programming languages. Second generation languages are characterized by broad usage, enormous software libraries, and the widest familiarity and acceptance. There is little debate that FORTRAN, COBOL, ALGOL, and (to some extent) BASIC are foundation languages by virtue of their maturity and acceptance.

FORTRAN has withstood 25 years of criticism and remains the premier programming language in engineering/scientific work. The original standardized version of FORTRAN (called "FORTRAN-66") provided a powerful tool for computational problem solving but lacked direct support of the structured constructs, had poor data typing, could not easily support string handling, and had many other deficiencies. The newer ANSI standard (called "FORTRAN-77") and the forthcoming "FORTRAN-88" standard correct some of the deficiencies found in earlier versions of the language. In many cases FORTRAN has been force-fit into application areas for which it was never designed, and much of the criticism of the language has been somewhat unfair. For number-crunching applications, FORTRAN remains the language of choice, but for system, real-time, or embedded product software applications, other languages provide compelling advantages.

COBOL, like FORTRAN, has reached maturity and is the accepted "standard" language for commercial data processing applications. Although the language is sometimes criticized for lack of compactness, it has excellent data definition capabilities, is largely self-documenting, and provides support for a wide range of procedural techniques relevant to business data processing.

ALGOL is the forerunner of many third generation languages and offers an extremely rich repertoire of procedural and data typing constructs. ALGOL has been used extensively in Europe, but has found little support (with the exception of academic environments) in the United States. The most commonly used version of the language, correctly termed ALGOL-60, has been extended to a more powerful implementation, ALGOL-68. Both versions of the language support the notion of block structuring, dynamic storage allocation, recursion, and other characteristics having a strong influence on the modern languages that have followed.

BASIC is a language originally designed to teach programming in a timesharing mode. The language was moving toward obsolescence in the early 1970s, but has experienced a rebirth with the advent of personal computers. There are hundreds of versions of BASIC, making it difficult to discuss benefits and deficiencies of the language.

11.4.3 Third Generation Languages

Third generation languages (also called *modern* or *structured* programming languages) are characterized by strong procedural and data structuring capabilities. The languages in this class can be divided into two broad categories, *general purpose high-order languages* and *specialized languages*. All general purpose high-order languages exhibit the technical characteristics discussed in Section 11.3. Specialized languages, on the other hand, have been designed to satisfy special requirements and have a syntax and form that is often unique.

GENERAL PURPOSE HIGH-ORDER LANGUAGES. The earliest general purpose high-order language (also a foundation language), ALGOL, served as a model for other languages in this category. Its descendants, PL/1, Pascal, Modula-2, C, and Ada, are being adopted as languages with potential for broad spectrum applications (i.e., for use in engineering/scientific, embedded products, commercial, and/or systems application areas).

PL/1 might more properly be categorized as a 2.5 generation language. It was the first true broad spectrum language, developed with a wide range of features that enable it to be used in many different application areas. PL/1 provides support for conventional engineering/scientific and business applications, while enabling specification of sophisticated data structures, multitasking, complex I/O, list processing, and many other features. Subsets of the language have been developed to teach programming (PL/C), for use in microprocessor applications (PL/M), and for systems programming (PL/S).

Pascal is a modern programming language developed in the early 1970s for teaching modern techniques (e.g., structured programming) in software development. Since its introduction, Pascal has found growing support from a broad audience of software developers and is used widely for engineering/scientific applications and systems programming (the language has been called "the FORTRAN of the 1980s"). Pascal is a direct descendant of ALGOL and contains many of the same features: block structuring, strong data typing, direct support for recursion, and other complementary features. It has been implemented on computers of all sizes.

Modula-2 is an evolutionary outgrowth of Pascal and (some would say) a possible alternative to the Ada programming language. Modula-2 couples direct implementation of design features such as information hiding, abstraction, and strong data typing with control structures to support recursion and concurrency. To date, the use of Modula-2 for industry applications has been limited, but early reports indicate that it may gain much wider acceptance.

The C programming language was originally developed as a language for operating system implementors. The Unix operating system is implemented in C. Today, however, a vast array of software products, embedded applications, and systems software has been built using the C language. C was developed for the sophisticated software engineer and contains powerful features that give it considerable flexibility. Cox [COX85] provides a poetic description of the language:

> One of my favorite hobbies is green wood working. A project begins not in the lumber yard with kiln dried wood, but in the forest. A straight-grained oak tree is cut down, and worked into rustic furniture with an awe-inspiring assortment of antique tools... .
>
> The tools of this hobby have a lot in common with the tools I use as a programmer. For example, the adze is a heavy blade on a four foot handle (like a hoe). It is a specialized tool, whose primary function is smoothing the rough surfaces of a split log. It is swung double-handed, standing astraddle the work. The razor sharp blade removes six-inch slabs of solid oak with a single blow, scant inches from unprotected feet and legs!
>
> I love that adze the way I love the C language. It is not a tool for fools and children. But in the hands of a skilled craftsman, it is capable of powerful, yet delicate work. Its potential for grave harm is so obvious that the danger provides the only safety mechanism; a healthy respect for what careless use can do!

Like other languages in this category, C supports sophisticated data structures and has reasonable typing characteristics, makes extensive use of pointers, and has a rich set of operators for computation and data manipulation. In addition, it enables the programmer to "get close to the machine" by providing assembler language–like features.

Ada is a language developed under contract to the U.S. Department of Defense as a new standard for embedded real-time computer systems. Pascal-like in structure and notation (but far more powerful and complex), Ada supports a rich set of features that include multitasking, interrupt handling, intertask synchronization and communication, as well as a set of unique features such as the Ada *package*. Ada has created and continues to generate much controversy. Adherents praise its rich language structure and the focus on the Ada environment for software engineering rather than language-related esoterica. Opponents worry about the complexity of the language, the current inefficiency of operational compilers, and the long learning curve. Only time will tell.

SPECIALIZED LANGUAGES. Specialized languages are characterized by unusual syntactic forms that have been especially designed for a distinct application. Hundreds of specialized languages are in use today. In general such languages have a much smaller user base than general purpose languages. Among the languages that have found application within the software engineering community are Lisp, PROLOG, Smalltalk, APL, and FORTH.

Lisp is a language especially suited to symbol manipulation and list processing encountered in combinatorial problems. Used almost exclusively by the artificial intelligence community, the language is particularly well suited to theorem proving, tree searches, and other problem-solving activities. Subprograms are implemented as functions that make heavy use of recursion. Because each Lisp function is a stand-alone entity, reusability can be achieved by creating libraries of primitive functions. In recent years, Lisp has been used to develop a wide array of expert systems and expert system "compilers." Lisp makes it relatively easy to specify facts, rules, and the corresponding inferences (implemented as Lisp functions) that are required for knowledge-based systems.

PROLOG is another programming language that has found widespread use in the construction of expert systems. Like Lisp, PROLOG provides features that support knowledge representation. Within the language a uniform data structure, called the *term*, is used to construct all data and all programs. Each program consists of a set of clauses that represent facts, rules, and inferences. Both Lisp and PROLOG are especially amenable to problems that treat objects and their relationships. For this reason, some people refer to Lisp and PROLOG as *object-oriented languages* (Chapter 9). In addition, the object-oriented nature of Lisp and PROLOG enable each to be applied within the context of the prototyping paradigm for software engineering.

Smalltalk, one of the first true object-oriented languages, introduces a control and data structure that is radically different from conventional programming languages. Smalltalk enables the programmer to define *objects* that combine a data structure and point to a set of *methods* (subprograms). Each object is an *instance* of a *class* of objects. Therefore, new objects can be easily created since they inherit all the characteristics of their class. Many industry observers feel that the object-oriented approach fostered by Smalltalk can lead to reusable program components that will greatly reduce development time (and size, measured in lines of code) for large software systems. Like Ada, Smalltalk is more than a programming language. The Smalltalk environment has been created to assist in the development of programs.

APL is an extremely concise and powerful language for array and vector manipulation. The language contains little support for structured constructs or data typing. APL does provide a rich set of computational operators and has gained a small but avid following for mathematical problem solving.

FORTH is a language designed for microprocessor software development. The language supports the definition of user-defined functions (implemented with post-fix (reverse-Polish) notation) that are executed in a stack-oriented manner for speed and memory efficiency.

From a software engineering standpoint, specialized languages provide both advantages and disadvantages. Because a specialized language has been designed to address a specific application, translation of requirements to design to code implementation can be facilitated. On the other hand, most specialized languages are far less portable and often less maintainable than general purpose languages.

11.4.4 Fourth Generation Languages

Throughout the history of software development, we have attempted to generate computer programs at higher and higher levels of abstraction. First generation programming languages worked at the machine instruction set level, the lowest possible level of abstraction. Second and third generation programming languages have raised the level at which we represent computer programs, but distinct and completely detailed algorithmic procedures still have to be specified. Over the past decade, *fourth generation languages* (4GLs) have raised the level of abstraction still higher.

Fourth generation languages, like all artificial languages, contain a distinct syntax for control and data structure representation. A 4GL, however, represents these structures at a higher level of abstraction by eliminating the need to specify algorithmic detail. For example, the statement

COMPUTE NET-PRESENT-VALUE AND RETURN-ON-INVESTMENT
FOR EXPENDITURES #5 AND #9.

is typical of a 4GL statement. The 4GL system "knows" how to compute the desired financial data and does so without requiring the software developer to specify the appropriate algorithms. It should be apparent that the "knowledge" described above is *domain-specific*. That is, the same 4GL would undoubtedly choke on:

COMPUTE THE ROOTS OF TRANSCENDENTAL EQUATION #3 AND APPLY THEM
TO PHYSICAL MODEL #4.

although another 4GL, designed specifically for the application domain implied above, might do the job nicely.

Fourth generation languages combine *procedural* and *nonprocedural* characteristics. That is, the language enables the user to specify conditions and corresponding actions (the procedural component) while at the same time encouraging the user to indicate the desired outcome (the nonprocedural component) and then applying its domain-specific knowledge to fill in the procedural details.

Martin ([MAR85], [MAR86]) presents a comprehensive discussion of 4GLs and develops the following broad categories.

QUERY LANGUAGES. To date, the vast majority of 4GLs have been developed for use in conjunction with data base applications. Such query languages enable the user to manipulate information contained in a pre-existing data base in a sophisticated manner. Some query languages require a complex syntax that is no simpler (and in some cases is worse) than a third generation language. For example [MAR85]:

list by region (87.act.sep.sales)
sum (87.est.sep.sales), (sum (sum (87.act.sep.sales))

However, other query languages available today offer a natural language interface that allows the user to state [INT86]:

For the eastern and western regions, how did actual sales for last month compare with forecasts?

Needless to say, the second approach would be favored by most users.

PROGRAM GENERATORS. Program generators represent another, somewhat more sophisticated, class of 4GLs. Rather than relying on a predefined data base as its point of focus, a program generator enables the user to create complete third generation language programs using (many claim) remarkably fewer statements. These *very high level programming languages* make heavy use of procedural and data abstractions (Chapter 6). Unfortunately for those working in the engineered products and systems domain, most of the program generators available today focus exclusively on business information systems applications and generate programs in COBOL.

OTHER 4GLS. Although query languages and program generators are the most common 4GLs, other categories exist. *Decision support languages* enable ''non-programmers'' to perform a variety of *what-if* analyses that range from simple, two-dimension spreadsheet models to sophisticated statistical or operations research modeling systems. *Prototyping languages* have been developed to assist in creating prototypes (Chapter 1) by facilitating the creation of user interfaces and dialogs and providing a means for data modeling. *Formal specification languages* (discussed in Chapter 5) can be considered 4GLs when such languages produce machine-executable code.

11.5 CODING STYLE

After source code is generated, the function of a module should be apparent without reference to a design specification. In other words, code must be understandable. Coding style encompasses a coding philosophy that stresses simplicity and clarity. In their landmark text on the subject, Kernighan and Plauger [KER78] state:

> Writing a computer program eventually boils down to writing a sequence of statements in the language at hand. How each of those statements is expressed determines in large measure the intelligibility of the whole....

The elements of style include internal (source code level) documentation, methods for data declaration, an approach to statement construction, and techniques for I/O. In the sections that follow, we consider each of these topics.

11.5.1 Code Documentation

Internal documentation of source code begins with the selection of identifier (variables and labels) names, continues with placement and composition of commenting, and concludes with the visual organization of the program.

Selection of meaningful identifier names is crucial to understanding. Languages that limit variable names or labels to only a few characters inherently obscure meaning. Consider the following three statements:

```
D = V*T
DIST = HORVEL*TIME
DISTANCE = HORIZONTAL.VELOCITY * TIME.TRAVELED.IN.SECS;
```

The BASIC language expression is undeniably concise, but the meaning of D=V*T is unclear unless the reader has prior information. The FORTRAN expression provides more information, but the meaning of DIST and HORVEL could be misinterpreted. The ALGOL statement leaves little doubt regarding the meaning of the calculation. These statements illustrate the way in which identifiers may be chosen to help document code.

It can be argued that "wordy" expressions (like the ALGOL statement above) obscure logical flow and make modification difficult. Obviously, common sense must be applied when identifiers are selected. Unnecessarily long identifiers do indeed provide a potential for error (not to mention a backache from sitting long hours typing at a development terminal). Studies [SHN80] indicate, however, that even for small programs, meaningful identifiers improve comprehension. In terms of the syntactic/semantic model discussed in Section 11.2.2, meaningful names "simplify the conversion from program syntax to internal semantic structure" [SHN80].

The ability to express natural language comments as part of a source code listing is provided by all general purpose programming languages. However, certain questions arise:

- How many comments are "enough"?
- Where should comments be placed?
- Do comments obscure logic flow?
- Can comments mislead the reader?
- Are comments "unmaintainable," and therefore unreliable?

There are few definitive answers to the above questions. But one thing is clear: *software must contain internal documentation*. Comments provide the developer with one means of communicating with other readers of the source code. Comments can provide a clear guide to understanding during the last phase of software engineering—maintenance.

There are many guidelines that have been proposed for commenting. *Prologue comments* and descriptive comments are two categories that require somewhat different approaches. Prologue comments should appear at the beginning of every module. The format for such comments is:

1. A statement of purpose that indicates the function of the module
2. An interface description that includes:
   a. a sample "calling sequence"
   b. a description of all arguments
   c. a list of all subordinate modules
3. A discussion of pertinent data such as important variables and their use, restrictions and limitations, and other important information

4. A development history that includes:
   a. module designer (author)
   b. reviewer (auditor) and date
   c. modification dates and description

An example of prologue comments is given in Figure 11.2.

Descriptive comments are embedded within the body of source code and are used to describe processing functions. A primary guideline for such commenting is expressed by VanTassel [VAN78]: "comments should provide something extra, not just paraphrase the code." In addition, descriptive comments should:

- describe blocks of code, rather than commenting on every line
- use blank lines or indentation so that comments can be readily distinguished from code
- be correct; an incorrect or misleading comment is worse than no comment at all

With proper identifier mnemonics and good commenting, adequate internal documentation is assured.

When a detailed procedural design is represented using a program design language (Chapter 6), design documentation can be embedded directly into the source listing as comment statements. This technique is particularly useful when implementation is to be done in assembler language and helps to ensure that both code and design will be maintained when changes are made to either.

The form of the source code as it appears on the listing is an important contributor to readability. Source code indentation indicates logical constructs and blocks of code by indenting from the left margin so that these attributes are visually offset. Like commenting, the best approach to indentation is open to debate. Manual indentation can become complicated as code modification occurs, and experiments [SHN80] indicate that only marginal improvement in understanding accrues. Probably the best approach is to use an automatic code formatter (a tool) that will properly indent source code. By eliminating the burden of indentation from the coder, form may be improved with relatively little effort.

11.5.2 Data Declaration

The complexity and organization of data structure are defined during the design step. The style of data declaration is established when code is generated. A number of relatively simple guidelines can be established to make data more understandable and maintenance simpler.

The order of data declarations should be standardized even if the programming language has no mandatory requirements. For example, declaration ordering for a FORTRAN module might be:

1. All explicit declarations

   INTEGER, REAL, DOUBLE PRECISION,...

```
C
C
C
C      TITLE:       SUBROUTINE NGON
C
C      PURPOSE:   THE PURPOSE OF TO CONTROL THE DRAWING OF NGONS.
C
C      SAMPLE CALL:  CALL NGON (KROW, IX, IY, KN)
C
C      INPUTS:       KROW   = IS THE LINE ON THE TABLET WHERE THE
C                                     NEXT LINE OF OUTPUT WILL BE PRINTED.
C                    IX        = X - COORDINATE OF THE LEFT END OF THE
C                                     BOTTOM SEGMENT
C                    IY        = Y - COORDINATE OF THE LEFT END OF THE
C                                     BOTTOM SEGMENT
C                    KN       = IS THE NUMBER OF THE LAST NGON
C
C      OUTPUTS:     KROW   = IS THE INCREMENTED ROW COUNTER
C                    KN       = IS THE INCREMENTED NGON COUNTER
C
C      SUBROUTINES REFERENCED:       1.)  DBNGON
C                                     2.)  ALPHA
C                                     3.)  ROWCOL
C
C      PERTINENT DATA:
C            KROW IS CHECKED TO SEE IF THE TABLET IS FULL.
C            IF IT IS THEN REPNT IS CALLED TO REFRESH THE SCREEN
C            AND PUT UP A NEW TABLET.  THE NGON COUNTER (KN) IS
C            INCREMENTED AND THE POINTER ARRAY PO IS WRITTEN
C            TO THE DISPLAY FILE.
C
C            A PROMPT IS THEN ISSUED FOR THE NUMBER OF
C            SIDES AND THE ORIENTATION OF THE NGON WITH
C            RESPECT TO THE X - AXIS.  THE ARRAY 'NG' IS LOADED
C            AND WRITTEN TO THE OBJECT FILE.
C
C            THE ROUTINE DBNGON DOES THE ACTUAL DRAWING.
C            IT REQUIRES THE NUMBER OF SIDES, THE LENGTH OF A
C            SIDE, THE ORIENTATION, AND THE COORDINATES OF THE
C            STARTING POINT AND IPEN.
C
C      AUTHOR:   M. WRIGHT
C
C      AUDITOR:  D. CURRIE
C
C      DATE:       10/30/86
C
C      MODIFICATIONS:
C
C            11/29/86  D.C.
C            CHANGES MADE TO ALLOW TABLES TO BE BUILT FOR REPNT
C
C            1/7/87     R.P.S.
C            ADD ERROR CHECKING COMMON 'SPECAL' AND ERROR HANDLING.

            SUBROUTINE NGON (KROW, IX, IY, KN)
            DIMENSION PO (10), NG (10)
            INTEGER  *2 ARG1, ARG2, ARG3, RPTFLG, RPTNUM
```

FIGURE 11.2
Code documentation.

423

2. All global data blocks

COMMON/block-name/...

3. All local arrays

DIMENSION array names and dimensions

4. All file declarations

DEFINE FILE, OPEN, CLOSE

Ordering makes attributes easier to find, expediting testing, debugging, and maintenance.

When multiple variable names are declared with a single statement, an alphabetical ordering of names is worthwhile. Similarly, labeled global data (e.g., FORTRAN common blocks) should be ordered alphabetically.

If a complex data structure is prescribed by design, commenting should be used to explain peculiarities inherent in a programming language implementation. For example, a linked list data structure in C or a user-defined data type in Pascal might require supplementary documentation contained in comments.

11.5.3 Statement Construction

The construction of software logical flow is established during design. The construction of individual statements, however, is part of the coding step. Statement construction should abide by one overriding rule: each statement should be simple and direct; code should not be convoluted to enhance efficiency.

Many programming languages allow multiple statements per line. The space saving aspects of this feature are hardly justified by the poor readability that results. Consider the following two code segments:

```
DO I = 1 TO N–1; T = I; DO J = I+1 TO N;     IF A(J) < A(T)
THEN DO T = J; END;     IF T<> I THEN DO H = A(T); A(T) = A(I);
A(I) = H; END; END;
```

The loop structure and conditional operation contained in the above segment are masked by multistatement-per-line construction. Reorganizing the form of the code:

```
DO I = TO N–1;
    T = I;
    DO J = I+1 TO N;
        IF A(J) < A(T) THEN ΔO
            T = J;
        END;
```

```
    IF T <> I THEN DO
        H = A(T);
        A(T) = A(I);
        A(I) = T;
        END;
    END;
END;
```

Here, simple statement construction and indentation illuminates the logical and functional characteristics of the segment. Individual source code statements can be simplified by:

- avoiding the use of complicated conditional tests
- eliminating tests on negative conditions
- avoiding heavy nesting of loops or conditions
- using parentheses to clarify logical or arithmetic expressions
- using spacing and/or readability symbols to clarify statement content
- using only ANSI standard features
- thinking: ''Could I understand this if I was not the person who coded it?''

Each of the above guidelines strives to support the dictum: ''keep it simple.''

11.5.4   Input/Output

The style of input and output is established during software requirements analysis and design, not coding. However, the manner in which I/O is implemented can be the determining characteristic for system acceptance by a user community. Input and output style will vary with the degree of human interaction. For batch-oriented I/O, logical input organization, meaningful input/output error-checking, good I/O error recovery, and rational output report formats are desirable characteristics. For interactive I/O, a simple, guided input scheme, extensive error-checking and recovery, human-engineered output, and consistency of I/O format become primary concerns.

Regardless of the batch or interactive nature of software, a number of I/O style guidelines should be considered during design and coding:

- Validate all input data.
- Check the plausibility of important combinations of input items.
- Keep input format simple.
- Use end-of-data indicators, rather than requiring a user to specify ''number-of-items.''
- Label interactive input requests, specifying available choices or bounding values.
- Keep input format uniform when a programming language has stringent formating requirements.
- Label all output and design all reports.

The style of I/O is affected by many other characteristics such as I/O devices (e.g., terminal type, computer graphics device, mouse, etc.), user sophistication, and communication environment. Wasserman [WAS81b] provides a comprehensive set of guidelines for "user software engineering and the design of interactive systems." These guidelines, applicable to both software design and coding, are summarized below:

1. Make the underlying aspects of the computer invisible to the user.
2. Make the program "bulletproof," that is, make it virtually impossible for the user to cause the program to end abnormally.
3. Notify the user if any request can have major consequences.
4. Provide on-line assistance in the use of the program.
5. Tailor input requirements to user skills.
6. Tailor output messages to the speed of output devices.
7. Distinguish among different classes of users.
8. Maintain a consistent response time.
9. Minimize extra work for the user in the event of an error.

Each of these guidelines should become an implicit software requirement for all interactive systems. Software should be designed to accommodate each and coded to implement a user software engineered interface.

11.6 EFFICIENCY

In well-engineered systems, there is a natural tendency to use critical resources efficiently. Processor cycles and primary memory locations are often viewed as critical resources, and the coding step is seen as the last point where microseconds or bits can be squeezed out of the software. Although efficiency is a commendable goal, three maxims should be stated before we discuss the topic further. First, efficiency is a *performance requirement* and should, therefore, be established during software requirements analysis. Software should be as efficient as is required, not as efficient as is humanly possible. Second, efficiency is improved with good design. Third, code efficiency and code simplicity go hand in hand. In general, don't sacrifice clarity, readability, or correctness for nonessential improvements in efficiency.

11.6.1 Code Efficiency

The efficiency of source code is directly tied to the efficiency of algorithms defined during detail design. However, coding style can have an effect on execution speed and memory requirement. The following set of guidelines can always be applied when detail design is translated into code:

- Simplify arithmetic and logical expressions before committing to code.
- Carefully evaluate nested loops to determine if statements or expressions can be moved outside.

- When possible, avoid the use of multidimensional arrays.
- When possible, avoid the use of pointers and complex lists
- Use "fast" arithmetic operations.
- Do not mix data types, even if the language allows it.
- Use integer arithmetic and Boolean expressions, whenever possible.

Many compilers have optimizing features that automatically generate efficient code by collapsing repetitive expressions, performing loop evaluation, using fast arithmetic, and applying other efficiency-related algorithms. For applications in which efficiency is paramount, such compilers are an indispensable coding tool.

11.6.2   Memory Efficiency

Memory restrictions in the large machine ("mainframe") world are generally a thing of the past. Virtual memory management provides application software with an enormous logical address space. Memory efficiency for such environments cannot be equated to minimum memory used. Rather, memory efficiency must take into account the "paging" characteristics of an operating system. In general, code locality or maintenance of functional domain via the structured constructs is an excellent method for reducing paging and thereby increasing efficiency.

Memory restrictions in the embedded microprocessor world are a very real concern, although low-cost, high-density memory is evolving rapidly. If minimal memory is demanded by system requirements (e.g., a high-volume, low-cost product), high-order language compilers must be carefully evaluated for memory compression features, or as a last resort, assembler language may have to be used.

Unlike other system characteristics that must be traded off against one another, techniques for execution time efficiency can sometimes lead to memory efficiency. For example, limiting the use of three- or four-dimensional arrays results in simple element access algorithms that are fast and short. Again, the key to memory efficiency is "keep it simple."

11.6.3   Input/Output Efficiency

Two classes of I/O should be considered when efficiency is discussed: I/O directed at a human or I/O directed to another device (e.g., a disk or another computer). Input supplied by a user and output produced for a user are efficient when information can be supplied or understood with an economy of intellectual effort.

Efficiency of I/O to other hardware is an extremely complicated topic and is beyond the scope of this book. From the coding (and detail design) standpoint, however, a few simple guidelines that improve I/O efficiency can be stated:

- The number of I/O requests should be minimized.
- All I/O should be buffered to reduce communication overhead.
- For secondary memory (e.g., disk), the simplest acceptable access method should be selected and used.
- I/O to secondary memory devices should be blocked.

- I/O to terminals and printers should recognize features of the device that could improve quality or speed.
- Remember that "super-efficient" I/O is worthless if it cannot be understood.

As we noted earlier in this chapter, I/O design establishes style and ultimately dictates efficiency. The guidelines presented above are applicable to both design and coding steps of the software engineering process.

11.7 SUMMARY

The coding step of software engineering is a process of translation. Detail design is translated into a programming language that is ultimately (and automatically) transformed into machine-executable instructions. Psychological and technical characteristics of a programming language affect the ease of translation from design and the effort required to test and maintain software. These characteristics may be applied to programming languages that fall into one of four language generations.

Style is an important attribute of source code and can determine the intelligibility of a program. The elements of style include internal documentation, methods for data declaration, procedures for statement construction, and I/O coding techniques. In all cases, simplicity and clarity are key characteristics. An offshoot of coding style is the execution time and/or memory efficiency achieved. Although efficiency can be an extremely important requirement, we should remember that an "efficient" program that is unintelligible has questionable value.

Coding lies at the kernel of the software engineering process. Critically important steps have preceded coding, relegating it to a somewhat mechanistic translation of a detail design specification. Equally important steps follow coding, and it is a discussion of these steps and related topics that constitutes the remainder of this book.

REFERENCES

[BAR84]   Barstow, D. R., H. E. Shobe, and E. Sandewall, *Interactive Programming Environments*, McGraw-Hill, 1984.

[COX85]   Cox, B., "Software ICs and Objective C," Productivity Products International, Sandy Hook, CT, 1985.

[FAI85]   Fairley, R. E., *Software Engineering Concepts*, McGraw-Hill, 1985.

[HAN78]   Brinch-Hansen, P., "Distributed Processes: A Concurrent Programming Concept," *CACM*, vol. 21, no. 11, November 1978.

[INT86]   "Intellect System Documentation," Artificial Intelligence Corporation, Waltham, MA, 1986.

[JEN74]   Jensen, K., and N. Wirth, *Pascal User Manual and Report*, Springer-Verlag, 1974.

[KER78]   Kernighan, B., and P. Plauger, *The Elements of Programming Style*, 2d ed., McGraw-Hill, 1978.

[KLA80]   Klatzky, R., *Human Memory*, 2d ed., W. H. Freeman and Co., 1980.

[LED81]   Ledgard, H., and M. Marcotty, *The Programming Language Landscape*, SRA, 1981.

[MAC80]   Mack, B., and P. Heath, eds., *Guide to Good Programming*, Halsted Press (Wiley), 1980.

[MAR85]   Martin, J., *Fourth Generation Languages*, vol. 1, Prentice-Hall, 1985.

[MAR86]   Martin, J., and J. Leben, *Fourth Generation Languages*, vol. 2, Prentice-Hall, 1986.

[PRA84]   Pratt, T., *Programming Languages*, 2d ed., Prentice-Hall, 1984.

[SHE81]   Shepard, S., E. Kruesi, and B. Curtis, "The Effects of Symbology and Spatial Arrangement on the Comprehension of Software Specifications," *Proc. 5th Intl. Conf. Software Engineering*, IEEE, San Diego, March 1981, pp. 207–214.

[SHN80]   Shneiderman, B., *Software Psychology*, Winthrop Publishers, 1980.

[VAN78]   Van Tassel, D., *Program Style, Design, Efficiency, Debugging and Testing*, 2d ed., Prentice-Hall, 1978.

[WAS81a] Wasserman, A., ed., *Software Development Environments*, IEEE Computer Society Press, 1981.

[WAS81b] Wasserman, A., "User Software Engineering and the Design of Interactive Systems," *Proc. 5th Intl. Conf. Software Engineering*, IEEE, San Diego, CA, March 1981, pp. 387–393.

[WEI71]   Weinberg, G., *The Psychology of Computer Programming*, Van Nostrand, 1971.

[WIL86]   Wileden, J. C., and M. Dowson, eds., Intl. Workshop on the Software Process and Software Environments, *ACM SIGSOFT Notes*, vol. 11, no. 4, August, 1986.

PROBLEMS AND POINTS TO PONDER

11.1 Do some research on natural language processing (a book by Harris entitled *Natural Language Processing* (Reston, 1985), is a good starting point) and write a position paper on the probability of natural language programming.

11.2 Much of the work in software psychology has centered on the characteristics of programming languages and their effect on the coding task. Write a paper that presents some of the more current work in this area.

11.3 Select one or more programming languages and provide examples of each of the psychological characteristics (e.g., uniformity, ambiguity, etc.) discussed in Section 11.2.

11.4 Select the one programming language that you feel best satisfies the software engineering traits discussed in Section 11.2.3. Would your choice change if the technical characteristics of the language were also considered?

11.5 Select one of the third generation languages discussed in Section 11.4.3. Prepare a brief summary of important language characteristics and write a small program that illustrates the language syntax.

11.6 Select any specialized language and prepare a summary of important characteristics and special features. Write a small program that illustrates language syntax.

11.7 Select any object-oriented language and prepare a summary of important characteristics and special features. Write a small program that illustrates language syntax.

11.8 Select any fourth generation language (see [MAR85]) and prepare a summary of important characteristics and special features. Write a small "program" that illustrates language syntax.

11.9 Expert systems applications have become an extremely "hot" topic. Research the Lisp and PROLOG languages and summarize their strengths and weaknesses in this application area. How are the languages similar? How do they differ?

11.10 Ada is a programming language with a wide variety of features. How is Ada different from programming languages such as Pascal or C? In providing your answer, focus on the three fundamental characteristics discussed in Section 11.3.

11.11   Ada has been the source of much controversy over the last few years. Summarize the arguments (pro and con) that have been presented in the literature.

11.12   List by priority those style guidelines that you feel are most important. Justify your selection. Are these guidelines language-dependent, i.e., do some languages obviate the need for a particular guideline?

11.13   Code and attempt to implement the procedural designs for corresponding problems in
–21   Chapter 6. You may use the programming language of your choice but remember the style and clarity guidelines discussed in this chapter.

FURTHER READINGS

Programming languages are fundamental to an understanding of computer science and should be understood both individually and in relationship to one another. Books by Pratt [PRA84] and Ledgard and Marcotty [LED81] satisfy both requirements nicely. A book by Smedema et al. (*The Programming Languages Pascal, Modula, CHILL and Ada*, Prentice-Hall, 1983) presents a thumbnail sketch of these important programming languages.

The *Elements of Programming Style* [KER78] remains *must* reading for all individuals who intend to generate source code. The authors have provided an extensive, annotated set of rules for coding (and design) that are well worth heeding. Books by Weiler (*The Programmer's Craft*, Reston, 1983) and Liffick (*The Software Developer's Sourcebook*, Addison-Wesley, 1985) provide additional information about style.

There is no "best" textbook that can be chosen from the hundreds that have been written about languages within any one of the language classes we have discussed. The following list contains a representative sample of source material for many of the programming languages discussed in this chapter:

FORTRAN:	Etter, D. M., *Problem Solving with Structured Fortran 77*, Addison-Wesley, 1984.
COBOL:	Medley, D., and R. Eaves, *Programming Principles with COBOL*, Southwest Publishing, 1985.
ALGOL:	Brailsford, D., and A. Walker, *Introductory Algol-68 Programming*, Wiley, 1979.
BASIC:	Cope, T., *Computing Using Basic*, Wiley, 1981.
PL/1:	Tremblay, J. P., et al., *Structured PL/1 (PL/C) Programming*, McGraw-Hill, 1980.
Pascal:	Koffman, E. B., *Problem Solving and Structured Programming in Pascal*, 2d ed., McGraw-Hill, 1985.
C:	Hancock, L., and M. Kreiger, *The C Primer*, McGraw-Hill, 1983.
Ada:	Cohen, N. H., *Ada as a Second Language*, McGraw-Hill, 1986.
Modula-2:	Joyce, E. J., *Modula-2*, Addison-Wesley, 1985.
Lisp:	Touretzky, D. S., *Lisp*, Harper & Row, 1984.
PROLOG:	Clocksin, W., and C. Mellish, *Programming in Prolog*, 2d ed., Springer-Verlag, 1984.
Smalltalk:	Goldberg, A., and D. Robson, *Smalltalk-80*, Addison-Wesley, 1983.
FORTH:	Katzen, H., *Invitation to FORTH*, Petrocelli, 1981.

An introduction to formal language theory can be found in *Jewels of Formal Language Theory* (A. Salomaa, Computer Science Press, 1981). This text surveys morphic representations, formal syntax specification, DOL languages, and many other topics. An equally rigorous treatment of these topics may be found in Pagan (*Formal Specification of Programming Languages*, Prentice-Hall, 1981).

An excellent anthology that contains many papers on the psychology of programming has been edited by Curtis (*Human Factors in Software Development*, 2d ed., IEEE Computer Society Press, 1985). Entire sections are dedicated to programming language characteristics, learning to program, problem solving and design, and many other topics.

CHAPTER

12

SOFTWARE QUALITY ASSURANCE

All of the methods, tools, and procedures described in this book work toward a single goal: *to produce high-quality software*. Yet many readers will be challenged by the question: "What is software quality?"

Philip Crosby [CRO79], in his landmark book on quality, discusses this situation:

> The problem of quality management is not what people don't know about it. The problem is what they think they do know....
>
> In this regard, quality has much in common with sex. Everybody is for it. (Under certain conditions, of course.) Everyone feels they understand it. (Even though they wouldn't want to explain it.) Everyone thinks execution is only a matter of following natural inclinations. (After all, we do get along somehow.) And, of course, most people feel that problems in these areas are caused by other people. (If only *they* would take the time to do things right.)

The placement of this chapter might lead a reader to infer that software quality assurance is something you begin to worry about after code has been generated. Nothing could be further from the truth! Software quality assurance (SQA) is an "umbrella activity" that is applied throughout the software engineering process. SQA encompasses: (1) analysis, design, coding, and testing methods and tools; (2) formal technical reviews that are applied during each software engineering step; (3) a multitiered testing strategy; (4) control of software documentation and the changes made to it; (5) a procedure to assure compliance with software development standards (when applicable); and (6) measurement and reporting mechanisms.

In this chapter, we shall examine the meaning of the elusive term *software quality*, and discuss the procedures and measures that help to assure that quality is a natural outcome of software engineering.

12.1 SOFTWARE QUALITY AND SOFTWARE QUALITY ASSURANCE

Even the most jaded software developers will agree that high-quality software is an important goal. But how do we define quality? A wag once said, ''Every program does something right; it just may not be the thing that we want it to do.''

There have been many definitions of software quality proposed in the literature. For our purposes, software quality is defined as:

> Conformance to explicitly stated functional and performance requirements, explicitly documented development standards, and implicit characteristics that are expected of all professionally developed software.

There is little question that the above definition could be modified or extended. In fact, a definitive definition of software quality could be debated endlessly. For the purposes of this book, the above definition serves to emphasize three important points:

1. Software requirements are the foundation from which *quality* is measured. Lack of conformance to requirements is lack of quality.
2. Specified standards define a set of development criteria that guide the manner in which software is engineered. If the criteria are not followed, lack of quality will almost surely result.
3. There is a set of *implicit requirements* that often goes unmentioned (e.g., the desire for good maintainability). If software conforms to its explicit requirements but fails to meet implicit requirements, software quality is suspect.

Software quality is a complex mix of factors that will vary across different applications and the customers who request them. In the sections that follow, software quality factors are identified and the human activities required to achieve them are described.

12.1.1 Software Quality Factors

The factors that affect software quality can be categorized in two broad groups: (1) factors that can be directly measured (e.g., errors/KLOC/unit-time) and (2) factors that can be measured only indirectly (e.g., usability or maintainability). In each case *measurement* must occur. We must compare the software (documents, programs, etc.) to some *datum* and arrive at an indication of quality.

McCall and his colleagues [MCC77] have proposed a useful categorization of factors that affect software quality. These *software quality factors*, shown in Figure 12.1, focus on three important aspects of a software product: its operational characteristics, its ability to undergo change, and its adaptability to new environments.

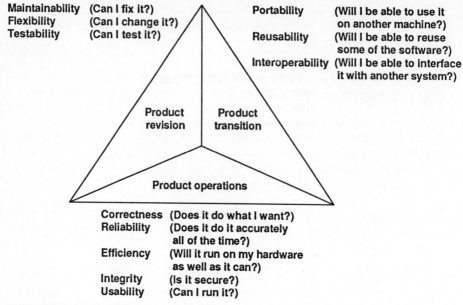

Maintainability (Can I fix it?)
Flexibility (Can I change it?)
Testability (Can I test it?)

Portability (Will I be able to use it on another machine?)
Reusability (Will I be able to reuse some of the software?)
Interoperability (Will I be able to interface it with another system?)

Product revision   Product transition

Product operations

Correctness (Does it do what I want?)
Reliability (Does it do it accurately all of the time?)
Efficiency (Will it run on my hardware as well as it can?)
Integrity (Is it secure?)
Usability (Can I run it?)

FIGURE 12.1
McCall's software quality factors [MCC77].

Referring to the factors noted in Figure 12.1, McCall provides the following descriptions:

- *Correctness.* The extent to which a program satisfies its specification and fulfills the customer's mission objectives.
- *Reliability.* The extent to which a program can be expected to perform its intended function with required precision. (It should be noted that other, more complete, definitions of reliability have been proposed (see Section 12.5).)
- *Efficiency.* The amount of computing resources and code required by a program to perform its function.
- *Integrity.* The extent to which access to software or data by unauthorized persons can be controlled.
- *Usability.* The effort required to learn, operate, prepare input, and interpret the output of a program.
- *Maintainability.* The effort required to locate and fix an error in a program. (This is a very limited definition (see Chapter 15).)
- *Flexibility.* The effort required to modify an operational program.
- *Testability.* The effort required to test a program to ensure that it performs its intended function.
- *Portability.* The effort required to transfer the program from one hardware and/or software system environment to another.

- *Reusability.* The extent to which a program (or parts of a program) can be reused in other applications. This is related to the packaging and the scope of the functions that the program performs.
- *Interoperability.* The effort required to couple one system to another.

It is difficult, and in some cases impossible, to develop direct measures of the above quality factors. Therefore, a set of metrics are defined and used to develop expressions for each of the factors according to the following relationship:

$$F_q = c_1 \times m_1 + c_2 \times m_2 + \ldots + c_n \times m_n$$

where F_q is a software quality factor, c_n are regression coefficients, and m_n are the metrics that affect the quality factor. Unfortunately, many of the metrics defined by McCall can only be measured subjectively. The metrics may be in the form of a checklist that is used to "grade" specific attributes of the software [CAV78]. The grading scheme proposed by McCall is a 0 (low) to 10 (high) scale. The following metrics are used in the grading scheme:

- *Auditability.* The ease with which conformance to standards can be checked.
- *Accuracy.* The precision of computations and control.
- *Communication commonality.* The degree to which standard interfaces, protocols, and bandwidth are used.
- *Completeness.* The degree to which full implementation of required function has been achieved.
- *Conciseness.* The compactness of the program in terms of lines of code.
- *Consistency.* The use of uniform design and documentation techniques throughout the software development project.
- *Data commonality.* The use of standard data structures and types throughout the program.
- *Error tolerance.* The damage that occurs when the program encounters an error.
- *Execution efficiency.* The run-time performance of a program.
- *Expandability.* The degree to which architectural, data, or procedural design can be extended.
- *Generality.* The breadth of the potential application of program components.
- *Hardware independence.* The degree to which the software is decoupled from the hardware on which it operates.
- *Instrumentation.* The degree to which the program monitors its own operation and identifies errors that do occur.
- *Modularity.* The functional independence (Chapter 6) of program components.
- *Operability.* The ease of operation of a program.
- *Security.* The availability of mechanisms that control or protect programs and data.
- *Self-documentation.* The degree to which the source code provides meaningful documentation.

- *Simplicity.* The degree to which a program can be understood without difficulty.
- *Software system independence.* The degree to which the program is independent of nonstandard programming language features, operating system characteristics, and other environmental constraints.
- *Traceability.* The ability to trace a design representation or actual program component back to requirements.
- *Training.* The degree to which the software assists in enabling new users to apply the system.

The relationship between software quality factors and the metrics listed above is shown in Table 12.1. It should be noted that the weight given to each metric is dependent on local products and concerns.

12.1.2 Software Quality Assurance

Quality assurance is an essential activity for any business that produces products to be used by others. Prior to the twentieth century, quality assurance was the sole responsibility of the craftsperson who built the product. The first formal quality assurance and control function was introduced at Bell Labs in 1916 and spread rapidly throughout the manufacturing world. Today, every company has mechanisms to ensure quality in its products. In fact, explicit statements of a company's concern for quality have become a marketing ploy during the past decade.

The history of quality assurance in software development parallels the history of quality in hardware manufacturing. During the early years of computing (1950s and 1960s), quality was the responsibility of the programmer alone. Standards for quality assurance for software were introduced in military contract software development during the 1970s and have spread rapidly into software development in the commercial world.

The role of software quality assurance (SQA) is illustrated schematically in Figure 12.2. SQA is part of a larger quality assurance function and encompasses activities that span many technical disciplines.

The scope of quality assurance responsibility might best be characterized by paraphrasing a popular automobile commercial: "Quality is Job #1." The implication for software is that many different constituencies in an organization have software quality assurance responsibility—software engineers, project managers, customers, salespeople, and the individuals who serve within the SQA group.

The SQA group serves as the customer's in-house representative. That is, the people who perform SQA must look at the software from the customer's point of view. Does the software adequately meet the quality factors noted in Section 12.1.1? Has software development been conducted according to pre-established standards? Have technical disciplines properly performed their roles as part of the SQA activity? The SQA group attempts to answer these and other questions to ensure that software quality is maintained.

TABLE 12.1

Quality factors and metrics

Quality factor / Software quality metric	Correctness	Reliability	Efficiency	Integrity	Maintainability	Flexibility	Testability	Portability	Reusability	Interoperability	Usability
Auditability				x			x				
Accuracy		x									
Communication commonality										x	
Completeness	x										
Complexity		x				x	x				
Concision			x		x	x					
Consistency	x	x			x	x					
Data commonality										x	
Error tolerance		x									
Execution efficiency			x								
Expandability						x					
Generality						x		x	x	x	
Hardware indep.								x	x		
Instrumentation				x	x		x				
Modularity		x			x	x	x	x	x	x	
Operability			x								x
Security				x							
Self documentation					x	x	x	x	x		
Simplicity		x			x	x	x				
System indep.								x	x		
Traceability	x										
Training											x

(Adapted from [ART85])

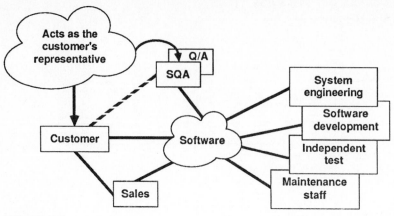

FIGURE 12.2
Software quality assurance.

12.1.3   SQA Activities

Software quality assurance comprises a variety of tasks associated with seven major activities: (1) application of technical methods, (2) conduct of formal technical reviews, (3) testing of software, (4) enforcement of standards, (5) control of change, (6) measurement, and (7) recordkeeping and reporting.

Software quality is designed into a product or system; it is not imposed after the fact. For this reason, SQA actually begins with the set of *technical methods and tools* that help the analyst to achieve a high-quality specification and a high-quality design. Measures of specification and design quality have already been discussed in this book (e.g., see Chapters 4 and 6).

Once a specification (or prototype) and design have been created, each must be assessed for quality. The central activity that accomplishes quality assessment is the *formal technical review*. The formal technical review (FTR) is a stylized meeting conducted by technical staff with the sole purpose of uncovering quality problems. In many situations, reviews have been found to be as effective as testing in uncovering defects in software. Reviews are discussed in Section 12.2.

Software testing combines a multistep strategy with a series of test case design methods that help ensure effective error detection. Many software developers use software testing as a quality assurance ''safety net.'' That is, developers assume that thorough testing will uncover most errors, thereby mitigating the need for other SQA activities. Unfortunately, testing, even when performed well, is not as effective as we might like for all classes of errors [JON81]. Software testing is discussed in detail in Chapters 13 and 14.

The degree to which formal *standards and procedures* are applied to the software engineering process varies from company to company. In many cases, standards are dictated by customers or regulatory mandate. In other situations standards are self-imposed. If formal (written) standards do exist, an SQA activity must be established to assure that they are being followed. An assessment of compliance to standards may be conducted by software developers as part of a formal technical review, or in situations where independent verification of compliance is required, the SQA group may conduct its own *audit*.

A major threat to software quality comes from a seemingly benign source: *changes*. Every change to software has the potential for introducing error or creating side effects that propagate errors. The *change control* process (a task that is part of software configuration management, covered in Chapter 15) contributes directly to software quality by formalizing requests for change, evaluating the nature of change, and controlling the impact of change. Change control is applied during software development and later, during the software maintenance phase.

Measurement is an activity that is integral to any engineering discipline. An important goal of SQA is to track software quality and assess the ability of methodological and procedural changes to improve software quality. To accomplish this, *software metrics* should be collected. Software metrics encompass a broad array of technical and management-oriented measures and are discussed in Section 12.4.

Recordkeeping and reporting for software quality assurance provide procedures for the collection and dissemination of SQA information. The results of reviews, audits, change control, testing, and other SQA activities must become part of the historical record for a project and should be disseminated to development staff on a need-to-know basis. For example, the results of each FTR for a procedural design are recorded and placed in a folder that contains all technical and SQA information about a module.

12.2 SOFTWARE REVIEWS

Software reviews are a "filter" for the software engineering process. That is, reviews are applied at various points during software development and serve to uncover defects that can then be removed. Software reviews serve to "purify" the software engineering activities that we have called analysis, design, and coding.

Freedman and Weinberg [FRE82] discuss the need for reviews this way:

Technical work needs reviewing for the same reason that pencils need erasers: *To err is human*. The second reason we need technical reviews is that although people are good at catching some of their own errors, large classes of errors escape the originator more easily than they escape anyone else. The review process is, therefore, the answer to the prayer of Robert Burns:

> O wad some power the giftie give us
> to see ourselves as others see us

A review—any review—is a way of using the diversity of a group of people to:

1. Point out needed improvements in the product of a single person or team;
2. Confirm those parts of a product in which improvement is either not desired or not needed;
3. Achieve technical work of more *uniform*, or at least more *predictable*, quality than can be achieved without reviews, in order to make technical work more *manageable*.

There are many different types of reviews that can be conducted as part of software engineering. Each has its place. An informal meeting around the coffee machine is a form of review, if technical problems are discussed. A formal presentation of software design to an audience of customers, management, and technical staff is a form of review. In this book, however, we focus on the *formal technical review* (FTR)— sometimes called a *walkthrough*. A formal technical review is the most effective filter from a quality assurance standpoint. Conducted by software engineers (and others) for software engineers, the FTR is an effective means for improving software quality.

12.2.1 Cost Impact of Software Defects

The obvious benefit of formal technical reviews is the early discovery of *software defects* so that each defect may be corrected prior to the next step in the software engineering process. For example, a number of industry studies (TRW, Nippon Electric, Mitre Corp., among others) indicate that design activities introduce between 50 and 65 percent of all errors (defects) during the development phase of the software engineering process. However, formal review techniques have been shown to be up to 75 percent effective [JON86] in uncovering design flaws. By detecting and removing a large percentage of these errors, the review process substantially reduces the cost of subsequent steps in the development and maintenance phases.

To illustrate the cost impact of early error detection, we consider a series of relative costs that are based on actual cost data collected for large software projects [IBM81]. Assume that an error uncovered during design will cost 1.0 monetary unit to correct. Relative to this cost, the same error uncovered just before testing commences will cost 6.5 units; during testing, 15 units; and after release, 67 units.

12.2.2 Defect Amplification and Removal

A *defect amplification model* [IBM81] can be used to illustrate the generation and detection of errors during the preliminary design, detail design, and coding steps of the software engineering process. The model is illustrated schematically in Figure 12.3. A box represents a software development step. During the step, errors may be inadver-

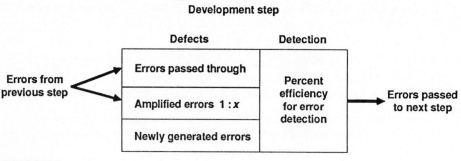

FIGURE 12.3
Defect amplification model.

tently generated. Review may fail to uncover newly generated errors and errors from previous steps, resulting in some number of errors being passed through. In some cases, errors passed through from previous steps are amplified (amplification factor, x) by current work. The box subdivisions represent each of these characteristics and the percent efficiency for detecting errors, a function of the thoroughness of review.

Figure 12.4 illustrates a hypothetical example of defect amplification for a software development process in which no reviews are conducted. Referring to the figure, each test step is assumed to uncover and correct 50 percent of all incoming errors without introducing any new errors (an optimistic assumption). Ten preliminary design defects are amplified to 94 errors before testing commences. Twelve latent errors are released to the field. Figure 12.5 considers the same conditions except that design and code reviews are conducted as part of each development step. In this case, ten initial preliminary design errors are amplified to 24 errors before testing commences. Only three latent errors exist. Recalling the relative costs associated with the discovery and correction of errors, overall cost (with and without review for our hypothetical example) can be established. Referring to Table 12.2 it can be seen that total cost for development and maintenance when reviews are conducted is 783 cost units. When no reviews are conducted, total cost is 2177 units—nearly three times more costly.

To conduct reviews, a developer must expend time, effort, and money. However, the results of the preceding example leave little doubt that we have encountered a "pay

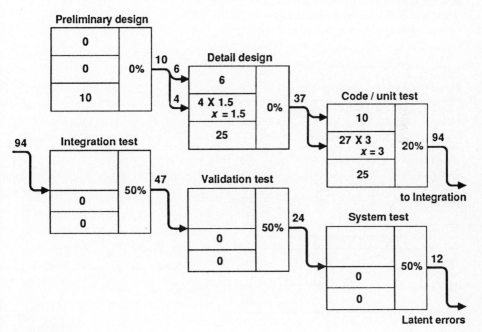

FIGURE 12.4
Defect amplification—no reviews.

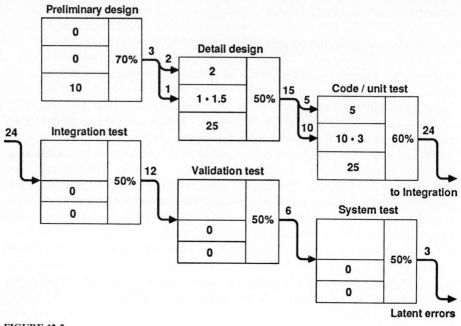

FIGURE 12.5
Defect amplification—reviews conducted.

TABLE 12.2
Development cost comparison

Errors found	Number	Cost unit	Total
Reviews conducted			
During design	22	1.5	33
Before test	36	6.5	234
During test	15	15	315
After release	3	67	201
			783
No reviews conducted			
Before test	22	6.5	143
During test	82	15	1230
After release	12	67	804
			2177

now or pay much more later'' syndrome. Formal technical reviews (for design and other technical activities) provide a demonstrable cost-benefit. They should be conducted.

12.3 FORMAL TECHNICAL REVIEWS

A formal technical review (FTR) is a software quality assurance activity that is performed by software engineering practitioners. The objectives of the FTR are: (1) to uncover errors in function, logic, or implementation for any representation of the software; (2) to verify that the software under review meets its requirements; (3) to assure that the software has been represented according to predefined standards; (4) to achieve software that is developed in a uniform manner; and (5) to make projects more manageable. In addition the FTR serves as a training ground, enabling junior engineers to observe different approaches to software analysis, design, and implementation. The FTR also serves to promote backup and continuity because a number of people will become familiar with parts of the software that they may not have otherwise seen.

The FTR is actually a class of reviews that include *walkthroughs*, *inspections*, *round-robin reviews*, and other small group technical assessments of software. Each FTR is conducted as a meeting and will be successful only if it is properly planned, controlled, and attended. In the paragraphs that follow, guidelines similar to those for a *walkthrough* ([FRE82], [YOU78]) are presented as a representative formal technical review.

12.3.1 The Review Meeting

Regardless of the FTR format that is chosen, every review meeting should abide by the following constraints:

* Between three and five people (typically) should be involved in the review.
* Advance preparation should occur but should require no more than two hours of work for each person.
* The duration of the review meeting should be less than two hours.

Given the above constraints, it should be obvious that an FTR focuses on a specific (and small) part of the overall software. For example, rather than attempting to review an entire design, walkthroughs are conducted for each module or small group of modules. By narrowing focus the FTR has a higher likelihood of uncovering errors.

The focus of the FTR is on a *product*—a component of the software (e.g, a portion of a requirements specification, a detailed module design, a source code listing for a module). The individual who has developed the product—the *producer*—informs the project leader that the product is complete and that a review is required. The project leader contacts a *review leader* who evaluates the product for readiness, generates copies of product materials, and distributes them to two or three *reviewers* for advance preparation. Each reviewer is expected to spend between one and two hours reviewing the product, making notes, and otherwise becoming familiar with the work. Concurrently, the review leader also reviews the product and establishes an agenda for the review meeting, which is typically scheduled for the next day.

The review meeting is attended by the review leader, all reviewers, and the producer. One of the reviewers takes on the role of the *recorder*, that is, the individual who records (in writing) all important issues raised during the review. The FTR begins with an introduction of the agenda and a brief introduction by the producer. The producer then proceeds to "walk through" the product (explains the material), while reviewers raise issues based on their advance preparation. When valid problems or errors are discovered, the recorder notes each.

At the end of the review, all attendees of the FTR must decide whether to (1) accept the product without further modification, (2) reject the product due to severe errors (once corrected, another review must be performed), or (3) accept the product provisionally (minor errors have been encountered and must be corrected, but no additional review will be required). The decision made, all FTR attendees complete a *sign-off*, indicating their participation in the review and their concurrence with the review team's findings.

12.3.2   Review Reporting and Recordkeeping

During the FTR, a reviewer (the recorder) actively records all issues that have been raised. These are summarized at the end of the review meeting and a *review issues list* is produced. In addition a simple *review summary report* is completed. A review summary report answers three questions:

1. What was reviewed?
2. Who reviewed it?
3. What were the findings and conclusions?

The review summary report takes the form illustrated in Figure 12.6. In general, this single-page (with possible attachments) form becomes part of the project historical record and may be distributed to the project leader and other interested parties.

The review issues list serves two purposes: (1) to identify problem areas within the product and (2) to serve as an *action item* checklist that guides the producer as corrections are made. An issues list that corresponds to the summary report is shown in Figure 12.7.

It is important to establish a follow-up procedure to assure that items on the issues list have been properly corrected. Unless this is done, it is possible that issues raised can "fall between the cracks."

12.3.3   Review Guidelines

Guidelines for the conduct of formal technical reviews must be established in advance, distributed to all reviewers, agreed upon, and then followed. A review that is uncontrolled can often be worse than no review at all.

Technical Review Summary Report

Review Identification:

Project: NC Real-Time Controller   Review Number: D-004
Date: 11 July 86   Location: Bldg. 4, Room 3   Time: 10:00 AM

Product Identification:

Material Reviewed: Detailed Design — modules for motion control

Producer: Alan Frederick

Brief Description: Three modules for x, y, z axis motion control

Material Reviewed: (note each item separately)
1. Detailed design descriptions: modules XMOTION, YMOTION, ZMOTION
2. PDL for modules

Review Team: (indicate leader and recorder)
         Name   Signature:

1. R. S. Pressman (Leader)   Roy S. Pressman
2. A. D. Dickerson (Recorder)   A. Dickerson
3. P.W. Brotherton   Paul W. Brotherton
4. M. Lambert   M. Lambert
5.

Product Appraisal:

Accepted: as is ( )   with minor modification (✓)
Not Accepted: major revision ( )   minor revision ( )
Review Not Completed: (explanation follows)

Supplementary material attached:

Issues list (✓)   Annotated Product Materials (✓)
Other (describe)

FIGURE 12.6
Technical review summary report.

Review Number: D-004
Date of Review: 07-11-86
Review leader: R.S. Pressman   Recorder: A.D. Dickerson

Issues List

1. <u>Prologues for module YMOTION, ZMOTION are not consistent
with design standards.</u> Purpose of the module should be
explicitly stated (reference is <u>not</u> acceptable) and data item
declaration must be specified.

2. <u>Loop counter for interpolation in X,Y,Z axes increments
one time too many for step motor control.</u> Review team
recommends a recheck of stepping motor specifications and
correction (as required) of the loop counter STEP.MOTOR.CTR.

3. <u>Typo in reference to current X position, X.POSITION, in
modules XMOTION and ZMOTION.</u> See marked PDL for specifics.

4. <u>PDL pseudo code statement must be expanded.</u> The
pseudo code statement: "Converge on proper control position
as in XMOTION" contained in modules YMOTION and ZMOTION
should be expanded to specifics for Y and Z motion control.

5. Review team recommends a modification to the "position
comparator" algorithm to improve run time performance.
Necessary modifications are noted in annotated PDL. Designer
has reservations about the modification and will analyze
potential impact before implementing change.

FIGURE 12.7
Review issues list.

The following represents a minimum set of guidelines for formal technical reviews:

1. *Review the product, not the producer.* An FTR involves people and egos. Conducted
   properly, the FTR should leave all participants with a warm feeling of accomplish-
   ment. Conducted improperly, the FTR can take on the aura of an inquisition. Errors should be pointed out gently; the tone of the meeting should be loose and constructive; the intent should not be to embarrass or belittle. The review leader
   should conduct the review meeting to assure that the proper tone and attitude is
   maintained and should immediately halt a review that has gotten out of control.
2. *Set an agenda and maintain it.* A malady of meetings of all types is *drift*. An FTR
   must be kept on track and on schedule. The review leader is charged with the responsibility for maintaining the meeting schedule and should not be afraid to
   nudge people when drift sets in.
3. *Limit debate and rebuttal.* When an issue is raised by a reviewer, there may not be
   universal agreement on its impact. Rather than spending time debating the question, the issue should be recorded for further discussion off-line.

4. *Enunciate problem areas, but don't attempt to solve every problem that is noted.* A review is not a problem-solving session. The solution of a problem can often be accomplished by the producer alone or with the help of only one other individual. Problem solving should be postponed until after the review meeting.

5. *Take written notes.* It is sometimes a good idea for the recorder to make notes on a wall board, so that wording and prioritization can be assessed by other reviewers as information is recorded.

6. *Limit the number of participants and insist upon advance preparation.* Two heads are better than one, but 14 are not necessarily better than four. Keep the number of people involved to the necessary minimum. In addition, all review team members must prepare in advance. Written comments (providing an indication that the reviewer has reviewed the material) should be solicited by the review leader.

7. *Develop a checklist for each product that is likely to be reviewed.* A checklist helps the review leader to structure the FTR meeting and helps each reviewer to focus on important issues. Checklists should be developed for analysis, design, code, and even test documents. A set of representative review checklists is presented in Section 12.3.4.

8. *Allocate resources and time schedule for FTRs.* For reviews to be effective, they should be scheduled as a task during the software engineering process. In addition, time should be scheduled for the inevitable modifications that will occur as the result of an FTR.

9. *Conduct meaningful training for all reviewers.* To be effective all review participants should receive some formal training. The training should stress both process-related issues and the human psychological side of reviews. Freedman and Weinberg [FRE82] estimate a one-month learning curve for every 20 people who are to participate effectively in reviews.

10. *Review your early reviews.* Debriefing can be beneficial in uncovering problems with the review process itself. The very first product to be reviewed might be the review guidelines themselves.

12.3.4   A Review Checklist

Formal technical reviews can be conducted during each step in the software engineering process. In this section we present a brief checklist that can be used to assess products that are derived as a part of software development. The checklists are not intended to be comprehensive but rather to provide a point of departure for each review.

SYSTEM ENGINEERING. The system specification allocates function and performance to many system elements. Therefore, the system review involves many constituencies that may each focus on their own area of concern (Figure 12.8). The software engineering (SWE) and hardware engineering (HWE) groups focus on software and hardware allocation, respectively. Quality assurance (QA) assesses system-level validation requirements (see Chapter 2) and field service examines the requirements for diagnostics. Once all reviews are conducted, a larger review meeting

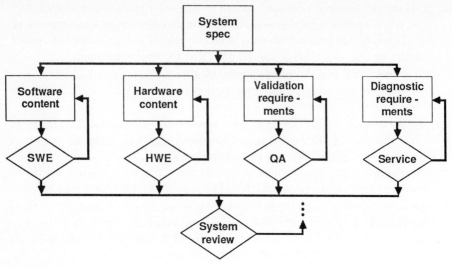

FIGURE 12.8
System review logistics.

with representatives from each constituency is conducted to assure early communication of concerns. The following checklist covers some of the more important areas of concern.

1. Are major functions defined in a bounded and unambiguous fashion?
2. Are interfaces between system elements defined?
3. Are performance bounds established for the system as a whole and for each element?
4. Are design constraints established for each element?
5. Has the best alternative been selected?
6. Is the solution technologically feasible?
7. Has a mechanism for system validation and verification been established?
8. Is there consistency among all system elements?

SOFTWARE PROJECT PLANNING. Software project planning develops estimates for resources, cost, and schedule based on the software allocation established as part of the system engineering activity. Like any estimation process, software project planning is inherently risky. The review of the *Software Project Plan* should attempt to establish the degree of risk. The following checklist is applicable.

1. Is software scope unambiguously defined and bounded?
2. Is terminology clear?
3. Are resources adequate for scope?

4. Are resources readily available?

5. Are tasks properly defined and sequenced? Is parallelism reasonable given available resources?

6. Is the basis for cost estimation reasonable? Has the cost estimate been developed using two independent methods?

7. Have historical productivity and quality data been used?

8. Have differences in estimates been reconciled?

9. Are pre-established budgets and deadlines realistic?

10. Is the schedule consistent?

SOFTWARE REQUIREMENTS ANALYSIS. Reviews for software requirements analysis focus on traceability to system requirements and representation consistency and correctness. A number of FTRs are conducted for the requirements of a large system and may be augmented by reviews and evaluation of prototypes as well as by customer meetings. The following topics are considered during FTRs for analysis.

1. Is information domain analysis complete, consistent and accurate?

2. Is problem partitioning complete?

3. Are external and internal interfaces properly defined?

4. Are all requirements traceable to system level?

5. Is prototyping conducted for customer?

6. Is performance achievable with constraints imposed by other system elements?

7. Are requirements consistent with schedule, resources, and budget?

8. Are validation criteria complete?

SOFTWARE DESIGN. Reviews for software design focus on data structure, program structure, and procedure. In general two types of design reviews are conducted. The *preliminary design review* assesses the translation of requirements to design and focuses on software architecture. The second review, often called a *design walkthrough*, concentrates on the procedural correctness of algorithms as they are implemented within program modules. The reviews occur in a sequence illustrated in Figure 12.9. The following checklists are useful for these reviews.

Preliminary design review

1. Are software requirements reflected in the software architecture?

2. Is effective modularity achieved? Are modules functionally independent?

3. Is program architecture factored?

4. Are interfaces defined for modules and external system elements?

5. Is data structure consistent with the information domain?

6. Is data structure consistent with software requirements?

7. Has maintainability been considered?

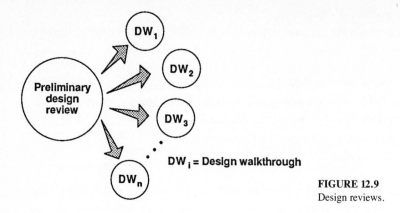

DW$_i$ = Design walkthrough

FIGURE 12.9
Design reviews.

Design walkthrough

1. Does the algorithm accomplish the desired function?
2. Is the algorithm logically correct?
3. Is the interface consistent with architectural design?
4. Is logical complexity reasonable?
5. Have error handling and ''antibugging'' been specified?
6. Is local data structure properly defined?
7. Are structured programming constructs used throughout?
8. Is design detail amenable to the implementation language?
9. Which are used: operating system or language-dependent features?
10. Is compound or inverse logic used?
11. Has maintainability been considered?

CODING. Although coding is a mechanistic outgrowth of procedural design, errors can be introduced as the design is translated into a programming language. This is particularly true if the programming language does not directly support data and control structures represented in the design. A code walkthrough can be an effective means for uncovering these translation errors. The checklist that follows assumes that a design walkthrough has been conducted and that algorithm correctness has been established as part of the design FTR.

1. Is design properly translated into code? (The results of the procedural design should be available during this review.)
2. Are there misspellings or typos?
3. Has proper use of language conventions been made?
4. Is there compliance with coding standards for language style, comments, module prologue?
5. Are incorrect or ambiguous comments present?

6. Are typing and data declaration proper?

7. Are physical constants correct?

8. Have all items on the design walkthrough checklist been reapplied (as required)?

SOFTWARE TESTING. Software testing is a quality assurance activity in its own right. Therefore, it may seem odd to discuss reviews for testing. However, the completeness and effectiveness of testing can be dramatically improved by critically assessing any test plans and procedures that have been established. In the next two chapters, test case design techniques and testing strategies are discussed in detail. A review of Chapters 13 and 14 is suggested prior to consideration of the following checklists:

Test plan

1. Have major test phases been properly identified and sequenced?

2. Has traceability to validation criteria/requirements been established as part of software requirements analysis?

3. Are major functions demonstrated early?

4. Is the test plan consistent with the overall project plan?

5. Has a test schedule been explicitly defined?

6. Are test resources and tools identified and available?

7. Has a test recordkeeping mechanism been established?

8. Have test *drivers* and *stubs* been identified, and has work to develop them been scheduled?

9. Has *stress testing* for software been specified?

Test procedure

1. Have both white and black box tests (see Chapter 13) been specified?

2. Have all independent logic paths been tested?

3. Have test cases been identified and listed with expected results?

4. Is error handling to be tested?

5. Are boundary values to be tested?

6. Are timing and performance to be tested?

7. Has acceptable variation from expected results been specified?

In addition to the FTRs and review checklists noted above, reviews (with corresponding checklists) can be conducted to assess the readiness of field service mechanisms for product software, to evaluate the completeness and effectiveness of training, to assess the quality of user and technical documentation, and to investigate the applicability and availability of software tools.

MAINTENANCE. The review checklists for software development are equally valid for the software *maintenance* phase (Chapter 15). In addition to all of the questions posed in the checklists, the following special considerations should be kept in mind:

1. Have side effects associated with change been considered?
2. Has the request for change been documented, evaluated, and approved?
3. Has the change, once made, been documented and reported to interested parties?
4. Have appropriate FTRs been conducted?
5. Has a final *acceptance review* been conducted to assure that all software has been properly updated, tested, and replaced?

12.4 SOFTWARE QUALITY METRICS

Earlier in this chapter, a set of qualitative factors for the "measurement" of software quality were discussed (Section 12.1.1). We strive to develop precise measures for software quality and are sometimes frustrated by the subjective nature of the activity. Cavano and McCall [CAV78] discuss this situation:

> The determination of quality is a key factor in every day events—wine tasting contests, sporting events [e.g., gymnastics], talent contests, etc. In these situations, quality is judged in the most fundamental and direct manner: side by side comparison of objects under identical conditions and with predetermined concepts. The wine may be judged according to clarity, color, bouquet, taste, etc. However, this type of judgment is very subjective; to have any value at all, it must be made by an expert.
>
> Subjectivity and specialization also apply to determining software quality. To help solve this problem, a more precise definition of software quality is needed as well as a way to derive quantitative measurements of software quality for objective analysis....Since there is no such thing as absolute knowledge, one should not expect to measure software quality exactly, for every measurement is partially imperfect. Jacob Bronkowski described this paradox of knowledge in this way: "Year by year we devise more precise instruments with which to observe nature with more fineness. And when we look at the observations we are discomfited to see that they are still fuzzy, and we feel that they are as uncertain as ever."

Other subjective measures for software quality have been proposed by Boehm [BOE78]. These are compared to McCall's metrics [MCC77], presented earlier in this chapter, in Figure 12.10.

In this section we examine a set of software metrics that can be applied to the quantitative assessment of software quality. In all cases the metrics represent indirect measures, that is, we never really measure *quality* but rather some manifestation of quality. The complicating factor is the precise relationship between the variable that is measured and the quality of software.

12.4.1 Halstead's Software Science

Halstead's theory of software science [HAL77] is "probably the best known and most thoroughly studied...composite measures of (software) complexity" [CUR80]. Software science proposes the first analytical "laws" for computer software.*

---

*It is important to note that Halstead's "laws" have generated substantial controversy. There is not universal agreement that these "laws" are correct.

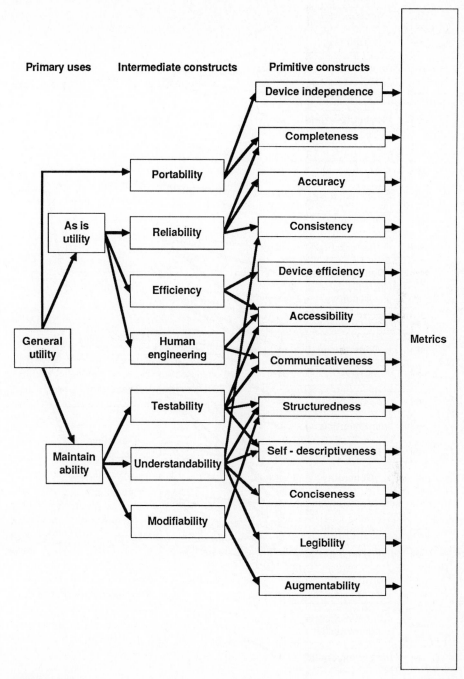

Boehm et al., model

FIGURE 12.10
Relating software quality characteristics (*Source*: William Curtis, ''Management and Experimentation in Software Engineering,'' *Proceedings of the IEEE*, vol. 68, no. 9, September 1980, p. 1147. Reprinted with permission.) Figure 12.10 is continued on page 454.

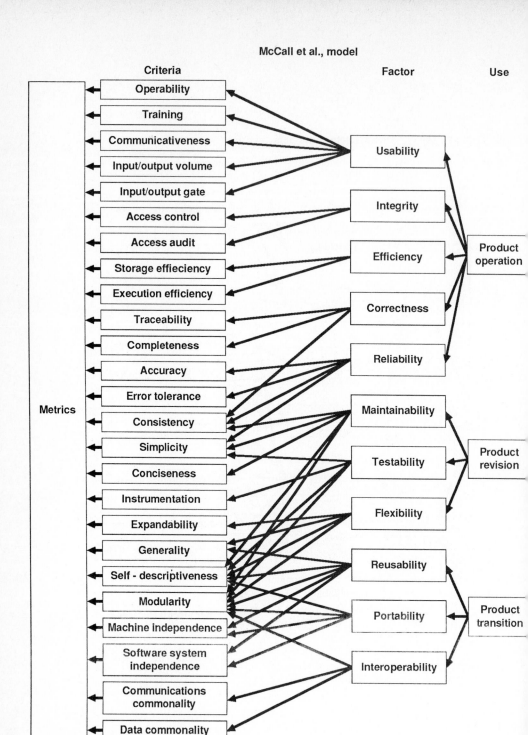

FIGURE 12.10
(*continued*)

Software science assigns quantitative laws to the development of computer software. Halstead's theory is derived from one fundamental assumption [HAL77]: "The human brain follows a more rigid set of rules (in developing algorithms) than it has been aware of...." Software science uses a set of primitive measures that may be derived after code is generated or estimated once design is complete. These are listed below.

n_1—the number of distinct operators that appear in a program
n_2—the number of distinct operands that appear in a program
N_1—the total number of operator occurrences
N_2—the total number of operand occurrences

To illustrate how these primitive measures are obtained, refer to the simple SORT program [FIT78] shown in Figure 12.11.

Halstead uses the primitive measures to develop expressions for the overall program *length*; potential minimum *volume* for an algorithm; the actual volume (number of bits required to specify a program); the *program level* (a measure of software complexity); *language level* (a constant for a given language); and other features such as development effort, development time, and even the projected number of faults in the software.

Halstead shows that length N can be estimated

$$N = n_1 \log_2 n_1 + n_2 \log_2 n_2$$

and program volume may be defined

$$V = N \log_2 (n_1 + n_2)$$

It should be noted that V will vary with programming language and represents the volume of information (in bits) required to specify a program. For the SORT module shown in Figure 12.11, it can be shown [FIT78] that the volume for the FORTRAN version is 204. Volume for an equivalent assembler language version would be 328. As we would suspect, it takes more effort to specify a program in assembler language.

Theoretically, a minimum volume must exist for a particular algorithm. Halstead defines a volume ratio L as the ratio of volume of the most compact form of a program to the volume of the actual program. In actuality, L must always be less than one. In terms of primitive measures, the volume ratio may be expressed as

$$L = \frac{2}{n_1} \times \frac{n_2}{N_2}$$

Halstead proposed that each language may be categorized by language level, l, which will vary among languages. Halstead theorized that language level is constant for a given language, but other work [ZEL81] indicates that language level is a function of both language and programmer. The following language level values have been empirically derived for common languages:

Interchange sort program

```
SUBROUTINE SORT (X,N)
DIMENSION X(N)
IF (N.LT.2) RETURN
DO 20 I = 2,N
    DO 10 J = 1,I
    IF (X(I).GE.X(J)) GO TO 10
        SAVE = X(I)
        X(I) = X(J)
        X(J) = SAVE
10 CONTINUE
20 CONTINUE
    RETURN
    END
```

Operators of the interchange sort program

Operator	Count
1 End of statement	7
2 Array subscript	6
3 =	5
4 IF ( )	2
5 DO	2
6 ,	2
7 End of program	1
8 .LT.	1
9 .GE.	1
n_1 = 10 GO TO 10	1
	$28 = N_1$

Operands of the interchange sort program

Operand	Count
1 X	6
2 I	5
3 J	4
4 N	2
5 2	2
6 SAVE	2
n_2 = 7 1	1
	$22 = N_2$

FIGURE 12.11

Operators and operands for a simple program. (*Source*: A. Fitzsimmons and T. Love, "A Review and Evaluation of Software Science," *ACM Computing Surveys*, vol. 10, no. 1, March 1978. © 1978, Association of Computing Machinery, Inc. Reprinted with permission.)

Language	Mean/l
English prose	2.16
PL/1	1.53
ALGOL/68	2.12
FORTRAN	1.14
Assembler	0.88

It appears that language level implies a level of abstraction in the specification of procedure. High-level languages allow specification of code at a higher level of abstraction than does assembler (machine-oriented) language.

Unlike many software metrics, Halstead's work is amenable to experimental verification. A large body of research has been conducted to investigate software science. A discussion of this work is beyond the scope of this text, but it can be said that good agreement has been found between analytically predicted and experimental results.

12.4.2 McCabe's Complexity Measure

A complexity measure of software proposed by Thomas McCabe [MCC76] is based on a control flow representation of a program. A *program graph*, illustrated in Figure 12.12, is used to depict control flow. Each circled letter represents a processing task (one or more source code statements); flow of control (branching) is represented with connecting arrows. (A more detailed discussion is presented in the following chapter.) For graph G in Figure 12.12, processing task a may be followed by tasks b, c, or d, de-

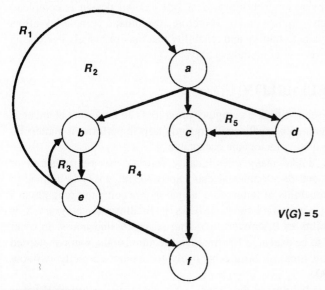

FIGURE 12.12
Control flow graph complexity.

pending on conditions tested as part of a. Processing task b is always followed by e, and both may be executed as part of a doubly nested loop (the curved arrows moving upward to b and a, respectively).

McCabe defines a software complexity measure that is based on the *cyclomatic complexity* of a program graph for a module. One technique (others are discussed in Chapter 13) that may be used to compute the cyclomatic complexity metric, $V(G)$, is to determine the number of regions in a planar graph (see McCabe [MCC76] or for more detail, Bondy and Murty [BON76]). A *region* may be informally described as an enclosed area on the plane of the graph. The number of regions is computed by counting all bounded areas and the unbounded area outside the graph. The graph in Figure 12.12 has five regions (noted as R_1 through R_5) and thus has a cyclomatic complexity metric, $V(G) = 5$.

Because the number of regions increases with the number of decision paths and loops, the McCabe metric provides a quantitative measure of testing difficulty and an indication of ultimate reliability. Experimental studies (e.g., [GRE76], [CUR79]) indicate distinct relationships between the McCabe metric and the number of errors existing in source code, as well as time required to find and correct such errors.

McCabe also contends that $V(G)$ may be used to provide a quantitative indication of maximum module size. Collecting data from a number of actual programming projects, he has found that $V(G) = 10$ appears to be a practical upper limit for module size. When the cyclomatic complexity of modules exceeded this number, it became extremely difficult to adequately test a module (see Chapter 13 for a discussion of test case design techniques).

The McCabe and Halstead metrics are representative of a growing "quantitative" approach to the measurement of computer software. Automated tools that assist in the computation of both metrics have been developed. The McCabe measure may be applied earlier in the software engineering process (after detail design is complete) than the Halstead approach (requires code). Therefore, cyclomatic complexity offers an evaluation tool for software testability and reliability that may ultimately become an important criterion for the review of module quality.

12.5   SOFTWARE RELIABILITY

There is no doubt that the reliability of a computer program is an important element of its overall quality. If a program repeatedly and frequently fails to perform, it matters little whether other software quality factors are acceptable.

Software reliability, unlike many other quality factors, can be measured or estimated using historical and developmental data. Software reliability is defined in statistical terms as "the probability of failure free operation of a computer program in a specified environment for a specified time" [MUS87]. To illustrate, program X is estimated to have a reliability of 0.96 over eight elapsed processing hours. In other words, if program X were to be executed 100 times and required eight hours of elapsed processing time (execution time), it would be likely to operate correctly (without failure) 96 times out of 100.

Whenever software reliability is discussed, a pivotal question arises: What is meant by the term *failure*? In the context of any discussion of software quality and reliability, failure is nonconformance to software requirements. Yet even within this definition there are gradations. Failures can be merely annoying or catastrophic. One failure can be corrected within seconds while another requires weeks or even months to correct. Complicating the issue even further, the correction of one failure may result in the introduction of other errors that ultimately result in other failures.

12.5.1 Measures of Reliability and Availability

Early work in software reliability attempted to extrapolate the mathematics of hardware reliability theory (e.g., [ALV64]) to the prediction of software reliability. Most hardware-related reliability models are predicated on failure due to *wear* rather than failure due to design defects. In hardware, failures due to physical wear (e.g., the effects of temperature, corrosion, shock) are more likely than a design-related failure. Unfortunately, the opposite is true for software. In fact, all software failures can be traced to design or implementation problems; wear (see Chapter 1) does not enter into the picture.

There is still debate over the relationship between key concepts in hardware reliability and their applicability to software. Although an irrefutable link has yet to be established, it is worthwhile to consider a few simple concepts that apply to both system elements.

If we consider a computer-based system, a simple measure of reliability is *mean time between failure* (MTBF) where

$$MTBF = MTTF + MTTR$$

(The acronyms MTTF and MTTR are *mean time to failure* and *mean time to repair*, respectively.)

In addition to a reliability measure, we must develop a measure of *availability*. Software availability is the percentage that a program is operating according to requirements at a given point in time and is defined as:

$$Availability = MTTF / (MTTF + MTTR) \times 100\%$$

The MTBF reliability measure is equally sensitive to MTTF and MTTR. The availability measure is somewhat more sensitive to MTTR, an indirect measure of the maintainability of software.

12.5.2 Software Reliability Models

In one of the most comprehensive treatments of software reliability to date, Musa and his colleagues [MUS87] describe software reliability models in the following manner:

> Software reliability models are used to characterize and predict behavior important to managers and engineers. In order to model software reliability, one must first consider the principle factors affecting it: fault generation, fault removal and the environment. Fault generation depends primarily on the characteristics of the developed code (code created or modified for the application) such as size and development process characteristics such as software engineering technologies and tools used, level of experience of personnel, etc.

Note that code can be developed to add features or to remove faults. Fault removal depends on time, operational profile, and the quality of the repair activity. The environment depends on the operational profile. Since some of the foregoing factors are probabilistic in nature and operate over time, software reliability models are generally random processes.

Software reliability models fall into two broad categories: (1) models that predict reliability as a function of chronological (calendar) time, and (2) models that predict reliability as a function of elapsed processing time (CPU execution time). Musa [MUS87] suggests that software reliability models based on elapsed processing time (execution time) show the best overall results.

Models that have been derived from hardware reliability work make the following assumptions: (1) the debugging time between error occurrences has an exponential distribution with an error occurrence rate that is proportional to the number of remaining errors; (2) each error discovered is immediately removed, decreasing the total number of errors by one; and (3) the failure rate between errors is constant [SUK78]. The validity of each of these assumptions can be questioned. For example, corrections of one error may inadvertently introduce other errors in the software, invalidating the second assumption.

Another class of reliability models is based on the internal characteristics of a program and computes a predicted number of errors that exist in the software. The models, based on the quantitative relationships derived as a function of software complexity measures (Sections 12.4.1 and 12.4.2), relate specific design or code-oriented attributes of a program (e.g., number of operands and operators or the cyclomatic complexity) to "an estimate of the initial number of errors to be expected in a given program" [HAL77].

Seeding models (e.g., [KNI85]) can be used as an indication of software reliability or, more practically, as a measure of the "error detection power" of a set of test cases. A program is randomly seeded with a number of known "calibration" errors [MIL72]. The program is tested (using test cases). The probability of finding j real errors of a total population of J (an unknown) errors can be related to the probability of finding k seeded errors from all K errors embedded in the code.

Much more sophisticated stochastic models for software reliability have been proposed in recent years (e.g., see [SHO83], [MIL85], and [MUS87]). For those readers who intend to study such models in greater detail, Iannino [IAN84] suggests a set of criteria for comparison and assessment:

Predictive validity. The ability of the model to predict future failure behavior based on data collected from the testing and operational phases.

Capability. The ability of the model to generate data that can be readily applied to pragmatic industrial software development efforts.

Quality of assumptions. The plausibility of the assumptions on which the mathematical foundation of the model is based and the degree of degradation of the model when the limits of those assumptions are reached.

Applicability. The degree to which a reliability model can be applied across different software application domains and types.

Simplicity. The degree to which collection of data to support the model is straightforward; the degree to which the mathematics and approach are intuitive; the degree to which the overall approach can be automated.

A discussion of the models to which these criteria apply requires a background in statistics and probability and is better left to textbooks dedicated to software reliability. The interested reader should refer to [SHO83] and [MUS87].

To date the results obtained from the pragmatic application of reliability models have been mixed. Further work remains to be done before such models can be widely used throughout the software engineering community.

12.6 A SOFTWARE QUALITY ASSURANCE APPROACH

Although few managers and practitioners would debate the need for software quality, many are disinterested in establishing formal SQA functions. The reasons for this seeming contradiction are many: (1) managers are reluctant to incur the extra up-front cost, (2) practitioners feel that they are already doing everything that needs to be done, (3) no one knows where to put such a function organizationally, and (4) everyone wants to avoid the ''red tape'' that SQA is perceived to introduce into the software engineering process.

In this section, we present a brief discussion of the most important concerns in instituting software quality assurance activities. For a more detailed presentation, see [DUN82] or [CHO84].

12.6.1 Examining the Need for SQA

All software development organizations have some mechanism for quality assessment. At the low end of the scale, quality is solely the responsibility of the individual who may engineer, review, and test software at any comfort level. At the high end of the scale, an SQA group is chartered with the responsibility for establishing standards and procedures for achieving software quality and assuring that each is followed. The real question for every software engineering organization is: ''Where on the scale do we sit?''

Before formal quality assurance procedures are instituted, a software development organization should adopt software engineering procedures, methods, and tools. This methodology, when combined with an effective paradigm for software development, can do much to improve the quality of all software produced by the organization.

We have already discussed the importance of formal review techniques, comprehensive test case design, and change control for software quality. In addition to these and other development activities, specific SQA activities can be conducted. The first step to be conducted as part of a concerted effort to institute software quality assurance procedures is an *SQA/SCM Audit*. The current ''state'' of software quality assurance and software configuration management (Chapter 15) is assessed by examining the following topics:

Policies. What current policies, procedures and standards exist for all phases of software development? Are they enforced? Is there a specific (management-supported) policy for SQA? Are policies applied to both development and maintenance activities?

Organization. Where does software engineering reside in the current organizational chart? Where does QA reside?

Functional interfaces. What is the current relationship between QA and SQA functions and other constituencies? How does SQA interact with formal technical reviews, with SCM, with testing activities?

Once the above questions have been answered, strengths and weaknesses are identified. If the need for SQA is apparent, a careful assessment of the pros and cons is undertaken.

On the positive side, SQA offers the following benefits: (1) software will have fewer latent defects, resulting in reduced effort and time spent during testing and maintenance; (2) higher reliability will result in greater customer satisfaction; (3) maintenance costs (a substantial percentage of all software costs) can be reduced; and (4) overall life cycle cost of software is reduced. As Crosby [CRO79] states, "Quality is free!"

On the negative side, SQA can be problematic for the following reasons: (1) it is difficult to institute in small organizations, where available resources to perform the necessary activities are not available; (2) it represents cultural change—and change is never easy; and (3) it requires the expenditure of dollars that would not otherwise be explicitly budgeted to software engineering or QA.

At a fundamental level, SQA is cost effective if:

$$C_3 > C_1 + C_2$$

where C_3 is the cost of errors that occur with no SQA program, C_1 is the cost of the SQA program itself, and C_2 is the cost of errors not found by SQA activities. It is important to note, however, that a more detailed analysis must also consider reduced testing and integration costs, reduced numbers of prerelease changes, reduced maintenance costs, and improved customer satisfaction.

12.6.2   SQA Planning and Standards

Once an organization has decided to institute SQA, a plan should be developed and standards should be acquired or developed. Dunn and Ullman [DUN82] present a list of tasks that should be addressed as part of any SQA plan:

1. system design review
2. software requirements specification review
3. preliminary design review
4. detail (module level) design review
5. review of integration test plan (Chapter 14)
6. code review

7. review of test procedures

8. audit of document standards

9. configuration control audit

10. test audit

11. defect data collection, evaluation, and analysis

12. tool certification

13. vendor and contractor oversight

14. record keeping

These and other topics are addressed in ANSI/IEEE Standard No. 730-1981—*Software Quality Assurance Plans*—available from the IEEE.

The SQA plan provides a road map for instituting software quality assurance. Table 12.3 presents a list of SQA related standards, published by the U.S. Department of Defense and other agencies, that will serve to guide the development of technical procedures for achieving software quality.

12.7   SUMMARY

Software quality assurance is an "umbrella activity" that is applied at each step in the software engineering process. SQA encompasses procedures for the effective application of methods and tools, formal technical reviews, testing strategies and techniques, procedures for change control, procedures for assuring compliance to standards, and measurement and reporting mechanisms.

SQA is complicated by the complex nature of software quality—an attribute of computer programs that is defined as "conformance to explicitly defined requirements." But when considered more generally, software quality encompasses many different product and process factors and related metrics.

TABLE 12.3
SQA standards

MIL-STD-1679A DOD-STD-2167	Encompass all aspects of software engineering
MIL-S-52779A	The basic SQA specifications for procurements
FAA-STD-018	SQA standard for the FAA
DLAM-8200.1	Defense Logistics Agency Manual contains guidelines for government audit of a contractor's SQA activities
DOD-STD-2168	A software quality evaluation standard
IEEE Std. 730	The IEEE standard for esablishing SQA plans

Software reviews are one of the most important SQA activities. Reviews serve as a filter for the software engineering process, removing defects while they are relatively inexpensive to find and correct. The formal technical review or walkthrough is a stylized review meeting that has been shown to be extremely effective in uncovering defects.

To conduct software quality assurance properly, data about the software engineering process should be collected, evaluated, and disseminated. Software quality metrics include both direct and indirect measures of software. Some metrics are the result of subjective qualitative assessment, while others are quantitative in nature. Software reliability models extend measurements, enabling collected defect data to be extrapolated into projected failure rates and reliability.

In summary we recall the words of Dunn and Ullman [DUN82]: "software quality assurance is the mapping of the managerial precepts and design disciplines of quality assurance onto the applicable managerial and technological space of software engineering." The ability to assure quality is the measure of a mature engineering discipline. When the mapping alluded to above is successfully accomplished, mature software engineering is the result.

REFERENCES

[ALV64]   von Alvin, W. H., ed., *Reliability Engineering*, Prentice-Hall, 1964.

[ART85]   Arthur, L. A., *Measuring Programmer Productivity and Software Quality*, Wiley-Interscience, 1985.

[BON76]   Bondy, J., and U. Murty, *Graph Theory with Applications*, North Holland, 1976.

[CAV78]   Cavano, J. P., and J. A. McCall, "A Framework for the Measurement of Software Quality," *Proc. ACM Software Quality Assurance Workshop*, November 1978, pp. 133–139.

[CHO84]   Chow, T. S., *Software Quality Assurance: A Practical Approach*, IEEE Computer Society Press, 1985.

[CRO79]   Crosby, P., *Quality Is Free*, McGraw-Hill, 1979.

[CUR79]   Curtis, W., et al., "Measuring the Psychological Complexity of Software Maintenance Tasks with the Halstead and McCabe Metrics," *IEEE Trans. Software Engineering*, vol. 5, March 1979, pp. 96–104.

[CUR80]   Curtis, W., "Management and Experimentation in Software Engineering," *Proceedings of the IEEE*, vol. 68, no. 9, September 1980.

[DUN82]   Dunn, R., and R. Ullman, *Quality Assurance for Computer Software*, McGraw-Hill, 1982.

[FIT78]   Fitzsimmons, A., and T. Love, "A Review and Evaluation of Software Science," *ACM Computing Surveys*, vol. 10, no. 1, March 1978, pp. 3–18.

[FRE82]   Freedman, D. P., and G. M. Weinberg, *Handbook of Walkthroughs, Inspections and Technical Reviews*, 3d ed., Little, Brown, and Company, 1982.

[GRE76]   Green, T. F., et al., "Program Structures, Complexity and Error Characteristics," *Computer Software Engineering*, Polytechnic Press, New York, 1976, pp. 139–154.

[HAL77]   Halstead, M., *Elements of Software Science*, North Holland, 1977.

[IAN84]   Iannino, A., et al., "Criteria for Software Reliability Model Comparisons," *IEEE Trans. Software Engineering*, vol. SE-10, no. 6, November 1984, pp. 687–691.

[IBM81]   "Implementing Software Inspections," course notes, IBM Systems Sciences Institute, IBM Corporation, 1981.

[JON81]   Jones, T. C., *Programming Productivity: Issues for the 80s*, IEEE Computer Society Press, 1981, pp. 13–20.

[JON86]   Jones, T. C., *Programming Productivity*, McGraw-Hill, 1986.

[KNI85]   Knight, J. C., and P. E. Ammenn, "An Experimental Evaluation of Simple Methods for Seeding Program Errors," *Proc. 8th Intl. Conf. Software Engineering*, IEEE, London, August 1985, pp. 337–342.

[MCC76]   McCabe, T., "A Software Complexity Measure," *IEEE Trans. Software Engineering*, vol. 2, December 1976, pp. 308–320.

[MCC77]   McCall, J., P. Richards, and G. Walters, "Factors in Software Quality," 3 vols., NTIS AD-A049-014, 015, 055, November 1977.

[MIL72]   Mills, H. D., "On the Statistical Validation of Computer Programs," FSC 72:6015, IBM Federal Systems Division, 1972.

[MIL85]   Miller, D. R., and A. Sofer, "Completely Monotone Regression Estimates for Software Failure Rates," *Proc. 8th Intl. Conf. Software Engineering*, IEEE, London, August 1985, pp. 343–348.

[MUS87]   Musa, J. D., A. Iannino, and K. Okumoto, *Engineering and Managing Software with Reliability Measures*, McGraw-Hill, 1987.

[SHO83]   Shooman, M., *Software Engineering*, McGraw-Hill, 1983.

[SUK78]   Sukert, A., and A. Goel, "Error Modelling Applications in Software Quality Assurance," *Proc. SQA Workshop*, ACM, San Diego, CA, November 1978, pp. 33–38.

[YOU78]   Yourdon, E., *Structured Walkthroughs*, 2d ed., Yourdon Press, 1978.

[ZEL81]   Zelkowitz, M., private communication, 1981.

PROBLEMS AND POINTS TO PONDER

12.1 Although the quality factors described in Section 12.1 are interesting at a macroscopic level, how would you assess the quality of a computer program if the source listing were dumped on your desk right now? Discuss both qualitative and quantitative aspects of your assessment.

12.2 Is it possible to assess the quality of software if the customer keeps changing his mind about what it is supposed to do?

12.3 Quality and reliability are related concepts but are fundamentally different in a number of ways. Discuss them.

12.4 Can a program be correct and still not be reliable? Explain.

12.5 Can a program be correct and still not exhibit good quality? Explain.

12.6 Why is there often tension between a software engineering group and an independent software quality assurance group? Is this healthy?

12.7 You have been given the responsibility for improving the quality of software across your organization. What is the first thing that you should do? What is next?

12.8 Besides errors, are there other countable characteristics of software that imply quality? What are they and can they be measured directly?

12.9 A formal technical review is effective only if everyone has prepared in advance. How do you recognize a review participant who has not prepared? What do you do if you are the review leader?

12.10 Some people argue that an FTR should assess programming style as well as correctness. Is this a good idea? Why?

12.11 Develop a small software tool that will perform a Halstead analysis on a programming language source code of your choice.

12.12 Research the literature and write a paper on the relationship of Halstead's metric and McCabe's metric to software quality (as measured by error count). Are the data compelling? Recommend guidelines for the application of these metrics.

12.13 Develop a software tool that will compute McCabe's metric (cyclomatic complexity) for a programming language module. You may choose the language.

12.14 Research the literature on software reliability and write a paper that describes one software reliability model. Be sure to provide an example.

12.15 The MTBF concept for software is open to criticism. Can you think of a few reasons why?

FURTHER READINGS

Crosby's book [CRO79] is an excellent management-level presentation on the benefits of formal quality assurance programs. Although it does not focus on software, Crosby's book is must reading for senior managers with software devlopment responsibility.

Dunn and Ullman [DUN82] present comprehensive guidelines for planning, establishing, and conducting the SQA function. Arthur [ART85] and Jones [JON86] present worthwhile discussions of software quality factors and quality metrics. In a book that is dedicated primarily to system testing, Beizer (*Software System Testing and Quality Assurance*, Van Nostrand, 1984) presents two excellent chapters on quality measurement and methods for achieving software quality. Chow's anthology [CHO84] on software quality assurance contains a number of excellent papers on measurement and tools.

Books by Shooman [SHO83] and Musa et al. [MUS87] contain detailed stochastic models for software reliability. A book by Kopetz (*Software Reliability*, Springer-Verlag, 1979) presents a less mathematical discussion of the subject. A special issue of the *IEEE Transactions on Software Engineering* (January 1986) is dedicated to recent research on software reliability modeling and verification.

CHAPTER
13

SOFTWARE
TESTING
TECHNIQUES

The importance of software testing and its implications with respect to software quality cannot be overemphasized. To quote Deutsch [DEU79]:

> The development of software systems involves a series of production activities where opportunities for injection of human fallibilities are enormous. Errors may begin to occur at the very inception of the process where the objectives...may be erroneously or imperfectly specified, as well as [errors that occur in] later design and development stages....Because of human inability to perform and communicate with perfection, software development is accompanied by a quality assurance activity.

Software testing is a critical element of software quality assurance and represents the ultimate review of specification, design, and coding.

The increasing visibility of software as a system element and the attendant "costs" associated with a software failure are motivating forces for well-planned, thorough testing. It is not unusual for a software development organization to expend 40 percent of total project effort on testing. In the extreme, testing of human-rated software (e.g., flight control, nuclear reactor monitoring) can cost three to five times as much as all other software engineering steps combined!

In this chapter, we discuss software testing fundamentals and techniques for software test case design. Software testing fundamentals define the overriding objectives for software testing. Test case design focuses on a set of techniques for the creation of test cases that meet overall testing objectives. In Chapter 14, testing strategies and software debugging are presented.

13.1 SOFTWARE TESTING FUNDAMENTALS

Testing presents an interesting anomaly for the software engineer. During earlier definition and development phases, the engineer attempts to build software from an abstract concept to a tangible implementation. Next comes testing. The engineer creates a series of test cases that are intended to "demolish" the software that has been built. In fact, testing is the one step in the software engineering process that can be viewed (psychologically, at least) as destructive rather than constructive.

Software developers are by nature constructive people. Testing requires that the developer discard preconceived notions of the "correctness" of the software just developed and overcome any conflict of interest that occurs when errors are uncovered.

Beizer [BEI83] describes this situation effectively:

> There's a myth that if we were really good at our jobs, there would be no bugs to catch. If only we could really concentrate, there would be no bugs. If only everyone used structured coding techniques [or the latest design method or avante garde programming language] or if all programs were specified in terms of "inverse-recursive produlations," then there would be no bugs. So goes the myth. There are bugs, the myth insists, because we are bad at what we do; and if we are bad at what we do, we should feel guilty about it. Therefore, testing and test case design is an admission of failure, which instills a goodly dose of guilt. And the tedium of testing is just punishment for our errors. Punishment for what? For being human? Guilt for what? For failing to achieve inhuman perfection? For failing to distinguish between what [someone] thinks and what he says? For failing to be telepathic? For not solving human communications problems that have been kicked around...for forty centuries?

Should testing instill guilt? Is testing really destructive? The answer to these questions is "No!" However, the objectives of testing are somewhat different than we might expect.

13.1.1 Testing Objectives

In an excellent book on software testing, Glen Myers [MYE79] states a number of rules that serve well as testing objectives:

1. Testing is a process of executing a program with the intent of finding an error.
2. A good test case is one that has a high probability of finding an as-yet undiscovered error.
3. A successful test is one that uncovers an as-yet undiscovered error.

The above objectives imply a dramatic change in viewpoint. They move counter to the commonly held view that a successful test is one in which no errors are found. Our objective is to design tests that systematically uncover different classes of errors and to do so with a minimum amount of time and effort.

If testing is conducted successfully (according to the objective stated above), it will uncover errors in the software. As a secondary benefit, testing demonstrates that software functions appear to be working according to specification and that performance requirements appear to have been met. In addition, data collected as testing is conducted provide a good indication of software reliability and some indication of software quality as a whole. But there is one thing that testing cannot do:

Testing cannot show the absence of defects; it can only show that software defects are present.

It is important to keep this (rather gloomy) statement in mind as testing is being conducted.

13.1.2   Test Information Flow

Information flow for testing follows the pattern described in Figure 13.1. Two classes of input are provided to the test process: (1) a software configuration that includes *Software Requirements Specification*, *Design Specification*, and source code; and (2) a *test configuration* that includes a *Test Plan and Procedure*, test cases, and expected results. In actuality the test configuration is a subset of the software configuration when the entire software engineering process is considered.

Tests are conducted and all results are evaluated. That is, test results are compared with expected results. When erroneous data are uncovered, an error is implied, and debugging commences. The debugging process (discussed in Chapter 14) is an unpredictable consequence of testing. An ''error'' that indicates a discrepancy of 0.01 percent between expected and actual results can take one hour, one day, or one month to diagnose and correct. It is the uncertainty inherent in debugging that makes testing difficult to schedule reliably.

As test results are gathered and evaluated, a qualitative indication of software quality and reliability begins to surface. If severe errors that require design modifica-

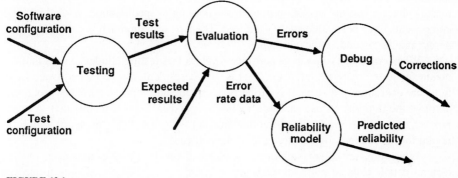

FIGURE 13.1
Test information flow.

tion are encountered with regularity, software quality and reliability are suspect, and further tests are indicated. If, on the other hand, software functions appear to be working properly and errors encountered are easily correctable, one of two conclusions can be drawn: (1) software quality and reliability are acceptable, or (2) tests are inadequate to uncover severe errors. Finally, if testing uncovers no errors, there is little doubt that the test configuration was not given enough thought and that errors do lurk in the software. These defects will eventually be uncovered by the users and corrected by the developer during the maintenance phase (when cost per fix can be 40 to 60 times the cost per fix during the development phase).

The results accumulated during testing can also be evaluated in a more formal manner. Software reliability models (Chapter 12) use error rate data to predict future occurrences of errors and, hence, reliability.

Each bubble of Figure 13.1 represents an exceedingly complex transform. Throughout the remainder of this chapter, we examine the concepts and processes that make test information flow comprehensible and test transforms understandable.

13.1.3 Test Case Design

The design of tests for software and other engineered products can be as challenging as the initial design of the product itself. Yet, for reasons that we have already discussed, software engineers often treat testing as an afterthought, developing test cases that may ''feel right'' but have little assurance of being complete. Recalling the objective of testing, we must design tests that have the highest likelihood of finding the most errors with a minimum amount of time and effort.

Over the past decade a rich variety of test case design methods have evolved for software. These methods provide the developer with a systematic approach to testing. More importantly, methods provide a mechanism that can help to assure the completeness of tests and provide the highest likelihood for uncovering errors in software.

Any engineered product (and most other things) can be tested in one of two ways: (1) knowing the specified function that a product has been designed to perform, tests can be conducted to demonstrate that each function is fully operational; (2) knowing the internal workings of a product, tests can be conducted to assure that ''all gears mesh''; that is, internal operation performs according to specification, and all internal components have been adequately exercised. The first test approach is called *black box testing* and the second, *white box testing*.

When computer software is considered, black box testing alludes to tests that are conducted at the software interface. That is, test cases demonstrate that software functions are operational, that input is properly accepted and output is correctly produced, and that the integrity of external information (e.g., data files) is maintained. A black box test examines some aspect of the fundamental system model (Chapter 5) with little regard for the internal logical structure of the software.

White box testing of software is predicated on the close examination of procedural detail. Logical paths through the software are tested by providing test cases that exercise specific sets of conditions and/or loops. The ''status of the program'' may be examined at various points to determine if the expected or asserted status corresponds to the actual status.

At first glance it would seem that very thorough white box testing would lead to "100 percent correct programs." All we need do is define all logical paths, develop test cases to exercise them, and evaluate results; that is, generate test cases to exercise program logic exhaustively. Unfortunately, exhaustive testing presents certain logistical problems. For even small programs, the number of possible logical paths can be very large. For example, consider the flowchart shown in Figure 13.2. The procedural design illustrated by the flow chart might correspond to a 100-line Pascal program with a single loop that may be executed no more than 20 times. There are approximately 100 trillion possible paths that may be executed!

To put this number in perspective, we assume that a *magic* test processor ("magic" because no such processor exists) has been developed for exhaustive testing. The processor can develop a test case, execute it, and evaluate the results in one millisecond. Working 24 hours a day, 365 days a year, the processor would work for 3170 years to test the program represented in Figure 13.2. This would undeniably cause havoc in most development schedules. Exhaustive testing is impossible for large software systems.

White box testing should not, however, be dismissed as impractical. A limited number of important logical paths can be selected and exercised. Important data structures can be probed for validity. The attributes of both black and white box testing can

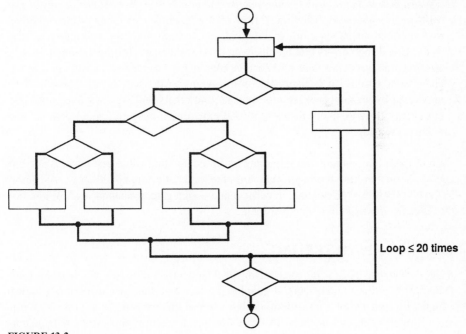

FIGURE 13.2
Problems with exhaustive testing.

be combined to provide an approach that validates the software interface and selectively assures that the internal workings of the software are correct.

13.2 WHITE BOX TESTING

White box testing is a test case design method that uses the control structure of the procedural design to derive test cases. Using white box testing methods, the software engineer can derive test cases that (1) guarantee that all *independent paths* within a module have been exercised at least once, (2) exercise all logical decisions on their *true* and *false* sides, (3) execute all loops at their boundaries and within their operational bounds, and (4) exercise internal data structures to assure their validity.

A reasonable question might be posed at this juncture: "Why spend time and energy worrying about (and testing) logical minutiae when we might better expend effort assuring that program requirements have been met?" Stated another way, why don't we spend all of our energies on black box tests? The answer lies in the nature of software defects (e.g., [JON81]):

- *Logic errors and incorrect assumptions are inversely proportional to the probability that a program path will be executed.* Errors tend to creep into our work when we design and implement function, conditions, or control that are out of the mainstream. Everyday processing tends to be well understood (and well scrutinized) while "special case" processing tends to fall into the cracks.
- *We often believe that a logical path is not likely to be executed when, in fact, it may be executed on a regular basis.* The logical flow of a program is sometimes counterintuitive, meaning that our unconscious assumptions about flow of control and data may lead us to make design errors that are uncovered only when path testing commences.
- *Typographical errors are random.* When a program is translated into programming language source code, it is likely that some typing errors will occur. Many will be uncovered by syntax-checking mechanisms, but others will go undetected until testing begins. It is as likely that a typo will exist on an obscure logical path as on a mainstream path.

Each of these reasons provides an argument for conducting white box tests. Black box testing, no matter how thorough, may miss the kinds of errors noted above. As Beizer has stated [BEI83]: "Bugs lurk in corners and congregate at boundaries." White box testing is far more likely to uncover them.

13.3 BASIS PATH TESTING

Basis path testing is a white box testing technique first proposed by Tom McCabe [MCC76]. The basis path method enables the test case designer to derive a logical complexity measure of a procedural design and use this measure as a guide for defining a *basis set* of execution paths. Test cases derived to exercise the basis set are guaranteed to execute every statement in the program at least one time during testing.

13.3.1 Flow Graph Notation

Before the basis path method can be considered a simple notation for the representation of control flow, called a *flow graph* (or *program graph*) must be introduced.[*] The flow graph depicts logical control flow using the notation illustrated in Figure 13.3. Each structured construct (Chapter 6) has a corresponding flow graph symbol.

To illustrate the use of a flow graph, we consider the procedural design representation in Figure 13.4a. Here, a flowchart is used to depict program control structure. In Figure 13.4b the flowchart is mapped onto a corresponding flow graph (assuming that no compound conditions are contained in the decision diamonds of the flow chart). Referring to Figure 13.4b, each circle, called a flow graph *node*, represents one or more procedural statements. A sequence of process boxes and a decision diamond can map into a single node. The arrows on the flow graph, called *edges*, represent flow of control and are analogous to flowchart arrows. An edge must terminate at a node, even if the node does not represent any procedural statements (e.g, see the symbol for the if-then-else construct). Areas bounded by edges and nodes are called *regions*. When counting regions we include the area outside the graph and count it as a region.

Any procedural design representation can be translated into a flow graph. In Figure 13.5, a program design language (PDL) segment and its corresponding flow graph are shown. Note that the PDL statements have been numbered and corresponding numbering is used for the flow graph.

When compound conditions are encountered in a procedural design, the generation of a flow graph becomes slightly more complicated. A compound condition occurs when one or more Boolean operators (logical OR, AND, NAND, NOR) are present in a conditional statement. In Figure 13.6, the PDL segment translates into the flow

---

[*]In actuality, the basis path method can be conducted without the use of flow graphs. However, they serve as a useful tool for illustrating the approach.

The structured constructs in flow graph form:

Sequence	If	While	Until	Case

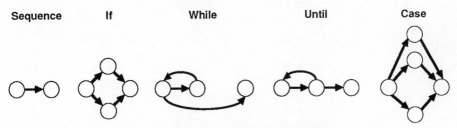

where each circle represents one or more nonbranching PDL or source code statements

FIGURE 13.3
Flow graph notation.

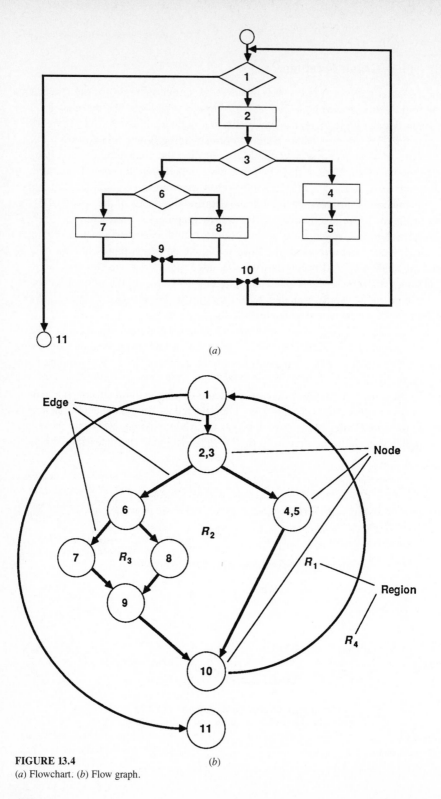

FIGURE 13.4
(a) Flowchart. (b) Flow graph.

474

Flow graph

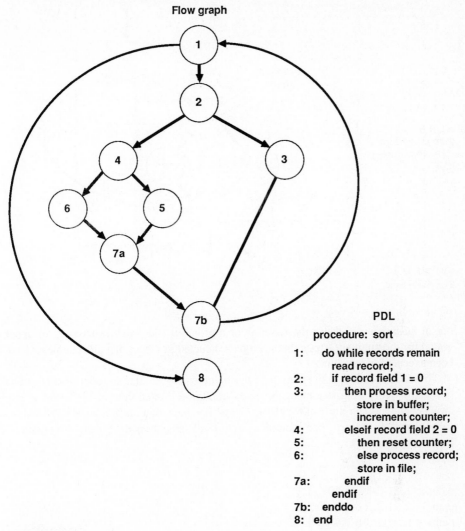

PDL

procedure: sort

1:     do while records remain
          read record;
2:     if record field 1 = 0
3:        then process record;
            store in buffer;
            increment counter;
4:        elseif record field 2 = 0
5:          then reset counter;
6:          else process record;
            store in file;
7a: endif
       endif
7b: enddo
8:    end

FIGURE 13.5
Translating PDL to flow graph.

graph shown. Note that a separate node is created for each of the conditions *a* and *b* in the statement IF *a* OR *b*. Each node that contains a condition is called a *predicate node* and is characterized by two or more edges emanating from it.

13.3.2 Cyclomatic Complexity

Cyclomatic complexity (Section 12.4.2) is a software metric that provides a quantitative measure of the logical complexity of a program. When used in the context of the basis path testing method, the value computed for cyclomatic complexity defines the num-

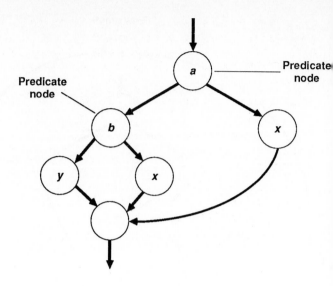

```
    .
    .
    .
IF a OR b
    then procedure x
    else procedure y
ENDIF
```

FIGURE 13.6
Compound logic.

ber of *independent paths* in the *basis set* of a program and provides us with an upper bound for the number of tests that must be conducted to assure that all statements have been executed at least once.

An independent path is any path through the program that introduces at least one new set of processing statements or a new condition. Stated in terms of a flow graph, an independent path must move along at least one edge that has not been traversed before the path is defined. For example, a set of independent paths for the flow graph illustrated in Figure 13.4b is:

path 1:   1-11
path 2:   1-2-3-4-5-10-1-11
path 3:   1-2-3-6-8-9-10-1-11
path 4:   1-2-3-6-7-9-10-1-11

Note that each new path introduces a new edge. The path

        1-2-3-4-5-10-1-2-3-6-8-9-10-1-11

is not considered to be an independent path because it is simply a combination of already-specified paths and does not traverse any new edges.

Paths 1, 2, 3, and 4 defined above compose a *basis set* for the flow graph in Figure 13.4b. That is, if tests can be designed to force execution of these paths (a basis set), every statement in the program will have been guaranteed to be executed at least one time and every condition will have been executed on its true and false sides. It should be noted that the basis set is not unique. In fact a number of different basis sets can be derived for a given procedural design.

How do we know how many paths to look for? The computation of cyclomatic complexity provides the answer.

Cyclomatic complexity has a foundation in graph theory and provides us with an extremely useful software metric. Complexity is computed in one of three ways:

1. The number of regions of the flow graph corresponds to the cyclomatic complexity.

2. Cyclomatic complexity, $V(G)$, for flow graph G is defined as

$$V(G) = E - N + 2$$

where E is the number of flow graph edges and N is the number of flow graph nodes.

3. Cyclomatic complexity, $V(G)$, for flow graph G is also defined as

$$V(G) = P + 1,$$

where P is the number of predicate nodes contained in flow graph G.

Referring once more to the flow graph in Figure 13.4b, the cyclomatic complexity can be computed using each of the algorithms noted above:

1. The flow graph has four regions
2. $V(G) = 11$ edges $- 9$ nodes $+ 2 = 4$
3. $V(G) = 3$ predicate nodes $+ 1 = 4$

Therefore, the cyclomatic complexity of the flow graph in Figure 13.4b is 4.

More importantly, the value for $V(G)$ provides us with an upper bound for the number of independent paths that compose the basis set, and, by implication, *an upper bound on the number of tests that must be designed and executed* to guarantee coverage of all program statements.

13.3.3 Deriving Test Cases

The basis path testing method can be applied to a detailed procedural design or to source code. In this section, we present basis path testing as a series of steps. The procedure *average*, depicted in PDL in Figure 13.7, will be used as an example to illustrate each step in the test case design method. Note that *average*, although an extremely simple algorithm, contains compound conditions and loops.

1. Using the design or code as a foundation, draw a corresponding flow graph. A flow graph is created using the symbols and construction rules presented in Section 13.3.1.

Referring to the PDL for *average* in Figure 13.7, a flow graph is created by numbering those PDL statements that will be mapped onto corresponding flow graph nodes. The numbering scheme is shown in Figure 13.8, and the corresponding flow graph appears in Figure 13.9.

```
PROCEDURE average;
    *  This procedure computes the average of 100 or fewer
       numbers that lie bounding values; it also computes the
       total input and the total valid.
    INTERFACE RETURNS average, total.input, total.valid;
    INTERFACE ACCEPTS value, minimum, maximum;
    TYPE value[1:100] IS SCALAR ARRAY;
    TYPE average, total.input, total.valid;
        minimum, maximum, sum IS SCALAR;
    TYPE i IS INTEGER;
    i = 1;
    total.input = total.valid = 0;
    sum = 0;
    DO WHILE value[ i ] <> –999 and total.input < 100
        increment total.input by 1;
        IF value[ i ] >= minimum AND value[ i ] <= maximum
            THEN increment total.valid by 1;
                    sum = sum + value[ i ];
            ELSE skip
        ENDIF
        increment i by 1;
    ENDDO
    IF total.valid > 0
        THEN average = sum / total.valid;
        ELSE average = –999;
    ENDIF
END average
```

FIGURE 13.7
PDL for test case design.

2. Determine the cyclomatic complexity of the resultant flow graph. The cyclomatic complexity, $V(G)$, is determined by applying the algorithms described in Section 13.3.2. It should be noted that $V(G)$ can be determined without developing a flow graph by counting all conditional statements in the PDL (for the procedure *average*, compound conditions count as 2 (number of logical operators)).

Referring to Figure 13.9,

$$V(G) = 6 \text{ regions}$$

$$V(G) = 17 \text{ edges} - 13 \text{ nodes} + 2 = 6$$

$$V(G) = 5 \text{ predicate nodes} + 1 = 6$$

3. Determine a basis set of linearly independent paths. The value of $V(G)$ provides us with the number of linearly independent paths through the program control structure. In the case of procedure *average*, we expect to specify six paths:

path 1:   1-2-10-11-13
path 2:   1-2-10-12-13
path 3:   1-2-3-10-11-13

PROCEDURE average;

* This procedure computes the average of 100 or fewer
  numbers that lie bounding values; it also computes the
  total input and the total valid.

INTERFACE RETURNS average, total.input, total.valid;
INTERFACE ACCEPTS value, minimum, maximum;

TYPE value[1:100] IS SCALAR ARRAY;
TYPE average, total.input, total.valid,
    minimum, maximum, sum IS SCALAR;
TYPE i IS INTEGER;

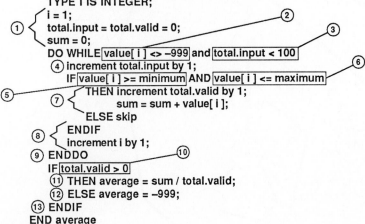

```
  i = 1;
① total.input = total.valid = 0;                      ②
  sum = 0;                                                        ③
  DO WHILE value[ i ] <> –999 and total.input < 100
  ④ increment total.input by 1;                              ⑥
     IF value[ i ] >= minimum AND value[ i ] <= maximum
⑤       THEN increment total.valid by 1;
   ⑦        sum = sum + value[ i ];
         ELSE skip
⑧    ENDIF
       increment i by 1;
⑨ ENDDO                        ⑩
  IF total.valid > 0
  ⑪ THEN average = sum / total.valid;
  ⑫ ELSE average = –999;
⑬ ENDIF
  END average
```

FIGURE 13.8
Identifying nodes.

path 4:   1-2-3-4-5-8-9-2-...
path 5:   1-2-3-4-5-6-8-9-2-...
path 6:   1-2-3-4-5-6-7-8-9-2-...

The ellipsis (...) following paths 4, 5, and 6 indicates that any path through the remainder of the control structure is acceptable. It is often worthwhile to identify predicate nodes as an aid in the derivation of test cases. In this case, nodes 2, 3, 5, 6, and
10 are predicate nodes.

4. Prepare test cases that will force execution of each path in the basis set. Data
should be chosen so that conditions at the predicate nodes are appropriately set as each
path is tested. Test cases that satisfy the basis set described above are:

Path 1 test case:
value(k) = valid input, where $k <$ i defined below
value(i) = -999 where $2 \leq i \leq 100$
expected results:
    correct average based on n values and proper totals
note: cannot be tested stand-alone; must be tested as part of path 4, 5, and 6 tests

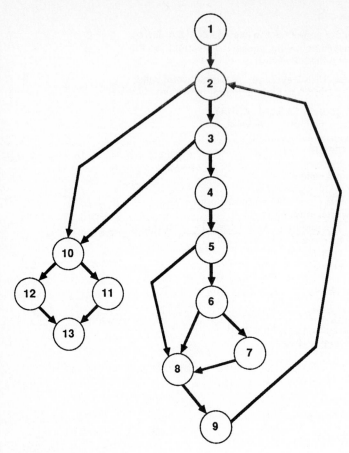

FIGURE 13.9
Flow graph of the procedure *average*.

Path 2 test case:
value(1) = −999
expected results:
average = −999; other totals at initial values

Path 3 test case:
attempt to process 101 or more values
first 100 values should be valid
expected results:
same as test case 1

Path 4 test case:
value(*i*) = valid input where *i* < 100
value(*k*) < minimum where *k* < *i*

expected results:
     correct average based on k values and proper totals

Path 5 test case:
value(i) = valid input where $i < 100$
value(k) > maximum where $k \leq i$
expected results:
     correct average based on n values and proper totals

Path 6 test case:
value(i) = valid input where $i < 100$
expected results:
     correct average based on n values and proper totals

Each test case is executed and compared to expected results. Once all test cases have been completed, the tester can be sure that all statements in the program have been executed at least once.

It is important to note that some independent paths (e.g., Path 1 in our example) cannot be tested in stand-alone fashion. That is, the combination of data required to traverse the path cannot be achieved in the normal flow of the program. In such cases, these paths are tested as part of another path test.

13.3.4 Graph Matrices

The procedure for deriving the flow graph and even determining a set of basis paths is amenable to mechanization. To develop a software tool that assists in basis path testing, a data structure, called a *graph matrix*, can be quite useful.

A graph matrix is a square matrix whose size (i.e., number of rows and columns) is equal to the number of nodes on the flow graph. Each row and column corresponds to an identified node, and matrix entries correspond to *connections* (an edge) between nodes. A simple example of a flow graph and its corresponding graph matrix [BEI83] is shown in Figure 13.10.

Referring to the figure, each node on the flow graph is identified by numbers, while each edge is identified by letters. A letter entry is made in the matrix to correspond to a connection between two nodes. For example, node 3 is connected to node 4 by edge b.

To this point, the graph matrix is nothing more than a tabular representation of the flow graph. However, by adding a *link weight* to each matrix entry, the graph matrix can become a powerful tool for evaluating program control structure during testing. The link weight provides additional information about control flow. In its simplest form, the link weight is 1 (a connection exists) or 0 (a connection does not exist). But link weights can be assigned other, more interesting properties:

- the probability that a link (edge) will be executed
- the processing time expended during traversal of a link
- the memory required during traversal of a link
- the resources required during traversal of a link

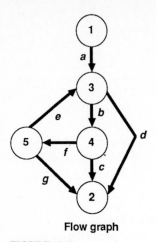

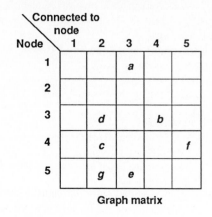

Flow graph

Graph matrix

FIGURE 13.10
Flow graph and corresponding graph matrix.

To illustrate, we use the simplest weighting to indicate connections (0 or 1). The graph matrix in Figure 13.10 is redrawn as shown in Figure 13.11. Each letter has been replaced with a 1, indicating that a connection exists (0s have been excluded for clarity). Represented in this form, the graph matrix is called a *connection matrix*.

Referring to Figure 13.11, each row with two or more entries represents a predicate node. Therefore, performing the arithmetic shown to the right of the connection matrix provides us with still another method for determining cyclomatic complexity (Section 13.3.2).

Beizer [BEI83] provides a thorough treatment of additional mathematical algorithms that can be applied to graph matrices. Using these techniques, the analysis required to design test cases can be partially or fully automated.

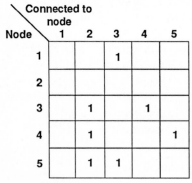

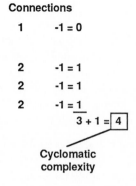

FIGURE 13.11
Connection matrix.

13.4   LOOP TESTING

Loops are the cornerstone for the vast majority of all algorithms implemented in software. And yet we often pay them little heed while conducting software testing.

Loop testing is a white box testing technique that focuses exclusively on the validity of loop constructs. Four different classes of loops [BEI83] can be defined: *simple loops*, *concatenated loops*, *nested loops*, and *unstructured loops* (Figure 13.12).

In addition to a basis path analysis that will isolate all paths within a loop, a special set of additional tests can be recommended for each loop type. These tests are intended to uncover initialization errors, indexing or incrementing errors, and bounding errors that occur at loop limits.

SIMPLE LOOPS. The following set of tests should be applied to simple loops, where n is the maximum number of allowable passes through the loop.

1. Skip the loop entirely
2. Only one pass through the loop
3. Two passes through the loop

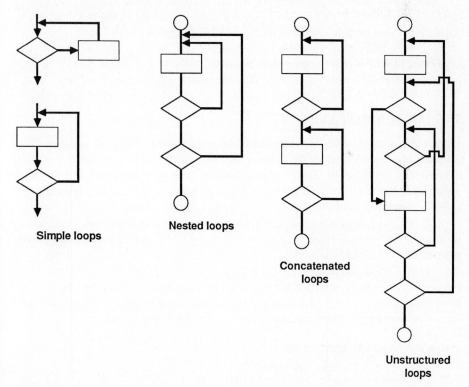

Simple loops

Nested loops

Concatenated loops

Unstructured loops

FIGURE 13.12
Loops.

4. m passes through the loop where $m < n$

5. $n - 1, n, n + 1$ passes through the loop

NESTED LOOPS. If we were to extend the test approach for simple loops to nested loops, the number of possible tests would grow geometrically as the level of nesting increases. This would result in an impractical number of tests. Beizer [BEI83] suggests an approach that will help to reduce the number of tests:

1. Start at the innermost loop. Set all other loops to minimum values.
2. Conduct simple loop tests for the innermost loop while holding the outer loops at their minimum iteration parameter (e.g., loop counter) values. Add other tests for out-of-range or excluded values.
3. Work outward, conducting tests for the next loop, but keeping all other outer loops at minimum values and other nested loops to "typical" values.
4. Continue until all loops have been tested.

CONCATENATED LOOPS. Concatenated loops can be tested using the approach defined for simple loops above, if each of the loops is independent of the other. For example, if two loops are concatenated and the loop counter for loop 1 is used as the initial value for loop 2, then the loops are *not* independent. When the loops are not independent, the approach applied to nested loops is recommended.

UNSTRUCTURED LOOPS. Whenever possible, this class of loops should be *redesigned* to reflect the use of the structured programming constructs (Chapter 6).

13.5   BLACK BOX TESTING

Black box testing methods focus on the functional requirements of the software. That is, black box testing enables the software engineer to derive sets of input conditions that will fully exercise all functional requirements for a program. Black box testing is *not* an alternative to white box techniques. It is, rather, a complementary approach that is likely to uncover a different class of errors than white box methods.

Black box testing attempts to find errors in the following categories: (1) incorrect or missing functions, (2) interface errors, (3) errors in data structures or external data base access, (4) performance errors, and (5) initialization and termination errors.

Unlike white box testing, which is performed early in the testing process, black box testing tends to be applied during later stages of testing (see Chapter 14). Because black box testing purposely disregards control structure, attention is focused on the information domain. Tests are designed to answer the following questions:

- How is functional validity tested?
- What *classes* of input will make good test cases?
- Is the system particularly sensitive to certain input values?
- How are the boundaries of a data class isolated?

- What data rates and data volume can the system tolerate?
- What effect will specific combinations of data have on system operation?

By applying black box techniques, we derive a set of test cases that satisfy the following criteria [MYE79]: (1) test cases that reduce, by a count that is greater than one, the number of additional test cases that must be designed to achieve reasonable testing, and (2) test cases that tell us something about the presence or absence of classes of errors rather than an error associated only with the specific test at hand.

13.5.1   Equivalence Partitioning

Equivalence partitioning is a black box testing method that divides the input domain of a program into classes of data from which test cases can be derived. An ideal test case single-handedly uncovers a class of errors (e.g., incorrect processing of all character data) that might otherwise require execution of many cases before the general error is observed. Equivalence partitioning strives to define a test case that uncovers classes of errors, thereby reducing the total number of test cases that must be developed.

Test case design for equivalence partitioning is based on an evaluation of equivalence classes for an *input condition*. An *equivalence class* represents a set of valid or invalid states for input conditions. Typically, an input condition is either a specific numeric value, a range of values, a set of related values, or a Boolean condition (yes or no). Equivalence classes may be defined according to the following guidelines:

1. If an input condition specifies a *range*, one valid and two invalid equivalence classes are defined.
2. If an input condition requires a specific *value*, one valid and two invalid equivalence classes are defined.
3. If an input condition specifies a member of a *set*, one valid equivalence class and one invalid equivalence class are defined.
4. If an input condition is *Boolean*, one valid class and one invalid class are defined.

As an example, consider data maintained as part of an automated banking application. The user can ''dial'' the bank using his or her microcomputer, provide a six-digit password, and follow with a series of keyword commands that trigger various banking functions. The software supplied for the banking application accepts data in the form:

    area code—blank or three-digit number
    prefix—three-digit number not beginning with 0 or 1
    suffix—four-digit number
    password—six-digit alphanumeric value
    commands—''check,'' ''deposit,'' ''bill pay,'' etc.

The input conditions associated with each data element for the banking application can be specified as:

area code: input condition, *Boolean*—the area code may or may not be present;
input condition, *range*—values defined between 200 and 999, with specific exceptions (e.g., no values > 905) and requirements (e.g., all area codes have a 0 or 1 as a second digit)

prefix: input condition, *range*—specified value > 200 with no 0 digits

suffix: input condition, *value*—four-digit length

password: input condition, *Boolean*—a password may or may not be present;
input condition, *value*—six-character string

command: input condition, *set*—containing commands noted above

Applying the guidelines for the derivation of equivalence classes, test cases for each input domain data item could be developed and executed. Test cases are selected so that the largest number of attributes of an equivalence class are exercised at once.

13.5.2 Boundary Value Analysis

For reasons that are not completely clear, a greater number of errors tends to occur at the boundaries of the input domain than in the "center." It is for this reason that *boundary value analysis* (BVA) has been developed as a testing technique. Boundary value analysis leads to a selection of test cases that exercise bounding values.

Boundary value analysis is a test case design technique that complements equivalence partitioning. Rather than selecting any element of an equivalence class, BVA leads to the selection of test cases at the "edges" of the class. Rather than focusing solely on input conditions, BVA derives test cases from the output domain as well [MYE79].

Guidelines for BVA are similar in many respects to those provided for equivalence partitioning:

1. If an input condition specifies a *range* bounded by values *a* and *b*, test cases should be designed with values *a* and *b*, just above and just below *a* and *b*, respectively.

2. If an input condition specifies a number of values, test cases should be developed that exercise the minimum and maximum numbers. Values just above and below minimum and maximum are also tested.

3. Apply guidelines 1 and 2 to output conditions. For example, assume that a "temperature vs. pressure" table is required as output from an engineering analysis program. Test cases should be designed to create an output report that produces the maximum (and minimum) allowable number of table entries.

4. If internal program data structures have prescribed boundaries (e.g., an array has a defined limit of 100 entries), be certain to design a test case to exercise the data structure at its boundary.

Most software engineers intuitively perform BVA to some degree. By applying the guidelines noted above, boundary testing will be more complete, thereby providing a higher likelihood of error detection.

13.5.3 Cause-Effect Graphing Techniques

In far too many instances, an attempt to translate a policy or procedure specified in a natural language into a software-based algorithm leads to frustration and error. Consider the following memo (believe it or not, it's real!) published in the Personnel Information Bulletin for the U.S. Army Corps of Engineers. The discussion centers on the procedure for determining employee holidays.

> Executive Order 10358 provided in the case of an employee whose work week varied from the normal Monday through Friday work week, that Labor Day and Thanksgiving Day each were to be observed on the next succeeding workday when the holiday fell on a day outside the employee's regular basic work week. Now, when Labor Day, Thanksgiving Day or any of the new Monday holidays are outside an employee's basic workweek, the immediately preceding workday will be his holiday when the non-workday on which the holiday falls is the second non-workday or the non-workday designated as the employee's day off in lieu of Saturday. When the non-workday on which the holiday falls is the first non-workday or the non-workday designated as the employee's day off in lieu of Sunday, the holiday observance is moved to the next succeeding workday.

There are few readers who would enthusiastically volunteer to test a computer program developed to implement the procedure described above.

Cause-effect graphing is a test case design technique that provides a concise representation of logical conditions and corresponding actions. (Under no circumstances will we attempt this on the memo presented above, leaving it instead to the adventurous reader.) The technique follows four steps:

1. *Causes* (input conditions) and *effects* (actions) are listed for a module, and an identifier is assigned to each.
2. A cause-effect graph (described below) is developed.
3. The graph is converted to a decision table.
4. Decision table rules are converted to test cases.

A simplified version of cause-effect graph symbology is shown in Figure 13.13. The left column of the figure illustrates various logical relationships between causes, c_i, and effects, e_i. The dashed notation in the right columns indicates potential constraining relationships that may apply to either causes or effects.

To illustrate the use of cause-effect graphs, we consider a variant of the utility billing example discussed in Chapter 6. Four causes are defined:

1:    residential indicator
2:    commercial indicator

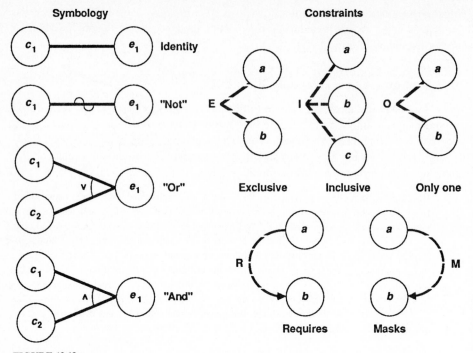

FIGURE 13.13
Cause-effect graphing.

3:    peak consumption > 100 KWH
4:    off-peak consumption ≥ 100 KWH

Based on various combinations of causes, the following effects may be listed:

101:    schedule A billing
102:    schedule B billing
103:    schedule C billing

A cause-effect graph for the above example is shown in Figure 13.14. Causes 1, 2, 3, and 4 are represented along the left side and final effects 101, 102, and 103 along the right side. Secondary causes are identified (e.g., causes 11, 12, 13, 14, etc.) in the central part of the graph. From the cause-effect graph, a decision table (Figure 13.15) can be developed. Test case data are selected so that each *rule* in the table is exercised. Obviously, if a decision table has been used as a design tool, cause-effect graphing is no longer necessary.

13.5.4 Data Validation Testing

Data validation testing encompasses a set of specialized test techniques that fill in the gaps left by other black box testing methods. Like other black box techniques, data

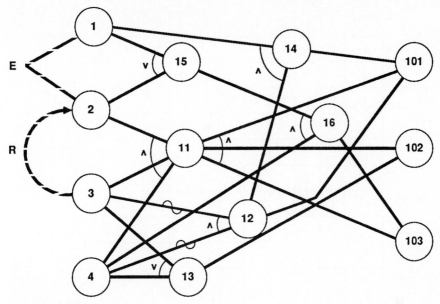

FIGURE 13.14
Cause-effect graph.

validation testing is heuristically directed. That is, a set of guidelines or checklists are provided to assist the tester, but no formal analysis or detailed algorithm is present.

The nature of human-machine interfaces has undergone significant change in the past few years. However, the vast majority of interactive systems still use a *second generation* interface—the user generates specific commands within a specific syntax and the system responds accordingly. Data validation testing should be applied to all command-driven systems with second generation interfaces.

When commands are typed using a keyboard, the interface software implements a string recognizer program that must be validated. The following data validation tests are appropriate:

1. Specify commands with incorrect syntax; use both blatant and subtle variations from correct form.

2. Provide syntactically correct input that is out of sequence or specified at the wrong time.

3. Type a partially correct command and then terminate the command entry.

4. Omit all commands; simply return.

5. Provide correct commands, but provide too much qualifying data.

6. Generate a system interrupt immediately after a command has been entered.

Commands are always *delimited* in some manner. That is, parentheses, brackets, commas, and other symbols are used to separate and group commands. The following tests may be conducted to validate delimiters:

		1	2	3	4	5	6	7	8	9		
Causes	1	1							0	1		
	2		1		1			1	1	0		
	3	0	1	0	1	0	1	1				
	4	0	1	0	1	1	0	1	1	1		
Intermediate causes	11		1		1			1				
	12	1		1								
	13					1	1					
	14	1										
	15								1	1		
	16								1	1		
Effects	101	1	1	1	0	0	0	0	0	0		
	102	0	0	0	1	1	1	0	0	0		
	103	0	0	0	0	0	0	1	1	1		

FIGURE 13.15
Decision table.

1. Specify a command with missing delimiters.
2. Use the wrong delimiter.
3. When delimiters are used to bracket information, use two correct but different delimiters to form right and left brackets.
4. Substitute one valid delimiter for another.
5. Verify that delimiter pairs are properly matched.

Specific data values, ranges of values, and selections from prespecified sets of data are all possible input modes for interactive systems. Equivalence partitioning (Section 13.5.1) and boundary value analysis (Section 13.5.2) are important complementary testing techniques for data validation.

13.6 PROOF OF CORRECTNESS

We have seen that testing can be used successfully to uncover errors, but (paraphrasing Dijkstra) it cannot be used to demonstrate program correctness. If an infallible prover of program correctness could be developed, test effort would be reduced substantially, the need for reliability models would disappear, and one of the major contributors to the software crisis—poor software quality—would be no more. Proofs of program correctness span a broad spectrum of sophistication. Manual correctness proofs, such as the use of mathematical induction or the predicate calculus, may have some value in the evaluation of small programs but are of little use when large software subsystems must be validated. As Anderson [AND74] states in his book on the subject: "...we are well aware that informal (manual) correctness proofs can easily contain errors and are no panacea for preventing or discovering all program errors."

If a general purpose method for proving software correctness is ever successfully developed, it will probably comprise the following:

- an easily applied and validated method for specifying assertions concerning the correct operation of the software
- a method for indicating variance from correct operation (errors)
- a technique for uncovering the cause of an error
- a fully automated approach that takes the source code or some other element of the software configuration (e.g., a design representation) as input

A number of automated approaches to proof of correctness for computer software have been developed during the past decade. Automated correctness provers, not to be confused with automatic testing tools, generally involve a formal specification of program logic. The specification can be developed by a *macrocompiler* that produces a symbolic representation of the software. Program correctness is "proved" by use of automated techniques (e.g., [SMI85]) whose foundation is derived from artificial intelligence theory and predicate calculus. Correctness provers for Pascal and Lisp programs have been developed. (These systems are currently limited to the evaluation of relatively small programs.) Recent work [BAS85] has attempted to assess the degree of uncertainty that can be attached to any representation of correctness. There is little argument that much work remains to be done before such systems can be practically applied to large-scale software.

13.7 AUTOMATED TESTING TOOLS

Because software testing often accounts for as much as 40 percent of all effort expended on a software development project, tools that can reduce test time (without reducing thoroughness) are very valuable. Recognizing the potential benefits, researchers and practitioners have developed a first generation of automated test tools. Miller [MIL79] describes a number of categories for test tools:

Static analyzers. These program-analysis systems support "proving" of static allegations—weak statements about a program's structure and format.

Code auditors. These special purpose filters are used to check the quality of software to insure that it meets minimum coding standards.

Assertion processors. These preprocessor/postprocessor systems are employed to tell whether programmer-supplied claims, called assertions, about a program's behavior are actually met during actual program executions.

Test file generators. These processors generate, and fill with predetermined values, typical input files for programs undergoing testing.

Test data generators. These automated analysis systems assist a user in selecting test data that make a program behave in a particular fashion.

Test verifiers. These tools measure internal test coverage, often expressed in terms that are related to the control structure of the test object, and report the coverage value to the quality assurance expert.

Test harnesses. This class of tools supports the processing of tests by making it almost painless to (1) install a candidate program in a test environment, (2) feed it input data, and (3) simulate by stubs the behavior of subsidiary (subordinate) modules.

Output comparators. This tool makes it possible to compare one set of outputs from a program with another (previously archived) set to determine the difference between them.

Dunn [DUN84] adds additional classes of automated tools to the above list:

Symbolic execution systems. This tool performs program testing using algebraic input, rather than numeric data values. The software being tested thus appears to test classes of data, rather than one specific test case. The output is algebraic and can be compared to expected results that are specified in algebraic form.

Environment simulators. This tool is a specialized computer-based system that enables the tester to model the external environment of real-time software and then simulate actual operating conditions dynamically.

Data flow analyzers. This tool tracks the flow of data through a system (similar in many respects to path analyzers) and attempts to find undefined data references, incorrect indexing, and other data-related errors.

Unfortunately, few testing tools are widely used. Most remain research vehicles rather than pragmatic support tools for software engineering. In the following paragraphs, we consider three representative testing tools. For a complete discussion of these and other automated tools, see Miller [MIL81] and Dunn [DUN84].

DAVE [OST76] is an automated test system that makes use of data flow and program graphing techniques (Section 13.3). The DAVE system is capable of accurately identifying many classes of program errors and *data flow anomalies* (e.g., data are referenced before being completely specified). The system is designed to evaluate FORTRAN programs and uses a sophisticated depth-first search algorithm to trace the flow of a specific variable. DAVE processes a subject program in a manner illustrated in Figure 13.16.

DISSECT [HOW78] is an automated test system that symbolically evaluates a program by creating algebraic predicates derived from representations of program input, control flow, and program output. Software may be "dissected" into individual sets of control paths. These sets, called *a system of predicates*, are used in the validation of computations within the program. In addition the system of predicates can be used as a basis for designing actual test case data.

Program mutation techniques [BUD80] provide an automated approach for determining the adequacy of test case data. An overview of the approach is described by the following steps:

1. For a program, P, a test case, T, is defined.
2. T is executed by P. If errors occur, the case has succeeded.
3. If no errors are uncovered by T, the program P is *mutated* by making subtle changes to the source code (e.g., a .LE. comparison becomes .LT.), and T is re-executed.
4. If the mutant program, P', gives the same results as P for the same test case T, then T does not have the sensitivity to distinguish the error purposely introduced into P'.

The above sequence of steps is executed automatically. The test system produces a series of reports and other information that help to measure the adequacy of a given test case. In addition, information obtained about mutants can be used as a tool in test case design.

Work on automated testing over the past few years can be discussed in two broad categories: (1) attempts to develop a stronger theoretical basis for the selection and execution of tests, and (2) increasing emphasis on artificial intelligence techniques to assist in software testing (or proof or correctness). An example of efforts that fall into the first category is the work of Clark and her colleagues [CLA85] on the selection and evaluation of criteria for path selection by automated tools. AI techniques applied to software testing span a broad array of approaches and are surveyed by Mostow and others [MOS85].

Although current usage of automated tools for software testing is limited, it is likely that application will accelerate during the next decade. Descendants of the first generation tools described in this chapter are likely to cause radical changes in the way we test software and the resultant reliability of computer-based systems.

13.8 SUMMARY

The primary objective for test case design is to derive a set of tests that have the highest likelihood of uncovering defects in the software. To accomplish this objective, two different categories of test case design techniques are used: white box testing and black box testing.

White box tests focus on the program control structure. Test cases are derived to assure that all statements in the program have been executed at least once during test-

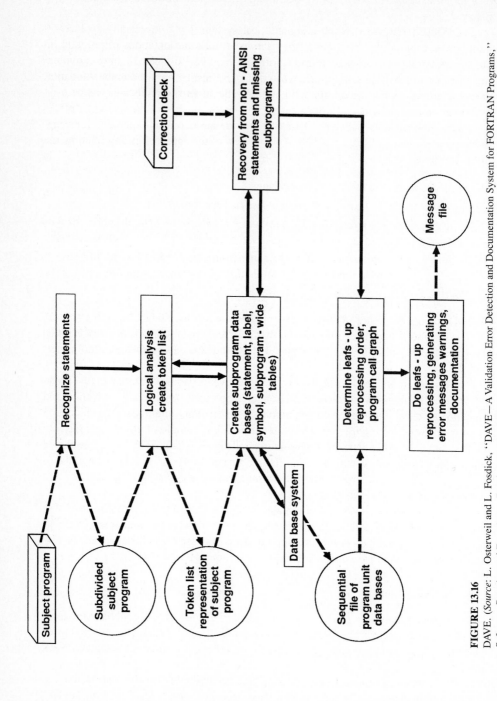

FIGURE 13.16

DAVE. (*Source*: L. Osterweil and L. Fosdick, "DAVE—A Validation Error Detection and Documentation System for FORTRAN Programs," *Software: Practice and Experience*. Reprinted with permission.)

494

ing and that all logical conditions have been exercised. Basis path testing, a white box technique, makes use of program graphs (or graph matrices) to derive the set of linearly independent paths that will assure coverage. Loop testing complements other white box techniques by providing a procedure for exercising loops of varying degrees of complexity.

Hetzel [HET84] describes white box testing as "testing in the small." His implication is that the white box tests we have considered in this chapter are typically applied to small program components (e.g., modules or small groups of modules). Black box testing, on the other hand, broadens our focus and might be called "testing in the large."

Black box tests are designed to validate functional requirements without regard to the internal workings of a program. Black box testing techniques focus on the information domain of the software, deriving test cases by partitioning the input and output domain of a program in a manner that provides thorough test coverage. Equivalence partitioning divides the input domain into classes of data that are likely to exercise specific software function. Boundary value analysis probes the program's ability to handle data at the limits of acceptability. Cause-effect graphing is a technique that enables the tester to validate complex sets of actions and conditions. Finally, data validation testing assures that interactive (command-driven) data are properly processed.

Automated tools have been developed for software testing but have not been used widely to date. The restricted scope of many tools and the difficulty in applying the more powerful tools have limited their utilization across most software engineering application areas. However, recent work in AI-based testing tools shows promise.

Experienced software developers often say, "Testing never ends, it just gets transferred from you [the developer] to your customer. Every time your customer uses the program, a test is being conducted." By applying test case design, the software engineer can achieve more complete testing and thereby uncover and correct the highest number of errors before the "customer's tests" begin.

REFERENCES

[AND74]   Anderson, R., *Proving Programs Correct*, Wiley, 1974.

[BAS85]   Bastani, F. B., "On the Uncertainty in the Correctness of Computer Programs," *IEEE Trans. Software Engineering*, vol. SE-11, no. 9, September 1985, pp. 857–864.

[BEI83]   Beizer, B., *Software Testing Techniques*, Van Nostrand Reinhold, 1983.

[BUD80]   Budd, T.A., R. DeMillo, R. J. Lipton, and F. G. Sayward, "Theoretical and Empirical Studies on Using Mutation Testing to Test the Functional Correctness of Programs," *Proc. 7th Annual Conf. on Programming Languages*, ACM, January 1980, pp. 220–233.

[CLA85]   Clarke, L., et al., "A Comparison of Data Flow Path Selection Criteria," *Proc. 8th Intl. Conf. Software Engineering*, IEEE, London, August 1985, pp. 244–251.

[DEU79]   Deutsch, M., "Verification and Validation," *Software Engineering*, R. Jensen and C. Tonies, eds., Prentice-Hall, 1979, pp. 329–408.

[DUN84]   Dunn, R., *Software Defect Removal*, McGraw-Hill, 1984.

[HET84] Hetzel, W., *The Complete Guide to Software Testing*, QED Information Sciences, Inc., Wellesley, MA, 1984.

[HOW78] Howden, W., "DISSECT—A Symbolic Evaluation and Program Testing System," *IEEE Trans. Software Engineering*, vol. 4, no. 1, January 1978, pp. 70–73.

[JON81] Jones, T. C., *Programming Productivity: Issues for the 80s*, IEEE Computer Society Press, 1981.

[MCC76] McCabe, T., "A Software Complexity Measure," *IEEE Trans. Software Engineering*, vol. 2, December 1976, pp. 308–320.

[MIL79] Miller, E., *Automated Tools for Software Engineering*, IEEE Computer Society Press, 1979, p. 169.

[MIL81] Miller, E., and W. E. Howden, *Software Testing and Validation Techniques*, 2d ed., IEEE Computer Society Press, 1981.

[MOS85] Mostow, J., ed., "Special Issue on Artificial Intelligence in Software Engineering," *IEEE Trans. Software Engineering*, vol. SE-11, no. 11, November 1985.

[MYE79] Myers, G., *The Art of Software Testing*, Wiley, 1979.

[OST76] Osterweil, L., and L. Fosdick, "DAVE—A Validation, Error Detection and Documentation System for FORTRAN Programs," *Software—Practice and Experience*, October–December 1976, pp. 473–486.

[SMI85] Smith, M. K., and R. M. Cohen, "Gypsy Verification System Status," *ACM Sigsoft Notes*, vol. 10, no. 4, August 1985, pp. 5–6.

PROBLEMS AND POINTS TO PONDER

13.1 Myers [MYE79] uses the following program as a self-assessment for your ability to specify adequate testing:

A program reads three integer values. The three values are interpreted as representing the lengths of the sides of a triangle. The program prints a message that states whether the triangle is scalene, isosceles, or equilateral.

Develop a set of test cases that you feel will adequately test this program.

13.2 Design and implement the program (with error-handling where appropriate) specified in Problem 13.1. Derive a flow graph for the program and apply basis path testing to develop test cases that will guarantee that all statements in the program have been tested. Execute the cases and show your results.

13.3 Can you think of any additional testing objectives that are not discussed in Section 13.1.1?

13.4 Apply the basis path testing technique to any one of the programs that you have implemented in Problems 11.13 through 11.21.

13.5 Specify, design, and implement a software tool that will compute the cyclomatic complexity for the programming language of your choice. Use the graph matrix as the operative data structure in your design.

13.6 Read Beizer [BEI83] and determine how the program you have developed in Problem 13.5 can be extended to accommodate various *link weights*. Extend your tool to process execution probabilities or link processing times.

13.7 Design an automated tool that will recognize loops and categorize them as indicated in Section 13.4.

13.8 Extend the tool described in Problem 13.7 to generate test cases for each loop category. It will be necessary to perform this function interactively with the tester.

13.9 Give at least three examples in which black box testing might give the impression that "everything's OK," while white box tests might uncover an error.

13.10 Will exhaustive testing (even if it is possible for very small programs) guarantee that the program is 100 percent correct?

13.11 Using the equivalence partitioning method, derive a set of test cases for the *Software Store* example described in Chapter 5.

13.12 Using boundary value analysis, derive a set of test cases for the patient monitoring system described in Chapter 5.

13.13 Using cause-effect graphing, derive a set of test cases for Executive Order 10358 described in Section 13.5.3. Good luck! For the adventurous: Attempt to design an algorithm that will implement the rules noted for the executive order.

13.14 Extend the guidelines for testing human-machine interfaces provided in Section 13.5.4. Develop a set of test cases that will fully exercise an interface that you regularly use, i.e., a PC-based word processor on a host-based editor.

13.15 Suggest the types of test case design techniques that you would use to test a new compiler. Explain your selections.

13.16 Write a paper that describes a software testing tool in detail. Focus on tools that are currently applied outside purely research environments.

FURTHER READINGS

A number of excellent books are now available for those readers who desire additional information on software testing. Myers [MYE79] remains a classic text, covering black box techiques in considerable detail. Beizer [BEI83] provides comprehensive coverage of white box techniques, introducing a level of mathematical rigor that has often been missing in other treatments of testing. In addition, books by Hetzel [HET84] and Dunn [DUN84] provide worthwhile supplementary information.

A detailed discussion of the basis path techniques can be found in McCabe's tutorial on testing (*Structured Testing*, IEEE Computer Society, 1983). Glass (*Real-Time Software*, Prentice-Hall, 1983) discusses specialized techniques for the testing and debugging of real-time systems.

Chapters by Miller ("Software Testing Technology: An Overview") and Saib ("Formal Verification") in Van Nostrand Reinhold's *Handbook on Software Engineering* (Vick and Ramamoorthy, eds., 1984) are good summaries of these complex topics. Miller and Howden (*Software Testing and Validation Techniques*, 2d ed., IEEE Computer Society Press, 1981) have edited an excellent anthology of papers on testing.

CHAPTER

14

SOFTWARE TESTING STRATEGIES

A strategy for software testing integrates software test case design techniques into a well-planned series of steps that result in the successful construction of software. As importantly, a software testing strategy provides a road map for the software developer, the quality assurance organization, and the customer—a road map that describes: the steps to be conducted as part of testing; when these steps should be planned and undertaken; and how much effort, time, and resources will be required. Therefore, any testing strategy must incorporate test planning, test case design, test execution, and resultant data collection and evaluation.

A software testing strategy should be flexible enough to promote the creativity and customization necessary to adequately test all large software-based systems. At the same time, the strategy must be rigid enough to promote reasonable planning and management tracking as the project progresses. Shooman [SHO83] discusses these issues:

> In many ways, testing is an individualistic process, and the number of different types of tests varies as much as the different development approaches. For many years, our only defense against programming errors was careful design and the native intelligence of the programmer. We are now in an era in which modern design techniques [and formal technical reviews] are helping us to reduce the number of initial errors that are inherent in the code. Similarly, different test methods are beginning to cluster themselves into several distinct approaches and philosophies.

These approaches and philosophies are what we shall call *strategy*. In Chapter 13 the technology of software testing was presented. In this chapter we focus our attention on the strategy for software testing.

14.1 A STRATEGIC APPROACH TO SOFTWARE TESTING

Testing is a set of activities that can be planned in advance and conducted systematically. For this reason a template for software testing—a set of steps into which we can place specific test case design techniques and testing methods—should be defined for the software engineering process.

A number of software testing strategies have been proposed in the literature. All provide the software developer with a template for testing and all have the following generic characteristics:

- Testing begins at the module level and works "outward" toward the integration of the entire computer-based system.
- Different testing techniques are appropriate at different points in time.
- Testing is conducted by the developer of the software and (for large projects) by an independent test group.
- Testing and debugging are different activities, but debugging must be accommodated in any testing strategy.

A strategy for software must accommodate low-level tests to verify that a small source code segment has been correctly implemented, as well as high-level tests that validate major system functions against customer requirements. A strategy must provide guidance for the practitioner and a set of milestones for the manager. Because the steps of the test strategy occur at a time when deadline pressure begins to rise, progress must be measurable and problems must surface as early as possible.

14.1.1 Verification and Validation

Software testing is one element of a broader topic that is often referred to as *verification and validation* (V&V). Verification refers to the set of activities that ensure that software correctly implements a specific function. Validation refers to a different set of activities that ensure that the software built is traceable to customer requirements. Boehm [BOE81] states this in another way:

> Verification: "Are we building the product right?"
> Validation: "Are we building the right product?"

The definition of V&V encompasses many of the activities we have referred to as software quality assurance (SQA).

Recalling the discussion of SQA in Chapter 12, software quality assurance may be viewed as the set of building blocks depicted in Figure 14.1. As reviews are conducted, definition and development tasks are filtered to assure the quality of each

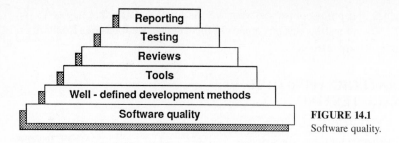

FIGURE 14.1
Software quality.

software engineering step. In a similar manner, analysis, design, and implementation (coding) methods act to enhance quality by providing uniform techniques and predictable results. Throughout the process, control applied to every element of a software configuration helps ensure the integrity of the whole. Testing provides the last bastion from which quality can be assessed and, more pragmatically, errors can be uncovered. But testing should *not* be viewed as a safety net (Figure 14.2). As they say, "You can't test in quality. If it's not there before you begin testing, it won't be there when you're finished testing." Quality is incorporated into software throughout the process of software engineering. Proper application of methods and tools, effective formal technical reviews, and solid management and measurement all lead to quality that is confirmed during testing.

Miller [MIL77] relates software testing to quality assurance by stating that "the underlying motivation of program testing is to affirm software quality with methods that can be economically and effectively applied to both large-scale and small-scale systems."

14.1.2 Organizing for Software Testing

For every software project, there is an inherent conflict of interest that occurs as testing begins. The people who have built the software are now asked to test the software. This

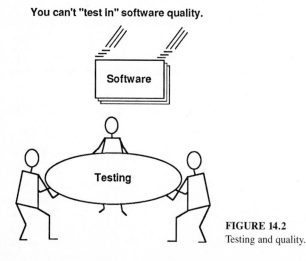

FIGURE 14.2
Testing and quality.

seems harmless in itself; after all, who knows the program better than its developers? Unfortunately, these same developers have a vested interest in demonstrating that the program is error-free, that it works according to customer requirements, and that it will be completed on schedule and within budget. Each of these interests mitigates against thorough testing.

From a psychological point of view, software analysis and design (along with coding) are *constructive* tasks. The software engineer creates a computer program, its documentation, and related data structures. Like any builder, the software engineer is proud of the edifice that has been built and looks askance at anyone who attempts to tear it down. When testing commences, there is a subtle, yet definite, attempt to "break" the thing that the software engineer has built. From the point of view of the builder, testing can be considered (psychologically) *destructive*. So the builder treads lightly, designing and executing tests that will demonstrate that the programs works, rather than uncovering errors. Unfortunately, errors will be present. And if the software engineer does not find them, the customer will.

There are often a number of misconceptions that can be erroneously inferred from the above discussion: (1) the developer of software should do no testing at all, (2) the software should be "tossed over the wall" to strangers who will test it mercilessly, and (3) testers get involved with the project only when the testing steps begin. Each of these statements is incorrect.

The software developer is always responsible for testing the individual units (modules) of the program, assuring that each performs the function for which it was designed. In many cases, the developer also conducts *integration testing*—the testing step that leads to the construction (and test) of the complete program structure. Only after the software architecture is complete does an independent test group become involved.

The role of an *independent test group* (ITG) is to remove the inherent problems associated with letting the builder test the thing that has been built. An independent test removes the conflict of interest that may otherwise be present. After all, personnel in the independent group team are paid to find errors.

However, the software developer does not turn the program over to the ITG and walk away. The developer and the ITG work closely throughout a software project to assure that thorough tests will be conducted. While testing is conducted, the developer must be available to correct errors that are uncovered.

The ITG is part of the software development project team in the sense that it becomes involved during the specification process and stays involved (planning and specifying test procedures) throughout a large project. However, in many cases the ITG reports to the software quality assurance organization, thereby achieving a degree of independence that might not be possible if it were part of the software development organization.

14.1.3 A Software Testing Strategy

The software engineering process may be viewed as the spiral illustrated in Figure 14.3. Initially, system engineering defines the role of software and leads to software requirements analysis, where the information domain, function, performance, con-

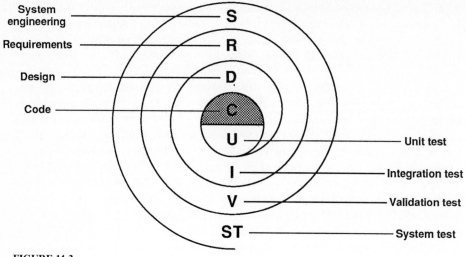

FIGURE 14.3
Testing strategy.

straints, and validation criteria for software are established. Moving in along the spiral, we come to design and finally to coding. To develop computer software, we spiral in along streamlines that decrease the level of abstraction on each turn.

A strategy for software testing may also be viewed in the context of the spiral (Figure 14.3). *Unit testing* begins at the vortex of the spiral and concentrates on each unit of the software as implemented in source code. Testing progresses by moving outward along the spiral to *integration testing*, where the focus is on design and the construction of the software architecture. Taking another turn outward on the spiral, we encounter *validation testing*, where requirements established as part of software requirements analysis are validated against the software that has been constructed. Finally, we arrive at *system testing* where the software and other system elements are tested as a whole. To test computer software, we spiral out along streamlines that broaden the scope of testing with each turn.

Considering the process from a procedural point of view, testing within the context of software engineering is actually a series of four steps implemented sequentially. The steps are shown in Figure 14.4. Initially, tests focus on each module individually, assuring that it functions properly as a unit. Hence the name *unit testing*. Unit testing makes heavy use of white box testing techniques, exercising specific paths in a module's control structure to assure complete coverage and maximum error detection. Next, modules must be assembled or integrated to form the complete software package. *Integration testing* addresses the issues associated with the dual problems of verification and program construction. Black box test case design techniques are most prevalent during integration, although a limited number of white box tests may be conducted to assure coverage of major control paths. Finally, validation criteria (established during the definition phase) must be tested. *Validation testing* provides final assurance that software meets all functional and performance requirements. Black box testing techniques are used exclusively during validation.

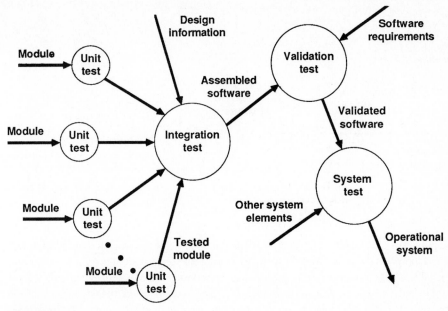

FIGURE 14.4
Software testing steps.

The last testing step falls outside the boundary of software engineering and into the broader context of computer system engineering. Software, once validated, must be combined with other system elements (e.g., hardware, people, data bases). *System testing* verifies that all elements mesh properly and that overall system function/performance is achieved.

In the sections that follow, each of the test steps is presented. Recalling our discussions of test case design techniques (presented in Chapter 13), it is important to note that each of the procedural steps in the testing strategy is coupled with appropriate test case design techniques so that effective software testing is accomplished.

14.2 UNIT TESTING

Unit testing focuses verification effort on the smallest unit of software design—the module. Using the detail design description as a guide, important control paths are tested to uncover errors within the boundary of the module. The relative complexity of tests and uncovered errors is limited by the constrained scope established for unit testing. The unit test is always white box–oriented, and the step can be conducted in parallel for multiple modules.

14.2.1 Unit Test Considerations

The tests that occur as part of unit tests are illustrated schematically in Figure 14.5. The module *interface* is tested to assure that information properly flows into and out of

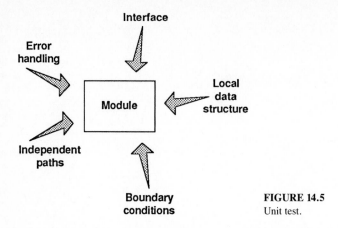

FIGURE 14.5
Unit test.

the program unit under test. The local *data structure* is examined to assure that data stored temporarily maintain their integrity during all steps in an algorithm's execution. *Boundary conditions* are tested to assure that the module operates properly at boundaries established to limit or restrict processing. All *independent paths* (basis paths) through the control structure are exercised to assure that all statements in a module have been executed at least once. And finally, all *error-handling paths* are tested.

Tests of data flow across a module interface are required before any other test is initiated. If data do not enter and exit properly, all other tests are moot. In his text on software testing, Myers [MYE79] proposes a checklist for interface tests:

1. Number of input parameters equal to number of arguments?
2. Parameter and argument attributes match?
3. Parameter and argument units systems match?
4. Number of arguments transmitted to called modules equal to number of parameters?
5. Attributes of arguments transmitted to called modules equal to attributes of parameters?
6. Units system of arguments transmitted to called modules equal to units system of parameters?
7. Number attributes and order of arguments to built-in functions correct?
8. Any references to parameters not associated with current point of entry?
9. Input only arguments altered?
10. Global variable definitions consistent across modules?
11. Constraints passed as arguments?

When a module performs external I/O, additional interface tests must be conducted. Again, from Myers:

1. File attributes correct?
2. OPEN statements correct?

3. Format specification matches I/O statement?

4. Buffer size matches record size?

5. Files opened before use?

6. End-of-file conditions handled?

7. I/O errors handled?

8. Any textual errors in output information?

The local data structure for a module is a common source of errors. Test cases should be designed to uncover errors in the following categories:

1. improper or inconsistent typing

2. erroneous initialization or default values

3. incorrect (misspelled or truncated) variable names

4. inconsistent data types

5. underflow, overflow, and addressing exceptions

In addition to local data structures, the impact of global data (e.g., FORTRAN COMMON) on a module should be ascertained (if possible) during unit testing.

Selective testing of execution paths is an essential task during the unit test. Test cases should be designed to uncover errors due to erroneous computations, incorrect comparisons, or improper control flow. Basis path and loop testing are effective techniques for uncovering a broad array of path errors.

Among the more common errors in computation are: (1) misunderstood or incorrect arithmetic precedence, (2) mixed mode operations, (3) incorrect initialization, (4) precision inaccuracy, and (5) incorrect symbolic representation of an expression. Comparison and control flow are closely coupled to one another (i.e., change of flow frequently occurs after a comparison). Test cases should uncover errors such as: (1) comparison of different data types, (2) incorrect logical operators or precedence, (3) expectation of equality when precision error makes equality unlikely, (4) incorrect comparison or variables, (5) improper or nonexistent loop termination, (6) failure to exit when divergent iteration is encountered, and (7) improperly modified loop variables.

Good design dictates that error conditions be anticipated and error-handling paths set up to reroute or cleanly terminate processing when an error does occur. Yourdon [YOU75] calls this approach *antibugging*. Unfortunately, there is a tendency to incorporate error handling into software and then never test it. A true story may serve to illustrate:

A major interactive design system was developed under contract. In one analysis module, a practical joker placed the following error-handling message after a series of conditional tests that invoked various control flow branches: ERROR! THERE IS NO WAY YOU CAN GET HERE. This "error message" was uncovered by a customer during user training!

Among the potential errors that should be tested when error handling is evaluated are:

1. Error description is unintelligible.
2. Error noted does not correspond to error encountered.
3. Error condition causes system intervention prior to error handling.
4. Exception-condition processing is incorrect.
5. Error description does not provide enough information to assist in the location of the cause of the error.

Boundary testing is the last (and probably most important) task of the unit test step. Software often fails at its boundaries. That is, errors often occur when the nth element of an n-dimensional array is processed, when the ith repetition of a loop with i passes is invoked, or when the maximum or minimum allowable value is encountered. Test cases that exercise data structure, control flow, and data values just below, at, and just above maxima and minima are very likely to uncover errors.

14.2.2 Unit Test Procedures

Unit testing is normally considered as an adjunct to the coding step. After source level code has been developed, reviewed, and verified for correct syntax, unit test case design begins. A review of design information provides guidance for establishing test cases that are likely to uncover errors in each of the categories discussed above. Each test case should be coupled with a set of expected results.

Because a module is not a stand-alone program, *driver* and/or *stub* software must be developed for each unit test. The unit test environment is illustrated in Figure 14.6. In most applications a driver is nothing more than a "main program" that accepts test case data, passes such data to the module (to be tested), and prints relevant results. Stubs serve to replace modules that are subordinate to (called by) the module to be tested. A stub or "dummy subprogram" uses the subordinate module's interface, may do minimal data manipulation, and prints verification of entry and returns.

Drivers and stubs represent overhead. That is, both are software that must be written (formal design is not commonly applied) but that are not delivered with the

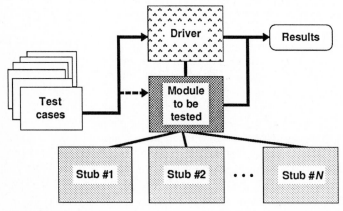

FIGURE 14.6
Unit test environment.

final software product. If drivers and stubs are kept simple, actual overhead is relatively low. Unfortunately, many modules cannot be adequately unit-tested with "simple" overhead software. In such cases, complete testing can be postponed until the integration test step (where drivers or stubs are also used).

Unit testing is simplified when a module with high cohesion is designed. When only one function is addressed by a module, the number of test cases is reduced and errors can be more easily predicted and uncovered.

14.3 INTEGRATION TESTING

A neophyte in the software world might ask a seemingly legitimate question once all modules have been unit tested: "If they all work individually, why do you doubt that they will work when we put them together?" The problem, of course, is "putting them together"—interfacing. Data can be lost across an interface; one module can have an inadvertent, adverse effect on another; subfunctions, when combined, may not produce the desired major function; individually acceptable imprecision may be magnified to unacceptable levels; and global data structures can present problems. Sadly, the list goes on and on.

Integration testing is a systematic technique for constructing the program structure while at the same time conducting tests to uncover errors associated with interfacing. The objective is to take unit-tested modules and build a program structure that has been dictated by design.

There is often a tendency to attempt *non-incremental integration*; that is, to construct the program using a "big bang" approach. All modules are combined in advance. The entire program is tested as a whole. Chaos usually results! A set of errors are encountered. Correction is difficult because isolation of causes is complicated by the vast expanse of the entire program. Once these errors are corrected, new ones appear and the process continues in a seemingly endless loop.

Incremental integration is the antithesis of the big bang approach. The program is constructed and tested in small segments where errors are easier to isolate and correct, interfaces are more likely to be tested completely, and a systematic test approach may be applied. In the sections that follow, a number of different incremental integration strategies are discussed.

14.3.1 Top-Down Integration

Top-down integration is an incremental approach to the construction of program structure. Modules are integrated by moving downward through the control hierarchy, beginning with the main control module (main program). Modules subordinate (and ultimately subordinate) to the main control module are incorporated into the structure in either a *depth-first* or *breadth-first* manner.

Referring to Figure 14.7, depth-first integration would integrate all modules on a major control path of the structure. Selection of a major path is somewhat arbitrary and depends on application-specific characteristics. For example, selecting the left-hand path, modules M_1, M_2, M_5 would be integrated first. Next M_8 or (if necessary for proper functioning of M_2) M_6 would be integrated. Then the central and right-hand control paths are built. Breadth-first integration incorporates all modules directly sub-

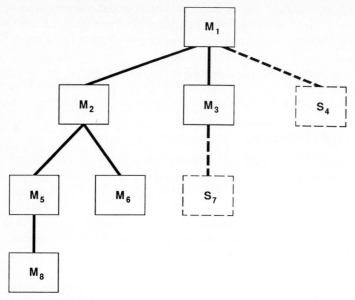

FIGURE 14.7
Top-down integration.

ordinate at each level, moving across the structure horizontally. From the figure, modules M_2, M_3, and M_4 (a replacement for stub, S_4) would be integrated first. The next control level, M_5, M_6, etc., follows.

The integration process is performed in a series of five steps:

1. The main control module is used as a test driver and stubs are substituted for all modules directly subordinate to the main control module.
2. Depending on the integration approach selected (i.e., depth- or breadth-first), subordinate stubs are replaced one at a time with actual modules.
3. Tests are conducted as each module is integrated.
4. On completion of each set of tests, another stub is replaced with the real module.
5. *Regression testing* (i.e., conducting all or some of the previous tests) may be conducted to assure that new errors have not been introduced.

The process continues from step 2 until the entire program structure is built. Figure 14.7 illustrates the process. Assuming a depth-first approach and a partially completed structure, stub S_7 is next, to be replaced with module M_7. M_7 may itself have stubs that will be replaced with corresponding modules. It is important to note that at each replacement, tests are conducted to verify the interface.

The top-down integration strategy verifies major control or decision points early in the test process. In a well-factored program structure, decision making occurs at upper levels in the hierarchy and is therefore encountered first. If major control problems do exist, early recognition is essential. If depth-first integration is selected, a complete function of the software may be implemented and demonstrated. For example, consider a classic transaction structure (Chapter 7) in which a complex series of interactive inputs are requested, acquired, and validated via an incoming path. The incoming path may be integrated in a top-down manner. All input processing (for subsequent transaction dispatching) may be demonstrated before other elements of the structure have been integrated. Early demonstration of functional capability is a confidence builder for both the developer and the customer.

Top-down strategy sounds relatively uncomplicated, but, in practice, logistical problems can arise. The most common of these problems occurs when processing at low levels in the hierarchy is required to adequately test upper levels. *Stubs* replace low-level modules at the beginning of top-down testing; therefore, no significant data can flow upward in the program structure. The tester is left with three choices: (1) delay many tests until stubs are replaced with actual modules, (2) develop stubs that perform limited functions that simulate the actual module, and (3) integrate the software from the bottom of the hierarchy upward. Figure 14.8 illustrates typical classes of stubs, ranging from the simplest (stub A) to the most complex (stub D).

The first approach (delay tests until stubs are replaced by actual modules) causes us to lose some control over correspondence between specific tests and incorporation of specific modules. This can lead to difficulty in determining the cause of errors and tends to violate the highly constrained nature of the top-down approach. The second approach is workable but can lead to significant overhead as stubs become more and more complex. The third approach, called *bottom-up testing,* is discussed next.

14.3.2 Bottom-Up Integration

Bottom-up integration testing, as its name implies, begins construction and testing with *atomic modules* (i.e., modules at the lowest levels in the program structure). Be-

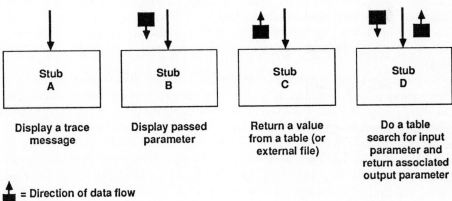

Stub A	Stub B	Stub C	Stub D
Display a trace message	Display passed parameter	Return a value from a table (or external file)	Do a table search for input parameter and return associated output parameter

■ = Direction of data flow

FIGURE 14.8
Stubs.

cause modules are integrated from the bottom up, processing required for modules subordinate to a given level is always available and the need for stubs is eliminated.

A bottom-up integration strategy may be implemented with the following steps:

1. Low-level modules are combined into *clusters* (sometimes called *builds*) that perform a specific software subfunction.
2. A driver (a control program for testing) is written to coordinate test case input and output.
3. The cluster is tested.
4. Drivers are removed and clusters are combined moving upward in the program structure.

Integration follows the pattern illustrated in Figure 14.9. Modules are combined to form clusters 1, 2, and 3. Each of the clusters is tested using a driver (shown as a dashed block). Modules in clusters 1 and 2 are subordinate to M_a. Drivers D_1 and D_2 are removed and the clusters are interfaced directly to M_a. Similarly, driver D_3 for cluster 3 is removed prior to integration with module M_b. Both M_a and M_b will ultimately be integrated with module M_c, and so forth. Different categories of drivers are illustrated in Figure 14.10.

As integration moves upward, the need for separate test drivers lessens. In fact, if the top two levels of program structure are integrated top-down, the number of drivers can be reduced substantially and integration of clusters is greatly simplified.

14.3.3   Comments on Integration Testing

There has been much discussion (e.g., [BEI84]) of the relative advantages and disadvantages of top-down vs. bottom-up integration testing. In general the advantages of one strategy tend to result in disadvantages for the other strategy. The major disadvantage of the top down approach is the need for stubs and the attendant testing difficulties that can be associated with them. Problems associated with stubs may be offset by the advantage of testing major control functions early. The major disadvantage of bottom-up integration is that "the program as an entity does not exist until the last module is added" [MYE79]. This drawback is tempered by easier test case design and a lack of stubs.

Selection of an integration strategy depends upon software characteristics and, sometimes, project schedule. In general a combined approach (sometimes called *sandwich testing*) that uses top-down for upper levels of the program structure, coupled with bottom-up for subordinate levels, may be the best compromise.

As integration testing is conducted, the tester should identify *critical modules*. A critical module has one or more of the following characteristics: (1) addresses several software requirements, (2) has a high level of control (resides relatively high in the program structure), (3) is complex or error-prone, or (4) has definite performance requirements. Critical modules should be tested as early as possible. In addition, regression tests should focus on critical module function.

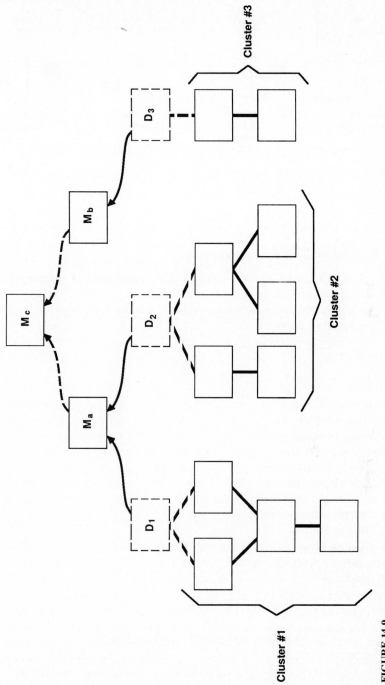

FIGURE 14.9
Bottom-up integration.

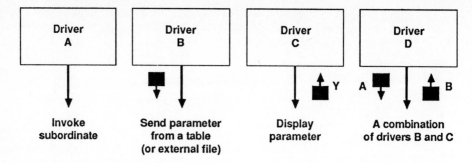

 = Direction of information flow

FIGURE 14.10
Drivers.

14.3.4 Integration Test Documentation

An overall plan for integration of the software and a description of specific tests are documented in a *Test Specification*. The specification is a deliverable in the software engineering process and becomes part of the software configuration. The following outline may be used as a framework:

1. Scope of Testing
2. Test Plan
   a. Test phases
   b. Schedule
   c. Overhead software
   d. Environment and resources
3. Test Procedure
   a. Description of test phase *n*
      (1) Order of integration
      (2) Purpose and modules to be tested
      (3) Special tools or techniques
      (4) Overhead software description
      (5) Test case data
   b. Expected results for test phase *n*
4. Actual Test Results
5. References
6. Appendices

The *Scope of Testing* summarizes specific functional, performance, and internal design characteristics that are to be tested. Testing effort is bounded, criteria for completion of each test phase are described, and schedule constraints are documented.

The *Test Plan* describes the overall strategy for integration. Testing is divided into *phases* and *subphases* that address specific functional and information domain characteristics of the software. For example, integration testing for a computer graphics–oriented CAD system might be divided into the following test phases:

- user interaction
  - —command selection
  - —drawing creation
  - —display representation
  - —error processing and representation
- data manipulation and analysis
  - —symbol creation
  - —dimensioning
  - —rotation
  - —computation of physical properties
- display processing and generation
  - —two-dimensional displays
  - —three-dimensional displays
  - —graphs and charts
- data base structure and content

Each of these phases and subphases (denoted by indentation) delineates a broad functional category within the software and can generally be related to a specific domain of the program structure.

The following criteria and corresponding tests are applied for all test phases:

Interface integrity. Internal and external interfaces are tested as each module (or cluster) is incorporated into the structure.

Functional validity. Tests designed to uncover functional errors are conducted.

Information content. Tests designed to uncover errors associated with local or global data structures are conducted.

Performance. Tests designed to verify performance bounds established during software design are conducted.

These criteria and tests associated with them are discussed in this section of the *Test Specification.*

A schedule for integration, overhead software, and related topics are also discussed as part of the *Test Plan* section. Start and end dates for each phase are established and "availability windows" for unit-tested modules are defined. A brief description of overhead software (stubs and drivers) concentrates on characteristics that might require special effort. Finally, test environment and resources are described. Unusual hardware configurations, exotic simulators, and special test tools or techniques are a few of the many topics that may be discussed in this section.

A detailed testing procedure that is required to accomplish the test plan (delineated above) is described in the *Test Procedure* section. Referring back to *Test Specification* outline items 3a and b, the order of integration and corresponding tests for each integration phase are described. A listing of all test cases (annotated for subsequent reference) and expected results is also included.

A history of actual test results, problems, or peculiarities is recorded in the fourth section of the *Test Specification*. Information contained in this section can be vital during software maintenance.

Like all other elements of a software configuration, the *Test Specification* format may be tailored to the local needs of a software development organization. It is important to note, however, that an integration strategy, contained in a *Test Plan*, and testing details, described in a *Test Procedure*, are essential ingredients and must appear.

14.4 VALIDATION TESTING

At the culmination of integration testing, software is completely assembled as a package; interfacing errors have been uncovered and corrected, and a final series of software tests—*validation testing*—may begin. Validation can be defined in many ways, but a simple (albeit harsh) indicator is that validation succeeds when software functions in accordance with the customer's reasonable expectations. At this point a battle-hardened software developer might protest: "Who or what is the arbiter of *reasonable expectations*?"

Reasonable expectations are defined in the *Software Requirements Specification*—a document (Chapter 4) that describes all user-visible attributes of the software. The specification contains a section called *Validation Criteria*. Information contained in that section forms the basis for a validation testing approach.

14.4.1 Validation Test Criteria

Software validation is achieved through a series of black box tests that demonstrate conformity with requirements. A test plan outlines the classes of tests to be conducted, and a test procedure defines specific test cases that will be used to demonstrate conformity with requirements. Both the plan and procedure are designed to ensure that all functional requirements are satisfied, all performance requirements are achieved, documentation is correct and human-engineered, and other requirements are met (e.g., transportability, compatibility, error recovery, maintainability).

After each validation test case has been conducted, one of two possible conditions exist: (1) the function or performance characteristics conform to specification and are accepted, or (2) a deviation from specification is uncovered and a deficiency list is created. Deviations or errors discovered at this stage in a project can rarely be corrected prior to scheduled completion. It is often necessary to negotiate with the customer to establish a method for resolving deficiencies.

14.4.2 Configuration Review

An important element of the validation process is a *configuration review*. The intent of the review, as illustrated in Figure 14.11, is to assure that all elements of the software configuration have been properly developed, are cataloged, and have the necessary de-

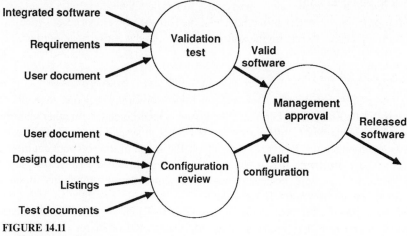

FIGURE 14.11
Configuration review.

tail to support the maintenance phase of the software life cycle. The configuration review, sometimes called an *audit*, is discussed in more detail in Chapter 15.

14.4.3 Alpha and Beta Testing

It is virtually impossible for a software developer to foresee how the customer will *really* use a program. Instructions for use may be misinterpreted, strange combinations of data may be regularly used, and output that seemed clear to the tester may be unintelligible to a user in the field.

When custom software is built for one customer, a series of *acceptance tests* are conducted to enable the customer to validate all requirements. Conducted by the end-user rather than the system developer, an acceptance test can range from an informal "test drive" to a planned and systematically executed series of tests. In fact, acceptance testing can be conducted over a period of weeks or months, thereby uncovering cumulative errors that might degrade the system over time.

If software is developed as a product to be used by many customers, it is impractical to perform formal acceptance tests with each one. Most software product builders use a process called *alpha and beta testing* to uncover errors that only the end-user seems able to find.

The alpha test is conducted at the developer's site by a customer. The software is used in a natural setting with the developer "looking over the shoulder" of the user and recording errors and usage problems. Alpha tests are conducted in a controlled environment.

The beta test is conducted at one or more customer sites by the end-user of the software. Unlike alpha testing, the developer is generally not present. Therefore, the beta test is a "live" application of the software in an environment that cannot be controlled by the developer. The customer records all problems (real or imagined) that are encountered during beta testing and reports these to the developer at regular intervals. As a result of problems reported during beta test, the software developer makes modifications and then prepares to release the software product to the entire customer base.

14.5   SYSTEM TESTING

At the beginning of this book, we stressed the fact that software is only one element of a larger computer-based system. Ultimately, software is incorporated with other system elements (e.g., new hardware, information), and a series of system integration and validation tests are conducted. These tests fall outside the scope of the software engineering process and are not conducted solely by the software developer. However, steps taken during software design and testing can greatly improve the probability of successful software integration in the larger system.

A classic system testing problem is "finger pointing." This occurs when an error is uncovered and each system element developer blames the other for the problem. Rather than indulging in such nonsense, the software engineer should anticipate potential interfacing problems and (1) design error-handling paths that test all information coming from other elements of the system, (2) conduct a series of tests that simulate bad data or other potential errors at the software interface, (3) record the results of tests to use as "evidence" if finger pointing does occur, and (4) participate in planning and design of system tests to insure that software is adequately tested.

System testing is actually a series of different tests whose primary purpose is to fully exercise the computer-based system. Although each test has a different purpose, all work to verify that all system elements have been properly integrated and perform allocated functions. In the sections that follow, we discuss the types of system tests [BEI84] that are worthwhile for software-based systems.

14.5.1   Recovery Testing

Many computer-based systems must recover from faults and resume processing within a prespecified time. In some cases a system must be fault-tolerant, i.e., processing faults must not cause overall system function to cease. In other cases a system failure must be corrected within a specified period of time or severe economic damage will occur.

Recovery testing is a system test that forces the software to fail in a variety of ways and verifies that recovery is properly performed. If recovery is automatic (performed by the system itself), reinitialization, checkpointing mechanisms, data recovery, and restart are each evaluated for correctness. If recovery requires human intervention, the mean time to repair is evaluated to determine whether it is within acceptable limits.

14.5.2   Security Testing

Any computer-based system that manages sensitive information or causes actions that can improperly harm (or benefit) individuals is a target for improper or illegal penetration. Penetration spans a broad range of activities: "hackers" who attempt to penetrate systems for sport, disgruntled employees who attempt to penetrate for revenge, and dishonest individuals who attempt to penetrate for illicit personal gain.

Security testing attempts to verify that protection mechanisms built into a system will, in fact, protect it from improper penetration. To quote Beizer [BEI84]: "The system's security must, of course, be tested for invulnerability from frontal attack—but must also be tested for invulnerability from flank or rear attack."

During security testing, the tester plays the role of the individual who desires to penetrate the system. Anything goes! The tester may attempt to acquire passwords through external clerical means; may attack the system with custom software designed to break down any defenses that have been constructed; may overwhelm the system, thereby denying service to others; may purposely cause system errors, hoping to penetrate during recovery; or may browse through public data, hoping to find the key to system entry.

Given enough time and resources, good security testing will ultimately penetrate a system. The role of the system designer is to make penetration cost more than the value of the information obtained through penetration.

14.5.3 Stress Testing

During earlier software testing steps, white box and black box techniques resulted in thorough evaluation of normal program functions and performance. *Stress tests* are designed to confront programs with abnormal situations. In essence, the tester who performs stress testing asks: "How high can we crank this up before it fails?"

Stress testing executes a system in a manner that demands resources in abnormal quantity, frequency, or volume. For example: (1) special tests may be designed that generate ten interrupts per second, when one or two is the average rate; (2) input data rates may be increased by an order of magnitude to determine how input functions will respond; (3) test cases that require maximum memory or other resources are executed; (4) test cases that may cause thrashing in a virtual memory management scheme are designed; (5) test cases that may cause excessive hunting for disk-resident data are designed. Essentially, the tester attempts to break the program.

A variation of stress testing is a technique called *sensitivity testing*. In some situations (the most common occur in mathematical algorithms) a very small range of data contained within the bounds of valid data for a program may cause extreme and even erroneous processing or profound performance degradation. This situation, illustrated in Figure 14.12, is analogous to a singularity in a mathematical function. Sensitivity testing attempts to uncover data combinations within valid input classes that may cause instability or improper processing.

14.5.4 Performance Testing

For real-time and embedded systems, software that provides required function but does not conform to performance requirements is unacceptable. *Performance testing* is designed to test run-time performance of software within the context of an integrated sys-

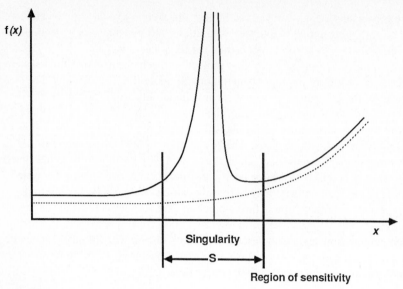

FIGURE 14.12
Sensitivity analysis.

tem. Performance testing occurs throughout all steps in the testing process. Even at the unit level, the performance of an individual module may be assessed as white box tests are conducted. However, it is not until all system elements are fully integrated that the true performance of a system can be ascertained.

Performance tests are often coupled with stress testing and often require both hardware and software *instrumentation*. That is, it is often necessary to measure resource utilization (e.g., processor cycles) in an exacting fashion. External instrumentation can monitor execution intervals, log events (e.g., interrupts) as they occur, and sample machine states on a regular basis. By instrumenting a system, the tester can uncover situations that lead to degradation and possible system failure.

14.6   THE ART OF DEBUGGING

Throughout Chapters 13 and 14, we have seen that software testing is a process that can be systematically planned and specified. Test case design can be conducted, a strategy can be defined, and results can be evaluated against prescribed expectations.

Debugging occurs as a consequence of successful testing. That is, when a test case uncovers an error, debugging is the process that results in the removal of the error. Although debugging can and should be an orderly process, it is still very much an art. A software engineer, evaluating the results of a test, is often confronted with a "symptomatic" indication of a software problem. That is, the external manifestation of the error and the internal cause of the error may have no obvious relationship to one another. The poorly understood mental process that connects a symptom to a cause is debugging.

14.6.1   The Debugging Process

Debugging is *not* testing, but always occurs as a consequence of testing.[*] Referring to Figure 14.13, the debugging process begins with the execution of a test case. Results are assessed and a lack of correspondence between expected and actual is encountered. In many cases, the noncorresponding data are a symptom of an underlying cause as yet hidden. The debugging process attempts to match symptom with cause, thereby leading to error correction.

The debugging process will always have one of two outcomes: (1) the cause will be found, corrected, and removed; or (2) the cause will not be found. In the latter case, the person performing debugging may suspect a cause, design a test case to help validate his or her suspicion, and work toward error correction in an iterative fashion.

Why is debugging so difficult? In all likelihood, the answer has more to do with human psychology (see the next section) than with software technology. However, a few characteristics of bugs provide some clues:

1. The symptom and the cause may be geographically remote. That is, the symptom may appear in one part of a program while the cause may actually be located at a

---

[*]In making this statement, we take the broadest possible view of *testing*. Not only does the developer test software prior to release, but the customer/user tests software every time it is used.

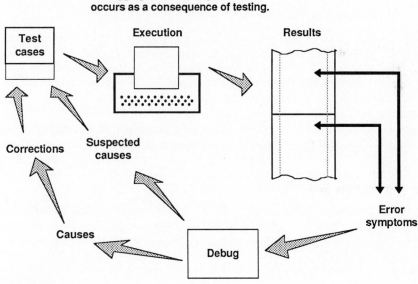

Debugging is *not* testing, but often occurs as a consequence of testing.

Test cases · Execution · Results · Corrections · Suspected causes · Causes · Debug · Error symptoms

FIGURE 14.13
Debugging.

site that is far removed. Highly coupled program structures (Chapter 6) exacerbate this situation.

2. The symptom may disappear (temporarily) when another error is corrected.

3. The symptom may actually be caused by nonerrors (e.g., round-off inaccuracies).

4. The symptom may be caused by human error that is not easily traced.

5. The symptom may be a result of timing problems rather than processing problems.

6. It may be difficult to reproduce input conditions accurately (e.g., a real-time application in which input ordering is indeterminate).

7. The symptom may be intermittent. This is particularly common in embedded systems that couple hardware and software inextricably.

During debugging we encounter errors that range from mildly annoying (e.g., an incorrect output format) to catastrophic (e.g. the system fails, causing serious economic or physical damage). As the consequences of an error increase, the amount of pressure to find the cause also increases. Often, pressure forces a software developer to fix one error while introducing two more.

14.6.2 Psychological Considerations

Unfortunately, there appears to be some evidence that debugging prowess is an innate human trait. Some people are good at it, and others are not. Although experimental evidence on debugging is open to many interpretations, large variances in debugging ability have been reported for programmers with the same educational and experiential background.

Commenting on the human aspects of debugging, Shneiderman [SHN80] states:

> Debugging is one of the more frustrating parts of programming. It has elements of problem solving or brain teasers, coupled with the annoying recognition that you have made a mistake. Heightened anxiety and the unwillingness to accept the possibility of errors increases the task difficulty. Fortunately, there is a great sigh of relief and a lessening of tension when the bug is ultimately...corrected.

Although it may be difficult to ''learn'' debugging, a number of approaches to the problem can be proposed. We examine these in the next section.

14.6.3 Debugging Approaches

Regardless of the approach that is taken, debugging has one overriding objective: to find and correct the cause of a software error. The objective is realized by a combination of systematic evaluation, intuition, and luck. Bradley [BRA85] describes the debugging approach in this way:

> Debugging is a straightforward application of the scientific method that has been developed over 2,500 years. The basis of debugging is to locate the problem's source [the

cause] by binary partitioning, through working hypotheses that predict new values to be examined.

Take a simple non-software example: A lamp in my house does not work. If nothing in the house works, the cause must be in the main circuit breaker or outside; I look around to see whether the neighborhood is blacked out. I plug the suspect lamp into a working socket and a working appliance into the suspect circuit. So goes the alternation of hypothesis and test.

In general, three categories for debugging approaches may be proposed [MYE79]:

- brute force
- backtracking
- cause elimination

The *brute force* category of debugging is probably the most common and least efficient method for isolating the cause of a software error. We apply brute force debugging methods when all else fails. Using a ''let the computer find the error'' philosophy, memory dumps are taken, run-time traces are invoked, and the program is loaded with WRITE statements. We hope that somewhere in the morass of information that is produced we will find a clue that can lead us to the cause of an error. Although the mass of information produced may ultimately lead to success, it more frequently leads to wasted effort and time. Thought must be expended first!

Backtracking is a fairly common debugging approach that can be used successfully in small programs. Beginning at the site where a symptom has been uncovered, the source code is traced backward (manually) until the site of the cause is found. Unfortunately, as the number of source lines increases, the number of potential backward paths may become unmanageably large.

The third approach to debugging—*cause elimination*—is manifested by induction or deduction and introduces the concept of *binary partitioning*. Data related to the error occurrence are organized to isolate potential causes. A ''cause hypothesis'' is devised and the above data are used to prove or disprove the hypothesis. Alternatively, a list of all possible causes is developed and tests are conducted to eliminate each. If initial tests indicate that a particular cause hypothesis shows promise, data are refined in an attempt to isolate the bug.

Each of the above debugging approaches can be supplemented with debugging tools. We can apply a wide variety of debugging compilers, dynamic debugging aids (''tracers''), automatic test case generators, memory dumps, and cross-reference maps. However, tools are not a substitute for careful evaluation based on a complete software design document and clear source code.

In many ways, debugging of computer software is like problem solving in the business world. Brown and Sampson [BRO73] have proposed a debugging approach, called ''The Method,'' that is an adaptation of management problem-solving techniques. The authors propose the development of a *specification of deviation* that describes a problem by delineating ''what, when, where, and to what extent?'' The specification is represented in the tabular format that follows:

Specification of deviation

Question	Is	Is not
What occurred?		
When?		
Where?		
To what extent?		

Each of the above questions (what, when, where, and to what extent) is split into *is* and *is not* responses so that a clear distinction between what has occurred and what has not occurred can be made. Once information about the bug has been recorded, a cause hypothesis is developed based on distinctions observed from the *is* and *is not* responses. Debugging continues using deductive or inductive approaches described earlier in this section.

Any discussion of debugging approaches and tools is incomplete without mentioning a powerful ally: other people. Weinberg's "egoless programming" concept (discussed earlier in this book) should be extended to egoless debugging as well. Each of us can recall puzzling for hours or days over a persistent bug. A colleague wanders by and in desperation we explain the problem and throw open the listing. Instantaneously (it seems), the cause of the error is uncovered. Smiling smugly, our colleague wanders off. A fresh viewpoint, unclouded by hours of frustration, can do wonders. A final maxim for debugging might be: "When all else fails, get help!"

14.7 SUMMARY

Software testing accounts for the largest percentage of technical effort in the software development process. Yet we are only beginning to understand the subtleties of systematic test planning, execution, and control.

The objective of software testing is to uncover errors. To fulfill this objective, a series of test steps—unit, integration, validation, and system tests—are planned and executed. Unit and integration tests concentrate on functional verification of a module and incorporation of modules into a program structure. Validation testing demonstrates traceability to software requirements, and system testing validates software once it has been incorporated into a larger system.

Each test step is accomplished through a series of systematic test techniques that assist in the design of test cases. With each testing step, the level of abstraction with which software is considered is broadened.

Unlike testing (a systematic, planned activity), debugging must be viewed as an art. Beginning with a symptomatic indication of a problem, the debugging activity must track down the cause of an error. Of the many resources available during debugging, the most valuable may be the counsel of other members of the software development staff.

The requirement for higher-quality software demands a more systematic approach to testing. To quote Dunn and Ullman [DUN82]:

What is required is an overall strategy, spanning the strategic test space, quite as deliberate in its methodology as was the systematic development on which analysis, design and code were based.

In this chapter, we have examined the *strategic test space*, considering the steps that have the highest likelihood of meeting the overriding test objective: to find and remove defects in an orderly and effective manner.

REFERENCES

[BEI84] Beizer, B., *Software System Testing and Quality Assurance*, Van Nostrand Reinhold, 1984.

[BOE81] Boehm, B., *Software Engineering Economics*, Prentice-Hall, 1981, p. 37.

[BRA85] Bradley, J. H., "The Science and Art of Debugging," *Computerworld*, August 19, 1985, pp. 35–38.

[BRO73] Brown, A., and W. Sampson, *Programming Debugging*, American Elsevier, New York, 1973.

[DUN82] Dunn, R., and R. Ullman, *Quality Assurance for Computer Software*, McGraw-Hill, 1982, p. 158.

[MIL77] Miller, E., "The Philosophy of Testing," in *Program Testing Techniques*, IEEE Computer Society Press, 1977, pp. 1–3.

[MYE79] Myers, G., *The Art of Software Testing*, Wiley, 1979.

[SHN80] Shneiderman, B., *Software Psychology*, Winthrop Publishers, 1980, p. 28.

[SHO83] Shooman, M. L., *Software Engineering*, McGraw-Hill, 1983.

[YOU75] Yourdon, E., *Techniques of Program Structure and Design*, Prentice-Hall, 1975.

PROBLEMS AND POINTS TO PONDER

14.1 Using your own words, describe the difference between verification and validation. Do both make use of test case design methods and testing strategies?

14.2 List some problems that might be associated with the creation of an independent test group. Are an ITG and an SQA group the same people?

14.3 Is it always possible to develop a strategy for testing software that uses the sequence of testing steps described in Section 14.1.3? What are possible complications that might arise for embedded systems?

14.4 If you could only select three test case design methods to apply during unit testing, what would they be and why?

14.5 Add at least three additional questions to each segment of the unit test checklist presented in Section 14.2.1.

14.6 The concept of "antibugging" (Section 14.2.1) is an extremely effective way to provide built-in debugging assistance when an error is uncovered.

(*a*) Develop a set of guidelines for antibugging.

(*b*) Discuss advantages of using the techniques.

(*c*) Discuss disadvantages.

14.7 Develop an integration testing stategy for the digital dashboard software described in Chapter 7. Define test phases, note the order of integration, specify additional test software, and justify your order of integration. Assume that all modules have been unit tested and are available.

14.8 How can project scheduling affect integration testing?

14.9 Is unit testing possible or even desirable in all circumstances? Provide examples to justify your answer.

14.10 Who should perform the validation test—the software developer or the software user? Justify your answer.

14.11 Develop a complete test strategy for the Home Security System described in Problems 4.7 to 4.15. Document it in a *Test Specification. Note*: it may be necessary to do a bit of design work first.

14.12 As a class project, develop a *Debugging Guide* for your installation. The guide should provide language- and system-oriented hints that have been learned through the school of hard knocks. Begin with an outline of topics that will be reviewed by the class and your instructor. Publish the guide for others in your local environment.

FURTHER READINGS

A detailed discussion on testing strategies can be found in books by Evans (*Productive Software Test Management*, Wiley-Interscience, 1984), Hetzel (*The Complete Guide to Software Testing*, QED Information Sciences, 1984), and Beizer [BEI84]. Each delineates the steps of an effective strategy, provides a set of techniques and guidelines, and suggests procedures for controlling and tracking the testing process.

For individuals that build product software, Gunther's book (*Management Methodology for Software Product Engineering*, Wiley-Interscience, 1978) remains a useful guide for the establishment and conduct of effective test strategies.

Deutsch's contribution to Jensen and Tonies' book ("Verification and Validation," *Software Engineering*, Prentice-Hall, 1979) provides a concise description of many important aspects of V&V. Lewis (*Software Engineering*, Reston, 1983) describes a "transform theory of software verification" that may be of interest to those who desire a rigorous view of testing. Methods for formal verification are presented in a special issue of *ACM Sigsoft Notes* ("A Formal Verification Workshop," August 1985). Recent advances in methods, tools and strategies are described in *Proceedings of a Workshop on Software Testing* (IEEE Computer Society Press, July, 1986).

Guidelines for debugging are contained in a book by Dunn (*Software Defect Removal*, McGraw-Hill, 1984). Beizer [BEI84] presents an interesting "taxonomy of bugs" that can lead to effective methods for test planning. Papers by Shen, Isoda, Fang, and LeBlanc (*COMPSAC-85 Proceedings*, IEEE, October 1985) discuss various aspects of the debugging process.

CHAPTER
15

SOFTWARE MAINTENANCE AND CONFIGURATION MANAGEMENT

Software maintenance has been characterized [CAN72] as an "iceberg": we hope that what is immediately visible is all there is to it. Realistically, we know that an enormous mass of potential problems and costs lies under the surface. The maintenance of existing software can account for over 60 percent of all effort expended by a development organization. The percentage continues to rise as more software is produced. On the horizon we can foresee "maintenance-bound" software development organizations that can no longer produce new software because all available resources are expended maintaining old software.

Uninitiated readers may ask why so much maintenance is required and why so much effort is expended. Rochkind [ROC75] provides a partial answer:

> Computer programs are always changing. There are bugs to fix, enhancements to add, and optimizations to make. There is not only the current version to change, but also last year's version (which is still supported) and next year's version (which almost runs). Besides the problems whose solutions required the changes in the first place, the fact of the changes themselves creates additional problems.

Because change is inevitable when computer-based systems are built, we must develop mechanisms for evaluating, controlling, and making modifications.

The second part of this chapter is dedicated to *software configuration management* (SCM)—an activity that manages change throughout the software engineering process. Because change can occur at any time, SCM activities are developed to identify change, control change, assure that change is being properly implemented, and report change to others who may have an interest.

It is important to make a clear distinction between software maintenance and software configuration management. Maintenance is a set of software engineering activities that occur after software has been delivered to the customer and put into operation. Software configuration management is a set of tracking and control activities that begin when a software development project begins and terminate only when the software is taken out of operation.

Throughout this book we have discussed a software engineering methodology. A primary goal of this methodology is to improve the ease with which changes can be accommodated and to reduce the amount of effort expended on maintenance. In this chapter, we discuss the specific activities that enable us to accomplish this goal.

15.1 A DEFINITION OF SOFTWARE MAINTENANCE

Upon reading the introduction to this chapter a reader may protest: "but I don't spend 60 percent of my time fixing mistakes in the programs I develop." Software maintenance is, of course, far more than "fixing mistakes." We may define maintenance by describing four activities that are undertaken after a program is released for use.

The first maintenance activity occurs because it is unreasonable to assume that software testing will uncover all latent errors in a large software system. During the use of any large program, errors will occur and be reported to the developer. The process that includes diagnosis and correction of one or more errors is called *corrective maintenance*.

The second activity that contributes to a definition of maintenance occurs because of the rapid change encountered in every aspect of computing. New generations of hardware seem to be announced on a 36-month cycle; new operating systems, or new releases of old ones, appear regularly; and peripheral equipment and other system elements are frequently upgraded or modified. The useful life of application software, on the other hand, can easily surpass ten years, outliving the system environment for which it was originally developed. Therefore, *adaptive maintenance*—an activity that modifies software to properly interface with a changing environment—is both necessary and commonplace.

The third activity that may be applied to a definition of maintenance occurs when a software package is successful. As the software is used, recommendations for new capabilities, modifications to existing functions, and general enhancements are received from users. To satisfy requests in this category, *perfective maintenance* is performed. This activity accounts for the majority of all effort expended on software maintenance.

The fourth maintenance activity occurs when software is changed to improve future maintainability or reliability or to provide a better basis for future enhancements.

Often called *preventive maintenance*, this activity is still relatively rare in the software world.

The terms used to describe the first three maintenance activities were coined by Swanson [SWA76]. The fourth term is commonly used in the maintenance of hardware and other physical systems. It should be noted, however, that analogies between software and hardware maintenance can be misleading. As we stated in the first chapter of this book, software, unlike hardware, does not wear out, and therefore the major activity associated with hardware maintenance—replacement of worn or broken parts—simply does not apply.

Some software professionals are troubled by the inclusion of the second and third activities as part of a definition of maintenance. In actuality the tasks that occur as part of adaptive and perfective maintenance are the same tasks that are applied during the development phase of the software engineering process. To adapt or perfect, we must determine new requirements, redesign, generate code, and test existing software. Traditionally, such tasks have been collectively called *maintenance*.

In fact, approximately half of all software maintenance is perfective, as illustrated in Figure 15.1. The percentages shown in the figure are based on Lientz and Swanson's [LIE80] study of 487 software development organizations. These data give the best information to date about the hidden proportions of the maintenance "iceberg."

15.2 MAINTENANCE CHARACTERISTICS

Software maintenance has until very recently been the neglected phase in the software engineering process. The literature on maintenance contains very few entries when compared to definition and development phases. Little research or production data have been gathered on the subject, and few technical approaches or "methods" have been proposed.

FIGURE 15.1
Distribution of maintenance activities.

To understand the characteristics of software maintenance, we consider the topic from three different viewpoints:

1. the activities required to accomplish the maintenance phase and the impact of a software engineering approach (or lack thereof) on the efficacy of such activities;
2. the costs associated with the maintenance phase;
3. the problems that are frequently encountered when software maintenance is undertaken.

In the sections that follow, the characteristics of maintenance are described from each of the perspectives listed above.

15.2.1   Structured versus Unstructured Maintenance

The flow of events that can occur as a result of a maintenance request are illustrated in Figure 15.2. If the only available element of a software configuration is source code,

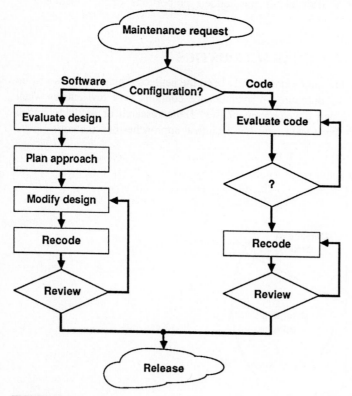

FIGURE 15.2
Structured versus unstructured maintenance.

maintenance activity begins with a painstaking evaluation of the code, often complicated by poor internal documentation. Subtle characteristics such as program structure, global data structures, system interfaces, performance, and/or design constraints are difficult to ascertain and frequently misinterpreted. The ramifications of changes that are ultimately made to the code are difficult to assess. Regression tests (repeating past tests to assure that modifications have not introduced faults in previously operational software) are impossible to conduct because no record of testing exists. We are conducting *unstructured maintenance* and paying the price (in wasted effort and human frustration) that accompanies software that has not been developed using a well-defined methodology.

If a complete software configuration exists, the maintenance task begins with an evaluation of the design documentation. Important structural, performance, and interface characteristics of the software are determined. The impact of required modifications or corrections is assessed and an approach is planned. The design is modified (using techniques identical to those discussed in earlier chapters) and reviewed. New source code is developed, regression tests are conducted using information contained in the *Test Specification*, and the software is released again.

This sequence of events constitutes *structured maintenance* and occurs as a result of the earlier application of a software engineering methodology. Although the existence of a software configuration does not guarantee problem-free maintenance, the amount of wasted effort is reduced and the overall quality of a change or correction is enhanced.

15.2.2 Maintenance Cost

The cost of software maintenance has increased steadily during the past twenty years. Figure 15.3 illustrates the past, current, and projected percentage of overall software budget expended on the maintenance of existing software. Although industry averages are difficult to ascertain and open to broad interpretation, the typical software development organization spends anywhere from 40 to 70 percent of all dollars conducting corrective, adaptive, perfective, and preventive maintenance.

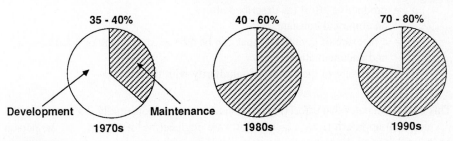

As a percent of software budget

FIGURE 15.3
Maintenance cost.

The dollar cost of maintenance is the most obvious. However, other, less tangible, costs may ultimately be a cause for greater concern. To quote Daniel McCracken [MCC80]:

> Backlogs of new applications and major changes that measure in years are getting longer. As an industry, we can't even keep up—let alone catch up—with what our users want us to do.

McCracken alludes to the maintenance-bound organization. One intangible cost of software maintenance is a development opportunity that is postponed or lost because available resources must be channeled to maintenance tasks. Other intangible costs include:

- customer dissatisfaction when seemingly legitimate requests for repair or modification cannot be addressed in a timely manner
- reduction in overall software quality as a result of changes that introduce latent errors in the maintained software
- upheaval caused during development efforts when staff must be "pulled" to work on a maintenance task

The final cost of software maintenance is a dramatic decrease in productivity (measured in LOC per person-month or function points per person month) that is encountered when maintenance of old programs is initiated. Productivity reductions of 40 to 1 have been reported [BOE79]. That is, a development effort that cost $25 per line of code to develop might cost $1000 for every line of code that is maintained.

Effort expended on maintenance may be divided into productive activities (e.g., analysis and evaluation, design modification, coding) and "wheel spinning" activities (e.g., trying to understand what the code does; trying to interpret data structure, interface characteristics, performance bounds). The following expression [BEL72] provides a model of maintenance effort:

$$M = p + K \exp(c - d)$$

where M = total effort expended on maintenance
p = productive effort (as described above)
K = an empirical constant
c = a measure of complexity that can be attributed to a lack of good design and documentation
d = a measure of the degree of familiarity with the software.

This model indicates that effort (and cost) can increase exponentially if a poor software development approach (i.e., a lack of software engineering) was used, and the person or group that used the approach is not available to perform maintenance.

15.2.3 Problems

Most problems that are associated with software maintenance can be traced to deficiencies in the way software was defined and developed. The classic "pay now or pay later" syndrome applies. A lack of control and discipline in the first two phases of the software engineering process nearly always translates into problems in the last phase.

Among the many classic problems that can be associated with software maintenance are the following:

- It is often exceptionally difficult to understand "someone else's" program. Difficulty increases as the number of elements in a software configuration decrease. If only undocumented code exists, severe problems should be expected.
- "Someone else" is often not around to explain. Mobility among software personnel is currently very high. We cannot rely upon a personal explanation of the software by the developer when maintenance is required.
- Proper documentation doesn't exist or is awful. Recognition that software must be documented is a first step, but documentation must be understandable and consistent with source code to be of any value.
- Most software is not designed for change. Unless a design method accommodates change through concepts such as functional independence or object classes, modifications to software are difficult and error-prone.
- Maintenance has not been viewed as very glamorous work. Much of this perception comes from the high frustration level associated with maintenance work.

All of the problems described above can, in part, be attributed to the large number of programs currently in existence that have been developed with no thought of software engineering. A disciplined methodology should not be viewed as a panacea. However, software engineering does provide at least partial solutions to each problem associated with maintenance.

A number of technical and management issues arise as a consequence of the problems associated with software maintenance. Is it possible to develop software that is well designed and maintainable? Can we maintain the integrity of software when it has to be modified? Are there technical and management approaches that can be successfully applied to software maintenance? These and other issues are discussed in the sections that follow.

15.3 MAINTAINABILITY

The characteristics described in the preceding section are all affected by the *maintainability* of software. Maintainability may be defined qualitatively as: the ease with which software can be understood, corrected, adapted, and/or enhanced. As we have stressed throughout this book, maintainability is a key goal that guides the steps of a software engineering methodology.

15.3.1 Controlling Factors

The ultimate maintainability of software is affected by many factors. Inadvertent carelessness in design, coding, and testing has an obvious negative impact on our ability to maintain the resultant software. A poor software configuration can have a similar negative impact even when the aforementioned technical steps have been conducted with care.

In addition to factors that can be associated with a development methodology, Kopetz [KOP79] defines a number of factors that are related to the development environment:

- availability of qualified software staff
- understandable system structure
- ease of system handling
- use of standardized programming languages
- use of standardized operating systems
- standardized structure of documentation
- availability of test cases
- built-in debugging facilities
- availability of a proper computer to conduct maintenance

In addition to these factors, we might add (half facetiously): the availability of the person or group that originally developed the software.

Many of the factors stated above reflect characteristics of hardware and software resources that are used during development. For example, there is no question that the absence of high-level language compilers (necessitating the use of assembler language) has a detrimental effect on maintainability. Other factors indicate a need for standardization of methods, resources, and approach. Possibly the most important factor that affects maintainability is planning for maintainability. If software is viewed as a system element that will inevitably undergo change, the chances that maintainable software will be produced are likely to increase substantially.

15.3.2 Quantitative Measures

Software maintainability, like quality or reliability, is a difficult term to quantify. However, we can assess maintainability indirectly by considering attributes of the maintenance activity that can be measured. Gilb [GIL79] provides a number of *maintainability metrics* that relate to the effort expended during maintenance:

1. problem recognition time
2. administrative delay time
3. maintenance tools collection time
4. problem analysis time
5. change specification time
6. active correction (or modification) time

7. local testing time
8. global testing time
9. maintenance review time
10. total recovery time

Each of the above metrics can, in fact, be recorded without great difficulty. Such data can provide a manager with an indication of the efficacy of new techniques and tools.

15.3.3 Reviews

Because maintainability should be an essential characteristic of all software, we must ensure that the factors noted in Section 15.3.1 are built-in during the development phase. At each level of the software engineering review process, maintainability has to be considered. During requirements review, areas of future enhancement and potential revision should be noted, software portability issues discussed, and system interfaces that might impact software maintenance considered. During design reviews, data design, architectural design, and procedural design should be evaluated for ease of modification, modularity, and functional independence. Code reviews should stress style and internal documentation, two factors that have an influence on maintainability. Finally, each test step can provide hints about portions of the program that may require preventive maintenance before the software is formally released.

Maintainability reviews should be conducted repeatedly as each step in the software engineering process is completed. The most formal maintenance review occurs at the conclusion of testing and is called the *configuration review.* The configuration review ensures that all elements of the software configuration are complete, understandable, and filed for modification control.

The software maintenance task itself should be reviewed at the completion of each effort. Methods for evaluation are discussed in the next section.

15.4 MAINTENANCE TASKS

Tasks associated with software maintenance begin long before a request for maintenance is made. Initially, a maintenance organization (de facto or formal) must be established, reporting and evaluation procedures must be described, and a standardized sequence of events must be defined for each maintenance request. In addition a recordkeeping system for maintenance activities should be established and review and evaluation criteria defined.

15.4.1 A Maintenance Organization

There are almost as many organizational structures as there are software development organizations. For this reason, ''recommended organizational structures'' for software development and software maintenance have been avoided in this book. In the case of maintenance, however, formal organizations rarely exist (notable exceptions are very large software developers), and maintenance is often performed on a catch-as-catch-can basis.

Although a formal maintenance organization need not be established, an informal delegation of responsibility is absolutely essential for even small software developers. One such schema is illustrated in Figure 15.4. Maintenance requests are channeled through a *maintenance controller* who forwards each request for evaluation to a *system supervisor.* The system supervisor is a member of the technical staff who has been assigned the responsibility to become familiar with a small subset of production programs. Once an evaluation is made, a change control authority (sometimes called a *change control board*) must determine the action to be taken.

The organization suggested above reduces confusion and improves the flow of maintenance activities. Because all maintenance requests are funneled through a single individual (or group), ''back door fixes'' (i.e., changes that have not been sanctioned and therefore can cause confusion) are less likely to occur. Because at least one individual will always have some familiarity with a production program, requests for changes (maintenance) can be assessed more rapidly. Because specific change control approval is implemented, an organization can avoid making changes that benefit one requester, but negatively impact many other users.

Each of the above job titles serves to establish an area of responsibility for maintenance. The controller and change control authority may be a single person or (for large program products) a group of managers and senior technical staff. The system supervisor may have other duties but still provides a ''contact'' with a specific software package.

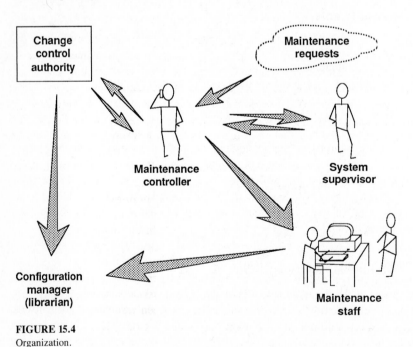

FIGURE 15.4
Organization.

When responsibilities are assigned prior to the start of maintenance activity, confusion is greatly reduced. More importantly, an early definition of responsibilities can temper any hard feelings that develop when a person is preemptively "pulled off" a development effort to conduct maintenance.

15.4.2   Reporting

All requests for software maintenance should be presented in a standardized manner. The software developer normally generates a *maintenance request form* (MRF), sometimes called a *software problem report*, to be completed by the user who desires a maintenance activity. If an error is encountered, a complete description of the circumstances leading to the error (including input data, listings, and other supporting material) must be included. For adaptive or perfective maintenance requests, a brief *change specification* (an abbreviated requirements specification) is submitted. The maintenance request form is evaluated as described in the preceding section.

The MRF is an externally generated document used as a basis for planning the maintenance task. Internally, the software organization develops a *software change report* (SCR) that indicates: (1) the magnitude of effort required to satisfy an MRF, (2) the nature of modifications required, (3) the priority of the request, and (4) after-the-fact data about the modification. The SCR is submitted to a change control authority before further maintenance planning is initiated.

15.4.3   Flow of Events

The sequence of events that occur as the result of a maintenance request are shown in Figure 15.5. The first requirement is to determine the type of maintenance to be conducted. In many cases a user may view a request as an indication of software error (corrective maintenance) while a developer may view the same request as adaptation or enhancement. If a difference of opinion exists, a settlement must be negotiated.

Referring to the flow shown in Figure 15.5, a request for corrective maintenance (error path) begins with an evaluation of error severity. If a severe error exists (e.g., a critical system cannot function), personnel are assigned under the direction of the system supervisor and problem analysis begins immediately. For less severe errors, the request for corrective maintenance is evaluated and categorized and then scheduled in conjunction with other tasks requiring software development resources.

In some cases an error may be so severe that normal controls for maintenance must be abandoned temporarily. Code must be modified immediately, without corresponding evaluation for potential side effects and appropriate updating of documentation. This *firefighting* mode for corrective maintenance is reserved only for "crisis" situations and should represent a very small percentage of all maintenance activities. It should be noted that firefighting postpones, but does not eliminate, the need for controls and evaluation. After the crisis has been resolved, these activities must be conducted to ensure that the present fixes will not propagate even more severe problems.

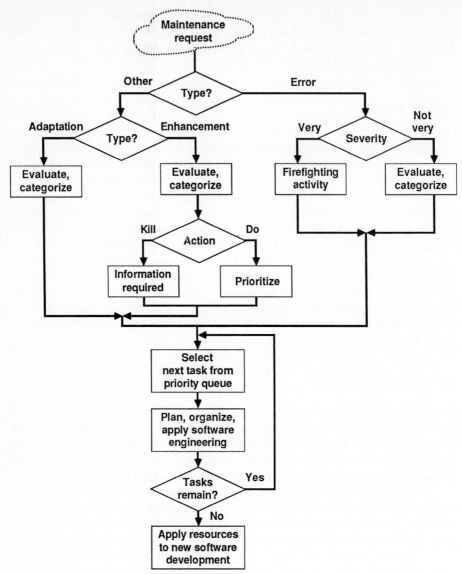

FIGURE 15.5
Priorities.

Requests for adaptive and perfective maintenance follow a different path. Adaptations are evaluated and categorized (prioritized) prior to being placed on a queue for maintenance action. Enhancements undergo the same evaluation. However, not all requests for enhancement are undertaken. Business strategy, available resources, the direction of current and future software products, and many other issues may cause a request for enhancement to be rejected. Enhancements to be made are also placed on the maintenance queue. The priority of each request is established and the required work is scheduled as if it were another development effort (for all intents and purposes, it is). If an extremely high priority is set, work may begin immediately.

Regardless of maintenance type, the same technical tasks are conducted. These maintenance tasks include: modification to software design, review, requisite code modification, unit and integration testing (including regression tests using previous test cases), validation tests, and review. In fact, software maintenance is actually software engineering applied recursively. Emphasis will shift with each maintenance type, but the overall approach remains unchanged. The final event in the maintenance flow is a review that revalidates all elements of the software configuration and assures that the MRF has, in fact, been fulfilled.

After the software maintenance task is complete, it is often a good idea to conduct a *situation review.* In general the review attempts to answer the following questions:

- Given the current situation, what aspects of design, code, or test could have been done differently?
- What maintenance resources should have been available but were not?
- What were the major (minor) stumbling blocks for this effort?
- Is preventive maintenance indicated by the types of requests being reported?

The situation review can have an important influence on the conduct of future maintenance efforts and provides feedback that is important to effective management of a software organization.

15.4.4 Recordkeeping

Historically, recordkeeping for all phases of the software engineering process has been inadequate. Recordkeeping for software maintenance has been nonexistent. For this reason we are frequently unable to assess the effectiveness of maintenance techniques, incapable of determining the quality of a production program, and unwilling to determine what maintenance really costs.

The first problem encountered in maintenance recordkeeping is to understand what data are worth recording. Swanson [SWA76] provides a comprehensive list:

1. program identification
2. number of source statements
3. number of machine code instructions
4. programming language used
5. program installation date
6. number of program runs since installation
7. number of processing failures associated with item 6
8. program change level and identification
9. number of source statements added by program change

10. number of source statements deleted by program change

11. number of person-hours spent per change

12. program change date

13. identification of software engineer

14. MRF identification

15. maintenance type

16. maintenance start and close dates

17. cumulative number of person-hours spent on maintenance

18. net benefits associated with maintenance performed

The above data are collected for each maintenance effort. Swanson proposes these items as the foundation of a maintenance data base that can be evaluated as described in Section 15.4.5.

More recent work on software maintenance metrics has focused on software characteristics that are most likely to affect frequency of maintenance and empirical models for predicting the amount of maintenance work based on other program characteristics. In a study of over 400 COBOL programs, Vessey and Weber [VES83] found that program complexity and programming style were the most significant factors in the occurrence of corrective maintenance. Using the COCOMO model (Chapter 3) as a basis [SCH85], the following model has been suggested as a predictor for the number of person-months, E.maint, expended on software maintenance annually:

$$E.maint = ACT \times 2.4 \times KLOC \exp(1.05)$$

where ACT is the *annual change traffic* defined as:

$$ACT = (KLOC \text{ for a system undergoing maintenance})/CI$$

where CI = number of source code instructions that are modified or added during one year of maintenance.

Although the results of clinical studies must be applied with caution, quantitative models provide one element of management control that has been missing for software maintenance.

15.4.5 Evaluation

An evaluation of software maintenance activities is often complicated by a lack of hard data. If recordkeeping is initiated, a number of measures of maintenance performance may be developed. Again from Swanson [SWA76], we present an abbreviated list of potential measures:

1. average number of processing failures per program run

2. total person-hours spent in each maintenance category

3. average number of program changes made per program, per language, per maintenance type

4. average number of person-hours spent per source statement added or deleted due to maintenance

5. average person-hours spent per language

6. average turnaround time for an MRF

7. percentage of maintenance requests by type.

These seven measures can provide a quantitative framework from which decisions on development technique, language selection, maintenance effort projections, resource allocation, and many other issues can be made. Clearly, such data can be applied to evaluate the maintenance task.

A number of studies have been conducted to assess the kinds of changes that are conducted during software maintenance and the impact of these changes on the maintenance task (e.g., [GUS85], [YEU85]). As more industry data become available, our ability to evaluate the efficacy of maintenance tools, techniques, and procedures will undoubtedly improve.

15.5 MAINTENANCE SIDE EFFECTS

Modification of software is dangerous. All of us have heard the following lament: "But all I did was change this one statement..." Unfortunately, each time a change is introduced to a complex, logical procedure, the potential for error grows. Design documentation and careful regression testing help to eliminate error, but maintenance *side effects* will be encountered.

When used in the context of software maintenance, the term *side effects* implies an error or other undesirable behavior that occurs as a result of modification. Freedman and Weinberg [FRE82] define three major categories of side effects, discussed in the following sections.

15.5.1 Coding Side Effects

A simple change to a single statement can sometimes have disastrous results. The inadvertent (and undetected) replacement of a "," with a "." had near-tragic consequences when flight control software for a manned space flight failed. Although not all side effects have such dramatic consequences, change invites error and error always leads to problems.

We communicate with a machine using programming language source code. The opportunities for side effects abound. Although every code modification has the potential for introducing error, the following changes [FRE82] tend to be more error-prone than others:

1. A subprogram is deleted or changed.

2. A statement label is deleted or modified.

3. An identifier is deleted or modified.

4. Changes are made to improve execution performance.

5. File open or close is modified.
6. Logical operators are modified.
7. Design changes are translated into major code changes.
8. Changes are made to boundary tests.

Coding side effects range from nuisance errors detected and remedied during regression testing to problems that cause software failure during operation. Again, we paraphrase Murphy's law: "if a change to a source statement can introduce error, it will."

15.5.2 Data Side Effects

The importance of data structure in software design was noted in Chapter 6. During maintenance, modifications are often made to individual elements of a data structure or to the structure itself. When data change, the software design may no longer fit the data and errors can occur. Data side effects also occur as a result of modifications made to software information structure.

The following changes [FRE82] in data frequently result in side effects: (1) redefinition of local and global constants, (2) redefinition of record or file formats, (3) increase or decrease in the size of an array or higher order data structure, (4) modification to global data, (5) re-initialization of control flags or pointers, and (6) rearrangement of arguments for I/O or subprograms. Data side effects can be limited by thorough design documentation that describes data structure and provides a cross reference that associates data elements, records, files, and other structures with software modules.

15.5.3 Documentation Side Effects

Maintenance should focus on the entire software configuration and not on source code modification alone. Documentation side effects occur when changes to source code are not reflected in design documentation or user-oriented manuals.

Whenever a change to data flow, design architecture, module procedure, or any other related characteristic is made, supporting technical documentation must be updated. Design documentation that does not accurately reflect the current state of the software is probably worse than no documentation at all. Side effects occur in subsequent maintenance efforts when an innocent perusal of technical documents leads to an incorrect assessment of software characteristics.

To a user, software is only as good as the documentation (both written and interactive) that describes its use. If modifications to the executable software are not reflected in user documentation, side effects are guaranteed. For example, changes in the order or format of interactive input, if not properly documented, can cause significant problems. New, undocumented error messages can cause confusion; outdated tables of contents, indices, and text can cause user frustration and dissatisfaction.

Documentation side effects can be reduced substantially if the entire configuration is reviewed prior to re-release of the software. In fact, some maintenance requests may require no change to software design or source code, but indicate a lack of clarity in user documentation. In such cases the maintenance effort focuses on documentation.

15.6 MAINTENANCE ISSUES

A number of important supplementary issues must be addressed during a discussion of maintenance. Frequently, we must maintain software that is poorly designed and documented. How do we proceed? Should preventive maintenance be conducted to improve the maintainability of working programs? Are there new philosophies to program development that may impact the maintenance phase? We discuss these issues in the sections that follow.

15.6.1 Maintaining "Alien Code"

Nearly every mature software development organization must maintain programs that were developed fifteen or more years ago. Such programs are sometimes called "alien code" because (1) no current member of the technical staff worked on development of the program; (2) no development methodology was applied and therefore poor design and documentation (by today's standards) exist; (3) modularity was not a design criterion and the concepts of structured design were not applied.

Early in this chapter we discussed the necessity for a *system supervisor*—a person who becomes familiar with a subset of production programs that may require maintenance. Familiarization with programs developed using a software engineering approach is facilitated by a complete software configuration and good design. What can be done with alien code? Yourdon [YOU75] provides a number of useful suggestions:

1. Study the program before you get into "emergency mode." Try to get as much background information as possible....
2. Try to become familiar with the overall flow of control of the program; ignore coding details at first. It may be very useful to draw your own (structure diagram) and high level flow chart, if one doesn't already exist.
3. Evaluate the reasonableness of existing documentation; insert your own comments in the (source) listing if you think they will help.
4. Make good use of cross reference listings, symbol tables and other aids generally provided by the compiler and/or assembler.
5. Make changes to the program with the greatest caution. Respect the style and formatting of the program if at all possible. Indicate on the listing itself which instructions you have changed.
6. Don't eliminate code unless you are sure it isn't used.
7. Don't try to share the use of temporary variables and working storage that already exist in the program. Insert your own variables to avoid trouble.
8. Keep detailed records of maintenance activities and results.
9. Avoid the irrational urge to throw the program away and rewrite it. [NOTE: This "urge" is sometimes both rational and practical.]
10. Do insert error checking.

Each of the above guidelines will help in the maintenance of old programs. However, there is a class of programs with control flow that is the graphic equivalent to a bowl of spaghetti, with "modules" that are 2,000 statements long, and three meaningful comment lines in 9,000 source statements, and no other elements of a software configuration. Incredibly, such programs may work for years, but when maintenance is requested the task may be untenable. In the next section we examine what can be done.

15.6.2 Preventive Maintenance

In maintenance situations for programs like the one described above, three options exist:

1. We can struggle through modification after modification, "fighting" the design and source code to implement the necessary changes.
2. We can redesign, recode, and test those portions of the software that require modification, applying a software engineering approach to all revised segments.
3. We can completely redesign, recode, and test the program.

There is no single "correct" option. Circumstances may frequently dictate the first option even if the second or third is more desirable.

Preventive maintenance of computer software is a relatively new and controversial issue. Rather than waiting until a maintenance request is received, the development or maintenance organization selects a program that (1) will remain in use for a preselected number of years, (2) is currently being used successfully, and (3) is likely to undergo major modification or enhancement in the near future. Then, option 2 or 3 above is applied.

The preventive maintenance approach was pioneered by Miller [MIL81] under the title "structured retrofit." He defined this concept as "the application of today's methodologies to yesterday's systems to support tomorrow's requirements." At first glance the suggestion that we redevelop a large program when a working version already exists may seem quite extravagant. Before passing judgment, we should consider the following points:

1. The cost to maintain one line of source code may be up to 40 times the cost of initial development of that line.
2. Redesign of the software architecture (program and/or data structure), using modern design concepts, can greatly facilitate future maintenance.
3. Because a prototype of the software already exists, development productivity should be much higher than average.
4. The user now has experience with the software. Therefore, new requirements and the direction of change can be ascertained with greater ease.
5. A software configuration will exist upon completion of preventive maintenance.

When a software development organization sells software as a product, preventive maintenance is seen in "new releases" of a program. A large in-house software developer (e.g., a business systems software development group for a large consumer products company) may have 500–2,000 production programs within its domain of responsibility. These programs can be prioritized by importance and then reviewed as candidates for preventive maintenance.

15.6.3 A "Spare Parts" Strategy

A classic characteristic of hardware maintenance is the removal of a defective part and its replacement with a spare part. The software prototyping concept (Chapter 4) can lead to the development of spare parts for programs. The prototyping concept is described by Spiegel [SPI81]:

> Software prototyping is a process (the act, study, or skill) of modeling user requirements in one or more levels of detail, including working models. Project resources are allocated to produce scaled down versions of the software described by requirements. The prototype version makes the software visible for review by users, designers and management....This process continues as desired, with running versions ready for release after several iterations.

If various prototype levels were developed, it might be possible to have a set of software *spare parts* [GIL81] that could be used when requests for corrective maintenance are received. For example, an analysis module might be designed and implemented in two different ways—one included in the working software. If that module failed, a spare part could be incorporated immediately.

Although the spare parts strategy for software does seem a bit unconventional, there is little evidence[*] that it is any more expensive when we consider all software engineering costs. However, further experience must be obtained before sweeping conclusions (pro or con) can be drawn.

15.7 SOFTWARE CONFIGURATION MANAGEMENT

Throughout this book, we have referred to a set of methods, procedures, and tools that are collectively called *software engineering*. The output of the software engineering process is information that may be divided into three broad categories: (1) computer programs (both source-level and executable forms), (2) documents that describe the computer programs (targeted at both technical practitioners and users), and (3) data structures (contained within the program or external to it). The items that compose all information produced as part of the software engineering process are collectively called a *software configuration*.

---

[*]It is interesting to note, however, that recent research indicates that there is a tendency for separate, independent teams of programmers to make the same mistakes when working from the same specification of a problem.

As the software engineering process progresses, the number of *software configuration items* (SCIs) grows rapidly. A *System Specification* spawns a *Software Project Plan* and *Software Requirements Specification* (as well as hardware-related documents). These in turn spawn other documents to create a hierarchy of information. If each SCI simply spawned other SCIs, little confusion would result. Unfortunately, another variable enters the process—*change*. Change may occur at any time, for any reason. In fact the First Law of System Engineering [BER80] states:

> No matter where you are in the system life cycle, the system will change, and the desire to change it will persist throughout the life cycle.

Software Configuration Management (SCM) is a set of activities developed to manage change throughout the software life cycle. SCM is a software quality assurance activity that is applied during all phases of the software engineering process. In the sections that follow, we examine major SCM tasks and important concepts that help us to manage change.

15.7.1 Baselines

Change is a fact of life in software development. Customers want to modify requirements. Developers want to modify technical approach. Management wants to modify project approach. Why all this modification? The answer is really quite simple. As time passes, all constituencies know more (about what they need, which approach would be best, and how to get it done and still make money). This additional knowledge is the driving force behind most changes and leads to a statement of fact that is difficult for many software engineering practitioners to accept: *Most changes are justified.*

A *baseline* is a software configuration management concept that helps us to control change without seriously impeding justifiable change. One way to describe a baseline is through analogy:

> Consider the doors to the kitchen of a large restaurant. To eliminate collisions, one door is marked OUT and the other is marked IN. The doors have stops that allow them to be opened only in the appropriate direction.
>
> If a waiter picks up an order in the kitchen, places it on a tray, and then realizes he has selected the wrong dish, he may change to the correct dish quickly and informally. If, however, he leaves the kitchen, gives the customer the dish, and then is informed of his error, he must follow a set procedure: (1) look at the check to determine if an error has occurred, (2) apologize profusely, (3) return to the kitchen through the IN door, (4) explain the problem, and so forth.

A baseline is analogous to the kitchen doors in the restaurant. Before a software configuration item becomes a baseline, change may be made quickly and informally. However, once a baseline is established, we figuratively pass through a swinging one-way door. Changes can be made, but a specific, formal procedure must be applied to evaluate and verify each change.

In the context of software engineering, we define a baseline as a milestone in the development of software that is marked by the delivery of a software configuration item and the approval of the SCI obtained by formal technical review (Chapter 12). For example, a preliminary design has been documented and reviewed. Errors are found and corrected. The approved preliminary design (program and data structure and supporting information) becomes a baseline. Further changes to the software architecture can be made only after each has been evaluated and approved (Section 15.8.2).

15.7.2   Software Configuration Items

We have already defined a software configuration item as information created as part of the software engineering process. In the extreme, an SCI could be considered to be a single section of a large specification or one test case in a large suite of tests. More realistically, an SCI is a document, an entire suite of test cases, or a named program component (e.g., a Pascal procedure or an Ada package).

The following SCIs become the target for configuration management techniques and form a set of baselines:

1. System specification
2. Software project plan
3. (*a*) Software requirements specification
   (*b* Executable or paper prototype
4. Preliminary user manual
5. Design specification
   (*a*) Preliminary design
   (*b*) Detail design
6. Source code listing
7. (*a*) Test plan and procedure
   (*b*) Test cases and recorded results
8. Operation and installation manuals
9. Executable programs
10. As-built user manual
11. Maintenance documents
    (*a*) Software problem reports
    (*b*) Maintenance requests
    (*c*) Engineering change orders
12. Standards and procedures for software engineering

In the next section we examine the SCM tasks that are applied to some or all of the SCIs noted above.

15.8   THE SCM PROCESS

Software configuration management is an important element of software quality assurance. Its primary responsibility is the control of change. However, SCM is also responsible for the identification of individual SCIs and various versions of the software, the auditing of the software configuration to ensure that it has been properly developed, and the reporting of all changes applied to the configuration.

Any discussion of SCM introduces a set of complex questions:

- How does an organization identify and manage the many existing versions of a program (and its documentation) in a manner that will enable change to be accommodated efficiently?
- How does an organization control changes before and after software is released to a customer?
- Who has responsibility for approving and prioritizing changes?
- How can we ensure that changes have been made properly?
- What mechanism is used to apprise others of changes that are made?

These questions lead us to the definition of four SCM tasks: *identification*, *change control*, *configuration auditing*, and *reporting*.

15.8.1   Identification

Identification is a software configuration management task that assures meaningful and consistent naming for all items in the software configuration. The term ''naming'' refers to an identification scheme that provides the following information:

1. SCI type (e.g, document, program, test case)
2. SCI name (e.g., *Design Specification*)
3. Project or product identification
4. Version number
5. Last release date

This information may be encoded and placed in a single SCI identification code or may be referenced as separate pieces of information.

Identification data may be maintained in an automated data base so that all relevant SCIs for a specific version of software may be acquired. For example, a software product builder must often support two or more different versions of the same basic product simultaneously. Let us assume that 400 copies of product P have been sold. Versions 2.0, 2.1, and the newest, 2.15, are currently installed. It is possible that changes may be made to any version, but not necessarily to all versions. How does the developer reference all modules, documents, and test cases for version 2.1? How does the marketing department know what customers currently have version 2.0? How can we be sure that changes to version 2.0 source code are properly reflected in corresponding design documentation? A key element in the answer to all of the above questions is identification.

A variety of automated tools (e.g., CCC, RCS, CMS) have been developed to aid in the identification (and other SCM) task. In some cases [TIC82], a tool is designed to maintain full copies of only the most recent version. To achieve earlier versions (of documents or programs), changes (cataloged by the tool) are "subtracted" from the most recent version. This clever scheme makes the current configuration immediately available and other versions easily available. Other SCM tools [CHR85] provide comprehensive management of all SCIs and provide support for all SCM tasks.

15.8.2 Change Control

For a large software development effort, uncontrolled change rapidly leads to chaos. *Change control*, the most important SCM task, provides a mechanism for the control of change. The change control process is illustrated schematically in Figure 15.6. A *change request** is submitted and evaluated to assess technical merit, potential side effects, overall impact on other system functions, and projected cost. The results of the evaluation are presented as a *change report* that is used by a *change control authority* (CCA)—a person or group who makes a final decision on the status and priority of the change. An *engineering change order* (ECO) is generated for each approved change. The ECO describes the change to be made, the constraints that must be respected, and the criteria for review and audit.

Some readers may begin to feel uncomfortable with the level of bureaucracy implied by the above process description. This feeling is not unjustified. Without proper safeguards, change control can retard progress and create unnecessary red tape. Most software developers who have change control mechanisms (unfortunately, many have none) have created a number of layers of control to help avoid the problems alluded to above.

Prior to an SCI becoming a baseline, only *informal change control* need be applied. The developer of the SCI in question may make whatever changes are justified by project and technical requirements (as long as changes do not impact broader system requirements that lie outside the developer's scope of work). Once the SCI has undergone formal technical review and has been approved, a baseline is created.

Once an SCI becomes a baseline, *project level change control* is implemented. To make a change now, the developer must gain approval from the project manager (if the change is "local") or from the CCA (if the change impacts other SCIs). In some cases, formal generation of change requests, change reports, and ECOs is dispensed with. However, assessment of each change is conducted and all changes are tracked and reviewed.

---

*Although many change requests are submitted during the software maintenance phase, we take a broader view in this discussion. A request for change can occur at any time during the definition and development phases of the software engineering process.

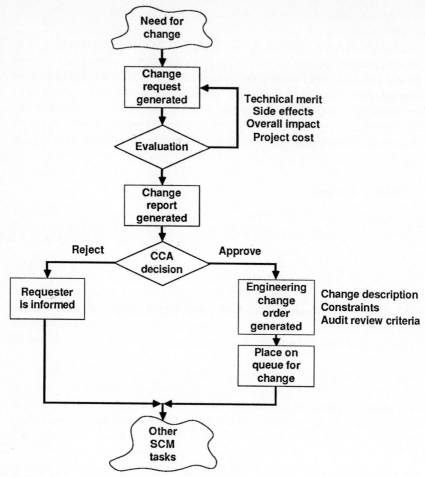

FIGURE 15.6
The change control process.

When the software product is released to customers, *formal change control* is instituted. The formal change control procedure has been outlined in Figure 15.6.

The change control authority (CCA) plays an active role in the second and third layer of control. Depending on the size and character of a software project, the CCA may comprise one person—the project manager—or a number of people (e.g., representatives from software, hardware, data base engineering, support, marketing, etc.). The role of the CCA is to take a global view, that is, to assess the impact of change beyond the SCI in question. How will the change impact hardware? How will the change impact performance? How will the change modify the customer's perception of the product? How will the change affect product quality and reliability? These and many other questions are addressed by the CCA.

15.8.3 Configuration Audit

Identification and change control help the software developer maintain order in what would otherwise be a chaotic and fluid situation. However, even the most successful change control mechanisms track a change only until an ECO is generated. How can we ensure that the change has been properly implemented? The answer is twofold: (1) *formal technical reviews* and (2) the *software configuration audit*.

The formal technical review (presented in detail in Chapter 12) focuses on the technical correctness of the SCI that has been modified. The reviewers assess the SCI to determine consistency with other SCIs, omissions, or potential side effects. A formal technical review should be conducted for all but the most trivial changes.

A software configuration audit complements the formal technical review by assessing an SCI for characteristics that are generally not considered during review. The audit asks and answers the following questions:

1. Has the change specified in the ECO been made? Have any additional modifications been incorporated?
2. Has a formal technical review been conducted to assess technical correctness?
3. Have software engineering standards been properly followed?
4. Has the change been "highlighted" in the SCI? Have the change date and change author been specified? Does the SCI identification reflect the change?
5. Have SCM procedures for noting the change, recording it, and reporting it been followed?
6. Have all related SCIs been properly updated?

In some cases the audit questions are asked as part of a formal technical review. However, when SCM is a formal activity, the SCM audit is conducted separately by the quality assurance group.

15.8.4 Status Reporting

Configuration status reporting (sometimes called *status accounting*) is an SCM task that answers the following questions:

1. What happened?
2. Who did it?
3. When did it happen?
4. What else will be affected?

The flow of information for configuration status reporting (CSR) is illustrated in Figure 15.7. Each time an SCI is assigned new or updated identification a CSR entry is made. Each time a change is approved by the CCA (i.e., a ECO is issued), a CSR entry is made. Each time a configuration audit is conducted, the results are reported as part of the CSR task. Output from CSR may be placed in an on-line data base

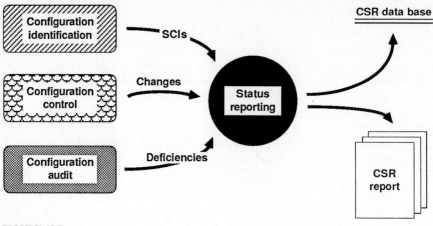

FIGURE 15.7
Status reporting.

[TAY85], so that software developers or maintainers can access change information by keyword category. In addition, an SCR report is generated on a regular basis and is intended to keep management and practitioners apprised of important changes.

Configuration status reporting plays a vital role in the success of a large software development project. When many people are involved, it is likely that "the left hand not knowing what the right hand is doing" syndrome will occur. Two developers may attempt to modify the same SCI with different and conflicting intents. A software engineering team may spend months of effort building software to an obsolete specification. The person who would recognize serious side effects for a proposed change is not aware that the change is being made. CSR helps to eliminate these problems by improving communication among all people involved.

15.8.5   SCM Standards

Over the past two decades a number of software configuration management standards have been proposed. Among the relevant standards are: MIL-STD-483, DOD-STD-480A, and MIL-STD-1521A. Although each of these standards refers to software developed for military applications, they serve as a good guideline (assuming some degree of simplification) for local standards that might be applicable to the commercial world. The interested reader should refer to [BER80] or [BRY80] for additional information.

15.9   SUMMARY

Maintenance, the last phase in the software engineering process, accounts for the majority of all dollars spent on computer software. As more programs are developed, a disturbing trend has emerged—the amount of effort and resources expended on software maintenance is growing. Ultimately, some software development organizations may become maintenance-bound, unable to embark upon new projects because all resources are dedicated to the maintenance of old programs.

Four types of maintenance are performed on computer software. Corrective maintenance acts to correct errors uncovered after the software is in use. Adaptive maintenance is applied when changes in the external environment precipitate modifications to software. Perfective maintenance incorporates enhancements requested by the user community. Finally, preventive maintenance improves future maintainability and reliability and provides a basis for future enhancement.

Technical and management approaches to the maintenance phase can be implemented with little upheaval. However, tasks performed during earlier software engineering phases define maintainability and have an important impact on the success of any maintenance approach.

Software engineering offers the key to improved maintenance productivity. With careful design, thorough documentation, and a complete series of reviews and testing methods, errors will be easier to diagnose and correct when they do occur.

Software configuration management is an umbrella activity that is applied extensively during the maintenance phase but also during software definition and development. SCM identifies, controls, audits, and reports modifications that will invariably occur while software is being developed and after it has been released to a customer. All information produced as part of the software engineering process becomes part of a software configuration. The configuration is organized in a manner that enables an orderly control of change.

The methods and techniques presented in this book have many goals, but one of the most important is to build software that is amenable to change. The items that compose a software configuration guide individuals who are unfamiliar with the software. Fewer person-hours will be expended on each modification or maintenance request. Resources will be freed to develop the new software that will be required for the increasingly complex systems, services, and products demanded by the advance of technology.

REFERENCES

[BEL72]   Belady, L. and M. Lehman, "An Introduction to Growth Dynamics," *Statistical Computer Performance Evaluation*, W. Freiberger, ed., Academic Press, 1972, pp. 503–511.

[BER80]   Bersoff, E. H., V. D. Henderson, and S. G. Siegel, *Software Configuration Management*, Prentice-Hall, 1980.

[BOE79]   Boehm, B., "Software Engineering—R&D Trends and Defense Needs," *Research Directions in Software Technology*, P. Wegner, ed., MIT Press, 1979, pp. 44–86.

[BRY80]   Bryan, W., C. Chadbourne, and S. Siegel, *Software Configuration Management*, IEEE Compter Society Press, 1980.

[CAN72]   Canning, R., "The Maintenance 'Iceberg,'" *EDP Analyzer*, vol. 10, no. 10, October 1972.

[CHR85]   Christian, K. B., and S. H. Zucker, "Automated Configuration Management of a DoD Satellite Ground System," *Proc. Conf. Software Maintenance—1985*, IEEE, November 1985, pp. 6–14.

[FRE80]   Freedman, D., and G. Weinberg, in *Techniques of Program and System Maintenance*, G. Parikh, ed., Winthrop Publishers, 1981.

[GIL79]   Gilb, T., "A Comment on the Definition of Reliability," *ACM Software Engineering Notes*, vol. 4, no. 3, July 1979.

[GIL81]   Gilb, T., in *Techniques of Program and System Maintenance*, G. Parikh, ed., Winthrop Publishers, 1981.

[GUS85]   Gustafson, D. A., et al., "An Analysis of Software Changes During Maintenance and Enhancement," *Proc. Conf. Software Maintenance—1985*, IEEE, November 1985, pp. 92–95.

[KOP79]   Kopetz, H., *Software Reliability*, Springer-Verlag, 1979, p. 93.

[LIE80]   Lientz, B., and E. Swanson, *Software Maintenance Management*, Addison-Wesley, 1980.

[MCC80]   McCracken, D., "Software in the 80s—Perils and Promises," *Computerworld* (special ed.), vol. 14, no. 38, September 17, 1980, p. 5.

[MIL81]   Miller, J., in *Techniques of Program and System Maintenance*, G. Parikh, ed., Winthrop Publishers, 1981.

[ROC75]   Rochkind, M., "The Source Code Control System," *IEEE Trans. Software Engineering*, vol. 1, no. 4, December 1975.

[SCH85]   Schaefer, H., "Metrics for Optimal Maintenance Management," *Proc. Conf. Software Maintenance—1985*, IEEE, November 1985, pp. 114–119.

[SPI81]   Spiegel, M., "Software Prototyping," Colloquium Series—Wang Institute of Graduate Studies, March 2, 1981.

[SWA76]   Swanson E. B., "The Dimensions of Maintenance," *Proc. 2nd Intl. Conf. Software Engineering*, IEEE, October 1976, pp. 492–497.

[TAY85]   Taylor, B., "A Database Approach to Configuration Management for Large Projects," *Proc. Conf. Software Maintenance—1985*, IEEE, November 1985, pp. 15–23.

[TIC82]   Tichy, W. F., "Design, Implementation and Evaluation of a Revision Control System," *Proc. 6th Intl. Conf. Software Engineering*, IEEE, Tokyo, September 1982, pp. 58–67.

[VES83]   Vessey, I., and R. Webber, "Some Factors Affecting Program Repair Maintenance," *CACM*, vol. 26, no. 2., February 1983, pp. 128–134.

[YUE85]   Yuen, C., "An Empirical Approach to the Study of Errors in Large Software Under Maintenance," *Proc. Conf. Software Maintenance—1985*, IEEE, November 1985, pp. 96–105.

[YOU75]   Yourdon, E., *Techniques of Program Structure and Design*, Prentice-Hall, 1975, p. 24.

PROBLEMS AND POINTS TO PONDER

15.1 Your instructor will select one of the programs that everyone in the class has developed during this course. Exchange your program randomly with that of someone else in the class. *Do not* explain or walk through the program. Next, implement an enhancement (specified by your instructor) in the program you have received.

    (*a*) Perform all software engineering tasks including brief walkthrough (but not with the author of the program).

    (*b*) Keep careful track of all errors encountered during testing.

    (*c*) Discuss your experiences in class.

15.2 Attempt to develop a software rating system that could be applied to existing programs in an effort to pick candidate programs for preventive maintenance.

15.3 Are corrective maintenance and debugging the same thing? Explain your answer.

15.4 Discuss the impact of high-level languages on adaptive maintenance. Is it always possible to adapt a program?

15.5 Should maintenance costs be incorporated in the software planning step? Are they?

15.6 Will the overall duration of the software life cycle expand or contract over the next decade? Discuss this issue in class.

15.7 Team project: Develop an automated tool that will enable a manager to collect and analyze quantitative maintenance data. Use Sections 15.3.2 and 15.4.4 as a source for software requirements.

15.8 Discuss the viability of a "spare parts" strategy. Consider both technical and economic issues.

15.9 For the practitioner: Relate a maintenance "horror story."

15.10 Research the literature in an attempt to find recently published papers, books, and, most important, quantitative data on software maintenance. Write a paper on your findings.

15.11 Why is the First Law of System Engineering true? How does it affect our perception of software engineering paradigms?

15.12 Design a data base system that would enable a software engineer to store, cross-reference, trace, update, change, etc. all important software configuration items. How would the data base handle different versions of the same program? Would source code be handled differently than documentation? How will two developers be precluded from making different changes to the same SCI at the same time?

15.13 Using the data base that you developed in Problem 15.12, design software to implement an SCM tool.

15.14 Research an existing SCM tool and compare it to the design you have developed in Problem 15.13.

15.15 Develop a rational identification scheme for software configuration items. The scheme must accommodate different version numbers.

15.16 Assume that you have CSA responsibility for a large software project. Develop a generic list of questions that you would ask while assessing the impact of a requested change.

15.17 What is the difference between an SCM audit and a formal technical review? Can their function be folded into one review? What are the pros and cons?

FURTHER READINGS

The literature on software maintenance has expanded significantly over the past few years. Although most books on the subject rehash software engineering procedures and methods that can be used both for new software development and maintenance, each offers important new insight into the maintenance process.

    Martin and McClure (*Software Maintenance*, Prentice-Hall, 1983) discuss the impact of fourth generation techniques on the maintenance process. Parikh (*Handbook of Software Maintenance*, Wiley-Interscience, 1986) discusses software maintenance using an effective question and answer format. Glass and Noiseux (*Software Maintenance Guidebook*, Prentice-Hall, 1981) present still another worthwhile treatment of the subject. Data collected by Lientz and Swanson [LIE80] remain the most comprehensive study on maintenance published to date.

Parikh's anthology (*Techniques of Program and System Maintenance*, Winthrop Publishers, 1981) and another anthology by Parikh and Zvegintzov (*Software Maintenance*, IEEE Computer Society Press, 1983) contain collections of papers on maintenance.

The literature on software configuration management is considerably less generous than that available for software maintenance. Books by Babich (*Software Configuration Management*, Addison-Wesley, 1986), Bersoff, Henderson and Siegel [BER80], and an anthology edited by Bryan et al. [BRY80] contain useful guidelines for management of the software configuration.

EPILOGUE

An engineering approach to the development of computer software is a philosophy whose time has come. Although debate continues regarding the ''right paradigm,'' the degree of automation, and the most effective methods, the underlying principles of software engineering are now accepted throughout the industry. Why, then, are we only recently seeing their broad adoption?

The answer, I think, lies in the difficulty of technology transition and the cultural change that accompanies it. As software engineering procedures, methods, and tools are adopted, a culture established in the 1960s and 1970s begins to change—and change is never easy. Even though most of us appreciate the need for an engineering discipline for software, we struggle against the inertia of past practice.

To ease the transition we need many things—an effective methodology, acceptance by practitioners, support from managers, and no small dose of education and ''advertising.''

Software engineering has not had the benefit of massive advertising, but as time passes the concept sells itself. In a way, this book is an ''advertisement'' for that concept.

The software engineering process has been described in a way that conjures visions of a vortex. The definition steps—system engineering, software project planning and software requirements analysis—reside on ''streamlines'' that grow progressively closer to the central core that we call *development*. Design and coding move us into the core and a series of testing steps pull us back out toward the boundaries. Finally, the maintenance phase starts the process over again. In this book we have come full circle.

You may not agree with every approach described in this book. Some of the techniques and opinions are admittedly controversial; others must be tuned to work well in different software development environments. It is my sincere hope, however, that *Software Engineering: A Practitioner's Approach* has delineated the problems we face, demonstrated the strength of a software engineering concept, and provided a framework of methods and tools.

When the first edition of this book was written, we were just entering the 1980s—the decade of software. The decade of the 80s is now almost behind us, but the challenge of software remains. Let us hope that the people who meet that challenge— software engineers—will have the wisdom to develop systems that improve the human condition.

INDEX